WITHDRAWN

CHARACTERIZATION AND INDIVIDUALITY IN WOLFRAM'S 'PARZIVAL'

CHARACTERIZATION AND INDIVIDUALITY IN WOLFRAM'S 'PARZIVAL'

BY

DAVID BLAMIRES

Lecturer in German in the
University of Manchester

CAMBRIDGE
AT THE UNIVERSITY PRESS
1965

PUBLISHED BY
THE SYNDICS OF THE CAMBRIDGE UNIVERSITY PRESS

Bentley House, 200 Euston Road, London, N.W.1
American Branch: 32 East 57th Street, New York, N.Y. 10022
West African Office: P.O. Box 33, Ibadan, Nigeria

CAMBRIDGE UNIVERSITY PRESS
1965

LIBRARY OF CONGRESS CATALOGUE CARD NUMBER:
65–14354

Printed in Great Britain by
Spottiswoode, Ballantyne and Co. Ltd.
London and Colchester

CONTENTS

lichkeiten.'[1] Then, in concise terms, he sums up Wolfram's achievement: 'Der Mensch findet seine eigene Lebensmitte. Er ist nicht mehr vor allem lebensgeschickt, brauchbar und einfühlsam, er repräsentiert auch nicht mehr nur das Allgemeinmenschliche schlechthin oder in einer ständischen Ausprägung, sondern er wird Person.'[2]

The technique of individualization does not suddenly first occur in Wolfram's *Parzival*, nor is it in fact completely developed there. Its growth can be illustrated by references to religious literature, the *Minnesang* and the epic in its various stages from pre-courtly works to the romances of Hartmann, Gottfried and Wolfram, but it is not until this last period that a genuine kind of individuality is unmistakable.

In religious literature the growth of individuality can be clearly illustrated by a comparison of Williram's translation of and commentary on the *Canticum Canticorum* (composed *c.* 1060) with that originating from the monastery of St Trudpert (written *c.* 1160, though this dating is disputed by some scholars, who would put it as far back as 1120). In his exposition Williram uses a single interpretation of the union of the *sponsus* with the *sponsa*. For him the bride of Christ is alone the Church—there is, however, one occasion when he says: 'Reginae dáz sínt dîe édelen sêla, dîe der sínt sponsae regis aeterni' (103), but this can scarcely be counted as a genuine exception, as 'dîe édelen sêla' is merely a collective plural referring to the Church at large—and the whole of the interpretation of the *Canticum* is a didactic exposition of the relationship of Christ with the Church, and any teaching about the Father and the Holy Ghost is virtually excluded. The bride of Christ is the *ecclesia*, which is interpreted in the sense of the institution of the Church with all its hierarchy of prophets, apostles and doctors, for whom the laity are merely *auditores*. In the hundred years intervening between Williram and the St Trudpert commentary the spiritual and intellectual atmosphere changes

---

[1] *Wandel des Menschenbildes in der mittelalterlichen Dichtung* (*WW*, III (Sonderheft), 1952/3), p. 43.

[2] *Ibid.* pp. 45 f.

radically. In the latter work the *sponsa* is interpreted as the Blessed Virgin, whose role in humanizing Christianity and overcoming the immense distance separating man from God can hardly be overestimated (cf. St Peter Damian, who calls the *Canticum* an 'epithalamium in laudibus [Mariae]'[1]), or as the souls of those who emulate her, since the *rex pacificus* rests 'swâ er uindet die wârun diemût unde die durcnahtigin kûsse, dc kît diemûtigiu sêle und kûskin lîp',[2] and what was before a collective plural has now become an individualized singular. The Virgin takes over the function of the *doctores* as the neck which joins together the head and the body, God and humanity, and in this respect she represents the spiritual fulfilment of the mystical union with the Godhead; this interpretation can, however, be transferred from her to the individual soul. This trend is pursued further by St Bernard, who speaks of the kiss, which the St Trudpert commentary identifies with Christ, as 'quod non est aliud nisi infundi spiritu sancto',[3] transferring the image to the individual, personal experience. Thus, the development of the interpretation begins with an ecclesiastical one, in which the order of the Church and the Christian community is all-important, becomes more direct and human when the Virgin assumes the function of the Church as mediator, and finally emphasizes the possibility of the union of the individual soul with the Holy Ghost. At this point mysticism becomes the most important contribution of the medieval Church to the development of Christianity, and the thirteenth and fourteenth centuries are its *Blüteʒeit*.

The trend towards individualization is also clearly noticeable in *Minnesang*. Perhaps more than with any other poet of *Minnesangs Frühling* the poems of Reinmar von Hagenau show the fine distinctions in mood of the *minne*-relationship, even though the *frouwe* herself may not emerge at all as an individual figure. Each poem is constructed on the basis of a particular *seelischer Vorgang*, and it is this which is individualized, though the process is evident

---

[1] *PL*, CXLIV, col. 558.
[2] *Das St. Trudperter Hohe Lied*, ed. Hermann Menhardt (Halle, 1934), p. 144.
[3] *PL*, CLXXXIII, *Sermones in Canticum Canticorum*, VIII, 2–3.

much more in the mind of the poet and his interpretation of the details of the *mĭnne*-relationship than in the depiction of the *frouwe*. There is, however, an individual approach to the problems of courtly love on the part of the more outstanding lyric poets: an intellectual, religious attitude in Hausen, ecstatic sensualism in Morungen, discontent with the barrenness of unrequited service in Hartmann, continual change and experimentation in Walther until he reaches the solution of *ebene minne*, rejection in favour of the more natural kind of love to be found in *nidere minne* in Neidhart.

In the early love-lyrics of the Kürenberger there is a reluctance on the part of the poet to express himself directly. Thus, of the fifteen strophes attributed to him eight are *Frauenstrophen*, two more are combined with two of these to form *Wechsel* (7.1 and 7.10 together, and 8.1 and 9.29 together), and one is in itself a *Wechsel* (8.9), leaving only four as independent *Männerstrophen*. Here the poet prefers an oblique kind of expression and uses the form of a generalization with which he may only implicitly identify himself; only on one occasion does he introduce a first person pronoun in the first line (9.21). The most indirectly expressed emotion is to be found in 9.17:

> Wîp unde vederspil   diu werdent lîhte zam;
> swer si ze rehte lucket,   sô suochent si den man.
> als warb ein schœne ritter   umb eine frouwen guot.
> als ich dar an gedenke,   sô stêt wol hôhe mîn muot.

The poem begins with a general statement which occupies half of the entire strophe (in 10.1 and 10.9 it is only the first line which constitutes the generalization or simile) and then continues with the baldest of statements transferring this generalization to *one* knight and *one* lady with the implication that this is the poet's experience. This, however, is never stated, and a first person pronoun is introduced only at the beginning of the last line. Like the other lyrics, this is simple, fresh and unsophisticated in both form and content, giving only a general impression and leaving much to the imagination.

Gradually this reticence which is the peculiar characteristic of the Kürenberger yields to a more personal, immediate expression of emotion. The poet becomes more aware of his own personality. Thus, a first person pronoun or adjective is found in the first line of eight of Johansdorf's twelve poems, in twenty-two of Morungen's thirty-three poems, and in fifteen of Hausen's seventeen poems. Each *Minnesänger* works on the same basic concept of courtly love, but elaborates and adapts it to suit his own particular interpretation of the *minne*-experience, and it is the individuality of his approach, his use of language and original imagery, which constitute his right to fame.

In the epic the different effect of individuality as a factor in characterization can be illustrated with great clarity. In such a poem as Pfaffe Konrad's *Rolandslied* the element of idealization is of the utmost importance in the author's purpose. The characters are sketched according to the moral judgement which Konrad passes on them, and any deviation from the ideal of a Christian hero is to be interpreted as a sign of moral weakness, even though this may be purely external in form. Thus, Genelun is individualized in a negative way, and his individuality is the mark of the sin of *superbia*. A comparison between the *Rolandslied* and the *Chanson de Roland* versions of the council scene brings out a sharp distinction in the characterizations of Guenes and Genelun. In the *chanson de geste* Guenes' advice is listened to with respect as he holds a place of honour at the court, and he speaks half-way through the council, after Roland and before Neimes. By contrast, in the German poem Genelun speaks at the end of the council after the other heroes have given their opinion, and his advice is given in deliberate opposition to what has preceded, not merely as one opinion among others as it appears in the French poem. In the *Chanson* Guenes is depicted, at least at first, as just one of the knights at the emperor's court, and although he is very early characterized as 'Guenes ... ki la traïsun fist' (178), this does not mean that he is singled out and individualized in the negative way of the *Rolandslied*. Julius Schwietering interprets this attitude by reference to the development in the evaluation of mercy and love, which occurs simultaneously with the emergence of individuality.

The basic difference between what he calls the Romanesque and the Gothic spirit lies in the negative appraisal of mercy and love on the part of the Romanesque and the positive appraisal on the part of the Gothic. Thus, in the *Rolandslied* the old heroic ideal prevails: 'nur Genelun zeigt hier eine weiche stelle, und ebendort keimt der judassaat'.[1] The Christian heroic ideal is so pronounced in the German epic that little distinction is made between the various heroes. The contention of Friedrich Maurer that 'Der Kaiser, die Fürsten, die Bischöfe werden sehr individuell gezeichnet in all den Einzelgestalten von Karl, Roland und Genelun, Olivir und Turpin bis zu dem Herzog Naimes und dem Bischof Johannes'[2] is exaggerated and misleading, since the individuality which exists is functional rather than an essential part of characterization. Thus, the Emperor Charlemagne is the main character of the poem and a well-defined, unmistakable portrait of him emerges, though on at least one occasion a descriptive phrase is applied both to him and to Marsilie, giving them the characteristic of being 'wise unt biderbe' (2864 and 4074). With the other warriors, however, no such clear picture appears, and even the distinction between Roland and Olivir, so important in the *Chanson*, is virtually obliterated, both being characterized by youthful impetuosity (1326 ff.), whereas the *Chanson* states: 'Rollant est proz e Oliver est sage' (1093).[3] The purpose of Pfaffe Konrad in writing his poem was to expound didactic ideas through a deliberate contrast between the imitable idealism of deeds of valour in the service of God and despicable wickedness in betraying these ideals. On this score individualization was completely unnecessary and might even have been harmful in the treatment of the theme. Slight differences between characters are possible if their function demands it, but otherwise they are construed as moral differences and as such are negatively valued.

Idealization is not only a specifically Christian feature in

[1] Julius Schwietering, *Der Wandel des Heldenideals in der epischen Dichtung des 12. Jahrhunderts* (*ZfdA*, LXIV, 1927), p. 139.
[2] In the introduction to his edition of the *Rolandslied* (Leipzig, 1940), p. 8.
[3] Cf. Eva-Maria Woelker, *Menschengestaltung in vorhöfischen Epen des 12. Jahrhunderts* (Berlin, 1940), pp. 36 f.

characterization: it occurs also in primarily secular epics and especially in courtly romances. In so far as all medieval literature has a didactic aim in portraying models of conduct and, in the widest sense, moral qualities, idealization plays an inevitable part in characterization. The result is that heroes are depicted in superlatives and hyperboles and tend to coalesce into an ideal type differentiated only by the deeds they perform. This is particularly the case in the portrayal of women, whose excellence is expressed in terms of a formula, though this does not emerge until courtliness becomes the most important form of literary expression, as until this time woman occupies a very inferior position in the Christian and feudal view of society. Early examples of this superlative description can be found in the *Rolandslied*, when Genelun speaks of his wife as 'deme aller schonisten wibe, / die ie dehein man gwan ze sinem libe' (1460 f.), though this statement is a sign of Genelun's moral weakness and has no real significance for his wife, who otherwise has no part in the poem; and in *Orendel*, where King Ougel tells his son that Bride is 'die schonste ob allen wiben' (224). With the rise of courtliness it becomes more frequent: of the second Isalde Kehenis says: 'dû mûst des vorwâre jên, / daz nî wart kein schôner wîp' (Eilhart's *Tristrant* 5682 f.); of Enite Hartmann writes: 'man saget daz nie kint gewan / einen lîp sô gar dem wunsche gelîch' (*Erec* 331 f.), and: 'dâ enwas dehein man, / er enbegunde ir vür die schœnsten jehen / die er hæte gesehen' (1741 ff.); he describes Laudine as 'ein wîp / daz er [sc. Iwein] nie wîbes lîp / alsô schœnen gesach' (*Iwein* 1308 ff.). These examples could easily be multiplied and serve to show the extent to which woman has become, in courtly literature, merely an ideal figure, a representative of feminine perfection, so that the knight's task can be seen in terms of Herzeloyde's demand to Gahmuret: 'nu êret an mir elliu wîp' (88.27).

Heroes as well as heroines are included in the ideal type described by superlatives. Thus, of Turpin it is said: 'Du bist der aller chunisten ain, / den diu sunne ie bescain' (4395 f.); King Rother is called 'der aller heriste man, / der da zv rome / ie intfinc die cronen' (10 ff.); Liupolt is described as 'der aller gestruiste man. / den

iesich hein romisc kuninc gewan' (55 f.). Of 'der arme Heinrich'
it is said:

> an dem enwas vergezzen
> nie deheiner der tugent
> die ein ritter in sîner jugent
> ze vollem lobe haben sol. (32 ff.)

But here a more detailed description is given later. In the superlatives applied to heroes the comment is usually of a more precise
nature than is the case with heroines and contains a limitation of
the perfection ascribed to them in that it is a special kind of
perfection relevant to their particular situation, as is evident from
the above examples.

A certain lack of differentiation between characters is observable
in the use of set expressions. Thus, in the *Rolandslied* the phrase
'ein helt chûne unt snel' is applied to Anshelm (126), to a heathen
(580), to Mantel (1627), to Witel (4128), to Egeriers (4537), to
Antel (8256), and an anonymous crowd from a variety of countries
are referred to as 'chûne unt snelle' (8071) as well. Moreover, the
adjectives used to describe the heroes of almost all the epics are so
general that they can be and are applied indiscriminately to all and
sundry. Thus, in the *Alexanderlied* Alexander is obviously singled
out for more detailed treatment and so, to a lesser degree, is Darius,
as his chief opponent, but the other heroes are not individualized
and are recognizable only by their function in the episodes in
which they occur. In the *Eneide* also the range of adjectives is
restricted, and Eneas, Turnus and Latinus are all referred to as 'der
hêre', 'der rîke' and 'der mâre', to mention only the most obvious
instances. There is a large number of conventional phrases of the
type 'der helt balt', but there is no clear system of values to dictate
their use. What differences do occur are on the whole external or
in terms of contrast, since there is scarcely any attempt at a psychological study of characters until the courtly epic proper.

Very frequently the lack of individuality is emphasized through a
description of or a speech on the part of two or more characters at
once. Darius, in one of his numerous letters in the *Alexanderlied*,

writes to 'zwein herzogen, di ime wâren lieb' (1594) and asks for their help, to which they reply in unison: 'Darius ist harte betrogen ...' (Strasbourg version 1614 ff.). This feature is characteristic of the *Rolandslied* too, where many sections of the action are performed by a group of undifferentiated princes. Thus, a group speaks together accepting Genelun's advice (2958 ff.); a number of princes swear *en masse* to Paligan that they will follow him to the death (7218 ff.); the external appearance of the princes is given in general, inclusive terms (1558 ff.). There is even one case where two important characters, Naimes and Anseis, are the subject of one description, are included in one category and differentiated only by name (8285 ff.). In *König Rother*, where by and large there is an attempt at individualization, though it does not proceed very much further than a distinction of types, as 'Berker der alde man', 'Asprian der riese', there is at the very beginning a description of the external appearance of all the heroes, 'eilf grauen ime do swŏren. / Daz si erme herren umbe die maget voren' (144 f.), which is prefaced by the statement: 'Sie trogen riterlich gewant. / alle geliche' (203 f.). This last phrase certainly underlines their splendid uniformity.

It is not until the epics of Hartmann, Gottfried and Wolfram that a psychological interest is found in characterization and an attempt is made to discuss conflicts and problems within a personality. Broadly speaking, the function of the twelfth-century epic had been until then that of social entertainment and of moral didacticism, in which the main centre of interest was the deeds of the hero and the way in which they exemplified an ideal to be aimed at. Apart from the obvious exception of the *Rolandslied*, however, the deliberately didactic purpose of the author in the secular epics was minimal, since all that the audience required was a good story. There was no question of dealing with the complexities of theology and philosophy in problems of human behaviour because this presupposed an awareness of individual psychology that was lacking even in contemporary learning, and the opposition of the courtly to the Christian morality was felt only by a limited number of clerics. Adventure for its own sake is the proper subject of the pre-courtly and, to a large extent, of the early courtly epic, in which the courtly idea is too new for problems within it and in its relationship with the world to have arisen.

Even in the early courtly epic external forces are at work moulding the plot, since it often does not develop logically from the personality of the characters concerned. In this respect the characters are not the centre of the action, they are not yet in control of the situations in which they are placed, they are still not fully *persons*. Thus, in the *Eneide* much of what Eneas does is as a result of external forces, of which *minne* is one. Even when he leaves Carthage it is not by his own wish, but he is compelled *malgré lui* to forsake Dido because 'die gode enlân mich hie niet sîn' (2031). Veldeke does not elaborate Eneas' character to account for his departure in the way that Wolfram explains Gahmuret's flight from Belacane through the inner processes of his personality. Similarly, in Eilhart's *Tristrant* the love-potion acts as an irresistible impulse from outside:

> alsô schîre sie in trang,
> dô dûchte sie beide sundir wang
> sie vorlorin alle ire sinne:
> sie musten ein ander minne.   (2353 ff.)

It is viewed more in the light of a sudden incursion into the lives of Tristrant and Isalde than as the culmination of a process which had begun some time before, as in Gottfried's re-interpretation. Here the description of the effect of the potion is deferred in order to show Brangæne's reaction on realizing what has happened, and although the magic provides the external reason for what then happens, the situation is carefully built up beforehand and is, as it were, merely confirmed by the potion.

The position of women in medieval society is closely linked with the emergence of individuality. The cult of the Blessed Virgin, which began to flower in the twelfth century as an essential part of the more human, imaginative approach to religion, had an influence on the position of women in general and was probably a contributory factor in the appearance of courtly love. Previously the role of woman had been that of a servant and of an inferior being. With the advent of courtliness her position is elevated, and the man takes on the part of servant. At first the woman is merely the object of a quest, as in *König Rother*, and all the *Brautwerbung* stories, but gradually she becomes an individual, an idealized representative of a sex. In early courtliness there is a mutuality about the *minne*-relationship with *dienst* being given by both knight and lady, but in the period of *hôhe minne* the lady is of importance in her moods and feelings primarily on account of the effect these have in the emotions of the knight who is serving her. This is true of the love-lyric, but in the epic, by contrast, the lady is not, except in the case of Ampflise, a distant, unreciprocating figure. Enite shares the responsibility for Erec's disgrace and rides before him as he ventures out to perform deeds of valour in order to rid himself of the stain on his character. The relationship of Tristan and Isot is one of mutual devotion, in which both are ennobled by their love for each other. In *Parzival* virtually all *minne*-relationships are consummated in marriage, in the union of a person with a person.

Idealization of both knight and lady is, despite Wolfram's concern to individualize, an essential part of his technique in characterization, but he nonetheless finds it possible to depict both Gahmuret and Anfortas in blameworthy situations without feeling obliged to justify their actions. His aim is not one of absolutely unqualified idealization. Of him, as of the Middle Ages in general, it can be said:

Wenn man es [sc. the Middle Ages] aber aus sich selbst heraus zu verstehen sucht, dann offenbart sich immer wieder, wie gerade in der als selbstverständlich hingenommenen Gebundenheit Individualität als in sich geschlossene Wesenseigentümlichkeit sich entfalten kann. Und dort, wo mittelalterliche Kunst am stärksten zu uns spricht, da erkennen wir nicht nur Normen und Ideale, sondern wir erleben Menschen, und wir erleben sie durchaus als Individualitäten.[1]

The preceding remarks illustrate the compass of differences which the element of individuality introduces into literature of all

[1] Woelker, *op. cit.*, pp. 226 f.

kinds and give a brief outline of the general trend in the development of the idea. The following chapters will examine the question in detail with respect to the chief characters in Wolfram's *Parzival*. Although the techniques used for characterization cannot be separated from what they express, it is primarily the understanding of man which is the subject of this study. The division of chapters therefore takes place according to the character under examination and not according to the methods employed in Wolfram's characterization as a whole. In dealing with the question of individuality, the aspects of character which come under the influence of idealization, typology and symbolism will all have their place and cannot in fact be rigidly separated from the discussion of individuality as such.

II

GAHMURET

INTRODUCTION AND SOURCES

THE first two books of Wolfram von Eschenbach's *Parzival* have occasioned much thought on the part of scholars, since they are only loosely connected with the material of the rest of the poem, and more particularly, because it is only here, in Wolfram's work, that the episodes related about Gahmuret are joined to the theme of the Grail. At an early stage, however, the *Conte del Graal* of Chrétien de Troyes, the main source of Wolfram's poem, had been enlarged by the addition of a prologue known as the Bliocadrans prologue, which attempted some account of the immediate background of Perceval's family so as to provide a wider setting for the unfolding of the main theme. Wolfram went much further than the French author of the prologue and created a detailed and virtually independent miniature epic to fulfil the same function. The history of Gahmuret is a self-complete entity in that it can be read and understood without necessarily being referred to the rest of the poem, but its aim was to depict Parzival's background in terms of his family heritage, and it thus adds greatly to the significance of Parzival's own history. From the point of view of the rest of the romance it is of considerable value, as a study in family relationships and the influence of heredity; indeed, an understanding of Wolfram's use of kinship motifs is essential to an appreciation of the poem as a whole. The complex genealogical patterns which form the framework of the romance clearly show the importance which he attached to family relationships, and the fact that the Gahmuret episodes occupy one eighth of the total work illustrates this even more strikingly. There is an amazing variety of characters in *Parzival*, but each of them is seen in terms of his relationship with the main character of the poem, Parzival, either directly or indirectly through Gawan or

14

Gahmuret. Despite this, Wolfram never allows his characterization to deprive the personalities he creates of their existence apart from their relationship with Parzival (or Gawan or Gahmuret). On the contrary, each character has a twofold existence—a genuine individuality of his own and a place in society. Through the fact that each character is so conceived the characterization of Parzival is enriched and deepened, since there is a system of relationships, which, while centring on Parzival, also ramify among themselves. A pattern is built up around the concept of individuality within a community, this latter being provided by the family of the Grail, the circle of the knights of the Round Table and the family of Artus.

The figure of Gahmuret is the feature which gives unity to books I and II, a fact which is all the more remarkable as Wolfram had no one written source for it. Friedrich Panzer[1] has investigated the question of sources with penetrating erudition and has discovered several literary and historical parallels as well as a multitude of motifs occurring in a variety of contexts; but the evidence is not of the first degree of relevance to Wolfram's purpose in composing a significant background for the Parzival story, since the great majority of the parallels are in external events and not first and foremost in the field of characterization, and the result of the combination of these findings is only a more or less conventional kind of hero. There are, however, two sources which gave Wolfram certain basic ideas for the development of books I and II, namely, Veldeke's *Eneide* and the *Conte del Graal* itself.

The similarity of plot between the *Eneide* and the first two books of *Parzival* has long been noticed and Wolfram's references to Veldeke and allusions to incidents in the *Eneide* in both *Parzival* and *Willehalm* make it more than probable that the *Eneide* helped to shape the history of Gahmuret.[2] The basis of both stories is the theme of a man who is forced to flee from the love of a noble queen and finds another lady to serve in another land. Gahmuret's flight

[1] Friedrich Panzer, *Gahmuret. Quellenstudien zu Wolframs Parzival* (*SB d. Heidelberger Akad. d. Wiss., phil.-hist. Kl.*, 1939/40).

[2] Cf. *Heinrichs von Veldeke Eneide*, ed. Otto Behaghel (Heilbronn, 1882), pp. ccxiv ff.

from Belacane takes place in the same stealthy way as Eneas leaves Dido (cf. *Parȥival* 55.12 and 22: 'daz wart verholne getân'; 'ich pin dirre verte ein diep'; *Eneide* 2027: 'verholenlîke alse ein dief'). There are, however, differences in the motivation. Both Gahmuret and Eneas are loth to leave their respective lovers, but Eneas is compelled by the will of the gods to go on to Italy (this was his intention even before possessing Dido, but he keeps silent about it) (1619 ff.), and later the power of the gods becomes so great that he has to depart against his will (1953 ff.), whereas Gahmuret is driven by his own innate emotions and by the lack of *rîterschaft* to seek adventure elsewhere. In the case of Gahmuret the relationship had progressed as far as marriage and the whole motivation is on a more satisfactory plane. Eneas is driven by an external force which is largely impersonal despite the fact that the gods are personified as his mother Venus and brothers Amor and Cupido, whereas the reason for Gahmuret's flight proceeds from his own nature and his need for *rîterschaft*. Moreover, Eneas' action is excused by his being subject to more powerful external forces, while Gahmuret is presented in a situation for which he bears the responsibility. This in itself marks a considerable step forward in the process of individualization.

In each case the hero of the poem finds a second lover and a marriage ensues. With Gahmuret the details of the marriage are rendered more complex on account of his previous marriage with Belacane and he cannot be completely exonerated from blame. Herzeloyde claims precedence over Belacane in virtue of possessing Christian baptism, but the question is in the end only resolved by resorting to the external judgement of a *Minnegericht*.

Apart from this parallel in the plots of *Parȥival* and the *Eneide* there are a few other points of comparison. The burial of Gahmuret (106.29–109.1) is conceived in terms which are very similar to the two long descriptions of the burials of Pallas (8235–8408) and Kamille (9385–9574) and contains references to a large variety of jewels, an epitaph and mention of the fact that the body was embalmed, features common to all three descriptions. In addition to this, there are notable resemblances between the tent which

Gahmuret erected outside Waleis (61.8 ff.) and the one which Dido gave to Eneas (9208 ff.).

The exploits of Eneas and Gahmuret are from the beginning of their adventures very similar. Both are compelled to leave their native countries in search of fulfilment of their existence, both fall in love with a queen whom they later desert only to marry another lady of noble birth. Gahmuret has in both cases to win his lady by fighting for her, whereas Eneas fights only for the hand of Lavine. In general terms, despite the difference that Gahmuret is virtually forced into marrying Herzeloyde, while with Eneas it is by his own will that he marries Lavine, the two histories provide strikingly similar plots, which are most plausibly accounted for if Wolfram used the *Eneide* as a basis for the Gahmuret story.

The figure of Gahmuret also owes much to parallel situations in the story of Perceval in Chrétien's poem and of Parzival in the later books of Wolfram's own work. There are affinities from the very beginning of the Gahmuret episodes, but they do not so much furnish a basis for the characterization of Gahmuret as show us Parzival's character developing, at least in part, from that of his father. This is, as it were, an example of heredity in reverse.

The relationship existing between mother and son is in both cases so intimate that the mother dies of a broken heart when her son leaves her and all other remaining supports have been taken away:

> Ce fu li doels que ta mere ot
> De toi quant departis de li,
> Que pasmee a terre chaï
> Al chief del pont devant la porte,
> Et de cel doel fu ele morte. (6394 ff.)

> dô ir erstarp Gandîn
> und Gâlôes der bruoder dîn,
> unt dô si dîn bî ir niht sach,
> der tôt och ir daz herze brach. (92.27 ff.)

In the case of Gahmuret his mother Schoette only dies when she loses her other son Galoes as well, but the death of both mothers occurs unknown to the sons and is reported to them later.

The closest analogy occurs with the sieges of Patelamunt and Biaurepaire, where the external situation and its significance are almost identical. Biaurepaire has been reduced by siege and famine to a state of dire necessity and the queen has to ask the help of Perceval to relieve her from the oppression of Clamadeus, who wishes to marry her against her will. Patelamunt is also in a state of siege and the queen requires assistance against the onslaughts of Hiuteger and Gaschier, who correspond to Clamadeus and Engigerons respectively. In both instances the town under siege is ruled by a queen of great beauty, who gains the love of the hero after he has vanquished the adversary, here Hiuteger and Clamadeus, in single combat. A further parallel may be drawn with the impetuous courage, simplicity of heart and directness to be found in both Perceval and Gahmuret, though with Perceval this may be occasioned to a greater extent by his youthful ignorance and innocence.

The structure of the love episodes in Gahmuret's story closely resembles that of Parzival's. Condwiramurs had a previous lover, Schenteflur, who died in her service in an attempt to protect her against the attacks of Clamide (there is no correspondence in the *Conte del Graal*), and Belacane also had a suitor, Isenhart, whom she tested to see if he was worthy to be her *friunt* and who was killed in a duel with one of her own princes, Prothizilas. One difference lies in the fact that the attacks on Patelamunt are made by the relatives of Isenhart led by Vridebrant, King of Scotland, as they believed that Belacane had caused Isenhart's death herself, whereas Schenteflur was the son of Gurnemanz, her uncle, and the assaults had been taking place beforehand. There is, however, a further parallel between the relationship of Belacane with Isenhart and that of Sigune with Schionatulander. Both knights were the virtually accepted lovers of the two ladies, but were being tested for their worthiness; the tests went too far and both Belacane and Sigune were stricken with grief that they had not acknowledged their lovers sooner. Sigune on the one hand remained faithful to the memory of Schionatulander, while Belacane accepted Gahmuret in Isenhart's place.

One or two other less important similarities can be traced. The entry of Gahmuret into Patelamunt is based on Parzival's passage through the crowd at Pelrapeire and both are led by the *marschalc* (18.17 ff. and 182.7 ff., cf. also Chrétien 1744 ff.). The *coucher* of the heroes is also described in much the same language for Gahmuret as for Parzival (35.7 ff. and 191.10 ff.). In addition there are various minor details common to both (the celebration of mass and the general conduct of the battle), but these have scarcely any significance at all, as they are part of the normal background of courtly romance in general.[1]

It is clear from the preceding paragraphs that Wolfram found much basic material for the character of Gahmuret in the *Eneide* and the histories of Perceval and his own Parzival. Most of the incidents are not original, but they derive their value from the way in which they are used to shed light on the character of Gahmuret and build up a consistent background which will enrich the personality of Parzival by reference to his heredity. The genius of Wolfram consists in taking the available conventional material and giving it poetic significance through the careful delineation of a character that was already present in embryo.

SYNONYMS

The ways used by Wolfram to refer to Gahmuret instead of repeating his name or using a pronoun constitute one method of shorthand characterization in that various facets of Gahmuret's personality are continually being impressed unobtrusively upon the consciousness of the audience, or reader. The synonyms which Wolfram employs cover a wide field and may be divided roughly into three groups, which deal with objective, external aspects, kinship motifs and psychological features.

There is a considerable number of terms referring to the external aspect of Gahmuret's situation on life, of which the most

---

[1] Much of the information of the paragraphs dealing with the connexions with Perceval and Parzival is taken from Maurice Wilmotte, *Le Poème du Gral et ses auteurs. Le Parʒival de Wolfram d'Eschenbach et ses sources françaises* (Paris, 1933). I have referred the incidents back to *Chrétien* where possible, but Wilmotte refers them only to *Parʒival*.

frequent are *hêr* and *hêrre*,[1] *helt*[2] and *gast*.[3] *Helt* is combined with
milte (18.5), *küene* (64.28), *unverʒaget* (12.4) and *von Anschouwe*
(41.17) on other occasions, and these adjectives and adjectival
expressions add an individual note to a word which, in pre-courtly
and early courtly epics, was the most frequently used for referring
to a male character. *Gast* is linked with *werde* (15.4, 22.25) and
with *küene* and *werde* together (42.19). The word *künec* is
employed after Gahmuret has married Belacane (53.13, 54.13,
85.10), and then the title *künec von Zaʒamanc*[4] which is extended
three times by the adjective *werde* (65.19, 73.3, 83.3) and once by
rûrec (93.30) on the occasion of Galoes' death. Four times he is
called *ritter* (16.19, 33.11, 37.14, 95.28) and in one instance his
youth and courtliness are indicated by the fact that he is called *der
ritter âne bart* (63.28), this being at the time of his splendid entry
into Kanvoleis. In addition there also occurs the term *wirt* which
is used after Gahmuret's marriage to Belacane (47.3, 48.6), but
also is found independently of this fact when Gahmuret receives
Herzeloyde (90.9) and after his marriage to her (100.4); on one
occasion it is combined with *hôhst* (45.23). Once, after Gahmuret
has been persuaded of Herzeloyde's right to have him as her
husband, he is referred to as *ir friunt* (99.29).

Wolfram's attraction to many aspects of pre-courtly life and
literature is shown here by his use of the words *wîgant*, *recke* and
degen, which were on the whole eschewed by the writers of the
high-courtly period since they belong more to the sphere of the
heroic epic. Wolfram, presenting his credentials: 'schildes ambet ist
mîn art' (115.11), consciously retains the vocabulary of an earlier
period which was more in accordance with his ideals, and thus
from this point of view he creates what is, for his day and audience,
an individual impression, as it must be interpreted as a sign of a
deep-rooted criticism of contemporary society and its ideals. Up
to the death of Gaschier Gahmuret is three times referred to as *der*

---

[1] 6.20, 14.15, 15.2, 19.10.20, 36.3, 59.29, 60.1, 68.30, 76.16, 82.22.

[2] 22.6, 30.7, 34.30, 35.7.18, 50.25, 53.21, 62.29, 63.10, 72.4.14, 92.16.

[3] 20.20, 23.30, 24.15, 26.1, 32.27, 33.12, 34.15, 35.9.14, 42.9, 43.13, 44.9, 70.26, 61.30.

[4] 62.16, 68.3, 69.1.25, 75.23, 79.27.

wîgant (5.23, 12.15, 39.1) and then once more in the description of his death on the field of battle (106.18). He is called *recke* immediately after meeting Belacane, when, during the night, he longs for *rîterschaft* (35.29), and after hearing of his brother's death he implicitly refers to himself as a *recke* when he renounces the anchor of his arms (99.15 f.). The word *degen* is combined with *guot* (30.4) and twice with *wert* (63.13, 64.7), the former being used at Gahmuret's reception in Patelamunt and the two latter on the occasion of his entry into Kanvoleis. These terms are well distributed through books I and II, though a considerable gap occurs over the greater part of book II, where Gahmuret is usually referred to in more conventional terms or as king of Zazamanc.

In addition to being linked, after his first marriage, with the land of Zazamanc Gahmuret is once qualified as *dirre Franzois* (37.17) and many times as coming from the kingdom of Anschouwe. It is by no means unambiguous what significance Wolfram attached to Anschouwe (which is generally taken to mean Anjou), and there is a great diversity of opinion among scholars about it. It is possible that the influence of the personality of Richard the Lionheart upon the formation of the character of Gahmuret, as postulated by Panzer and Snelleman,[1] may have led to the introduction of Anschouwe as the native country of Gahmuret, but this is mere conjecture. The frequency with which the term occurs, however, is a clear indication of its importance, and it is not only used with reference to Gahmuret, but also to Galoes and above all to Feirefiz.[2] Several times Gahmuret is mentioned as being an *Anschevîn*,[3] and then there are the variations *der junge Anschevîn* (11.1, 14.8, 17.9), *ein Anschevîn von hôher art* (21.13), *der von Anschouwe* (76.20) and *der helt von Anschouwe* (41.17). The application of the term to Gahmuret is found most in book I and then in later references in the Parzival story; there is a gap during the greater part of book II in which Gahmuret is usually called *der künec von Zazamanc*. The

---

[1] Panzer, *op. cit.* pp. 63 ff.; Willem Snelleman, *Das Haus Anjou und der Orient in Wolframs 'Parzival'* (Nijkerk, 1941), esp. p. 37.

[2] See the chapter on Feirefiz, p. 439.

[3] 6.26, 38.11, 40.2, 98.18, 106.6, 325.20.

word has, however, the value of a kinship motif, since it is used almost as a surname with both Gahmuret and Feirefiz, and it is this usage which leads Parzival to recognize Feirefiz as his brother.

Family relationships are, as has already been mentioned, important in the poem as a whole. In this respect Gahmuret is more significant as being the point of reference for Parzival as *Gahmuretes kint*, etc., but he is himself twice denoted as *fil li roy Gandîn* (10.15, 40.13). This is of small importance in comparison with the extent to which the relationship between Gahmuret and Parzival is exploited in the later part of the poem, but it provides an instance of the same technique being used at an early stage in the romance.

The third group of synonyms includes terms which give a little more information about the internal aspect of character, though many of these are conventional and will be immediately recognized as such. Thus, the adjective *wert* is combined with the name Gahmuret, with *man* and other nouns and occurs frequently.[1] Similarly, the word *küene* is found four times (54.17, 58.23, 59.14, 64.28). There are, however, several terms which express rather more meaning: *gehiure* (21.26, 38.21), *stolz* (37.18, 54.17. 74.25), *fier* (61.28, 81.11), *gevüege* (13.9), *reine* (107.4), *sigehaft* (38.10), *muotes rîch* (18.17), *der minnen geltes lôn* (23.7), *des site man gein prîse maz* (145.3), and the two symbolic references *der den anker treit* (79.15) and *der anker* (80.5), which will be treated in a different context. The use of the words *wert* and *küene* is purely conventional and cannot be given any further significance, but the others have more point and the ones which occur only once obviously can have greater weight attached to them as pin-pointing a particular aspect of Gahmuret's character.

DESCRIPTIVE PASSAGES

In the course of books I and II there are several passages of descriptive characterization, which may be divided into groups centring on particular events: first of all, Gahmuret's arrival in Patelamunt

[1] 14.11, 15.4, 22.25, 40.29, 55.11, 63.13, 61.18, 64.7, 65.19, 73.3, 83.3, 89.1, 117.15, 808.26.

(18.5–19.16 and 21.11–22.2); secondly, Gahmuret prepared for battle (36.11–37.7); then three passages dealing with his arrival in Kanvoleis (62.3–20, 63.2–25 and 64.22–30), once more readiness for the fray; and lastly, a summary of his many achievements up to the conclusion of the *vesperîe* (85.10–86.4). From this catalogue it can be seen that all these passages are intimately connected with Gahmuret's prowess as a knight and serve to emphasize his deeds. These form the principal method of characterization in this part of the poem, by a clear delineation of the pageantry and colour of the background against which they are set. Indeed, the two processes are so closely fused that neither of them can be regarded separately except to the detriment of a real understanding of the work. The descriptions form such an integral part of the unfolding of the action that they must be understood in this context as a completely natural, obvious technique for the poet to use. There is nowhere any suggestion that Wolfram as it were inserted these passages as a deliberate, conscious means by which to deepen the psychology of his hero. On the contrary, the descriptions are on the whole static and external in their points of reference, and all but one of them are exclusively concerned with his outstanding ability as a knight. The last one (85.10 ff.) is the only one which touches on the conflict of *minne* and *âventiure*, which is the corner-stone of Gahmuret's nature, and this is scarcely more than implicit in the context. Because of their place within the action these passages are not to be looked upon as a completely different mode of characterization, though there are certain features which they do bring out more clearly than is the case elsewhere by the very fact of pin-pointing, heightening, and slowing down the progress of the plot.

In discussing the various descriptions it would be both laborious and largely unprofitable to try to distinguish rigidly between those lines and phrases which refer solely to Gahmuret's external appearance and those which are concerned with portrayal of his inner character, with his moral position and his psychology. These two aspects must be viewed in conjunction with each other since they frequently, indeed almost always, overlap. Words which are applied to outward features, to clothing, battle-standards and so on, very often are meant as external signs of an internal condition.[1] It is a characteristic trait of medieval life and literature that a thing may appear in more than one function, that is, it can appear as itself and also as a symbol or outward manifestation of something else, some idea or quality. This is particularly true of religious literature, especially of mystical writings, and the medieval love of symbolism and allegory is patently obvious in such works as the *Physiologus* and the commentaries on the *Song of Solomon*, but it is by no means confined to the religious sphere. The dictum of St Irenaeus 'nihil vacuum neque sine signo apud Deum'[2] finds expression almost everywhere, as symbolism and allegory are the best medium for expressing philosophical, metaphysical and religious ideas to people unaccustomed to reading, but impressionable to visual imagery.

The idea that outward appearance correlates with inner character is so much taken for granted that it is difficult to find passages which explicitly state that this is so. It is rather through differences from the courtly ideal that this is made clear. Thus, for example, in Hartmann's *Iwein* the nakedness of Iwein symbolizes the fact that he is at this time lacking in all the attributes of courtliness (3231 ff., 3359 f.). Pfaffe Konrad, in his description of Genelun in the *Rolandslied*, implies by his criticism of the usage that exterior beauty can, for the courtly generation, normally be equated with uprightness of character: 'Under sconem schade luzet, / iz en ist nicht allez golt daz da glizzit' (1958 f.). Many other passages in other works imply, however, that a splendid appearance indicates worthiness of character (for example *König Rother* 203 ff., 218 ff., *Nibelungenlied* st. 63 ff., 343 ff., *Erec* 732 ff.).

[1] Cf. Helmut de Boor, *Geschichte der deutschen Literatur*, Bd. II. *Die höfische Literatur. Vorbereitung, Blüte, Ausklang* (Munich, 1953), p. 9. 'Wir begreifen höfische Dichtung nur, wenn wir uns darüber klar sind, daß für das Denken der Zeit eine unmittelbare Rückbezüglichkeit zwischen dem Innen und dem Außen besteht. Schönheit der Erscheinung ist Ausdruck eines schönen Innern; nur der edle Mensch kann schön sein.'

[2] Cf. Johan Huizinga, *The Waning of the Middle Ages* (London, 1924), pp. 183 f.

The many descriptions of Gahmuret's outward magnificence are therefore to be taken as implicit commentaries on his inner character. The exterior physical beauty is the manifestation of an inward nobility of soul. Although there are sections which treat his character in terms of a psychological approach, this occurs fairly infrequently. It must always be borne in mind that Wolfram was here only creating a background for the history of Parzival, where questions of psychology and inner development loom much larger, and too detailed a characterization of Gahmuret would have detracted from the actual purpose of the whole romance. Thus, Wolfram confines his attention to those aspects which serve to bring out the basic function of Gahmuret as the father of Parzival and illuminate the processes of heredity.

Just as it is undesirable to distinguish between internal and external features of characterization, the descriptions of him, retinue cannot be separated from the passages which refer to him alone and to his personal appearance. He is seen as the leader of a community, and this community reflects on his own character, strengthening his appearance by qualities and splendour which in the last analysis they derive from him. As far as it is possible, however, the references to Gahmuret alone will be treated separately in order to show the extent of the interdependence of the two.

Of the two passages which occur in connexion with Gahmuret's entry into Patelamunt one is concerned exclusively with him, the other only partially. The initial few lines of description depict him in terms of his heraldry, a feature to be dealt with at length in a later section, and the fact that these arms were gained from the caliph of Baldac on account of his prowess in battle against the two brothers Ipomedon and Pompeius is highly significant. The richness of the arms indicates the extent of Gahmuret's intrepidity, and they provide a point of recognition for the queen's marshal at the battle of Alexandrie, which is summed up in the line: 'sînen prîs dâ niemen widerwac' (18.16). The description succeeding this is introduced by a similarly evocative couplet, which with its two expressions *muotes rîche* and *behagenlîche*, gathers up the main traits of Gahmuret's character and sets forth his strength and confidence.

The second passage consists of a report by the burgrave to Belacane and is couched in more personal terms relating to Gahmuret alone. The burgrave portrays him in glowing language, primarily from his knowledge of Gahmuret's performance as a vassal of the caliph at the battle of Alexandrie, and after having characterized him as *ein degen fier* and mentioned his noble *Anschêvin* blood, breaks forth in a eulogy of his technique in battle:

> âvoy, wie wênic wirt gespart
> sîn lîp, swâ man in læzet an!
> wie rehter dar unde dan
> entwîchet unde kêret!
> die vînde er schaden lêret.
> Ich sach in strîten schône,
> dâ die Babylône
> Alexandrîe lœsen solten,
> unde dô si dannen wolten
> den bâruc trîben mit gewalt.
> waz ir dâ nider wart gevalt
> an der schumphentiure!
> da begienc der gehiure
> mit sîme lîbe sölhe tât,
> sine heten vliehens keinen rât.   (21.14 ff.)

To make a worthy end to this description, which is in itself a miniature characterization of Gahmuret in action, the burgrave proclaims that his fame extends over many lands.

These two passages provide the introduction of Gahmuret to the queen and the people of Patelamunt and are followed by a third, which depicts him ready for battle on behalf of Belacane (36.11–37.7). This is much the same as any description of a knight prepared for battle. There is little to mark his physical appearance as being in any way strikingly different from that of any other knight apart from the remark that his battle-tunic is of green *achmardî*, his cloak likewise, his horse's cover of green satin, his *schiltriemen* a dazzling belt of costly jewels and the buckle of *rôt golt, geliutert in dem fiure*. Previously to this we find the phrase: 'aldâ wîp unde man verjach, / sine gesæhn nie helt sô wünneclîch' (36.18 f.), but the effect of this pronouncement is cancelled out by the medieval predilection for hyperbole, which instead of making the hero unique, as it should by its literal sense, merely includes him in an ideal type. This statement, however, is immediately followed by the line: 'ir gote im solten sîn gelîch' (36.20), which while retaining the same intention of idealization imparts an individual note by the reference to the gods of the people of Zazamanc. The equation of the idealized knight with a god is a significant early foreshadowing of the incident in book III where the young Parzival confuses the first knights that he sees with the God about whom his mother had just been telling him. To the ignorant people of Zazamanc and the inexperienced Parzival the perfect knight incorporates their limited conception of a deity. Apart from this reference, however, it is purely the clothing which, in this particular context, distinguishes Gahmuret from the rest of his kind.

The description of Gahmuret on his entry into Kanvoleis (63.13 ff.) is similarly conceived in conventional terms. It could indeed scarcely be otherwise, since there were definite prescriptions for knightly appearance. Individualization is only possible in motivation and details of the action and where clothing makes outward differences evident. So far as physical appearance is concerned there is no need to individualize, as all that is required is that Gahmuret should measure up to the high standards of court-liness. Of this Hans Naumann writes:

> Der leibliche Wunschtyp verlangt Blondheit, Helläugigkeit, lichte Farbe der Haut ... Die große Manessische Minnesingerhandschrift gibt die Figuren von 468 Männern und Frauen der staufischen Zeit, wie sie sich vorstellt; davon sind 384 blond gemalt; 74 sind behelmt, verkappt, verschleiert oder verhüllt, so daß man den Typ nicht erkennt, 6 sind grau oder weiß als alte Leute, nur drei sind schwarz, darunter einer, der damit als Heide gekennzeichnet ist.[1]

[1] Hans Naumann, *Die Kultur im Zeitalter des Rittertums* (Potsdam, no date [1938]), p. 117.

We find that Gahmuret fits into this general picture: he has ruby, burning-red lips, blond curly hair, in build he is neither too fat nor too thin, and then comes the phrase which subsumes all courtly attributes: 'sîn lip was allenthalben clâr' (63.19). In addition to this we find details of his clothing—boots over his bare legs, a costly hat, a mantle of green velvet, a white tunic with a sable fur on top. Green and white were the main colours of his heraldic arms.

In the same context of the entry into Kanvoleis there occurs a further description by a young knight, who comes riding up and reports to the king of Spain that he has seen Gahmuret, but this adds little to what has already been observed. The adjectives *fier* and *küene* are applied to him, but otherwise the description is mainly heraldic and portrays the hero among his retinue as an opponent to be reckoned with.

The splendour of Gahmuret's physical appearance is emphasized in a passage describing him prepared for entering the *vesperie* at Kanvoleis (70.13 ff.). The greater portion of this is again heraldic in conception, but the costliness of his clothes and armour with their ornamentation of gold, precious stones, sable and rich furs from oriental sources is also stressed, and these features underline the position of worldly honour to which Gahmuret has attained. The brightness of his appearance, a further mark of his excellence, is depicted in striking imagery:

> ob i'n geprüeven künne,
> er schein als ob hie brünne
> bî der naht ein queckes fiwer.
> verblichen varwe was im tiwer;
> sîn glast die blicke niht vermeit:
> ein bœsez oug sich dran versneit. (71.11 ff.)

Apart from this, little is added to the previous descriptions.

The last description of Gahmuret alone (85.10 ff.) consists of a catalogue of his deeds as Kaylet sees them, such a formidable list of accomplishments that Kaylet is at a loss to understand why Gahmuret should be unhappy. His knightly prowess has now achieved a world setting: he has won the hand of Herzeloyde and her kingdom; Britons and Irishmen, men from France and Brabant recognize his supremacy; Brandelidelin, Lähelin, Hardiz, Schaffillor, all relied on Gahmuret to help them out of their difficulties; Razalic the Moor became his vassal. It seems to the outside observer that nothing more is necessary for Gahmuret's complete happiness, but in fact he is nonetheless unhappy. Later, this is clarified by reference to the conflict of *minne* and *âventiure*, but in all the descriptions mentioned above the sole theme is that of *âventiure*. The other side of Gahmuret's character is never explicitly depicted.

As a supplement to the descriptions referring specifically to Gahmuret the entries into both Patelamunt and Kanvoleis provide the background of a colourful retinue against which Gahmuret's own magnificence is set. His followers act as a reflection of his own achievement. Descriptions applied to them and particularly to their social and moral worth can be transferred from them to Gahmuret. Thus, the precise detail which is lavished on the procession indicates the extent of the power and respect which he enjoys and adds to the already considerable effect of the account of Gahmuret alone.

The cavalcade entering Patelamunt comprises ten mules, twenty squires riding after them, pages, cooks and boys, twelve high-born young men following, Saracens of good breeding and gentle conduct, eight horses veiled with taffeta (*zindâl*), a ninth bearing Gahmuret's saddle, a squire carrying his shield, a trumpeter, a drummer, flautists, three fiddlers, and last of all Gahmuret himself and his dearly beloved sailor. It is a motley train, consisting of men from both East and West, a fact which shows Gahmuret as accepted and honoured in both the Christian and the Islamic world. The expressions *stolz, wol geborn, guotiu zuht* and *süeze siten* all clearly demonstrate the nobility of conduct proper to the retinue of so worthy a knight as Gahmuret.

Similarly, his entry into Kanvoleis, where likewise he is not at once recognized, but creates a deep impression with his suite, is described in a combination of outward splendour and corresponding inward good breeding. His men are *kurtoys, stolz, vor missewende vrî*; there are both heathens and Frenchmen among them, and 'etslîcher mag ein Anschevîn/mit sîner sprache iedoch wol sîn' (62.5 f.). In this context we find that Gahmuret's followers speak of their leader's readiness to come to the assistance of those in trouble, a customary attribute of the knight errant, and this is succeeded by the first mention of Gahmuret as king of Zazamanc. The messenger who furnishes the queen with this information also remarks on their physical appearance: 'ir muot ist stolz, ir wât ist clâr, / wol gesniten al für wâr' (62.7 f.), before continuing with a description of the magnificent tent (see above, pp. 16f), which required thirty mules to carry it and of which he asserts to the queen: 'iwer krône und iwer lant / wærn niht derfür halbez phant' (62.19 f.). This is followed by a detailed survey of the actual entry into Kanvoleis, accompanied with great pomp, music and ceremony, and the loudness of the procession evidently indicates the importance of the central figure in it:

> die hellen pusînen
> mit krache vor im gâben dôz
> von würfen und mit slegen grôz
> zwên tambûre gâben schal:
> der galm übr al die stat erhal.
> der dôn iedoch gemischet wart
> mit floytieren an der vart:
> ein reisenote si bliesen. (63.2 ff.)

These various descriptions form the usual background for Gahmuret. It is true that we see him in isolation before the *vesperîe* at Kanvoleis and that he is singled out for individual treatment even in the description of his retinue, but this would have been of considerably less effect if the strong background of his followers had not been simultaneously sketched in. When he left Anschouwe at the beginning of his career his following was much smaller—sixteen *knappen*, four young men (8.2 ff.), five strong horses, and much gold and jewels too—but this is a possession which he is *given*: it is not his own rightful property and is therefore to be considered as external to his character, at least in the first instance. On the other hand, the retinues surrounding him at Patelamunt and Kanvoleis are the proof of his own endeavour and his rise in the world's favour. In this respect therefore they form an integral part of Gahmuret's personal history and deserve a fitting place in the descriptions which Wolfram considers necessary. The two are thus to be regarded as complementary and mutually dependent.

SYMBOLIC DEVICES

Wolfram in many places makes use of symbolic devices as an aid to characterization, and the most important example of this in connexion with Gahmuret is in the matter of heraldry. After having performed services of signal merit to the caliph of Baldac, Gahmuret is given a new set of arms in recognition, which are the sign of a deserved independence and are henceforth deployed so as to contribute towards an indirect characterization through symbolism.[1] The new arms mark the achievements of his career as forged by his own personality in isolation from his family.

They consist of: vert an anchor ermine with a rope or entwined round it. Of these the anchor is the most important feature and is a device by which Gahmuret is recognized both by other characters and by the audience. It occurs in twenty-one places as a point of reference. Sometimes it is merely one anchor, sometimes three, sometimes an unspecified number, but whatever it is, the basic meaning remains unchanged: it is the symbol of wandering and adventure in search of an undefined goal, as Gahmuret himself declares when he hears of his brother's death and is called to the throne of Anschouwe: 'der anker ist ein recken zil: / den trage und nem swer der wil' (99.15 f.). With this last line and the two which precede those just quoted—'ich sol mîns vater wâpen tragn: / sîn lant mîn anker hât beslagn'—Gahmuret realizes that

---

[1] The device of the *pantel*, which Panzer is anxious to connect with Richard the Lionheart, forms part of the arms inherited by Gahmuret from his father—'dez pantel, daz sîn vater truoc, / von zoble ûf sînen schilt man sluoc' (101.7 f.)—is mentioned only once and seems to be an additional device rather than a permanent part of his arms. Cf. also Snelleman, *op. cit.*, pp. 25 f.

his lot is now to re-assume the arms of his father and put away those of his own youthful, carefree *Wanderjahre*, to settle down as the ruler of a kingdom. The change of arms indicates Gahmuret's recognition of the need to change character. This is the last mention of the word with reference to Gahmuret and marks the end of his career apart from the last battle in which he loses his life. The anchor is sewn on his clothes—'hermîn anker drûf genæt' (14.27) —at the very beginning after he has received his arms, and the clothes which Belacane presents to him similarly bear the sign: 'anker die swæren / von arâbischem golde / wârn drûfe alser wolde' (23.4 ff.). In addition there are on each *ʒindâl drî härmîn anker lieht gemâl* (64.29), and his banners are likewise marked: 'drî härmîn anker dran sô fier / daz man ir jach für rîcheit' (59.8 f.). While, clearly, the anchor is a symbol of the *recke*, it is with Gahmuret, as this last quotation shows, also intimately bound up with the idea of wealth and power through the expressions which are employed in connexion with it, viz.: *lieht hermîn* (14.17), *von arâbischem golde* (23.5), *drî härmîn anker* (59.8, 64.29), *einen anker, dâ man inne vant / verwieret edel gesteine* (70.22 f.), *ʒobelîn* (71.3), *tiwer* (98.26). Such is the importance of the word that *anker* is used as an expression which simply means 'Gahmuret', as: 'dem anker volgete nâch der strûz' (72.8), 'der anker kom doch vor an in' (73.1), 'hie kumt der anker, fîâ fî' (80.5).

The anchor is the most telling feature of Gahmuret's arms, but there are several other noteworthy details, among which are the expressions connected with wealth and power just mentioned, of which *hermîn* and *ʒobel* are the most significant. Ermine was considered in Germany as a 'Wahrzeichen geistlicher und weltlicher Herrscherwürde'[1] and further comments are to be found: 'In der Dichtung gilt das Blendendweiß seines Pelzes [sc. the ermine's] als Sinnbild sittlicher Reinheit, vgl. die Wendung: 'Der Hermelin ihres Rufs.' 'Da der Pelz seiner Kostbarkeit wegen seit dem Mittelalter zur Verzierung des Fürstenmantels diente, wurde der Zusammenstellung *Hermelin und Purpur* fast sprichwörtlich. Von hier wurde *Hermelin* Sinnbild für monarchische Herrschaft

---

[1] *Trübners Deutsches Wörterbuch*, under 'Hermelin'.

überhaupt. ....'¹ Likewise *zobel* was emblematic of princely wealth and dignity, though not to quite the same extent as ermine. Trübner merely remarks: 'Bei seiner Kleinheit und Kostbarkeit dient es meist nur zu Verbrämungen.'² In Hartmann's *Erec* it is said: 'diz was der vürsten kleit' (2012), and the *Nibelungenlied* mentions it together with ermine among the clothes of the Burgundians at the reception of Sivrit (st. 575). Ermine occurs as an actual part of the arms of Gahmuret referring to the anchor, whereas sable is not so frequently used to refer to the arms, but is more often cited as the fur accompanying the arms. The distinction is in any case not an important one as both furs indicate much the same kind of thing and occur almost exclusively in the context of the arms.

The colour symbolism of the field of Gahmuret's arms is also illuminating. According to medieval ideas green is the colour of hope and joy and is transferred during the fourteenth and fifteenth centuries to signify the beginnings of love. In *Willehalm* we find the conjunction of the two ideas 'green' and 'joy' in the line: 'mir begruonet vröude nimmer mêr' (122.26), and in the *Passional*³ we find the passage:

> swer ouch mit rechter lêre
> die grûse des gelouben
> offenlîche und tougen
> prediget und lêret
> und got dar an êret,
> daz er an im kûne ist,
> des cleit sîn billich grûne,
> die in mit vreuden ummevân.   (4.20 ff.)

Both these references give examples of green being equated with joy. This use of green as a basis for Gahmuret's arms may therefore be assumed to give an additional emphasis to the positive, joyful

---

¹ *Ibid.*
² Under 'Zobel'.
³ Quoted in Wilhelm Wackernagel, *Die Farben- und Blumensprache des Mittelalters. Kleinere Schriften*, vol. 1 (Leipzig, 1872), p. 185.

aspect of his existence, which is the mark of a true courtly knight. Green is the colour of his horses' trappings, which are 'noch grüener denne ein smârât . . . und nâch dem achmardî var' (14.20 ff.), and his tunic is also of the same colour.[1]

Closely connected with the symbolism of the arms, yet separate from it, is the concept of the *adamas* (lit. diamond or steel), which Wolfram uses to denote Gahmuret's helmet, but does not define very closely. He describes it three times, as follows: 'ûf erde niht sô guotes was, / der helm, von arde ein adamas / dicke und herte, / ame strîte ein guot geverte' (53.3 ff.); 'dô schouwet er den adamas: / daz was ein helm' (70.20 f.); 'man bant im ûf den adamas, / der dicke unde herte was' (77.23 f.). Gahmuret's anchor *ʒimierde* is fastened on top of the *adamas* and is inlaid with jewels, but the *adamas* itself remains vague and obscure. The term *adamas* is used generally as a mark of excellence, as, for example: 'ganzer tugende ein adamas' (Heinrich von Morungen, *MF* 144.27); 'stæter triuwe ein adamas' (*Der arme Heinrich* 62); 'der ie ein rehter adamas / rîterlîcher tugende was' (*Iwein* 3257 f.), and this characteristic sheds light on the fact that Gahmuret's *adamas* possesses such virtue that its power and protection can only be destroyed by magic. Under normal conditions therefore Gahmuret's strength is such that he will always emerge as victor, and this is clearly seen throughout that part of the poem in which he appears. Further elucidation is to be derived from the younger Pliny's *Historia Naturalis*, book XX, where the words occur: 'adamantem opum gaudium, infragilem omni cetera vi et invictum, sanguine hircino rumpente'. This is supported by Isidore's *Etymologiae* XVI, 13: 'hic [sc. adamans] nulli cedit materiae, nec ferro quidem nec igni, nec umquam incalescit ... Sed dum sit invictus ferri ignisque contemptor, hircino rumpitur sanguine recenti et calido maceratus, sicque multis ictibus ferri perfrangitur.'[2]

---

[1] Perhaps it is merely coincidence that Wolfram should have chosen to use the word *achmardî*, a green silken material from Arabia, among the many other things which he mentions from the East, also for the cushion on which Repanse de schoye bears the Grail.

[2] See Ernst Martin, *Wolframs von Eschenbach Parʒival und Titurel* (Halle, 1900–3), vol. 2, pp. 104 f.

The narration of the cause of Gahmuret's death is in complete accord with these authorities:

> gunêrtiu heidensch witze
> hât uns verstoln den helt guot.
> ein ritter hete bockes bluot
> genomen in ein langez glas:
> daz sluoger ûfe den adamas:
> dô wart er weicher danne ein swamp.   (105.16 ff.)

This property of the *adamas* to withstand all normal attacks is the sign of Gahmuret's outstanding ability and at the same time offers a reason plausible to a medieval audience for his death. It is a feature with considerable power for unifying various traits of Gahmuret's character and accounting satisfactorily for his fall.

This heraldic and battle symbolism is a clear indication of individuality. Heraldry itself arose as a means for distinguishing knights in battle, and as such it is of great historical significance as well as being, for us, a method of characterization in a wide sense. Heraldry was not a matter of individuality *in vacuo*, nor is the individualization of Gahmuret, still less that of Parzival: family ties and the claims of heredity show themselves unmistakably in heraldic arms. Their individuality is, as everywhere in medieval culture, an individuality within the community.

GAHMURET IN ACTION

The most important part of the technique of any author's characterization is to be found in the expression of a personality through action and speech, as it is in the tensions of action and the workings of the mind that characters come to life. Description alone tends to remain static, whereas depiction in action gives a more adequate representation of the reality of a person's existence and, unless it is confined to one particular kind of action, allows of a fuller and rounder understanding of the character involved.

Gahmuret is viewed in a series of different situations in the poem, through which it is possible to see the development of the portrayal of his nature. Here there is a distinct difference between him and Parzival. The personality of Parzival is presented in its development from childhood to manhood and from an understanding of the world of Arthurian knights to an appreciation of human and religious values and an insight into the world of the Grail. Of course, these elements are latent in him from the beginning on account of his heredity, but we are allowed to see them unfold as the story progresses. With Gahmuret, on the other hand, we have a character which is already formed at the outset of the book (contrast the characterization of Riwalin, who is first of all depicted as a child, *Tristan* 245 ff.). With him we see a detailed exposition of character through action and are able to piece together times of information so as to form a more or less complete picture of a mature personality.

The introduction of Gahmuret into the poem occurs immediately after the prologue. Wolfram comments generally on the French custom of inheritance, explaining:

> der altest bruoder solde hân
> sîns vater ganzen erbeteil.
> daz was der jungern unheil,
> daz in der tôt die pflihte brach
> als in ir vater leben verjach.
> dâ vor was ez gemeine:
> sus hâtz der alter eine.   (5.4 ff.)

After having justified this practice, not in use in Germany, Wolfram tells how Gahmuret in this way lost land and castles. Following this particularization, in which he picks out Gahmuret with the three telling words *kiusche*,[1] *vrech* and *wîgant*, Wolfram describes the assembly of the princes of the realm, come to receive their fiefs from Galoes, and how they entreat the king to act in a spirit of *bruoderlîche triwe* towards Gahmuret. Interestingly enough, Gahmuret himself remains quite passive in this context. The king

---

[1] It is significant that Gahmuret should be described from the beginning by the word *kiusche*, since one of the striking features of Wolfram's ethical attitude is his development of the idea of *kiusche* as that which subsumes and epitomizes all virtue. Moreover, *kiusche* is essential to the knights who guard the Grail (493.23 f.), and Anfortas' suffering is caused through his having desired *minne* outside the bounds of *kiusche* (472.29 f.).

is moved by the pleas of the princes on his brother's behalf and makes a generous offer to share his wealth and let Gahmuret be his *ingesinde*. This, however, is not what Gahmuret was wanting, and he can contain himself no longer. He explains his poverty-stricken state and declares that had he wanted to become the king's *ingesinde* he would have spoken for himself. His aim is quite the opposite:

> ich wil kêren in diu lant.
> ich hân ouch ê ein teil gevarn.
> ob mich gelücke wil bewarn,
> so erwirbe ich guotes wîbes gruoz.
> ob ich ir dar nâch dienen muoz,
> und ob ich des wirdec bin,
> sô rætet mir mîn bester sin
> daz ichs mit rehten triwen phlege. (8.8 ff.)

This sets the tone for the rest of the romance in so far as it gives a concise account of the motivating forces of Gahmuret's existence —his delight in adventure and his service on behalf of *minne*. The king expresses his sorrow at his brother's intention to depart, but gives him all that he desires for his independence and praises his manly qualities. Gahmuret then takes leave from his mother, relating once more his purpose. The future is clouded with uncertainty, but the key to the eventual outcome of his adventures has been struck, and the first of three sorrowful departures has already taken place.

Gahmuret is first depicted in relation to his own family, reduced to an inferior position of poverty through outward circumstances beyond his control, but nonetheless exercising charity towards his brother and mother and receiving their tokens of love in return, though in smaller measure than was intended. Relationships are intimate, but restrictive because they do not coincide with Gahmuret's wishes. His character is shown in somewhat abstract terms in order to set the scene for the later course of events; his sense of adventure and his aim of service are not directed towards any known enterprise or person. His nature demands that he should serve as a knight and as a lover, and his behaviour is directed towards finding a suitable object of such service. His departure from his own family is the prototype of his later leave-takings, which take place for exactly the same reasons, that is, in order to find a more satisfactory object of his desire for both *minne* and *âventiure*. The parallel with Parzival's departure from Herzeloyde is obvious and the result in the case of the mother is the same (see above, p. 17).

The introduction of Gahmuret as one of a body of people who lost their possessions through the vicissitudes of inheritance might have led to Gahmuret's being represented as one of a type, but the particular circumstances surrounding the general case are sufficient to make it clear that this is not so. The details which ensue demonstrate that this is an occasion for him to show his character in its two developed forms. The depiction of his nature shows that all that was necessary was something to set in motion the intentions which were already there as an integral part of Gahmuret's make-up.

To what extent, however, does Gahmuret typify the courtly knight, whose aims of *minne* and *âventiure* are identical with his? Is there in fact anything which makes him more than a personification of these two forces? The *Erec* and *Iwein* of Hartmann von Aue are exercises in the search for *mâʒe*, and Gahmuret's adventures may also be looked upon in this light, but with the difference that he does not achieve, even at the end, a genuine balance between *minne* and *âventiure*. Wolfram's aim in this section of the poem is not first and foremost didactic, as Hartmann's always was and Wolfram's was later in the character of Parzival: rather, he was concerned to show the painful results of the forces of heredity, where *minne* and *âventiure* were equally strong. Gahmuret never finds a solution to the problem; this comes later with Parzival. The background to books I and II is courtly, as the figure of Ampflise more than anything puts beyond question, but it is not an attempt to depict courtly virtues as a model to follow. In this respect again Parzival progresses further than his father and moves through the courtly world to that of the Grail, so that Gahmuret is definitely subordinated to Parzival while yet being characterized as the ideal of the courtly knight.

After his departure from Anschouwe Gahmuret embarks on a journey to the East, knowledge of which had been given to the West by the Crusades, and spends the greater part of book I there, though not in the strict geographical sense, since the names of the lands and towns through which he passes are based on both genuine and fantastic geography and even include certain German-sounding names. The significance of the extent of Gahmuret's travels in general has been commented on at length by Marianne Wynn:

> We are led to believe that Gahmuret has explored lands so distant that their very names suggest the borderline between reality and fairyland. *Zaʒamanc* still suggests exotic distance to modern ears and we may assume that its evocative quality roused the imagination of the medieval audience whose known world was more restricted than ours, to an even larger extent. *Arâbî* cannot be identified, nor can *Zaʒamanc*[1] or *Pâtelamunt*. Commentators have regretfully admitted defeat trying to relate these and others to geographical reality. They omitted to consider whether they were ever meant to be identified. Unrelated to reality, side by side with names from the factual world, they fulfil a twofold narrative function—appealing to the sense of wonder by their evocative power and thus eliminating the need for direct description. Based on reality they would become poetically meaningless.[2]

Against this oriental background we see Gahmuret for the first time in action and are able to assess his qualifications as a knight. He becomes the vassal of the most powerful lord in the East, the caliph of Baldac, and immediately performs him a service of great merit in conquering the two lords of Babylon, Pompeius and Ipomidon, who had wrested Nineveh out of the caliph's hand. At this stage Wolfram is content merely to say: 'jâ nam nâch dienste aldâ den solt, / Gahmuret der werde man' (14.10 f.), and leaves the rest to his audience's imagination, but a longer account of his exploits at Alexandrie is given by the burgrave to Belacane when Gahmuret is presented to the queen (see above, pp. 26 f.). By the time Gahmuret arrives at Patelamunt he has visited a considerable

---

[1] Snelleman (*op. cit.*, p. 83) suggests it is an adaptation of 'Casa Mansa' and means 'the king's palace'.

[2] Marianne Wynn, *The Poetic Structure of Wolfram von Eschenbach's 'Parʒival'. A Study of the Natural Setting* (Diss. Cambridge, 1953), pp. 47 ff.

number of places—Marroch, Persîâ, Arâbîe, Dâmasc, Hâlap and
Arâbî—so that he 'establishes his chivalrous fame throughout the
East before the meeting with Belacâne.'[1] He learns of the reason
for the siege and at once offers his service (17.9 ff.). Although he
finds little of absorbing interest in Zazamanc, he takes up his
quarters there and makes a confident entry into the town to the
sound of much music. First of all he is received by the burgrave
and then presented to the queen, all of which takes place with great
enthusiasm. The queen is obviously overwhelmed with feelings of
love from the beginning, but this is stronger on her part than on
Gahmuret's, as becomes clearer later:

> der küneginne rîche
> ir ougen fuogten hôhen pîn,
> dô si gesach den Anschevîn.
> der was sô minneclîche gevar,
> daz er entslôz ir herze gar,
> ez wære ir liep oder leit:
> daz beslôz dâ vor ir wîpheit. (23.22 ff.)

Then comes the sign confirming the respect which she bears him:
'ein wênc si gein im dô trat, / ir gast si sich küssen bat' (23.29 f.).
In answer to her praises Gahmuret protests his readiness to remove
what has been or is causing her pain, but declares with humility:
'ich pin niht wan einec man' (24.25). Belacane explains about the
death of her lover Isenhart, which his people wrongly blame her
for and therefore are attacking Patelamunt, so that Gahmuret
knows what is at stake.

During this time his love for Belacane is aroused, and when she
waits on him at table her service displeases him. When night comes
and they take leave of each other on retiring to bed, the love which
earlier was unequal is now mutual:

> si nam urloup, dô gienc si dan
> aber hin wider für ir gast.
> des herze truoc ir minnen last.
> daz selbe ouch ir von im geschach;
> des ir herze unde ir ouge jach:
> diu muosens mit ir phlihte hân. (34.14)

[1] Marianne Wynn, *op. cit.*, p. 46.

The way in which this manifests itself physically in Gahmuret is described variously, showing the extent of joy and pain which *minne* causes him, both on its own account and because it conflicts with his desire for *âventiure*. He is unable to sleep for the emotional agitation:

> den helt verdrôz
> daz sô lanc was diu naht.
> in brâhte dicke in unmaht
> diu swarze Mœrinne,
> des landes küneginne.
> er want sich dicke alsam ein wit,
> daz im krachten diu lit.
> strît und minne was sîn ger. (35.18 ff.)

This last line sums up all the tensions in him at this time, as indeed generally. But Wolfram does not leave it at this: he describes the conflict in a number of ways, so as to emphasize the importance of it in Gahmuret's character:

> sîn herze gap von stôzen schal,
> wand ez nâch rîterschafte swal.
> Daz begunde dem recken
> sîne brust bêde erstrecken,
> sô di senwen tuot daz armbrust.
> dâ was ze dræte sîn gelust. (35.27 ff.)

At this stage the emotion is expressed in external forms, but it is none the less real for that, and although we find the usual contrast of *liebe* and *leit* expressed as: 'der helt was trûric unde frô' (34.30), the imagery which Wolfram uses afterwards is of a more personal nature. A comparison with the Condwiramurs episode points a contrast in that Parzival's first night in her castle was not spent in the same love-torments and that their love developed only afterwards.

The duel between Gahmuret and Hiuteger is dealt with very briefly. Gahmuret declares who he is in the battle, and Hiuteger immediately surrenders. Gaschier is disposed of in equally summary terms, and the capitulation of the entire opposing army ensues. The brevity of the combat unequivocally demonstrates Gahmuret's superiority both in actual technique and in moral worth. Moreover, he similarly overcomes Razalic, one of the Moorish princes, and becomes king of the land of Zazamanc by his marriage to Belacane. At this point the question of family relationships again emerges, as several of the participants on the opposing side are members of the family to which Gahmuret belongs, and the recognition of this fact makes further combat impossible. Gahmuret makes a generous settlement of the entire situation, sharing out gifts with exceeding liberality 'als al die boume trüegen golt' (53.18), and the guests then depart for their homes. The action here can do no more than extol Gahmuret's virtues as a warrior and a knight, and the last episode illustrates his nobility of mind and his generosity. There is otherwise little that can be expressed in such terms as to distinguish Gahmuret completely from all other heroes of this type who are successful in their enterprises and just towards their opponents.

A test comes at the end of the first book, after all the guests have returned. Gahmuret is driven to deceit in that he allows his people to believe he is planning an expedition to Azagouc, when he is actually contemplating deserting Belacane in search once more of adventure. The tension within him is extreme:

> daz er niht rîterschefte vant,
> des was sîn freude sorgen phant.
> Doch was im daz swarze wîp
> lieber dan sîn selbes lîp. (54.19 ff.)

The love of adventure is too much for him, and even though Belacane is twelve weeks pregnant he feels compelled to leave her, fleeing in secret because he cannot bear the thought of explaining his position to her, so great is his regard for her and his understanding of her sorrow and so great also is his moral cowardice. Consequently he writes a letter to inform her of what he has not the courage to tell her face to face. He confesses the unworthiness of his action in taking flight: 'ich pin dirre verte ein diep: / die muose ich dir durch jâmer steln' (55.22 f.), but tries to excuse himself on the grounds that Belacane is not baptized. The question of baptism had never arisen between them earlier, as the queen laments the fact after his flight and says she would willingly have been baptized and lived her life according to Gahmuret's religion. In his letter Gahmuret also gives a complete account of his heredity and incorporation into the Arthurian scheme, claiming descendance from the fairy Terdelaschoye's union with Mazadan, so that even though he does not himself remain with Belacane his son will know the kind of family to which his father belonged. The reason for Gahmuret's departure, however, lies deeper than the excuse which he gives would lead us to believe, since he himself is not convinced of the same argument when it is put to him by Herzeloyde. Adventure is the ruling feature of his life; all else is secondary. Where he has no opportunity for *rîterschaft*, *minne* alone cannot hold him. This is what makes him say of Ampflise: 'jâ diu ist mîn wâriu frouwe' (94.21), since it is with her alone that the full possibilities of *âventiure* are granted him. Once this is understood, the flight from Belacane and the difficulties of the marriage with Herzeloyde can be seen in their correct perspective.

The problem of *minne* becomes most acute with Herzeloyde after the *vesperîe* at Kanvoleis. Gahmuret has won the hand of Herzeloyde through his success at the tournament, but is unwilling to marry her, his first reaction being to remain faithful to Belacane despite his having deserted her. He denies the rumour that he left her on account of her black skin (perhaps here the statement of the *sponsa* in the *Song of Solomon* i. 5, 'Nigra sum, sed formosa', had a certain influence) and extols her purity and generosity towards him, while at the same time seeking to find reasons for his conduct:

> nein, ich muoz bî riwen sîn:
> ich sen mich nâch der künegîn.
> ich liez ze Pâtelamunt
> dâ von mir ist mîn herze wunt,
> in reiner art ein süeze wîp.
> ir werdiu kiusche mir den lîp
> nâch ir minne jâmers mant.
> si gap mir liute unde lant.

mich tuot frô Belakâne
manlîcher freuden âne:
ez ist doch vil manlîch,
swer minnen wankes schamet sich.
der frouwen huote mich ûf pant,
daz ich niht rîterschefte vant:
dô wânde ich daz mich rîterschaft
næm von ungemüetes kraft.
der hân ich hie ein teil getân.
nu wænt manc ungewisser man
daz mich ir swerze jagte dane:
die sah ich für die sunnen ane.
ir wîplîch prîs mir füeget leit:
si ist (ein) bukel ob der werdekeit.   (90.17 ff.)

In this passage Gahmuret realizes that his nature involves two contradictory elements, that the two cannot be satisfied together and yet that neither alone can be the essence of his existence. This is the heart of his problem, and when he is confronted with the decision of the knights in council as to what should be the issue of the problem (since it is impossible for Gahmuret to decide what is necessary for the later development of the plot according to the lines marked out by Chrétien on account of his desire to be faithful to Belacane (94.5 ff.)), he has to make a condition for his marriage to Herzeloyde, namely that he should be allowed to dispense with *huote* (cf. 90.29 f.) and also be able to take part once a month in tournaments. From the point of view of logical characterization this is an unsatisfactory conclusion, since it is effected by a *deus ex machina* amd overrides Gahmuret's genuine feelings of love towards the queen of Patelamunt despite the blackness of her skin and the fact of her not being a Christian. But while this means that Gahmuret here is to a certain extent the product of the exigencies of the plot, he is not made into a sheer puppet of the author. On the contrary, Wolfram does his utmost to make his action understandable and create a real and self-consistent character, not reducing him to the stature of a hero entirely conditioned by outward circumstances.

In his attempts to escape marrying Herzeloyde Gahmuret had

pleaded his previous marriage to Belacane and, in desperation, the
fact that a *vesperíe* had taken the place of the tournament, by which
he hoped that the queen of Waleis would allow him this way out
of his dilemma (95.14 ff. and 22 ff.), but Herzeloyde herself considered Ampflise as her more dangerous rival.

Ampflise[1] exerts a strong influence on Gahmuret's career without ever actually being personally introduced into the poem;
we are never shown her coming into immediate contact with
Gahmuret. Wolfram refers to her on several occasions, and during
the tournament at Kanvoleis she is represented by her chaplain
and three messenger princes (87.17 ff.). Her part in the poem is
that of Gahmuret's *Minneherrin*, to whom he owes a lasting loyalty
despite his vacillations at the time of his marriage with Herzeloyde.
Hans Naumann writes of her:

> Klar und deutlich steht Gahmuret jeweilig zwischen zwei streng
> geschiedenen Sphären, zwischen seiner jeweiligen Gattin und seiner
> Minneherrin Ampflise. Von Ampflise hat er sein Rittertum, für sie hat
> er sich zum Ritter erzogen, sie ist seine wahre Herrin, ihr gilt der
> Dienst seiner hohen Minne; tiefste Sehnsucht ruft ihn zu ihr (98.6).
> Als sie ihn heiraten will, kann er dies um der ritterlichen Idee willen
> verweigern (97.25), in deren Dienste er doch für sie steht. Rittertum
> und Frauendienst um die Minne Ampflisens sind ihm durchaus iden-
> tisch und zwingen ihn recht instruktiv zweimal, seine Ehefrau zu
> verlassen, nacheinander nämlich Belakanen und Herzeloyden, so innig
> er mit der anderen Seite seines Wesens diese in ehelicher Liebe liebt.
> Nicht die Existenz Ampflisens, die über alle Ehen hinweg seine Herrin
> bleibt, sondern die Belakanens, seiner ersten Frau, macht ihn zunächst
> so abweisend allen Eheabsichten Herzeloydens gegenüber. Schließlich
> stirbt er, entflohen den Gattinnen, im Ritterdienst Ampflisens, der
> allein ihm kein Problem ist.[2]

There is in fact no opposition between the idea of service to
Ampflise and marriage to Herzeloyde if the ideal of *hôhe minne*,
i.e. the relationship of a knight to a married lady not his wife, is
adhered to. Problems only arise when Ampflise, on the death of

---

[1] Snelleman, *op. cit.*, pp. 26 ff., considers that Aloysia, the youngest daughter
of Louis VII, was the historical model for Ampflise.

[2] *Op. cit.*, p. 138.

the king of France, requests Gahmuret to become her husband (77.1 ff.), thus dissolving the former type of relationship. This Herzeloyde will not tolerate: she has offered her hand in marriage to the winner of the tournament and cannot allow a former *Minneherrin* to usurp her rightful place. She regards Ampflise as being a more powerful opponent than Belacane, since the heathen queen is, for her, automatically disqualified through not possessing Christian baptism, but the relationship with a *Minneherrin* cannot be allowed to take the place of that with a wife. She in fact wants to assume the function of a *Minneherrin* (88.27) but under the conditions of marriage. This, however, does not happen: Gahmuret remains faithful to Ampflise, provided the relationship continues specifically as one of *hôhe minne*, and immediately after his marriage to Herzeloyde he sends word by the persuasive chaplain and the messengers that he will be Ampflise's knight, adding: 'ob mir alle krône wærn bereit, / ich hân nâch ir mîn hœhste leit' (98.5 f.). The *âventiure* of his life is inseparably bound with the ideal of *rîterschaft*, which he received from Ampflise (12.2 ff., 78.17 ff., 95.1 ff., 97.25 ff.), and not even the high estate of marriage can nullify this for him. So long as the two ideals of *minne* with *âventiure* and *minne* with marriage can be kept on different planes, the problem is—temporarily—solved. Ampflise causes the difficulty by wishing to become Gahmuret's acknowledged wife.

Wolfram gives no descriptions of Ampflise in physical terms apart from the instance in her letter to Gahmuret, when she claims: 'ich bin schœner unde rîcher [sc. than Herzeloyde], / unde kan och minneclîcher / minne enphâhn und minne gebn' (77.13 ff.). She is referred to variously as *sîn friundin* (12.11), a term which is more frequent and usual in pre-courtly literature, but is used here of a relationship which is specifically courtly, *küneginne*,[1] *rêgîn de Franze* (76.13, 88.3), *diu werde Franzoysinne* (88.26), *der Franzoyser künegîn* (94.18), *diu gehiure* (95.1), *frouwe*.[2] She is, like Belacane and Herzeloyde, an entirely worthy character, and this is stressed by her being called *diu werde küneginne* (70.2), *ein werdez wîp*

[1] 70.2, 76.7, 87.7, 94.8, 94.29, 97.14.
[2] 76.19, 87.11, 97.19.

(81.25), *diu werde Franʒoysinne* (88.26), *der kiuschen und der wîsen* (87.8), *der werden minne schanʒe* (88.4). Indeed Herzeloyde herself obliquely refers to her as *ein werdeʒ wîp*. In another place her *minne* is again called *werde minne* (77.16), and Gahmuret himself, in giving his reasons to Herzeloyde for his unwillingness to marry her, points out Ampflise's excellence: 'diu küneginne Amphlîse / wont an wîplîchen prîse' (94.29). It is from her that Gahmuret became *kurtoys* (325.27 ff.), and there is no attempt to diminish the ethical value of this courtly relationship, since even in this only genuine example of *hôhe minne* it is termed *werde minne*. It is an instance of the type of *hôhe minne* which dispenses with the need for physical fulfilment as Antikonie's words make clear:

> ich erbiutz iu durch mîns bruoder bete,
> daz ez Ampflîse Gahmurete
> mînem œheim ni baz erbôt;
> âne bî ligen. (406.3 ff.)

The knight's service is its own reward, and Gahmuret is never actually shown coming into contact with Ampflise. Her *minne* is nonetheless not to be despised (though Wolfram makes it obvious in the later part of his poem that it is to be superseded): it is merely on a different plane of experience and is judged on this plane according to its own ethical standards. It is a lasting relationship on the basis of *rîterschaft* and *dienst*: 'an sînem dienste lac gewin' (12.12); 'aldâ wart von Gahmurete / geleistet Ampflîsen bete, / daz er ir ritter wære' (78.17 f.); 'vart wider, sagt ir dienest mîn; / ich sül iedoch ir ritter sîn' (98.3 f.). Its place in Gahmuret's existence is not in opposition to the love of Belacane or Herzeloyde, but as a complement.

Once Gahmuret has married Herzeloyde his relationship with her is of the most intimate, but the force of adventure which had driven him away from Belacane also separates him from his second wife and leads to his death. In this instance, however, it is a call from outside, from his liege lord the caliph, which causes the separation. The love of adventure is the bane of Gahmuret, though it must be remembered that it is through the power of witchcraft that he is overcome (105.16 ff.) (see above, pp. 34 ff.). Husband and wife had in the meanwhile become so close to each other that Herzeloyde experiences the knowledge of her husband's death through a nightmare conceived in the most horrible form (but see also below, pp. 76 ff.), but death in battle is one that is entirely appropriate to Gahmuret's career and character.

All the incidents mentioned so far deal with the conflicting aspects of *minne* and *âventiure*, but there are occasions when these fade into the background for a short while and other emotions come to the fore. At the very beginning we saw the intimacy of the relationship between the two brothers of Anschouwe even though Gahmuret felt obliged to depart, and when he learns of Galoes' death immediately after his winning the tournament at Kanvoleis, his grief is intense. This and his remembrance of Belacane combine to create a mood of the utmost emotional stress:

> dô er vernam des bruoder tôt,
> daz was sîn ander herzenôt.
> mit jâmer sprach er disiu wort.
> 'wie hât nu mîns ankers ort
> in riwe ergriffen landes habe!'
> der wâppen teter sich dô abe.
> sîn riwe im hertes kumbers jach. (92.9 ff.)

Later he is quite unable to contain his sorrow:

> sîn kumber leider was ze grôz:
> ein güsse im von den ougen vlôz.
> er schuof den rittern ir gemach,
> und gienc da er sîne kamern sach,
> ein kleine gezelt von samît.
> die naht er dolte jâmers zît. (93.5 ff.)

While it is true that some features of this description are typical of scenes of great sorrow, the episode is a model of concise expression, in which the emotional bonds with Galoes are clearly indicated. Further literary description would have nullified the effect by overstatement, whereas the brevity of the scene and the departure of Gahmuret into the solitude of his own tent to spend the night there lamenting his loss give adequate emphasis to the reality of the emotion. In such a context individuality is best expressed by restraint, otherwise the result could so easily be banal and ungenuine.

Religious feeling in Gahmuret's character is purely conventional in its nature. We hear twice that he goes to mass, once before his battles in defence of Patelamunt (36.6 ff.) and once after the occasion of his brother's death (93.29 f.). Two other instances occur where Gahmuret speaks of God, but these are examples of conventional piety and there is no reason for attaching any special importance to them (8.16, 11.2). There is no attempt at anything more than the conventional, since this particular aspect of human experience is reserved for detailed treatment in the character of Parzival.

SPEECH AND CONVERSATION

Characterization through the medium of speech is an essential adjunct to the depiction of characters in action and allows direct access to the workings of the mind. It is therefore to be expected that the most important episodes in the poem will be highlighted by the dramatic effects of speech. Not all the speeches by any means are subjective or depictions of a psychological state; many of them are quite objective statements or questions which bring out for the benefit of the audience the reasons governing the progress of the plot. But on the whole they clarify the motives of the action and allow a greater proximity to the core of the problems being treated.

The introduction of Gahmuret into the poem is made deeply significant through the fact that he presents himself in his own words—an obvious example of immediate, personal characterization. He outlines his situation in material terms: 'sehzehen knappen ich hân, / der sehse von îser sint' (8.2 f.), and then asks his brother for four youths besides, stipulating that they should be 'mit guoter zuht, von hôher art' (8.5), so that they should be able to stand up to the rigours of his plans. Already he has had some experience of adventure, and now he declares his intention to go out into other countries in search of *âventiure* and *minne*. His aims are high: he is seeking to serve, and win *guotes wîbes gruoʒ*, is conscious of the claims of *rehte triuwe* and prays for God's guidance. At the same time he is humbly aware of the moral demands this places on him 'ob ich des wirdec bin' (8.13) and envies his brother for his success in *minne*. Again, later, he refuses to accept his brother's praise and says: 'hêrre, ir lobt mich umbe nôt, / sît ez iwer zuht gebôt' (9.17 f.).[1] His emotions are growing ever stronger:

> mîn herze iedoch nâch hœhe strebet:
> ine weiz war umbez alsus lebet,
> daz mir swillet sus mîn winster brust.
> ôwê war jaget mich mîn gelust?
> ich solz versuochen, ob ich mac.
> nu nâhet mîn urloubes tac. (9.23 ff.)

The force of his desires overcomes him and compels him to leave mother and brother in search of both *âventiure* and *minne*. As yet these feelings have not become completely clear to him, but he recognizes their presence, and to us they foreshadow the later developments of his life.

The main part of the exposition is given through the medium of speech, thus making it direct and vivid. The very first time that Gahmuret speaks, he establishes in our minds the basis of his nature and the character of his relationship with his brother. The princes have been interceding on his behalf with Galoes, but not in quite the way in which he himself desires, and so he impetuously interrupts with the remark: 'wolt ich ingesinde sîn / iwer oder decheines man, / sô het ich mîn gemach getân' (7.20 ff.). The very last thing he wants is his *gemâch* (contrast Erec). He explains the unenviable poverty of his position to Galoes and his dependence on his brother's generosity and then leaves the whole matter to the king's judgement, in which he has every confidence: 'nu prüevet dar nâch mînen prîs / (ir sît getriuwe unde wîs), / und râtt als ez

---

[1] Gahmuret's dislike of praise is a characteristic feature, which occurs again later in his history. When Kaylet acclaims his accomplishments in battle, he reacts with a similar combination of modesty and cussedness: 'dîn munt mir lobs ze vil vergiht' (50.17), and in a parallel situation he once more says: 'Mîn frouwe mac wænen daz du tobst, / sît du mich alsô verlobst' (86.5 ff.).

geziehe nuo' (7.23 ff.). He reminisces about their former exploits together and shows how he looks on Galoes as a model of knightliness for himself: 'ôwe wan het ich iwer kunst / und anderhalp die wâren gunst!' (8.25 f.). The respect which Gahmuret owes his brother is brought out even more when he hears of Galoes' death (see below, pp. 54 f.). In explaining his intentions to Galoes, Gahmuret declares: 'ich wil kêren in diu lant ...' (8.8), thus expressing his aim of achieving the ends of true knightliness (cf. Trevrizent's remarks to Parzival: 'swer schildes ambet üeben wil, / der muoz durchstrîchen lande vil' (499.9 f.)). The king is sorrowful to hear of Gahmuret's purposed departure, but he nonetheless gives him what he desires and more, so that Gahmuret is able to do as he wishes.

There exists also between Gahmuret and his mother Schoette an intimate relationship, which is sensitively dealt with on Gahmuret's leaving Anschouwe. The queen grieves that her son will be with her little longer as a source of comfort to her in her affliction from the death of her husband the king. Gahmuret tries to console her and commends her to God's care, asserting that no one can reproach him with causing her pain and explaining that he is now setting off in search of *ritterschaft* in order to gain honour for himself. The parting brings sorrow to them both, but Gahmuret is none the less compelled by his innate disposition to act in this way. His mother, interpreting *ritterschaft* as *hôhe minne*, accepts his intention gracefully and loads him with presents, telling him to let her know when he returns. To this Gahmuret replies that his future is uncertain and that he does not know where he will go, but he expresses his deep gratitude to both Galoes and her for their sterling generosity towards him in his plans. When he later hears of his brother's death, his first instinct is to enquire about his mother's welfare (92.24 ff.), only to learn that the deaths of her husband and elder son, combined with the separation from her younger son, were too much for her to bear.

The next few examples, chronologically, of Gahmuret in speech are connected with his defence of Patelamunt and are the concise questions and comments of a man of action. His first remarks to

Belacane are an enquiry as to the origin of the siege, which he is at a loss to understand, but as soon as he hears the reason for it he offers his service, and Belacane immediately accepts it. He is discountenanced at Belacane's demonstration of her gratitude through waiting on him at table and says that he is unaccustomed to such honour, adding that he might have asked more of her that night, but prefers to keep within the bounds of *mâʒe* (33.21 ff.). In battle, Gahmuret's actions speak louder than words and his reputation is the gauge of his worth when, on being demanded his name by Hiuteger, he replies in the briefest possible way: 'ich pin Gahmuret Anschevîn' (38.11), at which Hiuteger forthwith surrenders. Similarly the force of his personality, at the defeat of Gaschier, is such that he only needs to command him to go and ask the Scots to desist from battle for the whole conflict to be at an end (39.1 ff.).

The situation at the end of the battle illustrates Gahmuret's generosity of spirit towards his enemies. He requests both Razalic and Gaschier to kiss his wife as a sign of reconciliation (cf. *Nibelungenlied* st. 1113) and generally pardons many of his opponents since they are united by a common kinship, which precludes Gahmuret from exacting his otherwise legal claim to reparations. He liberates Killirjacac, kisses him himself, listens to his story and asks him to fetch Gaschier and Kaylet, with whom he also reconciles himself. He refuses to dispossess Kaylet and enquires what led him to become his opponent, which had happened through family connexions. In his conversation with Kaylet his gives a pregnant summary of his position:

> ich kom gestern, hiute bin ich hie
> worden hêrre überz lant.
> mich vienc diu künegîn mit ir hant:
> dô wert ich mich mit minne.
> sus rieten mir die sinne. (49.20 ff.)

and then continues with a friendly discussion of particular aspects of the battle, telling how he had recognized Kaylet by his plume and by the *sarapandratest* on his shield. All the speeches of this section are distinguished by the human approach, full of sympathy and magnanimity, which Gahmuret has towards all those whom he meets. Again he is shown as the paragon of the courtly knight, but it is through the details of his behaviour that we are led to an understanding of his supreme virtue. The same kind of attitude is to be found in a later conversation with Kaylet in book II, which is characterized by Gahmuret's unwillingness to take a superior position before the tourney at Kanvoleis: 'wir sulen haben einen muot' (68.6).

Almost all the remaining passages in which Gahmuret speaks are connected with the problem of the marriage to Herzeloyde. This crucial point of Gahmuret's life is heightened considerably through his thoughts and conflicting emotions being expressed in words, since he has to justify his whole attitude to Herzeloyde and is eventually forced to give way. The questions involved in this have already been treated in the previous section, as it proved impossible to separate completely the two aspects of action and speech, but after he has accepted the decision of the council of knights Gahmuret sums up his present situation and his duty towards the kingdom of Anschouwe. He realizes that both he and Herzeloyde must overcome their bereavement, rejoin the living and assume responsibility for the kingdom of his father. He exhorts Herzeloyde to rejoice and help him in retaining the vassalage of the kings and princes who are there until they consummate their marriage. These are the last words that Gahmuret speaks (99.8 ff.) and his remaining part in the poem is expressed, as is more in keeping with his character, in action—in his final combat in the service of the caliph.

MONOLOGUES

A small section of Gahmuret's characterization is achieved through the medium of monologue, a technique which is generally used to make explicit the inward, personal emotions of a character where this cannot be effectively accomplished through action or conversation. It is therefore an important medium for the individualization of key figures, since it transfers *self*-conscious emotions into the realm of *social* consciousness, that is, into the mind of the audience. Not all monologues possess this individualizing aspect, however, since many of them are conventional modes of expression and traditional forms of literary usage. To this category belongs the *Totenklage*, which is the only form of monologue that Wolfram makes use of for Gahmuret. This is an indication that the characterization of Gahmuret is not as advanced or complex as, for example, that of Herzeloyde (see below, pp. 93 ff.), but while the *Totenklage* is generally a conventional form, this does not mean that it has no depth of meaning.

The two instances of monologues in Gahmuret's case refer to the death of Galoes and show quite clearly the intimate relationship which existed between the two brothers. Emil Walker, in his study on the monologue,[1] quotes the following passage from H. Springer's dissertation on the Provençal *planch*,[2] which he then transfers, with certain reservations, to the *Totenklage* as found in the epic: ' Als stehende und für den Charakter der Gattung typische Grundgedanken weist der Planch in der Hauptsache drei Elemente auf: Klage über den erlittenen Verlust, Lob des Verstorbenen und Fürbitte für seine Seele.' These observations can be applied to Gahmuret's monologues, and the two taken together agree with the above analysis, but with a slight modification of the last feature. The three characteristics do not perhaps receive explicit expression, but the first monologue and the first line of the second correspond to the lament of the loss, are followed by an apostrophe of the hero and rounded off by the pious desire: 'nu erbarmet mich dîn güete' (92.22). Thus, it can readily be seen that the form used here is typical of the *Totenklage* in general.

Prefacing the actual words which Gahmuret utters are three lines which put these brief expressions of feeling in their context: ' Dô er vernam des bruoder tôt, / daz was sîn ander herzenôt. / mit jâmer sprach er disiu wort' (92.9 ff.). Then follows the first monologue, a second description, which emphasizes that: 'der

---

[1] Emil Walker, *Der Monolog im höfischen Epos. Stil- und literaturgeschichtliche Untersuchungen* (Stuttgart, 1928), p. 168.

[2] H. Springer, *Das altprovenzalische Klagelied* (Diss. Berlin, 1894), p. 18.

helt mit wâren triwen sprach' (92.16), and the second monologue. Apart from the use of the anchor symbol, there is nothing which cannot be characterized as a normal, conventional expression of grief at the death of a dear brother, no specifically unusual elements, no striking adjectives or telling phrases. But the brevity of the lament, the concise way in which the emotion is portrayed without any unnecessary words, are the very means by which Wolfram succeeds in making this incident realistic and convincing.

In comparison with Parzival, Gahmuret reveals little of his character through monologues, though the fact that he does use one kind of monologue shows that Wolfram was concerned to make him as individual a figure as possible, so far as this would not detract from the importance of Parzival. Gahmuret, like all the other characters of the poem, is subordinate to Parzival and because he is so near to the personality of Parzival he cannot be greatly individualized (other minor characters *can* be considerably individualized, provided they do not come into too close contact with the main hero, as for example Obie, Obilot, Antikonie). The *Totenklage* is therefore very much in place in Gahmuret's case, since it expresses inward emotion in a traditonal form and is in keeping with the rest of the characterization of Gahmuret as a man of actions rather than words. The relationship of Galoes and Gahmuret was a very close one, and as Galoes' death occurs at a moment of great emotional tension, when Gahmuret is deeply concerned about his broken relationship with Belacane and the claims of Herzeloyde, the *Totenklage* gives a natural and sufficient outlet for the pent-up feelings raging within him.

LETTERS

The use of letters as a method of characterization is more in the nature of a literary device than a purely natural medium of expression such as would be employed in oral story-telling. The letter presupposes a literary culture and is a method of communication within the framework of a literary work—a communication by proxy. Normally this is not a lengthy procedure (though one has only to look at the Strasbourg *Alexander* to find an obvious exception).

The letter which Gahmuret leaves behind for Belacane is an explanation for his conduct, but also contains a considerable amount of information about himself, his background and his heredity. This information is expository and provides the link between Gahmuret's family and that of Artus. Up to this point the only explicit communication on this score is to be found in the first 200 lines of the poem, where the details about Anschouwe occur. Gahmuret stresses this in his letter when he writes that their child will be 'erborn von Anschouwe' (56.1) and follows this up with details about the child's grandfather Gandin and his further ancestry, going back through Addanz and Lazaliez to Mazadan, whose marriage with the fairy Terdelaschoye resulted in the other great family of Artus through Brickus and Utepandragun. In this way Gahmuret (and therefore Feirefiz and Parzival) is brought into the framework of the Arthurian world. Gahmuret's history is itself realistic in tone and lacking in the supernatural fantasy often to be found in the basic material of Arthurian romance, and therefore this passage adds nothing to an understanding of *his* character; but it is of the utmost importance for the characterization of both his sons from the point of view of their incorporation into the Arthurian scheme. In this respect Gahmuret is of consequence in his function as father of Feirefiz and Parzival and not as the knight errant, the liberator of Patelamunt and the winner of the tourney at Kanvoleis. The genealogical pattern, while containing information about past relationships, has also prophetic significance in that references are made to ancestry in order to illuminate the future. The lines: 'ieslîcher sider krône truoc, / und heten werdekeit genuoc' (56.23 f.), are vivid indications of the kingdoms to which Parzival and Feirefiz are later to attain. Then, further, there is a clear prediction about Feirefiz' life: 'diu minne wirt sîn frouwe: / sô wirt ab er an strîte ein schûr, / den vînden herter nâchgebûr' (56.2 ff.). These are indeed the keynotes of Gahmuret's own life—service offered to his mistress, *minne*, and strong opposition to the enemy—which he prophesies for his son.

In addition, he considers it of importance that his son should know that his grandfather Gandin and also his great-grandfather lost their lives in pursuit of their knightly calling. Consistency in the motivating forces of the lives of father and son is again borne out in Wolfram's treatment of his material. Once more we can see the extent to which the character of Gahmuret is conceived in terms of a background for the story of Parzival and Feirefiz.

From the point of view of our appreciation of Gahmuret's own character, however, it is the other part of the letter which interests us. Gahmuret is conscious of his base action in forsaking Belacane, but tries to show that he has not left her merely for the sake of a whim and attempts to explain, for his own satisfaction as well as for hers, the forces which compelled him to his decision. His first reaction is to confess his guilt: 'ich pin dirre verte ein diep: / die muose ich dir durch jâmer steln' (55.22 f.). After this he gives his excuse, repeated at the end, that Belacane does not belong to the same *orden* as he does, and that if she did: 'sô wær mir immer nâch dir wê: / und hân doch immer nâch dir pîn' (55.26 f.). But it is not until he is faced with marriage to Herzeloyde that he gives a genuine emotional expression to the sentiments which he enter- tains towards Belacane. More than anything else this letter shows, for Gahmuret, his consciousness of having sinned against her, his own weakness in having to admit this through a letter rather than face to face, and a feeling of responsibility towards her and his unborn son—hence all the genealogical information. Here then are just the beginnings of what forms the principal theme of the latter part of book II in the encounter with Herzeloyde.

THE EPITAPH AND GAHMURET'S PART IN BOOKS III–XVI

Gahmuret's epitaph, engraved on his helmet the *adamas*, concludes his own story with a series of pithy comments on the outstanding features of his life, merely reiterating already known facts in a general panegyric, but his part in the poem does not end here. On the contrary, mention is made of him in various ways in all the succeeding books except books VII, X, XI and XII. This is mainly with respect to his being Parzival's father (cf. the expressions

Gahmuretes kint, Gahmuretes suon, fil li roy Gahmuret, among others), but Feirefiz is also characterized in similar terms. This type of reference is, however, of more importance for the portrayal of Parzival than of Gahmuret. It is used to emphasize the influence of heredity, for example: 'den twanc diu Gahmuretes art / und an geborniu manheit' (174.24 f.), here bringing out the love of tournaments and fighting, but in other places it is *minne* that is stressed, for example: 'done wolt in Gahmuretes art / denkens niht erlâzen / nâch der schœnen Lîâzen' (179.24 ff.).

In addition to these brief mentions of Gahmuret as a point of reference for both Parzival and Feirefiz, there are one or two longer passages where more is said about him. Of these the first is to be found in Cundrie's long tirade against Parzival for having omitted to ask Anfortas about his ailment, where she draws a vivid contrast between Parzival's behaviour and the exemplary conduct of Gahmuret:

> nu denke ich ave an Gahmureten,
> des herze ie valsches was erjeten.
> von Anschouwe iwer vater hiez,
> der iu ander erbe liez
> denn als ir habt geworben . . .
> geloubet von ir [sc. Herzeloyde]
> guoter mære,
> unt daz iwer vater wære
> manlîcher triwe wîse
> unt wîtvengec hôher prîse.
> er kunde wol mit schallen.
> grôz herze und kleine gallen,
> dar ob was sîn brust ein dach.
> er was riuse und vengec vach:
> sîn manlîchez ellen
> kund den prîs wol gestellen.   (317.11 ff.)

Here, in summarized form, we have a by no means repetitive sketch of Gahmuret. Indeed, there are certain features which are not found clearly expressed in the first two books. It is, for example, explicitly stated that Gahmuret 'kunde wol mit schallen', an accomplishment that was part of the stock-in-trade of the perfect knight (cf. *Der arme Heinrich* 71), but this is nowhere mentioned previously. Similarly, the description of him as being 'riuse und vengec vach' is an addition, if merely a verbal one, to the information given earlier in the poem. Otherwise these few lines take up the most important characteristic of books I and II and express them in different words—the connexion with Anschouwe, Gahmuret's freedom from *valsch*, his devotion to *triuwe* and his manly courage, his renown and his magnanimity. This passage is of significance from the point of view of the contrast between Parzival and Gahmuret. In this context more was obviously required than a casual reference to Gahmuret's character, which had been described quite a considerable time before and had probably faded in the memory of Wolfram's audience; hence the revivification in other words.

Another longer passage referring to Gahmuret is found at the time of Parzival's encounter with Trevrizent. Parzival learns a great deal about his father's adventurous life, since when Trevrizent was travelling in search of *âventiure* he on one occasion met Gahmuret. This was in Sibilje, where Gahmuret was already lodging when Trevrizent arrived. Trevrizent makes no secret of his youthful admiration for Parzival's father, rejoicing that he was able to meet him and sorrowing that 'der werde Anschevîn' was killed in battle at Baldac. He refers to him again as 'der werde vater dîn' (497.22) and describes him as being a paragon of manly beauty: 'man muose ouch mir für wâr dâ jehn / daz ni schœner mannes bilde wart' (497.28). Gahmuret visited Trevrizent's lodging and made him a gift of a jewel, a green stone out of which Trevrizent had had his casket made. Then, on his departure, he left Trevrizent his kinsman Ither, the king of Kukumerlant, as a servant and went off to the caliph of Baldac while Trevrizent continued to the Rohas. This early meeting of Gahmuret and Trevrizent establishes an unexpected connexion between Gahmuret and the family of the Grail previous to his marriage with Herzeloyde, and it is enhanced by the breadth of sympathy between the two knights and the mutual love and respect which they owe each other. The importance of Gahmuret's travel-history is stressed through our being reminded of it here, but it is seen as subordinate to Trevrizent's, for the latter covered a far greater expanse of country, including all the continents of the known world as well as many mythical places and, most important of all, the Grail territory.[1]

In book XV there occurs a further long eulogy of Gahmuret by Parzival in response to Feirefiz' telling him that the object of his travels was to find his father. This passage (751.2 ff.) describes Gahmuret in the most laudatory terms and concentrates again on his dual reputation in *strîten* and *minne*, concluding with a brief description of his death at the hands of Ipomidon outside Baldac. It gives Feirefiz all the information he desires about their father, and although it adds no further details to those already given up to this point in the poem, it is an impressive recapitulation of all that Gahmuret stands for.

The remaining allusions to Gahmuret are shorter and on the whole merely recount features expressed earlier. In the context of the Round Table, after Cundrie's departure, comes a further reference to Parzival's heritage (325.17 ff.), which is followed by a brief mention of Gahmuret's relationship with Ampflise, 'dâ von der helt wart kurtoys' (325.29). In book VIII Antikonie also alludes to this liaison, and her statement, particularly the words 'âne bî ligen' (406.6), makes clear that this was one of specifically courtly love. This latter reference, however, is as important for the light in which we are meant to see Antikonie's relationship with Gawan as for what it says about Gahmuret.

Gahmuret is generally cited as a paragon of knightly virtue as a point of comparison for other characters, not merely for Parzival. Thus, Artus sees Feirefiz' accomplishments in the sphere of *minne* as being due to capabilities inherited from Gahmuret (769.1 ff.). On another occasion Feirefiz is linked with the kinship of the Grail through his father, as Parzival informs Gawan (758.10 ff.); and Feirefiz himself speaks of his own knowledge of Gahmuret as a knight whom no other excelled (771.2 ff.).

[1] Marianne Wynn, *op. cit.*, pp. 51 ff.

But Gahmuret forms a point of comparison for others too, and Gawan, who knew him from the tourney at Kanvoleis (66.15 ff.), finds himself comparing Vergulaht in book VIII with both Parzival and Gahmuret on account of his splendid appearance (400.13 ff.). Later, when Gramoflanz forms one part of the comparison, it is Gahmuret's prowess in *minne* that is the point to note (687.1 ff.), though his brother Galoes and king Kyllicrates are mentioned also in the same context. Lastly, the beauty of the restored Anfortas is compared with Gahmuret's widely proclaimed handsome physique (cf. 63.13 ff.):

> und al den schœne was geslaht,
> unt des man Gahmurete jach
> dô mann în zogen sach
> ze Kanvoleiz sô wünneclîch,
> ir decheins schœn was der gelîch,
> die Anfortas ûz siechheit truoc. (796.10 ff.)

These features are not in any particular way outstanding, nor do they, apart from the longer description of Cundrie, strikingly complement the picture of Gahmuret gained from the first two books. Their function is strictly utilitarian and serves to underline aspects in the characters of other persons, especially of Parzival and Feirefiz, and to revitalize the picture of Gahmuret that was given earlier.

CONCLUSION

In conclusion we must note that the individualization of Gahmuret is limited by the role he is allotted in the poem as a whole. His function is to provide a significant background for Parzival's own story and character, and since Parzival derives his basic desire to be a knight from his father, the two have many features in common. Gahmuret, however, is in a subordinate position: his history is to a large extent founded on parallels with Parzival's and cannot be allowed to compete with the place that the latter must have in the poem. But while the fundamentals of his character are not essentially original, the way in which they are described and connected *is*, so long as this does not detract from the characterization of Parzival himself. Gahmuret's personality cannot be completely developed, since this is done in the characterization of Parzival, and thus it remains as a preliminary approach to the general problem which is treated in detail with that of his son.

Gahmuret is by no means a colourless character. We see him from many angles and in a variety of situations where he is able to show himself as an independent personality capable of taking the initiative and acting as a result of the forces of his own character and not, like Eneas on leaving Carthage, in obedience to some external power. He is presented in three quite different love relationships, only one of which is completely conventional in that it unambiguously portrays the ethos of courtly love (Ampflise). Of the other two, the relationship with Belacane shows Gahmuret, who in all other respects is the epitome of the true knight, in an ignoble position as he deserts her in search of *âventiure*. It is in any case unusual for such a relationship, between a black-skinned, pagan queen and a Christian knight, to be represented with such sympathy (cf. however the association between the queen of Sheba, whose name by tradition was Bilqis, and Solomon, from whose union it is reputed that a great emperor, by name Menelek, was born (1 Kings x. 1–13)). In the third relationship, with Herzeloyde, a distinctive feature is given through Gahmuret's unwillingness to marry the queen of Waleis and the fact that she takes the initiative in the relationship from the beginning (cf. Dido). These motifs form the basis of the action of Gahmuret's history and, although they can be paralleled with other similar incidents, the fact that Gahmuret's own nature, as developed by Wolfram, adequately accounts for their juxtaposition gives an element of individuality to the whole. In this same sphere of action a further example of individualization is provided by the details of Gahmuret's travel-history, specifying his achievements and thereby illustrating his prowess as a knight.

The action of the plot brings out a few general points about Gahmuret's character, but these would be largely ineffective were they not supported by the revelation of his character through dialogue. In this way a much more immediate picture of Gahmuret is established and the motive forces of his life are clearly shown, though not completely elucidated. Thus, he explains in great detail his reasons for wanting to leave Anschouwe, and this technique of self-presentation is extremely important in the creation of an individualized character. He shows the closeness of the bonds with his family, with his brother and his mother, but he has to break away from them in order to forge a reputation for himself. Outward circumstances provide him with the opportunity for this, but his character, his desire for *âventiure* and *minne*, are such that he would have had to leave his family at some time in any case in order to achieve this ambition. It is in his personal relationships that Gahmuret appears most clearly individualized. He is marked with a warmth of feeling, humanity and generosity at all times, even towards his enemies, and this makes him highly credible and real in a way that would be impossible if he had been shown merely as the type of the perfect knight. Through dialogue again he is able to reveal the complexities of his love relationships with Belacane, Ampflise and Herzeloyde. Had this not been so, the significance of these relationships would have been almost nullified and his entire career would have been just another of the episodic kind, where the hero proceeds from one adventure to the next with nothing to connect them except perhaps the technique of gradation. As it is, however, Wolfram is able to develop the three relationships, causing them to interact and showing Gahmuret's different reactions to each. Nevertheless it is true that none of them is very highly developed: the amount of information given to us about Ampflise is minimal and none of it creates a clear visual image; the delicate question of the moral basis of marriage in general as opposed to specifically Christian marriage is only just touched in Gahmuret's relationship with Belacane; and in his second marriage to Herzeloyde Gahmuret is so passive as to have almost lost his own personality, being compelled into a union that he did not genuinely desire. Thus we see the beginnings of an individualization that is not fully carried out. If the questions just mentioned had been treated in detail, the result would have been an epic of greatly increased length, and such was, clearly, impossible.

The many descriptive passages devoted to Gahmuret do not create a distinctive portrait of the hero (apart from the fact that his clothing is treated in some detail) since their function is to provide an idealized picture. This is achieved by a wealth of minor details that are almost entirely external in their application and could be employed for any worthy knight. Gahmuret's clothing is not a mark of individual character in the way that, for example, Cundrie's is or that of the wild man of Kalogreant's story (*Iwein* 418 ff.); it is merely the characteristic of the perfect hero. One important aspect of these descriptions concerns the differences in the extent and quality of Gahmuret's retinue as he progresses from Anschouwe to Patelamunt and Kanvoleis, as these illustrate his rise in worldly esteem. In his own personal description the use of the colour green for several items of his clothing ties up with the symbolic devices, which constitute a considerable degree of individualization.

The devices of the anchor and the *adamas* are among the most striking features in the portrayal of Gahmuret's character. Both form clear distinguishing marks for him in battle, and the *adamas* is an individualized token of superiority in knightly prowess which can only be eliminated by magic wrought on it.

A small amount of individualization is achieved in the use of synonyms. Most of them are conventional, but the quantity of them indicates a desire for variety. Some of them are significant in that they are normally avoided in courtly romances, as, for example, *wîgant*, *degen* and *recke*. This tendency of Wolfram to use the terminology of pre-courtly and heroic literature is characteristic of his desire to emphasize the importance of *schildes ambet* while on the quest for *minne* and, above and beyond this, implies his rejection of the usual values of courtliness. In view of this the names *wîgant*, etc. have a pronounced individual flavour. The use of the geographical background of Anschouwe and the kingdom of Zazamanc also helps in particularizing the hero, and his place in the complex system of kinship assures him a further individuality as a member of a group.

In the characterization of Gahmuret both traditional and individual traits are to be recognized. The conventional depiction of the hero provides a firm basis for the idealized representation of Gahmuret as the perfect knight, though this is modified through his being shown in an unworthy situation (his desertion of Belacane), which he does not attempt to remedy by accomplishing feats of great hardship, as Erec and Iwein do. Once the basis of perfection, with the above qualification, is firmly established it can be elaborated and individualized. This is done in a variety of ways, but it can be most successfully carried out where it is external in its point of reference, since here it does not prejudice the characterization and particularly the psychology of Parzival. Hence the use of the symbolic devices, which can in themselves be elaborated without necessarily securing a deeper validity than the first use of the symbol implies. Hence also the details of the travel-history and the battles, the use of kinship motifs and synonyms. When psychological characteristics are brought into the foreground, Wolfram has to be more careful. This is well illustrated by his use of monologue, where in Gahmuret's case he only makes use of a conventional type, the *Totenklage*, which allows him to present Gahmuret in an individual light, but without danger that he will outshine Parzival. Similarly, in his use of dialogue Wolfram goes as far as he can to individualize the problems with which Gahmuret is faced in his various relationships, but in none of them does he investigate the questions thoroughly or attempt any kind of solution.

From this analysis it is clear that Wolfram was striving for an individualized interpretation of Gahmuret's character, but had to guard against the possibility that Gahmuret might detract from Parzival if too highly particularized. His solution was to elaborate external features at considerable length while keeping the psychological aspects carefully subordinate to the characterization of Parzival.

III

HERZELOYDE

INTRODUCTION

IN considering the portrayal of Herzeloyde we are confronted with various problems concerning Wolfram's purpose in writing *Parzival* and his methods of depicting his characters. The two interlinked ideas of the Grail and the Arthurian world demand different techniques of characterization, since the figures of the Grail world have, on the whole, a definite function to fulfil in their relationships with Parzival, whereas those of the Arthurian community stand further away from him and the inner developments of his personality, and their appearances, while yet having significance for him, are episodic by nature. Those characters who come into close contact with Parzival are not highly individualized, since they might have jeopardized Parzival's unique position by detracting from his personality. On the other hand, those whom he seldom or never encounters can have a pronounced personal individuality on account of their belonging to a world which only initially influences him and from which he is called to the world of the Grail. W. J. Schröder writes about this feature of characterization in his study *Der dichterische Plan des Parzivalromans*,[1] having already mentioned the tendency of certain characters to fulfil a function:

Andererseits setzt die funktionale Bedeutung der Neigung zum Individualisieren und Realisieren naturgemäß starken Widerstand entgegen, der Dichter kann hier nur ein Weniges tun, wenn er nicht die Funktion stören will. Daraus ergibt sich, daß die Hauptfiguren typisch, Nebenfiguren in viel stärkerem Maße realistisch gezeichnet werden konnten und auch gezeichnet worden sind. Man vergleiche nur etwa Konduiramurs oder Herzeloyde mit den beiden Backfischen Obie und Obilot. Hier konnte so etwas wie Charakterschilderung möglich

[1] *Beitr.*, LXXIV, 1952, pp. 412 f.

werden. Humor und Stimmung breiten sich aus, die Lebenswirk-
lichkeit tritt uns frisch entgegen.

Schröder considerably overstates his case in implying that only the
individualized peripheral characters come to life, but the differences of portrayal which he mentions certainly have an effect in the
poem, though to a much smaller extent than he claims. If a person
has only one clear function, the tendency is that the characterization becomes 'typical', as is perhaps most obvious in the case of
Condwiramurs, but frequently the person has more than one
function, and the tendency is thereby diminished.

Herzeloyde appears in three distinguishable roles—as the queen of
Waleis, the wife of Gahmuret, and the mother of Parzival. The last
of these is the most important, and here there is an inclination to
portray Herzeloyde solely as a mother figure, but her roles as the
queen of Waleis and wife of Gahmuret are the factors which lead
up to this position and cannot be too rigidly separated from it.
Personal attributes are, however, not particularly clear, though
Wolfram tries as far as possible to make Herzeloyde's actions
psychologically understandable and allows himself to enlarge on
certain aspects of her individual existence. This task is not easy,
since Herzeloyde's life is always related to some other person, at
first to Castis (though this is not explained until book IX), then to
Gahmuret, who provides the bridge from her existence as the
queen of Waleis to what follows, and lastly to Parzival. Her
belonging to the Grail family is not made explicit until 455.19 ff.,
and although this is Parzival's only connexion, it receives next to
no amplification; in fact, the relationship appears to be a purely
external one, as the Grail has no significance whatsoever in
Herzeloyde's life. The only passage which sheds any light on the
subject is Trevrizent's explanation of the custom whereby members
of the Grail family marry into other ruling families or take over the
government of countries whose kings have died:

> sus gît man vome grâle dan
> offenlîch meide, verholn die man,
> durch fruht ze dienste wider dar,
> ob ir kint des grâles schar

mit dienste suln mêren:
daz kan si got wol lêren. (495.1 ff.)

The paucity of evidence on this score indicates that the link between the various functions of Herzeloyde is provided more by the development and by the needs of the plot than by a unified characterization. In short, the needs of the plot are in this case primary, and characterization is subordinate to them. This does not mean, however, that glaring discrepancies are apparent, but only that certain features are not fully developed.

In examining the actual processes of characterization it is worth noting initially one important variation from the *Conte del Graal*. In Chrétien's work the mother of Perceval is never named (cf. also *Ruodlieb*). This anonymity may well be a sign of fairy-tale origin, since in them names rarely occur (cf. *Peredur*), but it is a general difference between Chrétien and Wolfram that the former uses few names, while the latter's work is marked by a superabundance of them. Perceval's mother is anonymous in her function as a mother, appearing incidentally as *la veve fame*—though the first mention of this aspect is immediately connected with Perceval as it occurs as an attribute of the young boy: *li fix a la veve fame* (74)—and communicating the necessary information about Perceval's father. She is hardly ever referred to as an independent person in her own right: she is merely the mother figure of typical courtliness and orthodox piety. Wolfram's naming of Parzival's mother signifies one step away from impersonality in that, functional or personal, she at least possesses a name. The first part of the name 'Herze-' has an obvious meaning in view of the love that Herzeloyde bears towards Gahmuret and Parzival (cf. Wolfram's other compounds: *herzeleit, herzeminne, herzenleit, herzenôt, herzeroum, herzesêr*). The second part is probably an allusive variant of 'leide', since Herzeloyde spends the greater part of the time that she appears in the poem mourning the husband she has lost in battle and meets her death mourning her loss of Parzival.[1]

---

[1] Karl Bartsch, *Eigennamen in Parzival und Titurel* (*Germ. Stud.* II, Vienna, 1875), derives 'Herzeloyde' from an originally Germanic name Harchelildis/Harchehildis in the gallicized form Herceleude/Hercelaude, presupposing that

SYNONYMS

The synonyms used to refer to Herzeloyde, while being many in number, have not a very wide range of meaning. Strangely enough, Herzeloyde is never expressly referred to as a widow, in contrast to the French poem, but is most often merely called *diu künegîn* (*küneginne*).[1] She is first named half way through book II (84.9), at the time when she visits Gahmuret in his tent, anxious to have him as her husband. Until this time Gahmuret had viewed her solely as the organizer of the tournament; now, however, he comes into personal contact with her and is made to realize that the tournament was not just an opportunity for him to satisfy his general desire for *âventiure*, but had the aim of securing Herzeloyde a husband. At this particular point therefore it is necessary for Herzeloyde to emerge from her anonymity as the queen of Waleis and become a person with whom Gahmuret comes face to face. Once named, Herzeloyde is frequently thus referred to, and *vrou Herzeloyde* occurs four times in combination with the term *künegîn* (100.14, 103.3, 109.7, 122.23). She appears several times as just *vrou Herzeloyde*,[2] once as *vrou Herzeloyd diu rîche* (116.28), *des landes vrouwe* (113.27), and a multitude of times merely as *diu vrouwe*.[3] In addition to these conventional terms, various other nouns are applied to her: *wirtîn* (64.11), *magt* (95.28, 97.12), *wîp* (116.19).

A few expressions are to be found which impart a little more information than those already mentioned. Twice Herzeloyde is called *diu künegîn von Wâleis* (*von Wâleis diu künegîn*) (60.9, 64.11), once *diu Wâleisinne* (81.16) and once *diu werde Wâleisinne* (84.1). The use of the kingdom of Waleis as a point of reference for

Wolfram used a French source for the name, but this is not a very satisfactory explanation. Bodo Mergell, *Wolfram von Eschenbach und seine französischen Quellen. II. Teil. Wolframs Parzival* (Münster, 1943), p. 112, n. 2, suggests that the name includes 'die Vorstellung des Herzeleids und der *vroide*'.

[1] 61.3.29, 62.25, 64.5, 67.10, 69.24, 70.10, 77.11, 81.2, 82.30, 83.25, 86.29, 88.9.20, 93.23, 96.5, 99.30, 100.8, 101.10, 106.18, 111.6, 112.21, 113.1.5, 118.18, 119.9, 125.23, 126.3.24, 127.11.

[2] 84.13, 85.14, 94.2, 98.17. 99.21, 102.21, 105.6, 118.29, 128.16.

[3] 81.20, 83.27, 95.29, 101.16, 103.25, 104.25, 109.2.14.20, 110.11.23, 111.3.14.20.26, 112.6, 126.16, 127.1.

Herzeloyde is important for Parzival later, since he is frequently called *Wáleis*, thus contrasting with Feirefiz the *Anschevîn*. Just before the death of Gahmuret Herzeloyde is referred to as *küngîn über driu lant* (103.6), a name which marks the apex of her power, so soon to be ended. Wolfram alludes to this ironically at the beginning of book III when he says: 'frou Herzeloyd diu rîche / ir drîer lande wart ein gast' (116.28 f.).

A few phrases refer specifically to internal aspects of character, though almost all are conventional or idealistic. Thus, Herzeloyde is singled out for the excellence of her virtue as *die wîbes missewende vlôch* (113.12) and *ein wurzel der güete / und ein stam der diemüete* (128.27 f.),[1] and on another occasion she is called *diu vrouwe valsches laz* (128.20). The first of these expressions is used immediately after the birth of Parzival, the other two describe her at the time of her death. When she flees into the wilderness of Soltane, she is called *diu vrouwe jâmers balt* (117.7), an expression depicting her attitude after the death of Gahmuret, overcome with grief and determined to withdraw from the courtly world in order to protect Parzival from it; this is the most striking phrase applied to her. Other words are *gemeit* (81.24), a word generally shunned by courtly writers and therefore to that extent an indication of individuality, *gehiure* (88.13), *wîse* (110.29), *süeze* (434.3) and *junc* (451.6), of which the last two are used retrospectively after Herzeloyde's death.

DESCRIPTIVE PASSAGES

What we learn about Herzeloyde in descriptive passages is extremely sparse and lacking in precise visual imagery. Indeed, there is very little at all that specifically refers to her external appearance apart from general impressions. There are one or two brief references to her physical attributes and to the fact that she was 'ein maget niht ein wîp' (60.15, 84.6), and three longer passages give a rounder description. From this comparative lack of precise external features we can safely assume that the most important aspect of Herzeloyde lies in her function in the poem

---

[1] For a discussion of the significance of this phrase see below, p. 95 f..

and particularly in her relationship with the young Parzival, where a considerable elaboration is to be found.

The casual references (apart from those dealing with her virginity) are concerned exclusively with Herzeloyde's radiant beauty. The first shows its physical effect on Gahmuret:

> von dem liehten schîne,
> der von der künegîn erschein,
> derzuct im neben sich sîn bein:
> ûf rihte sich der degen wert,
> als ein vederspil, daz gert. (64.4 ff.)

This is taken up by the next passage, which intensifies the original impression of light by a striking hyperbole:

> vrou Herzeloyde gap den schîn,
> wærn erloschen gar die kerzen sîn,
> dâ wær doch lieht von ir genuoc. (84.13 ff.)

Later, in the description which forms an interlude during Gahmuret's absence in the service of the caliph of Baldac, there occurs the line: 'diu was als diu sunne lieht' (102.26). The use of the light metaphors goes back to the Bible, but there is a resurgence in the twelfth century under the influence of *Mariendichtung* and mystical literature, which is continued and expanded in the thirteenth century and later. The imagery of light is naturally directed towards expressing goodness and perfection, as Herzeloyde makes clear in teaching Parzival (119.18 ff.), and therefore is a mark of idealized characterization. It is applied also, among others, to Repanse de schoye—'ir antlütze gap den schîn, / si wânden alle ez wolde tagen' (235.17 f.)—and to Condwiramurs, who is called *diu lieht gemâl* and *diu lieht erkant*. In this same context of physical radiance we learn that Herzeloyde has a *minneclîcher lîp* (102.27), and in another place she soothes Kaylet's wounds with 'ir linden handen wîz: / an den lac der gotes flîz' (88.15 f.). In her anguish after hearing of Gahmuret's death she tears open her dress and shows her 'brüstel linde unde wîz' (110.25), the same adjectives being used here as before. None of these phrases creates an individualized visual picture of Herzeloyde; the result is merely a conventional idealization in terms of perfection in beauty, as is summed up in the phrase: 'si was gar ob dem wunsches zil' (102.30).

The longer descriptions expatiate on the excellence of Herzeloyde's bearing, firstly in a courtly setting, then in isolation from it in the wilderness of Soltane, and lastly after her death. There is a pronounced contrast between the first passage and the other two, but they are connected by the repetition of key words.

To begin with we have a description of Herzeloyde elaborating the idealized features already mentioned. We learn that she combines youth with magnificence and has 'freuden mêre dan ze vil' (102.29). She enjoys a good reputation in the world on account of her knowledge of good things, and her moral worth and purity receive nothing but praise. Just as Gahmuret is characterized by the word *kiusche* and Belacane's *kiusche* is so pure that it can represent baptism for her (28.14), so also Herzeloyde's virtue is subsumed under the term *kiusche*.[1] She loves her husband so greatly that it is of no consequence to her whether any other lady has so worthy a *friunt*. Added to these moral qualities is her high position as queen of the three countries of Waleis, Norgals and Anschouwe. The joy surrounding her at this time, however, is caused not by her fundamental character, but by various accidentals—by her love for Gahmuret and his reciprocation of it, by the worldly favour and renown accompanying this, and by the splendour of her position as queen of three lands. With the next description all these external causes for joy have been removed.

At the beginning of book III a complete contrast is found. Herzeloyde has left the world of courtliness 'durch des himiles ruom' (116.24) and become a stranger to her three countries, forsaking 'der erden rîhtuom', but being called, ironically, *diu rîche*. Similarly, the key word *freude* is taken up negatively by the line: 'si truoc der freuden mangels last' (116.30). The joy that formerly was hers is now expressed by an equally hyperbolical

---

[1] See above, p. 36, fn. 1.

grief, and she who was 'als diu sunne lieht' now finds a reversal of values:

> ein nebel was ir diu sunne:
> si vlôch der werlde wunne.
> ir was gelîch naht und der tac:
> ir herze niht wan jâmers phlac.　　　　(117.3 ff.)

This new situation is, however, not valued negatively since Herzeloyde's retirement from the world is motivated by *triuwe* (116.19), and in the middle of the description of her sorrow occur two lines which point forcibly to the positive side of her painful situation: 'der valsch sô gar an ir verswant, / ouge noch ôre in nie dâ vant' (117.1 f.). This passage taken together (116.28–117.6) marks the beginning of her purification from the ways of courtliness, a process which continues through Parzival's childhood until he finally leaves her.

The last descriptive passage is in the form of a *Totenklage* by Wolfram, apostrophizing Herzeloyde after her death on seeing Parzival depart into the world in search of Artus. For her there is now no further reason to live, since Parzival, her only remaining memory of Gahmuret, the centre of her existence and sole *raison d'être*, has gone. Wolfram takes up his comment from the introduction to book III: 'swer die [sc. armuot] durch triwe lîdet, / hellefiwer die sêle mîdet' (116.17 f.) with his initial remark: 'ir vil getriulîcher tôt / der frouwen wert die hellenôt' (128.23 f.). The *triuwe* to which Wolfram ascribes Herzeloyde's death is motivated on three levels—as faithfulness to the memory of Gahmuret, as a loving concern to protect Parzival from the dangers of a knight's life, and as the faithfulness to God of a religious recluse. It is this last aspect of religious *triuwe* which is most stressed in this passage. The lines quoted above are immediately followed by the phrase: 'ôwol si das se ie muoter wart!' (128.25), which with its similarity to the language of the cult of the Blessed Virgin Mary clearly emphasizes the religious excellence of her nature. This again is succeeded by a further eulogy of Herzeloyde, which attributes to her all goodness and humility:

'sus fuor die lônes bernden vart / ein wurzel der güete / und ein stam der diemüete' (128.26 ff.), and Wolfram laments that we, the poet and his audience, are not even related in 'der eilfte spân' to such virtue.[1]

ACTIONS

It is particularly difficult in treating the characterization of Herzeloyde to make a clear distinction between action and speech, since the two are closely linked, the one supplementing and explaining the other. Accordingly, the present section will merely sketch in the importance of Herzeloyde's position in the poem and leave the main discussion to the next section.

The threefold nature of Herzeloyde's part in the romance has already been mentioned. It now remains to be seen to what extent these various aspects cohere and how they affect the action of the poem.

First of all, the introduction of Herzeloyde into the poem is effected by the tourney at Kanvoleis. The queen offers herself and the lordship of her two lands to the knight who wins the day at her tournament, and, as is to be expected, Gahmuret is the successful knight whom the queen singles out for marriage. She had observed his arrival with keen interest, sitting at her window with her ladies, and after the tourney she is anxious to meet personally the knight on whom she had set her heart. Previously she had been troubled not to see the king of Zazamanc among the first to fight in the *vesperie*, but as soon as his armour had been fitted, he joined in and quickly outdid the rest. After the *vesperie* Herzeloyde goes to Gahmuret's tent and, in order to be able to show him the warmth of her welcome and the feelings motivating her visit, she has also, on his request, to kiss the other knights present, but she asserts her individuality through kissing only 'dies tâ wâren wert' (83.23). She has to persist in her initiative, since Gahmuret is reluctant to accept her offer on account of the fact that it was solely the desire for *rîterschaft* that brought him to Kanvoleis and also because of

---

[1] Cf. J. K. Bostock, *Der eilfte spân*, (*MLR*, LV, 1960). The whole question of Marian symbolism is treated below, pp. 93 ff.

his marriage with Belacane. Herzeloyde draws him closer to her
as they sit together:

> er saz für si sô nâhe nidr,
> daz sin begreif und zôch in widr
> anderhalp vast an ir lîp.
> si was ein magt und niht ein wîp,
> diu in sô nâhen sitzen liez. (84.3 ff.)

Moreover, she shows herself gracious to Gahmuret's entourage in
general, allows Brandelidelin to sit next to her and soothes Kaylet's
wounds with her 'linden handen wîz' (Kaylet is in any case her
aunt Rischoyde's husband), all these actions indicating her desires
towards Gahmuret. On the strength of the tournament she then
stakes her claim to Gahmuret in opposition to Ampflise and,
satisfied for the time being, departs.

More, however, is required than just this. Herzeloyde has to
take the leading part in the whole relationship, as Wolfram had
formed Gahmuret's character and history in such a way as to make
it impossible for him to act logically as the active lover of Herzeloyde, given the basis of his loyal relationship with Belacane.
Herzeloyde has to overcome Gahmuret's objections, founded on
his love for Belacane, in order to obtain her 'rights'; but although
the heathen queen's deficiency in Christian baptism should have
been sufficient to allow Gahmuret to dissolve his first marriage
without in any way staining his own character, the two have in the
end to resort to an impartial arbitration in order to reach a conclusion in the matter. But Herzeloyde's initiative presupposes a
certain individuality and is probably also an intentional contrast
with the normal *minne*-relationship. It can be paralleled with the
leading role of the lady in Wolfram's dawnsongs, where the knight
usually plays a subordinate, if not actually passive, part in the
development of the theme. Thus, in 3.1 it is the lady who speaks on
each occasion and who initiates the embraces; in 4.8 the exchanges
are invariably between the lady and the watchman; in 7.41 the
lady first complains at the coming of dawn and embraces her lover
before he has to depart, to which the knight reacts by assuming
the initiative, only finally to yield first place once more to the lady.

(By contrast 6.10 consists entirely of a warning on the part of the watchman, to which the knight replies, and commentary by the poet, the lady playing in this case an extremely passive role.)

In the first stage at least of Gahmuret's and Herzeloyde's married life Herzeloyde continues to give the lead:

> diu künegîn zir friunde sprach
> 'nu habt iuch an mîne phlege.'
> si wîst in heinlîche wege.
>
> ...
>
> juncfrouwen unt diu künegîn
> în fuorten dâ er freude vant
> und al sîn trûren gar verswant.
> entschumphiert wart sîn riwe
> und sîn hôchgemüete al niwe:
> daz muose iedoch bî liebe sîn.
> frou Herzeloyd diu künegîn
> ir magettuom dâ âne wart.
> die munde wâren ungespart:
> die begunden si mit küssen zern
> und dem jâmer von den freuden wern.   (99.30 ff.)

With this passage, marking the consummation of Herzeloyde's relationship with Gahmuret, the first section of her part in the poem is over. The two have come together from the ends of the earth, and from their union Parzival, the proper subject of the poem, is conceived. Gahmuret's function is now fulfilled: his separation from Herzeloyde and subsequent death in battle provide the necessary conditions for Parzival's boyhood.

A dream of extraordinary vividness and terror announces Gahmuret's death to Herzeloyde in a manner which illustrates the intimacy of their relationship. The form which the dream takes is reminiscent of the birth of Alexander in Lamprecht's poem (Strasbourg version 129 ff.), but the aim of the motif there—to indicate the divine origin of Alexander—is completely changed.[1]

---

[1] K. Lucae, *Über den Traum der Herzeloyde im Parzival* (ZfdPh, IX, 1877), implies that the idea of divine influence on the birth of Alexander is transferred to Parzival, but with Wolfram the motif is as important for illuminating the relationship between Gahmuret and Herzeloyde.

Gahmuret had been absent from Waleis half a year, and Herzeloyde's joy was based on the hope of his return. In the midst of this joy she is suddenly smitten by the effects of a terrible dream, whose supernatural character is confirmed by the news that Gahmuret's death had occurred as a result of heathen magic (105.16 ff.). The dream gives the lie to Herzeloyde's previous courtly existence, as Nora Schneider observes: 'In Bezug auf Herzeloyde bedeutet dieser Traum: Uebergang von der Gattin zur Mutter, ein Weg hinaus aus der höfischen Welt. Denn hier wird sichtbar, daß Herzeloydes höfische Unbeschwertheit nur Vordergrund war, und daß in Wirklichkeit ihr Wesen in Schwermut und Tiefsinn verwurzelt ist.'[1]

The lurid beginning of the dream, to the accompaniment of thunder and lightning, and the sensation of being lifted into the air among these various celestial manifestations, whose effect on Herzeloyde is described in some detail, is succeeded by a more personal depiction of her physical condition. Firstly a griffin comes and twists her right hand; then she has the feeling of nursing a serpent that tears apart her womb and of suckling a dragon that tears her heart out of her body and flies away never to be seen again. As Wolfram says: 'ez ist selten wîbe mêr geschehen / in slâfe kumber dem gelîch' (104.18 f.). Herzeloyde begins to weep and cry out in her sleep, is awakened by her maids and then faints on hearing from Tampanis, her husband's servant, of the death of Gahmuret.

The precise significance of all the dream imagery is not perfectly clear, but the dream itself requires a twofold interpretation, which sheds light on the relationships of Herzeloyde with both Gahmuret and her as yet unborn child. The position of the dream in the development of book II, between Wolfram's comment: 'dô brast ir freuden klinge / mitten ime hefte enzwei' (103.18 f.) and the news of Gahmuret's death, indicates a natural connexion between the dream and Gahmuret's end in battle, this being supported by Tampanis' report that he was killed as a result of heathen magic, which would serve as an explanation of the extraordinary

[1] Nora Schneider, *Erziehergestalten im höfischen Epos* (Diss. Bonn, 1935), p. 50.

phenomena of the dream. Thus, the heart is the seat of *minne*, and its being torn away by the dragon is symbolic of Herzeloyde's final separation from her husband; and in so far as *minne* is at this time the essence of her existence, the loss of her heart signifies the end of her courtly life. If she is to continue to live, the centre of her existence must be fixed elsewhere—on God and on Parzival.[1] At the same time, however, the dream must be interpreted with reference to Parzival, and this is possible because Herzeloyde identifies Parzival with Gahmuret, and the two are as it were one person for her (113.13 f.). Thus, in book IX, Trevrizent alludes to the dream in this way and equates Parzival with 'daz tier daz si dâ souc, / unt der trache der von ir flouc' (476.27 f.) on account of the cruel and thoughtless way in which he caused his mother's death, Parzival being at that time the unborn child in the womb. The dream is undeniably striking in its effect and in its twofold significance shows a greater individuality than its parallel or probable source in the *Alexanderlied*.

After Gahmuret's death some of his possessions are brought back to Kanvoleis, among them his tattered, bloodstained battle-tunic, which Herzeloyde wishes to wear, as she used to formerly on Gahmuret's return from tourneys (101.9 ff., 111.26 ff.), but she is prevented from doing this, and his spear and tunic are buried in the minster.

Herzeloyde's grief is slightly mitigated by the knowledge that she bears Gahmuret's child in her womb, although the physical suffering she endures at this time is extreme. Parzival's birth brings her near to death, but she recovers and rejoices to find her child is a boy, kisses him again and again, calls him 'bon fîz, scher fîz, bêâ fîz' and gives him to suck. She feels as though Gahmuret were with her again (113.13 f.), and this feeling strengthens the fact that

---

[1] The image of the heart is used frequently by Friedrich von Hausen (particularly in the crusading lyrics) for the seat of *minne*. In the poem 'Mîn herze und mîn lîp diu wellent scheiden' (*MF* 47.9), however, the *herze* is clearly subordinated to the *lîp*, which is serving God in a crusade. Transferring this idea from the knight to Herzeloyde, who is separated from Gahmuret, we find that courtliness alone is insufficient and that her personality is threatened with extinction unless she turns to an existence with more enduring values.

whereas the motherhood of Herzeloyde is emphasized to a far greater extent than any other aspect of her existence, it must none-theless be borne in mind that this is not her only attribute. Her motherhood cannot be too distinctly separated from Gahmuret's fatherhood, and it is her position as the wife of Gahmuret which provides the structural link between the ideas of books I and II and the Parzival story proper. While rejoicing at the birth of her son, Herzeloyde remembers the Virgin and the birth of Jesus, but her joy is continually mingled with pain and sorrow.

Herzeloyde's life in the wilderness of Soltane is motivated on several levels, not all of which are immediately expressed. Wolfram gives us to understand first of all that she has withdrawn from the courtly world for the sake of living a virtuous life in poverty (116.15 ff.): a life thus led for the sake of *triuwe* leads to heavenly bliss. She seeks out a place lacking in flowers and meadows to correspond with her *jâmer*, and here she educates Parzival in isolation from the world of knights in order to prevent him from being endangered by the same hazards to which his father succumbed. It is not until Parzival is ready to leave Soltane that Herzeloyde mentions that Lähelin had invaded his lands of Waleis and Norgals and won them from him. This last motivation is probably accounted for by the *Conte del Graal*, where Perceval's mother explains how his father's territories had been lost after the death of Uterpandragon (438 ff.). The account is rather imprecise, and Wolfram must have wanted to make clear how Herzeloyde had lost her lands without immediately prejudicing the moral reasons for her flight to Soltane, which are his innovation and mark Herzeloyde's individuality.

Herzeloyde's poverty is only relative to her wealth as queen of Waleis: she has in the wilderness farmers and cowherds who culti-vate her land and also several maidservants. Nevertheless, the life she and her followers lead is simple and far removed from all courtly influence, which is Herzeloyde's prime intention. Here she brings up Parzival alone, impressing on her servants the necessity for him never to learn about the ways of knights, disobedience to this command being punishable with death. Parzival is the sole reason for which she lives, and when she finds him listening to the song of the birds, a symbol of *freude*[1] which reminds her too forcibly of courtliness, she is overcome by an irrational desire to remove them (earlier Parzival had been moved to tears by birdsong, and Herzeloyde remembers this for a long time). She sends her farmers and cowherds out to kill the birds, but the birds are too quick for them. When Parzival innocently questions her action, she gives way and realizes the folly of it, admitting to having transgressed God's commands in what she had done. This gives her an opportunity to educate Parzival in religious matters and distinguish between good and evil in such a way as to make it possible for him to generalize on her remarks and mistake the knights for gods.

When Herzeloyde hears of the fateful meeting with the knights, she is terrified by Parzival's words and faints. On regaining consciousness her first reaction is to enquire where he had learnt about the knights, since she had thought she had reckoned with all the possibilities there were in the isolation of Soltane. She cannot face the thought of losing Parzival, who is at the centre of her life, and she racks her brain to discover a means of keeping him away from Artus' court. In the end she has to give way to his will, but she dresses him in fool's clothing in the hope that if people should mock at him he will return to her. She persuades him to stay the night before setting out and gives him advice as to how to behave with the various people he will be likely to meet. Then, on the following morning, she kisses him, runs after him and, realizing that all hope of his returning to her is illusory, she falls to the ground and dies, deprived of the only thing that gave her life meaning. She had done all she could to protect Parzival from falling a prey to the same stroke of fate as Gahmuret, but all fails.

---

[1] The connexion of birdsong with *freude* specifically is common in all courtly literature. Cf. Veldeke, *MF* 56.1, 62.25, 64.17, 65.28; Walther 45.37, 92.9, 110.27 (numbering according to Lachmann); in Provençal literature Bernart de Ventadorn's 'Can vei la lauzeta mover', Jaufre Rudel's 'Quan lo rossinhols el folhos' and Giraut de Bornelh's 'Er'ai gran joi que·m remembra l'amor', are three obvious examples. Moreover, the passage in the *Conte del Graal* (86 ff.) corresponding to the lines in *Parzival* also contains the idea of joy.

Herzeloyde's action is at bottom a selfish one, despite the fact that she genuinely believes it to be in Parzival's best interests, since she looks upon Parzival as a source of psychological support. From her very first appearance in the poem, her part is determined by a craving for dependence (hence the tournament). She finds her relationship with Gahmuret fulfils this and contents herself with Parzival when her husband is taken from her. Consequently, when she loses this last support, this last emotional bond, there is no longer any point of dependence for her. The initiative which she had taken with Gahmuret at the tournament has at its root the need for security and emotional dependence, which means that she cannot be fully individualized. Indeed, her character would have no relevance were it not for her relationships with Gahmuret and Parzival. When she loses both of them, she loses her own existence. Independence as at the beginning is impossible in view of her unbounded grief; nothing else can follow but death.

THE USE OF DIALOGUE

It is a sign of Herzeloyde's importance in the poem that by far the greatest part of her characterization is achieved through dialogue. Because of her weakness as an individual (apart from her exemplifying the concept of motherhood) it was necessary to emphasize her position by more than mere description. She is allowed to express herself directly, dramatically, and features of this kind greatly assist in creating a picture of her that is not purely conventional and does not represent her as a type.

Herzeloyde's remarks are all of interest for a study of her character, since very few of them are purely objective by nature. For convenience' sake they may be divided under the headings *minne*, courtliness and religion, but all three are interrelated and should be understood in conjunction with each other.

(i) In discussing the theory of *minne* with reference to Herzeloyde we need to distinguish between her *minne*-relationship with Gahmuret, in which she herself plays an active part, and the instruction about *minne* which she gives to Parzival. In the first case theory and practice are presented together; in the second she merely gives a few characteristic attitudes, which Parzival is not in a position to invest with a precise ethical meaning, as he is at the very beginning of his development and has no experience of what his mother has told him. Herzeloyde's instruction is understandable only to one already versed in the ideology and basic theory of *minne*.

From the moment Herzeloyde appears in the poem her attention is fixed on Gahmuret, and the first words which she speaks are also concerned with him, though she speaks to her followers, enquiring where the knight of whom she had heard so many wonders had come from. Because of Gahmuret's connexion with Belacane, of which indeed Herzeloyde is at first ignorant, the roles of seeker and sought are reversed. Normally the knight seeks the favour of the lady; here the lady seeks the service of the knight. This situation is paralleled by that of Dido and Eneas in Veldeke's *Eneide*, where Dido similarly offers her *dienest* to Eneas:

> Enêas der hêre,
> dem wele ich goet end êre
> ende dienste doen alsô vele,
> als he selve nemen wele.
> ich wele em bieden âne nôt,
> dat ich manne gebôt
> in dirre werlde noch nie,
> end wold er altoges wonen hie.
> . . .
> ich deile em lûde ende lant
> end allet dat ir hie gesiet. (535 ff.)

On another occasion Dido says: 'ich hân mîn dienest verloren' (2120), and Veldeke comments in one instance: 'her dienest was vele gereit / heren lieven gaste' (1636 f.). In early courtly literature the service between knight and lady is mutual, so that it is not only with Dido that the idea of service on the part of the lady is to be found. Veldeke writes also of Lavine: 'et ontbûdet Lâvîne / Enêâse den rîken / her dienest innelîke' (10794 ff.). In *Parzival*, however, it is only in the case of Herzeloyde that *dienst* on the part of the lady is explicitly mentioned: 'hêr, nu sît ir mîn. / ich tuon iu dienst nach hulden schîn' (96.7 f.).

Gahmuret has come to the tourney for the sake of *âventiure*, not for the sake of the lady who had promised her hand to the winning knight. The unusual situation ensures that Herzeloyde has to woo him and convince him of the rightness of becoming her husband. This involves removing the claims of two rivals, which Herzeloyde achieves by Christian logic in the case of Belacane and in Ampflise's case by the fact that she herself intends to assume the role of Gahmuret's *Minneherrin*, but under the conditions of marriage. She is conscious of being supported by the rules of the tournament which she arranged, as well as having a certain moral claim to Gahmuret's service:

> swaz mînes rehtes an iu sî,
> dâ sult ir mich lâzen bî:
> dar zuo mîn dienst genâden gert.
> wird ich der beider hie gewert,
> sol iu daz prîs verkrenken,
> sô lât mich fürder wenken. (87.1 ff.)

Later, in a further attempt to convince Gahmuret of his duty, she expresses the transcendental nature of *Minnedienst* in the serving of womankind in the one lady:

> nu êret an mir elliu wîp,
> und lât ze rehte mînen lîp.
> sît hie unz ich mîn reht genem:
> ir lâzet anders mich in schem. (88.27 ff.)

By this time Gahmuret is losing his powers of resistance and promises to do as she wishes.

All Herzeloyde's remarks at this stage are made in an awareness of her position as the educator of Gahmuret. So far he has only enjoyed the love of Belacane and the specifically courtly relationship with Ampflise, and Herzeloyde's task is to take him beyond this point and bring him to an understanding of a new doctrine of *minne* within the bounds of marriage, to educate him away from the self-centred love of an individual woman, Belacane, and the service of a distant, almost impersonal *Minneherrin*, Ampflise, to loving womankind in the one lady, herself, Herzeloyde, who can fulfil this function on account of her beauty and her consciousness of her position. This educative process is a long-lasting struggle for Herzeloyde.

After the tournament she goes to introduce herself to Gahmuret, being 'wirtîn überz lant' (83.14), but her advances are at first warded off. Slowly, however, she gains her will. She stresses to Gahmuret that her *minne* is superior to Belacane's on account of her baptism and that he should love her 'nâch unser ê: / wan mirst nâch iwerr minne wê' (94.15 f.). She also mentions her rival Ampflise and asks whether she is the obstacle to their union. On hearing Gahmuret's reply with its various reasons for his unwillingness, she is dissatisfied and returns impatiently: 'lât mich den lîp niht langer zern: / sagt an, wâ mite welt ir iuch wern?' (95.11 f.). This tension can only be removed through arbitration, and when the verdict is given in her favour, she triumphantly informs Gahmuret:

> hêr, nu sît ir mîn.
> ich tuon iu dienst nach hulden schîn,
> und füege iu sölher fröuden teil,
> daz ir nâch jâmer werdet geil. (96.7 ff.)

In this passage is expressed the essence of the new *minne*-relationship, which has more in common with the reciprocal service of early courtliness and Walther's demand for mutuality than with the virtually unrequited love-relationship of *hôhe minne*. Here, in Herzeloyde's interpretation of *minne*, the lady, in receiving the honour paid her by the knight, also gives him service in that she brings him the reward of *freude*, with its implications of the highest expectations of physical fulfilment, though this is not to be considered as a matter of course, but rather 'nach hulden schîn'. The education of Gahmuret is complete but for the consummation, which Herzeloyde soon remedies (99.30 ff.). The queen succeeds in her desires, but she has in return to grant Gahmuret a concession, the one which leads to his death: 'hêr, nemt iu selbe ein zil: / ich lâz iu iwers willen vil' (97.5 f.).

Gahmuret, in addition to claiming the right to a monthly tournament, asks to be freed from the necessity of *huote* (96.25 f.). About this courtly custom Hans Furstner writes: 'Die höfische Gesellschaft, wie sehr auch vom Dichter in der Problematik der *minne* einbezogen, wollte im tiefsten Grunde die *minne* als Dasein nicht anerkennen. Die *huote* und die *merkære* sind keineswegs etwa vom Gemahl der *frouwe* eingesetzt, um die Frau vor zu dreisten Annäherungen seitens des Ritters zu schützen: davon ist im Minnesang überhaupt nicht die Rede. Die *merkære* sind Repräsentanten der *liute*, der Gesellschaft, der Welt. . . .'[1] If this is so, then Gahmuret's demand is a denial of the courtly world— his relationship with Herzeloyde is not a courtly one, but on the contrary a human relationship—and an assertion that he has nc need of *huote* in order to preserve his *êre*. If Wolfram's new approach to the question of *minne* was not already perfectly clear, then this rejection of *huote* makes it obvious. The relationship between Gahmuret and Herzeloyde exceeds the limits of pure courtliness in that it is not based on *hôhe minne*, hence the initiative on Herzeloyde's part, hence the consummation in marriage, hence the mutual service. It is sharply contrasted with Gahmuret's liaison with Ampflise and clearly supersedes it. Herzeloyde's attitude is an individual one, a fact which must be strongly emphasized, and paves the way for a fuller treatment in the relationship of Parzival and Condwiramurs.

(ii) In book III Herzeloyde expresses to Parzival her understanding of courtliness, which has been radically changed as a result of Gahmuret's untimely death. Her attitude is largely negative, but we must beware of evaluating it in a completely negative fashion. Nora Schneider's analysis, admirable as it is in most respects, judges Herzeloyde's action after Gahmuret's death in the light of Gahmuret's morality and of the one-sided education which Parzival receives from her,[2] all of which may have its value if we look at the situation in modern terms, but this is not Wolfram's

---

[1] Hans Furstner, *Studien zur Wesensbestimmung der höfischen Minne* (Groningen/Djakarta, 1956), p. 64.
[2] *Op. cit.*, pp. 52 ff.

attitude. Nowhere does he seek to derogate from Herzeloyde's action, but considers it according to her own viewpoint and continually stresses the virtue of her *triuwe*. Nora Schneider writes:

> Die Tragik Herzeloydes aber ist es, ... daß sie sich aus *triuwe* zu Gahmuret an dem eigentlichen Sinn der *triuwe* vergeht. Sie bewahrt Gahmuret zwar ihre Liebe. Aber sie bringt es nicht fertig, sich selbst in dieser Liebe zu wandeln. Sie ist aus dem Rahmen der Zeit und des höfischen Raumes herausgetreten und entzieht sich der Verantwortung, die ihr aus der *triuwe* zu Gahmuret Parzival gegenüber erwächst.[1]

Surely, however, the case is that Herzeloyde has a different ideal before her, namely, that she can be most faithful to Gahmuret by attempting to spare Parzival a fate similar to the one which caused his father's death and by bringing him up in a state of youthful innocence. She unfortunately miscalculates the power of heredity, but her intention is nonetheless motivated by faithfulness to what she considers to be a higher ideal. The criticism that her behaviour is 'unhöfisch'[2] is true, but it was never intended to be courtly on account of her experience with Gahmuret; it cannot therefore be judged on these grounds. That she also acts 'unchristlich' and 'ungermanisch'[3] may be questioned. Herzeloyde's withdrawal from the world is in itself a neutral feature, and Wolfram is not trying to venture deliberately outside the limits of orthodox Christianity. Herzeloyde is *not* guilty of individualism in the sense of *superbia*, as the laudatory report of her death makes abundantly clear. The fact that Wolfram does not consider it necessary to insert references to specific practices of the Church in describing this period of Herzeloyde's life is solely an indication that his main concern is with the religious and not with the ecclesiastical, but he does not see them in opposition to each other (this point will be dealt with in more detail later). The 'un-Germanic' attitude of Herzeloyde (if such an epithet is at all relevant) as educator of Parzival is again explained by her different interpretation of her duties as the mother of Gahmuret's son. The whole question of

[1] *Op. cit.*, p. 54.   [2] *Ibid.*, p. 53.   [3] *Ibid.*

Parzival's education has to be seen and judged in the light of Herzeloyde's own sorrowful experience of Gahmuret's death. On settling in Soltane Herzeloyde tells her followers, on pain of death for disobedience, that they should not allow Parzival to learn about knightly society. When she then hears that he has become acquainted with knights, she immediately faints at the shock and on regaining consciousness enquires where he had learnt about them: 'sun, wer hât gesagt / dir von ritters orden? / wâ bist dus innen worden?' (126.6 ff.). She dimly realizes that from now on she will not be able to persist in the same anti-courtly spirit as had formed the basis of her previous existence in the wilderness, but she nevertheless dresses Parzival in fool's clothing in the hope that the mockery of the courtly world will drive him back to her. In this unstable frame of mind she gives Parzival various items of advice about courtliness, but they are all external and superficial, as her emotional distance from courtly practice is so great that she is incapable of imparting its ethical structure to Parzival. What she tells him presupposes a knowledge of the spiritual aspect of *minne* (which she herself had) to be comprehensible. Obviously, Parzival lacks this, and so it is impossible for him to find his way about the courtly world solely on a basis of this information.

Herzeloyde stresses the importance of greeting people generally and *guotiu wîp* in particular: 'du solt dich site nieten, / der werlde grüezen bieten' (127.19 f.); 'swâ du guotes wîbes vingerlîn / mügest erwerben unt ir gruoz, / daz nim: ez tuot dir kumbers buoz' (127.26 ff.). In the first place her advice is that Parzival should greet all he meets—a sign of good breeding—and this advice he follows to the letter. The second piece of advice is more circumscribed and is a limitation of the courtly ideal of honouring womankind in that the ladies must be *guot* whom Parzival greets. Walther also had made this kind of distinction in his attack on the normal conception of *minne*, and references to *guotiu wîp* frequently occur in his songs.[1] Earlier Herzeloyde had said: 'nu êret an mir

---

[1] Cf. the following passages, quoted according to Hermann Paul's edition (P) (Halle, 1945): 'Sich wænet maneger wol begên / sô daz er guoten wîben niht enlebe: / Der tôre kan sich niht verstên / waz ez vreude und ganzer wirde

elliu wîp' (88.27), implying her own worthiness to be honoured, and now she strictly defines her attitude towards courtliness by making a qualitative distinction with a high standard against which to measure womankind. The term *gruoʒ* is at times used as a circumlocution for *bî ligen*, but here it must be understood in its literal sense in view of the fact that Wolfram's ideal of *minne* is included in marriage and that this advice refers to woman in generic and not specific terms. Herzeloyde couples with this basic concept of the *gruoʒ*, which in *hôhe minne* is 'des Minnesängers höchstes Glück',[1] the mention of winning 'guotes wîbes vingerlîn', which is the outward sign of having reached the position to which the *gruoʒ* is only the first stage on the way. These two favours have to be *erworben* (a fact which Parzival later glosses over), and only after being *erworben* can they be followed by the kisses and embraces, of which his mother next speaks:

> du solt zir küsse gâhen
> und ir lîp vast umbevâhen:
> daz gît gelücke und hôhen muot,
> op si kiusche ist unde guot.   (127.29 ff.)

The last phrase ties up with Herzeloyde's previous injunction that the lady must be *guot*; here it is further emphasized by the use of the word *kiusche*. Herzeloyde's teaching consists purely of external, sensual forms, but the ideal state to which they are supposed to lead, if the advice is followed correctly, is not sensual, but spiritual. The term *gelücke* can be applied generally to sensual as well as to spiritual pleasure, but *hôher muot* is a state of mind or

gebe. / Dem lîhtgemuoten dem ist iemer wol / mit lîhten dingen, als ez sol: / swer wirde und vreude erwerben wil, / der diene guotes wîbes gruoʒ' (P 6.31 ff., L 96.9 ff.). 'swâ man noch wîbes güete maz, / dâ wart ir ie der habedanc' (P 20.7 f. L 92.16 f.). 'swer guotes wîbes minne hât, / der schamt sich aller missetât' (P 20.47 f., L 93.17 f.). 'Swer verholne sorge trage, / der gedenke an guotiu wîp: er wirt erlôst' (P 42.17 f., L 43.9 f.). 'Der alsô guotes wîbes gert als ich dâ ger, / wie vil der tugende haben solte!' (P 51.28 f., L 59.10 f.). 'Vrouwe, daz wil ich iuch lêren, / wie ein wîp der werlte leben sol: / Guotiu liute sult ir êren, / minneclîche an sehen und grüezen wol: / Eime sult ir iuwern lîp / geben vür eigen, nemet den sînen. / vrouwe, woltet ir den mînen, / den gæbe ich umbe ein sô schœne wîp' (P 28.17 ff., L 86.15 ff.).

[1] Furstner, *op. cit.*, p. 153.

a condition, a basic attitude towards the world of confidence and joyfulness. The external nature of Herzeloyde's advice contrasts curiously with the idealism of its imagined results, and its effect on the young Parzival serves to underline the extent to which she had lost touch with the spirit of the courtly world.

The teaching of Herzeloyde on *minne* is paralleled to a certain degree by her own behaviour towards Gahmuret, which itself is a deviation from the courtly norm. She goes to meet him in his tent, kisses him and 'dies tâ wâren wert' and embraces him closely (84.4 f.). Later it is mentioned that they exchanged greetings 'nâch zühte kür' (84.19). All the necessary external elements are present, though it is Herzeloyde, and not Gahmuret, who takes the initiative, as we have seen before.

Together with this advice about *minne* Herzeloyde counsels Parzival to avoid 'tunkel fürte', a habit he rigorously observes, and to follow the teaching of 'ein grâ wîse man' on matters of *ʒuht*. All in all, the advice centres on *minne* and *ʒuht*, two important features of courtly life, but the key problems of *êre*, the theme of the courtly epic as a whole, and *mâʒe* (the problem of reconciling conflicting ethical duties) are not touched upon. This lack is a further indication of Herzeloyde's spiritual separation from courtly society. Her emphasis on *ʒuht*, which Parzival learns later from Gurnemanz and which leads him to refrain from asking Anfortas the reason for his pain, is another example of advice given without the necessary spiritual background. For Herzeloyde this was obvious, as we can see from her own actions previous to her flight to Soltane, but her advice does not provide an effective point of departure for Parzival. *Zuht* is something which she does not feel herself qualified to instruct Parzival in; she merely indicates it as a *sine qua non* of courtly life and advises her son to seize the opportunity of instruction when it comes.

(iii) The comments which Herzeloyde makes on matters of religion are spiritual rather than ecclesiastical, since they refer to questions of doctrine more than the ritual practices of the Church. On one occasion, however, when she is endeavouring by all possible means to persuade Gahmuret to become her husband, she says: 'des toufes segen hât bezzer kraft. / nu ânet iuch der heiden-schaft' (94.13 f.), but here 'des toufes segen' is merely a synonym for 'Christianity' and does not imply, specifically, the rite of baptism. This does not mean that Wolfram is trying to create a dichotomy of spiritual and ecclesiastical affairs: for him the two are inseparable, and although the development of Parzival's character towards maturity shows the precedence in Wolfram's mind of the spiritual, this does not entail the assumption that the ecclesiastical is superseded. Indeed, where people are apparently spiritually equal, the ceremonial adjunct of baptism in the case of one is sufficient to weight the balance in that one's favour. Thus, although Wolfram writes of Belacane: 'ir kiusche was ein reiner touf' (28.14), Herzeloyde is able to dismiss (perhaps rather tendentiously) Gahmuret's objection that he is already married on the grounds that she herself possesses Christian baptism (cf. the importance of baptism in the incorporation of Feirefiz into the Grail family, where a similar spirituality is apparent without being accompanied by baptism). An arbitration is necessary not on account of the invalidity of Herzeloyde's claim, but because of Gahmuret's inability to come to a decision himself. To Gahmuret Herzeloyde is the representative of religious belief and, after his mother, who casts doubt upon God's purposes when Gahmuret leaves her, the first person to bring more than merely conventional religious formulas into the basic pattern of the poem.

Herzeloyde's other speeches are directed towards Parzival in answer to his question: 'waz wîzet man den vogelîn?' (119.10); they are the first formative element in the development of his religious ideas. Previously Wolfram had stated that Herzeloyde did not know the reason for her bitterness towards the birds, but in replying to Parzival she begins to doubt the rightness of her attitude: 'wes wende ich sîn gebot, / der doch ist der hœhste got? / suln vogele durch mich freude lân?' (119.13 ff.). In admitting that it is by God's command that the birds sing, she gives Parzival the opportunity to ask further: 'ôwê muoter, waz ist got?', in answer to which he receives his first religious instruction. This is given in the most rudimentary terms in a series of naïve contrasts between light and darkness, *triuwe* and *untriuwe*, which on account of their vagueness and descriptive rather than definitive nature allow Parzival to mistake for gods the knights he later meets in the forest. Beginning with the concept of light and using that as a basis, Herzeloyde describes the Incarnation, but without mentioning Christ by name. This last feature is characteristic of her individuality in that she avoids the normal terminology for Christ, and in not naming Him she gives an example of a lack of objectivity that is uncommon in medieval times and so makes it possible for Parzival, in his natural desire to objectify this abstract explanation, to transfer the image created by it in his mind to the knights. Herzeloyde continues by stating her confidence in God and counsels her son to pray to Him about his troubles, since 'sîn triwe der werlde ie helfe bôt' (119.24). Opposed to this God of light and salvation is the lord of hell, who is described in the exact contraries of what precedes: 'der ist swarz, untriwe in niht verbirt' (119.26). Parzival should turn his thoughts away from the devil and also (here she takes up the words of the prologue, which will be dealt with later in the chapter on Parzival) from *ʒwîvels wanc*, from lack of trust in God and lack of belief in His *triuwe*.[1]

Herzeloyde's explanation shows that her expression of religion is poetic and symbolic, not bound to dogma, though not contravening it. The imagery of light, with which Parzival becomes

---

[1] Since this chapter was first written an essay by Walter Johannes Schröder, *Die Soltane-Erʒählung in Wolframs Parʒival* (Heidelberg, 1963) has appeared which bears on the interpretation of Herzeloyde's character. While I am prepared to admit that there is a limited identification of Herzeloyde with the Virgin Mary and, as a logical extension of that, of Parzival with Christ, this is definitely and clearly subordinated to the individualizing trends visible in the characterization in general. I cannot follow Schröder's strictures on Herzeloyde's religion, which betrays no anti-Christian elements; one does not need to refer explicitly to the Trinity on every occasion in order to prove oneself a Christian. It is impossible for me at this stage to deal with Schröder's study at every point where I find myself in disagreement, especially as several of my divergences have the same basis as my disagreements with *Der dichterische Plan des Parʒivalromans*. I certainly do not think that 'Herzeloyde und Parzival sind rein dichterisch-fiktive Gestalten, sie sind in der Tat "Figuren", die so agieren, wie es das heilsgeschichtliche Urbild, das sie figurieren, vorschreibt' (p. 61).

intimately associated, is closely allied, in its connexion with the Incarnation, to the opening verses of St John's Gospel, the most mystical and symbolic of all the gospels. This advice is again, like that which Herzeloyde gave on *minne* and courtliness, insufficient in that Parzival is not in a position to evaluate and act upon it. All Herzeloyde's advice (except that on prayer—the one piece of concrete advice to strike home—which Parzival immediately puts into practice) requires enlargement before Parzival can understand it, and it is not until he meets Trevrizent that the religious teaching of his mother, the significance of which had hitherto evaded him, can be re-interpreted and presented to him in a way which speaks to his religious needs. Here again it is in a place of retreat and separation from the world that the religious values of Christianity are expounded to him.

Wolfram judges Herzeloyde according to her *intention* of educating Parzival away from the chivalric world, but in view of the fact that his life, once he has reached the brink of adolescence, leads into this world and then through it to the world of the Grail, we have to admit that this process of education is misleading. Herzeloyde reaches the height of her religious experience only *after* having lived fully in the courtly world (cf. also Gregorius), but she expects to be able to educate Parzival in such a way as to spare him the stage of experience in chivalry, and this hope is shattered. This pattern of deep spiritual awareness after active participation in the life of the courtly world is shared by and most clearly exemplified in Trevrizent, who exceeds the prowess of Gahmuret in his knightly career. Herzeloyde's standpoint, viewed objectively from outside, is deficient in its consciousness of the stages of development required of Parzival. In this case then Herzeloyde's role as educator is to be regarded in two opposing ways: firstly, as a praiseworthy attempt to guide Parzival away from every trace of chivalry, and secondly, as an unsuccessful endeavour to initiate him into courtliness, an endeavour which completely misleads him. This is the origin of the differing judgements of Herzeloyde's position as Parzival's educator, but both elements have to be taken into account. Wolfram emphasizes the first by expressing his own positive assessment of Herzeloyde's enterprise; the second becomes clear as Parzival blunders on from one encounter to the next, gradually learning the meaning of the very rudimentary and carelessly unqualified advice of his mother. The first is an expression of Herzeloyde's own character with its curious inconsistencies, since she spurs Parzival on to knightly activity in explaining how Lähelin had invaded and won his two lands of Waleis and Norgals, while at the same time trying to shield him from it by dressing him in fool's clothing; the second emerges as an unfortunate, but inevitable consequence of the first. This dual nature of her conduct dispels the possible conventionality of Herzeloyde's characterization and is in fact an individualizing element in her make-up.

MONOLOGUES AND MARIAN SYMBOLISM

The psychology of Herzeloyde is stressed at two critical points in her life by the use of monologues, which are found in two series— one dealing with her reactions on the death of Gahmuret, the other concerned with Parzival's departure from Soltane. These are her only monologues, but considerable effect is gained by this economy of usage, and these two periods of great emotional stress are made more significant through our being allowed to perceive the workings of her mind and spirit and see the mingling of personal with symbolic characterization.

The first group forms a complex of ideas best interpreted in a poetic sense: an attempt at literal interpretation would end in untold difficulties, as most of the references and allusions are in the nature of hints. Here Herzeloyde fuses together her relationship with Gahmuret and that with her unborn child. There is an aura of the *pietà* about the whole passage and also a similarity with the mystery of the mass of Christmas Day, when the birth and death of Christ are celebrated at one and the same time; but there is at this stage no explicit reference to the Virgin. However, the language Herzeloyde uses is reminiscent of the ways in which the Virgin's relationship with Christ and with the Holy Ghost (or the Father) would be portrayed, viz.: 'ich was vil junger danne er, /

und bin sîn muoter und sîn wîp' (109.24 f.). It is this identification of *muoter* and *wîp* that would lead to the idea of a comparison with the Virgin Mary.

This kind of statement, in which the same two persons in each *actually are* identified, would immediately bring to the mind of the medieval Christian the unique situation of the Virgin, who is both mother and bride to God as Christ and the Holy Ghost respectively. The lines quoted above look at the relationship from the inside as it were, from Mary's (Herzeloyde's) angle, whereas it is usual for the situation to be observed from the outside, the poet describing the mystery of God's twofold relationship with the Virgin. Thus, a passage in the *Litanei* dealing with the whole question of the theological position of the Virgin states: 'dv ne helfis uns, frowe, etislicher frist / vmbe den der din sun vnde din uater ist' (347 f.). Similarly, in a poem attributed to Walther the line is found: 'Er ist dîn kint, dîn vater und dîn schephære (P 107.15, L 36.25). Neither of these passages gives a perfect parallel with the lines from *Parʒival*, but the equation of either mother and wife or father and son would be unequivocally understood as an allusion to the Virgin and the Incarnation, and the parallelism which is here incomplete is supported by further allusions of a different kind later on in the poem.

Herzeloyde is therefore making a comparison of herself with the Virgin, and since Gahmuret and Parzival are expressions of human destiny on different planes and with different functions, neither of which invalidates the other, an analogy can be traced with the concept of Father and Son in the Godhead, both being united in the Virgin. Herzeloyde is at one and the same time the *mater dolorosa* and the *mater jocosa*, mourning the death of her son while at the same time bearing him in her womb, since at this time, and indeed later, Gahmuret-Parzival is one person for her. Herzeloyde is compelled to this identification, as her unborn child is all that she has left of what Gahmuret meant to her, and when Parzival is born, she is presented with a sense of their unity: 'si dûht, si hete Gahmureten / wider an ir arm erbeten' (113.13 f.).

Various later references substantiate this parallelism of Herzeloyde with the Virgin Mary, of which the clearest is when, after the birth of Parzival, Herzeloyde implicitly identifies herself with the Virgin with the Child Jesus at her breast. Her own purity and chastity is attested to by the fact that her previous marriage with Castis was never consummated and that she remained a virgin: 'si was ein maget, niht ein wîp' (60.15). This parallelism with the Virgin is again supported by Wolfram's comment after Herzeloyde's death, when he exclaims:

> ôwol si daz se ie muoter wart!
> sus fuor die lônes bernden vart
> ein wurzel der güete
> und ein stam der diemüete. (128.25 ff.)

Furthermore, Ither remarks on first seeing Parzival: 'gêret sî dîn süezer lîp: / dich brâht zer werlde ein reine wîp. / wol der muoter diu dich bar!' (146.5 ff.), which is echoed by a knight at Gurnemanz' castle: 'wol doch der muoter diu in truoc, / an dem des wunsches lît genuoc' (164.19 f.). Trevrizent also says of those named to the service of the Grail: 'wol die muoter diu daz kint gebar / daz sol ze dienste hœren dar!' (471.3 f.). The language used here is typical of that found in *Mariendichtung*. In Walther's *Leich*, for example, there is a similar statement, which shows the currency of the theme in contemporary poetry: 'Wol ir, daz si den ie getruoc, / der unsern tôt ze tôde sluoc! (P 94.45 f., L 4.16 f.). This theme 'ôwol der muoter' is a reminiscence of the words of St Luke xi. 27: 'Factum est autem, cum haec diceret, extollens vocem quaedam mulier de turba, dixit illi: Beatus venter qui te portavit, et ubera quae suxisti.' The theme of *wurʒel* and *stam* also occurs in the *Litanei*, which designates Mary as 'wurzel allir gute, / uon dir der ast blute' (295 f.) and declares that she is sprung from the root of Jesse: 'dv bist uze der wurzele iesse / ein gerte uz gesprungen' (210 f.), which has its origin in the prophecy of Isaiah xi. 1: 'Et egredietur virga de radice Jesse, et flos de radice ejus ascendit.' Wolfram's eulogy of Herzeloyde in the terms we are discussing would immediately be aligned by his audience with the position of the Blessed Virgin, and this is more important than the fact, which

Martin notes in his commentary, that *wurʒel* and *stam* are metaphors signifying the strength and power of Herzeloyde's moral qualities. The idealistic view of Herzeloyde's motherhood brought out by the preceding observations (despite the selfishness she may seem to have when seen in a modern psychological light or when judged from Gahmuret's standpoint, which is partially present in Wolfram's characterization) is maintained as the central aspect of her importance in the poem as a whole. When narrating her death immediately after Parzival's departure, Wolfram remarks only on her highest qualities and leaves us in no doubt of his own assessment of her when he mentions 'ir vil getriulîcher tôt' and the fact that she is going 'die lônes bernden vart', both of which link up with the beginning lines of book III (116.15 ff.). There is no hint of disapproval of Herzeloyde's attachment to Parzival. On the contrary, her actions are seen as those of a loving mother doing what she considers to be in her child's best interests.

The parallelism of Herzeloyde with the Virgin does not make her more of a personality in her own right. The function of the comparison is to emphasize the transcendent quality of human nature and the immediacy of the spiritual world through the medium of Christian symbolism. Thus, we have here a picture of Herzeloyde in universal terms, of an individual typifying one aspect of human personality with all its potentiality for perfection. The situation of the Virgin is, however, unique, and therefore the fact that phrases normally applied to the Virgin are transferred to Herzeloyde means that she is similarly to be seen as unique, at least in terms of poetic symbolism, if not in actual fact.

After this excursion on Marian symbolism we must return to a discussion of the monologues themselves. The main theme of the first series is the death of Gahmuret, and Herzeloyde expresses once more the extent of her joy at his splendour, now so sadly ended by his venturesome desires, but she is consoled at the knowledge of bearing in her womb the seed of his love and asks God to allow her to bring the seed to fruition. She complains that death has robbed her of too much in snatching Gahmuret away from her and dilates on his excellence, particularly on his success in love and on his compassion for noble ladies in distress, praising his manly loyalty and lack of deceit (but contrast his desertion of Belacane, where Gahmuret is conscious of guilt, while Herzeloyde never gives it a thought). Herzeloyde's sorrow at their separation is so great that she contemplates suicide, but turns away from it in her realization that she is bearing Gahmuret's child, whose death in this way would be a second death for Gahmuret. Her part is now to cherish her unborn child as that part of Gahmuret still living on. We are here seeing Herzeloyde wrestling with her desire to be true to her husband, a struggle which is resolved in the turning of her thoughts from death, both her own and Gahmuret's, to life continuing and the birth of their child. These monologues provide the first instance of Herzeloyde's deep religious awareness (the mention of baptism with regard to Belacane is merely a conventional assumption of the superiority of Christianity). Three times she asks for God's help, twice for the birth of her child and once to protect herself from the foolish torment of wanting to put an end to her life. We see her trying to answer Gahmuret's *triuwe* with an equally great loyalty on her own part.

Immediately following these monologues are two passages where Herzeloyde talks to her breasts, marvelling at her milk, which is already there before the birth of her son. For her it is a sign of *triuwe* and would have served for baptism, had she not already been baptized. Her *triuwe* is the equivalent of Belacane's *kiusche* (28.14), both being signs of a high personal morality which could have dispensed with the need for baptism. In her lamentation for Gahmuret Herzeloyde declares that she will pour over herself both milk and tears, doing this both 'offenlîch und tougen' (111.12) as a testimony to the world and as the expression of deep personal grief.

Perhaps of all the passages yet mentioned, whether monologues or otherwise, these two show most clearly the individuality of Wolfram's art. We are presented with a picture of intimate originality portraying a unique and moving scene in which both joy and sorrow, life and death, are combined in an unforgettable mingling of sadness and poetry. It is the visual quality of this section which makes it stand out in the memory.

Herzeloyde's religious awareness is further attested to by the last monologue of book II, where she alludes to the Virgin, with the Child Jesus at her breast. She then expatiates on the Atonement offered by Christ's death on the Cross and declares that if anyone should despise His love (*triuwe*), he would be in a grave situation at the time of judgement, however pure he might be. Here, as indeed later in the explanations she gives to Parzival, Herzeloyde underlines the importance of *triuwe* and uses, as elsewhere, highly pictorial language and vivid, visual imagery to express the human, this-worldly aspect of God's revelation to man in the Incarnation. Here we find Christ in His nearness to man because He was a man, and it is the human and not the transcendental aspects which are the object of Wolfram's description here. This human side of Christ only appears where mention is made of Mary, since she is the occasion for dwelling on it.

The last group of monologues is composed of two short passages introducing the *Dümmling* motif into the poem, which form a sharp contrast to the previous religious mood of what Herzeloyde had been saying and provide an example of the mingling of Wolfram's techniques. At this point all her thoughts are occupied with considering how she can best protect Parzival from the world of knights and so keep him still for herself, but she decides that she will give him what he asks unless it should be something evil. She resolves to make use of the habit that people have of mocking and laughing at others who are curiously dressed and to send Parzival out into the world in fool's clothing, and she is so self-centred in her aim that it is of little consequence to her that he should be 'geroufet unt geslagn' so that he might return to her. But despite all this preparation she has little confidence in her plan, so little in fact that when she sees Parzival ride away in the morning she falls to the ground and dies. Her idea of sending him out dressed like a fool is the last straw of hope to which she clings, but the little knowledge of courtliness which she imparts to Parzival shows that she realizes her precautions are likely to be of no avail whatsoever. The use of the monologue at this point stresses the depth of despair to which Herzeloyde has sunk in her last attempt to keep Parzival away from the perils of chivalry, giving at first hand a description of her intense emotion.

LATER REFERENCES

Many references are made to Herzeloyde after her death, but most of them are incidental and merely furnish a circumlocution for 'Parzival', but with the idea of inherited features included. Herzeloyde thus sets a standard for Parzival's behaviour, which he is not always able to reach. This kind of reference is scattered throughout the poem and is a method of keeping alive the mother-son relationship and Parzival's membership of the Grail family. The question of inheritance is made explicit, for example, at the meeting of Gawan and Parzival:

> da tet frou minne ir ellen schîn
> an den den Herzeloyde bar.
> ungezaltiu sippe in gar
> schiet von den witzen sîne,
> unde ûf gerbete pîne
> von vater und von muoter art. (300.14 ff.)

After the Good Friday meeting the following lines express the same idea, strengthening it by reference to the key theme of *triuwe*:

> hin rîtet Herzeloyde fruht:
> dem riet sîn manlîchiu zuht
> kiusch unt erbarmunge:
> sît Herzeloyd diu junge
> in het ûf gerbet triuwe,
> sich huop sîns herzen riuwe. (451.3 ff.)

Herzeloyde's *triuwe* is also quoted by Sigune (140.19) when she meets Parzival for the first time, and by Trevrizent when he informs him of his mother's death (476.25 and 499.23). Already what began as a periphrasis for 'Parzival' has developed into an enlargement on or confirmation of Herzeloyde's own character. Her relationship with other characters is also established more specifically. Sigune twice tells Parzival: 'dîn muoter ist mîn muome' (140.22 and 252.15). Wolfram informs us that Kyot read all the history of Titurel and his descendants, among whom was 'Anfortas, / des swester Herzeloyde was, / bî der Gahmuret ein kint / gewan' (455.19 ff.), this passage forming the first specific connexion of Herzeloyde with the Grail family. Trevrizent shows himself to be Herzeloyde's brother (475.19 and 497.24 f.), and at the very end of the poem Herzeloyde is mentioned with the other four children of Frimutel (823.17) with the comment: 'diu valscheit ûz ir herzen stiez.'[1]

It is solely in book IX that Herzeloyde's marriage with Castis is mentioned. This is in connexion with the explanation of the custom of the Grail knights in taking over the rule of lands that have no king, but it is not made particularly clear. We are told, however, that Castis (whose name suggests the idea of chastity) asked for the hand of Herzeloyde and was given her to marry, but that he died shortly afterwards on an expedition, but not before he had legally made over to her his lands of Waleis and Norgals. There is no further account of this relationship.

A further period of Herzeloyde's life is filled in by Sigune when she tells Parzival of his history. She adds to the facts already known that Orilus had left her, Sigune, in distress and that Herzeloyde had taken her as foster-daughter, from which she is able to recognize Parzival (140.15 ff.). When she mentions again at her second meeting with Parzival that Herzeloyde is her aunt, she also adds a word of praise: 'wîplîcher kiusche ein bluome / ist si, geliutert âne tou' (252.16 f.).

Other passages illustrate the young Parzival's relationship with her, but add little to our knowledge of Herzeloyde herself. While they are of much greater significance for the understanding of Parzival, they do keep alive our awareness of Herzeloyde's role in the poem long after she has ceased to be an active character herself.

---

[1] Earlier in the poem, at the second appearance of Sigune, we are told that Frimutel 'liez vier werdiu kint' (251.11). Schoysiane is probably the one who caused the miscount.

Certain additional material facts are given in these posthumous references, but there is nothing new in the psychology.

CONCLUSION

The preceding study has shown what methods of characterization are used for the depiction of Herzeloyde and demonstrated the wideness of their application. Perhaps the first thing that emerges from this is the diversity we find in a character W. J. Schröder sees fit to call 'typisch'. Herzeloyde's three roles as queen, wife and mother preclude her from being any one type exclusively, but one cannot go on to assert with Schröder: 'Wechselt die Funktion, spielt die Figur also eine doppelte Rolle, so tritt das Unlebendige, Maskenhafte besonders hervor.'[1] It is true that there is a marked difference between the Herzeloyde who woos Gahmuret and the mother-educator of Parzival, but there are several features which make this difference psychologically comprehensible and which provide links between the two aspects of Herzeloyde's character. At the beginning Herzeloyde represents a radically modified interpretation of courtliness; at the end she is seen in retreat from the courtly world, imbued with a deep religious faith. These two diametrically opposed views are not in any way synthesized; there is, on the contrary, a complete cleavage between them, marked by Gahmuret's death, and the severe emotional shock resulting from this acts as the point by which they are joined. Herzeloyde reacts violently against her former courtly life and determines to renounce it and live in austere simplicity, devoted to the task of bringing up her son in an isolated atmosphere unsullied by the danger and sorrow that courtliness could bring. While it is clearly Gahmuret's death which gives the psychological impetus for Herzeloyde's retirement into Soltane, there are several features which have a basis in both aspects of her existence. In her relationship with both Gahmuret and Parzival Herzeloyde is the dominant partner. With the former her dominance is partially caused by the plot, as Gahmuret could not both be faithful to Belacane and at

---

[1] *Der dichterische Plan*, pp. 411 f.

the same time consistently woo another wife, but since Herzeloyde also takes the initiative in organizing the tournament and, ostensibly, in withdrawing with Parzival from the world of chivalry, this must be seen as an essential component of her own character. In both relationships she is conscious of her task as educator, though this is primarily concerned with *minne* in Gahmuret's case and with religion in Parzival's. In both instances, however, there are elements of *minne* and religion; with Gahmuret the question of Belacane's lack of baptism is touched upon, with Parzival there is the important advice on courtliness. Each of Herzeloyde's relationships seeks emotional dependence. Her first *point d'appui* is a sensual *minne*-relationship, and this is changed into an equally self-conscious, religiously biased relationship with the child produced by it for the second. Her position as the wife of Gahmuret is the structural link between the episodes centred on the queen of Waleis and those dealing with the boyhood of Parzival.

When we consider the position of Perceval's mother in Chrétien de Troyes' poem, we are immediately struck by Herzeloyde's individuality in that she possesses a name and because the tenuous details of her life given by the French poet (420 ff.) are expanded into a long episode in which she is the leading figure. Her position in the poem gains a deeper meaning in view of the fact that her story occupies the whole of book II and part of book III and thus prevents her from appearing solely as the mother-figure of the story of Parzival's youth. Moreover, we are shown that it is her own personal decision to retire to Soltane; the pressure of external circumstances is not mentioned until Parzival is ready to leave her. Here again we have an instance of Herzeloyde's initiative in action. Curiously, however, the treatment of Herzeloyde's religious attitude is by no means as specific as that of Perceval's mother, who teaches her son about angels and devils, instructs him in prayer, describes churches and monasteries to him and tells him to visit them, and also gives him detailed, though conventional, teaching about Jesus Christ. But though Herzeloyde tells Parzival less, her expression of religion is not conventional, as is that of Perceval's mother, but naïvely personal and careless of the outward forms of ecclesiasticism. The individuality here is in the attitude, not in the elaboration of already existing traits.

Herzeloyde is conventionally courtly so far as the external descriptions of her are concerned, and no clear-cut visual image appears as a result of them; everything is in the most general and idealized of terms. Furthermore, her courtliness is scarcely more than superficial, as her reaction at Gahmuret's death goes to show, and she quickly sweeps aside any influences it may have had upon her. Her view of the nature of *minne*, however, imparts individuality to the kind of courtliness she exhibits. Her attitude contrasts sharply with that of Ampflise, as it does not include within it the ideal of *hôhe minne*. For Herzeloyde the *minne*-relationship must be physically consummated, and this consummation must be within the bounds of marriage. The fact that she takes the initiative in it is not an essential factor, but the whole relationship is a mutual one and she offers *dienst* also to Gahmuret as well as accepting his. These features are to be found in the early courtly theory of *minne* as found, for example, in Veldeke's *Eneide*, but Herzeloyde qualifies them in her advice to Parzival by limiting the relationship to one with *guotiu wîp*. As a further difference in her relationship with Gahmuret she can, on Gahmuret's demand, dispense with the custom of *huote*. To some extent these deviations from *hôhe minne* are general to Wolfram's conception of the nature of *minne* (except in the case of Ampflise), but they are perfectly in keeping with Herzeloyde's character as developed elsewhere. Thus, her religious attitude would account for the idea of the consummation of *minne* within marriage as well as the restriction of the relationship to *guotiu wîp*, and her taking the initative and offering her *dienst* is typical of her dominance in her relationships with other people in general. This interpretation of *minne* is, however, clearly an individual one and forms one of the cardinal aspects of her characterization.

Just as a considerable amount of individualization was achieved with Gahmuret in the symbolism of the anchor, etc., so Herzeloyde is individualized by the use of Marian symbolism. She is given in poetic form the same unique position which the Virgin enjoys in spiritual reality. This may mean that Herzeloyde tends to typify the idealized concept of motherhood, but the Marian symbolism is carefully elaborated and creates an individual picture of Herzeloyde on account of its high idealism, beyond which it is impossible to go, and because it is applied to no one else. In this way we have an individuality in symbolism just as in Gahmuret's case. The psychological problems—as, for example, a thorough evaluation of Herzeloyde's role as an educator, or her inconsistent attitude towards Parzival on his leaving Soltane—are merely outlined, since too detailed a treatment of them might have damaged the position of Parzival in the poem, and as he now has become an active participant, *he* must be the centre of interest and *his* problems must be spotlighted. The use of symbolism coincides with the use of monologues, and in the case of Herzeloyde the monologues are less conventional than Gahmuret's and are more extensive. They mark a considerable advance from the dialogue of Schoette and Gahmuret on the latter's departure from Anschouwe in that the monologue focuses Herzeloyde more than the dialogue focuses Schoette, since all attention is directed solely towards her. This is a further sign of individuality.

In conclusion, we have to note various aspects of characterization and cannot categorically say that Wolfram is more concerned with establishing an individual picture of Herzeloyde than with indicating the universal side of her character. Both elements are present in the work. People *are* emerging as individuals, but they are also shown in conventional form (through the courtly descriptions) and as transparencies for ideas and figures that are universal and eternal (through symbolism and idealization). It is to Wolfram's credit that we do not feel Herzeloyde to be either merely conventional, merely symbolic or merely an individual and that we are not conscious of any gulfs that cannot be spanned in the characterization.

IV

PARZIVAL

INTRODUCTION

THE characterization of Parzival is, clearly, the most complex of all the characters portrayed in the poem. His story is its main subject, and although Gahmuret, Gawan and Feirefiz also function as the hero of a particular book or books, he is quite properly referred to as *des mæres hêrre*. Moreover, since his story is so diversified and moves on several levels, it can scarcely be described without involving the other main characters too. Some aspects of his story will therefore be dealt with in chapters devoted more particularly to some other character. Thus, a discussion of the theme of *minne* appears in the chapter on Condwiramurs, while the subject of Parzival's guilt is treated mainly in the chapter on Trevrizent. The conclusion of the poem is investigated both in the present chapter and in the chapter on Feirefiz. Such a procedure has its drawbacks in a slight duplication of material as well as a possible fragmentation of interlinked themes, but the quantity of the subject-matter is so great that some subdivision is necessary for a systematic analysis of it. Wolfram's use of Chrétien with respect to Parzival is dealt with at appropriate stages in this chapter and the others, but I have concentrated on interpreting Wolfram's poem from the text as much as possible.

SYNONYMS

In the course of his history from childhood to the kingship of the Grail Parzival, as is to be expected, is referred to in a considerably greater number of ways than any other character of the poem. The patterns formed by this large variety of names are skilfully contrived so as to focus particular aspects of Parzival's complex personality at illuminating moments in the unfolding of the plot as well as to indicate the development of the hero from a carefree, innocent childhood to his solemn destiny of the kingship of the Grail. Many of the synonyms used are not in themselves interesting for the individual light they throw on his character, but their combination with others, some of which occur once or twice only, provides a basis of typical knighthood against which the more individual features of his characterization can be seen more clearly. At times Parzival may be viewed from one particular angle—as the *Dümmling*, as the Red Knight—but no one of these outweighs the others so as to make Parzival solely a type: there is too much variety for this to be possible.

The introduction of Parzival into the poem after the prologue (4.15–26) immediately gives some of the key aspects of his character: *er stahel; er küene, træclîche wîs; helt; er wîbes ougen süeʒe; wîbes herʒen suht; vor missewende ein wâriu fluht; den ich hie ʒuo hân erkorn; dem man dirre âventiure giht.* Already he is characterized by boldness, by a handsome appearance, a reputation in the eyes of women, by moral purity; but then Wolfram proceeds to depict a hereditary background to this through the history of Gahmuret, and Parzival is re-introduced only at the end of book II. In this section he is described by reference to Gahmuret as *sînes verhes samen* (109.27) and as *die werden fruht von Gahmurete* (110.15), a method which is continued throughout the course of the poem and which emphasizes the continuity of the personalities and exploits of father and son in the world of *âventiure* and *minne*. The very first reference occurs after Gahmuret's death when Herzeloyde turns her attention to the *kint, daʒ in ir lîbe stieʒ* (109.3), of whom it is said he will become *aller ritter bluome* (109.11). Then there are two references which link up with the synonyms used after the prologue—Wolfram's 'professional' terminology— *dem diʒ mære wart erkorn* (112.12) and *diss mæres sachewalte* (112.17).[1] From the beginning the elements of heredity (looking backwards) and destiny (looking forwards), together with the author's personal interest in the character whose story he is telling,

---

[1] Parzival is also called *des mæres hêrre* (338.7) at the beginning of the Gawan episodes, and towards the end of them, in the last line of book XIII, Wolfram declares: 'an den rehten stam diz mære ist komen.'

are present as essential functions of characterization. Thus, Parzival is never described essentially for what he is at any one moment, but also for what he has been and for what he will become.

In the sphere of kinship motifs he is connected with both father and mother (these two relationships are obviously the most important) and also with many other relatives, to whom he stands in the relationship of *neve*, a term with as wide a range of application as the word *cousin* in Shakespeare's time.

There are a fair number of variations on the basic theme of *Gahmuretes kint*, which is itself used unadorned seven times,[1] viz.: *des künec Gahmuretes kint* (293.23, 301.5), *des werden Gahmuretes kint* (117.15, 748.15), *des werden Gahmuretes suon* (808.26), *des stolzen Gahmuretes kint* (761.17), *Gahmuretes sun* (*suon*) (332.23, 434.4, 697.21, 781.3), *fil li roy Gahmuret* (122.28, 153.22, 156.20, 197.1, 809.30). These references occur throughout the poem, and while their point of reference is identical, their significance varies. Thus, the first few references up to the death of Ither point the contrast between Gahmuret and Parzival and have an ironic flavour about them because of Parzival's adolescent difficulties firstly in becoming aware of the existence of knights, secondly in finding out about the true nature of knighthood, and thirdly in adapting himself to this ideal by the painful process of making mistakes. The later references show the dependence of Parzival on his heritage of *âventiure* and *minne* and their importance in his life. Where Parzival departs from the Arthurian court to prove himself in face of Cundrie's denunciation, the references to Gahmuret again have an ironical touch about them. Usually, however, the linking of Parzival's adventures with Gahmuret's name creates a depth of meaning in Parzival's own development as the name reminds us of Gahmuret's many deeds of valour and of his prowess in courtly love. But while we realize that Parzival does not immediately succeed to his father's reputation in battle—he has to learn the formal values of fighting before his courage and ability can be completely positively evaluated—he excels it, eventually, in

---

[1] 212.2, 224.5, 333.15, 695.25, 700.15, 717.23, 742.14. This last instance includes both Parzival and Feirefiz.

minne and proceeds to a standard of practice more consonant with the ideals of the Church. This aspect of *minne* provides the connexion with Parzival's higher destiny, that of the kingship of the Grail, in which he surpasses the reputation of his father.

Just as important as these references are those to his mother. In this case the variations are: *Herʒeloyden kint* (747.25, 827.6), *Herʒeloyden suon* (745.21), *Herʒeloyde fruht* (451.3), *Herʒeloyden barn* (318.3), *der süeʒen Herʒeloyden barn* (434.3), *[der] den Herʒeloyde bar* (300.15, 333.29). The reference to Herzeloyde constitutes a sign of Parzival's calling to the Grail kingship, since she is a member of the Grail family; and here once more the reference sometimes emphasizes the rightness of Parzival's doing and of his movement towards the Grail and sometimes points the contrast between his behaviour and his calling and therefore the distance which this movement has to cover. In the so-called *Blutstropfenepisode*, however, Herzeloyde's name is invoked together with Gahmuret's to stress not merely the power of *minne* in Parzival's life, but more especially the accompanying pain: 'und ûf gerbete pîne / von vater und von muoter art' (300.18 f.). At the time of Cundrie's curse we are again reminded of Herzeloyde and of Parzival's failure to achieve the Grail kingship on his first visit to Munsalvæsche, and we hear soon afterwards how he sets out on 'schildes ambet nâch dem grâl' (333.27). The following two references are on the occasion of Parzival's approach to Trevrizent; and the last three emphasize Parzival's destiny while at the same time having an additional practical value in distinguishing the two sons of Gahmuret by allusion to their respective mothers. One synonym may have several values according to the context.

At other times Parzival is referred to, by Herzeloyde and by Wolfram, as *sun* (*suon*),[1] and Herzeloyde herself calls him *bon fîʒ, scher fîʒ, bêâ fîʒ*[2] (113.4), which Parzival quotes to Sigune as the only name he knows, from which his cousin deduces his identity (140.6). Sigune, in common with Artus, Gawan and Trevrizent,

---

[1] 112.7, 114.3, 117.19, 126.6, 127.25, 128.3.18, 317.19 (meaning in this last case Gahmuret's *sun*).

[2] The term *biax fix* is used very frequently by Chrétien.

calls Parzival *neve*, once qualifying it with *liep* (254.20) and once
with both *liep* and *guot* (141.14). Trevrizent has frequent recourse
to the word[1] and on occasion qualifies it with *liep* also (480.20,
497.21). Artus uses this form of address three times (708.2, 717.29,
755.28) and on the last occasion adds *von Kanvoleiʒ*. Gawan also
calls Parzival *neve* (708.16, 758.7, 759.2.26), adding in the last
instance the qualification *von Kingrivâls*. Towards the end of the
poem Trevrizent changes his mode of address to *swester sun unt
der hêrre mîn* (798.10), thereby indicating a change in the relationship though the ties of kinship are just the same. In connexion
with Feirefiz Parzival is referred to as *bruoder*.[2] The word *kint* is
used on a few occasions at the beginning of Parzival's story (118.27,
126.26, 144.9), and the fisherman with whom he spends the night
after his encounter with Jeschute obsequiously adds the adjective
süeʒe (143.5). Once he is called *kindelîn* (112.6), and towards the
end of the poem he and Feirefiz are known as *eins mannes kint*
(740.5).

These various expressions of kinship establish Parzival as an
individual within a large family with a considerable number of
different relationships to link him with the Grail family, with
representatives of heathendom and with the large Arthurian circle.
Parzival's place within a community is essential to his development
as an individual, as it provides a stable basis for him to develop the
different facets of his character.

An examination of the types of terminology used to characterize
Parzival underlines the fact of his development, both physical and
spiritual. Thus, at the beginning he is most frequently referred to
as *knappe* (*knabe*),[3] this being a translation of Chrétien's *vallés*.
The use of this term (with one exception[4]) extends only as far as
the combat with Ither, after which the word *man* is used: Parzival

---

[1] 447.28, 486.22, 488.21, 492.23, 494.1, 500.3.26.
[2] 760.10, 769.19, 771.22, 773.2, 793.4, 811.24,29, 818.16, 823.5.
[3] 113.29, 117.30, 119.9.16, 120.27, 121.1.4.21.29, 123.19, 124.1, 125.27, 128.14,
129.3.11.16, 130.26, 131.4.22, 132.25, 138.2.15.20.27, 139.25, 140.3, 142.19,
143.1.15.19, 144.17, 146.4, 147.9.19, 149.5, 150.3.23, 151.18, 153.3, 154.28. But
other words are used side by side with *knappe* so that in fact a gradual progress
from boy to man is shown. Cf. Mergell, *op. cit.*, pp. 67 f.
[4] *ein strenger knabe* (290.6), used in the *Blutstropfenepisode*.

has proved his manhood with this combat and henceforth can be referred to accordingly. But even here the term *knappe* is modified by the addition of descriptive adjectives: *wol getán* (129.5, 131.1), *wol geborn* (132.15, 149.25), *guot* (138.7, 155.4, 156.29), *mære* (139.9, 144.6, 157.17), *wert* (126.19), *snel* (124.11), *unverdrozzen* (139.1), *unbetwungen* (148.19). Behind the first two and the last two of these expressions lies the idea of the *Dümmling*, this being ironically expressed at the beginning as Parzival fails to live up to his high birth and causes pain through his ignorance, and being directly expressed at the end.

The *Dümmling* theme is important in Parzival's development right up to the time of his departure from the Arthurian court at the end of book VI and is treated in a number of ways.[1] On one occasion the word *tump* is combined with *knappe* (126.19), but it also stands alone (149.6, 161.25) and in combination with *man* (161.17, 162.1, 468.11, 473.13) and with the name *Parzivál* (155.19, 161.6). Other ways of expressing the same idea are given by the words *tôr* (133.16), used by Jeschute in explaining her plight to Orilus; *der knappe der vil tumpheit wielt* (124.16), on the occasion of Parzival's meeting with the knights in Soltane; *der tumpheit genôz* (142.13), after his departure from Sigune; *an dem was tumpheit schîn* (163.21), when Parzival shows at Gurnemanz' castle how he follows his mother's advice to the letter. In two instances the word *tœrsch* is used, once combined with *knabe* (138.9) and once with *Wâleise* (121.5).

The word *Wâleis* provides Wolfram with a means of continuing the *Dümmling* theme in a more subtle way as far as book VI, since at this first conjunction of *tœrsch* with *Wâleis* Wolfram, following Chrétien, who has a similar comment to make on the word *Galois* (242–8), interpolates:

> ein prîs den wir Beier tragn,
> muoz ich von Wâleisen sagn:
> die sint tœrscher denne beiersch her,
> und doch bî manlîcher wer. (121.7 ff.)

[1] Cf. Mergell, *op. cit.*, pp. 68 f., for the element of development. For a more detailed discussion of the theme see below, pp. 142 ff.

When the term *Wâleis* is interpreted in later passages with this in mind, it becomes clear that this idea illuminates the significance of further episodes. Thus, the name is used when Parzival does not consummate his marriage with Condwiramurs on the first night (though there are also other considerations here[1]) (202.19); when Parzival meets Sigune after his first visit to the Grail castle (251.25); in the *Blutstropfenepisode*, when Parzival's 'witze was der minnen pfant', a situation which Wolfram considers harmful;[2] and at Artus' court, more especially when Cundrie comes and pronounces her curse on Parzival.[3] Probably, however, the later examples of the use of *Wâleis* are neutral in this respect, since they occur towards the end of the poem when Parzival has quite overcome his *tumpheit* (699.1, 706.29, 763.21). If anything, they may be slightly ironical in pointing back to a time when Parzival was not so experienced, but this might be to push the equation *Wâleis* = *tump* too far. The use of the word *witze* in earlier synonyms— *der knappe an witzen laz* (144.11), *der dâ was witze ein weise* (167.9), *der helt mit witzen kranc* (169.15)—supports the *Wâleis* = *tump* theory when Cundrie eventually arrives at Artus' court, since she is referred to as *der witze kurtoys* (312.22) and *diu maget witze rîche* (313.1). Being in this situation (as also at the end of the poem) the messenger bringing news of Parzival's destiny, she is surrounded with an aura of authority, and the contrast between this and Parzival's *tumpheit* is underlined by the use of the same word *witze*, which takes up, this time in a positive sense, that aspect of Parzival's character which proved his undoing. Parzival is at this time, however, referred to by the term *Wâleis*, which makes Wolfram's deliberate opposition of Cundrie and his hero a subtler piece of artistry.

As reference to Parzival as a *Wâleis* keeps alive the notion of his *tumpheit*, so the term *der rôte ritter* (*der rîter rôt*) reminds one of Parzival's guilt in killing Ither and of the uncourtly way in which

---

[1] See below, pp. 241 f.
[2] 281.11, 293.29, 294.9.27, 295.3.15, 300.1.20, 301.26, 305.8.
[3] 307.23, 308.11, 310.9.13.24, 311.8.15, 315.16, 319.3, 326.12, 327.15, 328.2, 329.14, 331.3, 332.1.

he did it. This name is used many times from book III to book VIII[1] and is also modified into the forms *den man den rôten ritter hiez* (202.21), *den man dâ hiez den ritter rôt* (176.20, 206.16), *den der sich der rîter rôt | nante* (280.9 f.), *ein ritter allenthalben rôt* (383.24), *einer, der truoc wâpen rôt* (618.21). In one place Parzival is explicitly called *der Ithêrn vor Nantes sluoc* (559.9). Many of these references to Parzival characterize him as he passes across the background of Gawan's exploits, more or less anonymously— in one instance he is at the same time called *der ungenante* (383.25), and on another occasion *ein ritter . . . | bî rôtem wâpen unrekant* (398.4 f.). But after Trevrizent has freed him from the burden of his sin, he is only twice mentioned in this way, the stain on his character having been removed through penitence and absolution. The title *der ritter rôt* was formerly Ither's (145.16), and Parzival's assumption of it, together with Trevrizent's declaration: 'du hâst dîn eigen verch erslagn' (475.21), raises the question of relationships and Parzival's identity, a question which will be discussed at greater length below. But it should be noted that the application of the title to Parzival entails a measure of Ither's own knightly prowess as well as of Parzival's guilt and of his knightly inexperience at the start of his career.

Modes of address are another means whereby Parzival's development is indicated, though these are not very varied. They begin with the name *junchêrre*[2] and move via *junc vlætic süezer man* (141.5) on the part of Sigune and *lieber friunt* (146.5) and *friunt* (147.1) on the part of Ither (Wolfram also calls Parzival *mîn friunt* (144.4) in an aside) to the general term *hêrre* (*hêr*), which is used so many times that it is unnecessary to detail them. Meanwhile he is addressed again as *friwent* by Gawan (331.25) and as *helt* (270.25, 745.14.18, 747.20, 749.17) on various occasions by various people. These modes of address are given a pronounced emotive content when Parzival is cursed by Sigune: *gunêrter lîp, verfluochet man* (255.13), and by Cundrie: *ir vil ungetriwer gast*

---

[1] 170.6, 276.4.21, 278.25, 218.4, 221.6, 305.11, 307.18, 309.16, 315.9, 388.8, 389.4.29, 392.20.

[2] 123.8.15, 125.20, 131.9, 132.10, 145.10, 149.7.

(316.2), *gunêrter lîp, hêr Parʒivâl* (316.25). At other times they
have an ethical ring about them: *küene starker man* (266.4), *küener
degen balt* (267.2), both spoken by Orilus, acknowledging Parzival's superior strength; *werlîcher Parʒivâl* (743.14), *werlîcher man*
(744.29), *werlîcher helt* (745.3), the first being Wolfram's encouragement to Parzival in his fight with Feirefiz, the others being
spoken by Feirefiz himself, who also calls Parzival *vorhtlîch süeʒer
man* (748.26) and *werder helt* (749.17).

Very frequently Parzival is referred to as a *gast* and as a *helt*.
But Wolfram uses many other terms in addition, showing a
marked predilection for pre-courtly vocabulary in his choice of
synonyms for *helt*. Thus, *wîgant* is very popular;[1] *degen* also is
found frequently,[2] as often as not combined with the qualification
wert[3] or *ellens rîch*[4] or *balt*.[5] *Recke* also occurs (259.4, 706.11—
here a plural in which Parzival is included); and finally there is the
normal courtly term *ritter (rîter)*.[6] At the very end of the poem,
when he has succeeded to the Grail kingship, Parzival is given the
title of *künec* (802.22, 803.2, 804.19, 820.13) and called *wirt*.[7] The
pre-courtly terminology shows that Wolfram intended to dis-
sociate his hero from the contemporary trends of courtliness in
the sphere of *minne* and particularly from the (to Wolfram's mind)
reprehensible conduct of Gottfried's Tristan. In this way Parzival's
individuality is strongly asserted. But although Parzival is created

---

[1] 215.19, 245.24, 247.1, 252.9, 438.2, 456.23, 459.10, 706.5 (here the plural is
used referring to both Parzival and Gawan and is qualified by *küene*).

[2] 222.26 (*der junge degen unervort*), 302.21 (*der degen wert*), 306.22 (*der degen
snel*), 333.3 (*der degen wol getân*), 440.28 (*der degen snel*).

[3] 187.2, 191.30, 208.23, 213.3, 246.27, 265.27, 447.1.

[4] 185.22, 229.6 (here the basis is *gast*), 249.11 (*helt*), 256.4 (*gast*), 331.24 (*helt*).

[5] 213.3, 264.20, 293.6, 319.13, 435.3.

[6] 175.27, 203.27, 305.8, 424.18 (here it is *ein ritter*, whom Vergulaht, the teller
of the story, does not know by name), 619.18, 678.18.

[7] 796.27, 805.27, 813.12.24, 814.18, 815.1.4. Parzival is, however, earlier
referred to as *der junge stolʒe wirt gemeit* (208.27), as *des landes wirt* (212.11) and
as *künec* (268.4), but in these cases the kingdom in question is Pelrapeire, which
Parzival has gained through his marriage to Condwiramurs. Sigune also calls
him *künec ʒe Norgâls* (140.29) in describing his inheritance from Herzeloyde at
their first meeting. But these are just sporadic uses of the terms *wirt* and *künec*,
not consistent ones as those at the end of the poem are.

in some respects as the anti-type of Tristan,[1] this does not mean that his characterization—any more than that of Tristan—is that of a typical figure: both Gottfried and Wolfram have a too well developed sense of human psychology for this to be the case. A large number of other words and phrases are applied to Parzival to shed light on other aspects of his personality. Up to the conclusion of book VI the most popular of these words is *junc*, but Parzival's departure from Artus' court marks a real turning-point in his career and here he leaves his youthful immaturity behind.[2] His courtly idealized nature is further emphasized by the use of the expression *âne bart* (174.23, 211.16, 227.28, 307.7). *Süeʒe* is also found (166.28, 174.23), as are further examples of *wert*.[3] *Unverʒaget* (138.3, 209.28, 262.15 (where Orilus is also depicted in this manner), 331.20) takes up the words of the pro-logue, as does—negatively—the term *eins ʒagen muot* (181.28). *Stæte* occurs with a similar function (186.13, 202.3). Other ex-pressions bring out Parzival's ability as a knight: thus, *muotes hert* (208.1); *der sigehafte* (212.30), *der den sic hât* (213.29) after the battle with Clamide; *der snelle man* (243.28); *küene* (245.30, 263.9, 703.25, 706.29 (here combined with *stolʒ*)), *stark* (266.4, 265.11, 693.1), *rîch* (796.23); *kampfgenôʒ* (212.6, 688.13 (here *Gâwânes*), 689.10); *flins | der manlîchen krefte* (678.20 f.); *schûr der rîterschefte* (678.22). Many words and phrases are calculated to bring out Parzival's physical beauty, and in fact the very first one expresses his perfec-tion: *aller manne schœne ein bluomen kranʒ* (122.13), which excels the *bluome an mannes schœne* (39.22) applied to Kaylet. This is followed up by his being called *der an dem got wunsches het erdâht* (148.30), *den schœnsten man | der schildes ambet ie gewan* (209.11 f.),

---

[1] As Julius Schwietering has worked out the general principle in his article *Typologisches in mittelalterlicher Dichtung* in the Festgabe Gustav Ehrismann (Berlin/Leipzig, 1925), a principle which has been followed by many scholars since.

[2] 153.14, 165.16, 179.7, 181.21, 191.16.20, 193.17.21, 196.15, 198.13, 208.1, 242.25, 245.6.29, 247.13, 249.9, 265.11, 228.1, 229.9, 306.22, 308.1. Parzival's development is nevertheless gradual, as the change from *knappe* to *man* does not coincide with the abandonment of *junc*.

[3] 186.6, 203.27, 228.19, 229.21, 433.9, 646.15, 678.28, 706.7.17, 723.24, 730.26, 755.3, 771.23.

der schönste übr elliu lant (258.3), *der ûʒ erkorne* (619.14). Normally, however, the terms *wol gevar* (191.20, 245.6, 228.10, 698.20, 699.18), *wol geslaht* (242.21), *wol getân* (288.8), *lieht gevar* (196.8, 230.23), *lieht gemâl* (717.30), *gehiure* (390.7, 433.8, 709.2), *clâr* (696.15) express the extent of Parzival's handsome physique. Another set of references applies largely to his moral qualities, viz.: *der reine* (201.9), *der getriwe* (202.3), *der hôch gemuot* (267.9), *der valscheite widersaʒ* (249.1), *der valscheitswant* (296.1), *der geliutrten triwe fundamint* (740.6), *der kiusche vrävel man* (437.12). At the end of the poem he is most frequently called *der getoufte*[1] in opposition to Feirefiz, *der heiden*. In the sphere of *minne* he becomes *der dienst gebende* (195.9), *dienstman* (199.11, 740.21 (here the *dienstman* of both Condwiramurs and the Grail)), *âmîs* (200.5), *der minneclîche wine* (228.6), another term in vogue before the courtly period and at Wolfram's time disdained, *dem der minne was verselt* (287.6), used in the *Blutstropfenepisode*. The term *herʒen trût* is used once by Herzeloyde (117.24) and once by Condwiramurs (202.28), and *herʒen freude mîn* once by Condwiramurs (801.7).

Parzival's combat with Kingrun and Clamide in defence of Condwiramurs is kept in the audience's memory through reference to him as *der durch si dâ streit | mit Kingrûne und mit Clâmidê* (389.8 f.) and *der si lôste ê | von dem künege Clâmidê* (425.13 f.). One or two other synonyms do occur, but they add little to the significance of those already given.

It is clear from the above examples how great the scope of the synonyms used for Parzival is. They cover every side of his activity (and inactivity) and present the essential outlines of his character, showing his relationships with other personages and members of his family, his development from childhood to maturity, his prowess as a knight, his manly beauty, his ignorance and his guilt. No one kind of synonym predominates over the entire poem, but at particular periods certain aspects of his character are emphasized to the virtual exclusion of others. Thus, the impression we have is of a fully rounded personality and of

[1] 738.12, 739.23.27, 740.13, 741.1.26, 742.16, 743.9.23, 745.13.

the development of an individual. Parzival is not merely the embodiment of the perfect knight, since the Grail demands more than knighthood and since he has to acquire even this knighthood by his own experience; nor does he merely represent man in his search for the will of God, since earthly relationships have their importance and Parzival's life takes place among real people and not as in an allegory. It is rather through the many-sided personality of an individual that eternal, representative values are seen.

DESCRIPTIVE PASSAGES

More than anyone else in the poem Parzival undergoes a marked development, and this is reflected in the descriptions which Wolfram inserts in the course of the narrative. The descriptions of Gahmuret and Herzeloyde are, broadly speaking, static and centre on the one function of each character in the poem, the descriptions being varied according to whether they are more concerned with external appearance and actions or with the inner nature of the character. Both kinds of description are used for Parzival, and in a very concrete way they portray the stages of his growth. Even more than is the case with Gahmuret the descriptions of external appearance are a means whereby significant aspects of *personality* can be described.

The first description that we are given of Parzival after the various brief comments that Wolfram intersperses in his narration of the initial events of Parzival's life[1] deals with his physical beauty:

> dô lac diu gotes kunst an im.
> von der âventiure ich daz nim,
> diu mich mit wârheit des beschiet.
> nie mannes varwe baz geriet
> vor im sît Adâmes zît.
> des wart sîn lob von wîben wît.   (123.13 ff.)

This passage is the forerunner of all those later ones extending this praise of Parzival's appearance. Until Anfortas is healed of his

---

[1] Viz.: 'sîn lîp was clâr unde fier' (118.11), and the reference to him as 'aller manne schœne ein bluomen kranz' (122.13).

wound, Parzival is the *ne plus ultra* of manly beauty. Wolfram supports his assertion that God's handiwork is visible in Parzival— an indication of his essential goodness—by appealing to the authority of his source. Descriptions of Parzival's physical beauty and praise of his character occur throughout the poem. The next examples are found in the episode at Gurnemanz' castle, where one of the knights is so struck by Parzival's appearance that he spontaneously bursts into hyperbolic praise and eulogizes him as the perfection of humanity and knighthood (164.12 ff.). Another passage (168.24 ff.), very like this, contains a prophecy of the eventual success of his life on the part of the knights who receive him at the castle. His outstanding handsomeness is again noted and connected with Herzeloyde's own virtue in bringing so worthy an offspring into the world (cf. also 166.16), and the knights speak of the favour he will win in the sphere of *minne*, thus taking up the words of the first eulogy (123.18). The emphasis on Parzival's merit in the field of *minne* is extremely important, and its repetition here, before he is initiated into the elements of chivalry by Gurnemanz and first awakened to *minne* by Liaze, is characteristically well-placed. It is followed up by one or two similar comments when Parzival arrives at Artus' court, ready to be received into the company of the Round Table. This physical splendour, with the accompanying understanding that Parzival enjoys God's favour, provides the justification for his reception into this noble circle:

> dô truoc der junge Parzivâl
> âne flügel engels mâl
> sus geblüet ûf der erden.
>
> . . .
>
> gein sîme lobe sprach niemen nein:
> sô rehte minneclîcher schein.   (308.1 ff.)

A little later in the same episode Wolfram enlarges on this excellence by a comparison with the other knights, none of whom could reach the virtue displayed by Parzival. Youth, strength and shining beauty are his characteristics, and this brilliance is the mark of Parzival's *stæte* and furnishes Wolfram with a *point de départ* for a biting attack on faithless women. The imagery at this point becomes capricious and complex: Parzival's mouth is brighter than many a mirror in which women look at themselves; his complexion is compared with a pair of tongs which has the firm grasp (*stæte*) needed for scraping off undesirable *zwível*. The sense, however, remains clear enough, and the unusual imagery acts as a highly individual touch to the general description (311.9 ff.).

After this visit to Artus' court and the curse which Parzival suffers from Cundrie, eulogistic descriptions vanish, only to reappear at the end of book XIII, as Parzival becomes once more the hero of the story and a happy ending comes into sight. Gawan had been the subject of the last four books, and Wolfram now has to re-introduce Parzival and assure his excellence above that of Gawan. Thus, he is called 'flins / der manlîchen krefte', 'schûr der rîterschefte' (678.20 ff.), and his knightly reputation is hereby secured. Neither deceitfulness of heart nor dishonour are to be found in him. During the period of his degradation praise of this kind would have been out of place, but now that Parzival's success is no longer in the balance it can return, and his outstanding qualities are re-established here and in the Arthurian circle. He is praised also by Gramoflanz' army, gathered to support its leader against Gawan, and the same type of hyperbole is found here as in the previous passage:

> si jâhn in Gramoflanzes her
> daz ze keiner zît sô wol ze wer
> nie kœme rîter dechein,
> den diu sunne ie überschein:
> swaz ze bêden sîten dâ wære getân,
> den prîs mües er al eine hân.　　　　(709.5 ff.)

The descriptive passages detailed above deal with just one aspect of Parzival's personality—his striking appearance and fundamental beauty of character—and occur largely in connexion with his irruptions into knightly society, though the first passage of all essentially sets the tone for the whole of his story and not merely the Arthurian sections. They are found carefully embedded into the story as integral parts of it and serve to stress the outstanding nature of the hero at appropriate points in the development of the story. They do not themselves contribute towards the development, but rather show what is always present, even if at some times it is overlaid by other features of Parzival's character. An early description introduces the *Dümmling* theme as a conscious motif into the poem.[1] The decision to dress her son in fool's clothing constitutes Herzeloyde's last vain attempt to prevent Parzival from learning more about the knightly world in which his father was killed, but its main function is to symbolize Parzival's inner nature, to be the outward sign of his ignorance in matters both secular and religious. Thus, the traditional fairy-tale motif now receives a twofold psychological significance—for the light it throws on Herzeloyde and for its characterization of Parzival. The details of the clothing—the shirt and trousers of sackcloth, the pointed hood, the calfskin boots—are in themselves of little importance: all that is necessary is that they should be recognizable as fool's clothes. The theme is followed by a description of Parzival's difficulty in trying to put on his armour when preparing to fight with Ither (155.19 ff.). Here he is portrayed as *Parzival der tumbe*, and in his inexperience he presents an awkward picture, attempting to put on his helmet and greaves and failing at it. But at the end of the duel a more significant action is depicted. Parzival commits *rêroup* on Ither, takes off his armour and puts it on himself. Iwanet points out, to Parzival's chagrin, that he ought not to wear boots under his armour, but now put on a knight's clothing. Parzival's refusal to part with the clothes his mother gave him shows just how much he is still subject to her authority and unaware of his own potentialities and responsibilities, and he proceeds to put on the ill-gotten armour on top of his fool's clothes. The only thing that Iwanet refuses to let him do is to have a *gabilôt*: now that he has won the honours of knighthood, though

---

[1] Already one or two of the synonyms have foreshadowed it (121.5, 124.16, 126.19), but now the new clothes make Parzival's (temporary) role perfectly obvious. See also below, pp. 142 ff.

in a way that all deplore, he cannot be allowed to bear an uncourtly weapon. The action of donning Ither's armour is, to be sure, the sign of Parzival's attainment of knighthood, but the fact that he puts it on top of his other clothes shows unmistakably that his achievement is purely outward and formal. He has not yet comprehended the true nature of the knight's vocation, and indeed he is not accepted into the company of the Round Table until much later, when he has made good some of his former misdeeds and established a worthy reputation. Again, there is an overlapping of two stages of his development.

Parzival's uncourtly appearance and conduct are described in a passage where he is proceeding towards Nantes after having been left by the fisherman with whom he spent the previous night, and Wolfram particularly points out the contrast between Parzival's and Tristan's early background: 'in zôch dechein Curvenâl: / er kunde kurtôsîe niht, / als ungevarnem man geschiht (144.20 ff.). From here he goes on to describe Parzival's uncouth, battered appearance, his poor horse and reins, his old saddle and his complete destitution with regard to fine clothes, samite and ermine, coat and cloak. Here his poverty-stricken state is the result of a lack of education in courtly matters, but on the two other occasions on which his battered appearance is mentioned the reason for it is different. These descriptions are found in the *Blutstropfenepisode* (283.27 ff.) and when Parzival rejoins Artus in book XIV (702.12 ff.). The holes in his armour and the general damage to his equipment are the visible proof of his long periods of knightly activity, during which he has been establishing himself a reputation. They both occur just before Parzival comes into the Arthurian community, but in both cases he very soon departs again.

Changes of clothing are important in showing the beginning of a new stage in Parzival's career and occur, apart from the one mentioned above in connexion with Ither's death, at Gurnemanz' castle (164.2 ff. and 168.1 ff.), at Munsalvæsche (227.26 ff.), at Artus' court when Parzival becomes a member of the Round Table (306.10 ff.), in Trevrizent's cell (459.1 ff.), after the duels with Gawan (695.14 f.) and with Feirefiz (794.19 f.).

Immediately after his arrival at Graharz Parzival's fool's clothing creates a scare among the inhabitants, and they take it from him. The old misconceptions of courtly life are to be removed and a new process of education replace it. After a night's rest Parzival takes a bath and as it were washes away the misconceptions which characterized his past. Gurnemanz' attempts to instill courtliness into Parzival are more successful than Herzeloyde's earlier endeavour at education, and the new clothes which Parzival receives here are a mark of the enlightenment and of the progress that he is making towards the knightly ideal. His ignorance gradually fades into the background as he gains in knowledge, but it does not finally disappear until the end of book VI. Gold and satin, ermine and sable express the magnificence of Parzival's new status, and the red clothes that are the sign of the Red Knight, the legacy of Ither's reputation and Parzival's guilt, are represented by scarlet stockings and the crimson material of his cloak. A costly belt and brooch complete the array.

We must nonetheless bear in mind that Parzival's usual garb during this long period of many changes is Ither's red clothing, and this is referred to *en passant* on many occasions. In describing Parzival's duel with Clamide, Wolfram mentions how his horse wears red samite trappings over its armour and how Parzival himself carries a red shield and wears a red tunic. The distinctive colour provides an easy method of identifying Parzival wherever he is, either as a character in the background or as the hero of the episode that is then the main subject of the poem.[1] In any case, the memory of Ither is kept alive until book XII (618.21) despite the fact that Trevrizent absolves Parzival of his guilt at the end of book IX, and this is the most important aspect of the use of red clothing.

[1] Peter Wapnewski, *Wolframs Parzival. Studien zur Religiosität und Form* (Heidelberg, 1955), p. 63, writes about the significance of the colour red: '... ist Rot die Farbe der Sünde (weil des Blutes), der Liebe (weil des Blutes), der leiblichen Schönheit, der Freude, des Zornes, der Scham, des Krieges (Apokal. 6,4 reitet der Krieg auf rotem Roß ...), der peinlichen Gerichtsbarkeit, der Falschheit ... Man darf aber wohl dies alles auf einen Nenner bringen: Rot ist die Farbe des lebendigen Diesseits, seines Glanzes wie seiner Sündhaftigkeit.'

At the Grail castle a second change of clothing takes place, and again Parzival symbolically washes away the misdeeds of the past. He is given a mantle of silk from Arabi to wear, and all those present marvel at his brilliant appearance. Unfortunately for Parzival, this change of clothing is not permanent: its significance lies in its being an expression of graciousness on the part of the Grail family, made in the hope that the visitor will relieve their misery, but Parzival is unequal to the task and departs the next morning just as he arrived, but with the difference that now he bears the sword that Anfortas has given him as well as the one he took from Ither.

Another change of clothing is described when Parzival is received into the company of the Round Table (306.10 ff.). Cunneware looms large in this particular episode, as it is on her behalf that Parzival has in great measure won his knightly fame, having protected her against the attacks and insults of Keie (305.13 ff.). She has clothes brought for him made of silk from Nineveh, and as the cloak has no cord, she herself makes one and fits it in for Parzival. This gracious act is followed by Cunneware's gift of a costly belt, on which animal devices are expressed in precious stones, a ruby brooch and an emerald for the clasp at his neck. All this constitutes a reward for Parzival's initial compassion shown to Cunneware at his first visit to the Arthurian court and is a sign of his worthiness to be accepted into the gallant circle of knights. Moreover, the silks from Nineveh were to have been worn by Clamide, now Cunneware's prisoner, and Parzival's wearing of them is another way of showing Clamide's defeat. But the mere description of the new clothes is not enough, and Wolfram inserts a variety of eulogistic remarks into the story about Parzival's shining skin, his red mouth and the general impression that he makes on the assembled company:

> gekleidet wart der degen snel:
> dô was er fier unde clâr.
> swer in sach, der jach für wâr,
> er wære gebluomt für alle man.
> diz lop sîn varwe muose hân.   (306.24 ff.)

This comment on Parzival's excellence apart from his clothing underlines the significance of the change. The hero has now proved his knightly virtue, again (as at Gurnemanz' castle) washes off the stains of his previous reputation and puts on new clothes to symbolize his attainment. It is ironic that just at this point of attainment Cundrie comes to shatter Parzival's illusions and show him his failure, thus pointing forward to a worthier goal. Parzival has just put aside the weakness and insufficiency of his past, but is not now allowed to cling to the accomplishment of the Arthurian court as a sufficient, once and for all vocation: he has to go beyond it. He nevertheless leaves the court in a fine array, wearing brilliant white armour of the costliest kind and a tunic and battledress decorated with jewels (333.1 ff.). It is curious how the red clothing of Ither keeps cropping up despite the various changes of clothing that Parzival undergoes, and this shows that Wolfram definitely attached a certain symbolic value to the clothes in which he describes his hero at any given time. In any case he was not concerned about describing every single event in Parzival's travels or in creating an impeccable consistency about all that he described. The over-all *impression* had to have its unity; the details could be left to the exigencies of the moment.

A great contrast is found when Parzival meets Kahenis and his family on the Lenten pilgrimage. He is still wearing his splendid plumes and armour, and in these circumstances they represent his worldly concern and his *superbia* in vivid contrast to the humble pilgrims' sober grey. Wolfram succinctly points this out: 'in solhem harnasch er reit, / dem ungelîch was jeniu kleit / die gein im truoc der grâwe man' (447.5 ff.). A little later Kahenis' daughters note the difference once more and express the contrast as one of warm and cold. Parzival's magnificent armour is of no avail in keeping him warm against the cold and snow. This motif is taken up again in Trevrizent's cell, and the extreme cold of the season is a powerful link with that caused by the rising of the planet Saturn, which occasions such strange things as the 'sumerlîcher snê' (489.27) and is the origin of much of Anfortas' pain in that it makes his flesh become colder than snow. In this way the sufferings and guilt of Parzival and Anfortas are connected and symbolized by an accompanying coldness. Trevrizent takes Parzival into the inner recesses of his cell, where glowing coals keep the room warm. Here the young knight takes off his painful armour and rests from his long wanderings. His naked defencelessness reveals his spiritual impoverishment. Now he is ready to acknowledge his defection and to accept the warmth of Trevrizent's welcome, through which he is enabled to overcome his sin. This is all prefigured at his reception in the cell, though the actual absolution does not come until later; thus: 'al sîne lide im wurden warm, / sô daz sîn vel gap liehten schîn' (459.12 f.). And then Trevrizent puts on him a cloak so that he can keep warm, corresponding on the material level to the insight which he is to gain and the forgiveness he is to receive. In this way another important period in Parzival's life is spotlighted by an appropriate change in clothing.

The last two instances of the manner in which the technique of changing clothes deepens the significance of a change in attitude or experience occur with reference to the relationships between Parzival and Gawan and Parzival and Feirefiz respectively. The parallelism of the two duels is emphasized by this feature. Thus, at the beginning of book XIV Parzival is presented as the Red Knight, armed and ready for battle, though his shield seems rather the worse for wear, and as he departs from Artus' court at the end of the same book, prepared for his next adventure, which is the duel with Feirefiz, he seizes his armour and sets forth in pursuit of battle. At the end of each duel the result is the same: neither duel is concluded, but Parzival is acknowledged pseudo-victor in each case and is identified with Gawan and Feirefiz in a completely unmistakable fashion. This identification[1] is shown, furthermore, in the clothing which each pair of heroes puts on after the battle:

Parzival and Gawan (695.14 f.)	Parzival and Feirefiz (794.18 ff.)
dô truoc man dar in beiden	ein kameræer dar nâher gienc:
von tiwerr koste glîch gewant.	der brâht in kleider rîche,
	den beiden al gelîche.

[1] For a more detailed discussion of this identification see the section on 'The prologue and the duels' below, pp. 189 ff.

The identical clothes are an obvious expression of the identity in character which it is Wolfram's aim to bring out between the heroes. Once more we see the importance of clothing for emphasizing certain aspects of characterization. Hardly anything could be clearer in meaning than this last change in clothing.

Similarly, the deployment of Parzival's various horses points to a development in his character. He rides away from Herzeloyde on a *pfert*, i.e. a non-knightly horse, which he gets rid of when he takes possession of Ither's *kastelân* after their joust. This second horse betokens his ascent into the courtly world, while also reminding us of the shameful way in which he achieved this. In book IX, however, after Parzival's meeting with Sigune and the pilgrims this horse is killed as a result of the encounter with the Grail knight, whose horse, marked with the sign of the dove, Parzival then seizes. The fact that Trevrizent later reproves him for this robbery does not minimize the symbolic indication that Parzival is now in the process of emerging from the bonds of sin and acquiring the faith in God and the *diemüete* which will fit him for the kingship of the Grail. The symbolism of the horses points out his progress to his final goal; it is one of the indicators of his spiritual development, marking the crucial points of Ither's death and the sojourn with Trevrizent.

The descriptive passages applied to Parzival are none of them very long, and their number is not very large. Parzival's character is expressed most fully and deeply through the mediums of action and speech, and other methods of characterization should not be magnified out of proportion to their place and value. The significance of the contribution of descriptions to characterization is, within these limits, striking, emphatic and also tactful in that they indirectly, but none the less clearly, express the change in Parzival's experience, reflecting the individuality of his history.

MONOLOGUES

Much of the individualized characterization of Parzival is achieved through the medium of the monologue, whereby we are able to gain a considerable insight into the development of the hero from boyhood to maturity. Only about half of his monologues are taken over from Chrétien's poem,[1] the rest having either only a slight connexion with the subject-matter of the *Conte del Graal* or no point of contact whatsoever. From this we can see that Wolfram was concerned to portray Parzival's character in as much detail as he could in order to bring out the psychological depth in his development. Little space is wasted on descriptions of Parzival's appearance (they are usually just a few lines long); instead he is shown in action, in speech and in thought. It is the last medium of self-expression which interests us here, for through it the audience is able to appreciate directly the motivation of Parzival's actions and the finer aspects of his character.

The monologues are important for three main reasons: firstly, for showing Parzival's development from youth to maturity; secondly, for the light they shed on the problem of *minne*; and thirdly, for the understanding they give us of the spiritual side of Parzival's character. These distinctions are not, however, rigid, and the three aspects frequently coincide.

From the very beginning of Parzival's story, when he is first and foremost seen as the *Dümmling*, the boy who has everything to learn about the knightly life despite its being innate in him, we hear his thoughts and inquisitive questions. Even at this point his ignorance is made more immediate through the use of the monologue, and a point of comparison is given for us to assess the increase in depth of his later musings. Thus, we first (120.17 ff.) find him as a boy in the forest, bold and successful in hunting, but with memories of his mother's religious teaching ringing in his brain. On hearing the beat of horses' hoofs, his first thought is that it might be the devil approaching, and he is filled with confidence that he would easily be able to overcome him. Here too we have the first hint that, although he accepts unquestioningly the religious and moral teaching of his mother, the urge for a knightly

---

[1] Emil Walker, *Der Monolog im höfischen Epos*, pp. 237 ff. The following monologues have no correspondence in the *Conte del Graal*: 162.2 ff., 188.2 ff., 202.6 ff., 302.7 ff., 444.4 ff., 450.12 ff., 451.13 ff., 452.1 ff.

life is strong within him and leads him to belittle his mother's courage. He is full of natural confidence in his physical powers, but as soon as the knights actually appear he is so impressed by them that his thoughts of the devil are replaced forthwith by an assumption that the knights are gods. This first monologue illustrates the twofold nature of Parzival's character: his inborn longing for the knightly life, expressed by his physical ability, and his lifelong preoccupation with the antitheses of the spiritual life, with God and the devil. It is a telling irony that Parzival should imagine himself to be in a position to vanquish the devil at this point and then immediately wish to follow the knights that represent as it were the darker side of life to his mother and in doing so fall away from God through ignorance, inexperience and sin. Parzival's last monologue (732.15 ff.) shows the reverse of this experience when he is able to put his quest for the Grail and the releasing of Anfortas as his very first desire and duty.

The *Dümmling* theme is again touched on when Parzival, characterized as *der tumbe man*, contrasts the splendid appearance of Gurnemanz' castle, the towers of which he supposes to have been 'sown' there by Artus, with the poverty of the produce of his mother's farmers. This fantastic comparison, illustrative of both Parzival's *tumpheit* and Wolfram's humour, arises from the way in which Parzival sees the towers growing visually larger as he approaches Graharz and assumes that this rapid growth must be due to Artus' *heilikeit* and *sælde*, and possibly to a greater rainfall than was usual in Soltane! The fact that Parzival is misled by the mere appearance of Graharz into attributing such power to Artus, the irony of which the audience appreciates, suggests that the events due to take place at Gurnemanz' castle may also be misleading. There is a delicate hint of the relativity of Gurnemanz' instruction in courtliness, which is typical of Wolfram's technique of gradual revelation.

Intimately connected with Parzival's education by Gurnemanz is the monologue, Parzival's *Gedankenrede*, on viewing the elaborate ceremonial and seeing the members of the Grail family at Munsalvæsche. It is here that his *tumpheit* is most strikingly depicted, since it is in following Gurnemanz' counsel on the subject of *zuht* without a proper understanding of courtly life that Parzival falls into the sin of omission for which he is cursed in virtually identical terms by both Sigune and Cundrie: 'durch zuht in vrâgens doch verdrôz' (239.10). Gurnemanz' advice is in no way denigrated, since it was given 'mit grôzen triwen âne schranz' (239.12), but Parzival's following it in blind obedience is fateful. He supposes that he will be able to comprehend without asking any questions the various happenings in the castle, an attitude which accords well with his ignorance and imagined self-sufficiency which later becomes complete defection from God. He does not ask the question from any lack of compassion—the encounter with Sigune above all makes this clear—but it is his unquestioning obedience to all the precepts which will bring him to true knighthood that leads him astray. In this way we see unmistakably that Parzival's destiny reaches beyond the circle of Arthurian knights, since his obedience to courtly standards is just what jeopardizes his calling. It is extremely important that at this crucial moment in Parzival's career we are able to follow his inmost thoughts, his weighing up of the considerations which guide him to keep silence and his assumption that all will go as smoothly and satisfactorily at the Grail castle as at Graharz. Parzival is at this stage aware only of the question of obedience: he has not yet learned to be responsible to himself and make moral decisions. He has arrived at the Grail castle with a veneer of chivalry, which is all he is at this moment concerned about, and is quite unconscious of the guilt which lies upon him from having killed Ither and caused his mother's death. At the time of this monologue it is his desire to fulfil the demands of knighthood which causes him not to put the question to Anfortas. In book IX the emphasis changes, and the problem of guilt becomes all-important.[1]

Several of Parzival's monologues deal with the theme of *minne* and his relationship with Condwiramurs. The initial confusion of Condwiramurs with Liaze, where Parzival is thrown off balance

[1] For a detailed discussion of Gurnemanz' involvement in the question motif see below, pp. 343 ff.

on seeing the beauty of his future wife, and the long *Blutstrop-fenepisode* will be treated more fully in the chapter on Cond-wiramurs,[1] but two short monologues occur at the end of the *Blutstropfenepisode*, both in the nature of an *Orientierungsrede* (302.7 ff., 17 f.). Parzival is just recovering from his *minne*-trance, ended through Gawan's intervention, and wonders how he has returned to consciousness. After having been so deeply moved by the contemplation of Condwiramurs' beauty he questions his own worth in having won her love and liberated her from the impor-tunities of Clamide. He had found many bold hearts in direst woe, and now, how he does not know, Condwiramurs has been taken away from him. He has no knowledge of the fighting with Segramors and Keie and speaks, as it were to no one, about the loss of his spear, which he remembers having brought with him. The function of these monologues is to emphasize the extent of Parzival's withdrawal of his senses during the *minne*-trance. He had been completely abstracted from the world and given over entirely to the contemplation of the drops of blood on the snow, and after this his return to consciousness has to take place slowly with only a gradual realization of what had happened to him.

The most significant periods of Parzival's relationship with Condwiramurs are heightened by the use of the monologue, as at their first meeting and in book VI, where the destructive nature of *minne*, untempered by the quest of and obedience to the call of the Grail, is, despite all its depth and power, made perfectly clear. Similarly, the young couple's inexperience at the beginning of their marriage is singled out and given added meaning by a *Gedankenrede* on the part of Parzival. He muses on the question of physical consummation (202.6 ff.) and on the beauty and sensitivity of his relationship with Condwiramurs up to this point. He thinks of the years (a poetical exaggeration) of service devoted to her and the consolation which she gave him. All that he had desired was to touch the hem of her garment. She was an elevated figure, a paragon of feminine virtue to be admired and honoured, placed on a pedestal in the mind of the humbly worshipping

[1] See below, pp. 232 f., 250 ff.

knight. Now the distance between them is removed, and Parzival thinks that if he should sensually and excessively desire more than had been granted to him before, this would be to be guilty of *untriuwe*. He has to achieve a fitting transition from the former distant admiration of a *Minneherrin* to physical consummation with a wife, and this demands time and a change in attitude. He wonders whether he would be justified in causing Condwiramurs *arbeit* and thus in spreading a reputation of themselves that would be bad, but he comes to the conclusion that it is the opposite (*süeʒiu mære*) which is most suited to a *Minneherrin*. And so he remains in indecision, considerate, but timid and not quite ready both to give himself fully to Condwiramurs and to possess her in return.

The longest of Parzival's monologues occurs when, after the festivities and the union of lovers at Artus' court at the end of book XIV, he is faced with the necessity for deciding which is more important for him—the Grail or his wife. It is a moment of isolation for Parzival, a moment when his calling to the Grail kingship separates him completely from the Arthurian circle, establishes his destiny on a higher plane and spotlights his individuality. Before he is allowed to express his own thoughts on the whole topic, Wolfram inserts a few comments of his own to make clear what his hero's position is. Thus, he explicitly states that no other lady had won Parzival's heart but Condwiramurs:

> grôz triwe het im sô bewart
> sîn manlîch herze und ouch den lîp,
> daz für wâr nie ander wîp
> wart gewaldec sîner minne,
> niwan diu küneginne
> Condwîr âmûrs.   (732.8 ff.)

The monologue itself begins with a contrast between Parzival's inheritance and his present situation. *Minne* lies within the scope of his capabilities, but what has she now done to him? He himself was born as the fruit of *minne* between Gahmuret and Herzeloyde, so how does it come about that he now loses *minne*? Parzival is bewildered by the position in which he finds himself, and his thoughts follow each other in a series of mutually exclusive alternatives. The choice he has to make is between searching for the Grail, in which case he will be tormented by the thought of his wife's embraces and his separation from her, and returning to the joy of being with Condwiramurs, in which case he will have to let Anfortas continue in suffering. He recognizes that these two calls have unequal importance and that he could never become *hôhes muotes rîche* if he were to neglect his duty towards the Grail king. The only solution—and here Parzival shows his spiritual growth and conquest over the sin of *hôchvart* in that he *willingly* submits—is to place himself in God's hands (though the use of the word *gelücke* to denote the deciding power only paves the way for a more explicit statement that this is actually what Parzival means). He comes to the conclusion that it is his lot *not* to enjoy the consolations of *minne*, accepts it and declares that what henceforth happens to him is of no consequence: 'ich enruoche nu waz mir geschiht. / got wil mîner freude niht' (733.7 f.). The next passage shows the extent of Parzival's faithfulness to Condwiramurs. He postulates a situation in which physical separation and *zwîvel* might destroy their love so that the possibility would arise for him to love and serve another lady, but he immediately negates this with his own confirmation of what Wolfram had already mentioned, i.e. that no one, not even Orgeluse (619.11 f.), can secure his *minne* but Condwiramurs alone. Her power is so great that it displaces all thought of other ladies: 'nu hât ir minne mir benomn / ander minne und freudebæren trôst' (733.14 f.). Again he invokes *gelücke*, this time to grant joy to all those who desire finite joy, and then God to give joy to those from whose presence he is resolved to depart.

The placing of this monologue is illuminating. It occurs after the duel with Gawan and immediately before that with Feirefiz. Parzival's pseudo-victory over Gawan is to be linked with the finite joy which he now renounces for himself but asks God to grant to others. In showing himself 'superior' to Gawan he has proved his worth and is able to renounce earthly delights in order to attain to his destiny, and it is this resolve to put God's purpose first which gives him the moral superiority also over Feirefiz. He is now conscious of and prepared to accept the strictures which his calling to the Grail kingship lays upon him. The joy which he is to have is not *endehaft* and includes his union with his wife. It is only at this particular stage that the question of either *minne* or God arises, and once Parzival has made the right decision between them and their relative importance he is able to succeed to the kingship of the Grail and then bring his wife into it. The Grail here demands the sacrifice of *minne*, though only temporarily and to make the priorities clear. Parzival has now grown sufficiently in spiritual stature to be able to make it.

The young knight's stay at and departure from the Grail castle are also given further significance through the use of monologues. The dream, linking up with Herzeloyde's nightmare on the occasion of Gahmuret's death, which Parzival has causes him to wake up at dawn in the castle, quite at a loss to know where the servants were who should have helped him to dress. But he directly goes to sleep again, and when he wakes for the second time, he finds his armour ready for him to put on. He interprets the sufferings of his dream as an indication of the hardships that the day is to bring him and declares his willingness to serve his host in battle. This again stresses the positive side of Parzival's nature, his readiness to help, a further proof—if one should be wanted—that his failure to ask the question was not due to a lack of compassion. Moreover, he emphasizes his desire to serve Repanse de schoye, who had in her goodness lent him a cloak; but he makes clear that his admiration of her and his offer of service are called forth by his respect for her and not on account of *minne*. His faithfulness to Condwiramurs remains unblemished: 'wan mîn wîp de küneginne / ist an ir lîbe alse clâr, / oder fürbaz, daz ist wâr' (246.20 ff.). Parzival is very ready to do all he can to help and to show his concern for the Grail family, but something else prevents his success. Even after the page has passed judgement on him as he leaves the castle, Parzival has still absolutely no idea what it is that he is being vilified for (248.19 ff.). He imagines that it is cowardice that lies at the root of his trouble and declares to himself that those knights whose tracks he is following probably would be fighting on behalf of his host and that if he were to fight with them he would be able to stand up worthily to them. He would help them in their troubles, if only to merit his food and the sword that Anfortas gave him. And he concludes that because he bears the sword without merit, therefore people consider him a coward. Parzival shows himself here to be completely preoccupied with the plain, straightforward ethos of the knightly world. All his thinking is in terms of his own knightly and courtly achievement and is itself an explanation for his failure at Munsalvæsche.

The last group of monologues we have to discuss is perhaps the most important of all, occurring in book IX at the time of Parzival's growing awareness of his sinfulness, at the turning point in his story. The first of these (444.4 ff.) portrays him as he is being challenged by an unknown knight on account of his riding too near the Grail territory and shows him in a conciliatory mood, anxious to avoid giving offence and conscious that if he were to offend his cause would be entirely lost: 'ich wære unernert' (444.4). And indeed Parzival is driven away and loses his sword; his means of defence is taken from him, and his defeat is the physical side of his humiliation, a prelude to his voluntary spiritual humiliation, which follows later.

The next monologue (450.12 ff.) shows an advance in Parzival's condition. He has just met Kahenis and his family on their Good Friday pilgrimage of penance and is struck by the incongruity of his appearance with theirs. He is just beginning to realize what is demanded of him to see that his accent on the outward accomplishments of knighthood ill accords with the humility and poverty of spirit that the occasion merits. He recognizes that his riding is sadly out of tune with the walking of the knight's daughters, and decides that it would be better for him to separate from them. His thoughts begin with observations of the outward circumstances, then turn to the spiritual realities of which they are the manifestation. He contrasts their different attitudes: on the one hand the love that the knight and his family bear to God and the help that they expect and receive from Him, and on the other his *haȝ* towards God, Whom he accuses of withholding help from him and of not protecting him from sorrow. Parzival is in a rebellious mood and has not yet reached the stage where he can become reconciled with God, but at least he has realized *that* he is separated from God, and this realization marks the start of the eventual reconciliation. In parting from Kahenis he receives his good-will and realizes his own unworthiness to travel on with him.

Parzival's inner change now comes nearer the surface: 'sich huop sîns herzen riuwe' (451.8), and he thinks of the Creator of the world and of His power. He concentrates largely on those aspects of God's nature which have their origin in a feudal and knightly conception of Him,[1] and his attitude is, broadly speaking, that of a knight to his feudal lord. Thus, Parzival decides, as it were, that he will test God and give Him a chance to reveal His protecting power and overcome his (Parzival's) despondency. He expresses his readiness to serve God with shield and sword and prove himself worthy of God's *helfe* through his fighting-power, expecting that on this day, 'sîn helflîcher tac' (451.21), i.e. Good Friday, He will grant His *helfe* if this indeed lies within His power. Until this moment Parzival had had neither the desire nor the spiritual capacity for reconciling himself with God. He had been wholly concerned with knightly prowess to the complete exclusion of all else. The concern with prowess remains, but it is pushed towards the background, and its place is taken by the genuine desire to learn God's will.

The last stage before Parzival is ready to receive the instruction of Trevrizent immediately follows on the previous one, and Parzival entrusts himself completely to God's guidance. He reasons that if God is so powerful that He can guide horses, beasts and human beings, then he will praise Him for it. He will no longer rely on his own capacities and knowledge, but slacken his horse's

[1] H.-J. Koppitz, *Beobachtungen über das Verhältnis Wolframs von Eschenbach ȝur religiösen Tradition des Mittelalters* (Diss. Bonn, 1954), p. 20. '[Das Gottesbild] bei Wolfram [wird] durch solche [Züge] ergänzt, die Gott als den obersten Lehensherrn zeigen. Gott wird gleichsam ein ritterliches Gewand umgelegt.'

reins and let God guide him where He will, as is most fitting for his journey. Thus, Parzival overcomes his own selfish desires and reaches the point at which he can confess his guilt and unite his will to God's. All his rebelliousness fades into insignificance, and his *haʒ* dies into incipient confidence and trust before blossoming forth into love.

The preceding remarks show how carefully placed Parzival's monologues are and how they spotlight important stages in his development from the time of his earliest boyhood to the moment of his last decision about the priorities in his life when all his companions are celebrating their marriages. The *Dümmling* theme, the questions of *minne* and Parzival's relationship with God are all deepened by the use of the monologue in showing us Parzival's self-awareness and consciousness of his individuality. Particularly to be noticed is the fact that the two most important series occur when he has to part from the Arthurian world, after his encounter with Kahenis and after the festivities at the end of book XIV. Here his individuality is emphasized both in the psychological treatment of the event (through the monologues) and in the physical separation from the other inhabitants of the Arthurian world. The use of the monologues is an isolating factor and thus brings out the individuality of the character in question. The frequent use of it for Parzival underlines his particularly strong individuality.

PARZIVAL'S CHILDHOOD

Descriptions of the hero's childhood and its significance for his later, adult life are frequent enough in medieval German literature. Either before or roughly contemporaneous with Wolfram's *Parʒival* we find Lamprecht's *Alexander*, Hartmann's *Gregorius*, Gottfried's *Tristan* and even the *Nibelungenlied* which furnish details of the hero's childhood and youth as an illuminating preliminary to the story proper that the author intends to relate. Slightly later there are childhood stories of Hagene in *Kudrun* and the various attempts in the *Wolfdietrich* epics. Moreover, the epics of Charlemagne, which had formerly dealt with the maturity of the Emperor and especially the battle of Roncevaux, during the course of the thirteenth century develop stories of the boyhood of Charles. And, of course, Chrétien's *Conte del Graal* provides an introductory childhood episode too. All this indicates the growth of interest in the total career of the hero in question, in the light which details of childhood may shed on adult activities, adventures and character. It points towards the beginnings of interest in the development of a personality as opposed to a mere delight in adventurous exploits for their own sake. But the childhood episodes can be treated in a variety of ways, most of which are strictly in line with the concept of heroic or exemplary character. Thus, the burden of Lamprecht's description of the young Alexander is to illustrate from the very beginning the exemplary nature of his hero as a boy and to show through the taming of the horse Bucival that Alexander's superhuman strength and capabilities are his chief characteristics. All the information which Lamprecht gives is little more than an extension back into childhood of the mature 'wunderlîcher Alexander'. Thus, there is no real development of character, no gradual unfolding of personal attributes; everything is fully present from the start. The same is essentially true of Sivrit in the *Nibelungenlied*, though the *âventiure* describing his youth is more refined and more courtly than the corresponding passages dealing with Alexander.

In *Tristan* the *Vorgeschichte* assumes greater and more important proportions, and the tragic history of Tristan's parents furnishes a highly significant background for the hero's own personal development. The exemplary conception of the hero remains the controlling factor in the description, but in his depiction of the outstanding courtly accomplishments of Tristan and the breadth of his education Gottfried pursues his aim with great subtlety, finesse and lavish detail. Nevertheless all this is in the nature of a prelude to the main theme of the poem, the *minne*-relationship of Tristan and Isot. The initial episodes of Tristan's story display his noble character from the start and manifest the qualities which go to make up an *edelez herze*. They are essentially a preamble to fuller discussion of the principal theme, which emerges unambiguously from them and fulfils the intentions of the prologue. Hartmann's portrayal of Gregorius' boyhood provides a closer analogy with Parzival's, since here there is no straightforward progression from the characteristics of childhood and education to their fulfilment in maturity, but rather a reversal and breaking-away from the initial pattern of life. Hartmann's poem is imbued with an obvious didacticism and is concerned to point out the painful consequences of sin and heredity and the means whereby they may be overcome, but his technique is to write in strict antitheses and to be content with crude, sudden changes in psychological and emotional attitudes. For him the theme of the poem is the important thing; the didactic message comes first, the characterization has to be adapted to it.

How then does Wolfram's description of Parzival's childhood compare with these other cases?

In the first place it is clear that in one pre-eminent respect the childhood of Parzival is more similar to that of Gregorius than to Alexander's, Sivrit's or Tristan's, since his initial situation in life is not in direct line with his later development. Both Gregorius and Parzival have to break away from the way of life in which they are brought up; they each become conscious of the forces of heredity within them and leave monastery and forest respectively in order to discover the meaning of chivalry, but their solutions to the problems facing them are vastly different from each other.

The question of heredity is an important one for Parzival, and Wolfram's invention of the history of Gahmuret emphasizes the significance which it had for him. The constant reference to Parzival as *Gahmuretes barn* or *Herzeloyden kint* is a perpetual reminder of this, and it is no surprise to us that *art* and *gelust* soon combine to lead Parzival into pursuits that are as near chivalry as he can get. Herzeloyde's aim is to preserve Parzival at all costs from knowledge of the knightly world in which his father died, and she compels all her people, on pain of death for infringement, never to mention anything about knights to her son. One thing, however, she omits to do—she allows Parzival to play with bows and arrows—

and this little thing permits the development of innate, only half-realized desires and a gradual access to knightly life. Parzival learns how to kill birds with his home-made weapons, but cannot understand just what happens when they die, bursting forth with loud song. Nor does Herzeloyde realize straight away why it is that the birdsong causes Parzival such inexplicable sorrow until she has kept a careful watch on him and seen him gazing up into the trees to listen to the birds. Birdsong in the courtly lyric is closely connected with the idea of *freude* in *minne*,[1] and Wolfram tells us that Herzeloyde 'wart wol innen daz zeswal / von der stimme ir kindes brust. / des twang in art und sîn gelust' (118.26 ff.). Clearly Gahmuret, with his reputation as a lover (though one who was unable to settle with any of his three *frouwen*), is exerting an influence over Parzival despite all Herzeloyde's precautions. Nor do any of her attempts to get rid of the birds succeed, for Parzival with childish innocence demands, 'waz wîzet man den vogelîn?' (119.10), and Herzeloyde cannot but yield to the reasonableness of his question. Moreover, the fact that she considers her action to have been contravening God's command leads the enquiring Parzival to follow his first question by one of deeper import: 'ôwê muoter, waz ist got?' (119.17). In this way the various levels of his history are seen to be closely linked right from the beginning. A chain of cause and effect starting with the young boy's games with bows and arrows progresses through the first vague awakening of *minne* in him to the question which foreshadows the religious anguish of book IX. After this we hear how Parzival's physical development advances by leaps and bounds and how he is able to carry home singlehanded an ungralloched beast that would have been too much for a mule to carry. Here is the only example so far of any exemplary, idealized feature of Parzival's character, though just less than 100 lines further on Wolfram mentions his great physical beauty. Nevertheless, the emphasis is on the purely natural, normal activities and questions of Parzival as a boy, so that when he runs crying to Herzeloyde and cannot tell

---

[1] See above, p. 80, fn. 1.

her what it is that is causing him pain, Wolfram can point out that this is quite usual with children (118.21 f.).

Parzival's childhood is, therefore, in contrast with that of Tristan or Alexander, unmarked by any outstanding, idealized characteristics apart from the one already mentioned. But it is not the kind of childhood typical of a courtly knight, and it is this obvious aspect which is most important. The countrified upbringing of Parzival singles him out from the normal run of chivalrous heroes and creates an untypical and therefore individualized figure of him. Moreover, despite the fact that the basis of the idea is present in Chrétien's poem, the actual description of Parzival's early life in Soltane contains many more details, since Chrétien proceeds almost immediately to the encounter with the knights and its effect on Perceval, his mother and her *herceor*. These details form a series of incidents, remarks and questions, all of which give a more individualized, active picture of Parzival. This first section of the childhood story in Wolfram's poem establishes a proper setting for the later episode with the knights, and the reasons for it and Herzeloyde's command that her son should be kept in ignorance of all knightly matters are given at this point and not in the middle of the scene with the knights, as with Chrétien. But the whole section is embellished with individual touches so that it becomes important in its own right and as an essential, integral part of Parzival's entire history.

The episode with the knights Wolfram both abbreviates from Chrétien and constructs more tightly and logically, using the events he has already described to motivate more clearly Parzival's actions and reactions. Here we have the incident through which Parzival realizes more fully the dim awareness he had felt of another world to which he belongs. The young boy, on hearing the noise of the knights' approach, immediately thinks of the devil and feels challenged to overcome him, since he considers that his mother has probably exaggerated the danger from him. But as he stands there, alert for battle, three of the knights, *nâch wunsche var* (120.25), appear, and the bright splendour of their armour makes him connect them with the God Whom his mother had characterized in terms of light imagery instead. Terror is struck into his heart, and he falls to the ground beseeching God for help. When Karnah-karnanz arrives on the scene, Parzival is doubly convinced that he sees God before him and exclaims: 'nu hilf mir, hilferîcher got' (122.26). Karnahkarnanz straight away disclaims this title and tells the boy that he is in the presence of four knights, which then allows Parzival to ask, as he has already done with respect to God:

> du nennest ritter: waz ist daz?
> hâstu niht gotlîcher kraft,
> sô sage mir, wer gît ritterschaft? (123.4 ff.)

The knight then informs him of Artus and, after appraising Parzival, remarks, 'ir mugt wol sîn von ritters art' (123.11). The boy takes little notice of this, but goes on with his inquisitive questions about the knight's armour, which he compares with the rings that his mother's maids wear, an individualized comparison which is not found in Chrétien, though the succeeding remark, comparing the coat-of-mail with the hides of stags, is (273 ff.). Parzival's interest lies first and foremost in the external features of the knights he meets, and he connects everything he sees with something of which he has personal experience, however strange the point of comparison. This brings out the humorous side of the episode very well, though it has its serious content too. In the course of the encounter Parzival discovers a considerable amount of information about the knights, while they by contrast learn nothing of the two knights and the abducted lady they are pursuing, since Parzival ignores their questions and in any case can give them no answer. The annoyance which Chrétien's knights feel towards the even greater disregard of Perceval is toned down by Wolfram in the course of his abridgement. But though the knights find Parzival amusing and comical, they also notice his handsome appearance and its portent for the future.

Parzival's two questions about God and about knights are a clear sign from the start as to the two chief preoccupations of his life. It is, I think, significant that they should be placed in the order that they appear in the poem and that the former should be connected with the latter through misunderstanding. As the question about God is chronologically first, so it is also first in the ultimate theme of the poem as a whole. It is emblematic of Parzival's development that he confuses the knights with the simplified idea of God that he has imbibed from his mother and that his every endeavour up to the end of book VI should centre on the problem of chivalry rather than on God. Thus, the main theme of the whole poem—the problem of reconciling the claims of *schildes ambet* with a proper devotion to God—is already to be seen in the childhood episodes, where the conflict is seen in terms of a dual heredity, the claims of chivalry being represented by Gahmuret, whose influence Herzeloyde unsuccessfully attempts to frustrate, while Herzeloyde's role is to exemplify the virtues of *triuwe* especially in relation to God. Parzival's departure from Soltane, dressed as a fool and armed only with Herzeloyde's all too brief instruction about courtly life, plainly illustrates his desire to find out for himself about the knightly world. The death of Herzeloyde implies his rejection of religious values as the main criteria for living, and it is therefore only to be expected that in book IX Trevrizent will characterize Parzival's causing the death of his mother as one of the *zwuo grôze sünde* of which he is guilty. But with his departure the inexperienced boy begins his gradual progression in the sphere of chivalry and starts to assert his own individuality through his unwillingness to be content with the life his mother desires for him.

The main theme of the poem is already embryonically present in the childhood episodes, but it is important to note that Wolfram's treatment of it is completely suited to the understanding and capacity of a child. The incidents described are not such as might occur in adulthood but have been projected back into childhood and therefore appear exemplary, nor are they merely generalized descriptions of normal education, either for the courtly or for the religious life. They are, on the contrary, a highly individualized picture, full of details, of an unusual childhood which provides the *point de départ* for the story of Parzival and the Grail.

THE DÜMMLING THEME

Parzival's departure from Soltane dressed in *tôren kleider* is the event which makes the *Dümmling* theme explicit, though previous comments have heralded its appearance. The early reference in the opening lines of book I to the hero who is *træclîche wîs* is followed by a long series of synonyms varying this theme,[1] and Parzival's reaction to seeing the knights in the forest, which causes them to call him 'dirre tœrsche Wâleise' (121.5), is the first expression of the theme in the gradual unfolding of the story. Parzival's *tumpheit*, as Mergell has pointed out,[2] is portrayed in a very varied development and is 'keine in sich ruhende Schilderung, sondern ein Vorläufiges, das auf später sich vollendende Reife und Erfahrung weist.'

The *tôren kleider* symbolize Parzival's psychological state of complete inexperience in the ways of the world and betoken his rustic, uncourtly upbringing. Jeschute, when she is explaining to her husband Orilus what has happened to her, refers to Parzival as 'ein tôr' (133.16), mentioning at the same time his *gabilôt* and his countrified boots. The *gabilôt* is well known as a weapon unsuited to courtly uses, as Iwanet tells the young Parzival after he has killed Ither: 'ich enreiche dir kein gabilôt: / diu ritterschaft dir daz verbôt' (157.19 f.). But Parzival from the start is described as using it in his daily life in the forest, and it takes him a long time to discover that it is out of place in any proper knight's scheme of things. Thus, with Signe he unthinkingly demands whether Schionatulander met his end with a *gabilôt*, and Signe gently points out to him the antithesis between courtly combat and fighting with such a weapon (139.29 f.). Again later, when Parzival arrives at Nantes, Wolfram describes his appearance as being in complete contrast to courtly fashion and tells how instead of *suknî* and *surkôt*, garments whose French names indicate their courtly significance, he bears his *gabilôt*. In this way, since the weapon is mentioned on later occasions too (153.18, 155.6), the *gabilôt* becomes the emblem of Parzival's total ignorance of

---

[1] See above, pp. 110 f.   [2] *Op. cit.*, p. 68.

courtly etiquette and *savoir vivre*. Nonetheless, it is by means of this same instrument that he kills Ither and in doing so attains the rank of knight, but the *gabilôt* is erected on Ither's grave 'nâch der marter zil' (159.16), in the same way as the Cross signifies the Passion of Christ.[1] Thus, as Parzival's original desire to discover the nature of chivalry entails the death of his mother and the burden of sin that goes with it, so his achievement of chivalry brings with it the death of Ither, the second of the cardinal sins of which Trevrizent judges him guilty. His experience of the knightly world is fraught with transgressions against the moral law.

Similarly, considerable attention is paid to the actual *tôren kleider* themselves, as when Parzival has felled Ither he takes off the knight's armour, thus committing the sin of *rêroup*, and proceeds to put it on himself. Iwanet tries to tell Parzival that he should not wear the armour immediately on top of his *ribbalîn* and that he now ought to wear knightly clothing, but Parzival places such faith in everything he has derived from his mother, whether in the way of knowledge or in physical possessions, that he refuses to part with any of it. Wolfram's comment on Iwanet is characteristically humorous and emphasizes the knight's experience as against Parzival's blind following of his mother: 'daz dûhte wunderlîch genuoc / Iwâneten (der was kluoc)' (157.3 f.). Through this action of Parzival's we are shown how the boy's acquisition of knightly honour is merely external and that he understands nothing of the true ethos of chivalry. He merely presents a clumsily knightly appearance, while underneath he is really still a fool. This state of affairs persists until Parzival finds his way to Gurnemanz' castle, where his fool's clothing and untanned boots create a scare among the lord's servants who look after him. Soon, however, they overcome their embarrassment and amazement and do all they can to minister to his exhausted condition. Parzival receives a fine new set of clothes, all in the courtly fashion, and with this change in appearance he learns more about and properly assimilates the true essence of knightly conduct from the instruction that Gurnemanz gives him.

[1] *Parzival*, ed. Bartsch-Marti, I, p. 170.

But it is not solely in these obvious and largely external details that the *Dümmling* motif is expressed. Parzival's ignorance is shown in many more ways and permeates the whole of his development in changing form up to the end of book VI. To begin with, the young boy, dimly aware of his lack of knowledge in a strange world, relies blindly on the advice given him by Herzeloyde before he leaves her. As we have seen earlier, this advice presupposes some kind of awareness of the underlying ethos of courtliness for it to be properly comprehended, and this is precisely what Parzival lacks. He hears only the general advice and has no idea of how to apply it to particular situations, so that he applies it literally all the time to every situation he finds himself in. The various instances differ widely, of course, some of them being extremely serious and involving Parzival in danger and sin, while others are comically absurd in their absolute irrelevance to the conditions that obtain. In this way we get a skilful mingling of humour and comedy with elements of extreme gravity and even death. The *Dümmling* motif thus penetrates all levels of existence and contributes to the detailed, individualized picture of Parzival that Wolfram presents.

The first example of this comical adherence to the letter of Herzeloyde's advice occurs immediately after Parzival has left her and comes to a little stream—'den hete ein han wol überschritn' (129.8)—but which is *tunkel* because of the flowers and grass growing close to its brink. Accordingly, Parzival refrains from crossing it, not realizing that his mother's advice was given to help him in dangerous situations, where a deep river would usually be *tunkel*. Again, he rigorously applies the injunction: 'du solt dich site nieten, / der werlde grüeze bieten' (127.19 f.) to every person he meets, telling them that he does so at his mother's command. Thus, as he leaves Jeschute distraught at his violence, he adds: 'got hüete dîn: / alsus riet mir diu muoter mîn' (132.23 f.). There is an ironic flavour about the literal meaning of the greeting (it is in fact merely a literal rendering of the Old French 'deus vos sal', where the component words have more or less lost their original meaning), since Parzival has left Jeschute in such a position that she stands in need of God's help to escape from it. Even at such a tragic point in the story a humorous note is present and by its inappropriateness shows up all the more Parzival's complete incomprehension of what he has done. This juxtaposition of the serious and the comical is repeated when he meets Sigune and says, being now slightly more aware of the situation, but nonetheless full of youthful bumptiousness, 'er sî trûric od freuden var, / die bat mîn muoter grüezen gar. / got halde iuch' (138.25 ff.) (cf. also 138.5 ff.). In the course of the account of his wanderings before he arrives at Nantes Wolfram again points out that Parzival greets everyone, whether knight or merchant, informing them that he does it at his mother's advice (142.6 ff.), and he greets Ither in exactly the same terms: 'got hald iuch, riet mîn muoter mir' (145.9). Moreover, he reiterates the greeting to Iwanet (147.19 ff.) and to the assembled knights of the Round Table (147.30 ff.), and when he arrives at Graharz, he is still under the spell of Herzeloyde's words (163.25). This constant repetition of the formula, which is a well-known technique of humour, serves to underline the *Dümmling* motif in every episode of book III and to illustrate it on a fairly superficial, but nonetheless telling, level.

But the other instances in which Parzival follows his mother's instruction literally are far more significant in his growth as an individual, since they involve him in situations which have serious repercussions later.

THE JESCHUTE EPISODES

Herzeloyde had said to her son:

> sun, lâ dir bevolhen sîn,
> swa du guotes wîbes vingerlîn
> mügest erwerben unt ir gruoz,
> daz nim: ez tuot dir kumbers buoz.
> du solt zir küsse gâhen
> und ir lîp vast umbevâhen;
> daz gît gelücke und hôhen muot,
> op si kiusche ist unde guot.   (127.25 ff.)

As a result of this advice about how to win the favour of courtly ladies Parzival makes a dubious entrance into the realms of *minne*.

There is a careful gradation of his experiences in this sphere, which progress beyond the thoughtless brutality characteristic of the first Jeschute episode to the awakenings of a more sensitive, 'spiritual' type of *minne* with Liaze, which is fulfilled in his relationship with Condwiramurs, to whom he remains faithful throughout all his wanderings, so that the sensual temptations of Orgeluse can have no influence on him. In addition, Parzival offers his *dienest* through the mediation of Orilus to Cunneware de Lalant and to Ginover, but this *dienest* is free from any suggestion of true *minne*: it is merely a sign of the respect that the knight shows to a lady, and, incidentally, also to Artus.

Parzival's first encounter with Jeschute is the expression of a sheer blundering attempt to acquire the external tokens of *minne* from a lady. The crass recklessness of his action could scarcely be more dramatically or more clearly illustrated. He has nothing more than his mother's words to guide him, and as soon as he catches sight of Jeschute's ring, he remembers and immediately attempts to implement them. He is totally unmoved by the sensual attractions of Jeschute, though Wolfram depicts them in considerable detail and creates a beautifully individualized portrayal of a sleeping lady who is 'des wunsches âventiur' (130.10). As yet, he is insensitive to sexual emotions, and it never enters his head that he is doing anything that could be construed as unworthy or that any grave consequences will accrue from his action. Even in this episode there is an undercurrent of humour, since despite this rough and callous treatment of Jeschute Parzival puts himself into highly suggestive sexual situations, but takes no advantage of them, contenting himself instead with robbing the lady of her ring and brooch and then asking for food to still his hunger. Jeschute is at a loss to understand what is happening and can only conclude that he is a madman. She warns the boy of her husband's undoubted anger at what he has done, but Parzival further shows his utter incomprehension of the gravity of his deed and retorts: 'wê waz fürht ich iurs mannes zorn?' He then exacts another kiss from Jeschute and greets her as he leaves *ân urloup*, doing as his mother commanded.

Parzival's actions in this episode are, so far as his intentions are
concerned, quite amoral. There is no question of right or wrong
involved; he is merely obeying the commands of his mother in the
only way that he knows. Unfortunately obedience and stupidity
only combine to make him responsible for a complete dissolution
of Jeschute's and Orilus' mutual respect and love, since Orilus
assumes that the vanished ring and brooch mean that his wife has
had 'ein ander âmîs' (133.10). Nothing can convince him that for
Parzival they signify nothing more than they actually are, and he
consequently subjects Jeschute to a terrible humiliation, denying
her any of the normal privileges of marriage and forcing her to
ride on a broken-down, lean, unsaddled horse, wearing nothing
but a ragged shift, while he follows in all his knightly splendour.
Parzival had obviously not the least suspicion that anything like
this might occur as a result of his own action, as his compassion,
mingled though it is with curiosity, at the plight of Signe and
Schionatulander shows. For he is indeed capable of pity when he
meets a sorrowful situation. He is merely at this earlier stage
incapable of foreseeing any results to his actions. He acts as it
were in a vacuum, relating what he does to nothing but his mother's
advice.

In book V, after his visit to Munsalvæsche and his second
encounter with Signe, Parzival once more meets Jeschute, but
does not at first recognize her, so different does she look from when
he first saw her. Wolfram here gives as detailed a description of
Jeschute's appearance in distress as he does when Parzival first sees
her, so that the two descriptions form an antithesis to each other,
though the sensual element remains—'ir munt was rôt:/ der muose
alsölhe varwe tragen,/ man hete fiwer woldrûz geslagen' (257.18 ff.,
cf. 130.7 ff.). Parzival greets her (this time there is no reference
to Herzeloyde), and Jeschute answers by telling him that she has
seen him before and that her present misery originates from him.
The young knight immediately refutes Jeschute's accusation:

> jane wart von mîme lîbe
> iu noch decheinem wîbe

laster nie gemêret
(sô het ich mich gunêret)
sît ich den schilt von êrst gewan
und rîters fuore mich versan.
mirst ander iwer kumber leit.   (258.17 ff.)

With this refutation Parzival sets out his present position and
shows just how much he has developed and changed since the
time when he first met Jeschute. He has now learnt something
about the true nature of chivalry from both Artus and Gurnemanz
and can therefore see that if he had caused Jeschute's pitiful condition he would have acted against the spirit of knightly society.
His conclusion is, thus, that he himself has not acted in such a
way, at least not since he has been initiated into the knightly life.
It is not perfectly clear just when Parzival realizes Jeschute's
identity, but as soon as Orilus arrives on the scene he takes it upon
himself to fight him on Jeschute's behalf and to effect a reconciliation between them. In this way he manages to put right the painful
situation that he himself caused.

The significance of the episode is twofold. In the first place it
illustrates Parzival's increasing maturity and should be seen within
the context of his sins and his failure at Munsalvæsche. And
secondly, the encounter with Orilus indicates precisely Parzival's
achievement in terms of knightly strength and skill.

(i) The Parzival who meets Jeschute in book V is scarcely the
same person as robbed her of her ring and brooch in book III. It is
indicative of his present position that he does not recognize
Jeschute when he sees her, for he is not so far advanced in his
spiritual development as to be able to recognize when he has gone
astray or in fact sinned. It has to be pointed out to him that he is
responsible for what has gone wrong, however much he himself
is subjectively unaware of the wrong. The episode is preceded by
his fateful visit to Munsalvæsche and by his second encounter
with Sigune, who explains to him the fact of his failure at the
Grail castle and its significance; no indication is given, however,
of any means whereby this defection can be put right. When
Parzival therefore meets Jeschute again, he is made aware of his

guilt, and his newly won prowess enables him to try to reunite the husband and wife whose alienation he caused. This is already a step forward from the utter failure at Munsalvæsche, and through his success in wiping out the disgrace of his treatment of Jeschute a hint is given—and this is reinforced by the fact that Parzival swears his oath in Trevrizent's cell[1]—that the failure at Munsalvæsche will also be made good.

The increased maturity of Parzival is visible in several ways. The obvious difference lies in his deepened appreciation of courtly conduct, arising principally from his stay with Gurnemanz,[2] but also owing something to his tragic encounter with Ither. While on his first acquaintance with Jeschute Parzival knew nothing but a few external details of courtliness, he is now fully instructed in the values of chivalry and in a position to put them into practice. Moreover, he has also been initiated into the perfect experience of *minne* through his marriage with Condwiramurs and is now, therefore, able to appreciate from personal experience the gravity of his former conduct towards Jeschute. From the firm basis of his own *minne*-relationship he is able to do something to set Jeschute's aright. Similarly, Parzival's capacity for compassion is revealed to a far greater extent than had hitherto been the case. With Signe his pity had been overlaid largely by curiosity, and at Munsalvæsche it was stifled by excessive reliance on Gurnemanz' advice. Here, however, it comes clearly to the fore, unencumbered by other considerations, as Parzival is moved by Jeschute's pitiful state to alleviate her distress and force Orilus to take her back. From all this it is manifest that Parzival's understanding of *kurtôsie, minne* and *leit* is vastly increased.

(ii) The encounter with Orilus and subsequent defeat of that proud knight is a precise indication of Parzival's growing accomplishment as a knight. His conquest of Ither, much as it marked his achievement of knightliness, was sullied with the slaughter it entailed and the distress that it caused at the Arthurian court, particularly among the ladies. Further, Ither's reputation is

---

[1] See the chapter on Trevrizent, p. 312.
[2] See below, pp. 152 ff.

described in terms of *prís*, freedom from *valsch* or *untât*, *ʒuht*, *mannes triuwe*; in short, Ither is characterized by the moral virtues of chivalry. With Orilus the matter stands somewhat differently, since it is physical prowess that is his outstanding characteristic. When he returns to Jeschute's tent after Parzival's departure and finds that his wife has, as he thinks, betrayed him, he sets forth in some detail the extent of his knightly achievements, demonstrating through the self-assured boastfulness of his catalogue the aptness of his name, derived from the French 'Orgueilleus de la Lande'. From this speech of Orilus, made to Jeschute to justify himself against her supposed disdainful infidelity, we learn of his defeat of Jeschute's brother Erec at Karnant, an incident not recounted in Hartmann's *Erec*; of his killing Galoes, Gahmuret's elder brother and Parzival's uncle, which is mentioned in book II (80.6 ff.), though without reference to Orilus; of his defeat of Plihopliheri; of his defeat of eight knights of the Round Table at the tournament of Kanedic, at which he won the hand of Jeschute; of the death of Schionatulander (not mentioned by name, but referred to by Sigune also (141.8 f.)), which occurred that very morning. This redoubtable list of Orilus' successes combines well with the description of his marvellous appearance in book V (260.18 ff.) to show the excellence of the opposition that Parzival has to face. Wolfram speaks in hyperbolic language of their joust:

> newederhalp wart widersagt:
> si wârn doch ledec ir triuwe.
> trunzûne starc al niuwe
> von in wæten gein den lüften.
> ich wolde mich des güften,
> het ich ein sölhe tjost gesehen
> als mir diz mære hât verjehen.
> dâ wart von rabbîne geriten,
> ein sölch tjoste niht vermiten:
> froun Jeschûten muot verjach,
> schœner tjost si nie gesach.
> diu hielt dâ, want ir hende.
> si freuden ellende
> gunde enwederm helde schaden.   (262.16 ff.)

What great credit must then redound to Parzival's achievement when he succeeds in conquering Orilus!

The duel with Orilus stands in sharp contrast to that with Ither, though at this stage the importance of the encounter with Ither has been scarcely more than hinted at. In the first place Wolfram makes quite clear the fact that nothing stands in the way of Orilus and Parzival's fighting, whereas with Ither blood-relationship should have prevented them from duelling. Secondly, the fight is not brought to an end by death. This is an important aspect of all the duels that Parzival fights after his killing Ither: he conquers, but he does not spill blood, and therefore he wins credit through his greater humanity and compassion.[1] Thirdly, the duel is conducted according to the rules of chivalry: there is no question of either opponent's using underhand methods or uncourtly weapons such as brought Parzival his tragic success with Ither. Lastly, the duel with Orilus is fought with a particular aim—and, moreover, a very laudable one—in view; it is fought not merely to demonstrate knightly ability as such. The result of the whole episode is the rectification of an injustice, while the duel with Ither brought the external acquirement of knighthood, but at the same time involved Parzival more deeply in the bonds of sin.

The duel with Orilus has an unusual conclusion. Parzival refuses any of the 'liute, lant noch varnde guot' (267.10) that Orilus offers him in order to be relieved of the necessity of being reunited with Jeschute, but demands that he should go to Bertane and promise his, Parzival's, service to Cunneware, who suffered beating from Keie on Parzival's account, and also to Artus and Ginover, and he insists in addition that Orilus shall take back Jeschute. To this end he goes with the two to Trevrizent's cell and swears an oath to Jeschute's innocence, explaining how everything happened. Orilus thereupon accepts the *schumpfentiure* that has brought him *freude* (270.27 f.). returns with Jeschute to their tent, where the two are fully reconciled, and then proceeds to the

---

[1] Hermann John Weigand, *Three Chapters on Courtly Love in Arthurian France and Germany. Lancelot—Andreas Capellanus—Wolfram von Eschenbach's Parzival* (Chapel Hill, 1956), p. 28.

Arthurian court, which is gathered by the nearby Plimizœl, to give his sister Cunneware his *sicherheit* and to present Parzival's compliments to the king and queen. In this way Parzival's first breach of conduct after leaving Herzeloyde is brought to a satisfactory conclusion at the Arthurian court, which provides the standards and the background against which everything else is judged.

GURNEMANZ OF GRAHARZ

Parzival's stay at Gurnemanz' castle is fraught with singular significance for the course of his history. It occurs immediately after his killing of Ither and completes on the mental and spiritual level the process of his becoming a knight. The extent to which his defeat of Ither marks merely an external achievement of chivalry is shown by the fact that within the space of thirty lines between the panegyric on Ither and Parzival's reception at Graharz the young man is characterized four times by the word *tump* (161.6.17.25, 162.1). He is still very much under the influence of his mother's advice and refers to her on every possible occasion. He follows her instruction on greeting in the same way as previously (163.25) and twice tells Gurnemanz that his mother had told him to listen to the advice of a grey-haired old man (162.29 ff. and 163.15 f.). But the reliance on Herzeloyde is enlarged in this episode through references to matters other than those mentioned in her parting words, viz. to the fact that Herzeloyde's peasants have little success in agriculture since their corn doesn't reach the same height as the many towers of Graharz and to the fact that she likes her fill of sleep (162.2 ff. and 166.6 ff.), both colouring Parzival's naïveté with humour. Eventually, however, Gurnemanz tires of Parzival's constant reiteration of his mother's name and exclaims:

> ir redet als ein kindelîn.
> wan geswîgt ir iwerr muoter gar?
> und nemet anderr mære war.
> habt iuch an mînen rât:
> der scheidet iuch von missetât. (170.10 ff.)

Then follows the instruction of Gurnemanz on courtliness, which is meant to guide Parzival away from the snares of *missetât*, but leads him into sin at Munsalvæsche. This instruction forms the culmination of Parzival's visit to Graharz, the first part of which is taken up with an account of the welcome and hospitality extended to the young knight, of the care lavished on him in his exhausted condition and of the removal of the outward signs of his *tumpheit*, the fool's clothing. Once this is over, the scene is set for Gurnemanz to initiate Parzival into the ethos of the courtly world.[1]

Gurnemanz' instruction is given as a series of aphorisms on the various virtues of the courtly life and is divided into clearly differentiated sections, each setting forth some particular aspect of the whole. There are, thus, a series of interlinked remarks on (in the order in which they are mentioned) shamelessness; *erbärmde* and the corporal works of mercy, readiness to help those in distress; wealth and poverty; *mâze*; conversation; mercy and its relation to courage; cleanliness; *minne* and a proper attitude towards womankind. This advice is clearly articulated and covers the whole of courtly behaviour, though there are certain features which are not explicitly named, such as, for example, *stæte* and *zuht*. Missing completely from the list, however, is the cardinal virtue of *triuwe*, which we have seen to be of such importance for Parzival.[2] This omission is indeed the most fundamental feature of Gurnemanz' instruction, since it is *the* quality above all others that Parzival needs to manifest, though not acquire, as he has inherited it from his mother. But the fact that it is omitted now goes to show that a reliance solely on the courtly precepts of Gurnemanz will not suffice to bring Parzival to his ultimate goal in life, though it will, if rightly followed, assist him in his journey. The main interest of scholars, of course, has been devoted to Gurnemanz' fateful advice about not asking too many questions and its importance for Parzival's visit to Munsalvæsche, but it is necessary to examine the

---

[1] Cf. Siegfried Grosse, *Wis den wisen gerne bi. Die höfischen Lehren in Hartmanns Gregorius und Wolframs Parzival* (*DU*, XIV, vi, 1962), pp. 59 ff.

[2] Gottfried Weber, *Parzival. Ringen und Vollendung* (Oberursel, 1948), p. 27, n. 1; p. 176.

whole passage within its context, since the other pieces of advice also have their part to play in the young knight's story.

The chief of the courtly virtues is *zuht*, and Gurnemanz as the *houbetman der wâren zuht* (162.23) centres his attention on this subject, though he never actually mentions it in so many words. The whole of what he has to say must be seen in relation to Parzival's childish way of talking, his lack of any *savoir vivre* and simple tact, and it is clear that the old man feels that it is high time that someone taught the youth some of the more obvious habits of courtly society and wooed him away from his rustic and uncouth naïveté. Thus, his reference to *sich verschemn* is to be understood as an exaggeration of certain undesirable features that he had noticed in Parzival's behaviour, and the first essential is for the young man to overcome this. Any knight who neglects this *sine qua non* is well on the way to hell.

The courtly knight is pledged to the service of those in distress, especially ladies and orphans, and this aspect of courtly life is strongly emphasized by Gurnemanz at this point, once he has noted Parzival's noble bearing and appearance. In the exercise of the corporal acts of mercy he should practise both *milte* and *güete* and embrace *diemüete*. Generosity of spirit and kindness are here linked with what must be termed modesty or that unassuming reticence and lack of boastfulness which characterizes the perfect knight, for *diemüete* in this context is a courtly virtue and has none of the religious significance which attaches to the use of the word with reference to Parzival's guilt.[1] Later on in his instruction Gurnemanz reverts to the theme of compassion and counsels that pity and courage should go hand in hand. It is from his advice that a knight should accept his defeated opponent's *sicherheit* rather than put him to death that Parzival acts as he does towards Orilus and that he refuses to kill any of the knights whom he conquers in battle. We see from these utterances that Gurnemanz is at pains to open Parzival's consciousness to the ideal of compassion with those who require help and with those against whom

[1] Herbert Kolb, *Schola Humilitatis. Ein Beitrag zur Interpretation der Gralerzählung Wolframs von Eschenbach* (*Beitr.* (Tübingen), LXXVIII, 1956), p. 85.

the knight fights. He even puts this into a religious framework by declaring: 'swenne ir dem [i.e. the needy man] tuot kumbers buoz,/ sô nâhet iu der gotes gruoz' (171.3 f.). All of this should have formed an encouragement to Parzival in his visit to the Grail castle, for Anfortas is clearly a 'kumberhafte werde man' troubled by an 'unsüez arbeit'. Unfortunately, Gurnemanz' next few words lead off to the fateful advice and the context in which they are spoken becomes of no effect to Parzival.

The next section is concerned with the subject of mâʒe. Moderation combined with understanding is the key to true courtly behaviour, and after an introductory admonition about undue lavishness or miserliness Gurnemanz proceeds to enunciate the general principle 'gebt rehter mâze ir orden' (171.13). And in order to show that his remarks are to be understood with reference to what he knows of Parzival's previous life, Gurnemanz explicitly mentions this and instructs him to renounce unfuoge, the crudity and uncouthness of his former ways. Then follows the crucial line 'irn sult niht vil gevrâgen' (171.17), which in Gurnemanz' mind relates to the young knight's earlier life, but is misunderstood by Parzival with such disastrous results. As far as Gurnemanz is concerned, the young knight is a brash greenhorn and needs to learn something of the elementary rules of courtly conversation. He ought to desist from continually asking questions and to answer questions with due circumspection. Beyond this he should use his five senses to increase his knowledge and awareness. In itself this particular advice is perfectly sound and understandable and is something which Parzival stands in need of. It is only through its misapplication that it becomes dangerous.[1] Parzival does, however, remember it on an occasion other than his visit to Munsalvæsche, namely, at Pelrapeire, where he sits in complete silence waiting for Condwiramurs to address him on first being welcomed to the castle (188.15 ff.). Here the consequences of his reliance on Gurnemanz are nothing more than humorous, though the queen muses a great deal about his conduct before she eventually speaks.

[1] For a discussion of the later development of the question motif see below, pp. 343 ff.

In addition, Parzival's possession of *ʒuht* is stressed both by Wolfram (188.15) and by Condwiramurs (189.3), so that his demeanour on this occasion appears fully justified.

The last section of Gurnemanz' advice deals with the theme of *minne* and the behaviour of a knight towards womankind. It is introduced by a rather down-to-earth advice about the fact that a knight who has been wearing armour is liable to get dirty and that a good wash will make him 'minneclîch gevar' and the object of a woman's attention. This, in contrast to Herzeloyde's instruction, is the only piece of concrete action that Gurnemanz specifies: what he has to say is concerned with the generalities of knightly conduct towards women, with the moral basis of *minne*. A knight should be *manlîch* and *wol gemuot* and consequently full of *werder prîs*. The result of his devotion to women will be such that 'daz tiwert junges mannes lîp' (172.10); there is no mention of *gelücke* or *hôher muot*. Gurnemanz' thoughts on the relationship between the sexes are much further removed from the ideals of *hôhe minne* than those expressed by Herzeloyde or those exemplified in the story of Gahmuret. Indeed, what he says about honesty in love and his statement that

> man und wîp diu sint al ein;
> als diu sunn diu hiute schein,
> und ouch der name der heizet tac.
> der enwederz sich gescheiden mac:
> si blüent ûz eime kerne gar   (173.1 ff.)

constitute Wolfram's fundamental position on the subject and form the basis of the *minne*-relationship between Parzival and Condwiramurs. Thus, for this key relationship in Parzival's life, which is linked with his search for the Grail,[1] the knight derives his moral justification from Gurnemanz, and this soundest of his advice provides a firm, reliable *point d'appui* for Parzival throughout the course of his troubles and wanderings. Gurnemanz points out the moral obloquy which a knight can bring upon himself in the pursuit of *minne* if he does not at all times act honourably; he is particularly

[1] See below, pp. 244 ff.

anxious that Parzival should realize what the pitfalls are and thenceforth avoid them.

In addition to setting out this philosophy of courtly life Gurnemanz introduces Parzival to the religious rituals of the Church that his mother had totally ignored. It is significant that Wolfram should mention them at this point in connexion with Parzival's initiation into courtliness, whereas Chrétien had already introduced the subject in the parting words of Perceval's mother (567 ff.); for Wolfram's whole tendency is to stress the inward side of religious experience to the neglect of the usual outward ceremonial. The fact that the practice of going to mass, crossing oneself and so on are placed in the courtly context suggests that for Wolfram they are a necessary part of Parzival's experience, but one which he must eventually transcend. The courtly stage is, however, the period at which Parzival must learn about the norm of life before he is able to proceed to something higher.

Theoretical advice is the most important part of Gurnemanz' instruction, but he does also see to it that Parzival gets some practical experience. Having poked fun at him for the way he bears his shield, he takes the young man with some other knights out on to the jousting field and teaches him the rudiments of the tourney. Parzival quickly assimilates this new knowledge, being spurred on by 'diu Gahmuretes art / und an geborniu manheit' (174.24 f.), and at the end of the session the onlookers praise his accomplishment and valour and rejoicingly expect that Gurnemanz will give his daughter Liaze to Parzival for his wife. But despite the attractions of Liaze Parzival is not ready for marriage and follows in his father's footsteps in that 'er wolt ê gestrîten baz, / ê daz er dar an wurde warm, / daz man dâ heizet frouwen arm' (177.2 ff.). Accordingly, having learnt a great deal in the way of worldly experience and got rid of his *tumpheit* (188.16 f.), Parzival asks permission of Gurnemanz to depart. With reluctance the old man, to whom Parzival has become as a fourth son lost, hears his request and tells him of the catastrophes which have befallen his family, thus introducing the story of Condwiramurs, where the young knight is swiftly able to make good use of his newly learnt talents.

THE ARTHURIAN EPISODES

When Parzival on meeting the four knights in the forest of Soltane asks them, 'wer gît ritterschaft?' he receives the answer, 'daz tuot der künec Artûs' (123.6 f.). From this moment his aim is to find his way to the Arthurian court and become a knight. It is true, as Wehrli has pointed out,[1] that Wolfram's poem is both an Arthurian and a Grail romance in which the two elements have their own ethical and social standards, but the Arthurian section of the work, being subordinated to the Grail theme, has received little attention in comparison with the other problems of *Parȝival*, apart from the studies of Hildegard Emmel and Maria Bindschedler.[2] The fact is, however, that Parzival's history is linked with the Arthurian circle at quite crucial points of his career, and that his actions as a knight are constantly referred, if not to Artus, then to other figures at his court. It is therefore necessary to examine the particular significance of the Arthurian episodes in some detail and to evaluate them in relation to the characterization of Parzival.

According to the normal canons of Arthurian literature the position of Artus and his court is shown as an ideal against which the actions of particular knights are measured. Artus himself appears as the epitome of the just king whose achievements and accomplishments are beyond question and who presides in an almost detached majesty over the knights of the Round Table. This is the view of Chrétien and Hartmann,[3] but it is not completely the case with Wolfram. A certain measure of the traditional and idealized features of Artus is present, but Wolfram pokes fun at this in the initial lines of book VI, where he points out the unusual element of snow in the normal Arthurian scheme of life:

> Artûs der meienbære man,
> swaz man ie von dem gesprach,
> zeinen pfinxten daz geschach,

---

[1] Max Wehrli, *Wolfram von Eschenbach. Erzählstil und Sinn seines 'Parȝival'* (*DU*, VI, V, 1954), p. 30.

[2] Hildegard Emmel, *Formprobleme des Artusromans und der Graldichtung* (Bern, 1951); Maria Bindschedler, *Die Dichtung um König Artus und seine Ritter* (*Dt. Vjs.*, XXXI, 1957).

[3] Emmel, *op. cit.*, p. 93.

odr in des meien bluomenzît.
waz man im süezes luftes gît!
diz mære ist hie vast undersniten,
ez parriert sich mit snêwes siten.   (281.16 ff.)

In other words, Wolfram is not primarily concerned with the ideal
representation of Artus, but instead draws him into a more real
knightly world in which he also is involved. This is made clear
through Kingrun's comparison of Artus with Clamide to the
former's disadvantage:

> noch rîcher denne Artûs
> wær du helfe und urborn,
> und hetes dîne jugent bevorn.
> sol Artûs dâ von prîs nu tragn,
> daz Kai durch zorn hât geslagn
> ein edele fürstinne,
> diu mit herzen sinne
> ir mit lachen hât erwelt
> der âne liegen ist gezelt
> mit wârheit für den hôhsten prîs?   (221.16 ff.)

Where a comparison of this type occurs, Artus can no longer be
conceived in purely ideal terms. A humanization of the Arthurian
circle has taken place; its position is relativized by means of irony
and comparison, and this is possible because its function is no
longer quite the same as in other Arthurian romances on account
of the increased significance allotted to the Grail community by
Wolfram. Only because the Grail community provides the final
test of Parzival's endeavours and thus assumes the role in which
the Arthurian court is usually cast can the latter undergo a change
in its depiction and function. The relativization of Artus and his
court is, however, compensated for by a new 'menschliche
Atmosphäre'[1] and by the increase in importance of minor figures
such as Cunneware and Segramors and by the conscious deviation
from tradition in the person of Keie, who is normally seen as being
in the wrong vis-à-vis the main hero,[2] but whose essential werdekeit
Wolfram is at pains to justify (296.13 ff.). There is, therefore, in

---

[1] Ibid., p. 96.   [2] Ibid., p. 93.

Wolfram's portrayal of the Arthurian circle a clear process of individualization at work. The old pattern is no longer adhered to for its own sake, but is varied and developed in accordance with Wolfram's usual technique of individualization. And as the Arthurian figures—apart from Gawan, who will be discussed in a separate chapter—are peripheral to the main plot, their individualization offers no threat to the principal characters, but is there rather to enhance the history of Parzival.

The young knight's first face-to-face encounter with the Arthurian court occurs after the Jeschute episode in the royal capital of Nantes. Two of the characters, namely Artus, who is the immediate object of Parzival's quest, and Cunneware, who is later to play an important part with regard to his knightly exploits, have already been introduced by Wolfram in a speech of Orilus', along with other well- and lesser-known figures of the Arthurian circle (133.30 ff.), so that this episode is, in accordance with Wolfram's characteristic method, knitted into the framework of the whole story. But although the court in this way loses something of its majestic isolation, it nonetheless remains of such essential nobility that, in the words of the fisherman who gives Parzival lodging for the night, 'diu mässenîe ist sölher art, / genæht ir immer vilân, / daz wær vil sêre missetân' (144.14 ff.). These words appear as a warning, since Parzival's uncouth appearance is just such as to make the fisherman think the young man would give offence at the court, though Ither is not misled by his curious exterior, but straight away addresses him as *junchêrre* (145.10) and comments on his strikingly handsome body. The previous lines, however, are concerned to point the contrast between Parzival's appearance and conduct on the one hand and that of the Arthurian court and the typical courtly knight on the other. To this end Wolfram invokes Hartmann von Aue, then universally acknowledged as the foremost of German Arthurian poets, to protect the awkward, poorly dressed youth from the mockery of men, mentioning that the same could easily happen to Hartmann's own heroine Enite, who also appeared at the Arthurian court in a pitiful condition. The reference to Hartmann and the threefold repetition of *spot* (143.25, 144.3.4) accentuate the contrast that Wolfram wishes to make. A further allusion to Tristan underlines the consciously different approach of Parzival to the matter of courtliness: 'in zôch nehein Curvenâl: / er kunde kurtôsîe niht, / als ungevarnem man geschicht' (144.20 ff.). This lack of courtliness in Parzival is, as the words of Ither quoted above show, a more or less superficial aspect of his character, since at every turn the young man either is praised by the author for the excellence of his physical appearance (148.24 ff.) or evokes reactions of wonder on the part of those other characters with whom he comes into contact. Such are the reactions of Cunneware here and of a knight and members of Gurnemanz' court later (164.11 ff., 168.23 ff.). There are obviously present in Parzival qualities which make his ignorance in courtly matters of secondary importance.

The function of Cunneware in Wolfram's poem is enlarged from what he found in Chrétien, although the motif of Keus' assault on her and Perceval's insistence on the fact that all the knights whom he defeats should go to present his compliments to the *damoisele* are present in the French poem. Wolfram creates an individual of the lady through giving her a name, describes the episode in more detail and elaborates her history in the latter part of his work. However, in the scene now under consideration the function of Cunneware's action is to proclaim Parzival as the knight 'die den hôhsten prîs / hete od solt erwerben' (151.14 f.). This formulation thus points to an element of predestination, though only delicately foreshadowed, in the history of Parzival, and the fact that the young knight sends his conquered opponents Kingrun, Clamide and Orilus to her reminds one at many moments in the story of her prophetic role. In view of Parzival's crazy appearance at Artus' court it is natural that Keie should react to Cunneware's second-sight in the way he does, since her words must seem a mockery of Arthurian standards to the person with no knowledge of how the situation is to develop. Parzival, however, is deeply incensed by Keie's brutal treatment of both Cunneware and Antanor, 'der witzehafte tôr' (153.11), but is happily prevented by the throng around the queen from doing any damage here with his *gabilôt*, an ominous hint of what is to happen with Ither. But his later knightly endeavours are referred to it for a long time afterwards, and Keie's knowledge of how things seem on the surface, seen here and in the *Blutstropfenepisode*, is always contrasted with the true knowledge which sees deeper. The Cunneware episode of book III is brought to a fitting conclusion in book VI, where she is given in marriage to Clamide, whom Parzival defeated in the defence of Condwiramurs. In this way the first part of Parzival's career—as an Arthurian knight—is suitably rounded off, for the lady on whose account he has performed his deeds of knightly valour has her honour restored in a worthy marriage, and mercy is granted to the king who proved so great a torment to Condwiramurs. Parzival is now free to put the whole of his energy into the service of his wife and the search for the Grail; nothing remains to deflect him any longer from these two inextricably linked aims in his life. The merely Arthurian part of his career is now over; henceforth Parzival excludes himself from the Arthurian court and presses on unremittingly in his endeavour to win the Grail. No longer can he be content with serving more than one lady and performing feats of bravery of which the Arthurian circle is the arbiter, but he has to progress to a more penetrating appreciation of knightly life and its problems, which is symbolized in his struggle to reach the Grail and ask the so-called *Mitleidsfrage*.

The chief significance of the Arthurian scenes of book III lies in Parzival's encounter with Ither, the Red Knight, the king of Kukumerlant.[1] Margaret F. Richey has pointed out[2] that the figure of Ither is viewed in three different ways—as an enemy by Artus, as the possessor of the red armour which Parzival so naïvely covets as a token of knighthood, as the epitome of true knightliness to Ginover—and she has attempted to explain these differences in terms of an incomplete fusing by Wolfram of

---

[1] For arguments against the identification of Kukumerlant with Cumberland see M. O'C. Walshe, *Der Künec von Kukumerlant* (*Lond. Med. St.* I, 1937/9).
[2] Margaret F. Richey, *Ither von Gaheviez* (*MLR*, XXVI, 1931), pp. 318 ff.

elements from Chrétien's Chevalier Vermeil with the figure of Yder fil Nuc, the hero of a thirteenth century French verse romance. I do not wish to question Dr Richey's findings on this aspect of the problem, but it seems to me that the differences between Chrétien and Wolfram should first be explained by reference to Wolfram's changed conception of the character of Ither, that is, by reference to internal considerations in Wolfram's story. For we know that Parzival's killing of Ither has far more weight attached to it than Perceval's conquest of the Chevalier Vermeil. As one of Parzival's *ʒwuo gróʒe sünde* the slaughter of the Red Knight cannot be unequivocally accompanied by the shades of honour which attach to Perceval's 'vengeance' of the dishonour inflicted on the queen in Chrétien's poem, which leads her to commit suicide. The death of Ither according to Wolfram receives its stark importance through the fact that Ither is related to Parzival by kinship. As Trevrizent says: 'du hâst dîn eigen verch erslagn' (475.21). Chrétien's poem contains not a trace of this; there is hostility from both Artus and his queen towards the Chevalier Vermeil with the result that there can be rejoicing when Perceval kills him. Clearly, it would be too much of an unmotivated *volte face* for Wolfram to retain this episode unaltered, but later to evaluate it in such opposing terms. There must be some indication when it actually occurs that all is not well with the killing, and this Wolfram achieves by a reinterpretation of Ginover's role in the situation, since in the French poem she is the most vaguely delineated character in the episode—she is not even named—and has no more than a passive part to play. Thus, Ginover does not kill herself, the incident with the goblet and the wine is toned down and explained as an accident in contrast to the manifest brutality indulged in by the Chevalier Vermeil, and the queen and Ither are represented as enjoying an amicable relationship. All this shows a radical change, while the relationship between Artus and the Red Knight remains the same. Wolfram, however, does not feel concerned to justify or explain the differences in attitude between Ginover and Artus. Probably the various lovers of Ginover, with whom Artus had to contend, could be augmented in number without any feeling of impropriety on the part of the audience of the Arthurian romances, though it is only by reading between the lines that Ither can be cast in this role; there is no explicit statement by Wolfram that this is so. Since, therefore, Ginover expresses grief at Ither's death immediately after its occurrence, this fact (together with Trevrizent's own intimate relationship with Ither) makes comprehensible Wolfram's reassessment of its significance in book IX. Without Ginover's reaction to the situation in book III the changed evaluation of Ither's death in book IX would have appeared abrupt and senseless. As it is, it is crucial for a proper understanding of Wolfram's treatment of the Grail story.

The Ither episode marks Parzival's crashingly ignorant irruption into the Arthurian world. All that he is concerned about is to be made a knight, understood in the crudest and most naïve of terms, and he is totally unmoved by causing Ither's death and by the finer elements of knightly conduct, partially because he is under the delusion that Ither is in fact his inherited enemy Lähelin (154.25 f.), about whom both Herzeloyde and Sigune had told him.[1] He blunders into a delicate situation, wreaks havoc everywhere and rides away once he has acquired some external display of knightliness in the shape of the Red Knight's armour. His whole behaviour is marked by his childish desire to possess some palpable token of knighthood; he has no idea that more is involved than this. So little does he understand of the knightly world that when he arrives at the court he causes great amusement by saying: 'ich sihe hie mangen Artûs: / wer sol mich ritter machen?' (147.22 f.). His eagerness is such that not even Artus can hold him back for a proper initiation into the ways of knightly life. Parzival rejects the king's promise to prepare him for knighthood the following morning and insists on his desire for the Red Knight's armour, which he so naïvely covets. This desire lacks any clear will to do Ither harm; Parzival's intention is selfish covetousness barely tinged by the idea of righting a former wrong done him by

[1] Cf. Wolfgang Harms, *Der Kampf mit dem Freund oder Verwandten in der deutschen Literatur bis um 1300* (Munich, 1963), p. 151.

Lähelin. He is attracted merely by the bright armour. Once he has won the object of his immediate desire, he happily and unconcernedly leaves the Arthurian court, no longer worried about becoming a knight on Artus' terms.

Parzival does not understand the nature of the conflict between Ither and Artus, but his lack of understanding evokes different responses in the various characters. Ither himself recognizes Parzival's innate nobility and uses the ignorant youth to present his version of the unfortunate clash with the goblet at the court and to challenge one of the knights to win back the symbol of his claim to Bertane. Artus feels himself in an unpleasant position *vis-à-vis* Ither, he wishes to regain the goblet, but expresses a sense of responsibility towards the inexperienced boy with his desire to have Ither's armour. He points out that it is not in his power to grant Parzival's wish and hesitates to allow him to fight with Ither, whether for his armour or for the goblet. Keie on the other hand looks at the matter in a severely practical way, and the importance which he attaches to the recovery of the goblet leads him to consider both Parzival and Ither as expendable. It is Iwanet, however, who first instructs Parzival in some of the rules of knightly conduct and acts as his guide and mentor from his initial appearance at Nantes. He takes him at the beginning into Artus' presence, and at the end he gratefully receives the goblet from Parzival, while at the same time providing for a decent burial for Ither. He helps Parzival to put on his newly won armour and explains that he cannot as a knight make use of the *gabilôt* any longer, but must stick henceforth to sword and spear. This reference to the *gabilôt* and the *rêroup*, which is strangely permitted by Artus, provides two obvious points from which the gravity later ascribed to Parzival's deed can be partially supported.

This first Arthurian episode contains many important elements in the development of Parzival's history. It shows with considerable complexity and subtlety the tragicomedy of Parzival's desire to become a knight, though this is only the first stage of the process, in which he wins the external trappings and nothing more. But in winning them he unwittingly loads upon himself the burden of Ither's death, the full significance of which is only revealed in book IX. When Parzival puts on Ither's armour over his fool's clothing, he shows with devastating clarity his solely external apprehension of knighthood; but the next time he visits the Arthurian court all this has changed.

It is a mark of how much Parzival has matured and become wiser in the ways of the courtly world that in the Arthurian scenes of book VI the roles of seeker and sought are reversed. Parzival's conquests of his knightly opponents—Kingrun, Clamide and Orilus—have come to Artus' notice through the former's insistence that all his defeated foes should declare their service to Cunneware and Artus, and they have shown the king the extraordinary extent of Parzival's achievements. Artus, therefore, embarks on a search for the young knight, determined to invite him to the Round Table, and now, of course, Parzival has so widened and deepened his experience that he is perfectly suited for this honour—apart from one thing, whereby Cundrie disrupts the whole of Parzival's imagined happiness. But he is now fully aware of the true ethos of the courtly society into which he desires entrance: Gurnemanz has seen to this and assisted his passage from boyhood to manhood. With Condwiramurs he has found the rare delight of *minne* and remains unswervingly devoted to her. He has put right his injury to Jeschute. In all these he has manifested the true spirit of courtliness. Only at Munsalvæsche, a territory beyond the reach of the Arthurian court, has he failed.

Book VI, in which the Arthurian circle plays its most important part in Parzival's life, begins with the so-called *Blutstropfenepisode*, where Parzival's love for Condwiramurs is shown in a unique manner. This episode stands in an ironical parellelism with the later part of the book, namely, Cundrie's denunciation, for in both instances it is claimed that Parzival has disgraced the Round Table. In the first, however, a justification is made and accepted; in the second the claim is acknowledged and Parzival departs from the scene.

The *Blutstropfenepisode* is rich in layers of meaning: the motif of dishonour to be intensified later is introduced; Keie's brutality

towards Cunneware and Antanor is avenged; Parzival meets
Gawan, the paragon of Arthurian knighthood, whose career is
paralleled with his own.

The dishonour motif starts with the reactions of Cunneware's
garȝûn to meeting Parzival *verdâht* at the sight of the drops of
blood on the snow and sitting on his horse, holding his spear
erect as if ready for a joust. But the importance of these reactions
is minimized by a depreciation of the page: 'sîne kurtôsîe er dran
verlôs' (28.11), together with a curious reference to his lady's
being *lôs*. If this is to be understood in the normal meaning of *lôs*,
the statement is strangely at variance with the general portrayal of
Cunneware. Bartsch-Marti suggest that it should be taken in the
sense of 'schalkhaft',[1] which fits in better with the passage as a
whole, though this particular clause is inserted as a parenthesis and
as such need not have any deep significance. On seeing Parzival,
the *garȝûn* dashes back to the court, shouting out his horror at
what he has seen and declaring that 'tavelrunder ist geschant'
(284.21). The impetuous Segramors sees here a golden opportunity
to display his knightly prowess, and his part in the episode is
described with highly individualized detail—his disturbing Artus
and Ginover in bed for permission to deal with the stranger, the
reference to the Rhine, the description of the tinkling bells on
his horse and armour. But despite all his enthusiasm and endeavour
Segramors gains nothing, but is instead knocked by Parzival into
the snow and defeated. Keie then picks up the dishonour motif,
'tavelrunder hât unêre' (290.16), and begs permission to see what
he can do, which Artus readily grants. Keie, however, suffers in a
more extreme way than Segramors and ends up with a broken
right arm and left leg, though Parzival is all the time unconscious
of what he is doing and hears the news with surprise from Gawan.
In fact, as soon as he hears that Artus is in the vicinity, he remembers
Keie's beating of Cunneware and declares he must avenge it.
Wolfram, on the other hand, now that Keie has met with his punishment from Parzival, proceeds to a full-scale justification of Keie's

---

[1] *Parȝival*, ed. Bartsch-Marti, I, p. 303.

conduct and character in complete contrast with the traditional view of Keie,[1] and of this Wolfram is fully aware (cf. 296.21).

What is the purpose of this justification of Keie? One of the reasons for it may be found in Wolfram's own personal circumstances and his experiences of the rabble at the Landgrave of Thuringia's court, the 'ingesinde . . . daz ûzgesinde hieze baz' (297.17 f.), which leads to his declaration that the prince could have done with a Keie to deal with the throng. But there are two other grounds which are more closely knit into the framework of the plot, i.e. Wolfram's view of the *Blutstropfenepisode* as expressing a type of *minne* which is dangerous unless linked with a whole-hearted devotion to the Grail,[2] and the subsequent denunciation of Parzival by Cundrie, which demands some kind of preparation and justification from earlier events. In the first case the attempts of Segramors and Keie may be seen as justifiable actions, since their effect, though unconscious, is to break through Parzival's trance. And this can be so despite the asseveration of Kolb that they sinned in that they had 'in der Minne eines anderen Vernünftigkeit gesucht und damit nur bewiesen, daß Vernunft und Maß ihnen selber fehlten';[3] for this view is concerned to point the contrast between Segramors and Keie on the one hand and Gawan on the other, which is a different level of interpretation. This ties up with the second reason for the justification of Keie, namely, the dishonour motif as elaborated by Cundrie, since the two knights act as they do from loyalty towards Artus. If, therefore, Keie's action is approved, Parzival by implication is not completely justified in his, and Cundrie's outcry 'tavelrunder ist entnihtet' (314.29) is prepared for and supported from another source. Thus, a considerable change in the characterization of Keie can be seen as contributing towards a more complex depiction of Parzival. The individual traits in Keie serve the more detailed portrayal of the main hero.

From the preceding remarks it emerges that the second aspect

[1] See above, p. 159.   [2] See the chapter on Condwiramurs, pp. 250 ff.
[3] Herbert Kolb, *Die Blutstropfenepisode bei Chrétien und Wolfram* (*Beitr.* (Tübingen), LXXIX, 1957), p. 389. This remark is, however, directed at Saigremors and Keus in the French poem.

of the *Blutstropfenepisode*, the encounter between Keie and Parzival, is seen in two contrasting ways. Keie's former brutality towards Cunneware is avenged by Parzival, though the latter is unaware of having done so, while at the same time Keie's interference in the situation is condoned. It is the fact of the *minnetrance* which makes these two sides of the matter possible, for in this way the brutality is avenged without the duality in Keie's role becoming glaringly obvious. Wolfram's justification of him is an attempt to overcome this duality, and in large measure it is successful. There are no hard feelings left about Keie's first act.

The rest of book VI illustrates with great clarity the relativity of the Arthurian court in Parzival's history. Artus recalls the injury done to him by Parzival as well as the honour, but the latter outweighs the former to such an extent that he can invite Parzival to join the sodality of the Round Table. He also does him the honour of allowing him to kiss Ginover, and with this the queen expresses her forgiveness of his killing Ither. It seems then that Parzival has reached the height of his achievement in the Arthurian world, but at just this moment Cundrie appears and destroys everything.

Immediately Cundrie links the reputation of both Artus and Parzival, attacking the position of him who is traditionally the embodiment of knightly perfection:

> fil li roy Utpandragûn,
> dich selbn und manegen Bertûn
> hât dîn gewerp alhie geschant.
> die besten über alliu lant
> sæzen hie mit werdekeit,
> wan daz ein galle ir prîs versneit.
> tavelrunder ist entnihtet:
> der valsch hât dran gepflihtet.
> künc Artûs, du stüent ze lobe
> hôhe dînn genôzen obe:
> dîn stîgnder prîs nu sinket,
> dîn snelliu wirde hinket,
> dîn hôhez lop sich neiget,
> dîn prîs hât valsch erzeiget.

tavelrunder prîses kraft
hât erlemt ein geselleschaft
die drüber gap hêr Parzivâl.   (314.23 ff.)

By pointing out the enormity of Parzival's failure at Munsalvæsche Cundrie declares that he is completely unworthy of being
a member of the Round Table.[1] The deeds of chivalry undertaken
by Parzival between his two appearances at the Arthurian court
are shown not to be sufficient and unquestioned in allowing him
to join their fellowship. The demands of the Grail world are such
that a failure in it, for Parzival at least, necessitates a cleavage also
with the world over which Artus rules. However, Cundrie's
denunciation in face of Artus' willingness to receive Parzival into
their circle is an indication that more is required of him than that
he should merely be considered for membership of the Round
Table; he has to progress to something higher.

One might have considered that after Parzival's departure from
the Arthurian court and in view of its relativity in his scheme of
life Artus and the Round Table would fade into oblivion, but this
is not so. Books XIV and XV see two more occasions on which
Parzival and the Arthurian circle come into meaningful contact;
and as books III and VI have shown Parzival unworthy of association with the Round Table, so the latter books demonstrate his
rehabilitation.

In Parzival's history book XIV marks the equality he has won
with Gawan through the duel,[2] and this is celebrated in the
presence of Artus and Ginover. Wolfram has himself agreed with
the judgement of the wise and experienced men of both Gawan's
and Gramoflanz' retinue that Parzival is the one 'der dâ den prîs
genomen hât' (695.6), and when Artus arrives on the scene, his
presence being required for the duel between Gawan and Gramoflanz, Wolfram says:

Artûs bôt im êre
unt dancte im des sêre,

---

[1] Cundrie's denunciation is dealt with at greater length on pp. 347 ff.
[2] For a discussion of the significance of the duel between Parzival and Gawan
see below, pp. 200 ff.

daz sîn hôhiu werdekeit
wær sô lanc und ouch sô breit,
daz er den prîs für alle man
von rehten schulden solte hân.   (698.25 ff.)

Parzival himself recalls the previous occasion on which he had
been at Artus' court and points out the striking opposition between
these two encounters with Artus:

> hêrre, do ich iuch jungest sach,
> dô wart ûf d'êre mir gerant:
> von prîse ich gap sô hôhiu pfant
> daz ich von prîse nâch was komn.
> nu hân ich, hêr, von iu vernomn,
> ob ir mirz saget âne vâr,
> daz prîs ein teil an mir hât wâr.
> swie unsanfte ich daz lerne,
> ich geloubtez iu doch gerne,
> wold ez gelouben ander diet,
> von den ich mich dô schamende schiet.   (699.2 ff.)

These words show a very changed attitude in Parzival, brought
about principally by his stay with Trevrizent. He is no longer
full of the spirit of pride and indignation which characterized his
departure from the Arthurian court and his conduct for long
afterwards. He has learnt the kind of humility demanded of a
knight who is to succeed to the kingship of the Grail, and he now
asks for moral support in his return to the Round Table and his
striving for the Grail. This rehabilitation with Artus appears as a
necessary preliminary to Parzival's attaining the Grail kingship,
and indeed if now he has regained that 'rîterlîcher prîs' which
Sigune declared he had lost at Munsalvæsche (255.26 f.), he is
surely well on the way to establishing his succession to Anfortas.
Confirmation is, however, delayed until book XV, for Parzival has
further tests to undergo before this can happen.

Meanwhile, there is the little episode of Parzival's interference
in the duel between Gawan and Gramoflanz. In book XIV
Parzival is no more than a subsidiary figure: the main subject is

the love of Gramoflanz for Itonje, Gawan's sister, and the complications which arise through divided loyalties. Parzival requests permission from Gawan to take over his part in the duel against Gramoflanz, owing to Gawan's grave physical weakness, but the latter refuses him, whereupon Parzival takes the law into his own hands, steals a march on Gawan by getting up earlier on the morning for which the duel is fixed and enters the fight in Gawan's place. Gramoflanz is almost defeated by the time Gawan arrives on the scene together with Artus, Brandelidelin, Bernout de Riviers and Affinamus von Clitiers, who then stop the fight. Artus reproves Parzival for having stepped in in such an underhand way, but he nonetheless continues to express his admiration for Parzival to Gramoflanz' men:

> der mit iwerm hêrren vaht,
> dem was der sig wol geslaht:
> er ist Gahmuretes kint.
> al die in drîen heren sint
> komn von allen sîten,
> dine vrieschen nie gein strîten
> deheinen helt sô manlîch:
> sîn tât dem prîse ist gar gelîch.   (717.21 ff.)

The force of this episode is to show that Artus is still the master of the courtly world, and it is he, not Parzival, who succeeds in solving the Gawan-Gramoflanz-Itonje problem by recourse to the all-powerful nature of *minne*.[1] Artus remains supreme in this territory, and as the Arthurian court settles down to its rightful celebrations, Parzival feels himself less and less in tune with them, remembers Condwiramurs and quietly steals away from them. He is nearing the end of his long search for the Grail.

One last Arthurian episode is necessary before the conclusion can be reached: Feirefiz must also be initiated into the Round Table as a prelude to his acceptance into the Grail family and his marriage with Repanse de schoye. Thus, after Parzival's last test, his duel with Feirefiz, he takes his half-brother off to Artus' court

[1] This is treated in more detail in the chapter on Gawan, p. 433

to see 'frouwen schîn ... unt grôze wünne, / von iwerm werden künne / mangen rîter kurtoys' (753.26 ff.). He sees the court as the proper centre of their knightly activities: 'wir vinden unsern rehten art, / liut von den wir sîn erborn, / etslîches houbt zer krôn erkorn' (754.18 ff.). The Arthurian circle had been lamenting the absence of Parzival, and when he again appears they welcome him and Feirefiz into their midst, and Artus arranges a *hôchgezît* for the reception of Feirefiz into the Round Table. In this way everything is prepared for the conclusion. Parzival has come out unscathed from his duel with Feirefiz, and they have celebrated their meeting at the Arthurian court. Parzival has reached that position in which Cundrie can proclaim his succession to the kingship of the Grail: 'daz epitafjum ist gelesen: / du solt des grâles hêrre wesen' (781.15 f.). The Arthurian court, here as elsewhere, provides a measure of Parzival's achievement, and it is therefore appropriate and necessary that Cundrie should give her message here where she also fulminated her denunciation. Parzival's *strîten* for the Grail has turned into *erstrîten*, and he mentions in this context Trevrizent's words:

en franzoys er zin allen sprach
als Trevrizent dort vorne jach,
daz den grâl ze keinen zîten
niemen möht erstrîten,
wan der von gote ist dar benant.
daz mære kom übr elliu lant,
kein strît möht in erwerben:
vil liut liez dô verderben
nâch dem grâle gewerbes list,
dâ von er noch verborgen ist.   (786.3 ff.)

From this it is apparent that Parzival has now attained that summit of knightly perfection from which he can be *benant* to the Grail.[1] The matter of being *benant* is now seen in its proper relation to knightly endeavour.

The Arthurian scenes are clearly important stages in Parzival's development; their function is to point out one particular level of

[1] See also the chapter on Trevrizent, pp. 320 f., 326 f., and 340 ff.

meaning in his career. Book III shows his first, only outwardly successful attempt to acquire the trappings of knighthood. In book VI his accomplishments are recognized by his reception into the Round Table, while at the same time his falling-away from the Grail is publicized. Book XIV rehabilitates him with the courtly world, and book XV sees him ready to proceed to the kingship of the Grail. In this way the Arthurian circle points the way beyond itself to the Grail.

SIGUNE

Much of the characterization of Parzival is achieved through a careful gradation of the hero's many encounters with personages of the Arthurian and Grail worlds, which pinpoint his condition at particular stages in his development. Among these the meetings with Sigune are of the utmost importance, and they occur at critical moments of Parzival's story, so that we can look upon Sigune as the index of what he has or has not accomplished.

It is striking that Wolfram took up the one episode in the *Conte del Graal* (3420–3690) occurring immediately after Perceval's ignominious departure from the Grail castle, individualized his hero's *germaine cousine* by giving her a name, transformed the one incident into a series of four encounters and made Sigune one of the most important characters of the whole poem. The first two meetings (138.9–142.2 and 249.11–255.30) derive largely from the matter of Chrétien's poem, though with considerable elaborations, but the third and fourth meetings in the crucial ninth book and on Parzival's return with Condwiramurs to the Grail castle respectively are Wolfram's own invention. The importance which he attached to Sigune is obvious when we consider Wolfram's attempt to create another epic with Sigune and Schionatulander as the central figures in the *Titurel* fragments.

The function of Sigune in *Parzival* is to tell Parzival about his own nature, to acquaint him with the reality of *leit* and its meaning within the courtly ethos and to show him a *minne*-relationship in which *triuwe* is so strong that the lovers are united beyond death with each other and with God. The religious mood of all four

174

situations in which Sigune is portrayed elevates the concept of
minne from the purely secular to the religious sphere, and in this
way she is able to furnish Parzival with an understanding both of
the transcendent values of *minne* and of the necessity for trust in
God and a humble acceptance of His will. She is able to pierce to
the heart of Parzival's condition each time he meets her. In order
to demonstrate precisely the significance of each of their meetings
we must first investigate Sigune's own personality, the situations
in which she is depicted and the way in which they were caused.
We shall then the more easily see her importance for Parzival's
growth in self-awareness and progress towards the kingship of
the Grail.

On two occasions (253.10 ff. and 436.4 ff.) Wolfram alludes
disparagingly to Lunete's advice to Laudine in Hartmann's *Iwein*
(1793 ff.), which suggests that we are meant to see Sigune as an
anti-type of Laudine, as the lady who remains faithful to her lover
—let alone her husband and lord—beyond death, in the same
way as we may see Condwiramurs as the anti-type of Gottfried's
Isot. Sigune is a paragon of feminine virtue and constancy, and it
is this moral excellence which enables her to enlighten Parzival,
pass judgement on him and finally pardon him.

The first encounter is closely linked with the immediately
preceding Jeschute episode by the fact that it was Orilus who
killed Schionatulander. Only the barest outline of Schionatulander's death is given, but we learn that it occurred in Sigune's
service and that she bitterly regrets not having granted him earlier
the fulfilment of her *minne*. She takes upon herself the blame for
his death:

> ich hete kranke sinne,
> daz ich im niht minne gap:
> des hât der sorgen urhap
> mir freude verschrôten. (141.20 ff.)

She mentions, mysteriously, that 'ein bracken seil' was the
ultimate cause of his death, and this is further explained not in
Parȝival but towards the end of the *Titurel* fragments (st. 150 ff.).

Sigune's love for the dead Schionatulander is viewed therefore as 'Büße, Sühne, und Läuterung'[1] and, in addition, as that loyalty between lovers which continues beyond death. It is very definitely of a religious nature, although its origin is in fact secular, and it represents an even more thorough-going faithfulness than Herzeloyde's devotion to the memory of Gahmuret.

Of further importance for an understanding of Sigune's knowledge and authority is the fact that her mother died whilst she was still a child and that she, together with Schionatulander, was brought up by Herzeloyde (141.13). She therefore remembers how Herzeloyde used to call Parzival 'bon fîz, scher fîz, bêâ fîz' and is able to tell him his name and many details of his ancestry and kin. In her hermit-like seclusion and the spiritual aspect of her *minne*-devotion she is a parallel figure to Trevrizent and prepares Parzival for the long scene in book IX where he confesses his guilt, learns the secrets of the Grail and is absolved.

To begin with Parzival finds Sigune in rocky surroundings with Schionatulander lying in her lap. He has just acquitted himself disgracefully with Jeschute, but is quite unconscious of having done anything shameful. Now he sees an example of true *minne* and of the *leit* which this so often brings with it; and to make the picture more poignant the attitude in which we find Sigune is that of the *pietà*.[2] By contrast with the previous episode Parzival displays the more positive, compassionate side of his nature, though he is still hampered by youthful tactlessness and naïveté. He can appreciate the sorrow that Sigune is suffering, but he cannot see that it is a similar kind of suffering that he himself has inflicted through ignorance on Jeschute (he is, of course, as yet unaware of the consequences of his treatment of Jeschute with her husband). But the most important aspect of his character that Sigune evokes *is* his capacity for compassion, and Parzival, having greeted her according to his mother's injunction, enquires with insatiable,

[1] Friedrich Maurer, *Leid. Studien zur Bedeutungs- und Problemgeschichte besonders in den großen Epen der staufischen Zeit* (Bern/Munich, 1951), p. 118.
[2] Julius Schwietering, *Sigune auf der Linde* (ZfdA, LVII, 1919/20), p. 142, notes that the artistic representation of the *pietà* is first found in the second half of the fourteenth century, but the *concept* was evidently known long before then.

selfish curiosity who has wounded the knight, who shot him,
whether it was done with a *gabilôt* (the uncourtly weapon which is
all he knows of), and again who has killed him. Without waiting
for an answer he goes on to say that he would gladly go and
fight him. Elements of desire to win fame and knighthood enter
into Parzival's offer, but it is nonetheless mainly motivated by
compassion. Sigune is quick to notice this and praises him for
his virtue. She brings out all the finer aspects of his nature and
prophesies a brilliant future for him, even before she learns his
identity. Above all she equates the compassion that he bears her
on account of Schionatulander with the quality of *triuwe*: 'du bist
geborn von triuwen, / daz er dich sus kan riuwen' (140.1 f.). The
importance of this is stressed throughout Parzival's three encounters with Sigune alive. She herself is the epitome of *triuwe*, of love
and faithfulness and devotion to God, and she continually dwells
on it in her conversations with Parzival, telling him about his
mother's virtue (140.19)[1] and briefly mentioning how Gahmuret
was killed whilst fighting for Parzival and how 'sîne triwe er nie
verscherte' (141.4). Thus, Parzival's inheritance is firmly established, and, moreover, Sigune declares 'er trüege den gotes vlîz'
(140.5). She is first and foremost concerned with Parzival's
attitude, with his reactions in elemental situations, and only
secondly does she turn towards more factual matters and ask
Parzival his name.

Until this moment each has been dealing with the other as an
unknown person, and in fact until now Parzival has not been aware
of his individual identity. The only names that he has known are
the affectionate names his mother had called him, but from this
Sigune proceeds to tell him his real name, to give him a conscious
existence as a separate person. In Chrétien's poem[2] Perceval
guesses his name, not knowing whether he is right or wrong
(3573 ff.), and his identity is not made explicit until after his visit
to the Grail castle, and at the same time the name that he gives

---

[1] Cf. also: 'sît Herzeloyd diu junge / in het ûf gerbet triuwe' (451.6 f.).

[2] For Chrétien's technique see R. R. Bezzola, *Le sens de l'aventure et de
l'amour* (Paris, 1947), pp. 33 ff.

himself is changed into a condemnation: 'Perchevax li chaitis' (3582). Wolfram places the episode earlier in his hero's career and thus makes the responsibility that Parzival bears towards Anfortas a personal one and not merely the result of ignorance, as tends to be the case with Perceval. Moreover, he *receives* his name as a deliberate and significant act on the part of a character wielding a certain spiritual authority, and the name is emphasized by being interpreted: 'Parzivâl—rehte enmitten durch—right through the middle' (i.e. an indication of the genuineness of Parzival's nature and vocation). In this way Parzival is quite clearly individualized and made the focus of attention.

Once Parzival has learnt his name, he can be told his family history, his ancestry on the one hand from Anschouwe, on the other from Waleis and Norgals. Signune then relates her own plight to Parzival's through the exploits of the two brothers Lähelin and Orilus, the former having robbed Parzival of his two rightful lands, the latter having killed her lover Schionatulander. This is all she considers it necessary for him to know at this stage. In no way does she predict or foreshadow Parzival's visit to the Grail castle: that is his affair and something over which she has no control or knowledge. All that is required here is to sketch the bare outline of Parzival's geographical background—there is no mention of either Herzeloyde's or Gahmuret's name—and to show the basis of compassion and willingness to come to the assistance of those in trouble, which Parzival makes clear by two offers, on first seeing Sigune and on preparing to depart. Both characters undergo a parallel development: each new meeting with Sigune gives an added depth to her particular occupation as she strives towards a fulfilment of her *triuwe*, and each time that Parzival meets her he has undergone a change and has moved further along his painful journey from ignorant boyhood to maturity and consciousness of his vocation.

Parzival's second meeting with Sigune takes place immediately after his departure from the Grail castle. Sigune has moved, together with Schionatulander (no explanation being given of how this happens), from the forest of Brizljan, the forest *par excellence* of the courtly world, to the Grail forest. Both she and Parzival have taken a step away from their purely courtly existence, and henceforth their deeds are surrounded with a deeper religious atmosphere. The different surroundings symbolize a different plane of events in Parzival's career.

Sigune is depicted in the attitude of a tree-saint with Schionatulander lying in her arms. Again *triuwe* is greatly emphasized in the episode, but with the difference that this time it is herself, and not Parzival, who is the object of the description. By his conduct in the Grail castle Parzival has shown himself defective in *triuwe*— *so far as the outward manifestation is concerned*—in the sense in which Sigune had been understanding the term (*triuwe* = compassion), and so it is appropriate that here Sigune's virtue should be extolled. Thus, she is introduced with the striking visual image: 'vor im ûf einer linden saz / ein magt, der fuogte ir triwe nôt' (249.14 f.). Her doleful appearance is such that Wolfram declares that anyone unmoved by it would be characterized by *untriuwe*, and he then continues with customary hyperbole: 'al irdisch triwe was ein wint, / wan die man an ir lîbe sach' (249.24 f.). Later he makes a pointed reference to Laudine's inconstancy and then proudly announces: 'hœrt mêr Sigûnen triwe sagn' (253.18). This is very closely connected with Wolfram's polemics against unfaithful women: 'ich meine wîp die wenkent / und ir vriuntschaft überdenkent' (311.23 f.), and under this head he rejoices in attacking a lady of his own acquaintance (in the excursus placed between books II and III, particularly 114.10 f.) and the heroines of both *Tristan* and *Iwein*, evidently considering it his moral duty to show his audience an exemplary figure: 'Sigûne gerte ergetzens niht, / als wîp die man bî wanke siht, / manege, der ich wil gedagn' (253.15 ff.). Sigune's excellence in *triuwe* gives her the necessary authority for condemning Parzival's inaction at the Grail castle:

> ir truogt den eiterwolves zan,
> dâ diu galle in der triuwe
> an iu bekleip sô niuwe.
>
> . . .
>
> ir lebt, und sît an sælden tôt. (255.14 ff.)

We must be clear, however, that the concept of *triuwe* has undergone a development here. The *triuwe* in which Parzival is defective is no longer just the equivalent of compassion, as it had been in the couple's first meeting, since Parzival's first words to Sigune are concerned with her distress:

> frouwe, mir ist vil leit
> iwer senelîchiu arebeit.
> bedurft ir mînes dienstes iht,
> in iwerem dienste man mich siht.   (249.27 ff.)

Parzival's failure to ask the question at Munsalvæsche was thus not the result of a lack of compassion, but went deeper than that.[1] Sigune does not explain to Parzival what it was that lay at the root of his inaction: she is merely concerned to make his failure clear to him. The conversation between the two develops in a completely natural way as Sigune enquires where Parzival had been that he should be travelling in such unfrequented and dangerous parts. She then gathers from his description that he has been at Munsalvæsche and, having recognized him by his voice, tells him how great his destiny is. The thought that Parzival might possibly not have put the question to Anfortas has never entered her mind:

> lieber neve, geloube mir,
> so muoz gar dienen dîner hant
> swaz dîn lîp da wunders vant:
> ouch mahtu tragen schône
> immer sælden krône
> hôhe ob den werden:
> den wunsch ûf der erden
> hâstu volleclîche:
> niemen ist sô rîche,
> der gein dir koste mege hân,
> hâstu vrâge ir reht getân.   (254.20 ff.)

But when Parzival admits that he has not asked the question, she curses him in no uncertain terms, though her ground for this is

---

[1] The whole matter of the *Mitleidsfrage* is discussed at length in the chapter on Trevrizent, pp. 301 ff.

still that Parzival should have shown compassion: 'iuch solt iur wirt erbarmet hân' (255.17). There is a distinct difference in the interpretation that Signe places on the concept of *triuwe* and that which Wolfram intends for Parzival.[1] For Signe it is based on compassion, and she condemns Parzival for an act of omission for which he had the necessary fundamental constitution. For Parzival *triuwe* subsumes his relationship with God as well as his relationship with man, of which its expression here is compassion and love. There is an ambiguity in this episode on account of the difference between potential *triuwe*, which Parzival possesses, and actual *triuwe*, which is lacking in his relationship with Anfortas. It is not until book IX that the whole concept is satisfactorily explained in all its wealth of meaning. The important thing is Parzival's realization of his guilt. He straightaway declares to Signe his desire to mend his ways, but she leaves him comfortless, telling him that this is impossible and that he lost both honour and knightly fame at Munsalvæsche. He has failed both the family of the Grail and the knights of the Round Table, but he has to wait until book VI before Cundrie pronounces her (as it were) official and definitive curse upon him.

In this second episode Signe imparts a large amount of information to Parzival about the Grail castle and various members of the Grail family. She does this, however, *before* she learns her visitor's identity, and—contrary to what de Boor says[2]—she does not link Parzival with the Grail family or mention that his mother is a member of it. She contents herself with stating that the castle can only be found unwittingly and presumes that Parzival does not know of it. Then, having told its name and its situation in Terre de Salvæsche, she explains how Titurel passed it on to his son Frimutel, who on dying left four children,[3] of whom three are greatly suffering. She proceeds by naming Anfortas and Trevrizent, describing how the former is a complete invalid and the

---

[1] For a fuller and more analytical discussion of the meaning of *triuwe* see below, pp. 195 ff.

[2] Helmut de Boor, *Geschichte der deutschen Literatur*. Bd. II. *Die höfische Literatur. Vorbereitung, Blüte, Ausklang* (Munich, 1953), p. 99.

[3] Schoysiane must already have died.

latter spends his life in poverty and penitence. Nowhere does she say that Herzeloyde and therefore Parzival belong to the Grail family, nor does she inform Parzival of his mother's death, as the *germaine cousine* does in the *Conte del Graal* (3593 ff.): this is left to Trevrizent. Parzival's guilt is only gradually revealed to him through making him aware one by one of individual acts through which he becomes guilty. At this stage it is the failure to ask Anfortas the cause of his ailment that it is Sigune's function to bring out.

A further piece of information that Sigune gives in this episode concerns the sword that Anfortas gave to Parzival. The sword, magnificent in appearance and power, is the symbol of Parzival's vocation and was used by Anfortas before God physically injured him and thus singled him out as unfit to remain king of the Grail. In passing it on to Parzival, Anfortas chooses him as his successor, but Parzival is not sufficiently mature to respond to the gift by asking the fateful question, and the response is needed to give full meaning to the gift of the sword as a symbol. Sigune elaborates on the extraordinary powers of the sword and its origin, which are little more than picturesque additions, but also mentions 'des swertes segen' (253.25), which, if Parzival possesses it, will lead him to victory in battle and to his ultimate goal, though she suspects that Parzival does not know the *segens wort* (254.15). These comments clarify the symbolism of the sword in connecting the *segen* with the question that would have relieved Anfortas' suffering. Failure to put the question means lack of the *segen* and the impossibility of reaching the ultimate goal. The sword, however, is not minimized in its symbolizing Parzival's calling—we are told later, at the beginning of book IX, where repentance and the will to fulfil his vocation are now in sight: 'daz swert gehalf im prîss bejac' (434.30)—but without the *segen* it cannot take Parzival the whole way.

We now come to the third meeting, which takes place at the beginning of book IX before the Good Friday encounter with Kahenis and Parzival's sojourn with Trevrizent. The religious atmosphere is intensified, and Sigune is presented in the guise of a *klôsnærinne*, as a foreshadowing of the hermit life that Trevrizent habitually leads. Parzival is, as always, on the search for *âventiure* when he comes upon Sigune's new hermit call, where Schionatulander now lies buried and Sigune prostrates herself in grief upon his coffin. The circumstances of Sigune do not, however, correspond exactly with those of the usual medieval hermit, as both Wolfram in his descriptions and Parzival in his questions show. Sigune does not fulfil the external conditions of a hermit's life, but her actions go far beyond them in her dedication to *minne*. Thus, although she bears a psalter in her hand, she never hears mass: her life is, on the contrary, a continual penitence, and it is this fulfilment of the rule in spirit that distinguishes her life. Later, thinking of all that he knows about hermits, Parzival scolds Sigune and demands for whose sake she wears a ring, since love is prohibited to monks and nuns, and she explains that she wears it as a sign of her pure devotion to the memory of Schionatulander. In other words, what Sigune stands for is not purely religious, but a fusion of the worldly with the religious.

She has again undergone both a spiritual and a physical change. When she first appears in the poem, Wolfram mentions her long dark tresses (138.18), but does not enter into any further physical description until the second encounter, when Parzival notices that she has lost all her hair and also her colour and strength (252.30 ff.). At this third meeting he sees that her once red mouth has now become pale as well and that she is wearing a hair-shirt next to her skin underneath the grey cloak of penitence. All this emphasizes Sigune's progress in spirituality.

Again, the concept of *triuwe* is of the utmost importance in this episode. In his introductory remarks Wolfram describes how Sigune has dedicated her virginity and her joy to God because of her love for Him (435.14) and also because of her former, ever continuing *triuwe* (435.18), thus combining secular and spiritual love. And after he has permitted himself an attack on Lunete's advice, Wolfram in a rhetorical question praises Sigune's faithfulness in comparison with the joy about which he had been talking. Her *triuwe* derives its virtue from the extreme sorrow and hardship which she is undergoing in her acts of penitence. In describing her devotion to Schionatulander, Sigune explains the purpose of the ring which she is wearing as being her guide in God's law and a bond of her *triuwe* (440.13 ff.). She tries to make unmistakably clear the inseparable link between her faithfulness to Schionatulander and her love for God, and although her devotion to her lover is always the first or external aspect of her *triuwe*, she also says on one occasion to Parzival: '[got] gilt getriulîch urbot' (438.16). *Triuwe*, in this episode, has become quite definitely more than merely the basis of compassion: it is now the foremost expression of love for God, in which love for one's fellow man is included.

At the point where *triuwe* and *minne* converge Parzival and Sigune are united in *leit*. Sigune's whole existence is founded on her sorrowing at the death of her lover: 'durch minne diu an im erstarp, / daz si der fürste niht erwarp, / si minnete sînen tôten lîp' (436.1 ff.). Similarly, Parzival feels himself subject to great suffering on account of his separation from Condwiramurs:

> ich liez ein lant da ich krône truoc,
> dar zuo dez minneclîchste wîp:
> ûf erde nie sô schœner lîp
> wart geborn von menneschlîcher fruht.
> ich sen mich nâch ir kiuschen zuht,
> nâch ir minne ich trûre vil. (441.6 ff.)

But the parallelism goes even further in that while both are suffering on account of a secular transcendental relationship (with Schionatulander and Condwiramurs respectively), they also have corresponding spiritual sufferings, on the one hand for God, on the other for the Grail. Thus, on this occasion Parzival and Sigune are coming together again after the estrangement that Sigune's curse had brought about. Both have undergone a further development which unites them.

Parzival had been cursed three times—by the servant at the Grail castle, by Sigune and by Cundrie; and since then his lot has been to wander over the face of the earth searching for ways in which to prove his knightly worth and rectify the damage he had caused at Munsalvæsche. He had been separated from the normal places of courtly activity, wandering through pathless country, forest and waste land.[1] Signe, like Herzeloyde, had also withdrawn from courtly society and was suffering great hardship:

> ir dicker munt heiz rôt gevar
> was dô erblichen unde bleich,
> sît werltlîch freude ir gesweich.
> ez erleit nie magt sô hôhen pîn:
> durch klage si muoz al eine sîn.   (435.26 ff.)

Her hut is bare of all joy, and Parzival finds nothing there but 'jâmer grôz' (437.18). The two are united by the mark of *leit*. In the previous two episodes the main stress had lain on the compassion that Parzival shows Signe, but here the compassion is mutual. The situation forms an introduction to the main part of book IX, to Parzival's stay with Trevrizent, and because Parzival has himself reached the stage of recognizing his insufficiency and need of help, Signe is able to reconcile herself with him, take back the harsh words she had poured on him earlier and direct him on to a path which might lead him back to Munsalvæsche. She sympathizes with him in his predicament and now actively helps him to find his way back to his vocation. It is at this point that the change in his fortunes begins, since the request that he makes of Signe prepared the way for his sojourn with Trevrizent:

> 'Ich warp als der den schaden hât,'
> sprach er. 'liebiu niftel, [gip mir] rât,[2]
> gedenke rehter sippe an mir,
> und sage mir ouch, wie stêt ez dir?
> ich solte trûrn umb dîne klage,
> wan daz ich hœhern kumber trage
> danne ie man getrüege.
> mîn nôt ist zungefüege.'   (442.1 ff.)

[1] Cf. Marianne Wynn, *op. cit.*, p. 218: 'For chivalrous society ... existence in chaotic wilderness meant uncourtly living, a life cut off from the civilising influence of chivalry, transgressing against its fundamental law of "diu mâze".'

[2] Cf. Parzival's first words to his uncle (456.29 f.).

Here Parzival gives verbal expression to his compassion, which had previously been only in the parallelism of their respective situations, and immediately after this Sigune commends him into God's hands. Her connexion with the life of the Grail through the fact that once a week, on Saturday night, Cundrie brings her food from the Grail now enables her to give Parzival a positive directive in following her tracks. This advice is already a hint of the favourable conclusion of Parzival's story, since we know it is Cundrie who pronounced the curse on him in the first place. The fact that both she and Sigune are intimately connected with the Grail family means that Sigune's advice to follow her is what puts Parzival back on to the right path to the fulfilment of his destiny. Moreover, Wolfram rounds off the episode after Parzival's departure with a comment which recognizes his hero's change in attitude: 'ich wæne er het gevrâget baz, / wær er ze Munsalvæsche komn, / denne als ir ê hât vernomn' (443.2 ff.). Despite this encouraging remark he nevertheless prefaces these three lines with the grim and seemingly final statement: 'sus wart aber der grâl verlorn. / al sîner vröude er dô vergaz' (442.30 f.). The rest of the poem, however, proves that the Grail was not lost once and for all.

It is in this third meeting that the depth of Sigune's relationship with Schionatulander is most fully explored. The intensification in Sigune's ascetic life evokes Parzival's tart surprise at seeing her wearing a ring in these circumstances. Sigune explains her devotion to her lover and protests her purity of intention. Whilst Schionatulander was still alive, their love was never physically consummated, and Sigune thus still preserves the high virtue of virginity. The important aspect of their relationship is the way in which Sigune has transfigured it into a spiritual marriage analogous to that of the nun with Christ. She wears the gebende that is the privilege of married women, and her ring is the sign of her faithfulness to her dead lover. Because she did not give herself to Schionatulander while he was alive, she now gives herself to him in death:

mîner jæmerlîchen zîte jâr
wil ich in minne gebn für wâr.

der rehten minne ich pin sîn wer,
wand er mit schilde und ouch mit sper
dâ nâch mit ritters handen warp,
unz er in mîme dienste erstarp.
magetuom ich ledeclîche hân;
er ist iedoch vor gote mîn man.   (440.1 ff.)

This relationship, with its emphasis on the spiritual unity of the two lovers and the insignificance of the unaccomplished physical union, is analogous to Parzival's early relationship with Condwiramurs in its expression of *triuwe*.[1] The latter relationship is a genuine marriage on all levels, and Sigune's constancy is a powerful example to Parzival to keep his faith to Condwiramurs, which as yet has not been seriously questioned. It is the transcendental nature of both relationships that is important, and the unity between each couple is essentially undisturbed despite the fact that Sigune is externally separated from Schionatulander in time and Parzival from Condwiramurs in space. The essence of the relationship continues in face of this.

A motif which occurs in the three meetings already discussed is the moment of recognition that is found in all. Here again a development is apparent. In the first encounter Sigune recognizes who Parzival is from the names that his mother used to call him, and from this she goes on to give him a picture of his immediate family and her own plight. In the second meeting the two meet as strangers until suddenly Sigune recognizes Parzival by his voice, after which she directly enquires whether he has fulfilled what she knows to be his destiny. Parzival is so blinded by the consequences of his inaction at Munsalvæsche that Sigune has to explain to him the circumstances of their earlier meeting, and only then does he realize her identity. When for the third time they meet it is once more as strangers, but now it is Parzival who first recognizes with whom he is talking (admittedly after having heard Schionatulander's name), and then Sigune realizes from his appearance (440.26 ff.) who her companion is.

---

[1] See below, pp. 238 ff.

The final 'meeting' occurs as the result of Parzival's own initiative: on his return to the Grail castle with Condwiramurs he remembers the whereabouts of Sigune's cell and goes in search of her. This marks the fulfilment of their relationship, since Parzival finds Sigune in complete awareness of her identity at a time when he is swiftly moving towards the culmination of his career. The first three encounters are fortuitous, the last deliberate. Their progress runs as follows: (i) ignorance—Parzival learns his name through Sigune's recognition of 'bon fîz, scher fîz, bêâ fîz'; (ii) guilt—Sigune recognizes Parzival and reveals his guilt to him; (iii) repentence—Parzival recognizes Sigune and receives her forgiveness; (iv) fulfilment of *triuwe*—Parzival deliberately seeks out Sigune and finds her united in death with Schionatulander. In the first two cases we see the initiative being taken by Sigune, as Parzival is prevented from this through immaturity and sinfulness. In the last two cases Parzival takes the initative, as he approaches absolution from his sin and the fulfilment of his search. The question of recognition is carefully geared into this progressive scheme and acts as an index of Parzival's spiritual development.

The last scene in which Sigune appears (804.8–805.10) shows her in the fulfilment of her destiny, which is both paralleled and contrasted with Parzival's. She has reached perfect union with Schionatulander in her death at prayer, while Parzival is perfectly united with Condwiramurs in life and in the achievement of his vocation. Schionatulander's body lies uncorrupted in its coffin (one need only think of the many legends about the uncorrupted bodies of dead saints to realize its significance with regard to the relationship between the two lovers), and Parzival orders Sigune's body to be laid with his. The scene is one of mourning and tragedy, though for Sigune the *leit* is now over, and so also is Parzival's. Great festivities take place, and everything ends in the happiness that is the supreme characteristic of the Arthurian romance at its conclusion.

Sigune's existence is, as we have seen, closely related to that of Parzival in its meaning, but her story is an independent one and has a theme which, while illuminating Parzival's career at crucial moments, retains its own individual characteristics. It has in fact two significances: one for itself as the depiction of a love that continues beyond death, and one as an example for Parzival of constancy. It is the great merit of this subplot that it never becomes merely the recounting of *âventiure* for *âventiure*'s sake (as with pre-courtly or late-courtly literature) or degenerates into purely symbolic representation (as with post-courtly allegories). The different physical situations of Sigune's story, of which only the first two are given in Chrétien's poem, give it an individual character and intrinsic meaning of its own, and the way in which Wolfram enlarges upon his data and deepens their significance with a wealth of subtle connexions between his key themes of *minne*, *triuwe*, *leit* and belief in God serves to emphasize its individuality. Parzival's meetings with other characters always involve an exchange, and this means that both sides of the relationships which are described in the course of the poem must be given a certain individuality in order to provide an interdependence between Parzival and those he meets. On occasions he is more dependent on the characters he meets than they are on him. His relationship with Sigune is a case in point, since it is he who benefits from the encounters, and therefore the impetus for the enlightenment which he receives must come from Sigune.

Sigune's function in the poem underlines the continuity of Parzival's experience from the time of his boyhood departure from Soltane up to the moment of his accession to the kingship of the Grail. She brings out the essential points in Parzival's development, and, although other characters (for example Cundrie, Trevrizent and Condwiramurs) provide a deeper insight into this development at one particular time, this is her most important contribution to the poem. The *spiritual* side of Parzival's nature is shown in miniature through his encounters with her.

THE PROLOGUE AND THE DUELS

The prologue of *Parʒival* is remarkable for the number of obscurities and difficulties of interpretation which it presents, but it is not my purpose here to undertake a detailed investigation into all the questions it raises. It is provocatively rich in ideas and imagery, and it is almost certainly its function to be understood in more than one sense, some points illuminating Wolfram's own work (though not in an unambiguous way), while others constitute both criticism of and reference to the works of Gottfried and Hartmann. Moreover, it is unlikely that any completely satisfactory solution will ever be found to the problems posed by the prologue despite the large amount of time and energy devoted to it by many scholars.[1] What I am concerned with here is not these technicalities, but the light that the prologue sheds on the characterization of Parzival.

The first set of problems revolves around the meaning of the terms *ʒwîvel*, *stæte*, *unstæte* and *unverʒaget mannes muot*.

Stæte and *unstæte* are obvious antitheses, and those persons who espouse either the one or the other exclusively in their lives are destined either for heaven or for hell respectively. Thus, as Heinrich Hempel has pointed out, *stæte* is 'constancy in moral good' and *unstæte* 'constancy in evil'.[2] If *unstæte* merely meant 'inconstancy with respect to moral good', this would not in itself be sufficient for mortal sin, since it would leave room for good also where the inconstancy was, temporarily, overcome.

With the terms *ʒwîvel* and *unverʒaget mannes muot* also a contrast and a definite opposition are apparent, but the two are not antithetical in the exclusive sense of *stæte* and *unstæte*. Nor can one easily parallel *ʒwîvel* with *unstæte* and *unverʒaget mannes muot* with *stæte*, since they are not absolutes representing the extremes

---

[1] Cf. Heinz Rupp, *Wolframs Parʒival-Prolog* (*Beitr.* (Halle), LXXXII (Sonderband), 1961). Despite Hennig Brinkmann, *Der Prolog im Mittelalter als literarische Erscheinung* (*WW*, XIV, 1964), I do not think scholars have been mistaken in seeing a relationship between the ideas of the prologue and those of the story.

[2] Heinrich Hempel, *Der ʒwîvel bei Wolfram und anderweit*, in the Festgabe Karl Helm (Tübingen, 1951), p. 181: '*Unstæte* ist jedoch bei ihm nicht, wie das Präfix *un-* eigentlich erwarten läßt, der kontradiktorische Gegensatz der *stæte* als der Beharrung im Guten, also Unstetigkeit, Mangel an Festigkeit zum Guten. Diese ist ja noch keine Todsünde. Wolfram meint aber mit seiner *unstæte*. Schlimmeres, er nennt so den konträren Gegensatz der *stæte*, also "Stetigkeit im Bösen".'

of moral conduct like *stæte* and *unstæte*. The positive side of the antithesis, *unverʒaget mannes muot*, requires less treatment than the term *ʒwîvel* since the range of its meaning is not so wide. Broadly speaking, it represents the moral basis of the courtly knight's character, the spirit of affirmation in the face of all difficulties, the spirit of *hôher muot*. It is not such a specific or thorough-going concept as that of *stæte*, but it can be and is present in people even when they are beset by *ʒwîvel*.

The meaning of the word *ʒwîvel* requires more detailed treatment. Wolfram uses the term (and allied grammatical forms) fourteen times in the course of his poem,[1] and from the contexts in which it occurs a considerable range of meaning is apparent. In the first place, however, we must take into account the overtones which the word has from its use in Hartmann's *Gregorius*. The connexion between this poem and Wolfram's *Parʒival* has been carefully investigated by Hermann Schneider,[2] who has shown that Wolfram was in some measure writing an anti-*Gregorius*. In Hartmann's poem *ʒwîvel* is seen as *desperatio*, as despair, in which a man considers his sin so great as to be unforgivable by God and which in effect constitutes the rejection of God's will and purpose in one's life. This, together with *vürgedanc*, or *praesumptio*, the sin of deferring recognition of one's guilt and the need for reconciliation with God until the hour of death, is one of the sins against the Holy Ghost. For Hartmann *ʒwîvel* is a lasting thing, forming a permanent source of separation between man and God, and as such it is 'ein mortgalle zem êwigen valle' (167 f.). In another place Hartmann writes of 'zwîvel ... der manigen versenket' (64 f.) and continues:

> swer sich bedenket
> houbethafter missetât
> der er vil lîhte manige hât,

---

[1] I am indebted here as in many other places to Alfred Senn and Winfried Lehmann, *Word-Index to Wolfram's Parʒival* (Madison, 1938).

[2] Hermann Schneider, *Parʒival-Studien* (*SB d. Bayr. Akad. d. Wiss., phil.-hist. Kl.*, Jg. 1944/46, Munich, 1946), section I. Cf. also Wapnewski, *op. cit.*, pp. 19 ff., who expands Schneider's original thesis.

sô tuot er wider dem gebote,
und verzwîvelt er an gote
daz er sîn niht enruoche,
ob er genâde suoche,
und entriuwet niemer wider komen:
sô hât der zwîvel im benomen
den wuocher der riuwe.
daz ist diu wâre triuwe
die er ze gote solde hân:
buoze nâch bîhte bestân.
wan diu vil bitter süeze
twinget sîne vüeze
ûf den gemeinlîchen wec:
der enhât stein noch stec,
mos gebirge noch walt,
der enhât ze heiz noch ze kalt.
man vert in ânes lîbes nôt
und leitet ûf den êwigen tôt. (66 ff.)

Elsewhere Gregorius warns his mother of the danger of *ʒwîvel*:

gesprechet niemer mêre alsus:
ez ist wider dem gebote.
niht verzwîvelt an gote:
ir sult vil harte wol genesen. (2696 ff.)

It is clear from these examples that *ʒwîvel* is regarded as the mortal sin *par excellence*, but there is in fact no character in *Gregorius* who actually falls prey or succumbs to either of the two sins against the Holy Ghost, as the studies of Gabriele Schieb (only partially) and Hildegard Nobel[1] have shown. The torments of *ʒwîvel* are felt only by Gregorius' mother and not by Gregorius himself, and the problems of *ʒwîvel* as such—not its temptations— are not really dealt with at all in Hartmann's poem. In fact, *Gregorius* is more satisfactorily interpreted by reference to popular ideas and the structure of the poem than by recourse to medieval theology.[2]

[1] Gabriele Schieb, *Schuld und Sühne in Hartmanns Gregorius (Beitr.*, LXXII, 1950); Hildegard Nobel, *Schuld und Sühne in Hartmanns 'Gregorius' und in der frühscholastischen Theologie (ZfdPh*, LXXVI, 1957).

[2] Cf. the criticisms and suggestions of K. C. King, *Zur Frage der Schuld in Hartmanns* Gregorius (*Euph.* LVII, 1963).

Nonetheless, in the first two lines of *Parʒival* Wolfram unmistakably takes up the theme of *ʒwîvel*, and a comparison shows that these lines are a paraphrase of the idea expressed in *Gregorius* 166–9:

Ist zwîvel herzen nâchgebûr,	der [zwîvel] ist ein mortgalle
daz muoz der sêle werden sûr.	zem êwigen valle,
	den nieman mac gesüezen
	noch wider got gebüezen.

Thus, the phrase 'daz muoz der sêle werden sûr' renders the idea behind the words 'den nieman mac gesüezen', pointing to hell as the reward for a life conquered by *ʒwîvel*.[1] But Wolfram's conception of *ʒwîvel* differs from Hartmann's in that he considers even *ʒwîvel* can be overcome. Wolfram was concerned to combat the extreme asceticism of Hartmann's view of life as expressed in *Gregorius* and at the same time to explore the theme of *ʒwîvel* properly, telling the story of a man who succumbs to it, but nevertheless is not damned, but on the contrary attains to the highest calling that a man may have, i.e. the kingship of the Grail. Thus, although Wolfram accepts the basic equation *ʒwîvel* = *desperatio*, he does not consider *ʒwîvel* to be the sole and permanent occupier of the soul, as the image of the magpie indicates.

The fact that Wolfram in *Parʒival* is writing an anti-*Gregorius* is shown by a parallelism in the histories of the two heroes. The forces of heredity in both heroes are so strong as to lead them from their isolation in monastery and forest respectively into the knightly world which their fathers inhabited. Both then commit their grave sins: Gregorius forms an incestuous union with his mother; Parzival kills Ither and fails to ask Anfortas the cause of his ailment. Both heroes are then consumed with anger at God, to Whom they attribute all their misfortunes. Thus, Hartmann writes of Gregorius: 'er was in leides gebote. / sînen zorn huop er hin ze gote'

---

[1] Hempel, *Der Eingang von Wolframs Parʒival* (*ZfdA*, LXXXIII, 1951/2), p. 169, interprets the *muoʒ* of *Parʒival* (1.2) as possibility, not certainty, while Rupp, *op. cit.*, p. 33, prefers the straightforward *muß* and also sees *sûr werden* as meaning 'schwere Mühe machen, Schwierigkeiten bereiten, eine bittere Sache sein'.

(2607 f.); and Parzival declares, after having been cursed by Cundrie: 'hât er [i.e. God] haz, den wil ich tragn' (332.8), and later, at his meeting with Trevrizent: 'ouch trage ich hazzes vil gein gote: / wand er ist mîner sorgen tote' (461.9 f.). It is at this point, however, that the analogy between the two heroes breaks down and Wolfram writes an anti-*Gregorius*. Hartmann had been unable to cope with the psychological possibilities offered by Gregorius' initial defiance of God and merely depicts a rapid change from anger to abject penitence,[1] in which *zwîvel* in its thorough-going sense has barely a part. Wolfram, on the other hand, accepts the challenge and shows in great detail the processes of the change in Parzival's attitude and how his defiance gradually disappears and acceptance of God's will takes its place. Thus, the analogy diverges at its most significant point and demonstrates with supreme clarity the firmer grasp that Wolfram had of the fineness of human problems.[2] We see, therefore, that the key-word which provides the link between *Gregorius* and *Parzival* also proves to be the point at which the radical difference of the two authors' approach to life is most forcibly expressed. Wolfram takes over the form of the word *zwîvel* from Hartmann, accepting the basic meaning of *desperatio*, but he extends it and modifies it as well as giving a clear example of its actual presence in his hero's life, as opposed to its mere proximity to the problems of Hartmann's hero. Given this polemical relationship with Hartmann, we now have to consider the variety of meaning which Wolfram attaches beyond this to the term *zwîvel*.

Of the fourteen occurrences of the word in Wolfram's poem three only (excluding the instance in the prologue) refer to Parzival. Thus, Herzeloyde counsels her son to turn away from the devil and *zwîvels wanc* (119.28). Trevrizent, in answering Parzival's question about the man (Cain) who deprived his grandmother (the earth) of her virginity, begins by saying: 'von dem zwîvel ich iuch nim' (464.8). And lastly, when Parzival is

---

[1] Schneider, *op. cit.*, pp. 21 f.

[2] Hartmann, however, dealt with a question closely allied to that of *Gregorius* in *Der arme Heinrich*, where his solution to the problem of *superbia* displays a marked advance in his thought.

mediating on a choice between his call to the Grail and his allegiance to Condwiramurs, he thinks:

> stüend unser minne, mîn unt ir,
> daz scheiden dar zuo hôrte
> sô daz uns zwîvel stôrte,
> ich möht wol zanderr minne komn.   (733.10 ff.)

These three uses of the word[1] cover a wide range of meaning.

The first reference, to *zwîvels wanc*, immediately connects up with the prologue in that *zwîvel* and hell—or more specifically the devil, *der helle wirt* (119.25)—are placed on the same level. Here the meaning is primarily a spiritual one, and the connexion with *wanc* signifies uncertainty in the relationship with God, defection and disloyalty. In the prologue, however, it is the whole *bîspel* of the magpie that is associated with the idea of *wenken*, and there is nothing of the value-judgement that pervades the idea of *zwîvels wanc*. This concept is found embedded in a passage where the same kinds of antitheses are used as in the prologue. The opposition of light and darkness here has just the same significance as in the prologue, but the metaphysical terms are different and only one side of the antithesis is elaborated. In the earlier context it is *unstæte* that is associated with *swarz*, but in [Herzeloyde's exposition of faith *untriuwe* assumes this function. In this particular sense *untriuwe* and *zwîvel* are synonyms.

Triuwe is perhaps *the* key-word in the poem and includes a wide range of meaning, but the correspondence, in opposites, between it and *zwîvel* is striking. In the first place, it bears the Germanic and feudal connotation of loyalty in service. Parzival, for example, declares to Kahenis: 'ich diende eim der heizet got' (447.25), and his whole relationship with God up to the time of his meeting with Trevrizent has this as its basis. When God does not fulfil what Parzival considers to be His obligations to himself, he withdraws his service, being convinced of the reciprocal nature of the relationship—as indeed the feudal arrangement was— his attitude becomes one of hatred, and he falls into a state of defection.

[1] The complete list of instances of the word is as follows: 1.1, 119.28, 199.19, 311.22.26, 349.30, 350.30, 371.4, 411.26, 464.8, 519.1, 661.19, 712.28, 733.12.

In the second place, *triuwe* has the meaning of 'love' in the sense of God's love for human beings and is in this way connected with *minne*. Thus, Trevrizent advises Parzival: 'sît getriwe ân allez wenken, / sît got selbe ein triuwe ist' (462.18 f.); and later he continues:

> von dem wâren minnære
> sagent disiu mære.
> der ist ein durchliuhtec lieht,
> und wenket sîner minne nieht. (466.1 ff.)

In both these passages God's constancy and faithfulness are emphasized—'ân allez wenken', 'wenket ... nieht'. This use of the word *wenken* clearly ties up with *zwîvels wanc* and shows that *triuwe* is to be seen as the negation of *zwîvel*. In conjunction with the idea of *triuwe* as love we may note by way of contrast that Parzival bears 'hazzes vil gein gote', which is the mark of his defection, of his *zwîvel*.

Thirdly, the idea of belief, intimately linked with the concept of a feudal relationship with God, is expressed by the word *triuwe*, predominantly in book IX, where the religious aspect of Parzival's development receives its most detailed treatment.[1] The word *geloube* has none of the implications of a personal relationship such as are given by the term *triuwe*, and its opposite *ungeloube* has a similar limitation of meaning. Parzival's development is essentially a matter of growth in relationships, both with God and with his fellow men. It is not merely a spiritual growth, but is also human, moral and secular. This aspect could not have been dealt with under the headings of *geloube* and *ungeloube* on account of the restriction of these terms to the sphere of the purely spiritual. But the pair of words *triuwe* and *zwîvel* have the range of meaning necessary for Wolfram's purpose[2] and deepen the significance of Parzival's history, which might otherwise, like that of Gregorius, have received a solely spiritual treatment.

---

[1] Cf. Wapnewski, *op. cit.*, pp. 194 f.

[2] Helen Adolf, *The Theological and Feudal Background of Wolfram's 'zwîvel'* (*JEGP*, XLIX, 1950), examines this in some detail. I have leaned very heavily on her for my information.

We must now turn to the third instance of the use of the word *zwîvel* with respect to Parzival (733.12), where a sense of defection, disloyalty and lack of *triuwe* is postulated as a possibility in his love for Condwiramurs. Here the reference is to an earthly relationship, albeit one in which a transcendental power, that of *minne*, is evident. The difference lies in the fact that in this relationship *zwîvel* is considered as possible, but does not appear as an actuality, as it does in the case of Parzival's relationship with God. At this level of conduct, where *minne* is the ruling power, Parzival remains faithful and is characterized by a lasting *stæte*, which not even Orgeluse can overcome (619.3 ff.).

The second example of the reference of *zwîvel* to Parzival (464.8) bears, broadly speaking, the meaning of 'ignorance' in the sense of ignorance of God's dealings with men and of man's original sin. A certain element of doubt is also implied in Parzival's question to Trevrizent, which his uncle immediately counters by insisting upon the truth of what he is saying. His answer deals ostensibly with the one point—the virginity of the earth— but its application reaches further, and Trevrizent uses the simple question that Parzival had put to him to probe more deeply into the soul of his penitent and discourses upon the particular sin of which he supposes Parzival to be guilty.[1] Trevrizent's guess at the particular sin proves to be wrong, but his sermon retains its point, since the sin of Cain is the archetype of all murder and of the killing, witting or unwitting, of one's kin. Trevrizent tries to show Parzival the effect of Eve's sin through the inheritance of Cain, and in so doing he gives a closer parallel to Parzival's sin than would be expected of some-one who by his own account was unaware of Parzival's identity. For upon Parzival lies the sin of having killed his blood-relation Ither.

Parzival's ignorance, here, is the expression of his separation

---

[1] Helen Adolf, *op. cit.*, p. 300: '. . . original sin is not explained by reporting the disobedience of Eve . . ., but by presenting her sinful offspring, and this procedure proves to be appropriate: although Parzival is innocent of the manslaughter which Trevrizent has in mind, yet all his sins against man are caused by lack of love and should therefore be dealt with under the fifth commandment: thou shalt not kill.'

from God. It is not so much a conscious defection, a witting sin, as the consequence of human sinfulness in general. But while the particular sins which it engenders are less reprehensible because unwitting, the guilt from them remains, and satisfaction has to be made for them. Ignorance, both of knightly procedure and of his opponent's kinship with himself—this latter fact is not, however, revealed until Parzival's meeting with Trevrizent (475.21 and 498.13 f.)—allows Parzival to kill Ither. And ignorance again permits the duels between Parzival and Gawan and Feirefiz respectively, though by this time Parzival has become reconciled with God and accepts His purpose willingly. The lesser *zwîvel*, ignorance, is still in danger of leading to further sin, but mutual *triuwe* between God and Parzival prevents a sinful act from taking place.

In all three instances of *zwîvel* mentioned in connexion with Parzival an element of the concept of *triuwe*, or *untriuwe*, is present. *Zwîvels wanc* is aligned with *untriuwe* as a spiritual concept; *zwîvel* appears as a possible annihilator of Parzival's and Condwiramurs' mutual *triuwe*; and *zwîvel* (ignorance) arises to cut across the *triuwe* binding together members of the same family.

At this point it becomes necessary to examine to what extent the concepts of *zwîvel* and *triuwe* have relevance for an understanding of other characters in their relationship with Parzival. This involves a closer study of the question of Parzival's identity, i.e. his relationship with Ither, Gawan and Feirefiz (and, incidentally, with Gahmuret). These three figures are of the utmost importance for an understanding of Parzival's development, and, more particularly, the duels which Parzival fights with each spotlight the stages of his (in the widest sense of the word) spiritual journey. The significance of Ither, Gawan and Feirefiz is made clear by the fact that Parzival is identified with each of them at the time of the duels. There is also, as with Hartmann in his Arthurian romances and unlike pre-courtly literature, a definite gradation of the episodes and their meaning within the context of Parzival's development, beginning with the duel with Ither and ending with that with Feirefiz. These three encounters serve the primary aim of projecting important aspects of Parzival's character and of plotting the stages of his growth. The identification of Parzival with Ither is less direct and more general than that with the other two heroes, but it is perhaps more striking, and its effect is felt longer. The death of Ither is seen in the light of Cain's murder of Abel and illustrates the power of original sin (among other things) in human life.[1] The kinship between Parzival and Ither is, however, very distant—Gandin, Parzival's grandfather, and Ither are cousins twice removed—but nonetheless Trevrizent asserts the extreme gravity of blood-guilt and tells Parzival: 'du hâst dîn eigen verch erslagn' (475.21). This sin weighs heavily on Parzival, and the reader is kept alive to its importance through Parzival's assumption of the name *der rôte ritter*, which had formerly been Ither's. It is Gurnemanz who confers this name upon him:

> der wirt erkante den ritter rôt:
> er dersiufte, in derbarmt sîn nôt.
> sînen gast des namn er niht erliez,
> den rôten ritter er in hiez.   (170.3 ff.)

This name is a mark both of knightly power and of guilt and is one of the more important synonyms applied to Parzival up to his encounter with Trevrizent. This first duel is the means whereby Parzival acquits himself worthy of knighthood, but it is also the first clear instance of blood-guilt. Thus, far from being perfect and idealized from the outset of his career, Parzival at this point incurs his first guilt. He is aware of Ither's name, but knows nothing of their kinship. The knightly honour which he gains through vanquishing Ither is valid, but tainted through its being achieved by means of a *gabilôt*. Merely knightly honour and blood-guilt are here inextricably linked. The mortal sin now committed is a foreshadowing of the religious *zwîvel* which later besets Parzival. Ignorance, here as everywhere, lies at the root of his sin, and Trevrizent's reference to *zwîvel* in this sense (when Parzival enquires about the virgin earth) reaches back in its relevance to all

---

[1] Wolfgang Mohr, *Parzivals ritterliche Schuld* (*WW*, II, 1951/2), p. 150.

the sins which Parzival is guilty of since his departure from Herzeloyde. It is normal human sinfulness, the consequences of original sin, which cause Parzival, albeit unwittingly, to sin in particular cases, of which his killing of Ither is the outstanding example and the symbol, as it were, of all his sins through ignorance. Ignorance and *zwîvel* are closely linked, but there is in the poem a progression from harmful ignorance—at this time Parzival's sole interest is in knightly activity: spiritual values remain entirely outside the field of his self-interest—to ignorance which is harmless because of an overriding trust in God's will, a progression from sinfulness to innocence.

The death of Ither marks the end of Parzival's primitive innocence. When Parzival kills him, he loses this quality, and, although he does not become fully conscious of the extent of his sin until Trevrizent explains it, he realizes through the mourning of the Arthurian court that he has deprived it of one of its dearest members. Of Ither's personality we are told almost nothing apart from the fact that he is a paragon of knighthood. We cannot ascribe any *zwîvel* to him personally, but he is the medium through which Parzival's *zwîvel* first becomes manifest. Already, before meeting Ither, Parzival had committed sin in causing his mother's death (of which again he first becomes aware through Trevrizent) and in separating Jeschute from Orilus (which he is able to make good later), but blood-guilt becomes a powerful motif in depicting Parzival's development, and Ither's death subsumes all his sins of commission, from which Trevrizent releases him. Ither represents the idea of *mannes triuwe* (160.23), and by killing him Parzival shows his own lack of it, and, the deed done, he puts on Ither's clothing, in which the colour is the red of blood and thus of sin.[1]

A second identification occurs when Gawan is equated with Parzival after the duel which they fight in book XIV.[2] Parzival, on hearing Artus' messengers call out to Gawan by name, stops

[1] Wapnewski, *op. cit.*, p. 63.

[2] For a discussion of Parzival's duels with Gawan and Feirefiz, cf. also Wolfgang Harms, *op. cit.*, pp. 154 ff. Xenja von Ertzdorff, *Höfische Freundschaft* (*DU*, XIV, vi. 1962), pp. 39 ff. deals with the quality of Parzival and Gawan's relationship.

fighting and sorrowfully declares: 'ich hân mich selben überstriten' (689.5); and when Gawan learns who his opponent is, he also cries out:

> dîn hant uns bêde überstreit:
> nu lâ dirz durch uns bêde leit.
> du hâst dir selben an gesigt,
> ob dîn herze triwen phligt. (689.29 ff.)

The career of Gawan is to be seen as a parallel to Parzival's, the adventures of the latter not being fully narrated, but rather briefly hinted at. Gawan's adventures also show a gradation from the time at which the two heroes are confronted by Cundrie and Kingrimursel at the Arthurian court, each being accused of unworthiness, to the moment when they meet in combat. At this point Gawan is facing the prospect of a duel with Gramoflanz, and this Parzival undertakes for him, showing in this way that he is now taking over what had been Gawan's role in the poem. At Artus' court both heroes are calumniated, and, united again with Artus after their duel, they have in the meantime proved their worth and demonstrated their *triuwe*. It must be pointed out, however, that although there is a gradation in Gawan's *adventures*, there is no development in Gawan's *character* to compare with that of Parzival.

The motifs of the prologue are taken up both positively and negatively with Gawan in that he succumbs at various times to *zwîvel*, but is also characterized by the adjective *unverzaget*. The term *zwîvel* has here, however, a more limited sense and none of the religious depth that we find in its use with reference to Parzival, but usually indicates uncertainty or vacillation. The first instance is found when Gawan meets Meljanz von Liz' army as it is proceeding to besiege Bearosche, and he is confronted with doubt as to whether he should join in this or whether he might thereby fail to be at Schanpfanzun at the time fixed by Kingrimursel (349.30 ff.). At the next instance it is Gawan who—so he is told—frees Obilot from *zwîvel* (371.4), i.e. from uncertainty in face of the siege of Bearosche, even from disconsolateness at not having previously been the object of a knight's devotion. The last example occurs when Artus comes at Gawan's request in order to be present for his duel with Gramoflanz: 'Artûs Gâwâne den zwîvel brach' (661.19). But when it comes to the point of his duel with Parzival, it is no longer *zwîvel* which stands in the forefront. We have to remember all the time that the prologue deals with antitheses, not solely with *zwîvel*, and that *triuwe*, although it is not mentioned until 2.1, is of extreme importance as the practical, if not at this point explicitly stated, antonym of *zwîvel*. It is *triuwe* that is at stake when Gawan and Parzival fight. This positive side of the antitheses of the prologue is shown by the application of the term *unverzaget* to Gawan as well as to Parzival. Thus, the word occurs in the episode with Antikonie (426.11), at Schastel marveil (564.25, 582.8, 584.28), at the time of Artus' arrival at Bearosche (678.7), and at the combat with Gramoflanz (703.16 and 704.12).

As in all three duels under discussion there is in the one between Gawan and Parzival a strong element of ignorance, but this time it is the heroes' mutual ignorance of the other's identity. Both have come so far that they know the sin involved in killing one of their own kin. The relationship of the opponents is, however, no nearer than that of Parzival and Ither: indeed, it is even more distant, as Gawan is Brickus' great-grandson, whereas Ither was his grandson. Both heroes are now characterized by the possession of *triuwe*: 'gein ein ander stuont ir triwe, / der enweder alt noch niwe / dürkel scharten nie enpfienc' (680.7 ff.). They have both proved their valour and moral worth, thus removing the stain on their characters, but neither has yet succeeded to his due inheritance. Parzival does not overcome Gawan, but realizes the identity of his opponent at the point in the duel at which he is winning the upper hand, the realization coming as the intervention of providence from outside. The result of the duel implies a victory for Parzival, as Wolfram states, although in actual fact no such victory takes place: 'der dâ den prîs genomen hât. / welt irs jehn, deist Parzivâl' (695.6 f.). Gawan is not vanquished: his achievement stands unblemished for himself. The point is that Parzival goes beyond it. He has achieved *triuwe* in all the things which are the mark of the courtly knight, and his quasi-victory over Gawan (since this is what it is from his point of view) indicates this achievement. But the fact that the heroes come to a draw in their duel means in the first place that they are protected by providence from mortal sin and blood-guilt on account of their *triuwe*, and secondly that their careers and personalities are parallel and not in opposition to each other. Parzival's career continues beyond Gawan's, and so far as Wolfram's poem is concerned Gawan fades out of the story after he has gained his reward at Artus' court in marrying Orgeluse. Parzival continues his journey to his inheritance and encounters Feirefiz on the way.

Of all the characters in the poem Feirefiz is most obviously connected with the ideas of the prologue through the image of the magpie:

> gesmæhet unde gezieret
> ist, swâ sich parrieret
> unverzaget mannes muot,
> als agelstern varwe tuot.
> der mac dennoch wesen geil:
> wand an im sint beidiu teil,
> des himels und der helle. (1.3 ff.)

Wolfram makes this connexion at the birth of Feirefiz at the end of book I, while the image of the magpie and the opposition of black and white remain fresh in the audience's mind. Thus, we are told:

> Diu frouwe an rehter zît genas
> eins suns, der zweier varwe was,
> an dem got wunders wart enein:
> wîz und swarzer varwe er schein.
>
> . . .
>
> als ein agelster wart gevar
> sîn hâr und och sîn vel vil gar. (57.15 ff.)

And after the duel, some 20,000 lines later, Feirefiz' magpie-like appearance provides the means whereby Parzival recognizes him: 'der heiden schiere wart erkant: / wander truoc agelstern mâl' (748.6 f.). Feirefiz is mentioned at various points throughout the poem (317.4, 328.29, 519.3, 589.10) so that when he appears in book XV as an active participant in the story he is remembered by the audience. Similarly, the contrast of black and white in his skin is remarked on once or twice in the middle of the poem (317.9 f., 328.16 f.).

Feirefiz is not connected by the use of the word *zwîvel* also with the prologue, but by the word *unverzagt*. Thus, Parzival refers to him as 'ein helt unverzagt' (746.14), their fight is reported by Gawan as being 'ein strît unverzagt' (759.20), and Feirefiz' many journeyings are also characterized as *unverzagt* (735.1). In this way he is linked with the positive terminology of the prologue. *Triuwe* again is strongly emphasized in the duel between Parzival and Feirefiz, but the element of *zwîvel* is present too, although it is not mentioned explicitly. In Feirefiz the two motifs of the fraternal duel and of the opposition between *zwîvel* and *triuwe*, between paganism and Christianity, are most fruitfully combined. Both the positive and the negative terms of the prologue are taken up and elaborated.

The identity of Parzival and Feirefiz is stressed more than any other that Wolfram is concerned to establish. Before the duel actually takes place, Wolfram expends much energy in building up the idea of identity and indicating its importance. First of all he declares that it is impossible to distinguish between the pagan (Feirefiz) and the Christian (Parzival), and this point has its significance when Feirefiz is admitted into the Grail family; thus:

> ieweder des andern herze truoc;
> ir vremde was heinlîch genuoc.
> nune mac ich disen heiden
> vom getouften niht gescheiden. (738.9 ff.)

After this religious assertion Wolfram continues by stressing the physical, family bonds that make them one: 'ich muoz ir strît mit triwen klagen, / sît ein verch und ein bluot / solch ungenâde ein ander tuot' (740.2 ff.); and he goes on to equate the bond between brothers with that between man and wife: 'si wârn doch bêde niht wan ein. / mîn bruodr und ich daz ist ein lîp, / als ist guot man unt des guot wîp' (740.28 ff.). All these statements occur before the duel is broken, and after it Feirefiz reiterates the sense of these assertions, but including Gahmuret also within the idea, when he says to Parzival: 'beidiu mîn vater unde ouch duo / und ich, wir wâren gar al ein, / doch ez an drîen stücken schein' (752.8 ff.). Later he asseverates in a triple formula the clear identity between himself and Parzival, echoing the latter's words after his fight with Gawan: 'mit dir selben hâstu hie gestriten. / gein mir selbn ich kom ûf strît geritn, / mich selben het ich gern erslagn' (752.15 ff.). The duel with Feirefiz marks the culmination of the scheme of gradation. Parzival's fight with Gawan ends because Parzival fortuitously hears Gawan's name and realizes then with whom he is fighting. He himself says: 'ich hân mich selben überstriten' and deplores the fact that he has been fighting with Gawan, the epitome of knighthood. After this insight and self-recognition, having overcome that part of himself which is dedicated to *minne* and *âventiure* and nothing else, Parzival is able to muse on his obligations towards Condwiramurs and the Grail and resolve to give the Grail priority. Following on this clarification of Parzival's position, Wolfram can then introduce the encounter with Feirefiz, stating the terms of the identity in his function as author and narrator. Then it is Feirefiz who assumes the place that Parzival had had *vis-à-vis* Gawan. It is Feirefiz who would not have fought against Parzival, had he been aware of his identity, and who thus takes upon himself the blame for the event of the duel. Feirefiz confesses to guilt, and Parzival does not this time reproach himself with fighting.

In book XV the contrast between Parzival and Feirefiz is brought out by the use of the synonyms *getoufter* and *heiden* respectively, and this is in some measure carried over into book XVI, where, however, a variety of other synonyms are used for Feirefiz. The application of the term *zwîvel* to Feirefiz refers above all to his paganism, since immediately following the identification of the two brothers Wolfram writes:

> der touf sol lêren triuwe,
> sît unser ê diu niuwe
> nâch Kriste wart genennet:
> an Kriste ist triwe erkennet. (752.27 ff.)

This lack of the *triuwe* of Christianity is Feirefiz' outstanding lack. For his knightly *triuwe* he can be accepted into the company of the Round Table, but he is unable even to see the Grail, and on this account he complains, his words reminding us of Parzival's earlier defection from God: 'Jupiter mîme gote / wil ich iemmer hazzen tragn, / ern wende mir diz starke klagn' (812.28 ff.).

At the time of the heroes' meeting Feirefiz is in search of *minne* (736.6 ff., 20 ff.), and it appears later that he is not constant in his service of noble ladies, but rather follows in the footsteps of his father Gahmuret. Three queens—Olimpie, Clauditte and Secundille—have received his service, but this is on a plane with his worship of heathen gods, as Parzival makes clear when he tells Feirefiz what he has to do in order to receive baptism and marry Repanse de schoye: 'Jupiter dînen got / muostu durch si verliesen / unt Secundillen verkiesen' (815.6 ff.). In marrying Repanse Feirefiz acquires *stæte* in both love and religion.

But while it is true that Feirefiz is defective in religion and *minne* at the time of the duel, it is at the same time asserted that both the heroes are the epitome of *triuwe*, though this will have to be understood in the broader connotation of moral, not of spiritual, worth. Thus, both brothers are called 'der geliutrten triwe fundamint' (740.6), and later Wolfram comments: 'dâ streit der triwen lûterheit: / grôz triwe aldâ mit triwen streit' (741.2 f.). But the main point about the duel is the fact that it takes place under the divine judgement and the divine mercy: 'zurteile stêtz in beiden / vor der hôhsten hende' (744.22 f.). The duel theme has reached its conclusion, and the sword which Parzival won from Ither breaks on Feirefiz' helmet. Condwiramurs and the Grail do more to help Parzival than either Jupiter or Juno and Secundille do for Feirefiz. Thus, the outcome of this duel indicates Parzival's maturity and fitness for the position to which he has been called. The result of the duel is achieved by divine intervention, as Parzival is now sufficiently imbued with the power of *triuwe*, of trust in God's purpose, for God to prevent him from committing a crime in ignorance. Feirefiz represents the religious defection of Parzival and also the vacillation between *Minneherrinnen*, of which Parzival has never been guilty. Feirefiz, like Gawan, is not conquered, but it is quite obvious who is meant to be the 'victor', if such we can call him. The wheel has now turned full circle, the blood-guilt which began with Ither is now expiated, and Parzival can proceed untainted to the kingship of the Grail. And although Feirefiz is at first the symbol of Parzival's past, he too is incorporated into the Grail family, forsaking the *zwîvel* of paganism and embracing the *triuwe* of Christianity.

The prologue begins with the dread possibility that *zwîvel* can lead a man to hell. The rest of the poem shows how the main hero falls a victim to *zwîvel*, wrestles with his fate, becomes reconciled with God and finds himself spiritually mature enough to succeed to the kingship of the Grail. This maturity is characterized by *triuwe*, and after his own development has been seen in its uncertain course, Parzival, beset by *zwîvel* (though never by *unstæte*) but never completely deserted by innate *triuwe* and usually marked by *unverzagetheit*, meets his chequered brother and in his quasi-defeat of him overcomes the sins and inadequacies of his own past. He then leads his brother into the highest position that he could hold within the Grail family apart from the actual kingship itself. On the way to this conclusion we also see how Parzival first equals the perfection of which Gawan is the epitome and then transcends it. Thus, we are given—in deliberate contrast to Hartmann's view—a solution to the problem of *zwîvel* which remains within the world and affects a fitting union of service to the world and service to God. Hartmann's answer to this problem had been a traditional, clerical one, whereas Wolfram's achieves a real synthesis between secular and religious values despite the fact that he attributes this greatest of all spiritual sins to his hero. In Wolfram's poem we have a visible demonstration of the conquering of the most heinous of all sins being crowned with the achievement of perfection.

This solution that Wolfram gives is an individual's solution and marks the end of a time of personal searching and finding on the part of Parzival, but it does not neglect the question of the community. By the device of Parzival's identification with Ither,

Gawan and Feirefiz the most distant members of the human family are incorporated into Parzival's destiny, their own callings being independent, unsuperseded parts in a large whole. It is surely the purpose of Wolfram's complex genealogies to point out that all human beings are members of one family, and the inclusion of the pagan Feirefiz in this system foreshadows the theme of *Willehalm*, of the common humanity of pagans and Christians. Parzival's story, the question of *zwîvel* and *triuwe*, is a particular, individual example of what is all men's vocation.

BOOK XVI

Little remains to be said about the conclusion of Parzival's story in book XVI, since the problems with which the poem as a whole deals have been solved by the end of book XV—at least, so far as the problems of Parzival himself are concerned. The final book is where the actual consummation of the plot is described and celebrated. Parzival now puts the question: 'œheim, waz wirret dier?' (795.29), and with this fulfilment of the formal requirement Anfortas is cured and Parzival takes his place as king of the Grail. The reunion of Parzival with Condwiramurs ensues; we hear of Sigune's reconciliation with Schionatulander in death; Feirefiz is baptized and marries Repanse de schoye. Wolfram declares that he has told the true histories of the five children of Frimutel and in addition furnishes a short *Ausblick* on the story of Loherangrin, who succeeds his father in the service of the Grail. The theme of *gote und der werlde gevallen* is brought to a satisfactory end: knighthood is vindicated, *minne* transformed and purified, the Grail is struggled for and, through God's will, attained.

CONCLUSION

Since Parzival is *des mæres hêrre* it is to be expected that his character will be revealed in the greatest detail, with the subtlest complexity and with the highest degree of individualization. This is, in fact, the chief feature of Parzival's story, namely, that it is presented from many angles and with varying degrees of intensity so that a completely rounded, coherent and vital personality emerges. The dynamism of his character is shown to us not solely in its final maturity, but principally in its development from childhood onwards, and is provided with a *Vorgeschichte* telling of his father and a briefly indicated continuation in the story of his son Loherangrin. In this way Wolfram gives a total view of Parzival, dealing with every important aspect of his life—knightly exploits, *minne* and marriage, religion and morals—and the treatment of these themes is such that something of the elusiveness and ambiguity of a real, living person reaches out from the pages of a romance to the reality and depth of human experience in the reader.

On the level of the plot the character of Parzival is revealed largely through encounters with subsidiary figures. It is striking, however, that although these encounters serve the primary purpose of bringing out some important aspect of Parzival's development, they also express clearly articulated, complete stories of their own with recognizable beginnings and ends. Thus, the subplot centred on Jeschute and Orilus has as its subject the lovers' relationship which Parzival first destroys and then restores. Sigune has her own story as well as being involved in Parzival's. Similarly, Trevrizent's *raison d'être* is his penitence for Anfortas, though his importance as Parzival's confessor looms much greater in the poem. The history of Anfortas is described in more detail than would be necessary merely for an understanding of Parzival's role in releasing him from his misery. The episode of Clamide's unsuccessful siege of Pelrapeire and Condwiramurs is rounded off by his later marriage to Cunneware, which also satisfactorily ends the small, but significant part that she plays in Parzival's career. In this way the minor characters, and also those major ones who are inevitably subordinated to Parzival, maintain an existence of their own which goes beyond their actual encounters with Parzival and their significance for his history. Their colourful individual stories contribute to the brightness of Parzival's, while the peculiar nature of the latter's response to their problems and situations brings out their individuality too. In contrast with Chrétien, with whom many of the characters of his poem appear in one single episode and no other, Wolfram tends to expand the role of his minor characters so that they impinge on Parzival at more than one point in the story. The classic example of this is Wolfram's creation of four Sigune episodes from the one meeting of Perceval with his *germaine cousine*. This is further underlined by the idea of kinship that runs through so many of the relationships between the various personages of the poem, by which Wolfram aims to show the immense ramifications of human action, which are such that any act affects other members of the great human family. Thus, there can be no absolute independence. This is the burden of Wolfram's investigation of the question of *hôchvart*.[1]

The characterization of Parzival is effected by many of the methods used for other figures in the poem, though generally these are intensified. Thus, the synonyms used to refer to him are wider in their application than those of any other character and cover the entire range of his activity. They sum up the variety of aspects of his personality and spotlight particular features at significant moments in the story. There is no danger that Parzival might fall into any one category or express any one type of hero. If anything, he might rather stand as a prototype for mankind itself struggling to make sense of a mysterious and complex world, and as such he must break the confines of any one type. Only through being a complete individual, through plumbing the depths of his particular nature, can he illustrate the intensity of human experience.

The descriptive passages are used to show both permanent features of Parzival's appearance and a development in his character. Descriptions of his great beauty and his strong physique occur from the childhood episodes on and indicate his nobility and innate excellence. But other passages, especially those in which changes of clothing are portrayed, serve to represent on a physical plane the spiritual development which is taking place in his character. He is not described once and for all in idealized terms (though clearly idealization plays a large part), but the particular stages of his life are signified by the differences of emphasis in the descrip-

---

[1] See the chapter on Trevrizent, *passim*.

tions that occur, which contribute to the schemes of gradation so evident in the poem.

The chief means of characterization is through the progression of the plot, i.e. through action and speech, whether in conversation or in soliloquy. Through Parzival's own words we gain a detailed impression of his ideas, hopes and problems. Here description on the part of the author fades into the background and Parzival speaks for himself (though Wolfram occasionally adds a word of comment to pinpoint a situation). Here, then, is an emphasis on the character as the important thing. For this the author steps back a moment, though in Wolfram's case we do not forget his presence for long. We are allowed to see the workings of the hero's mind directly, without the interposition of the poet's comment. This insight is greatest, of course, in the monologues, which stress the element of individuality the most, and in this way we know Parzival's thoughts at particularly meaningful stages of his career. The theme of *minne* especially is dealt with in this manner at many points, most of all in the *Blutstropfenepisode* and at the end of book XIV. Book IX is rich in interior monologues on the question of Parzival's sin. Thus, the two poles of his experiences— *minne* and God—are brought into prominence and express the highly individualized nature of his problems. We have some idea of the increased individuality with which Parzival is viewed when we realize that eight of his monologues have no correspondence in the *Conte del Graal*. The monologue obviously concentrates attention on the character in question, and the isolation of him in this way is a plain indication of his individuality, his separation from the courtly and Arthurian worlds. This is especially true of the long monologue at the end of book XIV, where Parzival decides once more to leave Artus and his court.

The use of symbolic devices most frequently serves to point out the peculiar nature of Parzival's vocation and thus to illustrate his individuality. The dream motif, occurring in books II and IX, connects Parzival with his father Gahmuret, but also acts as a symbolic representation of his sin in leaving his mother. In this way the death of Herzeloyde gains in meaning. Similarly, the *rôter ritter* motif emphasizes the position that Ither's death holds in Parzival's career and keeps its significance alive long after it has taken place. Again, Parzival's two swords, the one robbed from Ither, which breaks in his duel with Feirefiz, and the other given by Anfortas as a token of protection in battle and a sign that he might be chosen for the Grail kingship, highlight specific incidents in his career in a most fitting manner. Analogous to this is the deployment of Parzival's horses. The most important of the symbolic devices is, however, the identification of Parzival in turn with Ither, Gawan, Feirefiz and Gahmuret and the significance of his duels with the first three. In one way, therefore, but not in every respect, Ither, Gawan and Feirefiz symbolize stages in Parzival's development, though in addition they have their own stories. The career of each hero represents a part of Parzival's, and such individual traits as the other knights possess contribute towards the greater individuality of *des mæres hêrre*. The peculiar ambiguity of Ither's relationship with the Arthurian court reflects on Parzival in his development; the knightly perfection of Gawan and the extraordinary brilliance of Feirefiz in battle are taken up by Parzival as he outdoes them in duelling; the 'defeat' of Feirefiz shows Parzival's final conquest of *zwîvel*. Symbolism here shows the intertwining of the various characters' careers and exploits in a similar fashion to the kinship motifs which proliferate in the poem. It becomes clear that the individuality which leads to physical and spiritual isolation, to *hôchvart* and *Gotteshaβ*, to a complete ignorance about times and seasons, to wandering in forests far from the joys of courtly life, must be condemned as contravening both the norms of courtliness and the ideals of religion. But individuality is right and proper when integrated into a scheme of personal relationships and a true knowledge of the meaning of knightly activity. This is clearly demonstrated in the final court scenes at Munsalvæsche, where Parzival's special vocation, his rightful individuality, is fulfilled in the presence of the entire Grail community.

In the concluding lines of book XVI Wolfram describes the theme of the poem as 'wie Herzeloyden kint den grâl / erwarp, als im daz gordent was, / dô in verworhte Anfortas' (827.6 ff.), but in the course of his tale Wolfram deals with aspects of Parzival's career, which, though finally subsumed under the Grail theme, constitute important subjects in themselves and provide the manifold gradations and levels of development in Parzival's character. Thus, we find a remarkable complexity and overlapping of themes —the *Dümmling* motif, the pursuit of *schildes ambet* and *âventiure*, the courtly world of Artus and the Round Table, the theme of *minne*, the development of religious ideas, the quest of the Grail. All of these have their own importance in the story, and while some of them may evince a greater degree of conventionality than others, the total effect is strikingly individual in its solution to the problems posed by the courtly society of Wolfram's day, for Wolfram took issue with both Hartmann and Gottfried in their very different assessments of courtliness. The dualism of Hartmann's world, represented by his Arthurian romances on the one hand and by *Gregorius* and, to a lesser extent, *Der arme Heinrich* on the other, was unacceptable to Wolfram, and both his *Parzival* and his *Willehalm* are expressions of his attempts to overcome this dualism of the religious and the secular.[1] His feud with Gottfried, though extending to other topics also, is concerned in *Parzival* primarily with the treatment of *minne*.

What therefore constitutes Wolfram's main divergences from contemporary tradition and in what respect do they show Parzival's individuality? They may be divided into the following categories: (i) the childhood episodes and their relation to the traditional idea of the hero; (ii) the treatment of *minne*; (iii) the portrayal and function of the Arthurian court; (iv) the problem of *gote und der werlde gevallen*. It is immediately apparent that these points are of fundamental importance in German literature of the courtly period. Wolfram's treatment of them, exemplifying poetic genius and an original mind, constitutes his great contribution to medieval literature.

[1] The articles of H. B. Willson on the religious aspects of *Erec* (*GR*, XXXIII, 1958) and *Iwein* (*MLR*, LVII, 1962) present an unconvincing view of the nature of the two poems.

(i) The childhood episodes show an expansion of what was already present in Chrétien's poem, but there is a closer linking of the various motifs which occur there with the later incidents of the story and the development of Parzival. The most important feature of this part of the poem is the fact that Parzival's youth is *not* shown in purely idealized terms, but represents a stage *out of which* he has to grow. This is in contrast to the childhood episodes of most medieval epics, where they merely comprise a projection of important aspects of the hero's mature character back into childhood, so that the childhood episodes appear as exemplary incidents from which a straightforward progression (sometimes also a development) into the main story can take place. In the case of Parzival the childhood episodes are extensively adapted, elaborated and individualized from what Chrétien wrote and form the beginning of a long and carefully graduated progression in Parzival's career, whereby his initial anti-courtly upbringing yields to a positive courtly phase, which in its turn is surpassed by the world of the Grail. These introductory episodes form a genuine study of childhood: the boy Parzival is not merely an adult in miniature, as is often the case in medieval literature. Nor is Wolfram's account devoted solely to description of external action: he attempts in a variety of ways to portray something of what goes on in the boy's mind. This attempt at an individualized portrait stands in contrast to the conventional idealization characteristic of childhood stories. Moreover, it sets the tone for the rest of Parzival's characterization, for although idealized features— for example his physical appearance, his prowess in battle—are evident in the story, his career in general is marked by a succession of subjective vicissitudes which he only gradually overcomes. Parzival only towards the end of the poem becomes the exemplary hero: he is not just *wîs*, he is *træclîche wîs* (4.18). The childhood episodes provide a setting from which Parzival has to make a conscious break to assert himself and his individuality. And this break, though entailing *sünde*, is a necessary step in his realization of his destiny.

(ii) Wolfram's conception of *minne* diverges sharply from that of *hôhe minne*, as expressed in the courtly lyric, for all the *minne*-relationships in the poem tend towards marriage as a natural consummation and nowhere more so than in the case of Parzival and Condwiramurs. Wolfram's derogatory remarks about Hart-mann's Laudine and his portrayal of Condwiramurs as a kind of anti-Isot also clearly indicate Wolfram's conscious difference from the other leading epic poets of his time. Parzival makes rapid progress in *minne* after his initial *faux pas*, and his relationship with Condwiramurs is characterized by a constancy and *kiusche* which not even Orgeluse can shake. Although a certain sensuality is apparent in the adventures of Gawan, Parzival and Condwira-murs show a youthful tenderness and shyness and a mutual respect which is far removed from the brash sensuality of Perceval and Blancheflor. Purely courtly *minne* takes up only a small part of Wolfram's range of description. In its place we find a type of *minne* which can be spoken of in connexion with the Grail itself and which can be sincerely maintained in a religious setting. This is clearly an important individualizing factor in the depiction of Parzival and of Condwiramurs.

(iii) Even the Arthurian circle shows marks of individuality in Parzival's story, as Wolfram at various points consciously diverges from the norm. It still maintains its function as a standard of conduct, but as the Grail exemplifies the standard to a greater degree the Arthurian court can be shown in a different light. Thus, we find the insolence of Keie toned down, the perfection of the Arthurian world questioned and given an ironic comment, and these features contribute also towards the individuality of Parzival in that the court still forms the significant background for several important stages of Parzival's life.

(iv) Most important among Wolfram's innovations is, how-ever, his treatment of the key problem of *gote und der werlde gevallen* and his development of the Grail as the symbol of this synthesis. This constitutes the great achievement of his poem and illustrates the individuality of Parzival in the deepest of human problems. For we are shown in detail the changes in him from childish innocence, through sin and despair, to a belief in God which finds fulfilment in remaining in the world, not in renouncing it. The finest and subtlest signs of this development are revealed to us throughout the poem, culminating in the long sojourn with Trevrizent, in which Parzival's *sünde* and his attitude to life are most penetratingly investigated. Here more than anywhere else the contrast between Chrétien and Wolfram is most clearly shown and the individuality of the latter most lucidly demonstrated. With the French poet the episode is brief and conventional in its religion; with Wolfram the episode becomes the most important in the whole work and the diagnosis one in perfect accord with the complex problems of the individual involved. Moreover, the way in which Parzival's own effort, his struggling for the Grail, is combined with an acceptance of God's grace shows how Wolfram investigated the problem of *gote und der werlde gevallen* more exhaustively than did Hartmann in *Der arme Heinrich*, which is perhaps the latter's most balanced view of the question. Nevertheless Hartmann's poem must still be considered a religious work, and its emphases are religious despite its avoidance (except for the B text) of a monastic conclusion; it remains within the conventional religious pattern. Wolfram by contrast treats the problem with much greater detail, and his use of the Grail as the symbol of synthesis indicates a more unified and less one-sided solution. One is just as much aware of the world in *Parzival* as one is of God; the same could not be said of *Der arme Heinrich*.

The characterization of Parzival is, to say the least, exceedingly complex. It includes strong elements of idealization (principally in the descriptions and in Parzival's knightly prowess); symbolism is present in many details, particularly as a means of indicating his predestination to the Grail; but the greatest part is taken up by individualization. Parzival may perhaps be taken as a representative of humanity struggling for a balance between the claims of God and the claims of the world, but as Wolfram describes his story it is as an individual seeking a particular destiny that we see him. At all points his psychology is investigated in the utmost detail. Theme twists round theme in a pattern of beautiful, coherent complexity. Character is linked with character in a variety of

unexpected, sometimes only dimly explained ways. The individuality of Parzival comes out most clearly in his single vocation to
the kingship of the Grail, for while he is identified with both Gawan
and Feirefiz towards the end of the poem neither of these two heroes,
exemplary though they are in their own ways, can attain also to
the kingship: they have their own paths marked out for them.
Only Parzival can become *des grâles hêrre*, and he cannot be
satisfied until he actually reaches this goal.

V

CONDWIRAMURS

INTRODUCTION

PERHAPS more than any other figure in Wolfram's *Parzival* Condwiramurs unites traits of symbolism and idealization with the features of an individualized character. At times she is idealized to represent the height of beauty and courtly bearing, since her intimate relationship with Parzival destines her to become queen of the Grail, and only the utmost purity is worthy of that noble position. Wolfram never loses sight of this elevated concept and elaborates it with a careful parallelism between Parzival's search for the Grail and his love for his wife. Condwiramurs' relationship with Parzival is such that her existence is completely dependent on his. In fact, it is only through her dependence on Parzival that she receives an existence of her own, since her refusal to yield to the advances of Clamide could only have led to her death, had she not succeeded in securing the assistance of Parzival as her protector. This dependence is so marked that Condwiramurs acts as a mirror of Parzival's development, and in their relationship Wolfram is able to realize his ideal of *minne* as best expressed in the bond of marriage, an ideal which is to be found in an incompletely developed form in Hartmann's *Erec* and *Iwein* and most clearly in Wolfram's own anti-dawnsong 'Der helden minne ir klage' (5.34), but which is not the ideal of courtliness proper in Provence and northern France. In this relationship, and in many other details, the characterization of Condwiramurs transcends what might easily have been a merely conventional idealization of the courtly lady. She is also more than just the wife of Parzival: she is a symbol of his destiny, and in this role she makes an appearance in almost every book of the poem from book III onwards, though rarely as an active participant in the unfolding drama.

R. R. Bezzola, in his book *Le sens de l'aventure et de l'amour*, contrasts Wolfram's treatment of incidents and characters with that of Chrétien in the *Conte del Graal* and reaches the following conclusion: 'Le fait est que nous avons à faire là à un esprit entièrement différent de celui du poète champenois, à un art qui s'éloigne de la poésie pure en substituant à la valeur poétique, symbolique des noms et des choses, une valeur déjà fortement logique et allégorique.'[1] On the same page he describes the values assigned to names in the following terms:

'Le XIIIe siècle, avec sa forte tendance rationaliste, ne se contentera pas de ce symbolisme discret [i.e. that of Chrétien], sensible seulement aux esprits courtois par excellence. Il précise. Sans aller jusqu'à citer les noms transparents que portent les chevaliers de la *Queste du saint Graal* ou les personnages du *Roman de la rose*: Amant, Bel-accueil, Malebouche et ainsi de suite, il suffit de songer à Wolfram d'Eschenbach. La dame veuve devient *Herʒeloyde*, la *mater dolorosa*, l'amie de l'Orgueilleux de la Lande deviendra *Jeschute*, la pucelle offensée par Keu, *Cunneware*, la mystérieuse cousine de Perceval, *Sigune*.'

For Bezzola Condwiramurs is the 'nom symbolique par excellence',[2] and he allows himself to be blinded by his admiration for the 'symbolisme discret' of Chrétien to the fact that Wolfram has a more highly developed plan for his poem, in which the form of names as well as the number of them plays a part. This admiration leads him to apply, mistakenly, the same criterion of judgement to both Chrétien and Wolfram. Wolfram is anxious to give his characters an identity, if only by the fact of their having a name, and where he alters a name, as in this case, we must assume a purpose in it. The name Blancheflor, as well as being common in courtly literature, occurs as the name of Tristan's mother in Gottfried's poem, and it is clear from Wolfram's alteration that he is seeking to avoid a possible comparison between his own concept of *minne* as expressed in Condwiramurs and that of Gottfried as shown in Blancheflor. Thus, the name Condwiramurs has two significations: firstly, it indicates Wolfram's intention to individualize and differentiate her from Chrétien's Blancheflor despite the

---

[1] *Op. cit.*, p. 60.   [2] *Ibid.*

fact that he chooses a highly symbolic name for her, thereby stressing that this aspect of her personality is to be paramount; and secondly, it implies conscious dissociation on the part of Wolfram from the theory of *minne* expressed by Gottfried in the person of Blancheflor.

The meaning of the name Condwiramurs is to be understood as 'to lead, or bring, love', being based on the French *conduire* and *amor(s)*. Twice in the text there occurs the germanized form *Condwîr(e)n âmûrs* (327.20, 508.22), and of the twelve instances of the use of the word *condwieren* or related words four specifically mention *minne* in connexion with it, viz.: 'ir minne condwierte / mir freude in daz herze mîn' (495.22 f.)—Trevrizent telling Parzival of his service to a lady in his youth; 'diu minne condwierte / in sîn manlîch herze hôhen muot' (736.6 f.)—referring to Feirefiz; 'durch der minne condwier / ecidêmôn daz reine tier / het im ze wâpen gegebn / in der genâde er wolde lebn, / diu küngîn Secundille' (741.15 ff.)—again referring to Feirefiz; 'swelhiu sîner minne enphant, / durch die freude ir was gerant, / unde ir schimpf enschumphiert, / gein der riwe gecondewiert' (155.15 ff.)—referring to Ither after his death at the hands of Parzival. In two other cases the connexion with *minne* is unmistakable, even though the word is not specifically used, viz.: 'nu wart gecondwieret / Parzivâl zer künegîn. / diu tet im umbevâhens schîn, / si druct in vast an ir lîp' (199.22 ff.)—after the defeat of Kingrun; 'dô frou Enîte / sîner freude was ein condewier' (401.12 f.)—referring to Erec. The six other references are either general or apply to the field of battle.[1] There can be no doubt from the examples quoted that the meaning of Condwiramurs adduced above is the one intended by Wolfram, particularly as one of them refers to Parzival at the time when he has just proved himself worthy of Condwiramurs' love by defeating one of her grimmest opponents.[2]

[1] 174.12 f., 511.28, 593.4 ff., 696.15 ff., 820.28 f., 821.27 f.
[2] The etymology of Bartsch in his study *Eigennamen in Wolframs Parzival und Titurel* avoids this obvious interpretation, pointing out that names could not be formed in French by the combination of infinitive plus noun and ignoring the fact that if Wolfram created the name he need not be bound by the French rules of word-formation, and puts forward the etymology 'coin de voire amors' =

Condwiramurs is first and foremost important for showing *one* side of Parzival's character as it develops, namely, the power of *minne* in his life. This means that Wolfram had to create a more than purely functional character in order to give a clear emphasis to the significance of the idea of *minne* in relation to the state of marriage, while at the same time being careful not to enlarge it with so much detail that it might detract from the portrayal of Parzival.

Condwiramurs is introduced into the poem as an active participant in the story in book IV. By this time Parzival has already encountered Jeschute, Sigune, Ither and Gurnemanz, and from these various meetings he has learnt a little about the courtly world, enough in fact to put together his experiences of *minne*, *leit*, *âventiure*, *zuht* and *mâze*, all of which he now needs, and use them for what is required of him in his relationship with Condwiramurs. Book IV marks Parzival's first successful assimilation of the ideals of courtliness; all his previous experiences had been lacking in some respect. These ideals are modified to the extent that Wolfram unites them in the ideal of marriage, and Condwiramurs is the person round whom they revolve and in whom they are realized. The first culmination of the poem is reached in book IV with the theme of *minne*, but is not concluded here, since the final union of *minne* and the Grail is not reached until book XVI.

Condwiramurs is presented in book IV at the right psychological moment, but she had already been mentioned at the end of book III. Gurnemanz tells Parzival of the death of his son Schenteflur in the service of Condwiramurs:

> dâ Cundwîr âmûrs
> lîp unde ir lant niht wolte gebn,
> in ir helfer flôs sîn lebn
> von Clâmidê und von Kingrûn.　　(177.30 ff.)

It is of obvious importance, and a careful foreshadowing of what is to come, that Gurnemanz says to Parzival: 'ir sît mîn vierder

---

'Ideal der wahren Liebe'. Cf. also Wolfgang Kleiber, *Zur Namenforschung in Wolframs Parzival* (*DU*, XIV, vi, 1962), p. 86.

sun verlorn' (177.14), and that Parzival, as his adopted son, manages to succeed where Schenteflur had failed. The situation of Condwiramurs' distress is then already briefly sketched in before Parzival actually comes to take an active part in relieving it. This previous mention provides a close structural connexion between the Gurnemanz episode and the whole of book IV, and this is strengthened by the existence, established later on, of kinship between Condwiramurs and Gurnemanz (the relationship of niece to uncle) and of the intimate friendship between Condwiramurs and Liaze, by whom Parzival was first aroused to love.

SYNONYMS

As is the case with all the main characters of the poem, Condwiramurs is referred to by a variety of synonyms. Many of these are conventional terms, but some do add a distinctive touch, though they may not be of profound significance, to the general impression that one has of her.

Most frequently Condwiramurs is simply called *künegîn* (*küneginne*), and this occurs so often that there is no need to list them. In a few cases it is qualified as *von Pelrapeir diu künegîn* (283.21, 295.6, 302.4, 619.8, 734.11), in one case merely reversed as *die künegîn von Pelrapeire* (293.11), and in another phrased as *der man giht | der krôn ʒe Pelrapeire* (425.6 f.). The two other variations are *des landes küneginne* (186.25) and *diu küneginne rîche* (188.20). Another series of synonyms is based on the word *vrouwe*, which also occurs frequently both alone[1] and with qualifications as follows: *des landes frouwe* (188.9), *diu frouwe jâmers rîche* (194.9), *Brôbarʒære vrouwe* (220.1). Lastly in this group indicating social position comes the term *wirtîn*, which is used at the beginning when Condwiramurs receives Parzival (187.11, 188.29, 189.7) and at the end of the poem when she welcomes Feirefiz (806.27, 816.1).—The character of the country of Brobarz is not elaborated beyond the fact that to reach it one has to ride

---

[1] 186.12, 187.1, 189.15, 190.10.17, 192.18, 193.23, 195.13, 196.3.17, 223.17, 302.7, 805.12, 807.10.

through 'wilde gebirge hôch' and that Pelrapeire, the capital, is situated by a swiftly flowing stream (180.15 ff.). The name Pelrapeire is the German form of the French Biaurepaire, meaning 'beautiful dwelling', a fitting name for the seat of such a paragon of courtly virtue as either Blancheflor or Condwiramurs.

Among the synonyms indicating kinship there occurs, first of all, Condwiramurs' relation with her father as *des künec Tampenteires parn* (211.1) and *Tampenteires kint* (808.27); in another place she is simply called *sîn kint* (180.27). The reference to Tampenteire is not especially illuminating for an understanding of the character of Condwiramurs (contrast the significance of the reference to Parzival as *fil li roy Gahmuret* and *Herzeloyde fruht*), as little is told us of Tampenteire himself. All that Wolfram relates is concerned with Pelrapeire, of which he says: 'der künec Tampenteire / het si gerbet ûf sîn kint, / bî der vil liute im kumber sint' (180.26 ff.), and later: 'sîn [i.e. Parzival's] sweher Tampenteire / liez im ûf Pelrapeire / lieht gesteine und rôtez golt' (222.15 ff.). In another place Condwiramurs herself says: 'mîn vater Tampenteire / liez mich armen weisen / in vorhteclîchen vreisen' (194.18 ff.). These comments explain solely how the desperate plight of Condwiramurs came about, but tell us nothing of the character of Tampenteire that adds to the inherited background of Condwiramurs' personality. Rather, it is an example of Wolfram's delight in names, kinship motifs and the creation of innumerable minor characters, this last factor being in itself a slight move towards individualization in that minor characters and not an anonymous crowd fill the background.

At other times it is Condwiramurs' relationship with Parzival that is stressed. She is referred to as his *wîp* in several different passages scattered through various parts of the poem,[1] and on two occasions this is combined with *küneginne* (246.20, 743.25). The only other reference in terms of a relationship is at the very end of the poem where Condwiramurs is called *sîn* [i.e. Loherangrin's] *muoter wol getân* (804.5). Thus, we see her in three different

---

[1] 202.23, 212.30, 246.20, 283.19, 295.5, 467.27, 732.2, 742.29, 743.25, 781.17, 799.9.

relationships—with her father, with her husband (predominantly), and with her son Loherangrin. This in itself is proof of a personality which extends beyond the one relationship with Parzival, though of course the third one is by its very nature inseparable from the second.

A third category of synonyms includes words and phrases describing qualities of character or appearance. The phrase *diu lieht gemâl* (which is also often used to refer to other female characters, but usually on only one occasion, and which is applied, in its masculine form, most consistently to Parzival) occurs five times (619.9, 732.2, 740.20, 801.33) and in one of these cases is amplified as *die kiuschen lieht gemâl* (742.28). In another instance Condwiramurs is described by the phrase *diu lieht erkant* (811.1).[1] From this use of the imagery of light, influenced by the language of mysticism,[2] we can see Wolfram's unmistakable intention of creating a highly idealized portrayal of Condwiramurs.

Besides using the word *kiusche*, as noted above, Wolfram several times at the beginning of the poem refers to Condwiramurs as *magt*,[3] once with the addition of the adjective *wert* (189.21), and later she is called *disiu magetbæriu brût* (202.27). The use of the term *friwendinne* (202.3) in connexion with the first marriage night is an example of Wolfram's inclination towards the ideas and terminology of pre-courtly and early courtly society and serves as a mark of his individual approach to the ideals of court-

---

[1] In his book *Die Kultur im Zeitalter des Rittertums*, Hans Naumann writes in a different vein about the 'ungeheure Lichtfreude, ... die sich aus dem Germanischen über das Angelsächsische und den Heliand herverfolgen läßt' as follows: 'Leibliche Schönheit ist für den höfischen Menschen Licht und Glanz und zugleich Quelle von Licht und Glanz, der schöne höfische Mensch trägt so etwas wie einen Heiligenschein um sich, und die ritterlichen Dichter äußern sich darüber oft in wundervollen Versen (Parz. 638). Licht ist Leben, Freude, Gradmesser der Schönheit, das beliebteste Attribut für Menschen, Blumen, Dinge aller Art. Licht ist Farbe, Antlitz, Leib, Haut, Augen, Hände, Mund. Licht ist viel gottgemäßer also bloße Schönheit an sich; ist Gott schön bei Chrestiens, so ist er bei Wolfram lichter als der Tag und *ein durchliuhtec lieht* (Parz. 119; 446)' (p. 187). The two views of Germanic and mystical influence are not mutually exclusive and probably both played their part in the light imagery of *Parzival*.

[2] See above, p. 71.

[3] 188.7, 190.17, 192.3, 193.7.15, 198.26, 202.22.

liness (cf. *MF* 13.21, 32.14, 39.25). In addition Condwiramurs is described by several other longer phrases, viz.: *diu junge süeʒe werde* (223.1), *daʒ werde wîp* (223.11), *daʒ werde süeʒe clâre wîp* (293.9),[1] *diu treit den bêâ cûrs* (327.19), *daʒ minneclîchste wîp* (441.7) and *diu geflôrierte bêâ flûrs* (732.14).[2] Both phrases containing French words occur in a position of rhyme with *Condwîr(en) âmûrs*, and the use of French is a device lending colour to and emphasizing the terms, this being particularly true in the last case, where the highest epithet that can be applied to the noun is itself derived from the noun in question.[3]

From the above remarks it is clear that Wolfram's prime aim is the creation of a character whose ideal nature knows no bounds. This could easily have resulted in a conventional idealization of the type 'she was the most beautiful of all women', but Wolfram intensifies the character of this formula and by his use of other words referring to Condwiramurs tries to create an individualized picture of her as well, though it is plain that the process of idealization tends to become increasingly abstract and that of individualization increasingly particular, thus introducing an element of conflict into both aim and method. This will be pursued in later sections of this chapter.

DESCRIPTIVE PASSAGES

An examination of the various descriptive passages dealing with Condwiramurs yields rather a meagre supply of points of

---

[1] On the use of the word *clâr* Kluge's *Etymologisches Wörterbuch* (Berlin, 1957) comments: 'Lat. *clarus* "hell" hat, vielleicht z.T. durch Vermittlung von frz. *clair* ... mnl. *claer* ergeben, das in rhein. Denkmäler des 12. Jh. eindringt, von Heinrich v. Veldeke nach Thüringen getragen, *nun seit Wolfram v. Eschenbach als mhd. klâr häufig wird.*' Wolfram uses the word very frequently—104 times as against 58 for *schœne*—and this is a marked feature of his language.

[2] The phrase *ein bêâ flûrs* is used also of Orgeluse (508.21), where she is described as 'aller wîbes varwe ein bêâ flûrs', but this is immediately followed by the qualification: 'âne Condwîrn âmûrs / wart nie geborn sô schœner lîp.'

[3] Cf. 'er bluome an mannes schœne' (39.22)—Kaylet; 'der aller ritter bluome wirt' (109.11)—the young Parzival; 'aller manne schœne ein bluomen kranz' (122.13)—again Parzival; 'Wiplîcher kiusche ein bluome / ist si' (252.16 f.)—Herzeloyde. It is obvious from these references that the word *bluome* is used as a term of the highest praise.

individualization. In the first place, the number of such passages is few, and they are usually fairly short. In addition, there is little that aims at establishing a particularized visual portrait of her. Such description as there is is in terms of courtly *Minnesang*, but with the difference that Wolfram makes copious use of allusion to and comparison with other heroines of literary distinction and states that the beauty of Condwiramurs surpasses them all. Thus, Wolfram proclaims his own individuality through polemics against the heroines of Hartmann and Eilhart, and the individuality of Condwiramurs through the fact that she is *not* more beautiful than all women, *but* more beautiful than certain specifically named heroines whose beauty was considered exemplary. There is no one long introductory passage of description such as Chrétien employs for Blancheflor (1795–1829), but a series of shorter ones with imagery which is, on the whole, symbolic and idealized. We are not given one single complete impression of Condwiramurs; rather, our view of her grows with the development of the action.[1]

Thus, we are told in concrete terms that when Condwiramurs first receives Parzival

> ein minneclîch antlützes schîn,
> dar zuo der ougen süeze sîn,
> von der küneginne gienc
> ein liehter glast, ê sin enpfienc. (186.17 ff.)

Here again we can observe the importance of light imagery in creating an ideal, and this is followed by a further reference to the queen's 'glastes schîn' (187.18) and a series of comparisons with others. A single line informs us that when Parzival and Condwiramurs kissed 'die munde wâren bêde rôt' (187.3). In another

---

[1] It may be mentioned here that there is nothing in Wolfram's characterization of Condwiramurs in the initial description which equals Chrétien's original touch in the following passage: 'Et la pucele vint plus cointe / Et plus acesmee et plus jointe / Que espreviers ne papegaus' (1795 ff.). The differences between Blancheflor and Condwiramurs are largely accounted for by differences in the aim of the authors, and it is of little importance to try to score off the one against the other, as Germanists tend to do for Wolfram and Romance scholars for Chrétien. Both are masters in their own fields, but their fields *are* different.

section we learn of her: 'diu truoc den rehten bêâ cûrs. / der name
ist tiuschen schœner lîp' (187.22 f.), to which Wolfram adds:

> ez wâren wol nütziu wîp,
> die disiu zwei gebâren,
> diu dâ bî ein ander wâren.
> dô schuof wîp unde man
> niht mêr wan daz si sâhen an
> diu zwei bî ein ander.
> guote friunt dâ vander.   (187.24 ff.)

In a completely different context, at Parzival's third meeting with
Sigune, he refers to Condwiramurs as 'dez minneclîchste wîp' and
says: 'ûf erde nie sô schœner lîp / wart geborn von menneschlîcher
fruht' (441.7 ff.). This last statement that Condwiramurs' beauty
excels that of *all* others does not occur until a long time after it
has been compared with that of other explicitly named heroines,
and therefore it is in the nature of a conclusion rather than an
unqualified hyperbole. It is, nevertheless, true that all these pieces
of information about Condwiramurs are very general, and that the
visual image of her emerging from them is not an individual one,
but symbolic of perfection and intensely idealized.

In the comparison with Liaze the following lines are to be found:

> Lîâzen schœne was ein wint
> gein der meide diu hie saz,
> an der got wunsches niht vergaz
> (diu was des landes frouwe),
> als von dem süezen touwe
> diu rôse ûz ir bälgelîn
> blecket niwen werden schîn,
> der beidiu wîz ist unde rôt.   (188. 6 ff.)

The idealization of the line 'an der got wunsches niht vergaz' is
amplified by a simile in the language and imagery of *Minnesang*.
References to the rose and the dew occur separately a great number
of times in the songs of *Minnesangs Frühling*, but the conjunction
of the two in one image is absent at this early period,[1] but a poem
wrongly attributed to Walther von der Vogelweide contains the

---

[1] I discount von Kraus' emendation of the Kürenberger's simile to 'als der
rôse in touwe tuot' (8.22) since the MS. has 'an dem dorne'.

line: 'dîn munt ist rœter dan ein liehtiu rôse in touwes vlüete' (P 106.13, L 27.29), and Ulrich von Winterstetten has an image which closely approximates to Wolfram's: Touwic rôse gen der sunnen, diu sich ûz ir belgelîn / hât zerspreitet, stât diu wîzer liljen nâhe bî.'[1] But it must be remembered that this is considerably later than the period at which Wolfram was writing. The poets of *Minnesangs Frühling* rarely used precise, particularized nature-imagery, as the effect they were aiming at was the evocation of a general mood. By contrast, Wolfram's image is developed by a close description of the rose emerging from the dew and displaying the fresh brightness of its white and red hues. This is certainly a mark of individualization (cf. the originality of imagery in Wolfram's lyrics, of which, referring to two of them in particular (3.1, 4.8), A. T. Hatto writes that it is 'fine and mature by any standards'[2]), but it is in the extension of a symbol, not in characterization as such.

An essential part of Wolfram's description of Condwiramurs is formed by the numerous allusions he makes to other female characters in his own work and to the heroines of Eilhart von Oberg and Hartmann von Aue. This includes a measure of individualization, as has already been noted. Thus, Wolfram writes:

> Condwîr âmûrs ir schîn
> doch schiet von disen strîten:
> Jeschûten, Enîten,
> und Cunnewâren de Lâlant,
> und swâ man lobs die besten vant,
> dâ man frouwen schœne gewuoc,
> ir glastes schîn vast under sluoc,
> und bêder Isalden.
> ja muose prîses walden
> Condwîr âmûrs.   (187.12 ff.)

---

[1] Carl von Kraus, *Liederdichter des 13. Jahrhunderts* (Tübingen, 1952), Song 11.3.1 f. Cf. also Wahsmuot von Kunzich VII.1.3 ff.; Der von Wildonje III.2.3 f.; König Wenzel von Böhmen 1.3.1 f. Mergell, *op. cit.*, p. 72, n. 7, refers also to *Parz.* 305.23, *Wh.* 195.5, *Tit.* 110.1, but these are more like the pseudo-Walther.

[2] A. T. Hatto, *On Beauty of Numbers in Wolfram's Dawnsongs* (*MLR*, XLV, 1950), p. 188.

Wolfram had devoted much care to his description of Jeschute, as
it was she who was the unhappy object of Parzival's first venture
in *minne*. In a passage of nearly thirty lines Wolfram describes
how Parzival finds her 'ligende wünneclîche, / die herzoginne
rîche, / glîch eime rîters trûte' (129.29 ff.). It is a picture of
Jeschute at a significant moment, in an unusual situation, with
careful attention to detail:

> Diu frouwe was entslâfen.
> si truoc der minne wâfen,
> einen munt durchliuhtic rôt,
> und gerndes ritters herzen nôt.
> innen des diu frouwe slief,
> der munt ir von einander lief:
> der truoc der minne hitze fiur.
> sus lac des wunsches âventiur.
> von snêwîzem beine
> nâhe bî ein ander kleine,
> sus stuonden ir die liehten zene.
> ich wæn mich iemen küssens wene
> an ein sus wol gelobten munt:
> daz ist mir selten worden kunt.
> ir deckelachen zobelîn
> erwant an ir hüffelîn,
> daz si durch hitze von ir stiez,
> dâ si der wirt al eine liez.
> si was geschicket unt gesniten,
> an ir was künste niht vermiten:
> got selbe worht ir süezen lîp.
> och hete daz minneclîche wîp
> langen arm und blanke hant.   (130.3 ff.)

Here we have an idealized picture of the courtly lady in concrete
terms emphasizing the physical and sensual aspect of her perfection. Wolfram refers to several details of her appearance, and
having once created a picture of this kind, he would have found it
well-nigh impossible to make another detailed portrait surpassing
it, and so he is content to leave this in his audience's memory and
state, with obvious effect, that Condwiramurs' beauty excels even
this. This is a much more satisfactory method than the repetition

of several physically idealized descriptions, since it furnishes criteria of idealized beauty in particular terms, and as a result Condwiramurs' appearance and character do not need to be limited by any details at all: they merely extend infinitely beyond the descriptions of the other heroines.

Wolfram uses Hartmann's skill in depicting Enite in a similar fashion. Enite is described by several hyperboles as the height of perfection: 'diu was ein diu schœniste maget / von der uns ie wart gesaget' (310 f.); 'man saget daz nie kint gewan / einen lîp sô gar dem wunsche gelîch' (331 f.); 'ich wæne got sînen vlîz / an si hâte geleit / von schœne und von sælekeit' (339 ff.); 'der wunsch was an ir garwe' (1700); 'man gesach nie ritterlîcher wîp' (1707); 'dâ enwas dehein man, / er enbegunde ir vür die schœnsten jehen / die er hæte gesehen' (1741 ff.). Besides this wealth of superlatives Hartmann lavishes a considerable amount of detailed description and imagery on Enite. He compares the beauty of her body with that of the swan and the appearance of the lily among thorns (329 f., 336 ff.) and stresses the contrast between her poverty-stricken condition and her great beauty, sparing no pains to make its excellence clear. The effect of Enite's splendour on the knights of the Round Table is such that 'si ir selber vergâzen / und kapheten die maget an' (1739 f.). Wolfram's technique in using Hartmann's efforts as a basis for his own chief heroine is a subtle device of great effect. The magnificence of Condwiramurs is made unassailable because it is not presented in concrete terms, and there are therefore no specific points of comparison which other poets could seize on.

Again, Wolfram refers to the two Isaldes of Eilhart and makes use of them in the same way as Enite. Eilhart's descriptions, however, deal not so much with physical appearance as with courtly bearing. Thus, the first Isalde is depicted as follows:

> ferre man sie bekande,
> ouch lobete man sie genûg:
> swâ man gûter vrauwin gewûg,
> dâ behîlt sie eine den prîs.
> sie was behegelich unde wîs,

an allen setin wol getân,
ouch kunde sie wol begân
êre unde vromigheit:
sie was mit zuchtin gemeit.
zu ir nam daz ganze rîche rât.
sie was die beste arzât
die in dem lande inne was.
von irer hulfe genas
manch sêre sîchir man:
daz von ir wîsheite quam. (1036 ff.)

She is another heroine whose external appearance and moral character are described as unblemished. The description is more general than Hartmann's, but it contains the same kind of claim to perfection. Isalde, Tristrant's wife, is described by Kehenis in the most general terms, but using the same sort of hyperbolic formula:

geselle, wolle wir hene gân
daz dich die vrauwin entvân,
sô machstû mîne swestir sên.
dû mûst des vorwâre jên,
daz nî wart kein schôner lîp.
sie mochte wol eines koninges wîp
wesin âne lastir. (5679 ff.)

Within his own work Wolfram refers also to Cunneware, Liaze, Orgeluse and the ladies of Ginover's entourage, but there is here a difference in the technique. Cunneware and Liaze are presented before Condwiramurs makes her first appearance in the poem, and neither is described in superlatives. On the other hand Orgeluse and Ginover's ladies are compared with Condwiramurs, and not vice versa: the effect is that they are seen to approach the height of beauty which Condwiramurs represents, not that Condwiramurs excels them. Both these comparisons occur long after the introduction of Condwiramurs into the poem (508.19 ff., 645.24 ff.) and therefore have no part in establishing her idealized character.

Of the other two characters little is said. Cunneware is portrayed as 'diu fiere und diu clâre' (151.12), her mouth is *minneclîch*, her hair is fair, curly and falls in long tresses. Otherwise nothing

more is said of her. Liaze is described at greater length in four short
insertions into the progress of the plot. She is first called *schœn*
(175.25), then further details are given. When Parzival meets
Liaze, Wolfram tells us:

> iedoch kuster se an den munt:
> dem was wol fiwers varwe kunt.
> Liâzen lîp was minneclîch,
> dar zuo der wâren kiusche rîch. (176.9 ff.)

Later we hear of her 'blanken hende linde' (176.18), and at the
beginning of book IV Wolfram relates how Parzival cannot help
thinking of 'der schœnen Liâzen, / der meide sælden rîche, / diu
im geselleclîche / sunder minn bôt êre' (179.26 ff.). The significance
of these two references to Cunneware and Liaze is by no means as
great as those to Jeschute, Enite and the Isaldes. Condwiramurs
quickly usurps the place of Liaze in Parzival's affections, and his
regard for Cunneware was based on compassion, not on *minne*.
The comparisons merely add weight to the assertion of Condwiramurs' absolute supremacy.

With reference to the figure of Liaze and Parzival's initial
confusion of Condwiramurs with her, there is a parallel situation
in Eilhart's *Tristrant*, where Tristrant, on meeting the second
Isalde, imagines he has found his previous love again: he dachte
'ich habe Isaldin vlorn: / Isaldin habe ich wedir vunden' (5690 f.).[1]
Parzival has been so moved by his acquaintance with Liaze that
when he meets Condwiramurs he instinctively thinks of her:

> der gast gedâht, ich sage iu wie,
> 'Liâze ist dort, Liâze ist hie.
> mir wil got sorge mâzen:
> nu sihe ich Liâzen,
> des werden Gurnemanzes kint.' (188.1 ff.)

The difference is that, while the second Isalde is merely a substitute
for the first, Condwiramurs is the person through whom Parzival

---

[1] Hans Eggers, *Literarische Beziehungen des Parzival zum Tristrant Eilharts
von Oberg* (*Beitr.*, LXXII, 1950). Emil Walker, *op. cit.*, p. 56.

is able to fulfil the love which was awakened in him by Liaze. In other words, Condwiramurs marks an advance on Liaze, whereas the second Isalde was, if anything, no more than a second-best. Thus, behind the equation of Liaze and Condwiramurs there is a distinct differentiation.[1]

Two other allusions, one early and the other late, indicate Condwiramurs' worthiness to be queen of the Grail, since they consist in comparisons with Repanse de schoye. The first occurs after Parzival has woken up for the second time in the Grail castle, when he compares his wife with the lady who lent him his cloak, namely, with Repanse, whose immaculate purity allows her to bear the Grail: 'mîn wîp de küneginne / ist an ir lîbe alse clâr, / oder fürbaz, daz ist wâr' (246.20 ff.). The other reference is at the conclusion of the poem just before Repanse and Feirefiz are united, where it is Condwiramurs' beauty against which Repanse's is measured: 'Cundwîr âmûrs diu lieht erkant / vil nâch nu ebenhiuze vant / an der clâren meide velles blic, (811.1 ff.). In both cases it is the Grail family, or rather its foremost representative, which provides the point of comparison, and by the end of the poem Condwiramurs has become this representative in her capacity as wife of Parzival and therefore as queen of the Grail.

The descriptions applied to Condwiramurs are unmistakably idealistic in intention and remarkably unspecific in their content. Wolfram's aim was to create an ideal beyond which nothing was possible, and by refusing to limit the beauty of Condwiramurs by describing her in particular terms he was able to realize this ideal. Individualization is impossible in this context and only occurs in the comparisons and in the extension of symbols: it would be foolish to expect anything further.

ACTION

More individualization is possible in the way Condwiramurs' character is revealed through the action of the poem. From the

---

[1] Mergell, *op. cit.*, p. 65, sees in Parzival's relationship with Liaze (and also later with Condwiramurs) a repetition of Gahmuret's problem 'strît und minne was sîn ger' (35.25) in his relationships with Belacane and Herzeloyde.

very first time she is mentioned at the end of book III we gain the impression of a character similar to Herzeloyde in the initiative she takes with her lover. She is a self-possessed person and in her obvious devotion to Parzival does not relinquish her identity in the effort of being a harmonious partner. After playing her part in book IV, she recedes into the background, as Parzival does in the Gawan books, but intermittent references keep her personality alive to the audience.

For a considerable time, however, Condwiramurs remains a passive character. Gurnemanz has introduced the situation into which Parzival enters by his reference to Condwiramurs' refusal to surrender herself and her lands, but she herself does not appear until Parzival has offered his service and been welcomed at Pelrapeire. A maid informs the queen of his arrival, and she is brought 'mit grôzer zuht' (186.30) by her uncles to the head of the steps leading to the palace, where she greets Parzival with a kiss and offers him her hand to lead him to a seat. Then, realizing her obligation as hostess and recognizing that Parzival will not open the conversation of his own accord,[1] she thanks him for his offer of service and explains to him and her uncles the plight in which she finds herself, as a result of which Kyot and Manpfiljot fetch provisions, which the queen shares out among her starving retinue, keeping only a small portion to be divided between herself and her guest.

The first thing which breaks this otherwise completely courtly depiction of Condwiramurs is her nocturnal visit to Parzival, which Wolfram exonerates from all blame by his assurance at the very beginning: 'ez prach niht wîplîchiu zil: / mit stæte kiusche truoc diu magt, / von der ein teil hie wirt gesagt' (192.2 ff.). He explains carefully that the queen was not seeking 'sölher minne / diu sölhen namen reizet / der meide wîp heizet' (192.10 ff.), but that she was so oppressed by the strain of battle and the death of those who had gone to help her that she could not sleep at night and therefore was looking for assistance and friendly advice. This

---

[1] See also above, pp. 155 f., and for a longer discussion of this point see below, pp. 256 f.

is all made plain before Wolfram embarks on the narration of the episode. He then proceeds ironically to describe Condwiramurs as if she were setting out on an expedition in search of love and uses the language of the battle-field (*werlîchiu wât, kampflîcher*) to point the contrast between the external appearances and her real intention, which is perfectly clear. Leaving all her household asleep, she slips quietly into the room when Parzival is sleeping and kneels down before his bed. Here again Wolfram emphasizes that neither the queen nor Parzival thought of sleeping together and that Condwiramurs was overcome with shame that she might be doing something contrary to convention. However, her grief is so great that her tears fall on Parzival, and he awakes at the sound of her weeping. At first he construes her action as a mockery of him, but then he asks her to sit by him or lie with him in bed, and, having received the assurance that he will not struggle with her, Condwiramurs takes the latter course and asks him *ʒühteclîche* if he will listen to her tale of woe. She explains the distress of her situation and manages to enlist Parzival's aid by mentioning Liaze, whose name immediately provokes him to offer his help and protection. When day comes, the dawnsong situation is as it were reversed, as it is Condwiramurs who has to depart in order that her visit should remain unknown to all but herself and Parzival, and she leaves thanking her guest profusely for his offer.

The depiction of this episode is more refined than in Chrétien's poem, where Blancheflor makes no conditions before joining Perceval in his bed, and the two spend the night 'bouche a bouche, bras a bras, / .... tant qu'il ajorna' (2068 f.). In addition to omitting the sensual detail of the *Conte del Graal*, Wolfram makes Parzival give an unconditional pledge of assistance to Condwiramurs, whereas Perceval defers judgement until the morrow and then makes the provision:

> Mais se je l'ochi et conquier,
> Vostre drüerie vos quier
> En guerredon, qu'ele soit moie;
> Autre guerredon n'en prendroie. (2103 ff.)

The essential feature which Wolfram is concerned to bring out in his treatment of the episode is that of Condwiramurs' moral purity and Parzival's innocence and willingness to help.[1]

Before Parzival joins battle, he attends mass with Condwiramurs—a conventional preparation for fighting. Then, after his success against Kingrun, Condwiramurs embraces him closely and, having declared she will become wife to no one else, helps to take off his armour. A feast ensues, and the couple spend the night together, though both of them are so imbued with the refinements of *zuht* as well as being inexperienced that they do not consummate the marriage. Afterwards, nonetheless, Condwiramurs puts on the coif that is the mark of the married woman and transfers the possession of her castles and territories to Parzival. The next two days and the third night they also spend together, and some of Parzival's intentions are realized, but described in cautious terms by Wolfram. With this scene Condwiramurs fades out of the book as an active character. Having taken the initiative in commencing the relationship with Parzival, she has little left to do, and the rest of book IV is devoted to a description of Parzival's prowess in battle on her behalf. Only at the end does Parzival return to her, and after a passage dilating on their mutual love he asks for leave to find out how his mother is, and Condwiramurs refuses to deny him it.

Until book XVI Condwiramurs makes no further active appearance in the poem. At this point she rides off joyfully towards Munsalvæsche to rejoin Parzival and become queen of the Grail, having learnt from a messenger that her 'klagendiu nôt' (797.3) is now over. Kyot and his companions take her to the forest in Terre de salvæsche where Segramors had been overcome by Parzival in a joust, to the spot where Parzival had been *verdâht* at the sight of the drops of blood on the snow—a meeting-place with an obvious symbolic meaning. Here she makes an encampment with her retinue, and it is here where

---

[1] Mergell, *op. cit.*, p. 75, n. 11, characterizes Wolfram's *Menschendarstellung* as one 'die nicht psychologischen Realismus' (as Chrétien 2128 ff.) 'sondern sittliche Norm erstrebt'.

Parzival comes to take her with him to the Grail castle. When he arrives, Kyot has to waken Condwiramurs by beating on the flap of the tent, and Parzival finds her in bed with their two children Loherangrin and Kardeiz. Condwiramurs, although 'si hete niht wanz hemde an' (800.30), jumps out of bed and embraces and kisses Parzival in her joy at seeing him again. After spending the rest of the morning together—Wolfram expresses it thus: 'ich wæne er kurzwîle pflac / unz an den mitten morgens tac'(802.9 f.)—king and queen hear mass, take their leave amid much sorrow on the part of Condwiramurs' retinue and make their way to Munsalvæsche. On the journey they come to the place where Sigune had been mourning her dead lover and find that she too has died. Parzival arranges the burial of the lovers, and Condwiramurs laments Sigune's death: she herself had been brought up as a child by Sigune's mother Schoysiane. After this the couple continue on their way, the queen being accompanied by an armed *templeis* from Patrigalt, and they are received at Munsalvæsche. Condwiramurs greets Feirefiz and Anfortas with a kiss, rejoicing at the king's restored health, and she embraces Repanse de schoye too. Having removed her travelling clothes and put on her *gebende*, she reappears in splendour:

> nu, diz was et âne strît,
> daz hôrt od spræch ze keiner zît
> ie man von schœnrem wîbe.
> si truog ouch an ir lîbe
> pfellel den ein künstec hant
> worhte als in Sârant
> mit grôzem liste erdâht ê
> in der stat ze Thasmê.   (808.1 ff.)

After this Feirefiz leads her into the assembled company, which she merely graces with her presence as the action draws to its close. All that is needed is that she should share in the joy and ceremony of Parzival's accession to the kingship of the Grail.

The above analysis shows that so far as the *action* of the poem is concerned Condwiramurs is only of importance in book IV, where she stimulates the further development of the plot and in particular Parzival's realization of the meaning of *minne*. Having once fulfilled this essential function, she becomes a passive character contributing little more to the action, but joining in the final celebrations as an indispensible participant, as the *kone reine* (495.10) to whom the king of the Grail alone is entitled. Nevertheless, although in the action as such Condwiramurs' role is not very great, there are significant features in the treatment of the theme of *minne* which are developed more through speech and comment and which make Condwiramurs a key figure for understanding the poem as a whole.

THE THEME OF MINNE

Wolfram's treatment of the theme of *minne* is one of his most interesting contributions to medieval poetry. The ideas of courtly love had reached Germany from Provence and northern France and had exercised a profound influence on literature in general. But even in poets such as Friedrich von Hausen, several of whose poems are modelled metrically and thematically on Provençal and French originals, there is a tendency towards the refinement of sensuality and a greater awareness of the conflict with specifically Christian ideals. Thus, for example, Hausen writes:

> doch klage ich daz
> daz ich sô lange gotes vergaz:
> den wil ich iemer vor in [sc. frouwen] haben,
> und in dâ nâch ein holdez herze tragen.   (*MF* 47.5 ff.)

Similarly, Hartmann von Aue, in his *Minnesang*, reacts eventually against the general concept of courtly love on account of his preoccupation with ethical and didactic matters and especially with the reconciliation of God and the world, and also on account of the barrenness of unrequited service of courtly ladies. On this last score he writes:

> Ze frowen habe ich einen sin:
> als sî mir sint als bin ich in;
> wand ich mac baz vertrîben
> die zît mit armen wîben.   (*MF* 216.37 ff.)

And in a crusading poem he asks Christ to help him renounce the sensual pleasures of the world:

> nû hilf mir, herre Krist,
> der mîn dâ vârend ist,
> daz ich mich dem entsage
> mit dînem zeichen deich hie trage. (*MF* 210.19 ff.)

Walther also experiments with various interpretations of *minne* in an attempt to find some balance between the *Minnedienst* which is its own reward and the natural sensual pleasure of *nidere minne*, showing again a dissatisfaction with the orthodox expression of the ideal of *minne*. These three poets exemplify in lyric forms a trend of thought which underlies the material of the three great German writers of Arthurian romances, namely, the problem of *minne* in its relationship with society and the world. All three poets, Hartmann, Gottfried and Wolfram, to some extent and for different reasons reject the concept of courtly love proper, and this process is the most radical with Wolfram.

In his lyrics Wolfram gives expression to several key ideas which he develops in his epics. The dawnsong form allows him to deal at length with the sensual aspect of *minne*, and it is clear from them that he feels the necessity for the physical fulfilment of love. However, the consummation of love under the conditions of the dawnsong, conceived as a genre of courtly love-poetry, is adulterous and illicit, and Wolfram's whole nature is directed towards the beauty, the transforming power and entirely worthy nature of love. This feeling he gives vent to in his anti-dawnsong, where the line 'ein offen süeze wirtes wîp kan solhe minne geben' (6.9) strikes at the very foundation of courtly love in favour of something more honourable in intention and more in harmony with the religious atmosphere of the period. Referring to this sentiment, M. F. Richey writes of Wolfram: '... he sees marriage love as a part of the great social order, honoured in the sight of men. Its legality sets it higher than the love which has recourse to guile.'[1] This viewpoint is so universalized in *Parʒival* that it is possible to

---

[1] M. F. Richey, *Essays on the Mediaeval German Love Lyric* (Oxford, 1943), p. 93.

make the categoric statement that 'all love relationships aim at marriage as their consummation',[1] provided that an exception is made in the case of Ampflise, who specifically represents the *Minneherrin* of courtliness proper. Thus, as H. J. Weigand points out,[2] Gahmuret marries Belacane and then Herzeloyde, Orilus is married to Jeschute, Clamide to Cunneware, Meljanz to Obie, Gawan to Orgeluse, Gramoflanz to Itonje, Cundrie to Lischoys Gwelljus, Sangive to Florant of Itolac, Feirefiz to Secundille and, after her death, to Repanse de schoye, and Parzival to Condwiramurs. 'Furtive passion'[3] such as is known in courtly love proper is to be found only in the relationships of Gramoflanz with Itonje, the most striking case of Gahmuret and Ampflise, and in Gahmuret's brother Galoes (8.17 ff.).

The *minne*-relationship between Parzival and Condwiramurs is naturally the one through which Wolfram develops his highest ideas on the subject, but it is not obvious from the beginning how he will finally shape them. The first night the lovers spend together after Parzival has defeated Kingrun is one occasion on which there is a certain ambiguity as to what Wolfram meant. However, by the end of the poem the situation has become very much clearer, and the departure from *hôhe minne* is unmistakable.

Wolfram's reassessment of *minne* does not involve a complete rejection of courtly love, even in the case of Condwiramurs. In fact, Parzival's first contact with her is prefaced by his offer of service in terms of the courtly ideal:

> dô sprach er 'frowe, hie habt ein man
> der iu dienet, ob ich kan.
> iwer gruoz sol sîn mîn solt:
> ich pin iu dienstlîchen holt.' (182.25 ff.)

This general statement is made to one of Condwiramurs' attendants, but it is this offer of service which allows Condwiramurs to seek Parzival at night and ask him for assistance, assistance which he readily promises without making the condition of *drüerie* that

---

[1] Weigand, *op. cit.*, p. 33.
[2] *Ibid.*, p. 34.
[3] *Ibid.*

Perceval demands, should he be successful in his venture. There is a complete lack of sensuality about this first phase of Condwiramurs' and Parzival's acquaintance which is in accord with the spirit of *hôhe minne* represented in Germany by the lyrics of Reinmar von Hagenau, but the reason for it is quite different. In the first place the two lovers are inexperienced in matters of love: 'si heten beidiu kranken sin, / er unt diu küneginne, / a, bî ligender minnen (193.2 ff.), and in the second Wolfram is concerned to put this episode of Condwiramurs' request for help in the best possible moral light. This last reason Wolfram emphasizes time and again (192.2 f., 192.9 ff., 192.20). Thus, the prime reason for their renouncing the sensual delights of *minne* is not adherence to the rules of *hôhe minne*, but simply the fact that neither of them has been actively aroused by the power of sexual love. Their relationship is in marked contrast to that of Perceval and Blancheflor, who undergo no development in their understanding of love. They are both presented as having more experience than Parzival and Condwiramurs: Blancheflor makes no conditions before joining Perceval in bed, and as she has already related her distress to him, they can spend the rest of the night undisturbed in each other's embraces; Perceval on the following morning demands her *drüerie* as a reward for his eventual success against Clamadeus and Engigerons. They are thus presented from the beginning as fully developed in the sphere of love. Parzival and Condwiramurs, on the other hand, only gradually come to realize the meaning of their love and consummate it. In this respect their relationship is more individualized than that of Perceval and Blancheflor.

This initial stage of the *minne*-relationship between Parzival and Condwiramurs with service and youthful inexperience as its focal points is easily understandable. The next stage, exemplified by the second night of abstinence, after the battle with Kingrun, presents greater difficulties in view of the later developments, in which *minne* and married love are completely identified. Still they do not physically consummate their love for each other, though the term *bî ligen* indicates this, and this was what they consented to (201.19f.). It seems that Wolfram is using the episode to demonstrate their virtue, *not* in an ascetic sense, which would be far from his intention, but rather to show their courtly qualities of *zuht*, *mâze* and *kiusche*. Wolfram writes of Parzival: 'er lac mit sölhen fuogen, /des nu niht wil genuogen / mangiu wîp, der in sô tuot' (201.21 ff.), and by the words immediately following he indicates his sympathy for Parzival's delicacy of feeling in this situation. Condwiramurs is here a completely passive character (contrast Herzeloyde and Gahmuret): she had taken the initiative in asking Parzival's protection, but now she waits for him to make the next move, as indeed she does throughout the rest of the poem. Parzival is now in a quandary. Until this moment he had been content merely with touching her clothes, and inordinate desire for more ('ob ich nu gîtes gerte' (202.13)) seems to him a sign of *untriuwe*. For the time being, therefore, he refrains from consummating the marriage, but this causes Condwiramurs no undue anxiety: 'si wânde iedoch, si wær sîn wîp' (202.23) (cf. also the second Isalde, with whom this is also the case). The relationship of Parzival and Condwiramurs is not based on the idea of *hôhe minne*, but on the reality of mutual affection: 'si wâren mit ein ander sô, / daz si durch liebe wâren vrô, / zwên tage unt die dritten naht' (202.29, ff.). This emphasis on *liebe*, meant as a contrast to *minne*, is paralleled in the love poems of Walther and is a further point of similarity in the two poets' conceptions of the nature of love. After initially abstaining from physical fulfilment, Parzival remembers his mother's advice: 'du solt zir kusse gâhen / und ir lîp vast umbevâhen' (127.29 f.), and also Gurnemanz' remark: 'man und wîp diu sint al ein' (173.1), and the two consummate their love so that 'der alte und der niwe site / wonte aldâ in beiden mite' (203.9 f.).

Although some aspects of Wolfram's treatment of *minne* can be interpreted in the light of *hôhe minne*, it is interesting to note, as Carl Wesle has shown, that 'Die Liebe Parzivals zu Condwiramurs wird nie als hohe Minne bezeichnet, dagegen mehrmals als werte Minne (223.25, 302.10, 743.26).'[1] This fact links up closely with Herzeloyde's counsel to Parzival about *guotiu wîp*[2] and makes

---

[1] Carl Wesle, *Zu Wolframs Parzival* (*Beitr.* LXXII, 1950), p. 22.
[2] See above, pp. 87 ff.

evident the moral quality which the relationship of the two lovers has. In the first two cases of *werde minne* referred to above it is Parzival who refers to Condwiramurs' love in this way; in the third case it is Wolfram who states that it is so. There is, however, a further reference by Clamide, not noted by Wesle, where he also, in his attempt to gain the love of Condwiramurs, talks about 'ir werden minne' (204.12), which shows that even here there is an ethical tinge to the concept. It must nevertheless be pointed out that not too much stress can be laid on the specific term *werde minne*, as it is also twice used with respect to Ampflise,[1] where there is no shadow of doubt that the relationship is one of *hôhe minne*. Furthermore, the love of Gramoflanz and Itonje is called 'ir werden minne tougen' (724.23), and that of Lischoys and Cundrie—or rather Cundrie's love for Lischoys—is characterized as 'ir werden minne' (730.5). It is clear, nonetheless, from the context and from the general development of the idea that a special significance attaches to the particular relationship of Parzival and Condwiramurs, and this is not dependent merely on the use of the term *werde minne*.

Although the main things that we learn about Condwiramurs' love are in terms of its effect on Parzival, it is essential to note that the power of *minne* residing in her is derived from her constancy, which provides Parzival with a prop of absolute security and which is a positive attitude on her part, so taken for granted by Wolfram and by Parzival that it need not be continually referred to. With regard to Clamide as a secondary character, this power of *minne* is completely involuntary, and Condwiramurs is merely the passive medium through whom it is manifested: her personality in this case is irrelevant. In her relationship with Parzival the emotion is mutual, and Condwiramurs' love must be understood as a continual conscious force grounded in her as well as in Parzival:

> ir minne stuont mit sölher kraft,
> gar âne wankes anehaft.

[1] See above, pp. 46 f.

si het ir man dâ für erkant,
iewederz an dem andern vant,
er was ir liep, als was si im.   (223. 3 ff.)

The connexion of *minne* with the Grail has already been touched upon and is of cardinal importance in understanding Wolfram's attitude. Wesle points out that, with the exception of the *Blutstropfenepisode*, all Wolfram's references to Condwiramurs after book IV are independent of Chrétien[1] and are almost without exception connected with the Grail.[2] Trevrizent reveals to Parzival that only the king of the Grail may have a wife (495.9 f.) and that the virtue of purity in *minne*, the lack of which causes Anfortas' suffering, is required of him:

er [sc. Anfortas] gerte minne
ûzerhalp der kiusche sinne.
der site ist niht dem grâle reht:
dâ muoz der rîter unt der kneht
bewart sîn vor lôsheit.
diemuot ie hôchvart überstreit.   (472.29 ff.)

The relationship of Parzival and Condwiramurs has a firm moral basis, as the preceding paragraphs show, and the combination of purity in *minne* with the essential purity of the Grail is developed by constant references throughout the poem. For Parzival the fundamental problems are the balance of *minne* and *âventiure* (the unsolved problem of Gahmuret) and the search for the Grail, under which heading the claims of religion and the world are subsumed. In Condwiramurs all these converge: *minne* and *âventiure* are at harmony in the service of womankind and the Grail. This structural unity of the themes of *minne* and the Grail is not to be found either in Chrétien's unfinished poem or in the French so-called continuations of the *Conte del Graal*, a fact which, as Hermann Schneider remarks, is 'der beste Beweis dafür,

---

[1] *Op. cit.*, p. 27.

[2] Mergell, *op. cit.*, p. 81, writes: 'Aus dieser Verinnerlichung der deutschen Minnehandlung ist zu verstehen, daß später unabhängig von der Quelle neben Parzivals Streben nach dem Gral immer die Sehnsucht nach Condwiramurs als unversiegbare seelische Kraft betont wird.'

... wie verhüllt des Dichters [i.e. Chrétien's] Fortsetzungs-
absichten geblieben waren.'[1] This feature of Wolfram's work,
combined with the depth of the religious significance of Parzival's
growth to maturity, constitutes the most important difference
between his poem and those of Chrétien and his continuators.

Parzival's faithfulness to Condwiramurs and his search for the
Grail are intimately linked by the *nôt* which both cause him. A
gradual progression can be discerned in the importance which
each of these has for him, as initially his *nôt* is more on account of
minne, then there is a balance between them, which finally gives
way to an overwhelming concern with the Grail. To begin with,
in the *Blutstropfenepisode*, it is his *nôt* on account of *minne* which
prevails:

> sîne gedanke umben grâl
> unt der küngîn glîchiu mâl,
> iewederz was ein strengiu nôt:
> an im wac für der minnen lôt.   (296.5 ff.)

But when, at the end of book VI, Parzival rides away from the
Arthurian court after being cursed by Cundrie, Wolfram merely
juxtaposes Parzival's thoughts about Condwiramurs with his
intentions of searching for the Grail, mentioning them in that
order (333.23 ff.), and this vagueness of priority marks the transition to the stage where the Grail takes first place in his mind.

The change is first shown in book VII, where Parzival's actions
are seen as a contrast to Gawan's. In speaking to a number of
knights outside Lippaut's castle, he lays upon them the task of
winning the Grail for him, but he then goes on to say:

> ob mîner bete niht ergêt,
> sô vart dâ Pelrapeire stêt.
> bringt der küngîn iwer sicherheit,
> und sagt ir, der durch si dâ streit
> mit Kingrûne und mit Clâmidê,
> dem sî nu nâch dem grâle wê,
> unt doch wider nâch ir minne.
> nâch bêden i'emer sinne.   (389.5 ff.)

---

[1] Schneider, *Parʒival-Studien*, p. 50.

The same task is laid upon Vergulaht (425.2 ff.), but when Parzival once more meets Sigune he dwells in more detail on his yearning for Condwiramurs, though in the end he sees the Grail as causing him greater pain.

> der grâl mir sorgen gît genuoc.
> ich liez ein lant da ich krône truoc,
> dar zuo dez minneclîchste wîp:
> ûf erde nie sô schœner lîp
> wart geborn von menneschlîcher fruht.
> ich sen mich nâch ir kiuschen zuht,
> nâch ir minne ich trûre vil;
> und mêr nâch dem hôhen zil,
> wie ich Munsalvæsche mege gesehn,
> und den grâl . . .   (441.5 ff.)

Here again Parzival is full of *sorgen* and *trûren*, and at the next point, in Trevrizent's cell, he intensifies the use of a comparative, *mêr*, with the expression of his *nôt* to a superlative:

> mîn hôhstiu nôt ist umben grâl;
> dâ nâch umb mîn selbes wîp:
> ûf erde nie schœner lîp
> gesouc an keiner muoter brust.
> nâch den beiden sent sich mîn gelust.   (467.26 ff.)

Again there is a hyperbolic description of Condwiramurs, in almost identical terms to the preceding one, and again Parzival yearns for both his wife and the Grail.

In the next reference, which is part of a long passage spoken by Orgeluse to Gawan, Parzival refuses Orgeluse's offer of her *minne* and her lands, explaining that 'er hete ein schœner wîp' (619.4) and stressing once more: 'der grâl mir anders kumbers giht' (619.12). In this case the Grail has become all-important, while Condwiramurs remains as a point of security in his life, unshakable by the attempts of others to usurp her place. At this stage Parzival is completely sure of Condwiramurs, and his *nôt* appears to be only on account of the Grail. He is sufficiently aware of his destiny to be able to resist the temptations of Orgeluse, but in the next instance, at the end of book XIV, he sees an insoluble conflict between his duty towards the Grail in healing Anfortas and his love for his wife. He is reminded of the power of *minne* and the fact that he is 'ûz minne erborn' (732.17) and questions his loss of it in his long separation from Condwiramurs. If *minne* has so long kept him separated from her, there can be no value for him in still remaining faithful to this personified goddess; the clear alternative is for Parzival to place his faith in God and perform his duty towards Anfortas. He tries to weigh up the situation:

> sol ich nâch dem grâle ringen,
> sô muoz mich immer twingen
> ir kiuschlîcher umbevanc,
> von der ich schiet, des ist ze lanc.
> sol ich mit den ougen freude sehn
> und muoz mîn herze jâmers jehn,
> diu werc stênt ungelîche. (732.19 ff.)

He sees that *minne* is not playing an active part in his life and comes to the conclusion: 'got wil mîner freude niht' (733.8). But Parzival is so loyal in his love for Condwiramurs that the thought of 'ander minne' is made impossible, even though if he were completely separated from her he would like to have another love. He finally determines to continue his struggle for the Grail and renounce the claims of *minne*, which until now has only brought him separation from his wife, prays God for *freude* for all others and declares: 'ich wil ûz disen freuden varn' (733.20). The claims of the Grail prevail.

But although Parzival has resolved to fulfil his higher mission, Condwiramurs is still there to help him. It is, however, Wolfram as the author, and not Parzival, who continues the essential unity of the two aims of Parzival's life, and this occurs at the point of highest tension in the poem, at the duel of Parzival with his brother Feirefiz, where Wolfram inserts a plea of his own:

> daz wende, tugenthafter grâl:
> Condwîr âmûrs diu lieht gemâl:
> hie stêt iur beider dienstman
> in der grœsten nôt dier ie gewan. (740.19 ff.)

And in a second interjection he underlines the saving power of Condwiramurs and the Grail: 'ob im nu niht gehelfen megen / Condwîr âmûrs noch der grâl' (743.12 f.). Parzival has now risen to his destiny, and the time has come for him to be re-united with his wife. At the time of his 'grœste nôt' Parzival had renounced her love from his side, but the power of love which nevertheless remains with her, since she is unaware of Parzival's decision, overcomes the conflict. Cundrie, who had pronounced the curse on Parzival in the first instance, returns and explicitly unites Condwiramurs with her husband:

> daz epitâfjum ist gelesen:
> du solt des grâles hêrre wesen.
> Condwîr âmûrs daz wîp dîn
> und dîn sun Loherangrîn
> sint beidiu mit dir dar benant. (781.15 ff.)

All the *nôt* of separation, of yearning for these two goals and of the conflict which overwhelms Parzival as he approaches the Grail for the second time is now finally overcome, and Condwiramurs is able to rejoin him at the Grail castle.

The idea of Condwiramurs' involvement in Parzival's *nôt* is not the only way in which she is brought into intimate relationship with the Grail. A further point of connexion is provided through the medium of *âventiure*, as when, for example, Parzival sets out from Artus' court:

> Condwier âmûrs
> dîn minneclîcher bêâ cûrs,
> an den wirt dicke nu gedâht.
> waz dir wirt âventiure brâht!
> schildes ambet umben grâl
> wirt nu vil güebet sunder twâl
> von im den Herzeloyde bar. (333.23 ff.)

This is in fact the basis of the deeper relationship which comes to the fore in times of stress, though it is only expressed shadowily owing to the prevalence of the religious mood in the idea of salvation through the Grail. Another instance of this connexion

occurs when Liddamus informs us in book VIII of his encounter
with Parzival, at which he was made to promise to seek the Grail for
Parzival and, if he should be unable to do it within a year, to go to
Condwiramurs and swear her fealty. In this case obedience to
Condwiramurs is counted the very next best thing to winning the
Grail and provides Parzival with a link at second hand during the
time of the separation. One further record of this type of link is
given when the *schifman* relates to Gawan that Parzival's exploits
are told at Pelrapeire, since he exacts promises of fealty from those
knights whom he overcomes, and that 'er reit hie vorschen umben
grâl' (559.18).

One last type of reference simultaneously to Condwiramurs and
the Grail is made by Clamide, when he tells Parzival of his
immeasurable *herzeleit* at losing Condwiramurs. His hyperbolic
assertion that the greatest wealth in the world together with 'des
grâles werdekeit' (326.25) would not be enough to compensate for
the loss of Condwiramurs is perhaps all the more impressive as
we know the importance Wolfram attaches to the Grail and as the
Grail is, in any case, out of Clamide's reach. Such then is the
power which Condwiramurs is able to exert over men.[1]

The constant parallelism of Condwiramurs and the Grail has
obvious implications which are supported by the connexion which
is made between *minne* and God through their mutual identification with *triuwe*. Thus, Trevrizent counsels Parzival: 'sît getriwe
ân allez wenken, / sît got selbe ein triwe ist' (462.18 f.), and
Wolfram asserts in an excursus on the nature of love in book X:
'reht minne ist wâriu triuwe' (532.10). Carl Wesle has made this
point of connexion very clearly: 'Wenn irdische Minne den Wert
der Treue in sich trägt ..., hat sie etwas gemein mit der *gotes
minne*, steht nicht in Gegensatz zu ihr, ist vielmehr ihr irdisches
Abbild. ... So ist die Treue, die Parzival in den langen Jahren
Condwiramurs bewahrt, ein Band, das ihn auch in diesen Jahren
der Gottentfremdung immer noch mit Gott verbindet.'[2] Condwiramurs' passive role, of which Parzival is largely unaware, is to
provide him with a constant feeling of security and also to furnish

---

[1] See below, pp. 254 ff.　　　　[2] *Op. cit.*, p. 31.

a link with God through *triuwe*. Thus, in this way she serves his individuality. This identification of *minne* and God with *triuwe* is one more point towards the understanding of Condwiramurs as a transcendental figure. Wolfram has invested her with a deep symbolism which goes far beyond the mere idealization of a *Minneherrin*. She has become a mediator between the transcendental powers of God as expressed through the symbol of the Grail and of the world as expressed through *minne*. It is this meaning attached to her personality which motivates the emphasis on purity in her relationship with Parzival and the stress on parallelism with the Grail. The two are in perfect harmony only when Parzival has fulfilled his destiny, released Anfortas and become king of the Grail in his stead. And as the Grail is described only in general and idealized terms, so Condwiramurs is represented as the height of perfection in love, beyond which nothing else is possible.

THE *BLUTSTROPFENEPISODE*

The power of the bond of *minne* between Parzival and Condwiramurs is most forcibly presented in Parzival's state of being *verdâht* at the sight of three drops of blood on the snow, which remind him of his wife's beauty. Sinking deeper and deeper into thought until he becomes completely unaware of the external world, he muses on the juxtaposition of the colours:

> dô dâhter 'wer hât sînen vlîz
> gewant an dise varwe clâr?
> Cundwier âmûrs, sich mac für wâr
> disiu varwe dir gelîchen.
> mich wil got sælden rîchen,
> sît ich dir hie gelîchez vant.
> gêret sî diu gotes hant
> und al diu crêatiure sîn.
> Condwîr âmûrs, hie lît dîn schîn.
> sît der snê dem bluote wîze bôt,
> und ez den snê sus machet rôt,
> Cundwîr âmûrs,
> dem glîchet sich dîn bêâ curs:
> des enbistu niht erlâzen.'   (282.26 ff.)

It is of extreme importance that even at this juncture, where one might have imagined the power of *minne* to exert such an influence of itself, Parzival is conscious of its religious implications. To begin with, snow is itself an unusual feature in Arthurian romance, as Wolfram himself ironically points out (281.16 ff.). The physical aspect of the situation is such that Parzival immediately comes to the conclusion that God wishes to crown him with happiness, and he praises Him and all His creatures for it.

I have already noted (see above, p. 245) that the first instance of the connexion of Condwiramurs with the Grail occurs in this episode, so that again she is viewed not merely as symbolic of the power of *minne* alone, but also in terms of spiritual values. The purely religious aspect of the phenomenon of abstraction from the external world is quoted by Eduard Wechssler from Hugo of St Victor's *De arce Noe morali* (III.8): '[Charitas] oblivionem quoque generat, quia, dum totam animi intentionem ad desideria aeternorum trahit, omnium, quae transeunt, memoriam ab animo funditus evellit. Insensibilem reddit, qui dum mentem per internam dulcedinem medullitus replet, quidquid exterius amarum infertur, contemnit, quasi non sentiatur.'[1] In the same place Wechssler writes: 'Diese Sehnsucht nach der Gottheit entrückt den mystisch Liebenden der jeweiligen Umwelt. Von Bernhard v. Clairvaux wird erzählt: "Die Sinne fanden sich so gebunden, daß er sehend nicht sah, hörend nicht hörte, noch auch schmeckend einigen Geschmack empfand".' From the parallelism of the religious and the secular phenomena of being *verdâht*[2] and from the explicit references made to God and to the Grail, it is plain that Wolfram assigned great importance to this episode, and the fact that it is referred to twice afterwards (586.16 ff., 802.1 ff.) is a confirmation of this.

The motif of the drops of blood on the snow goes back to a Celtic source and is in its original form slightly different from what

---

[1] Edward Wechssler, *Das Kulturproblem des Minnesangs* (Halle, 1909), p. 253.

[2] Wechssler, *ibid.*, also quotes examples from *Minnesang* where no religious mood is evident: Hausen, *MF*, 46.3 ff., Gutenburg, *MF*, 76.14 ff., Reinmar, *MF*, 163.18 ff., Walther, P 64.25 ff., L 41.37 ff.

we find in Wolfram. Of this first form E. Windisch writes: 'In der irischen Sage Longes mac n-Usnig ... sieht Derdriu, wie ein Rabe vom Blute eines Kalbes auf dem Schnee trinkt, und sagt, der eine Mann würde ihr lieb sein, an dem sich die drei Farben fänden, das Haar wie der Rabe, die Wange wie das Blut, der Leib wie der Schnee.'[1] After this he adduces the variation in *Peredur*, which, though influenced by the French Arthurian tradition, was composed on a basis of 'the same ancient traditions, both oral and written, as provided Chrétien with the outlines of his stories'.[2] The variation of the motif in *Peredur*[3] has altered the comparison so that it refers to a woman and not to a man; the blood is that of a duck killed by a she-hawk, which is driven away by the clatter of Peredur's horse, only to have its place taken by a raven. There are nonetheless three points of comparison remaining. In Chrétien's version one point of the comparison has disappeared, as also in Wolfram's—there is no raven to remind the hero of the colour of his mistress' hair. This is a case of the continental adaptation of what the Celts considered the height of beauty to one in line with their own conception, which did not include black hair.[4] This again is an instance of the idealized depiction of Condwiramurs and of the assimilation of an individual to a conventional ideal, though this is the case in Chrétien's poem first of all, and Wolfram merely takes over the ideal from him.

Parzival's loss of his senses at being reminded of his wife by the three drops of blood on the snow is described by several expressions—*sich verdenken* (283.16), *unversunnen* (283.17, 287.9, 288.9), *diu ʒuct im wiʒʒenlîchen sin* (283.22), *sus hielt er als er sliefe* (283.23), *dem der minne was verselt* (287.6). This state is of such intensity that it can be broken only with great difficulty and immediately returns the moment Parzival catches sight of the drops of blood again. In a long apostrophe to *frou minne* (291.1 ff.) Wolfram deplores the deleterious effects of her power in causing Parzival

---

[1] E. Windisch, *Das keltische Britannien bis ʒu Kaiser Arthur* (*Abhandl. d. sächs. Ges. d. Wiss., phil.-hist. Kl.*, XXIX, 1912), p. 133.

[2] Gwyn Jones and Thomas Jones, *The Mabinogion* (translation) (London, 1957), p. xxix.

[3] *Ibid.*, pp. 199 ff.   [4] See above, p. 27.

to lose his reason. This demonic power has been described by Herbert Kolb in a comparison of the corresponding episodes in Chrétien and Wolfram using one of Chrétien's lyrics as a *point de départ*:

> Was Chrétien von Troyes in seinem Lied der Minne ['D'amor ne sai nule issue'] bloß konstatierend nachgesagt hatte, stellenweise sogar mit Einverständnis und Ergebenheit, das wird in Wolframs Munde, gegründet auf persönliche Erfahrung und Urteilsfähigkeit, zur ungehemmten Anklage: die Minne verdirbt Maß und Vernunft und ist darum der bestehenden Daseinsordnung im höchsten Grade bedrohlich und gefahrbringend! Wie kaum ein anderer weltlicher Autor der literarisch ungemein lebendigen Jahrzehnte um 1200 hat Wolfram von Eschenbach das Destruktive der Minne gesehen und angefeindet, sei es, daß er als Epiker die größere Umsicht und Weitsicht besaß, sei es, daß ihm die Erlebensfähigkeit und Leidensbereitschaft in der Minne in geringerem Maß zu eigen war, sei es, daß seine durch und durch konservative Einstellung zu den Fragen des Lebens und der Literatur ihn von vornherein mit einem scharfsinnigen Mißtrauen gegen die heraufkommende und allzu oft sogleich in Mode und Libertinage ausartende Minne ausstattete.[1]

This love, despite the perfection of Condwiramurs, is dangerous because Parzival has not yet realized that his duty towards the Grail should be dominant in the unity of desire for it and for his wife: 'an im wac für der minnen lôt' (296.8). If he is to be true to his destiny, he cannot allow himself to lose his senses through yielding to the overwhelming force of *minne* when it is possible through worldly wisdom and through a conscious choice on his own part to overcome it. This is the purpose of Gawan's action in spreading the cloak over the drops of blood—to demonstrate that the power of *minne* can be nullified by the power of human reason and knowledge—and Gawan, as 'der tavelrunder hôhster prîs' (301.7), is the sole person to see this and is at the same time qualified to perform the action.[2] This is not, however, the only reason for

[1] Herbert Kolb, *Die Blutstropfen-Episode bei Chrétien und Wolfram* (*Beitr.* (Tübingen), LXXIX, 1957), p. 373.

[2] Kolb, *op. cit.*, p. 374. This article has been criticized from the Romance point of view by Erich Köhler, *Die drei Blutstropfen im Schnee. Bemerkungen zu einem neuen Deutungsversuch* (*GRM* (*NF*), IX, 1959), but while it clarifies the

his action. Gawan has himself also experienced this kind of *nôt* with Queen Inguse de Bahtarliez and acts out of a feeling of sympathy for Parzival, whom he wishes to free from this painful state, but over and above this he wants to reconcile Parzival with Artus, as the king himself intended.

In this episode we are shown that Condwiramurs' *minne* exercises a dangerous influence in Parzival's life unless subordinated to his call to the Grail. *Minne* can be a positive force only in subjection to this and in combination with Parzival's own freedom of will and consciousness of choice. Where it overwhelms from outside, as it were, its effect can only be negative and harmful. Thus, Wolfram's view is that *minne* may not be the only force in Parzival's life; it must, in fact, play a secondary part, subject to his destiny to the Grail kingship, while at the same time being an unconscious basis of security. In effect Wolfram's attitude is a restatement of the conflict between *minne* and *êre*, which involves a redefinition of the idea of *minne* and a deepening in religious significance of the concept of *êre*.

CONDWIRAMURS AND CLAMIDE

The destructive power of *minne* is seen most clearly in the relationship between Condwiramurs and Clamide. This relationship, if indeed it can be called one, is not mutual, but although Condwiramurs remains completely passive in it, the power of *minne* manifest in her exerts as much influence on Clamide as on Parzival, as his several references to her make obvious. This power of Condwiramurs indicates the universality of her love and is merely exemplified in the relationship with Clamide.

The hyperbole with which Clamide tries to express what

position of Chrétien it does not do justice to Wolfram. But Bezzola, *op. cit.*, p. 26, has even less sympathy for Wolfram and fails to take into account any difference in Wolfram's literary aims when he deplores his 'manque de tact': 'Ce manque de tact, cette manœuvre suivie d'autres ruses destinées à rappeler à la réalité Perceval, désespéré de voir sa vision s'évanouir, rabaissent presque Gauvain au rang de ceux qui l'ont précédé, Sagremor et Keu. Entre leur attitude et la sienne, il n'y a pas de différence essentielle.'

Condwiramurs means to him has already been mentioned, and his emotion is so excessive that he is firmly convinced that Condwiramurs will yield to his siege of Pelrapeire:

> Condwîr âmûrs wil mich hân,
> und ich ir lîp und ir lant.
> Kingrûn mîn scheneschlant
> mir mit wârheit enbôt,
> si gæbn die stat durch hungers nôt,
> unt daz diu küneginne
> mir büte ir werden minne.   (204.6 ff.)

Consequently, the despair into which he is plunged on being defeated by Parzival is equally excessive:

> ich trage den lebendigen tôt,
> sît ich von ir gescheiden bin,
> diu mir herze unde sin
> ie mit ir gewalt beslôz,
> unt ich des nie gein ir genôz.   (213.23 ff.)

Later, having been dispatched by Parzival to Artus' court, he gives rein to his emotion again:

>   minne mangels nôt
> lestet ûf mich sölhen last,
> mir ist freude gestîn, hôhmuot gast.
> Condwîr âmurs frumt mich grâ.
> Pilâtus von Poncîâ,
> und der arme Jûdas,
> der bî eime kusse was
> an der triwenlôsen vart
> dâ Jêsus verrâten wart,
> swie daz ir schepfær ræche,
> die nôt ich niht verspræche,
> daz Brôbarzære frouwen lîp
> mit ir hulden wær mîn wîp,
> sô daz ich se umbevienge,
> swiez mir dar nâch ergienge.   (219.20 ff.)

In this relationship Condwiramurs' passivity is much more marked than with Parzival. Here the demonic power of *minne* is released with almost annihilating results, since there is nothing whatsoever to temper it and nothing positive with which it can be combined. The whole situation with Clamide illustrates the lengths to which a man will go to express the fervour of his passion and the disastrous results which this has on his personality, dragging it down to the depths of despair, as the last hyperbole referring to Pontius Pilate and Judas makes starkly and terrifyingly plain. If this is the power of *minne*, even in such a virtuous figure as Condwiramurs then it must be tamed and transformed by subjection to a higher power. With Parzival this is the Grail; with Clamide there is none, and the result is bitter torment until he is later united with Cunneware.

CONVERSATION AND MONOLOGUES

It is mainly through the medium of speech that a certain proportion of individuality can be imparted to the characterization of Condwiramurs. Thus, the initiative taken by her in her relationship with Parzival is amplified in this way, and she is able to give expression to the thoughts and emotions which gave rise to it, thereby establishing her character on a firmer basis. A large part of her speeches is, however, in terms of exposition of the situation in which she finds herself at the beginning of book IV, but the psychology of her character as such is not elaborated. This is typical of her role in the poem—that of the embodiment of an ideal and not, when once the adventure of Pelrapeire has been solved, as an active participant in the furtherance of the plot.

Condwiramurs' first words concern her reception of Parzival. She is uncertain of her position as hostess, and in an important monologue in which Wolfram attempts to justify Parzival's silence she considers the reasons for the embarrassment. Her first conclusion is that Parzival despises her on account of her weakness, but she quickly realizes that there is a genuine reason for his behaviour—the rules of courtly decorum:

> nein, er tuotz durch einen list:
> er ist gast, ich pin wirtîn:
> diu êrste rede wære mîn.

dar nâch er güetlîch an mich sach,
sît uns ze sitzen hie geschach:
er hât sich zuht gein mir enbart.   (188.28 ff.)

In fact Parzival's silence is as a result of Gurnemanz' instruction which is explicitly stated by Wolfram, and is ascribed to Parzival's perfect *zuht* (188.15 ff.).[1] Condwiramurs, however, explains to Parzival that she and her household have not been used to receiving guests and, more particularly, to hearing their greetings and offers of service, and she adds sadly: 'des hât mîn herze sich gesent' (189.12), but then immediately enquires where Parzival had come from. This speech presents her as the perfect hostess, realizing her obligations towards her guest, apologizing for the embarrassment of his reception and at the same time implicitly thanking him for his offer of service, after which she puts her own troubles temporarily on one side in order to show a personal interest in Parzival's previous doings. On hearing them, Condwiramurs praises him for achieving in one day a journey which took her own messenger two, and then outlines her connexions with Gurnemanz and his family. This provides a suitable transition to her own plight, since while she was with Gurnemanz she spent 'manegen sûren tac' (189.30) with Liaze lamenting their sorrows. She begs Parzival to endure their lot for the night, in doing which he

[1] Wesle, *op. cit.*, p. 16, describes the difference between Chrétien's and Wolfram's treatment of the scene as follows: 'Wolfram will Parzivals Verhalten nicht nur entschuldigen, sondern vollständig rechtfertigen. Condwiramurs bricht das Schweigen, aber nicht wie Chrestiens' Blancheflor, weil sie merkt, daß Parzival es auf keinen Fall tun wird und sie als die Klügere ihm helfen muß, sondern weil sie zu der Einsicht kommt, daß es auch wirklich an ihr ist, zuerst zu sprechen. . . . Bei Chrestiens hat Perceval v. 1727–30 das Mädchen, das sich auf sein Klopfen am Fenster gezeigt hatte, um Einlaß und Obdach gebeten; dann hat man ihn eingelassen, die Herrin der belagerten Stadt hat ihn v. 1835–45 höflich begrüßt und willkommen geheißen: jetzt ist es in der Tat an Perceval zu sprechen, Blancheflor ist ganz in ihrem Recht, daß sie darauf wartet. Wolframs Parzival hat aber 182.25 gar nicht um Obdach gebeten, sondern seine Hilfe angeboten: er steht von vornherein in ganz anderer Rolle vor Condwiramurs. Sie sitzt nicht vor einem Gast, der sie um Obdach gebeten, dessen Bitte sie bereits zugesagt und den sie willkommen geheißen hat, sondern vor einem Mann, der ihr in ihrer Bedrängnis Hilfe angeboten, auf dessen Angebot sie noch mit keiner Silbe geantwortet und gedankt hat. Und an dieses Anerbieten knüpfen ihre Worte nun auch an.'

will partly serve his previous host, and declares that they are suffering from severe starvation. This completes the first part of the exposition, presenting Parzival with an analysis of the situation in general terms, but neither explaining how this has come about nor asking for assistance, despite Parzival's clear offer.

Condwiramurs' secret nocturnal visit to Parzival concludes the exposition and clarifies several aspects of her personality. Her first concern is, as Wolfram reiterates, that the bounds of virtue shall not be transgressed, and she demands of Parzival that he shall observe the rules of *ére* and *mâ*z*e* and not attempt to possess her, if she joins him in bed. It is her privilege as a *Minneherrin*, though not yet acknowledged as such, to stipulate these conditions, since it is the *frouwe* who raises the knight to her level and not vice versa. After apologizing for causing Parzival loss of sleep as well as sorrow, she immediately sets out the details of her situation— how Clamide and Kingrun had devastated her lands and castles except for Pelrapeire, how Tampenteire had left her an orphan in the most distressing circumstances and half or more of her kinsmen, princes and followers had died in her defence. The situation has now become so critical that she feels she would rather kill herself than sacrifice her virginity and become Clamide's wife, as it is he who killed her lover Schenteflur, Liaze's brother. At this point a strange mingling of roles takes place, since Condwiramurs is virtually a Liaze-substitute for Parzival, and for Condwiramurs Parzival takes the place in her affections of Schenteflur. Both still partly dwell in the past—a sign of a new relationship not yet conscious of its own individuality. The queen accepts Parzival's offer of assistance, but it is Kingrun, the slayer of many of her knights, and not Clamide, whom she first commissions Parzival to dispose of for her, as she knows he is coming the following day with the intention of conquering her for his lord's pleasure. Again she declares she would rather throw herself from the heights of her palace walls into the moat below than allow Clamide to win her virginity by force. In this way she would prevent him from realizing his boast that she would become his wife. Parzival's promise of unconditional help then virtually concludes the episode, as Condwiramurs receives it as simply as it is given, without her thanks being expressed. This is in contrast to Perceval's demand of *drüerie* in the event of his success. Condwiramurs' gratitude for Parzival's success with Kingrun is as unselfconscious and touching as her acceptance of his offer: 'si sprach "in wirde niemer wîp / ûf erde decheines man, / wan den ich umbevangen hân"' (199.26 ff.).[1] Her response is as unconditional as was Parzival's offer, and what she had before denied him she now grants unstintingly, once he is willing to accept.

This love of Condwiramurs, which is so generous as to allow Parzival to leave her, in the first place to see 'wiez umbe mîne muoter stê' (223.19) and secondly to search for the Grail, forms a constant and unwavering background to the rest of the poem until in the final reunion it comes once more to the fore. Condwiramurs rejoices at what she implies as being Parzival's return to her, not her going to him (although this is what actually happens). They meet at an intermediate place, at that spot where Parzival had been bereft of his senses at the sight of the three drops of blood on the snow, a place of great symbolic significance, and Condwiramurs rejoices: 'mir hât gelücke dich / gesendet, herzen freude mîn' (801.6 f.). Their long separation had given her ample justification for grievance, but she forgets it all:

> nu solt ich zürnen: ine mac.
> gêrt sî diu wîle unt dirre tac,
> der mir brâht disen umbevanc,
> dâ von mîn trûren wirdet kranc.
> ich hân nu des mîn herze gert:
> sorge ist an mir vil ungewert. (801.9 ff.)

This last passage sums up best the main feature of Condwiramurs, namely, her dependence on Parzival. Everything else is subject to this: she owes her physical existence to Parzival's protection, and the development of her character in terms of *minne* transcending *hôhe minne* is inseparable from the psychology of Parzival; it is through him that she receives her existence. No other figure is so dependent or so little individualized.

[1] A very probable reference to Isot and the ordeal. Cf. *Tristan* 15706 ff.

CONCLUSION

Several points emerge from the above analysis, and, as in the case of Gahmuret and Herzeloyde, they bear witness to the variety of tendencies in Wolfram's poem. The question of individualization is closely linked with the use of symbolism, which forms a bridge to what Condwiramurs' function in the poem demands, namely, idealized characterization.

In the first place, Condwiramurs is seen almost entirely in her relationship with Parzival: she is the complement of that part of him which is governed by *minne*, and as such she is dependent on him, and he also on her, to a degree that is seen in no other character. To be sure, she is mentioned in connexion with other characters—Tampenteire, Gurnemanz and Liaze, Kingrun and Clamide, Kyot and Manpfiljot, Kardeiz and Loherangrin—but these are almost all fleeting references. Only with Clamide is anything resembling a second 'relationship' present, and here Condwiramurs is an extremely passive character. None of these secondary connexions, apart from the one with Clamide, is sufficiently developed so as to form an integral, decisive part of her personality. This means that she is seen in very much the same light the whole of the time.

But although Condwiramurs is presented solely in terms of *minne*, this is by no means a conventional presentation, for Wolfram's adaptation of the courtly ideal is a marked individualization of the concept of *hôhe minne*. The initiative taken by Condwiramurs in going to Parzival's bedside is not, however, of the same quality as the lead given by Herzeloyde in her wooing of Gahmuret, since in the former case Parzival has already offered his service and Condwiramurs is now merely claiming it, though in an unconventional manner. There is no real reversal of roles such as occurs with Herzeloyde. The difference in Parzival's and Condwiramurs' situation is made by their youthful innocence and by the intensely 'moral' quality of their relationship. The uniqueness of this particular evaluation of *minne* is primarily due to the connexion of *minne* with the Grail, and thus the two lovers are both unique and both dependent on the other for a realization of their love. Since Parzival is the main character of the poem,

Condwiramurs is to a far greater extent dependent on him than he on her. The Grail is Parzival's destiny, into which is incorporated Condwiramurs as the perfect wife. Nonetheless this uniqueness of Condwiramurs in the relationship is not in the first instance due to her personality as such, but rather to her function. If she is to be included in the family of the Grail, which demands both purity and perfection, her character must be developed so as to fulfil this possibility. This very dependence of Condwiramurs on Parzival and on his final destiny is in itself the feature which makes her more than a conventional heroine and in this sense an individual figure.

Condwiramurs is individualized in one way by being idealized, since she represents the *ne plus ultra* of idealized characterization. She is not unique in being beautiful, but its quality makes her unique as it surpasses that of all others. Idealization in its ultimate form requires transcendence, and Wolfram achieves this in the case of Condwiramurs by comparison, by stating the degree of beauty of other heroines, which is limited by description even though the authors may claim that their heroines are 'the fairest in all the world', and by saying that that of Condwiramurs excels them all. This ideal is unrestricted in its scope as it is not limited by descriptions in concrete terms; it is not particularized, and the visual imagery which occurs in combination with it is only to a very small extent distinctive.

The process of idealization achieves its effect largely through the medium of symbolism and allusion. The name 'Condwiramurs' is the key example of this and is followed up by the rose and light symbolism expressing the transcendent nature of her character. Similarly, the use of the term *bêâ flûrs* as a synonym for Condwiramurs is also symbolic. The process is extended by a wealth of allusion to other heroines and by such a characteristically symbolic episode as that of the drops of blood on the snow. The effect of this is to create an individually symbolic and not a visually individualized figure, in which the separate symbols and allusions form the individual traits of the character. In this way the 'universality' of the character, in respect of the high calling of womankind to perfection, is evident, while at the same time the symbols used imply an objective reality as their basis.

On the direct level of 'realistic' characterization, whether in speech or in action, Condwiramurs is not highly individualized. Because she is the character with the most intimate connexion with Parzival, too great an individualization would probably have detracted from that of Parzival himself. In view of this the treatment of Condwiramurs has to be sensitive and in more delicate tones than the characterization of Parzival. This allows Condwiramurs to take the leading role in the nocturnal visit, and in this scene Wolfram goes into the motivation in great detail and presents an adequate exposition of Condwiramurs' plight. This is one case where a certain amount of individuality was possible, and it gives a more solid foundation to the character than idealization alone would have done. Again, Condwiramurs' action in putting on the *gebende* after the first marriage night is a further mark of individualization, though this has to be taken symbolically as well. Finally, the scene of reunion, where Parzival greets Condwiramurs as she lies in bed in her tent, is another example of the possibility of an individual touch being put to the description. On the whole, however, Wolfram refrains from adding too much detail, except where it is not damaging to the plot or to the character of Parzival, and concentrates on the depiction of Condwiramurs as a perfect figure.

In conclusion, we have to note the opposition of realism and individualization to idealization and symbolism. Of these the most important is idealization, which is portrayed through the use of symbolism and allusions. These are themselves individualized, and an intricate complex of symbols is thus created, but individualization in terms of realistic character-portrayal is strictly limited so as not to encroach upon the importance of the main character, Parzival. Thus, we can see the two aspects of realism and idealization with individualizing factors applied to both in varying measure.

VI

ANFORTAS

INTRODUCTION

As Anfortas appears as a participant in Parzival's history he is the most passive of all the main characters of the poem. All the other figures contribute towards Parzival's social and spiritual development, but Anfortas remains apart. It is on him that Parzival's growth is tested, first of all in book V, where the young hero's *sünde* prevents him from relieving Anfortas from his suffering, and secondly in book XVI, where Parzival remedies his former defection and restores Anfortas to health. Thus, the Grail king cannot contribute directly and actively towards Parzival's progress, since he fills the position which constitutes Parzival's goal. Through descriptions of his ailment and his earlier history we and Parzival learn what qualities are demanded of the man called to assume the kingship of the Grail. Anfortas serves as a warning example to Parzival of the results of disobedience to the demands of *diemüete* and *kiusche*.[1] In him we see the culmination of the theme of *leit* in the poem. Other characters—Sigune, Jeschute, Herzeloyde, and Parzival himself—also exemplify this, but Anfortas is the most important since he has failed in his vocation, and the full extent of *leit* is made manifest in him. The *leit* which Parzival endures is of a different order from that of Anfortas and is less than it, since Parzival can take the initiative in ridding himself of the weight of his sin and suffering, can confess and be absolved, whereas Anfortas is in the position that he can do nothing to alleviate his pain, but must wait to have it alleviated for him.

[1] H. B. Willson, *The Grail King in Wolfram's 'Parzival'* (*MLR*, LV, 1960), goes further and declares: 'He represents symbolically mankind in its fallen state, having broken the law of God' (p. 554), continuing this with a religious allegorical interpretation which I am unable and unwilling to follow.

But although Anfortas emerges primarily as the chief representative of *leit* in the poem, his character is enlarged in many ways and a variety of themes are touched on as we learn more about him. Parzival's ultimate destiny becomes clearer to us; we see the importance of *minne* and knightly activity; the dark, mysterious figure of the Fisher King passes before us; beauty and moral goodness are seen to be allied to each other. Through these features Anfortas appears as more than a mere symbol of suffering and becomes an individual with an independent personality.

SYNONYMS

The synonyms which are used to refer to Anfortas give some indication of the different aspects of his character, though they do not express a striking variety. There is a gradual introduction of his individual personality which begins anonymously in book V, when Parzival asks to be directed to a lodging for the night and Anfortas gives him directions to his own castle of Munsalvæsche. In the very first instance he is called a *weideman* (225.3), but the subsequent references in this context mainly call him a *vischære* (225.13, 226.1.25, 227.3, 229.20). Trevrizent refers to this occupation of Anfortas' during the period that Parzival spends in his cell and calls him by the same name (491.14). He explains to his nephew that the king can now neither walk nor ride, lie down nor stand upright, and so he takes exercise in fishing, in a leaning position, though he has little success at it. At least, this is the explanation that Wolfram gives of the Fisher King motif, which he took over from Chrétien.

In the many studies devoted to the sources of the material found in the Grail story this motif of the Fisher King looms large. Notable among the attempted explanations is that of Jessie L. Weston,[1] recently taken up again by H.-J. Koppitz,[2] but it has nothing of fundamental importance to say about the character of the Grail king in the person of Anfortas. The questions we have to

---

[1] Jessie L. Weston, *From Ritual to Romance* (Cambridge, 1920), ch. IX.

[2] H.-J. Koppitz, *Beobachtungen über das Verhältnis Wolframs von Eschenbach zur religiösen Tradition des Mittelalters* (Diss. Bonn, 1954), pp. 154 f. *et al.*

tackle here are those of literature, not anthropology, and though the studies of source material of this kind make fascinating reading, they very much tend to detract from the immediate questions which a work of art should put to its public, namely, the literary and human value of the work under discussion. It is possible that the story of the Fisher King may represent a fertility myth and that the fish is a symbol of wisdom, that the name of the Fisher King lived on, but the idea behind it grew obscure, and that Wolfram (and the other poets who dealt with the Grail material) attempted a rationalization of this name; but this is a postulation the accuracy of which in all probability can never be determined. What we *do* know, however, is that an episode occurs in *Parzival* where the Grail king is presented as a fisherman. We now have to evaluate this episode within the framework of the other incidents in the poem, particularly of those in which Anfortas appears. In fact, the episode fits into the poem without need for recourse to the anthropological motif of the Fisher King. It may seem mysterious and strange that the Grail king should go fishing, but it is not incomprehensible, and the element of mystery suitably corresponds to that surrounding the nature of the Grail itself. To explain the role of Anfortas in the poem with the main emphasis on the Fisher King hypothesis would be to do an injustice to Wolfram's work, since the fundamental interest of the poem lies in the treatment of Parzival's spiritual development, and the question motif has more significance for him than for Anfortas. Rather it should be the obvious meaning of the poem, the form of the journey as a mirror of a character's development, the interplay of the knightly and the Grail worlds, that provide the basis for the interpretation of the poem. This is the immediately apparent, self-consistent pattern that the poem displays, and this was what Wolfram and his public considered to be the subject of the work. *Parzival* is first and foremost a work of art; any anthropological considerations are purely incidental.

Similarly, the researches of Julius Schwietering embodied in his article *Der Fischer vom See Brumbane*[1] are concerned more with an

[1] *ZfdA*, LX, 1923.

attempt to throw light on the nature of the Grail than with the characterization of Anfortas as such. However true the conclusions that Schwietering reaches may be, it is extremely unlikely that Wolfram was conscious of the mystical significance of the 'angling fisherman' in the early Christian period and deliberately set it in his story with this background in mind. Parallels between Wolfram's descriptions and the practices of other times and places are numerous, but before they can be credited as sources, some mode of transference has to be established between the postulated source and Wolfram. If this is lacking, there seems little justification for taking a hypothesis into account when discussing characterization, which is exclusively a matter of explicit intention on the part of the author. Wolfram, though conversant with very many literary works of his day, is hardly likely to have had access to the thought of the first Christian centuries, and his audience must have been in the same position. It is much more probable that the incident of the 'angling fisherman' was treated by Wolfram as a mysterious event needing no further explanation, and not as a mystical event pointing to the pseudo-eucharistic drama of the Grail.

Wolfram spends little time describing Anfortas' occupation as a fisherman, and it is clear that he attaches no great significance to it. Its only purpose, so far as we can see from what Trevrizent tells Parzival (491.6 ff.), is to provide him with some opportunity for relaxation. His physical suffering is such that all the usual forms of knightly activity are impossible; fishing is all that remains as an alternative to hunting. But Trevrizent says that Anfortas is taken to Brumbane for the sake of the good air, by which his followers hope to alleviate his suffering. As a consequence of this, Trevrizent continues, a report has arisen that he is a fisherman, though he has in actual fact little success in it. From the evidence of the text, therefore, Anfortas' fishing is motivated by the desire of his family and retinue to relieve his suffering, and the report that he is a fisherman is, if we follow Trevrizent's version of the theme, a picturesque, but insignificant, detail.

The most common synonyms used for Anfortas are the terms

wirt,[1] *künec*,[2] *bruoder*[3] and *œheim*.[4]   Other terms extend the area
of social position and family ties, viz.: *hêrre* (248.28, 474.8. 477.21,
478.17, 616.13), *swâger* (819.10), *sun* (478.3), *vogt* (478.4). From
the instances quoted here it is plain that the basis of characterization
of Anfortas is to be found in his royal position and family relationships. These functional details, however, form only part of the
picture: the rest is given through adjectives and descriptive phrases.
Immediately the importance of Anfortas' suffering becomes
apparent, as in one of the first references to him at the lake of
Brumbane he is characterized as *trûric* (225.18), and this epithet
occurs several times in the course of the poem.[5] It is extended
elsewhere as *jâmers rîch* (230.30), *freuden lœre* (252.1), *helfelôs*
(330.29), *niht der geile* (491.18). The other adjectives applied to
Anfortas express the basically good side of his nature despite his
sin against the moral laws of the Grail, and he is called both *wert*
(248.24, 479.28, 781.25, 823.23) and *süeȝe*.[6] *Guot* also appears
(816.11), as do *junc* (479.28) and *frî* (478.29), while after his
restoration to health particularly he is characterized as *clâr*
(617.7, 810.7, 811.17, 823.23), the adjective most frequently used
by Wolfram to indicate excellence in physical beauty.[7] Other
words used are *gehiure* (734.8) and *balt* (820.28), both of which
are used in combination with *süeȝe*.

The references given above show the outstanding features of
Anfortas' personality. The preponderance of the term *wirt*
emphasizes the importance of this particular relationship with
Parzival at the time when the latter should have seized the opportunity to heal his host, and the significance of their kinship is

[1] 229.7, 230.15.26.30, 231.1, 233.24.27, 236.11, 237.7, 239.24, 240.7.18, 241.3,
242.12.22, 247.29, 248.21, 251.19.23, 252.1, 255.17, 256.2, 330.28, 441.24, 473.15.19,
484.26.
[2] 389.2, 472.21, 479.3, 480.3.25.27, 481.5, 482.28, 483.5, 484.8, 490.10.24,
491.2.20, 494.13.24, 493.7.17, 519.12, 616.13.19, 781.27, 788.21.
[3] 251.16, 477.19, 478.5.8.17, 480.15, 497.3.
[4] 479.11.25, 489.29, 491.30, 501.1, 795.29.
[5] 253.21, 256.2, 491.18, 783.20, 794.26, 795.27.
[6] 240.7, 433.25, 441.23, 479.11, 489.29, 519.27, 734.8, 781.25, 819.2, 820.28,
821.3.
[7] See above, p. 225, fn. 1.

brought out by the frequent use of the word *œheim*. For everyone Anfortas is known in his capacity as king, but his relationship with Trevrizent is noted with several uses of the term *bruoder*. The rest of the words in which aspects of Anfortas' character—as opposed to his position—are shown, are used of him by all the characters.

DESCRIPTIVE PASSAGES

The characterization of Anfortas is achieved largely through the medium of description, either on the part of the author or on the part of one of the other characters. Thus, what we learn about him is mainly historical. When Parzival meets him at Brumbane and Munsalvæsche, his active life is past (until after the putting of the *Mitleidsfrage* and his restoration to health), and he appears as a passive, suffering figure. This situation requires elucidation for the full impact of the meaning to strike the audience, and long passages are devoted to this by those who know the background of Anfortas' plight. Thus, Sigune, Trevrizent and Orgeluse provide us and Parzival with the necessary information, though Anfortas himself also contributes some comments on his position.

His physical appearance is that of a king, and this is the first thing that Wolfram mentions when he introduces him anonymously at Brumbane:

> der het an im alsolch gewant,
> ob im dienden elliu lant,
> daz ez niht bezzer möhte sîn.
> gefurriert sîn huot was pfâwîn.   (225.11 ff.)

By this superlative description Wolfram leads up to the depiction of the magnificence of the Grail palace in accordance with his aim of creating a world of splendour beyond that of the normal courtly world, one in which the height of knightly prowess is combined with a deep spiritual awareness. The Grail palace is Anfortas' habitual setting, and its splendour is the external sign of the nature of the kingship of the Grail and of the whole Grail community. The castle presents an impregnable appearance as Parzival enters, and inside it displays a wealth of decoration and furniture—a blaze of lights from a magnificent chandelier, a marble fireplace, a proliferation of couches. In the midst of this we find Anfortas, whose ailment necessitates great fires and warm clothes to secure him a minimum of comfort. Generous lengths of sable, the softest that can be found, are needed for both the outside and the lining of his mantle, and on his head he wears a double sable hood with an Arabian border and a ruby on top. At this point nothing specific is said about the nature of his illness, but the strange picture he presents adds mystery to the scene and shows that it is more than an ordinary illness.

At the end of the story (795.30 ff.) a corresponding description is given of Anfortas' restoration to health, though here all account of clothing is omitted, the description concentrating on physical radiance. Until this point Parzival had been the epitome of beauty, but now Anfortas surpasses him and also, into the bargain, Absalom, Vergulaht of Ascalun and Gahmuret at the time of his entry into Kanvoleis. These comparisons serve the same function as those of Condwiramurs with Isalde, Jeschute and Cunneware.[1] Absalom's beauty was proverbial in the Middle Ages and is referred to also in other works.[2] Vergulaht's handsome appearance is described at the beginning of book VIII:

> sîn blic was tac wol bî der naht.
> sîn geslähte sante Mazadan
> für den berc ze Fâmorgân:
> sîn art was von der feien.
> in dûhte er sæhe den meien
> in rehter zît von bluomen gar,
> swer nam des küneges varwe war.
> Gâwânen des bedûhte,
> do der künec sô gein im lûhte,
> ez wære der ander Parzivâl,
> unt daz er Gahmuretes mâl
> hete alsô diz mære weiz,
> dô der reit în ze Kanvoleiz.   (400.6 ff.)

[1] See above, pp. 228 ff.

[2] Cf. Rudolf von Ems, *Weltchronik*, 27000 ff.; Johannes Rothe, *Der Ritterspiegel*, 262; Chrétien de Troyes, *Conte del Graal*, 4792 (where the king of Escavalon is described as more beautiful than Absalom); *Lucidarius* (*DTM*), p. 73, 11.18 ff. Cf. Werner Fechter, *Absalom als Vergleichs- und Beispielfigur im mhd. Schrifttum* (*Beitr.* (Tübingen), LXXXIII, 1961).

Mention is explicitly made of Gahmuret's entry into Kanvoleis again, of which an account has already been given.[1] The description of Vergulaht makes use of the same light imagery that we find in this picture of Anfortas. His beauty is such that Wolfram finds the French word *flôrî* gives a more vivid impression that any German word he could find. Anfortas' skin begins to gleam (796.5 f.), and his sudden change is attributed to the power of Christ as shown in the stories of St Silvester and of Lazarus.[2] The illustration of Lazarus lends a certain support to the idea that Parzival's history is in a sense modelled on the life of Christ and that the Grail kingdom is as it were the Kingdom of God on earth. In any case, this final description of Anfortas both begins and ends with a religious tone, and this gives weight to what happens both for Anfortas and especially for Parzival, since it is unmistakably shown here that a full reconciliation has taken place between God and Parzival, as it is God's power which heals Anfortas through the mediation of Parzival.

Through the other descriptions of Anfortas we learn about the nature and cause of his ailment. This information is not given all at once, but progressively, explaining as much as is necessary for Parzival to know at each stage of his development. Thus, apart from the description already quoted of Anfortas' physical appearance, the only other thing we are told when Parzival sees the king in the Grail palace is: 'ez was worden wette / zwischen im und der vröude: / er lebte niht wan töude' (230.18 ff.). At this point Parzival has no idea of the possible significance of asking Anfortas the so-called *Mitleidsfrage*; nor indeed has the audience. But at least it is clear to all that something is going on which is quite literally a matter of life and death and that it evokes feelings of compassion. At this level Parzival could have responded—his capacity for pity has been demonstrated—but more is involved than this, though neither he nor the audience is explicitly aware of it at that time.

[1] See above, pp. 27 ff.
[2] The legend of St. Silvester and the bull was probably known to Wolfram through the *Kaiserchronik*, 8200 ff. Cf. especially 10303 ff.

Parzival's second meeting with Sigune gives him his first glimpse of the meaning of Anfortas' suffering, though the information given is rather sketchy. Until this moment Anfortas had remained nameless. At Munsalvæsche Parzival had known him merely as the *wirt*, but now Sigune tells Parzival Anfortas' name, thus bringing out his individuality and making Parzival aware of a personal involvement in the situation at the Grail castle, refusing him the possibility of escape and excuse through anonymity. She tells him also how Anfortas can do nothing but lean and how his brother Trevrizent lives a life of poverty for the sake of Anfortas' sin. More Sigune does not say directly about Anfortas, except to indicate, though not precisely, that the *Mitleidsfrage* has deep significance for his illness; why this is so she does not say. Thus, Parzival is left with the knowledge that he has committed a terrible 'sin', but he is ignorant of the exact nature of it. He has to wait until he meets Trevrizent to learn more about this, about his relationship with Anfortas and the reasons for the latter's plight.

In the course of Parzival's long interview with Trevrizent he is told in detail about Anfortas' history. The hermit has just finished giving Parzival instruction in the elements of Christianity, dwelling especially on the theme of *superbia* and sin, and he now proceeds to explain Anfortas' situation with this in mind. The cause of his sufferings is to be found in *hôchvart*, and his particular sin is against the virtue of *kiusche*, which for Wolfram subsumes all others:

> er gerte minne
> ûzerhalp der kiusche sinne.
> der site ist niht dem grâle reht:
> dâ muoz der rîter unt der kneht
> bewart sîn vor lôsheit.
> diemuot ie hôchvart überstreit. (472.29 ff.)

But for the intervention of a few words on the Grail community Trevrizent immediately pursues his explanation with a sorrowful comment on the irruption into the Grail castle of an unknown knight (whom *we* know to have been Parzival), who failed to speak to Anfortas about his misery. These general remarks show how much both Anfortas and Parzival are the victims of *superbia*, and it is only later that a differentiation is made with regard to the precise sins which are the outcome of the basic one of pride. Here, as in the encounter with Sigune, the matter of compassion comes to the fore: 'daz sol iuch unde mich armen / immer mêr erbarmen, / umb sîn herzebære nôt' (472.23 ff.), but this idea of compassion clouds the issue at stake. An analysis of the 'sins' of Anfortas and Parzival shows that both have the same root, and so long as this is the case it is impossible for Parzival to release the king.

One extremely important point arises from Trevrizent's initial discourse, namely, the fact that *kiusche* is one of the supreme requirements of the Grail king, and in this Parzival has not up to this moment failed and does not fail afterwards. The matter is not pursued here, but has to wait until book XII before any further light is shed on it. This occurs in a long speech by Orgeluse, where she explains to Gawan various details about the knights who have served her. It then emerges that it was she in whose service Anfortas was maimed (616.11 ff.), and it is significant that in the same speech, at the end of her outburst, Orgeluse mentions that Parzival has spurned her *minne* and remained true to Condwiramurs (619.3 ff.). This passage shows the contrast between Anfortas and Parzival very clearly in the matter of *kiusche*, and the fact of Parzival's constancy in love and avoidance of harmful escapades compares more than favourably with the known failing of Anfortas in this one respect, which is the first requirement of the Grail king. It is a strong indication that when Parzival has overcome his other sins nothing will stand in his way to the kingship of the Grail.

After this general exposition of Anfortas' situation Parzival reveals his identity, confesses to having killed Ither and learns the enormity of his crime from Trevrizent, who then proceeds to give a much lengthier account of Anfortas' career, complete with details of how he was maimed and what has been done in the attempt to cure him. First of all, he describes how Anfortas, as the eldest son of the family, became king of the Grail on the death of Frimutel and was worthy of the crown. When he reaches physical maturity, however, *minne* took a firm hold on him, and he chose a lady to serve who he thought was worthy, but of whom Trevrizent obviously has a different opinion, though he disdains to speak further of it. Nevertheless Anfortas gained fame in her service both for his bravery and for his success in battle. But one day, while he was out alone in search of *âventiure* and joyfully pursuing his desire for *minne*, a pagan from Ethnise met him in a joust and inflicted an incurable wound on him in his sexual organs by means of a poisoned spear, being confident that by his valour he could seize the Grail. Despite the pain Anfortas managed to kill the pagan, but he returned to the castle pale and weak as a result of the wound. A doctor removed the fragments of the spear from the wound, and immediately Trevrizent vowed to abstain from all knightly activity, from meat, wine, bread and all animal food, in the attempt to relieve Anfortas from his suffering through God's help.

It is clear from the long account then given of all the attempts to cure Anfortas that his ailment has the same significance as the leprosy with which the Armer Heinrich is afflicted. The wound is the external sign of the spiritual disfavour that Anfortas has incurred in the sight of the Grail. Both Anfortas and the Armer Heinrich are guilty of *superbia*, and the cures of both are occasioned by the mediation of some other person ready to turn his will to God's purpose.

In the attempt to cure Anfortas the Grail community has resort to everything known to medieval medicine, but none of the remedies of the medical books are of any avail. Nor are the waters of the four rivers flowing from the Garden of Eden, nor the rod which the Sibyl required Eneas to have in order to protect himself against the stench of hell and to ensure his subsequent departure from there,[1] nor the blood of the pelican, whose alleged habit of feeding its young with blood from its breast caused the bird to be regarded as a symbol of the crucified Christ, nor the heart of the unicorn, nor the carbuncle to be found beneath its horn, nor the

Cf. *Eneide*, 2786 ff., 2854 f.

herb *trachonté*. Finally the family falls down in devotion to the Grail and discovers written on it the news that the king's illness will end when a knight comes and asks what is ailing him. The knight must on no account be warned by anyone about asking the question, otherwise it will be of no effect. To release Anfortas from his suffering the question must be spontaneous and take place on the first night of the knight's arrival. If he puts the question at the right time, he is to succeed to the kingship of the Grail, having been guided to it by the hand of God, through Whom Anfortas' torment will be ended. Anfortas' sin is, however, so great that although he may be cured from his illness he will never again be worthy to continue as the Grail king. Until the knight comes, his wound is treated with spikenard, theriac and the smoke of aloes, but nothing gives him any comfort.

After Parzival has learnt all his information and has heard Trevrizent's laments about the knight who failed to ask the question, he confesses to having been that knight, and Trevrizent, curiously at pains to minimize the gravity of Parzival's omission, then tells him about the influence of the planet Saturn on Anfortas' condition. When this planet reaches its zenith, and also at the time of the full and the new moon, the pain from his wound increases. The rise of Saturn causes the phenomenon of summer snow and affects the king with cold more intense than frost. His flesh becomes colder than snow, and the only way for him to obtain relief is to have the poisoned spear laid on the wound, whereby the heat of the poison counteracts the cold and drives the frost out of his body. This is the explanation of the bleeding spear that Parzival sees at Munsalvæsche. The only person able to remove the frost from the spear is Trebuchet, who also knows the spell which gives power to the sword presented by Anfortas to Parzival on his first visit to the Grail castle. A spell which Trebuchet learnt from Anfortas' sword endows him with the skill of making two silver knives, by which the frost can be removed, and the drops which fall off the spear have such virtue that they cause asbestos to burn. The cold and the snow, together with the rise of Saturn and also— as we are told later (789.4 ff.)—with those of Mars and Jupiter,

show the more than purely physical nature of Anfortas' suffering.[1]
The cold is a sign of exclusion from the norms of both the courtly
and the Grail worlds. This is shown in Parzival's story in the
Blutstropfenepisode, where he is separated by the power of *minne*
from the Arthurian world, and in the important Good Friday
scene and the sojourn with Trevrizent, where Parzival is cut off
from contact with the rest of the world by the fact of his own sin.
This exclusion is the mark of *superbia*, of which both Anfortas
and Parzival are guilty, and as the whole significance of the poem
revolves round the destinies of the two kings of the Grail, the
questions of loyalty to one's vocation and acceptance of God's
will, the sufferings of these two characters are deepened through
their cosmic connexions.

Book XVI brings the consummation of the poem—the restoration of Anfortas to health and the accession of Parzival to the
kingship of the Grail. The fortunes of the two are clearly closely
linked, but now a third is joined to them—that of Feirefiz. Many
scholars have laid emphasis on the parallelism of the careers of
Gawan and Parzival, but as Wolfram draws to the conclusion of
his work, he finds little room for Gawan, but instead elaborates
the connexions between Parzival, Feirefiz and Anfortas. At the
beginning of book XVI Wolfram gives another description of
Anfortas' suffering, though he adds nothing of great significance
to his previous descriptions apart from a long catalogue of stones
decorating the bed on which he rests. If any meaning is to be
attached to this catalogue (leaving aside the possibility that
Wolfram merely wished to exhibit his vast knowledge once more),
I think it may be found in a deliberate parallelism between Feirefiz
and Anfortas, since the importance of the power of precious stones
for Feirefiz is forcibly brought out in the description of the duel
between him and Parzival (743.5 ff.). This parallelism has, however, more the function of isolating Parzival from the trinity of
characters than of focusing attention on any deeply significant
unity between Feirefiz and Anfortas. Nevertheless, at one point

[1] Marianne Wynn, *Scenery and Chivalrous Journeys in Wolfram's* Parzival
(*Spec.*, XXXVI, 1961), pp. 406 ff.

in the conclusion the three characters are linked in the excellence of chivalry: 'dâ sâzen dem grâle bî / der aller besten rîter drî, / die dô der schilde pflâgen' (815.17 ff.), and it is to be noted that Gawan is not one of the three. The conclusion of the poem stresses the pre-eminence of the Grail world, in which Anfortas still has a high place despite his earlier failure.

SPEECHES

Although much of the characterization of Anfortas is achieved through descriptive passages, a good part of it, especially towards the end of the poem, is given through what Anfortas himself says. The value of these sections varies considerably, however, and some parts contribute much more than others towards the establishment of a concrete personality.

To begin with there are the directions that Anfortas gives the wandering Parzival, who is looking for lodging for the night. Anfortas declares that he knows of no other place within a radius of thirty miles apart from a house that stands nearby, to which he invites the young knight. He gives him to understand that he will be his host when he returns in the evening and warns Parzival to take care not to lose his way. When he receives Parzival later at Munsalvæsche, he again shows his hospitable spirit by asking him to sit next to him, after which he presents Parzival with the sword that is a sign of his vocation to the Grail, explaining how he himself had used it in the course of his exploits and how it will protect Parzival in battle. These four speeches all show Anfortas in a position where he, the most passive of all the main characters in the poem, takes the initiative and acts with great *triuwe* (225.23) towards Parzival, providing him with even more than he asks, but his effort to obtain release nonetheless fails. The healing power which he knows Parzival to possess cannot be elicited in this way, and he is forced to remain as he was before and to wait. It becomes clear that the sufferer cannot himself remove the *leit* which he bears: all that he can do is to wait with patience until he is released by some power outside and beyond himself.

The main part of the characterization of Anfortas, both through speech and through descriptions, occurs in retrospect with regard to the first climax of the poem in Parzival's visit to Munsalvæsche in book V. The two chief protagonists of the action are ignorant of each other's identity, and the reader or listener shares this ignorance so far as the identity of Anfortas is concerned. The whole episode is shrouded in mystery, but the fact of Anfortas' *leit* is given due prominence, so that nothing else really disturbs the picture. The motif of the *Mitleidsfrage* (though as yet the idea of the question as such with respect to the Grail has not been introduced) dominates the scene, and it is not until later that the more complex issues come to the fore explaining the spiritual basis of Anfortas' suffering and the weight of original sin and pride on Parzival's side, which lead him to refrain from putting the question. The only indication that we have here of the magnitude of Anfortas' disobedience to his vocation is that he recognizes that his suffering is in accordance with God's will—'ê daz mich got / ame lîbe hât geletzet' (239.26 f.)[1]—but this requires considerable expansion before its meaning becomes quite clear. At this stage, however, where the *Mitleidsfrage* takes first importance and subsumes all the other aspects of the encounter, Wolfram intercalates his own feelings and intensifies Parzival's omission, making it obvious that the *Mitleidsfrage* was demanded by the outward circumstances, which are all that anyone involved in the action or in observing the action can see at the time:

> ôwê daz er niht vrâgte dô!
> des pin ich für in noch unvrô.
> wan do erz [sc. the sword] enpfienc in sîne hant,
> dô was er vrâgens mit ermant.
> och riwet mich sîn süezer wirt,
> den ungenande niht verbirt,
> des im von vrâgn nu wære rât. (240.3 ff.)

---

[1] Mergell, *op. cit.*, p. 213, points out that 'Gott selbst hat an Anfortas gehandelt' and declares: 'Diese Verschiedenheit in der Auffassung der Anfortas-Handlung —bei Chrétien rationale äußere Motivierung, bei Wolfram ethisch vertiefte, religiöse Deutung—ist der Vertiefung aller Handlungen im Bereich des Grals und der Gralsippe verwandt.'

After this episode Anfortas withdraws from the action of the poem until book XVI. This opens with a long speech by him describing his own position, and as such it is of first importance, since it shows an awareness of self and of a distinct personality. For when a character speaks about himself either in monologues or to other people, this usually expresses an individuality emerging from the functional nature of playing a part in an unfolding plot.

In this speech three points are made. (i) Anfortas begins by making a connexion between the possession of *triuwe* and the capacity for compassion: 'ich weiz wol, pflægt ir triuwe, / so erbarmet iuch mîn riuwe' (787.9 f.). *Triuwe* in this context means more than love and loyalty in the merely human sense and expresses something of the spiritual bond between man and God that is evident in the use of the word with reference to Parzival. And here there must be an implicit reference to Parzival, since he is shortly to release Anfortas from his suffering. A contrast is thus made between Parzival's spiritual condition on his first visit to Munsalvæsche and his later spiritual maturity, this difference being expressed by a growth in *triuwe*. Anfortas' statement is not, however, meant to imply that his immediate family and following do not possess *triuwe*, but is to be understood in the context of the despair which permeates all the speech and which leads the king to question the devotion of those who serve him.

(ii) Anfortas has reached the depths of despair in his misery and no longer cherishes any hope that he might be cured. His only desire is that he might die, but the court because of their *triuwe*—as Wolfram says—insists on keeping him alive by taking him into the presence of the Grail, which has the power of preventing him from dying. This life-giving force of the Grail has been mentioned earlier by Trevrizent to Parzival (480.25 ff.) and this is what causes Anfortas to despair. His *leit* makes it impossible for him to have any pleasure in living, and his being taken into the presence of the Grail removes his hope of release through dying. Anfortas tells his family that if they refuse to let him die, they also will perish, but they maintain their faith that the knight will come and relieve him.

(iii) Anfortas lays great stress on his knightly achievements. He implores the court to let him die 'durch des helmes art / unt durch des schildes orden' (787.20 f.) and reminds them how he devoted himself with honour and success to knightly pursuits and to their service. In his present condition he is incapacitated from knightly activity and can no longer be a worthy lord and master to them. He claims that he has forfeited the right to be their lord because he can no longer fulfil these knightly duties.

In his speech Anfortas sums up the qualities required of the Grail king—the need for *triuwe*, which in Parzival's case is bound up with the *Mitleidsfrage*, but which involves a right spiritual development exemplified in the moral sphere by the virtue of *kiusche*; the life-and-death nature of the laws governing the Grail king; and the need for excellence in chivalry. These points must be borne in mind as the essential basis for the kingship of the Grail. Anfortas exemplifies them negatively through failure (though he does not fail in everything); Parzival at the end of his career exemplifies them positively. Each time both Anfortas and Parzival have to be remembered.

The next speech of Anfortas, directed to Parzival after his arrival at Munsalvæsche, consists of a plea that he should end his misery by allowing him to die when a week has elapsed from his last seeing the Grail. He refers to Parzival's previous visit and again makes the connexion between *triuwe* and compassion, lending emphasis to his words by the use of the rhyme with *riuwe*. But Parzival does not put an end to Anfortas' *leit* in the way that the latter expects, but—contrary to all that we have been told about the fact that the *Mitleidsfrage* must be put on the first night of the knight's visit and that it must take place spontaneously without the assistance of any other person—Parzival proceeds to ask the question and cures Anfortas by so doing. The reason for this difference in approach to the *Mitleidsfrage* is explained by Parzival's action immediately before asking the question:

> sîn venje er viel des endes dar
> drîstunt zêrn der Trinitât:
> er warp daz müese werden rât
> des trûrgen mannes herzesêr. (795.24 ff.)

This clarifies the nature of the *Mitleidsfrage* and shows that it is a symbol for something greater and deeper. The connexions that I have indicated between *triuwe* and compassion strongly support this interpretation of the question, and the fact that it is Parzival's spiritual condition which is of prime importance, i.e. the extent to which he is consciously acting in the spirit of *triuwe* in its God-centred sense, is borne out by the repetition of the situation in which the question can be asked. If it were merely the question as such that generated the power of healing, then much of the deeper meaning of the entire poem would be lost. But the fact that Parzival is conscious that he is merely the instrument through which God can restore Anfortas is plainly stated at this point, whereas it was completely lacking at the time of his first visit to Munsalvæsche. On the first occasion the question was not put, but on the second it can be and is put because *triuwe* is the all-important basis of the question's power. The rules governing the asking of the question are the external features which preserve the form of the situation, but the rules are transcended by the virtue of *triuwe*.

Once Anfortas has been cured, he retires from the centre of attention and activity, while still retaining a position in the conclusion of the action. It is he who realizes that Feirefiz is unable to see the Grail because he is unbaptized, and by first questioning Feirefiz and then mentioning the matter to Parzival he sets in motion the final stage of the story, where Feirefiz is incorporated into the Grail community and receives Repanse de schoye in marriage. Anfortas sees that Feirefiz is in love with his sister and tells him that she has never before caused anyone pain and that no knight has ever ridden in her service. Her sharing Anfortas' *leit* has partially caused the pallor and sadness of her appearance. But although Anfortas can tell Feirefiz all this, he is unable to do anything further for him. He points out that Parzival now wields the authority in the Grail community and that he may be able to help Feirefiz.

Anfortas' last speech occurs in connexion with Feirefiz' request that he should go with Repanse and himself to India and gives a concise summary of Anfortas' position and future intentions. In being restored to health he has laid aside the *hôchvart* which caused his suffering and returned to pursuing the virtue of *diemüete*. He gives his blessing to Feirefiz and Repanse, but says that he must now renounce all wealth and love of women. Nevertheless his aim is to exercise his knightly skill, but this time in the service of the Grail and never in the service of any lady, though he has learnt not to bear them any ill-will despite the pain of his own experience. Anfortas has reached a state of purity once more, and now he must pay the Grail the service which is its due and in which he previously failed. In his last comment on Anfortas Wolfram shows his achievement of this aim in the attainment of *kiusche*:

> der werde clâre Anfortas
> manlîch bî kiuschem herzen was.
> ordenlîche er manege tjoste reit,
> durch den grâl, niht durch diu wîp er streit. (823.23 ff.)

CONCLUSION

The characterization of Anfortas is neither extensive nor very detailed. Like all the other characters his importance as a person is intimately linked with the role he plays in Parzival's destiny. His history is a parallel to Parzival's, but is clearly differentiated from it in those aspects which impinge on Parzival's career. Anfortas' *untriuwe*—for his *unkiusche*, his *hôchvart*, is defection before the Grail and before God—is made concrete in his suffering and acts as a reflexion of Parzival's own *untriuwe*. Parzival proves his own possession of *triuwe* by releasing Anfortas from his suffering. But although Anfortas presents to Parzival both a goal and a mirror of failure and although his story must necessarily be a function of Parzival's, he does retain a modicum of individuality. He is more than a mere figure and more than a mythical personage looming up from an anthropological mist. He belongs to a complex group of relationships and has more than one side to his character, though this emerges largely through the accounts of other characters, and when Parzival's story is ended he continues with a distinct career of his own, pursuing the demands of his own personality. The fact that the poem does not end on the accession of Parzival to the Grail, but concludes with a glimpse into the future of various characters shows that it is not Parzival's story alone which interests the author. The characters are sufficiently alive for him to want to relate a little of the future existence of Feirefiz and Repanse de schoye, of Anfortas, of Loherangrin. To this extent the individuality which they have is real and continues beyond the compass of their immediate function in the history of *des mæres hêrre,* Parzival.

VII

TREVRIZENT

'ich wil inz herze hin zuo dir.'

THESE words which *frou âventiure* utters at the beginning of
book IX (433.2) in her arresting altercation with the author
acutely sum up Wolfram's intentions in writing this pivotal
section of his poem. He is now out to expound the fundamental
ideas underlying his conception of the story of Parzival and the
Grail. It is, however, an exposition which has given rise to the
most varied and controversial interpretations among scholars, but
while many of them disagree violently with the conclusions reached
by other scholars, there is a basic unanimity among them on the
fact that book IX is the crucial portion of the whole work. Essentially through the person of Trevrizent (though Parzival's
encounters with Sigune and with Kahenis and his family constitute a preparation) Wolfram attempts to deal with two major
problems—the nature of the Grail and the Grail community, and
the question of Parzival's guilt. It is not my purpose here to
investigate the many theories which have been propounded about
the physical nature of the Grail and its origin or to examine in
detail the theology of Trevrizent's teaching *except in so far as they
shed light on the characterization of Trevrizent or of Parzival.*
Wolfram's theological presuppositions have been the subject of
many monographs and articles in recent years,[1] and it would lead
far beyond the boundaries of the present study to reassess this

---

[1] For example Benedikt Mockenhaupt, *Die Frömmigkeit im Parzival Wolframs
von Eschenbach* (Bonn, 1942); Julius Schwietering, *Parzivals Schuld. Zur Religiosität Wolframs in ihren Beziehungen zur Mystik* (*ZfdA*, LXXXI, 1944); Gottfried
Weber, *Parzival. Ringen und Vollendung* (Oberursel, 1948); Friedrich Maurer,
*Leid. Studien zur Bedeutungs- und Problemgeschichte besonders in den großen Epen der
staufischen Zeit* (Bern/Munich, 1951); Wolfgang Mohr, *Parzivals ritterliche Schuld*
(*WW*, II, 1951/2); Walter Johannes Schröder, *Der Ritter zwischen Gott und Welt*

problematic question. Similarly, the speculations about Wolfram's Grail point to fields of study outside the scope of an examination of character-portrayal, and I have accordingly steered my way past rather than through them.

It is inevitable in a discussion of the characterization of Trevrizent that most aspects of Parzival's personality will need to be treated. Indeed, this is necessarily so, since the main function of Trevrizent in the poem is to provide information and to teach. It is under his guidance that Parzival is enabled to see the reasons for his guilt and to overcome it, and from him he finds out about the mysteries of Munsalvæsche and his vocation to the kingship of the Grail. Thus, Schwietering's contention that Parzival's character develops through his encounters with the other personages of the poem[1] is seen to be especially true in the case of his meeting with Trevrizent. The present chapter will therefore comprise a discussion of some of the problems of Parzival as well as a treatment of the character of Trevrizent, which in any case must go further than the limits of book IX alone. But even from book IX it is clear that Trevrizent is more than a prosaic, dry purveyor of interesting facts and more than an impersonal confessor. Wolfram is at pains to integrate Trevrizent into his highly populated knightly world and adds a mass of details in order to create a carefully individualized figure comparable with his other major characters. He has a distinct personality of his own apart from being the means whereby Parzival discovers his true self. The rest of this chapter will be an attempt to portray this personality in detail.

A comparison of the Trevrizent episodes in *Parʒival* with

(Weimar, 1952); Peter Wapnewski, *Wolframs Parʒival. Studien ʒur Religiosität und Form* (Heidelberg, 1955); P. B. Wessels, *Wolfram ʒwischen Dogma und Legende (Beitr.* (Tübingen), LXXVII, 1955); Herbert Kolb, *Schola Humilitatis. Ein Beitrag ʒur Interpretation der Gralerʒählung Wolframs von Eschenbach (Beitr.* (Tübingen), LXXVIII, 1956); H.-J. Koppitz, *Wolframs Religiosität. Beobachtungen über das Verhältnis Wolframs von Eschenbach ʒur religiösen Tradition des Mittelalters* (Bonn, 1959); Hugo Kuhn, *Parʒival. Ein Versuch über Mythos, Glaube und Dichtung im Mittelalter (Dt. Vjs.,* XXX, 1956); to mention only the more important ones.

[1] Julius Schwietering, *Die deutsche Dichtung des Mittelalters* (Potsdam, n.d. [1932)], p. 164.

Chrétien's depiction of the encounter between Perceval and the hermit uncle in the *Conte del Graal* shows from the very beginning the extent of Wolfram's elaborations and the increased significance of the part of the hermit uncle in the German poem. At the most rudimentary level the difference is shown through the fact that the 300 lines which Chrétien devotes to the incident are developed into a complex spiritual encounter covering 2100. Admittedly Wolfram generally expands the basis he finds in Chrétien, and often the expansion is filled with copious asides and garrulous digressions, but the instruction which the young Perceval receives from his uncle is pitifully sparse in comparison with the generous, and sometimes almost gratuitous, information with which Trevrizent showers Parzival. In order to appreciate properly the extent of Wolfram's contribution to the Grail legend here, we must first consider and analyze the material which Chrétien offered him.

CHRÉTIEN'S HERMIT

The actual meeting of Perceval with his uncle in Chrétien's work is immediately preceded by his encounter with three knights and their ladies, who are performing their customary acts of penitence for Good Friday. The fact that Perceval is bearing arms—an action to be avoided at all costs 'au jor que Jhesucris fu mors' (6260)—affords one of the knights the opportunity to inform Perceval of the holy day and to tell him that he should be venerating the Cross and bewailing his sins. He then continues with a short account of the Incarnation, mentioning the Blessed Virgin twice and telling of the conception of Christ by the Holy Ghost and of His dual nature as both man and God. He stresses that God became man and died 'por nos pechiez' (6274) and that His death rescued His friends from hell and brought the dead to life. After this follows a brief attack on the Jews, who through the Crucifixion did themselves irreparable harm, while at the same time bringing about the salvation of the believers. He concludes by declaring that all who believe ought on this day to do penance and by reiterating the obligation not to bear arms.

Thereupon Perceval asks where the company have come from

and what they have been doing and receives the reply that they have been seeking counsel and making their confession to 'un preudome', 'un saint hermite' (6303). On hearing this, Perceval is moved to tears, and the knight gives him directions to the hermit's abode.

Sighing deeply over his culpability towards God and weeping tears of repentance, Perceval makes his way to the hermitage, where he finds the hermit, a priest and a server just beginning to celebrate mass in a little chapel. The hermit notices Perceval's copious tears and calls to him, whereupon the young knight falls to his knees at the hermit's feet and begs his counsel. On being requested straight away to make his confession, he tells of his five years' wandering in unbelief and lack of love for God, only to be asked further why this should be so and to be told to pray for God's mercy. In answer Perceval recounts his visit to the Rois Pescheor and views all his suffering as stemming from the fact that he did not ask about the bleeding lance nor about the person for whom the Grail was brought in procession and that he never made amends for this, but rather persisted in ignoring God, from which he could not expect any mercy. The hermit's reaction to all this is to demand his penitent's name, and on hearing it he proceeds to recall an earlier sin of which Perceval is guilty, namely, that of causing his mother's death through his abrupt departure from her as a boy, and he regards this sin as being of such a quality that it prevented Perceval from asking the questions at the Grail castle. He says explicitly that Perceval was unaware of having committed this sin—'uns pechiez dont tu ne sez mot' (6393)—and thereby mitigates its gravity, though he does not attempt to excuse it. It is interesting to note at this point that there is a certain ambiguity about Chrétien's account of the death of Perceval's mother, since when the departing boy turns round to take a last look he sees his mother 'pasmee en tel maniere / Com s'ele fust cheüe morte' (624 f.). If we are meant to believe the hermit's statement, then we must attach considerable weight to the phrase 'com se', which would exculpate Perceval from complete aware-ness of the situation. But the earlier statement, despite the 'com se', contains a broad hint of the sin that is to be exposed later on. We should also note that the confession with the hermit has been prepared for by Perceval's encounter with his *germaine cousine*, the *pucele soʒ le chaisne*, who informed him of the sinfulness of his omissions at the Grail castle and of the fact that his departure caused his mother's death (3545 ff.). The hermit traces all Perceval's sufferings back to the sin of causing his mother's death and declares that they would have been much worse, had not the power of his mother's intercession led God to guard Perceval from death and prison. He sums everything up by saying that in the Grail castle 'Pechie[z] la langue te trencha' (6409).

At this point the hermit takes it upon himself to explain that the service of the Grail is conducted for his brother and that Perceval's mother is sister to them both. The *riches Pescheor*, he mentions *en passant*, is the son of the Grail king. The latter is, however, so saintly ('espiritax' 6426) that he needs nothing to keep him alive except a single host, which is borne in the Grail and apparently receives its virtue from it. For twelve years (MS. A says 'fifteen') he has lived in this manner, never going out of the room. In the face of all this sanctity the hermit desires Perceval to repent of his sins.

Perceval takes heart from the knowledge that the hermit is his uncle and assures him that he will repent. The hermit then lists a large number of things that Perceval is to do. Firstly, he should go to church every morning before doing anything else and let nothing stand in his way; he should go as soon as he hears the bell or before, if he is already up. In this way he will gain great profit. At mass he should stay until the priest has completely finished. And from the exercise of prayer he will derive both honour and salvation. He should love, trust and worship God, honour wise men and women and stand up in the presence of priests, which pleases God on account of the humility which it shows. He is to help damsels, widows and orphans to the best of his ability. All these things he should do for his sins, if he wishes to receive the graces which he had previously, and Perceval gladly accepts his direction.

The hermit whispers a prayer into Perceval's ear that contains names of God such that he should not reveal them except on pain of death. The service then follows, and at the end Perceval venerates the Cross and bewails his sins, thus taking up the advice of the knights and their ladies whom he met at the beginning of the episode. The succeeding two days he spends with the hermit, sharing his abstemious way of life, abstaining from all meat and eating only chervil, lettuce, cress, millet and barley and oat bread and drinking pure spring water. His horse, also taken care of, feeds on straw and barley. Perceval learns of God's death and crucifixion on Good Friday and communicates worthily on Easter Day. At this point the narrative breaks off the story of Perceval and returns to Gauvain.

This brief sketch of Perceval's encounter with his hermit uncle, containing a discussion of Perceval's religious problems in intimate connexion with certain details about the Grail, has been and still is the object of widely varying interpretations, particularly as to the nature of the Grail and the bleeding lance. It is not necessary for us, here, to come to any conclusion about the origin of these important symbols, but we must be aware that the Grail is 'tant sainte chose' that it and the host which it bears have sustained and comforted the life of the old king for twelve years. Whatever the nature of the Grail, whether it is originally a Celtic symbol related to the idea of the magic cauldron, or the *paropsis*, the platter from the Last Supper, or a relic,[1] to mention only three of the possibilities which have been suggested, it is in Chrétien's poem seen in such a setting as to be associated with the eucharistic sacrifice of the host. This fact is important, as the mood of the whole episode is concentrated on Perceval's sin and reinforced by the symbolism of Good Friday, the Cross and the mass, which all derive their meaning from the fact that Christ died in order that a believing mankind should be released from its sin. The purely religious suppositions of the episode, apart from the vexed question

---

[1] Paul Imbs, *L'Élément religieux dans le Conte del Graal de Chrétien de Troyes* in *Les Romans du Graal aux XIIe et XIIIe siècles. Colloques internationaux du Centre National de la Recherche Scientifique* (Paris, 1956), pp. 40 ff.

of the Grail, which, according to Frappier, is surrounded by 'une ambiguïté adroite',[1] are quite straightforwardly orthodox, and we can agree with Imbs, when he says: 'La christologie de Chrétien de Troyes est très simple, très traditionelle, mais avec une note paulinienne qui met l'accent sur le péché.'[2] The pattern of confession and penitence and the rules for Christian living which the hermit enjoins upon him for when he leaves his retreat are firmly situated in an ecclesiastical setting, in which the clergy, the church and the celebration of mass are essential elements. The hermit assumes the basis of Christian dogma on the Incarnation, given Perceval earlier by the penitent knight, and merely stresses that the young man should implore God's mercy. He adds nothing in the way of dogma, but offers Perceval a whole series of pieces of concrete advice as to how to profit in his spiritual life. In brief, this advice consists in the exercise of humility and penitence in acts of charity towards God and his neighbour. The visible acts of charity towards his neighbour are, in fact, identical with the conduct expected of a courtly knight:

> Preudome et preudefeme honeure,
> Contre les provoires te lieve;
>
> . . .
>
> Se pucele aïde te quiert,
> Aiue li, que miex t'en iert,
> Ou veve dame ou orfenine.
> Iceste almosne est enterine,
> Aiue lor, si feras bien. (6460 ff.)

The latter part of this advice had already been given Perceval in much the same words by Gornemant (1656 ff.). The only unusual part of Chrétien's *aperçu* of the Christian life is to be found in the account of the prayer whispered by the hermit in Perceval's ear, which, under the guise of names of God, probably represents a form of esoteric knowledge. Otherwise the type of religion that Chrétien presents is one of practical moral and ritual precepts.

---

[1] Jean Frappier, *Le Graal et l'hostie. Conte del Graal, v. 6413–6431 (ibid.)*, p. 75.

[2] Imbs, *op. cit.*, p. 46.

There does not seem to exist for him anything of the problems of *gote und der werlde gevallen*, which looms so large in the conceptions of Wolfram.

The question of Perceval's guilt, of his five years spent in alienation from God, is related to three sins in particular, namely, (i) that he did not ask why the lance was bleeding, (ii) that he did not ask for whom the service of the Grail took place, and (iii) that he caused the death of his mother through leaving her as a boy. This threefold exposition of Perceval's guilt is given also by his *germaine cousine* in exactly the same order with the same explanation that the chronologically first sin was of such a kind that it made it spiritually impossible for Perceval to ask the two questions at the Grail castle. No reference is made either by the *germaine cousine* or by the hermit to Gornemant's advice about not talking too much (1648 ff.), although Chrétien uses this as a justification for Perceval's conduct at the time of his visit (3343 ff.). The hermit sees the solution to Perceval's problem in repentance and a return to the ordered Christian life, and in his view compassion is the virtue which can bring about such a change in the knight's life:

> Se de t'ame pitié te prent,
> Si aies vraie repentance. (6440 f.)

And indeed it is perfectly in place to interpret Perceval's three major sins in terms of a lack of compassion, though with the Grail and the bleeding lance there is clearly present a strong element of irrationality and mystery. Some of the obscurities of this episode might have been clarified, if Chrétien had been able to finish his poem, but it is very probably the case that the obscurities were intentional and that the audience was deliberately mystified. The episode as we have it was in all probability meant to stand for itself.

Bodo Mergell, commenting on Burdach's 'Versuch, auch Chrestiens Gralfrage als Mitleidsfrage zu interpretieren',[1] is too predisposed to Wolfram to credit the French poet with even the beginnings of an interpretation of the Grail questions in the light

---

[1] Mergell, *op. cit.*, p. 142, n. 48.

of compassion. It is scarcely a matter of 'Wolframs Deutungen
... bereits in den Percevalroman hineinzutragen' when the words
are in fact already there. The fact that Chrétien suggests that
Perceval can overcome his guilt by embracing *pitié*—though
admittedly this aspect is not developed further—surely points out
that a lack of *pitié* is somehow linked with his not asking the
questions, and it is reasonable to assume that Perceval's attitude
towards his mother's fainting and subsequent death, which is used
as the reason for his later failure, was also caused by a lack of *pitié*.
I am far from wanting to attribute to Chrétien a complete motivation in these terms, since other elements clearly outweight this,
but the idea is definitely present in embryo. Wolfram's interpretation is not quite as much his own as Mergell would like it to be.
Mergell's analyses of Wolfram's every deviation from Chrétien in
terms of a broader outlook, a deeper conception of the poem as a
whole, an additional subtle touch, etc. are too much like those of
a man who sees what he wishes to find for them always to be
convincing.

The picture presented of the hermit is one of the strictest
orthodoxy. He is carefully placed in the context of ecclesiastical
rectitude, appearing in the company of clergy and showing great
deference towards them in his instruction to Perceval. He himself
is shown as a typical hermit, living a holy life in isolation from the
world, eating the abstemious fare prescribed for Lent, revered by
those in the world who know him, and obviously in the possession
of profound knowledge about the Grail and its entourage and
about the ways of God. There is, however, despite the explicit
use of the word *confession*, no unambiguous statement that the
uncle is either a priest or a layman. But as there is no question of
absolution being given and as a priest is mentioned as being present
also, it seems likely that he is a layman. All in all, there is nothing
very extraordinary about the religious content of the passage in
general.

With Wolfram, however, things are different. His hermit is, in
modern terms, 'quite a character' and has a background which
includes considerable experience in the knightly world as well as a

deep spiritual insight. Furthermore, he gives Parzival a much more thorough grounding in Biblical and Christian teaching with special reference to his particular sins, and he seems to be an almost inexhaustible purveyor of knowledge about the Grail and its community, while at the same time doing nothing to divest the Grail of its essential mystery. He is aware of himself as an individual with a particular background and a particular vocation, whereas Chrétien's hermit appears detached and, despite the uncle-nephew relationship, impersonal, as the priest in the confessional is impersonal. We must now proceed to a detailed study of Wolfram's Trevrizent, using the *sainz hermite* as a point of comparison.

DESCRIPTIVE PASSAGES

In accordance with Wolfram's method of incorporating his characters into the total fabric of his poem through mentioning them at various stages in the development of the story, Trevrizent appears at points in the poem which have no correspondence in the *Conte del Graal*, where the role of the *sainz hermite* is confined to the episode described above. In *Parzival* Trevrizent is introduced into the poem gradually, before he commands the stage in book IX. In this way Wolfram ensures him an existence which is more than merely functional.

He is first introduced indirectly, i.e. by being named and described, not by being physically active in the plot, and this occurs in Parzival's second meeting with Sigune. (There is a clear link in knowledge and spirituality between Sigune and Trevrizent, just as there is between the *germaine cousine* and the *sainz hermite*.) Sigune is telling her cousin about the members of the Grail family and mentions merely that of the children of Frimutel:

> der vierde hât armuot,
> durch got für sünde er daz tuot.
> der selbe heizet Trevrizent.   (251.13 ff.)

This immediately sets the tone for everything further connected with Trevrizent. The fact that he has adopted a life of poverty and penitence is an obvious pointer towards his ability to deal with

Parzival's sins at a later stage. Here, however, nothing more is said, but soon afterwards Trevrizent is mentioned again, though only as a passive character in the background, when Orilus has been defeated in a duel to re-establish Jeschute's honour. A third brief description is given by Kahenis quite some time later, just before Parzival spends his lengthy stay in the hermit's fastness, and this takes up and amplifies Signe's comment:

> iu ensitzet niht ze verre vor
> ein heilec man: der gît iu rât,
> wandel für iwer missetât.
> welt ir im riwe künden,
> er scheidet iuch von sünden. (448.22 ff.)

Trevrizent's basic function is now set out. He is a holy man to be resorted to for advice and with the power to relieve penitents from the burden of their sins.

The next passage (452.13 ff.), which introduces Trevrizent properly into the action of the poem, refers back to the visit of Orilus, and this reference has its purpose in suggesting that as Parzival was able to make amends about his gross behaviour towards Jeschute he will also be able to rectify his more serious sins. Wolfram's use of parallelism is amply demonstrated elsewhere in the poem. The passage continues with a catalogue of all the types of food and drink that Trevrizent has forsworn, which includes wine, bread, fish and meat. This is the outward form of a life dedicated to a heavenly salvation, achieved through fasting and sorrow and a struggle with the devil. The passage concludes with the statement that from him Parzival is to learn the secret lore of the Grail, which serves as a *point de départ* for Wolfram's long excursus about Kyot. It is characteristic of the intertwining of the themes of the Grail and Parzival's guilt that Kahenis sends Parzival off to Trevrizent in order to be absolved from sin, but that when he arrives there Wolfram mentions only the matter of discovering the nature of the Grail. The two themes are, as we have seen also in Chrétien, virtually inseparable: the one is the necessary explanation of the other.

The next and last descriptive passage (495.7–499.10) is of a very different order from the preceding ones. It is, in the first place, a passage of self-description and as such reveals a consciousness of individuality that is absent in Chrétien. The previous passages in Wolfram have been either statements by the author or statements by another person in the poem. Here, however, Trevrizent speaks on his own account, for himself, and tells about a part of his life that only he knows. This narration of his adventures as a young knight is the second way in which this passage differs from those that go before. It is of great importance in creating another dimension of Trevrizent's character and making him into a rounded, whole figure with a past as well as a present, and a past into the bargain that makes sense of the present. The passage occurs in the midst of an account of the customs governing the Grail community and, in particular, the prohibition of *minne* to all the Grail knights apart from the king. Trevrizent launches forth into a history of his own reckless youth and *wilde âventiure* and describes how the love of a worthy lady took hold of him and compelled him to undertake all kinds of extravagant exploits in her service, disdaining the normal art of the tournament, and how he won his reward of *freude* through the fiercest of battles with both pagan and Christian knights. For this lady he travelled over the three known continents of the earth, visiting a vast number of places, some corresponding to known geography, others being invented by Wolfram to indicate exotic regions, and others again belonging to the Grail territory and therefore being outside the range of the normal knight. In covering so many places and countries, Trevrizent has acquitted himself worthy of the name of knight (499.9 f.). As Marianne Wynn says:[1] 'The greater the distance covered, the more fantastic the countries visited, the more illustrious is the knight. Trevrizent is a member of the Grail kinship and his chivalrous deeds must therefore surpass those of Gahmuret. Thus his travel-history reveals even greater wonders than Gahmuret's.' In the course of these fantastic journeyings Trevrizent meets Parzival's father, Gahmuret, at Sibilje and mentions

[1] *Poetic Structure*, p. 50.

briefly his grief at Gahmuret's death in Baldac. These few lines about Gahmuret are especially important, since they constitute Parzival's main source of knowledge about his father, and, like most of his discoveries, they come from Trevrizent. (The only direct statement to Parzival that is found earlier occurs when Sigune tells him that his father was an Anschevin (140.25).) Trevrizent displays his great regard for Gahmuret, which was probably a kind of hero-worship, since the Grail knight was at that time still beardless. But more important than his meeting Gahmuret (though this establishes at a very early date the connexion between Gahmuret's kin and the Grail community) is the fact that Gahmuret gave Ither to him as a servant. This close personal relationship with Ither helps to explain that heavy emphasis that Trevrizent puts on Parzival's killing him. This point will be touched upon later; here it need only be noted that Gahmuret and Ither are grafted into the Wolframian system of relationships and that this significant connexion is made by Trevrizent in the course of a description of things important to him in his youth. The facts that Trevrizent tells us in this passage are important also for Parzival's growing awareness of himself and his destiny and for the audience in its endeavour to link the significance of the many strands of action in the poem. In relating his experiences as a young knight, Trevrizent adds to his qualifications for dealing with Parzival's particular problems, since he shows that he has first-hand knowledge of knightly life and that he too, like both Anfortas and Parzival, is involved in the guilt due to disobeying the divine command: 'über daz gebot ich mich bewac / daz ich nâch minnen dienstes pflac' (495.13 f.). Trevrizent's suitability for helping Parzival in his distress is, therefore, clearly established.

The description of Trevrizent's knightly career must be understood in the context of the synthesis between God and the world which forms the basic theme of Wolfram's poem. Because Trevrizent has personal experience of the ways of knightly society and of God's ways through his life as a hermit, he is able both to absolve Parzival from his sins and to give him knightly advice

(501.17 f.). This enlargement of Trevrizent's personality constitutes Wolfram's major divergence from Chrétien at this point and is one which brings out the individuality of Wolfram's characterization in opposition to the type characterization of Chrétien in this particular instance. However, the knightly adventures of Trevrizent and Anfortas in search of *minne* form a complete contrast to those of Parzival, who remains constant to Condwiramurs throughout his wanderings. Both Trevrizent and Anfortas have sinned against the ideal of *minne* which Wolfram sets up, and their 'solution' is therefore an other-worldly one, whereas Parzival has a justified relationship and therefore does not need to renounce the world in any way. Thus, the sin of Parzival is to be looked for outside the sphere of *minne* and mere knightly activity, in which he is pre-eminent.

SYNONYMS

The range of synonyms used for Trevrizent is not extensive, but it includes everything that appears elsewhere as a part of his character. Wolfram sees him as more than just the saintly hermit of Chrétien's work, though this aspect is obviously paramount.

To begin with, there are a variety of expressions used to create a basis of sanctity. Of these the word *einsidel* is the one first used (268.30), and it is repeated in book IX (456.5), where it describes Trevrizent on Parzival's arrival at his cell. The penitent knight, as we can only expect from him, refers to *ein heilec man* (448.23), when he offers Parzival advice as to what he should do on this Good Friday morning. These two expressions are the most precise indications of Trevrizent's eremitical existence, but there are two others, which are very closely allied, though of wider significance, namely, the phrase *der guote man*[1] and the adjective *kiusche*.[2]

The synonym *der guote man* in its literal meaning of 'the good man', i.e. a man of high moral virtue, presents no problem whatsoever. But there have been, and still are, scholars who wish to connect this with the Cathar idea of the *perfectus* or the *bons om*,

[1] 457.2, 458.25, 460.19, 476.23, 487.24, 799.13.
[2] 452.15, 459.22, 472.12, 493.9.

since they see in Trevrizent's religious teaching and practice an analogy with the Cathar heresy. The factors which have led (or rather, misled) some critics of Wolfram on to this dangerous path are contained in his elaborations and additions to Chrétien's account and consist of such topics as lay confession, fasting and the neutral angels. The attempt to solve the question of lay confession, which lies at the root of the problem, by recourse to Catharism only leads into a theological jungle from which there is no return. The manifest contradictions between the text and the Cathar theory force Zeydel, the latest exponent of the doctrine,[1] into the most extraordinary muddled thinking in modern *Parzival* research. It is not my intention to refute Zeydel or the Cathar case here, as this task has been signally accomplished by P. B. Wessels,[2] who explains Trevrizent's theology in a much more acceptable fashion by reference to contemporary orthodox dogma and popular legend. We may, therefore, understand the term *der guote man* as a purely factual statement of Trevrizent's moral worth and link it with the idea of his sanctity.

The word *kiusche* is, like *der guote man*, not a specifically religious term, but refers to moral purity and is normally found in Wolfram's writing as the word which subsumes all other moral values.[3] It is, nevertheless, used in three instances in a plainly religious context—firstly, in connexion with Trevrizent's fasting (452.15); secondly, in the description of the hermit's religious possessions, i.e. the altar, the casket and his books; and thirdly, just before he makes his celebrated speech on *hôchvart* (472.12). The fourth example of its use occurs when Trevrizent is describing Anfortas' misery and the attempts of the Grail community to heal his wound. In all these cases the word is used in such a way that Trevrizent's moral and spiritual authority is emphasized at the particular point in question. It is a more general variant on the

---

[1] Edwin H. Zeydel, *Wolframs Parzival, 'Kyot' und die Katharer* (*Neoph.*, XXXVII, 1953), pp. 25–35.

[2] P. B. Wessels, *Wolfram zwischen Dogma und Legende* (*Beitr.* (Tübingen), LXXVII, 1955), pp. 112–24. Cf. also Oskar Katann, *Einflüsse des Katharertums auf Wolframs Parzival* (*WW*, VIII, 1957/8), pp. 321–9.

[3] See the chapter on Gahmuret, p. 36, fn. 1.

theme of Trevrizent's high spiritual stature, and the fact that it is used significantly for other characters helps to link Trevrizent's moral superiority with the more ordinary moral worth of others, thereby protecting him against the complete spiritual isolation that would otherwise be his chief characteristic. It is important that Trevrizent should appear in as many ways as possible as an integral member of the Grail family, and it is in the use of such small touches as the use of an adjective (which are significant through multiplication) that Wolfram frequently makes the matter of kinship real. The use of one adjective is perhaps in itself not very striking, but when it is supported by other similar little indications, the total effect is quite clear. Wolfram retains and intensifies the high esteem that attaches to Chrétien's hermit, but he also takes care that the esteem does not necessitate a complete isolation of character.

The kinship motifs which form so vital a part of the whole poem are made explicit in the use of the word *œheim*, though it occurs only twice (488.4, 799.1), being qualified the first time by the addition of the intimate adjective *liep*. This first instance is the only occasion on which Parzival calls his uncle anything but *hêr* (*hêrre*), the normal term of address, which he uses both before and after the two have discovered each other's identity.[1] Normally Wolfram refers to Trevrizent as *der wirt*, a word of very general application[2] and one which is used frequently for many of the other male characters at some time or other. The kinship relationship between Parzival and Trevrizent is obviously important in Wolfram's scheme, so that at first sight it seems odd that it should not be made more explicit in the synonymy. The fact is, however, that the emphasis is always put on Parzival, and the relationship is underlined through frequent reference to him as *neve*.[3] Despite the closeness of the relationship a certain distance is maintained

---

[1] 452.25, 456.29, 457.5, 460.2.6.18, 461.3, 464.2, 467.12, 474.30, 475.4, 486.27, 488.4.20, 500.5.13.19.

[2] 457.11.21, 458.26, 459.5.9.20, 460.1, 461.27, 464.7, 467.19, 468.1.18.23, 472.18, 474.26, 475.14, 485.3.21.23, 486.15.21, 487.27, 488.3, 492.2.23, 494.15.19, 500.1.11.26, 501.12.22.

[3] See above, p. 109.

between the uncle and the nephew in that Parzival, even after he has learnt of their relationship, continues to address his uncle as *ir* and *hêrre*, and the one occasion on which he uses the word *œheim* is, in fact, combined with *hêrre*. Trevrizent, on the other hand, changes to the *du* form of the verb immediately he realizes Parzival's identity and from then on always calls him *neve*. The initiative and outgoing warmth of understanding and sympathy during the whole of book IX belong to Trevrizent. It is he who has to break down the barriers between them, and it is only gradually that he is able to help the young man and be accepted by him. The spiritual gulf between them is one of Parzival's making, and it is merely indicative of the true state of his poverty and of his personal relationships that he should with one timid utterance of the word *œheim* begin to realize his own failure and follow the path Trevrizent points out to him.

Trevrizent's function as Parzival's spiritual director is further stressed when he characterizes himself as *râtes iwer wer* (475.3), *dîn râtes wer* (489.21) and *dîn wandels wer* (502.26). Could there be a greater personal awareness of his role as a guide to Parzival, as an embodiment of spiritual security and a representative of God's forgiveness? This self-awareness that Trevrizent possesses marks his individuality in a way that a mere description on the part of the author would not. He speaks for himself, and in so doing he expresses the true depths of his personality and his concern for Parzival and his particular problems. Despite his laity he is an expert *Seelsorger* and manifests that clear individuality which, paradoxically, true devotion to God as the *summum bonum* only enhances.

One more synonym remains to be treated—that of *leie* (462.11). Hans Naumann[1] has shown that constructions with *doch*, *swie* and *swâ* plus the subjunctive (as 'doch ich ein leie wære') are definitely used in a concessive sense and do not imply an unreal condition, so that we can be sure of Trevrizent's laity. But this laity does not allow of any introduction of rank heresy, as some

---

[1] Hans Naumann, *Doch ich ein leie wære* (*Arch.*, CLXXXVIII, 1951), pp. 116–17.

scholars have too readily assumed.[1] The matter of lay confession was not uncommon in the twelfth and thirteenth centuries, and although the practice was permitted only in extremity and the confession had to be repeated to a priest as soon afterwards as possible, there was nonetheless, according to the teaching of Albertus Magnus, a certain absolution present: 'Sed tamen absolutio quaedam est hic, sc. quae fit merito unitatis ecclesiae.'[2] Trevrizent certainly does not exclude the priesthood from his conception of religious life, so that he cannot be accused of inveighing against the established ecclesiastical system. Indeed, as Parzival is about to leave him at the end of book IX, he counsels him to pay particular respect and service to the priesthood (502.7 ff.). The fact that both Trevrizent and Wolfram in general are concerned with personal religious life does not mean that they spurn the ecclesiastical order of their time. Their views are meant to be seen within this framework. The concentration of Trevrizent on the pursuit of *diemüete* is surely stressed by the fact of his laity; the issue is not intended to be complicated by it. Wolfram did not want Trevrizent and Parzival to be separated through belonging to different *ordines*; he wanted to create a unity between them based on their belonging to the same family and their sharing the same type of spiritual problems. Trevrizent is, in book IX, manifestly more advanced in religion than Parzival, but his holiness is personal in the same way as his relationship with Parzival is personal; it is not a holiness deriving from a particular office. His laity is therefore an individualizing factor, since if he had been a priest his sanctity would have been more usually associated with the priesthood and not with his own personal qualities. Through stressing Trevrizent's laity Wolfram is able to show that he is more concerned with analysing Parzival's problems than with presenting a picture of orthodox dogma (though at almost all points his picture is orthodox) such as would be expected from a priest. At all times we are made aware that Trevrizent is speaking from his own spiritual experience, whereas a priest could at this period only be

---

[1] See above, pp. 296 f.   [2] Wessels, *op. cit.*, pp. 114 f.

regarded as speaking representatively for the Church and not in his own personal capacity. Trevrizent's laity must consequently be looked upon as a clear indication of his individuality.

TREVRIZENT AND THE QUESTION OF PARZIVAL'S GUILT

At Parzival's meeting with Kahenis, the old knight tells him that a holy man will give him advice, convert him from his former offences and, if he shows sorrow for them, deliver him from his sins (448.23 ff.). A little further on Wolfram declares that from Trevrizent Parzival will learn the secret lore of the Grail (452.29 ff.). The two matters are obviously interrelated and nowhere more so than in the so-called *Mitleidsfrage*,[1] which Parzival failed to put to Anfortas on his first visit to Munsalvæsche. This failure, together with the many other misdeeds and sins of Parzival, is the crux of the entire poem, and many scholars have racked their brains and spilt much ink about it with the result that much light has been shed on individual aspects of the problem, though many would not regard it, even now, as being satisfactorily solved. In recent years painstaking attention has been paid to the theological background of Trevrizent's pronouncements and particularly to Augustinian conceptions of sin, penitence and satisfaction.[2] In general this research has met with approval, though there is at least one dissident voice.[3] It would, however, go far beyond the bounds of this study to discuss in detail the theological points involved. As Schwietering so rightly points out, 'Es geht ja nicht um einen wissenschaftlichen Traktat sondern um Dichtung'.[4] We should not expect from Wolfram an expert's knowledge of theological subtleties for which there is no clear evidence that it was available to him. Even if Wolfram's disclaimers of book-knowledge (115.25 ff., *Wh.* 2.19 ff.) are not to be understood

---

[1] I do not intend by the use of the term *Mitleidsfrage* to prejudge the meaning of the question by which Anfortas can be released, but use it merely as a form of shorthand. For a full discussion of the problem see below, pp. 342 ff.

[2] See the contributions by Maurer and Wapnewski mentioned in note 1, p. 283 above.

[3] That of Herbert Kolb. See his review of Wapnewski's book (*Euph.* LII, 1958, pp. 82–94).

[4] Julius Schwietering, *Parzivals Schuld* (*ZfdA*, LXXXI, 1944/5), p. 64.

literally,[1] their purpose is surely to indicate that the meaning of his work is to be found within it and not by introducing ideas from outside. Wolfram chose to write a *poem* in order to express his ideas about human life; he did not sum them up in a mathematical or astrological formula, nor did he define them in a philosophical or theological treatise. First and foremost he was interested in people; there can be no doubt about this from the great store he sets on names and on personal encounters. Parzival's meeting with Trevrizent is developed in a most delicate and sympathetic manner, revealing similarities between the two at many points and showing how deeply a personal encounter can go. Wolfram uses theology only as a means of expressing an 'echte Begegnung' (to use a term of Buber's), not as an end in itself.

Trevrizent stands last and most important in the line of Parzival's educators—Herzeloyde, Gurnemanz, Sigune, Trevrizent. In this class of educators Sigune holds a special position, since Parzival meets her at four successive stages in his career and learns quite clear, positive things from her to meet the immediate situation. The teachings of Herzeloyde and Gurnemanz are abstract generalizations, and from following them without discrimination Parzival goes completely astray and indeed, through a mistaken reliance on Gurnemanz' advice: 'irn sult niht vil gevrâgen' (171.17), fails to ask the fateful *Mitleidsfrage*. Gurnemanz' advice is designed to teach Parzival the proper rudiments of courtly life and as such is a perfect summary of knightly requirements. But since Parzival is destined for a higher calling than that of a mere courtly knight, the instruction of both Herzeloyde and Gurnemanz is insufficient and *verhängnisvoll:*

Herzeloyde hat Parzivals Blick auf das Fernste, auf Gott, gerichtet, ohne ihm den Weg durch das Rittertum zu ebnen. Gurnemanz hat Parzivals Blick auf das Nächstliegende, auf das Rittertum, eingeengt, ohne ihm den Weg über die höfische Bildungswelt hinaus zu zeigen zu seiner sittlichen Vollendung. Beide haben nicht den richtigen und Parzivals Entwicklung gemäßen Weg der Erziehung eingeschlagen.[2]

[1] Cf. Hans Eggers, *Non cognovi litteraturam* (*zu Parzival 115, 27*) in the Festgabe Ulrich Pretzel (Berlin, 1963).
[2] Nora Schneider, *Erziehergestalten im höfischen Epos*, p. 66.

Gurnemanz had prefaced his instruction with the sentence:

> habt iuch an mînen rât:
> der scheidet iuch von missetât   (170.13 f.)

but now, in book IX, the old knight says of Trevrizent:

> der gît iu rât,
> wandel für iwer missetât.
> welt ir im riwe künden,
> er scheidet iuch von sünden.   (448.23 ff.)

Through these two parallel passages we are immediately conscious of the vastly different planes of life with which Gurnemanz and Trevrizent are concerned. The former occupies himself solely with the ethical presuppositions of courtliness; the latter brings human behaviour into the realms of the religious. From Gurnemanz' point of view Parzival would be protected from *missetât* if he followed his advice. It follows from this that, according to the courtly ethic, Parzival is not guilty of any moral wrong in not asking the *Mitleidsfrage*, so there is, from the same standpoint, nothing amiss in Parzival's admission to the Round Table. From the point of view of the Grail community, however, Parzival's failure must be reckoned *sünde* and, moreover, *sünde* of the deepest possible dye.[1] When Cundrie overwhelms Parzival with her curses and makes no bones about his depravity, she explicitly declares: 'da erwarb iu swîgen sünden zil' (316.23). His *sünde* is so enormous that, despite the fact that it is no misdeed according to courtly standards,

> tavelrunder ist entnihtet:
> der valsch hât dran gepflihtet.
>
> . . .
>
> tavelrunder prîses kraft
> hât erlemt ein geselleschaft
> die drüber gap hêr Parzivâl,
> der ouch dort treit diu rîters mâl.   (314.29 ff.)

---

[1] The word *sünde* covers a wide range of meanings, as Maurer (*op. cit.*, pp. 143 ff.) has pointed out. If at this stage it cannot be strictly defined in the religious sense, it nonetheless denotes an extremely grave misdeed.

Further on Cundrie tells Parzival quite plainly: 'sîn [sc. Anfortas'] nôt iuch solt erbarmet hân' (316.3), taking up in almost identical terms the execration that Sigune had hurled on him a little earlier (255.17). Parzival's apparent lack of compassion is seen by both Cundrie and Sigune as an affront to the circle of Arthurian knights —'ze Munsalvæsche an iu verswant / êre unt rîterlîcher prîs' (255.26 f.)—but it is more than just this, and this extra significance is the crux of the matter.

Parzival's reaction to Cundrie's curse marks the crisis of his life. He is forced at this point to make a decision of his own instead of relying blindly upon the advice of others. He realizes that Gurnemanz' instruction must somehow have been inadequate for him, but though he muses on the failure caused by adhering to the courtly virtue of *zuht* and cannot understand why it should have led him into his present plight, he does not rail against Gurnemanz' wholly excellent character.[1] The root of the problem is to be found in the depths of Parzival's own character, but in face of his inability to comprehend the curse that has befallen him he concludes that God is the originator of all his troubles. In answer to Gawan's commending him to God as he sets out on his journey, he launches into a tirade against Him:

> 'wê waz ist got?
> wær der gewaldec, sölhen spot
> het er uns pêden niht gegebn,
> kunde got mit kreften lebn.
> ich was im diens undertân,
> sît ich genâden mich versan.
> nu wil i'm dienst widersagn:
> hât er haz, den wil ich tragn'.   (332.1 ff.)

Parzival's reaction is to refuse to take personal responsibility for his moral failure and to turn away from trust in God. With this decision boyhood immaturity and unquestioning acceptance of all advice given him come to an end, but in their place a spirit of rebellion arises. Parzival considers that God has unjustifiably

---

[1] See Hilda Swinburne, *Parzival's Crisis* (*MLR*, L, 1955), p. 184.

spurned his earnest efforts to serve Him and is not the genuine bestower of mercy that he had imagined. He regards their relationship as one demanding reciprocity, more or less in terms of a feudal relationship between a lord and his knights. Since, according to Parzival's view, God has failed in His duty of protecting His subjects, Parzival feels that he can legitimately sever his bond. His consequent journeys and adventures consist in an abortive attempt to realize his self-sufficiency, going to the very extreme of defiance. This *Gotteshaß*, the sin of *superbia* or *hôchvart*, of complete egocentricity, lies at the centre of Parzival's conversations with Trevrizent. It is not so much Parzival's individual sins that are the subject of Trevrizent's instruction as his spiritual state in general. Where the individual sins are discussed, they are dealt with in the light of Parzival's present condition and not merely for their own sake. Book IX must be interpreted according to its total content and in the light of its place in the poem as a whole, not by means of a detailed and perhaps over-literal discussion of certain 'key-passages'.

If we look at Chrétien's assessment of Perceval's guilt, we shall immediately realize the extent to which Wolfram differs. Kellermann's illuminating coinage of 'Schuldautomatismus'[1] denotes the simple fact that because Perceval by his departure caused his mother's death, therefore he was unable to ask the two questions at the Grail castle. Perceval's reaction to the curse of the *laide damoisele* is merely to prove his worth through performing deeds of knightly valour (cf. Erec and Yvain). There is no outburst comparable to that of Wolfram's Parzival. Wolfram clearly rejects Chrétien's interpretation of Perceval's guilt as a total explanation, but uses the *données* of Chrétien's story to elaborate Parzival's defection and widen its scope. The emphasis is moved from the particular failure at the Grail castle to the basis of Parzival's character in general, of which the particular 'sins' are the outward manifestation and which contains almost from the beginning the seeds of *hôchvart*.

[1] W. Kellermann, *Aufbaustil und Weltbild Chrestiens von Troyes im Perceval-roman* (Halle, 1936), p. 109.

In order to evaluate more clearly Trevrizent's position in help-ing Parzival to grow into a right relationship with God and learn more about the Grail, we must first examine the immediately preceding episodes which lead up to their encounter, since they amount to about one quarter of the whole book (552 lines as against 2100).

After Wolfram's introductory remarks, which are calculated to refresh the audience about the poem's real hero, regaled as they have been with the adventures of Gawan, we learn how Parzival meets his cousin Sigune for the third time. On recognizing Parzival Sigune straight away goes to the point and enquires: 'wie stêtz iu umben grâl?' (440.30). This prompt question under-lines the fact, which we must never forget, that Parzival's primary occupation, upon which all else depends, is his search for the Grail.[1] Everything has to be viewed in the light of this, not least the religious problem of his guilt. Sigune realizes that Parzival has mellowed and become more acutely aware of his own insuffi-ciency, and this enables her to reconcile herself with him, offering him advice as to what to do.[2] She answers his request for help by reminding Parzival of Him 'dem aller kumber ist bekant' (442.10) and by directing him to follow Cundrie's tracks, in the hope that this might lead him back to the Grail. This plan is thwarted through the intervention of one of the *templeisen*, who attacks Parzival as he approaches too near the Grail territory. But although his onslaught does in fact prevent Parzival from pene-trating once more into Munsalvæsche, the Grail knight is knocked down a ravine, from where he makes his escape, and Parzival takes possession of his horse, since his own has been killed in the process. The outcome of this joust suggests again that Parzival's fortunes are on the turn. To be sure he does not manage to return into the Grail country proper, but he secures a Grail horse for his

---

[1] For a fuller discussion of the significance of Parzival's third encounter with Sigune see the section on *Parzival and Sigune* in the chapter on Parzival, pp. 182 ff.

[2] See Benedikt Mockenhaupt, *Die Frömmigkeit im Parzival Wolframs von Eschenbach* (Bonn, 1941/2), p. 87.

pains, and this can be reckoned as the first tangible fruit of Parzival's gradual change and as a foretaste of the Grail itself.

There then follows a further period of wandering of undetermined length before Parzival meets, one snowy morning, the knight Kahenis, his wife and two daughters, all dressed in the garments of penitents. There could scarcely be a greater contrast than this between the simple, poor penitential garb of the pilgrims and the deliberate finery of Parzival's armour to mark the spiritual differences of the two on this Good Friday. The starkness of the contrast reveals how far, despite the signs of change already noted and apparent, Parzival is still removed from an acceptance of obedience to God's will. Kahenis, filled with the spirit of devotion to 'got . . ., den man durch uns anz kriuze hienc' (448.11 f.) and distressed at Parzival's unseemly appearance, immediately points out to him the wrongness of wearing armour on such a holy day. The young knight, very significantly, pleads ignorance as the extenuation of his apparel, but goes on to state his position in brief, but quite unambiguous terms, virtually repeating his original outburst to Gawan. The grey knight in his reply shows himself deeply concerned for the state of Parzival's soul, answering his obstinate excuses by dwelling on the fact of God's love for man as expressed in the Crucifixion, commemorated on the day of their meeting, on Good Friday. He tries to show that Parzival's claims are contradicted by experience, thus indicating obliquely that if there is any defect in Parzival's relationship with God the fault must be on Parzival's side. In conclusion he advises him to seek advice and absolution from a holy man living not very far away.

Kahenis' daughters, however, whose physical beauty greatly attracts Parzival, direct their father's attention to the young knight's bodily needs, frozen as he is with his armour. There is a continual mingling of the physical and the spiritual in this episode, the one reflecting and emphasizing the other, since Parzival's physical condition is seen as the outward manifestation of his inner state of mind and soul. The cold from which he suffers is emblematic of his spiritual deprivation and his exclusion from both the Grail and Arthurian circles. It is at this point that he is associated most closely with Anfortas and his sin, since the Grail king also suffers keenly from intense bodily cold as a result of his wound, and the extent of his pain is measured by increases in cold more bitter than frost and by the presence of snow in summer. When Parzival's obvious discomfort has been brought to Kahenis' attention, he offers to take him to his tent and share his food and comfort, but Parzival feels unable to accept his warm hospitality, so alien does he feel his own mood and appearance to be:

> er dâhte 'ob ich erwinde,
> ich gên ungerne in dirre schar.
> dise meide sint sô wol gevar,
> daz mîn rîten bî in übel stêt,
> sît man und wîp ze fuoz hie gêt.
> sich füegt mîn scheiden von in baz,
> sît ich gein dem trage haz,
> den si von herzen minnent
> unt sich helfe dâ versinnent.
> der hât sîn helfe mir verspart
> und mich von sorgen niht bewart'.   (450.12 ff.)

In this interior monologue Parzival expresses a sense of shame for his position. The obvious piety of the grey knight and his family is having its impact on him in that he is becoming ever more acutely conscious that it is he who has failed God and not vice versa. Nevertheless Parzival is not sufficiently advanced in his awareness to be able to accept the knight's help and thereby identify himself with Kahenis' belief and devotion. Instead he takes polite leave of them and rides away. Their comments, however, have not gone unheeded. Parzival's thoughts, influenced by the power of *triuwe* inherited from his mother, turn to sorrow for his unhappy state. Then, brought to the point where he can of his own strength do nothing further, he entrusts himself to God's will by allowing his horse a free rein. The horse takes him 'nâch der gotes kür' (452.9) to Trevrizent.

The encounters with Sigune and Kahenis have prepared Parzival very thoroughly for the two linked purposes of his meeting with Trevrizent. Firstly, he is now sufficiently contrite to come to terms with his sinfulness; and secondly, he has reached the stage at which he can be initiated into the secrets of the Grail. These two questions are dealt with in direct, personal terms, in which theological concepts are used for clear and practical ends. Trevrizent is attempting to put across a religious *attitude*, one of *diemüete*, rather than give a series of carefully formulated dogmas. He proceeds with an inner, if not always an obvious, logic from one point to another in his conversation with Parzival until the latter finds himself able to confess the sin most weighing on his conscience. Trevrizent the whole time acts and speaks in a generous spirit, inviting confidence and gently probing into the recesses of Parzival's religious consciousness. From the beginning he is characterized by a welcoming nature and treats Parzival with the great courtesy that befits a true host, despite the fact that he has little physical comfort to offer. But these acts of kindness—the invitation to come inside from the cold and warm himself by the fire,[1] taking care of Parzival's horse, giving him a cloak to keep himself warm, digging up roots for them to eat—are indicative of a welcome which is spiritual as well. With the same meticulous care Trevrizent deals with Parzival's spiritual needs.

As soon as Parzival arrives at Trevrizent's cell, the hermit shrewdly realizes the basis of *hôchvart* underlying the young man's behaviour. He takes up Kahenis' remark that Parzival ought not to be bearing arms on such a holy day and expresses a sentiment that might well have come from Friedrich von Hausen:[2]

> hât iuch âventiure
> ûz gesant durch minnen solt,
> sît ir rehter minne holt,
> sô minnt als nu diu minne gêt,
> als disses tages minne stêt:
> dient her nâch umbe wîbe gruoz.

---

[1] The physical warmth that Trevrizent offers Parzival immediately links up with the symbolism of heat and cold mentioned above, pp. 274 f. The fire (456.15) and the *glüendige koln* (459.7) are signs of Trevrizent's spiritual knowlege, which he is now inviting Parzival to share. The warmth that Parzival gains and the light which then gleams from his skin foreshadow the spiritual benefit which he will later derive.

[2] *MF* 47.5 ff., quoted above, p. 238.

Parzival's priorities are all wrong, and Trevrizent loses no time in putting him on to the right path. This clear assessment of the situation in terms of *hôchvart* sets the tone for the rest of Parzival's stay with Trevrizent and is never lost sight of. It forms a constant background for the revelation of Parzival's particular sins, although it is not frequently explicitly taken up again. The most outstanding example of *hôchvart* is, of course, Anfortas, whose sin is even more heinous than that of Parzival himself. But more of this later.— Parzival accepts Trevrizent's judgement with great decorum in view of the pilgrims' advice, and the accusation elicits a corresponding admission, from which the first practical change in him takes place: 'hêr, nu gebt mir rât: / ich bin ein man der sünde hât' (456.29 f.). Trevrizent in answer gladly takes up Parzival's cause, but first makes a diversion to find out how the knight had made his way to him. The initial step has been made; there is now time for a few more narrative and explanatory details before the question is gone into more deeply.

This first interlude (457.5–460.27) serves a multiple purpose. In the first instance Trevrizent tells Parzival a few details about the knight who directed him to his cell, and by the information he gives he establishes—if there had previously been any doubt in the matter—Kahenis' *bona fides*. In a few swift strokes Wolfram presents a miniature of the knight's character, family background and history, creating—as is his usual practice—a named individual out of Chrétien's anonymous, typical figure. Kahenis acts at this stage as a contrast-figure to Parzival in two respects particularly. Parzival himself refers to him as *der selbe valsches frie*, whereas Cundrie in her curse had imputed *valsch* to the young knight[1] (though it should be remembered that before this incident of the curse Wolfram had twice (249.1, 296.1) praised Parzival's lack of *valsch*). Furthermore, Trevrizent says of Kahenis: 'der ist werdeclîcher fuore al wîs' (457.12), while he later on explains Parzival's defection at Munsalvæsche as being caused by *tumpheit*.[2] The *Dümmling* motif is such an important part of the characterization of Parzival, particularly up to book VI, that its overtones

---

[1] 314.30. See above, p. 169.   [2] See below, pp. 350 ff.

echo on into book IX with the result that this contrast between him on the one hand and Kahenis and Trevrizent on the other fits clearly and beautifully into the pattern of the whole poem.

Following this information about Kahenis, Parzival is prompted to ask whether his appearance frightened Trevrizent or caused him *leit*. This question, which betokens Parzival's concern lest he should have occasioned any unnecessary anxiety or harm and which is a practical sign of his growing humble spirit, also offers Trevrizent an excellent opportunity for telling him something of his former life and thus for establishing a link between them with regard to their common knightly background. He starts by saying that a bear or a stag would alarm him more than a man, since the life of a hermit is not his natural occupation, and from this he goes on to relate how he also used to be a knight in pursuit of *hôhe minne*, like Parzival, living his life in such a way as to obtain *genâde* from a lady. But he tells also of a fall from grace through cherishing *sündebærn gedanc* in opposition to *kiusche*. This dark hint of Trevrizent's past remains mysterious even when it is amplified later on, as we never learn the name of the lady who corrupted his virtue. For the time being, however, it serves as a sufficient (though as it happens a wrong) justification for Trevrizent's life as a hermit. The few details that Wolfram gives are typical of his method of characterization, for rarely does he give a complete picture of an important character in one go. His manner is usually to paint in his portrait gradually, making a few strokes at a time, and in his way he gives a more convincing characterization, since the reader feels that he is getting to know a real, well-rounded person and not being presented with a ready-made image that undergoes no modification or development. It is, however, the initial fact of Trevrizent's past sin which interests us here, since this clearly puts him, in one respect, on a level with Parzival and enables the latter more easily to confess his sin, knowing that Trevrizent has also been in the same position. The parallelism is important in that we are shown a Trevrizent who has conquered sin, and the thought cannot be far from the reader's mind that what Trevrizent has achieved must be reckoned with also for Parzival.

This thought is reinforced by the recounting of another incident. Parzival, in catching sight of a casket on Trevrizent's altar, remembers his previous visit and what happened then:

> dar ûffe Parzivâles hant
> swuor einen ungefelschten eit,
> dâ von froun Jeschûten leit
> ze liebe wart verkêret
> unt ir fröude gemêret. (459.26 ff.)

The fact that on this occasion Parzival was able to make good the injury he inflicted on Jeschute gives the reader reason to believe that what he accomplished then he is likely to repeat. Thus Wolfram, without making any direct statement to encourage it, provides the reader with two hints as to what the outcome of Parzival's sojourn with Trevrizent will be.

Parzival, at the same time as he recognizes the casket, recalls that he had taken a spear from Trevrizent's cell, with which he fought both Keie and Segramors when he was *verdâht* at the sight of the three drops of blood on the snow, and he is curious to know how long ago it was since he took it. Trevrizent's answer, guaranteed by his counting according to the use of the psalter, calculates the time between Parzival's two visits to his cell at four and a half years and three days. This provides an easy link with the next section of Parzival's spiritual confession, since he attempts to give some account of his activities during this time and thereby pinpoints more specifically the *sünde* to which he had confessed only in general terms.

Parzival now becomes more fully conscious of his desolation of spirit and the burden of sorrow that he bears and tells Trevrizent of the two sins which most oppress him—his failure to join in worship at any church or monastery, and his hatred towards God as the originator of all his troubles. These two sins express two intimately connected aspects of Parzival's condition: the *haʒ gein gote* is the root of his sin, his basic attitude towards life; the failure to go to church[1] is the outward manifestation of it, the flower which

---

[1] The failure to go to church is not very clearly motivated as an important sin. Gurnemanz, though he teaches Parzival the rudiments of church ritual, does

the root has nourished and produced. The *haʒ gein gote* is the sin of *ʒwível*, the lack of trust in God, the sin against *triuwe* or *caritas*, which arises from egocentricity, or, as Gottfried Weber puts it, the 'unbereinigter Geltungswille des um sich selbst kreisenden Ichs',[1] the sin of *hôchvart* or *superbia*. All these are variations, with slightly different emphases or from slightly differing angles, of the same basic theme of *ʒwível* as it is described in the prologue,[2] a theme which winds its way through the whole of the poem and cannot be forced into the terms of a short definition. Indeed, it is only through reading the whole poem that one can come to an understanding of what Wolfram means by *ʒwível*, and this is, accordingly, a complex and all-embracing idea.

In outlining his estrangement from God and its history, Parzival declares: 'ichn suochte niht wan strîten' (461.8), a statement which reminds one of Parzival's heritage from Gahmuret, of whom Wolfram wrote that 'strît und minne was sîn ger' (35.25) and whose life consisted in an unsuccessful attempt to balance these two opposing facets of his personality. The parallelism of Gahmuret's and Parzival's careers at this point is quite striking, since it is the exclusive desire that both have for *strîten* which leads them astray—Gahmuret to his death in battle, Parzival to his entanglement in the affairs of the knightly world and consequent alienation from God. In following in his father's footsteps Parzival fails to be true to his full heritage, which includes his membership of the Grail family through his mother Herzeloyde. To be sure, he is seeking for the Grail—this is mentioned continually—but he is seeking it with his father's methods alone despite the fact that Sigune has told him that he can only reach the Grail castle *unwiʒʒende* (250.29 f.). Parzival imagines that he can rehabilitate himself in the usual manner of Arthurian heroes by performing

---

not lay upon him the duty of attending mass in the course of giving his advice, and the lives of both Sigune and Trevrizent are led apart from the normal conventions of churches and monasteries. The mention of this particular failure does make it clear, however, that Wolfram was not against the orthodox practices of the Church, as some critics occasionally have claimed.

[1] Gottfried Weber, *Parʒival. Ringen und Vollendung* (Oberursel, 1948), p. 43.
[2] See above, pp. 189 ff.

knightly deeds demanding great bravery, but in his case more is at stake than mere knightly *êre*: there is a spiritual disgrace which cannot be solved precisely in this way. This fact Trevrizent points out when he tells the young knight: 'irn megt im [sc. God] ab erzürnen niht' (463.1). But this is far from meaning that all *strîten* must be avoided as being out of place: on the contrary, Wolfram's purpose in writing the poem was to show how the knight can fulfil his vocation as a knight, but must undertake it in a proper spirit of submission to God's will. Only if Parzival accepts the idea of *strîten* in this spirit can he win the crown of glory in the shape of attainment to the kingship of the Grail. At this point in the narrative, however, Parzival is far from having the right attitude towards knightly endeavour and harbours a host of misconceptions about God, which it is Trevrizent's task to help put right.

Parzival's condition, as expressed in this last complaint and confession (460.28–461.26) with its mingling of pain, desperation and incomprehension of all that has happened, is marked by a self-righteous attempt to justify his actions. He thinks little of God's *helfe* if this is the way in which it is manifested:

> ist mîn manlîch herze wunt,
> od mag ez dâ vor wesen ganz,
> daz diu riuwe ir scharpfen kranz
> mir setzet ûf werdekeit
> die schildes ambet mir erstreit
> gein werlîchen handen,
> des gihe ich dem ze schanden,
> der aller helfe hât gewalt,
> ist sîn helfe helfe balt,
> daz er mir denne hilfet niht,
> sô vil man im der hilfe giht.　　　　(461.16 ff.)

With Parzival so full of resentment at his lot Trevrizent has a delicate task to win him over to a proper understanding of God's purposes and to show him just where he has gone wrong. In the case of Chrétien's Perceval the young knight is already prepared to submit himself wholeheartedly to the hermit's care on his arrival at the cell; his encounter with the three pilgrim knights and their ladies has turned his obstinacy into contrition, and he is able to confess, receive advice and be absolved in one short, continuous process. Wolfram's treatment of this basic material, however, aims at a much more detailed analysis of Parzival's change of mood, beginning with the defiance of his *zwîvel* and working very gradually through to an acceptance of God's will. Parzival, on his arrival at Trevrizent's cell, is neither completely in the grip of *hôchvart* nor completely ready to admit to his sins, but wavers between the two, endeavouring bit by bit to confess the various sins that weigh on his soul. In this situation Trevrizent has continually to be seeking Parzival's confidence,[1] listening with sympathy, though also with sorrow, probing gently ever more deeply into the recesses of Parzival's awareness, explaining spiritual and theological matters in order to shed light on the young man's particular problems. Here, more than anywhere else in the poem, the process of individualization is most clearly seen in the contrast between Chrétien and Wolfram. Where Chrétien, broadly speaking, is more concerned with the narrative content of his material and prefers that his characters should show themselves principally through the action of the plot, Wolfram shows himself interested primarily in the development of characters as persons, as individuals. For this reason he dwells at much greater length than Chrétien on the question of motivation with respect to Parzival's failures and develops this—as opposed to merely depicting it—through the medium of dialogue, whereby the reality of Parzival's experience is expressed at first hand and in a wholly natural and convincing manner in the alternation of conversation, question and answer, statement and response. Through the dialogue we see Parzival gradually bring his problems into the open, groping tentatively towards the eventual disclosure of his failure at Munsalvæsche, which is the culmination of his conscious sin, aided all the time by the ministrations and explanations of Trevrizent, whose character is also slowly unfolded in the process, but with

---

[1] Walter Henzen, *Das 9. Buch des Parzival. Überlegungen zum Aufbau* in the Festgabe Karl Helm (Tübingen, 1951), p. 201.

the distinction that the changes in his character have already taken place in the past and are not presented as developments in book IX. In this way two complex personalities emerge before us: one of them, Trevrizent, has already translated the generality of the ideal into the particularity of the individual life, and it is his chief task to assist Parzival to make this real for himself also. A transition has to be made from seeing and recognizing the essence of truth to accepting and incarnating it. And because Wolfram's solution cannot be a *Patentlösung* for an existential situation, the ways in which Trevrizent and Parzival deal with their problems necessarily depend on their individual situations.

Trevrizent's reaction to Parzival's statement of his present spiritual position is to try to put Parzival's feudal attitude towards God into proper terms and to teach him the true meaning of *triuwe*. He describes his own experience of God's love, and he immediately identifies himself with Parzival in asking for God's help for them both. He emphasizes time after time that it is God's nature to help (461.30, 462.10 ff., 28). In order to make this clearer, he mentions also how much God has done for man in taking upon Himself man's flesh (462.22 ff.), thus providing a concrete instance of God's care for mankind. The two climaxes of this first section are the equations of God with *triuwe* and with *wârheit*—'sît got selbe ein triuwe ist' (462.19), and 'got heizt und ist diu wârheit' (462.25), which is followed later by a description of God as 'der wâre minnære' (466.1). These statements form the kernel of Trevrizent's teaching and are elaborated with reference to Parzival's *haʒ* and *ʒwîvel*.

Although Parzival has not yet confessed to any particular sinful acts (apart from his failure to go to church), he has quite roundly admitted to that state of soul from which the particular sins spring. Trevrizent accordingly proceeds with a detailed response to this underlying sinfulness, and the response is long because he recognizes the gravity of Parzival's attitude. Whatever particular sins he has been led to commit because of it, he must now be shown a better spiritual state to which he can attain. Hence Trevrizent launches forth into a panegyric of God's constancy, His love and reliability, which—in stark contrast to Parzival—is free from all vacillation: 'ern kan an niemen wenken' (462.28). He therefore counsels Parzival to be 'getriwe ân allez wenken' (462.18) and says: 'nu lêret iwer gedanke, / hüet iuch gein im an wanke' (462.29 f.). Parzival's *ʒwîvel*, the basis of his failure, is viewed here in terms of a general defection from God, as *falscher list* (462.20) and *falschiu fuore* (462.26), a completely wrong and improper attitude and one entirely at variance with what God Himself is.

Having now firmly established a general understanding of God's true nature, Trevrizent goes on to give a series of parallels to Parzival's present condition—the fall of Lucifer and his consequent damnation, the creation of Adam and Eve and the fall of man through Eve's agency, the story of Cain and Abel. In this context Trevrizent outlines the fact of original sin and the possibility of salvation from it through the death of Christ:

> Von Adâmes künne
> huop sich riwe und wünne,
> sît er uns sippe lougent niht,
> den ieslîch engel ob im siht,
> unt daz diu sippe ist sünden wagen,
> sô daz wir sünde müezen tragen,
> dar über erbarme sich des kraft,
> dem erbarme gît geselleschaft,
> sît sîn getriuwiu mennischeit
> mit triwen gein untriwe streit.
>
> . . .
>
> der pareliure Plâtô
> sprach bî sînen zîten dô,
> unt Sibill diu prophêtisse,
> sunder fâlierens misse
> si sagten dâ vor manic jâr,
> uns solde komen al für wâr
> für die hôhsten schulde pfant.
> zer helle uns nam diu hôhste hant
> mit der gotlîchen minne.   (465.1 ff.)

Trevrizent's instruction, far from being merely a 'kleine summa theologiae', as Ehrismann thought,[1] is carefully tailored to his

---

[1] Gustav Ehrismann, *Über Wolframs Ethik* (*ZfdA*, XLIX, 1908), p. 434.

penitent's measurements, as Helen Adolf has pointed out.[1] So far (and indeed for quite some time still) Trevrizent is unaware of Parzival's identity and can therefore only proceed on the basis of the information the young knight gives him, together with his own inferences from it. The purpose of his preliminary remarks is to give a forceful Biblical example of how *der menschen nît* arose, and in choosing the example of Cain he gives a close parallel to Parzival's own killing of Ither, which has, however, not yet been mentioned. The sin of Cain serves as the prototype of the grave human sins caused by a lack of love and is a warning example to Parzival in his present state of *haʒ gein gote*. But after having heightened the significance of Parzival's *ʒwîvel* by placing it in the context of Biblical parallels, Trevrizent is more concerned to point the way to a solution, provided by God's mercy through the atoning death of Christ, the truth of which is attested not only by Christian teaching, but also by the prophecies of Plato and the Sibyl. He exhorts Parzival to be converted from his former ways, to turn to an attitude of humility and to accept the fruits of God's love. He describes God in terms which echo Herzeloyde's original instruction to Parzival at the beginning of book III, using the same imagery of light and darkness:

> Von dem wâren minnære
> sagent disiu süezen mære.
> der ist ein durchliuhtec lieht,
> und wenket sîner minne nieht.
> swem er minne erzeigen sol,
> dem wirt mit sîner minne wol.
> die selben sint geteilet;
> al der werlde ist geveilet
> bêdiu sîn minne und ouch sîn haz.
> nu prüevet wederz helfe baz.
> der schuldige âne riuwe
> fliuht die gotlîchen triuwe:
> swer ab wandelt sünden schulde,
> der dient nâch werder hulde. (466.1 ff.)

---

[1] Helen Adolf, *The Theological and Feudal Background of Wolfram's 'ʒwîvel'* (*JEGP*, XLIX, 1950), p. 300.

The matter is presented to Parzival *for his free choice*; the alternatives are shown—on the one hand, rejection of God and its consequences in the pains of hell; on the other, conversion of spirit and its reward.

But Trevrizent has still not reached the end of what he has to say: a final warning has yet to be given in the strongest terms. The object of his warning is *gedanc*, which he identifies with the diabolical darkness of Herzeloyde's teaching (cf. 119.25 ff.). In a threefold formula he inveighs against thought as being deprived of the light of the sun, as being locked up from all creatures, and as darkness without light. Moreover, no thought is swift enough to avoid temptation, and the implication is clear enough that where there is temptation there is an obvious possibility of sin. Nor is Trevrizent content to let the matter rest with an onslaught on *gedanc*: he also includes acts arising as a result:

> sît got gedanke speht sô wol,
> ôwê der brœden werke dol!
> swâ werc verwurkent sînen gruoz,
> daz gotheit sich schamen muoz,
> wem lât den menschlîchiu zuht?
> war hât diu arme sêle fluht? (466.29 ff.)

Trevrizent is here attacking those aspects of man's actions which arise not from the pure agency of faith, not from complete trust in God, but from the self-opinionated egoism of man's fallen nature, i.e. from the workings of *hôchvart*. He sees before him a knight who, through misunderstanding, ignorance and deliberate wilfulness, has come to rely solely on his own judgement as a sufficient criterion for action, and he is therefore compelled to present Parzival with the alternative of submission to God's will, of distrust of the natural motions of the human spirit. The term *gedanc* subsumes all man's self-willed activity, and by aligning it with the symbolism of darkness Wolfram plainly indicates its opposition to all that lies within the divine purpose. With this as his final emphasis the hermit once more invites Parzival to renounce his former ways.

Parzival thanks Trevrizent for having told him about God's just dealings with men—he is experiencing a change of attitude—and tells him that he has spent all his youth attempting to express *triuwe*, but with *kumber* as his only reward. From this point *kumber* becomes a *Leitwort* that crops up in a variety of con-nexions, and Trevrizent immediately takes it up and links it with *sünde*, when he encourages Parzival not to keep his sorrow secret, but to tell him more and so enable him to give further advice. Parzival slips over the question of sin for the time being, since he has not yet reached the stage at which he can confess it, but instead tells of his *hôhstiu nôt* about the Grail and his concern for Cond-wiramurs. At last we have come to the point where the Grail is the centre of attention, for here, although Parzival at first avoids any further probing into it, *kumber* and *sünde* are combined with a more detailed discussion of *diemüete* and *hôchvart*.

Trevrizent, whose encyclopedic knowledge exceeds that of any other of Wolfram's characters in this poem, now proceeds to impart the information about the Grail that Parzival and the curious reader long to know, and what he says rests on the authority of personal knowledge: 'ich weizz und hânz für wâr gesehn' (468.16). His first utterance is calculated to discourage Parzival from his search and has an ironic flavour about it, since he is unaware of the fact that he is facing the future Grail king; for that matter, neither does Parzival know that he is destined to it, as his later outburst shows (472.8 ff.). Only the audience must suspect what is the goal of Parzival's endeavour.

The Grail premisses are now put forward by Trevrizent in all their simplicity: 'jane mac den grâl nieman bejagn, / wan der ze himel ist sô bekant / daz er zem grâle sî benant' (468.12 ff.). The linking of the two elements of *bejagn* and predestination is impor-tant, and the formula is repeated in almost identical words at the end of book XV (786.5 ff.). Trevrizent takes it up once more in book XVI (798.24 ff.), but omits the reference to predestination, though it is hard to say exactly why. The emphasis in book IX is obviously on the role the call has to play in the attainment to the Grail kingship, and this ties in beautifully with all that Trevrizent has been saying to Parzival previously. The initiative lies at all times with God, not with man. Any attainment to the kingship depends on obedience to God's calling and cannot be won through man's own willing. Once Trevrizent has made this clear and mentioned that he has himself seen the Grail, a natural opportunity occurs for Parzival to volunteer an account of his own visit, but Wolfram in two succinct lines recounts that he deliberately kept silent about it, asking instead for more information.

The Grail and everything which happens around it derive their ethical meaning, partially if not perhaps wholly, from the twin concepts of *diemüete* and *kiusche*, whose close relation to each other, though it cannot be expressed with absolute precision, is indubitable.[1] On the ethical level the Grail is, in Friedrich Ranke's words, the 'Stein der Demut',[2] against which the conduct of the neutral angels, the Grail knights, Anfortas, Trevrizent, Repanse de schoye, Feirefiz and Parzival is measured. In some cases the success or failure is described in terms of *kiusche* or *unkiusche*, in others in terms of *hôchvart* or *diemüete*, but the two pairs are complementary: they are merely slightly different viewpoints of a generalized ethical ideal.

The physical properties of the Grail are depicted and deepened through their connexion with the symbolism of the phoenix and the eucharist. For the Grail, which is a stone of great purity with a mysterious name in 'ein von Wolfram wohl bewußt verdrehtes und vieldeutiges Latein',[3] possesses a miraculous life-giving

---

[1] Wapnewski, *op. cit.*, p. 141.

[2] Friedrich Ranke, *Zur Symbolik des Grals bei Wolfram von Eschenbach* (*Triv.*, IV, 1946), p. 28. Cf. also Willy Krogmann, *wunsch von pardîs* (*ZfdA*, LXXXV, 1954/5), where Wolfram's *lapsit exillîs* is interpreted in the light of the *lapis exilis* of the *Iter ad paradisum* (see Kinzel's edition of Lamprecht's *Alexander*, p. 382).

[3] Helmut de Boor, *Die höfische Literatur. Vorbereitung, Blüte, Ausklang*, p. 102. The physical nature of the Grail and its possible sources are not proper subjects for this study in themselves. The examination of Chrétien's descriptions certainly sheds light on what Wolfram wrote, but this tells us more *how* Wolfram came to his interpretation rather than *why*. One thing, however, is important, namely, the fact that Wolfram explains and interprets his physical description of the Grail, while Chrétien merely describes and allows his reader to draw his own conclusions. Wolfram is anxious to 'demythologize' certain aspects of his under-

property such as the phoenix demonstrates in its death in the fire and subsequent resurrection from the ashes in a condition more splendid than before. Those who look upon the Grail are preserved from death during the ensuing week and are kept thus in a state of perpetual youth. The statement that even if a man looked at the stone for two hundred years he would not go grey is a rhetorical flourish not meant to be taken too literally, for we have already heard of the handsome old man, Titurel, who is 'noch grâwer dan der tuft' (240.30), and later on Parzival asks Trevrizent about the man who was 'al grâ bî liehtem vel' (501.21). The descriptions of Titurel mention his grey hair as an indication of his great age, but his youthful spirit is attested by his physical beauty and radiance. The power of the Grail can thus be regarded as a primarily spiritual one, which manifests itself also through physical characteristics. The image of the phoenix is also intended spiritually, since it was commonly understood as an image of Christ, as the *Jüngerer Physiologus*[1] tells. This passage about the phoenix by implication sets the Grail in the context of Christian symbolism, which is strengthened by the lines which follow.

The Grail is now closely associated with the eucharist, with the heart of the Christian sacramental tradition. Earlier, on the occasion of Parzival's visit to Munsalvæsche, it had appeared in a setting very strongly, but by no means completely, reminiscent of liturgical processions,[2] and in addition we are told that it is visible only to the baptized (813.17 ff.). The association of the Grail with the host of the eucharist already appears in Chrétien's poem (6422 ff.), where it has aroused much scholarly thought on account of its vagueness. Wolfram takes over the motif and places it firmly in the context of the events of Good Friday. On this day, which is the day of Parzival's visit to Trevrizent, a dove from heaven brings 'ein kleine wîze oblât' (470.5) and places it on the Grail,

standing of the Grail in order to demonstrate more clearly his ethical goal, which is his paramount objective.

[1] Friedrich Wilhelm, *Denkmäler deutscher Prosa des 11. und 12. Jahrhunderts* (Munich, 1960), p. 28. Cf. Wapnewski, *op. cit.*, pp. 60 ff.

[2] Cf. W. J. Schröder, *Der dichterische Plan des Parzivalromans* (*Beitr.*, LXXIV, 1952), pp. 435 ff. I do not agree with Schröder's elaborations.

thereby giving it the power to provide all earthly kinds of food
and drink, from which the Grail sodality are enabled to live.
Parzival has already experienced the wealth of food and drink the
Grail supplies, so that no further description is needed here.
Wolfram's purpose at this point is to transfer the fairy-tale motif
of the *Tischlein-deck-dich* into the realms of the religious and
particularly into the symbolism of the eucharist, though not
attempting to divest the Grail of any of its former associations. In
this way it becomes a nexus of complementary significances, while
the main emphasis is laid on the sacrificial death of Christ, commemorated on Good Friday and made visible and re-enacted in
the sacrifice of the mass. The properties of the Grail are thus made
dependent on the power of the host that the dove brings, the host
that is the supreme manifestation of *diemüete* and *kiusche*, since
God Himself was humble enough to take on human flesh and
allow Himself to be crucified for the salvation of mankind and is
now humble enough to reveal Himself under the outward form of
the host. It is through a death to the old self that the new and
transfigured self can arise. On this cardinal issue all the imagery of
book IX is concentrated.[1]

After Trevrizent has narrated these various details about the
nature of the Grail, he continues with a description of the vocation
to the Grail, which occurs through the appearance on the end of
the stone of the name of 'swer dar tuon sol die sælden vart'
(470.26). The irrevocability of this calling is indicated by the
fact that the letters cannot be obliterated, the mysterious nature of
it by the fact that the letters disappear before one's eyes as soon
as one has read them. In the course of his remarks Trevrizent
outlines how those who are called to the Grail are then liberated
from *sündebære schanden* and on dying enter the bliss of paradise.
An ironical twist is given to Trevrizent's ejaculation: 'wol die
muoter diu daz kint gebar / daz sol ze dienste hœren dar!' (471.3 f.),

---

[1] Cf. Herbert Kolb, *Schola Humilitatis*, pp. 112 f. Kolb's interpretation of
Parzival in terms of the hero's development in humility has been amplified by
Walter Henzen, *Zur Vorprägung der Demut im Parʒival durch Chrestien* (*Beitr.*
(Tübingen), LXXX, 1958).

as he is still unaware of Parzival's identity. These words provide another slight indication of Parzival's predestination to the Grail in that they tie up with the Marian symbolism already noted in the chapter on Herzeloyde.[1] The honour that is paid to the high moral worth of Herzeloyde through this device reflects also on Parzival, since he is singled out from the rest of humanity by the allusion, though to what particular calling is not yet stated. The exclamations of Ither (146.5 ff.) and the knight at Gurnemanz' castle (164.19 f.) are preparatory parallels for the isolation of Parzival for his particular calling, and in their close connexion with the events of the life of Christ they must be regarded more as heightening the individual aspects of Parzival's character by symbolic references than as being individualizing traits in themselves. This is, of course, true of the Christian symbolism of the Grail in general.

As a conclusion to his comments at this stage Trevrizent tells Parzival of the lot of the neutral angels, the first guardians of the Grail. This passage, together with Trevrizent's 'revocation' in book XVI (798.6 ff.), constitutes one of the most difficult problems of *Parzival* research in that Trevrizent's two utterances are so diametrically opposed. Here, in book IX, the hermit refers to the neutral angels in very favourable terms as 'die edelen und die werden' (471.19) and hints that God may well have forgiven them their offence, though he disclaims any precise knowledge as to what actually did happen to them. It is not at all clear why Wolfram should have introduced the neutral angels into the poem in this way. Mergell[2] interprets the lot of the neutral angels and Parzival's destiny as showing the dual aspects of God's nature as mercy and justice, both of which are necessary for any real value to be set on the other. Thus, if Parzival (and also Anfortas) are to receive the fruits of God's mercy, this must be freed from any sentimentality through justice being expressed in the form of punishment—on the neutral angels. While, therefore, Parzival is experiencing the sorrows of alienation from God, the neutral angels must, in order to show a balance and a contrast, be viewed with a certain favour,

---

[1] See above, pp. 93 ff.   [2] *Op. cit.*, pp. 199 ff.

though forgiveness cannot be definitively meted out to them; and when, at the end, Parzival attains the Grail kingship, the punishment that the neutral angels were already known earlier to have received can be published as an example of God's impartiality and justice. This interpretation makes sense within its own limits, but there is at least one serious drawback to it, even if one accepts the basic argumentation as plausible. The weakness lies in the fact that the actions involving the neutral angels on the one hand and Parzival and Anfortas on the other can hardly serve as balancing points for each other when their functions within the whole complex of the poem are so disparate in importance. The role of the neutral angels in the poem is a far too minor one for there to be any genuine balance between their fate and that of Parzival. Nevertheless, in the absence of any more convincing argument which accepts 798.11–22 as an integral part of the poem, Mergell's thesis does demonstrate a certain modicum of logic in Wolfram's two perplexing accounts.

Wapnewski's answer to the problem is to interpret the whole of the 'revocation' (791.1–30) as an interpolation or later insertion by Wolfram in order to correct his previous heretical statement about the neutral angels.[1] This is an extreme solution, but one which does justice to the facts. No one could accuse Wapnewski of neglecting the text at this point: his painstaking exegesis leads him inescapably to his honest conclusion. In the absence of such esoteric knowledge on the subject as Mergell seems to possess, it is perhaps the only conclusion one can reach.

If we accept the later passage as an interpolated correction, we have nonetheless to make sense of the earlier statements. The task of the neutral angels in guarding the Grail has to be seen in the light of what the Grail is—a symbol of *diemüete*. The neutral angels have failed in not aligning themselves with God; they are guilty of only a lesser *hôchvart* than that of Lucifer, though they have not actively sinned. Their punishment is, therefore, to guard

---

[1] *Op. cit.*, pp. 151–73. Cf. also Bernard Willson, *Wolframs neutrale Engel* (*ZfdPh*, LXXXIII, 1964), who characteristically connects the neutral angels with St Bernard's works.

the symbol of that quality of which they themselves stand in need.[1] That the neutral angels should as a punishment guard what is otherwise considered as *erden wunsches überwal* (235.24) is explicable by reference to the difference in earthly and heavenly values, whereby 'the assignment to the Grail, it being of the earth, would come to the angels as a demotion too steep for our imagination to grasp'.[2] This interpretation in the light of *diemüete* does full justice to the passage on the neutral angels in book IX and fits beautifully into the developing pattern of the whole book. It forms a fitting conclusion to this section of Trevrizent's instruction.

Parzival has so far maintained a comparative silence, only giving information where requested and asking short and pointed questions. His role has been that of a listener, Trevrizent's that of a teacher. Now, however, Parzival feels sufficiently bold to make a comment of his own volition, declaring his prime interest in battle:

> mac rîterschaft des lîbes prîs
> unt doch der sêle pardîs
> bejagen mit schilt und ouch mit sper,
> sô was ie rîterschaft mîn ger.
> ich streit ie swâ ich striten vant,
> sô daz mîn werlîchiu hant
> sich næhert dem prîse.
> ist got an strîte wîse,
> der sol mich dar benennen,
> daz si mich dâ bekennen:
> mîn hant dâ strîtes niht verbirt. (472.1 ff.)

The question of predestination and Parzival's desire to win the Grail through the performance of acts of knightly prowess is once more raised[3] and this time with the suggestion, coming from Parzival's own lips, that the two may be combined in his own person. The young knight is gradually becoming aware of his own destiny in terms that are much less defiant, though he still thinks

---

[1] Ranke, *op. cit.*, pp. 28 f.

[2] Hermann J. Weigand, *Wolfram's Grail and the Neutral Angels: A Discussion and a Dialogue* (*GR*, XXIX, 1954), p. 95. Weigand also mentions similar cases to be found in the *Lucidarius*.

[3] See above, pp. 173, 320 f., and below, pp. 340 ff.

that he knows best how God ought to deal with him. At this point, however, only the audience suspects the outcome, for Trevrizent is still talking to an unknown penitent, and it is not until book XV that Cundrie announces that Parzival's name has appeared on the *epitafjum* (781.15 f.). It is therefore entirely to be expected that Trevrizent, here expressly described as *kiusche*, should take up Parzival's remarks with a reproof to beware of *hôchvart*, lest his youth should lead him astray, for 'hôchvart ie seic unde viel' (472.17). Trevrizent's tears, which interrupt the flow of his speech, betoken how deeply moved he is at the thought of his brother Anfortas, about whom he is now to tell Parzival. Anfortas' plight is meant to serve as a warning example to Parzival of the depths of misery to which *hôchvart*, which here takes the form of *lôsheit*, can lead. At the same time Parzival is led ever closer to the problem of his own failure, since Trevrizent recounts with sorrow how *ein tumber man* came *unbenennet* to Munsalvæsche and went away again without ever asking about *des wirtes schaden* (473.12 ff.). But Trevrizent does not connect this unknown knight with Parzival. Instead he follows a private theory and adds an account of Lähelin's joust with Lybbeals of Prienlascors at Brumbane, whereby through *rêroup* he acquired a Grail horse very similar to the one Parzival has come riding on. In fact, Trevrizent is under the illusion that the young man so heavily oppressed by sin is Lähelin, and his desire to be certain is so great that he eventually asks Parzival point blank who he is.

This passage is very carefully built up with a whole host of essential details preceding it. We see now the function that the Grail horse has that Parzival wins from the Grail knight earlier in book IX. From here the confusion with Lähelin occurs, and the fact that Lähelin is guilty of *rêroup* leads Parzival to confess to his own *rêroup* and the killing of Ither, while at the same time informing Trevrizent of his penitent's identity. It is important that Parzival should reveal his identity—through declaring his father's name, in whose knightly footsteps he wills to follow—and confess his killing of Ither at the same time, for this particular sin, which is one of those that Trevrizent calls *grôze sünde* (499.20), requires a knowledge of Parzival's identity for a proper evaluation. For this sin, together with the death of Herzeloyde, is a sin against Parzival's *sippe*, the gravity of which Trevrizent finds himself called upon to emphasize with all possible force.

The killing of Ither marks the first climax in the discussion of Parzival's sin and changes the whole perspective of the book, for while Trevrizent had formerly been dealing with an unknown knight and Parzival only with conscious sins, now the hermit suddenly discovers who Parzival really is, and this discovery transforms their relationship so that Parzival's sins appear in a new and proper light. In other words, the individual aspects of Parzival's troubles come to the fore, and the whole tone of the conversation becomes more urgent and serious. Trevrizent becomes himself involved in Parzival's sin, because the two are bound together by the bonds of *sippe*. This closer, more intimate relationship is expressed through Trevrizent's adoption of the *du* form of the verb in addressing his nephew. The new relationship is revealed first of all through the person of Gahmuret, but Trevrizent at the earliest opportunity shows that their relatedness derives from Herzeloyde by calling Parzival *lieber swester suon* (475.19), and in so doing he informs the young man that he is his uncle. A little later he gives Parzival many more precise details about the entire Grail family and thus amplifies the original information Parzival had received from Sigune (251.1 ff.). All these facts both give Parzival a knowledge of his family, of which he was previously scarcely aware, and provide the basis for a partial explanation of his sin. Thus, Trevrizent's dual role as a source of information about the Grail and the Grail family and as Parzival's confessor is further underlined.

Parzival's confession that he killed Ither is introduced in an almost casual way: he admits it in a kind of parenthesis, since his consciousness is concentrated on the *rêroup*, which he knows to be a sin according to courtly ethics. He then inserts that it was Ither whom he killed and on whom the *rêroup* was committed. Thus, once he has made clear the fact that he is not Lähelin, he confesses to having committed *rêroup*, which he characterizes as *sünde*

(475.8), mentions Ither's name and then describes how he committed the crime. He is not aware of any particular sin in the killing of Ither as such. Moreover, he himself gives as his excuse: 'genam ich ie den rêroup, / sô was ich an den witzen toup' (475.5 f.). It was a sin he committed in ignorance.[1]

Trevrizent without hesitation takes up Parzival's confession and, ignoring the matter of rêroup, of which the young man is well aware, proceeds to interpret the killing of Ither, prefacing his remarks with an exclamation of despair: 'waz râtes möht ich dir nu tuon?' (475.20). This emphasis on Ither's death is one of Wolfram's major divergences from Chrétien, for whom the episode of the chevalier vermeil is in no wise connected with the question of Perceval's guilt and who is not described as being related to the young knight. Wolfram's metamorphosis may be explained in three complementary ways: (i) it takes up an undeveloped motif of Chrétien's—the offence against courtly society —and sets it firmly in the context of Parzival's guilt as a whole; (ii) Ither's death is incorporated into Wolfram's pattern of the sippe, the importance of which is thereby heavily stressed; (iii) it broadens the scope of Chrétien's motivation in terms of the death of the veve fame alone and thereby makes the over-simplification of Schuldautomatismus impossible. These three elements are so closely intertwined that it is not easy to talk about any one without involving the other two, and it is in any case necessary to bear in mind the other aspects of Parzival's sin during the discussion of any particular one, since the understanding of the problem depends on an acceptance of the total complexity.[2]

The inclusion of the killing of Ither as one of Parzival's ʒwuo grôʒe sünde widens the sphere of Parzival's responsibility in such a way as to embrace his activity as a courtly knight. His sin is not

---

[1] The significance of the killing of Ither is already indicated at the time when it actually occurs, as Wolfram himself comments: 'sît dô er sich paz versan, / ungerne het erz dô getân' (161.7 f.).

[2] Wolfgang Mohr, in his article Parʒivals ritterliche Schuld (WW, II, 1951/2), interpreting the problem of guilt in the light of Parzival's sin in killing Ither, is careful to emphasize that he regards his view only as a partial explanation, not as a total one (p. 156, n. 14).

seen as one-sidedly 'spiritual', consisting in *zwîvel*, from which every other particular sin arises. On the contrary, the very person from whom Parzival won his claim to knighthood is one against whom he sinned most gravely, though unwittingly. Thus, from the moment of proving himself as a knight Parzival is involved in the mesh of sin. And it is nonetheless a sin of importance, though it was committed in ignorance. Moreover, the killing of Ither, together with the causing of Herzeloyde's death, is not directly linked by Wolfram with Parzival's failure at Munsalvæsche in that the one is the cause of the other. Rather are all the various sins seen as manifestations of Parzival's general sinfulness, some of which are unconscious and some of which are deliberate and wilful, but all of which are in different ways offences against *triuwe*.[1]

Trevrizent does not deal with the problems raised by Ither's death all at once. His first reaction, highly personal and emotional, is to stress Parzival's most intimate relationship with Ither:

> du hâst dîn eigen verch erslagn.
> wiltu für got die schulde tragn,
> sît daz ir bêde wârt ein bluot,
> ob got dâ reht gerihte tuot,
> sô giltet im dîn eigen leben.
> waz wilte im dâ ze gelte geben,
> Ithêrn von Kaheviez? (475.21 ff.)

He then continues with a panegyric on Ither and the effect that his death must have had on those ladies whom he served, echoing the lamentations that Ginover earlier poured forth (160.3 ff.). But it is not until after he has told Parzival of his mother's death, of Anfortas' suffering, its cause and cure, and learnt about Parzival's omission of the *Mitleidsfrage* that he eventually returns to Ither and describes how Gahmuret had left Ither as Trevrizent's *kneht* in the latter's days as a knight. This little twist in the story again serves the purpose of integrating the relationships of all the characters in the poem into one complex whole, though here there is no more emphasis on the *sippe* as such. There is, however, a close *personal* relationship evident between Trevrizent and Ither,

---

[1] Mockenhaupt, *op. cit.*, p. 68.

which imparts a special pathos to Trevrizent's words and makes
them the expression of an individual emotion. The degree of kinship between Parzival and Ither—Parzival's grandfather Gandin
and Ither are cousins twice removed—is made more real through
the addition of the details of Trevrizent's close friendship with
Ither, for the somewhat bald statement announcing their kinship in
Trevrizent's earlier outburst needs a few individual touches to
create a living relationship out of something that might well have
otherwise seemed artificial and arbitrary. Out of this deep personal
experience Trevrizent formulates a second time Parzival's sin
against Ither:

> nu riwet mich mîn knappe rôt,
> durch den si mir grôz êre bôt.
> von Ithêr du bist erborn:
> dîn hant die sippe hât verkorn:
> got hât ir niht vergezzen doch,
> er kan si wol geprüeven noch.
> wilt du gein got mit triwen lebn,
> sô solte im wandel drumbe gebn.
> mit riwe ich dir daz künde,
> du treist zwuo grôze sünde:
> Ithêrn du hâst erslagen,
> du solt ouch dîne muoter klagen. (499.11 ff.)

Why does Trevrizent so emphasize Parzival's sin in killing
Ither and causing his mother's death? This question has to be seen
in relation to the other sins of which Parzival is guilty—*hôchvart*
(456.6 ff. and *passim*), failure to go to church (461.4 ff.), *haʒ gein
gote* (461.9 ff.), failure to ask the *Mitleidsfrage* (473.13 ff.), the
rêroup of Ither (475.5 ff.). With the exception of the *rêroup* of Ither,
which really falls within the scope of his being killed and is therefore accounted for, these sins can be made good:[1] Parzival can
become *dêmüetic*, he can pay respect to the priesthood and attend
the holy mysteries, his *Gotteshaß* can be turned to confidence;
though the matter of the *Mitleidsfrage* is not so easy to put right,
and the death of Herzeloyde and Ither cannot be undone. It is for
this reason that Trevrizent stresses them so much and counsels

[1] Cf. Mohr, *op. cit.*, p. 155.

wandel. The question of *hôchvart* has been treated with as much care as is possible, and Trevrizent detects a change in Parzival's spirit as a result of his teaching about God's true nature and of his providing a few warning examples. But the only answer to the problem of Ither and Herzeloyde and the *Mitleidsfrage* is to accept them for the sins that they are and to repent.

One of the main difficulties that scholars have wrestled with, particularly over the last twenty years, has been the interpretation of Parzival's sins in the light of whether they are consciously or unwittingly committed. Theological issues have consequently become of prime importance with the doctrines of Augustine taking the foremost place.[1] The studies that have followed these lines have the considerable merit of placing Wolfram's ideas fairly and squarely in an orthodox context; they provide a theological and an intellectual justification of Wolfram's view of the human problem of sin, which is very necessary. For Wolfram, however, these intellectual subtleties were—if they indeed ever occurred to him—secondary. He was concerned with the concrete realities of life and with the mystery surrounding the problems of sin and suffering. In this connexion some words of Friedrich Maurer's hit the nail on the head:

> Es muß auffallen . . ., wie wenig es Trevrizent darauf ankommt, ob Parzival subjektiv schuldig geworden ist oder nicht, ob er bewußt gefehlt hat oder nicht; ja daß er überhaupt weder im Fall der schweren und bewußten Sünden noch im Fall der unwissentlich begangenen sich des Näheren auf eine Erörterung der Sünden einläßt; daß er auch gar nicht daran denkt, Parzival ausführlich etwa einen Mangel an *triuwe* oder das 'Überhören der Stimme des Herzens' oder eine andere Schuld vorzuwerfen und sie zu beklagen. Vielmehr scheint es ihm nur darauf anzukommen, Parzival über das Rechte zu belehren, ihn vom Verharren in der Sünde und im Zustand des Nichtwissens und Nichtvermögens abzuhalten und ihm zu helfen, die richtige Haltung gegenüber seinen Verfehlungen einzunehmen, Trevrizent tut das im ersten Fall der echten und schweren Sünden durch seine Gotteslehre und Heilslehre; er tut es im zweiten Fall der Unreife und des Nichtwissens durch seine Belehrungen über den Tod der Mutter, den Tod

---

[1] Foremost among these are the studies of Wapnewski and Maurer.

Ithers und vor allem über den Gral. Das Ziel ist in beiden Fällen das gleiche, wieder in Übereinstimmung mit der Lehre Augustins: Auflockerung des Sünders, Erzeugung von Reue, Bußbereitschaft und demütiger Gesinnung gegenüber Gott.[1]

The killing of Ither is an act which Parzival does not recognize as sinful until Trevrizent informs him, but it is no less a sin for that. Wolfram's point in stressing it is to show that Parzival has to come to terms with the basically inexplicable problem of suffering which does not arise as a direct result of one's own personal action and of responsibility for actions of the wrongness of which one is unaware. This also applies to Parzival's failure at Munsalvæsche, though other factors are involved here which will be treated below. All this is the way of the world, as Trevrizent exclaims as soon as he hears of the killing of Ither:

> 'ôwê werlt, wie tuostu sô?'
> sprach der wirt: der was des mærs unfrô.
> 'du gîst den liuten herzesêr
> unt riwebæres kumbers mêr
> dan der freud. wie stêt dîn lôn!
> sus endet sich dîns mæres dôn.'   (475.13 ff.)

If we turn back to Trevrizent's account of the sin of Cain now, we shall find the context of Christian thinking into which the killing of Ither fits. For the *rêroup* of Ither corresponds to the murder of Abel 'umb krankez guot' (464.17) and is an instance of *der menschen nît*, which has continued ever since, man's descent from Adam being the vehicle of sin. But this continuing chain of sin is broken by the power of Christ's incarnation through the body of a virgin: 'sîn getriuwiu mennischeit / mit triwen gein untriwe streit' (465.9 f.). The only way to be freed from the chains of sin is to turn away from wickedness to trust in God's mercy. It is perhaps at first sight surprising that the atoning death of Christ receives such scant treatment at Wolfram's hands as it does. One would do Wolfram an injustice if one asserted that he neglects it, but the fact remains that it is mentioned somewhat obliquely

---

[1] Maurer, *Leid*, p. 149.

without explicit use of the name of Christ and three times only in the course of the whole of book IX.[1] The longest passage is contained in the episode with Kahenis before Parzival even confesses his *sünde*; the two subsequent passages are only slight and carefully incorporated into broader statements of God's love. The reason for this 'minimization' of or, at least, lack of emphasis on Christ's death is to be found in the development of the Grail as a symbol of salvation. The theme of the whole poem is that of *gote und der werlde gevallen* (cf. 827.19 ff.); this is the salvation towards which Parzival progresses, and as Mockenhaupt so clearly points out: 'der Gral ist die Synthese'.[2] This is why so much stress is placed on Parzival's visit to Munsalvæsche and particularly on his failure to ask the *Mitleidsfrage* and why everything in book IX builds up to Parzival's confession that he did not ask the question. Thus, with reference to the matter of the Atonement, we find the religious motif being subordinated to the poetic one. Wolfram is able to deal with Parzival's problems up to a certain point on a spiritual level, but it is not his intention to deal with it solely in this way since his avowed purpose is to maintain the world's favour while at the same time seeing to it that the soul is not lost through the body's fault. It is therefore evident that the profoundest matters should centre on the Grail, which is neither an exclusively religious or Christian nor an exclusively secular symbol, but one in which both are united.

Before I go on to discuss the *Mitleidsfrage* in more detail, there are a few comments to be made on the death of Herzeloyde and the position this holds in the total context of Parzival's guilt. The motif comes, of course, from Chrétien, but it is very much modified by Wolfram. In the first place, Wolfram rejects the crudity of Perceval's departure in the knowledge that his mother has fallen to the ground 'com s'ele fust cheüe morte' (625) and portrays Herzeloyde's death as occurring with Parzival in a state of ignorance about it. In fact Parzival only learns of it when Trevrizent tells him, extremely abruptly, after he has indicated the enormity

---

[1] 448.2–18 (Kahenis), 464.24–30 and 502.14–5 (both Trevrizent).
[2] *Op. cit.*, p. 113.

of the killing of Ither. But while the circumstances of Herzeloyde's death are mitigated, Parzival's responsibility for it is emphasized. It irrupts into his consciousness in a totally unprepared way and is aligned with the killing of Ither, for together they form the *zwuo grôʒe sünde*, about which Trevrizent's advice is:

> nim buoz für missewende,
> unt sorge et umb dîn ende,
> daz dir dîn arbeit hie erhol
> daz dort diu sêle ruowe dol. (499.27 ff.)

Herzeloyde's death is highlighted by reference to the mysterious dream which she had when Gahmuret was killed in battle (103.25 ff.), which Trevrizent interprets as an allegorical representation of Parzival's departure and its consequences. In this way the importance of Parzival's responsibility for Herzeloyde's death is placed a long way back in the narrative and foretold even before Parzival is born. If anything ties up with Augustinian doctrine, then this depiction of Parzival's primeval guilt and involvement in original sin must be reckoned as part of it.[1] But despite the fact that Trevrizent deals with the sins connected with both Ither and Herzeloyde under the same heading, the death of Herzeloyde is not elaborated in terms corresponding with the deeply personal tone of the hermit's remarks about Ither. The emphasis of guilt has been shifted very weightily from the death of Chrétien's *veve fame* to the killing of Ither. In all Trevrizent devotes no more than thirteen lines to Herzeloyde (476.12 f., 24–30, 499.22–5), whereas his very first speech about Ither covers more than twice that. This all points to an obvious dissatisfaction on Wolfram's part about his source. He certainly rejects Chrétien's *Schuldautomatismus*, but he also seems to be unhappy about the motif as such and avoids dealing with it except in the rather indirect, allegorical dream. This forms a striking contrast to the personal detail apparent in the evaluation of the Ither episode. One is therefore led to the conclusion that the emphasis on Herzeloyde's death is more formal (and in deference to the source, since Wolfram could scarcely have

---

[1] Cf. Augustine, *Confessiones*, I, 6 and 7.

eradicated the motif entirely) than real. It has the air of being an appendage to the discussion about Ither. Trevrizent does not explain to Parzival just how his departure caused Herzeloyde's death, nor does he attempt to give it a deeper psychological significance. He merely states that it happened and leaves Parzival and the reader to infer its meaning in the total context of Parzival's guilt. Mention has been made earlier about the significance of Parzival's departure for Herzeloyde,[1] and it is clear from the poem as a whole that Herzeloyde's character and actions are viewed in the light of *triuwe*.[2] Moreover, the entire poem also revolves around the theme of *triuwe* (cf. 4.9 ff.), so that it is legitimate to interpret Parzival's sin at this point as a sin against *triuwe* despite the fact that Wolfram makes no explicit reference to it here. We can agree with Mockenhaupt when he says that Parzival

lebt rein in seiner puren, gut angelegten, aber noch untermen-schlichen Naturhaftigkeit. Parzival hatte doch bemerkt, daß sein bloßes Bekanntwerden mit dem Rittertum eine lange Ohnmacht der Mutter zur Folge hatte und daß ihr nachher noch sein ausführlicher Bericht tiefsten Schmerz bereitete—kein Wort des Verständnisses oder der Teilnahme kommt über seine Lippen. Schon hier versäumt er die Mitleidsfrage. Er kennt nur sein Verlangen. Hätte er *triuwe* gehabt, so hätte er nimmer den gewiß berechtigten und auch nicht länger hinauszuschiebenden Ausritt mit der Rücksichtslosigkeit betrieben und vollzogen, die nun seine erste Sünde ausmacht. Unwissenheit entschuldigt zwar—wo sie selber unverschuldet ist; aber hier handelt es sich um eine rein aus naturhaft selbstischem Trieb hervorgehende Rücksichtslosigkeit, für deren Folgen man die Verantwortung vor Gott trägt.[3]

In this way Parzival's responsibility for the death of his mother and for his failure to put the *Mitleidsfrage* are linked together not mechanically (as with Chrétien), but *psychologically*. Essentially, Parzival's sin against Herzeloyde is one of self-centredness, but it is hard to understand, given the conflict of Parzival's heredity from Gahmuret and his upbringing by Herzeloyde, how he could

[1] See above, pp. 80 f.
[2] See above, pp. 73 ff.
[3] *Op. cit.*, pp. 66 f.

have acted otherwise. The point is, however, that as soon as Parzival makes a decision on his own account (i.e. to discover the truth about the knightly world and to join its ranks) and ceases to rely absolutely on the guidance and experience of others, he too becomes involved in the problem of sin.[1] But in this particular case it seems that Wolfram did not want to give more than the briefest indication of its significance, since it forms a background for the more important questions of the killing of Ither and the *Mitleidsfrage*. We must now turn our attention to this latter problem.

Once Trevrizent has informed Parzival of his mother's death, he continues with a long speech about the Grail family, mentioning Schoysiane, Sigune, Repanse de schoye, Frimutel and Anfortas, but dwelling especially on the latter and his particular plight. After outlining all the attempts to cure Anfortas, Trevrizent describes how they saw written on the Grail that a knight was to come and put an end to Anfortas' misery through the asking of a question. No one was to warn the knight about the necessity to ask the question, otherwise the question would lose its power and the king's ailment remain as it was before. If the question was put at the right time, the knight was to succeed to the kingship of the Grail and Anfortas be released from both his suffering and his office. At this point Trevrizent refers back to his previous statement about the unknown knight who failed to ask the king about his suffering (473.12 ff.) and emphasizes much the same things— that the question is concerned with compassion for the king's misery, that the knight refrained from putting the question out of *tumpheit*. In the earlier statement stress is laid on *sünde*, here it is *unprîs* and a lack of concern about *grôze sælde* that are mentioned. Undoubtedly Trevrizent has not forgotten the matter of *sünde*, but the immediate context of his second statement deals more with the Grail family than with Parzival's religious condition. This second passage does not need to reiterate the question of sin, since Parzival is obviously able to supply this knowledge from the previous statement. It would have been too repetitious on

[1] *Ibid.*, pp. 77 and 227.

Wolfram's part to have done this explicitly. As it is, however, the situation has changed since the first statement, when Trevrizent was completely unaware of Parzival's identity. Now he knows whom he is addressing, but he does not know that this person is in fact the person against whom his remarks are directed. And still Parzival feels himself insufficiently ready to admit his guilt. An interlude follows in which the two men forage for food for themselves and the Grail horse, and when Trevrizent eventually goes to the horse and expresses his sorrow at the horse's hunger, especially because it bears Anfortas' emblem, Parzival plucks up courage to confess:

> hêrre und lieber œheim mîn
> getorst ichz iu vor scham gesagn,
> mîn ungelücke ich solde klagn.
> daz verkiest durch iwer selbes zuht:
> mîn triwe hât doch gein iu fluht.
> ich hân sô sêre missetân,
> welt ir michs engelten lân,
> so scheide ich von dem trôste
> unt bin der unerlôste
> immer mêr von riuwe.
> ir sult mit râtes triuwe
> klagen mîne tumpheit.
> der ûf Munsalvæsche reit,
> unt der den rehten kumber sach,
> unt der deheine vrâge sprach,
> daz bin ich unsælec barn:
> sus hân ich, hêrre, missevarn.　　　　(488.4 ff.)

The motif of the *Mitleidsfrage* has now undergone three stages of progression. In the first instance it appears as it were in the abstract in the context of Trevrizent's disquisition on human sin, for neither the hermit nor Parzival is aware of the other's identity. Secondly, it recurs in the context of the Grail and the problems concerned with it, and here dramatic irony plays a great part, since although Trevrizent knows he is talking *to* Parzival, he does not know that he is talking *about* him. In the third case, Parzival himself takes control and admits to the sin that Trevrizent had

been describing to him. This progression is of the utmost importance, as through it we see a development in Parzival's character.
We see how he comes to Trevrizent burdened with the weight of
sin, but unable to cope with it, unable to analyse it and take
measures accordingly. In the course of his stay with the hermit
he gradually discovers the root of his troubles and is enabled to
confess his sins, first in general terms, then specifically, beginning
with the easier one and working through to the confession of his
failure at Munsalvæsche, which troubles him more than anything
else because he cannot understand it.

Trevrizent's reaction to Parzival's confession is one of heartfelt
grief, bursting forth with an exclamation equivalent to 'Do you
know what you're saying? Are you in your right senses?' But
he does not leave the young knight psychologically isolated at this
crisis of his life: his use of the first person plural and the pronoun
bêde demonstrates his most intimate care and sympathy for
Parzival in that he includes himself in the advice he offers:

> der wirt sprach 'neve, waz sagestu nuo?
> wir sulen bêde samt zuo
> herzenlîcher klage grîfen
> unt die freude lâzen slîfen,
> sît dîn kunst sich sælden sus verzêch.' (488.21 ff.)

At the end of this first couple of sentences we see that he slides over
into the second person singular, and from this point all his comments are addressed directly and specifically to Parzival. But
although Trevrizent has continually emphasized the enormity of
this particular sin both before and after Parzival's admission of it,
his words now seem curiously muted:

> dune solt och niht ze sêre klagn.
> du solt in rehten mâzen
> klagen und klagen lâzen.
> diu menscheit hât wilden art.
> etswâ wil jugent an witze vart:
> wil dennez alter tumpheit üeben
> unde lûter site trüeben,

dâ von wirt daz wîze sal
unt diu grüene tugent val,
dâ von beklîben möhte
daz der werdekeit töhte.
möht ich dirz wol begrüenen
unt dîn herze also erküenen
daz du den prîs bejagtes
unt an got niht verzagtes,
so gestüende noch dîn linge
an sô werdeclîchem dinge,
daz wol ergetzet hieze.
got selbe dich niht lieze:
ich bin von gote dîn râtes wer. (499.2 ff.)

And in a later passage Trevrizent tells Parzival with reference to this failure at Munsalvæsche: 'die sünde lâ bî dn andern stên' (501.5). In other words, this sin belongs to the same category as the killing of Ither and the causing of Herzeloyde's death, for which the hermit's advice is, as we have already noted, to repent and pursue the soul's salvation. Apart from this there is no concrete act of reparation that Parzival can make. The tone of Trevrizent's remarks is muted because Parzival has in fact already responded to the preceding spiritual instruction by renewing his relationship with God in the spirit of humility that his uncle has counselled and therefore stands in no further need of being admonished and set upon the right path. But in addition to the muted tone Trevrizent goes so far as to suggest the possibility of Parzival's undoing the sin he committed at the Grail castle, though here he does link it with the overcoming of *zwîvel*: 'daz du . . . an got niht verzagtes' (489.15 f.).

Gottfried Weber argues[1] that this faint hope which Trevrizent holds out to Parzival is the subject of the lie to which he confesses in book XVI (798.6 f.) and that Trevrizent is forced into it in order to preserve Parzival from falling into a more perilous state of despair. Thus, according to Weber, Trevrizent's basic position in book IX is (i) that the Grail can only be won (*bejagt*) by someone who is known in heaven to be called to do this (*benant*), and

[1] Weber, *op. cit.*, pp. 70, 151 ff.

(ii) that Parzival is *not* called to do it. Thus, Trevrizent's only logical counsel is: 'nim buoz für missewende ...' (499.27). He can, therefore, react in book XVI to Parzival's winning of the Grail by saying: 'grœzer wunder selten ie geschach ...' (798.1) and proceed to confess his 'lie'. This means, then, that book IX has to be seen in terms of an Augustinian answer to the question of *zwîvel* and that Trevrizent only aids Parzival to a realization of the synthesis of *gote und der werlde gevallen* in so far as he sets forth a proper attitude of *diemüete* as a basis for the synthesis which Parzival has to win through the sweat of his brow in co-operation with God's mercy, which is the Thomist answer of book XVI. The difficulty about this argument is, as Wapnewski has pointed out,[1] that Trevrizent's 'lie' in fact corresponds to what is found out to be true; in other words, it is only a *subjective* 'lie', a 'lie' according to Trevrizent's postulated earlier *imperfect* knowledge. This interpretation of book IX and Trevrizent's function in it belies Wolfram's statement about 'penetrating to the heart of the matter' (433.2) and is curiously at variance with Trevrizent's asseverations (which Wolfram nowhere in the course of book IX casts any doubt on) that he knows what he is talking about and has his knowledge from personal experience (464.9 f., 468.16), since, if Weber's thesis is correct, according to the ultimate truth, Trevrizent does not know what he is talking about.

That the 'lie' refers to the neutral angels has rather more to commend it, since the phrase 'wiez um in [sc. the Grail] stüende' (798.7) occurs also both before and after Trevrizent speaks about the neutral angels in book IX (468.22, 471.29). The difficulty here is the sense that one should give to the words 'durch ableitens list' (798.6). For why should Trevrizent's account of the neutral angels be calculated to lead Parzival away from the Grail? There is something which Wapnewski does not answer, and the text at this point gives no help at all, for Parzival immediately jumps in with his wish to be called by God to win the Grail by *strîten* (472.1 ff.). Perhaps really the only preference to be given to the claim that Trevrizent's revocation refers to the neutral angels is the fact that

---

[1] *Op. cit.*, p. 155.

here we know that medieval theology stated that the neutral angels were damned and not left with a suspended judgement about their lot.

But the text is so full of ambiguous and contradictory statements both about the Grail premisses and about the lot of the neutral angels that it is impossible to come to a clear view of what Wolfram meant. The only thing that is in any way clear is the fact that Trevrizent did not reckon with an *erstrîten* of the Grail by Parzival, though he knew that this was theoretically possible. His main concern was to arouse a spirit of *diemüete* in Parzival.

None of this ties in very well with the premisses about the asking of the *Mitleidsfrage*, which seems to indicate a now-or-never approach to it. Wapnewski[1] attempts to explain this inconsistency by reference to Trevrizent's statement that a knight (whom we know to have been Parzival) came *unbenennet* to Munsalvæsche (473.12 ff.)—that is, he came before his name had appeared on the Grail as the saviour of Anfortas and therefore this visit does not really count. This theory makes nonsense of Parzival's failure, since if he were not at that time *the* knight destined to release the king there would be no reason to consider his not asking the question as a failure at all. If he were not at that time *called* to the Grail, all the distress shown by the inhabitants and by Trevrizent would be vacuous and mistaken. How could Parzival be held responsible—as he quite clearly is—for an action which would have had no value on account of his not being *named* to do it? The matter requires a different kind of approach, and if we wish to understand it properly we have to ascertain the nature and purpose of the *Mitleidsfrage* and the significance of Parzival's failure.

As a starting point let us take Mockenhaupt's statement that an understanding of Parzival's guilt depends on the acceptance of the question motif as an integral part of the Grail story and of the fact that the neglect of this question brings with it a corresponding guilt.[2] Chrétien's treatment of this motif shows clear signs that it was originally a fairy-tale motif, since neither of the two questions Perceval should have asked contains more than a hint of a moral

---

[1] *Op. cit.*, p. 102.   [2] Mockenhaupt, *op. cit.*, p. 73.

function. The motif in the French poem has been characterized as a *Neugierfrage* in contrast to the term of *Mitleidsfrage* for Wolfram. Wolfram's conception involves a deepening of the fairy-tale motif through investing it with moral significance,[1] but he does not lose sight of the other elements with all their mystery and complexity.

We must first of all examine the question motif as it appears in book V and only afterwards take into account what is said later in elucidation. There are two things in which Parzival is interested at Munsalvæsche—firstly, Anfortas, and secondly, the marvellous nature of the Grail and everything that surrounds it. But it is primarily the mystery and wonder of what is happening around him that compel Parzival's attention, and Wolfram describes his reaction as follows:

> wol gemarcte Parzivâl
> die rîcheit unt daz wunder grôz:
> durch zuht in vrâgens doch verdrôz.
> er dâhte 'mir riet Gurnemanz
> mit grôzen triwen âne schranz,
> ich solte vil gevrâgen niht.
> waz op mîn wesen hie geschicht
> die mâze als dort pî im?
> âne vrâge ich vernim
> wiez dirre massenîe stêt.'   (239.8 ff.)

It is plain that Parzival's immediate and spontaneous action would have been to ask about what he saw before him, but he remembers Gurnemanz' fateful advice (171.17 ff.) and falls back on this to cover himself and evade any responsibility that might accrue from a possible wrong action. This reaction is taken over from Chrétien, who motivates Perceval's silence in exactly the same way, but adds the illuminating comment:

> Si criem que il n'i ait damage,
> Por che que j'ai oï retraire
> Qu'ausi se puet on bien trop taire
> Com trop parler a la foie[e].   (3248 ff.)

[1] *Ibid.*, pp. 71 ff.

Wolfram also adds a comment of his own after he has described
how Anfortas gives Parzival a sword for protection in battle and
mentions his disability, thus giving the young man a further push
to ask the question:

> ôwê daz er niht vrâgte dô!
> des pin ich für in noch unvrô.
> wan do erz enpfienc in sîne hant,
> dô was er vrâgens mit ermant.
> och riwet mich sîn süezer wirt,
> den ungenande niht verbirt,
> des im von vrâgn nu wære rât. (240.3 ff.)

From the passages quoted above and the context in which they
occur one cannot be too specific about the nature of the question.
As far as Parzival is concerned, it is a matter of 'wiez dirre
massenîe stêt' and not a clear *Mitleidsfrage* that he envisages, and
he neglects to ask the question *durch zuht*. His reliance on the
advice of Gurnemanz provides merely an external and subjective
justification. We must therefore assume that Parzival has failed to
comprehend the import of Gurnemanz' advice and that his neglecting the question must have an explanation arising from this failure.
If Gurnemanz' instruction can be summed up under one heading,
that of *mâze* must immediately spring to mind, and this is the
aspect of courtliness which Parzival only learns late. He is all too
prone to avoid taking action through observing the letter of any
advice he is given, whether it be Herzeloyde's or Gurnemanz',
and through observing the letter he sins against the spirit. And so,
referring to the *zuht* which prevents Parzival from asking the
question Mockenhaupt writes:

> ... *durch zuht*, wie ihm der Dichter ausdrücklich zugesteht, und
> unter Berufung vor allem auf eine empfangene Weisung, entzieht er
> sich der Notwendigkeit, der Forderung des Augenblicks gemäß zu
> handeln, in der ausgesprochenen Erwartung (239, 14–17), die Lösung
> der Rätsel werde sich schon von selber einstellen. ... er unterläßt [die
> Frage] ganz deutlich aus Schüchternheit und Unsicherheit, nicht, weil
> er aus der Beherrschung der Situation heraus überschaute, daß hier

das von Gurnemanz geratene diskrete, aber aufmerksame Schweigen am Platze wäre . . . die Zucht, die die Maßlosigkeit des Lebenstriebes bändigen soll, wird schuldhaft, sobald sie den Menschen hindert, in eigenem Namen zu handeln und für seine Taten und Unterlassungen persönlich einzustehen.[1]

This explains one level of motivation with specific reference to Gurnemanz' advice, but in addition to understanding that it is through a misapplication of this advice that Parzival falls into sin we have to discover some reason for the misapplication, and it is at this point that we see the impossibility of summing the whole matter up under one heading. It is dangerous to have too rationalistic an approach to a problem with so many ramifications, for Wolfram himself presents a large variety of viewpoints.[2]

In the passage quoted above (240.3 ff.) Wolfram shows that the question is, *inter alia*, though primarily, a *Mitleidsfrage*,[3] since he mentions in this context both Anfortas' ailment (239.26 f., 240.8) and the fact that this arouses pity in him (240.7). But at the time the question ought to have been put its significance is shrouded in mystery. Neither the audience nor the hero is properly aware of what is really happening, though the audience cannot but realize that something momentous is at stake. It is only after the event that its significance is revealed and then only gradually and from a variety of angles. To begin with, the rest of Parzival's stay at Munsalvæsche only impresses on him the fact that some terrible

---

[1] Mockenhaupt, *op. cit.* pp. 77 f.

[2] For the matter of Gurnemanz' advice see also above, pp. 153 ff. The omission of *triuwe* from Gurnemanz' catalogue of virtues makes it possible for Parzival to attempt to justify himself by reference to Gurnemanz, to whom he nonetheless attributes 'grôze triwen âne schranz' (239.12). We, however, do not accept Gurnemanz as a sufficient authority. Moreover, his omission of *triuwe* from his instruction strengthens us all the more in our understanding of the importance of *triuwe* in the asking of the question.

[3] I cannot agree with Gerhard Bauer, *Parzival und die Minne* (*Euph.*, LVII, 1963), who declares that 'Parzivals nicht gestellte Frage ist keine "Mitleids"-Frage, sondern eine Neugierfrage' (p. 81). The matter is not a purely subjective one for Parzival. Moreover, Bauer's conclusion that Parzival's 'Schuld' consists in 'seine alles übrige übertönende überstarke Minnebindung an Condwiramurs' (p. 96) is eccentric, to say the least.

calamity has overtaken him; just what it is he does not know. His sleep is disturbed by *strengiu arbeit* and premonitions of *künftigiu leit* (245.1 ff.) so painful as to rival the sufferings of Herzeloyde in her dream of Gahmuret's death. Parzival muses to himself about the meaning of his pain and declares his readiness to help both Anfortas and Repanse de schoye in any *urliuges nôt*. He is not lacking in ability or courage, as is plain from the whole poem as well as in what he says here, but he does not connect the sufferings of his dream with anything that he might have failed to do previously. He decides to leave Munsalvæsche, but finds no one in the castle and consequently departs in a state of confusion and shouting, only to receive the execrations of the *knappe* at the drawbridge, who tells him that he has lost *vil prîss* through not having opened his mouth and put the question to his host (247.26 ff.). Everything is phrased in very general terms, and Wolfram's subsequent comment (248.6 ff.) merely informs us of the fact that Parzival's visit to the Grail castle was like the throw of a die which could have brought either *freuden* or *sorgen* and that now he has to pay the price of his failure. This is, of course, all part of the technique of telling a good story: the audience's attention must be secured and kept in suspense; the author who is in command of his material must build up the tension and not give everything away at the moment it occurs. Wolfram is an adept at this technique, and as he only bit by bit reveals the secrets of the Grail, so he only gradually illuminates the nature of the *Erlösungsfrage*.

Parzival's meeting with Sigune adds a little more to what we partially know. Immediately Sigune realizes that Parzival has been at Munsalvæsche, she assumes that he has in fact asked the question and released Anfortas from his suffering. The matter appears so natural to her that she does not reckon with the possibility that Parzival has not asked it, and she can only talk about the splendour and perfection of worldly goods that he would have as king of the Grail. When the young man admits that he has not asked the question, her rejoicing turns to dismay and curses, and Parzival becomes conscious of what he has done. Sigune's first reaction centres on Parzival's failure in face of the *wunder* of Munsalvæsche and she mentions the *snîdnde silbr und bluotec sper*, the latter of which connects up with the motif of *la lance qui saine* and the second question in Chrétien's romance. This is mentioned again by Cundrie (316.27), but it is never properly incorporated into the complex of events around the Grail, and evidently Wolfram was at a loss to know its real significance. It is a feature of his source that Wolfram was reluctant to omit completely, but did not know what to do with if he retained it.[1] But Sigune goes on to make the meaning of the question much clearer:

> gunêrter lîp, vervluochet man!
> ir truogt den eiterwolves zan,
> dâ diu galle in der triuwe
> an iu bekleip sô niuwe.
> iuch solt iur wirt erbarmet hân,
> an dem got wunder hât getân,
> und het gevrâget sîner nôt.
> ir lebt, und sît an sælden tôt. (255.13 ff.)

Parzival declares his readiness to make reparations, but Sigune rules that out and says in addition that Parzival lost both *êre* and *rîterlîcher prîs* at Munsalvæsche.

In this passage the idea of the *Mitleidsfrage* is clearly enunciated. Sigune does not state an exact formula that Parzival should have uttered, but merely says that he should have asked about the Grail king's suffering. Cundrie, when she denounces Parzival in the presence of the Arthurian court, reinforces this interpretation of the question as a *Mitleidsfrage* by asking Parzival specifically to tell her 'war umb irn [sc. Anfortas] niht siufzens hât erlôst' (315.20) since 'sîn nôt iuch solt erbarmet hân' (316.3). But Cundrie is not primarily interested in the question *qua Mitleidsfrage*, but rather in the matter of publishing Parzival's disgrace to the community which has accepted him in its midst. The rest of

---

[1] Werner Richter, *Wolfram von Eschenbach und die blutende Lanze* (*Euph.*, LIII, 1959), pp. 367–79. In book IX (489.22 ff.) Trevrizent does ask Parzival if he has seen the *sper*, about which he then gives information, but it is not a genuine part of the question motif, although it is put in the context of Anfortas' suffering.

what she says will be discussed later. Trevrizent's understanding of the question, however, is expressed mainly, but not exclusively, in terms of compassion on each occasion that he says anything about the visit to Munsalvæsche. Speaking of the unknown knight, he says:

> der selbe was ein tumber man
> und fuorte ouch sünde mit im dan,
> daz er niht zem wirte sprach
> umben kumber den er an im sach.
> ich ensol niemen schelten:
> doch muoz er sünde engelten,
> daz er niht frâgte des wirtes schaden. (473.13 ff.)

A little later he tells Parzival that if he possesses *triuwe*, the Grail king's pain ought to cause him pity (477.29 f.). Further on, in a much longer exposition of the conditions governing the asking of the question, he formulates it quite specifically as 'hêrre, wie stêt iwer nôt?' (484.27), which appears in book XVI as 'œheim, waz wirret dier?' (795.29). It is clear, therefore, especially with the formulations here given that in its *form* the question to be put to the Grail king is a *Mitleidsfrage* and that Sigune, Cundrie and Trevrizent interpret its content, at least partially, as such. But it is equally clear that, although the question is characterized as a *Mitleidsfrage*, it is not a mere lack of compassion which prevents Parzival from asking it, for Wolfram shows him as being capable of compassion on at least two occasions before he visits Munsalvæsche, viz. when he kills the singing birds and when he first meets Sigune. We therefore have to seek an explanation elsewhere.

Cundrie's denunciation of Parzival goes much further than merely outlining Parzival's failure as a sin against the Grail community: it views the failure as threatening the very being of the knightly Arthurian society to which Parzival belongs. For as heaven decrees that Parzival shall be condemned to hell, so earth correspondingly sees him as 'ir heiles pan, ir sælden fluoch, / des ganzen prîses reht unruoch' (316.11 f.). And then Cundrie attacks his deficiency in *manlîchiu êre* and *werdekeit* and brands him for the *valsch* his conduct exemplifies, contrasting him unfavourably with

both his brother Feirefiz and his father Gahmuret, who are
renowned for the virtues in which he is conspicuously lacking:

> ich wil ûf iwerem houbte swern,
> gît mir iemen des den eit,
> daz grœzer valsch nie wart bereit
> necheinem alsô schœnem man. (316.16 ff.)

There can be no doubt that Parzival has forfeited all that he
possessed of knightly honour. His reputation is swept away
completely through his negligence at Munsalvæsche. But although
this is the case, it is only through the intervention of Cundrie that
the Arthurian court feels itself affected. It remains all the time a
passive observer of Parzival's fate and itself takes no initiative in
passing any judgement. Parzival attempts to justify his position,
though he is only dimly aware of what he has done and what has
happened to him, and has recourse once more to Gurnemanz'
advice:

> sol ich durch mîner zuht gebot
> hœren nu der werlte spot,
> sô mac sîn râten niht sîn ganz:
> mir riet der werde Gurnemanz
> daz ich vrävellîche vrâge mite
> und immer gein unfuoge strite. (330.1 ff.)

Then, without being forced by any member of the court to leave,
he deliberately excludes himself from the Arthurian circle until
such time as he has re-established his reputation. Through the
fact that Parzival's failure is considered to dishonour the Round
Table as well as himself, we are led to the assumption that the
guilt he incurs at the Grail castle must be considered *inter alia* as a
breach of that perfection of knightly conduct to which he is called.
Starting from this point, we can now consider Trevrizent's interpretation of Parzival's defection.

Parzival's failure at Munsalvæsche is the key event of the whole
Grail story. It is examined by Trevrizent in a spiritual context and
with constant reference to God, for Parzival's offence goes further
than disrupting the knightly community to which he belongs: it

affects the very essence of his personal moral and spiritual welfare. Trevrizent interprets the offence in terms of *tumpheit*, first calling the unknown knightly visitor to Munsalvæsche 'ein tumber man' (473.13) and then following it up with the comment:

> sît im sîn tumpheit daz gebôt
> daz er aldâ niht vrâgte,
> grôzer sælde in dô betrâgte.　　　　(484.28 ff.)

Furthermore, Parzival, when he actually comes to the point of confession, takes up this motif in asking Trevrizent to bewail his *tumpheit* (488.15). This explanation puts us to some confusion, since in book IV, just as Parzival first meets Condwiramurs, there occur the remarkable lines:

> sîn manlîch zuht was im sô ganz,
> sît in der werde Gurnemanz
> von sîner tumpheit geschiet
> unde im vrâgen widerriet,
> ez enwære bescheidenlîche,
> bî der küneginne rîche
> saz sîn munt gar âne wort.　　　　(188.15 ff.)

And a little earlier Wolfram mentions that Parzival 'tumpheit âne wart' as a result of Gurnemanz' instruction (179.23). This clearly compels us to interpret the two uses of the word *tumpheit* in two rigorously separated senses. The *tumpheit* from which Gurnemanz delivers the young Parzival is that lack of *savoir vivre* which is revealed in the development of the *Dümmling* theme, and we must therefore assume that Parzival's failure at Munsalvæsche cannot be explained primarily as an offence against courtly society. At the most it can be an offence the consequences of which constitute an affront to courtly society. For, as Heinz Rupp points out,[1] after the Gurnemanz episode Wolfram refrains from applying the word *tump* to Parzival in his capacity as author and thus does not call into question the specifically knightly aspect of his character. Instead it is left to Trevrizent, as the wielder of spiritual authority,

---

[1] Heinz Rupp, *Die Funktion des Wortes tump im 'Parzival' Wolframs von Eschenbach* (GRM (NF), VII, 1957), p. 101.

to describe his failure in terms of *tumpheit*. The *tumpheit* which inhibits Parzival's asking of the question is therefore spiritual. We must, however, guard against the tendency to restrict the spiritual to the purely religious and ecclesiastical. Trevrizent may be a hermit and holy enough to see clearly God's purposes, but he is also a member of the family in whose care the Grail, the symbol of the synthesis between God *and the world*, rests. And the *Mitleidsfrage* also must be viewed in the terms of this synthesis and not solely as a specifically religious matter.

This spiritual *tumpheit* consists in a lack of right reason according to Cundrie, for she flings the curse at Parzival:

> daz iu der munt noch werde wan,
> 'ich mein der zungen drinne,
> als iuz herze ist rehter sinne!' (316.4 ff.)

And Trevrizent supports this view too:

> . . .
> sît dîn kunst sich sælden sus verzêch.
> dô dir got fünf sinne lêch,
> die hânt ir rât dir vor bespart.
> wie was dîn triwe von in bewart
> an den selben stunden
> bî Anfortases wunden?' (488.25 ff.)

Thus, Parzival's guilt derives from his inability or rather refusal to act naturally and spontaneously, to make a decision on his own responsibility, to act according to the particular circumstances and thus according to the dictates of reason. As a result of this his innate *triuwe* is hindered from expression, and he thus also sins against the conception of *triuwe* which runs like a golden thread the whole of the way through the poem. The sin against *triuwe* as the key to the understanding of the *Mitleidsfrage* has often been stressed[1] and rightly so, for, as Mockenhaupt says: 'Nur dies ist

---

[1] For example Schwietering, *Parzivals Schuld*, pp. 59 ff.; Mockenhaupt, *op. cit.*, pp. 66 ff.; Mergell, *op. cit.*, pp. 97 f. Cf. also Bernard Willson, *Das Fragemotiv in Wolframs Parzival* (*GRM* (*NF*), xii, 1962), who relates Gurnemanz' advice interestingly to St Bernard's views on *curiositas* and *humilitas*, which can be reconciled by *caritas*.

wesentlich, daß in dem Epos, welches ganz den *gróȥen triuwen*
(4.10) gewidmet ist, einzige Sünde der Verstoß gegen die *triuwe*
sein kann, und bereits beginnt sich uns der Sinn des Entwick-
lungsweges Parzivals aufzuklären: er soll zur *triuwe* erzogen werden.'[1] Both Sigune (255.14 ff.) and Trevrizent (477.29 f., 488.28
ff.) indicate that Parzival's defection was caused by a lack of *triuwe*,
and, of course, the whole of the religious instruction which
precedes Parzival's confession of failure centres on the subject of
triuwe with particular emphasis on the *triuwe* God manifests
towards man. We must therefore assume an intimate connexion
between the *tumpheit* and the lack of *triuwe* which Trevrizent
laments in Parzival. Wolfram, however, does not work out explicitly what this connexion is.

Wapnewski, loyal to his thesis that Parzival's guilt can be
explained by reference to the teachings of St Augustine, sees
Parzival's failure as the

> konsequenter Ausdruck habitueller Sündhaftigkeit ... Ein andrer,
> nicht belastet mit der Blutschuld, wäre in seinem Schweigen *durh ȥuht*
> nur unreif gewesen. Parzival aber sündigt dadurch, daß er sündig **ist.**
> **Er hat den Gral bereits verloren, bevor er ihn durch sein**
> **Schweigen verliert.** Das Nichtfragen ist nur Bestätigung dafür,
> daß er, der als Prädestinierter zum Gral finden konnte, ihn im Stande
> der Sünde nicht **erringen** kann.'[2]

Parzival's *tumpheit* is the equivalent of *ignorantia*, 'jene Störung
der geistigen Kräfte des Menschen, die das Symptom für seine
Gott-Verlassenheit bilden und ihrerseits der Anlaß neuer sünd-
hafter Handlungen, also Sündenstrafe und Sünde sein kann'.[3] It
is clear from the text that Parzival has already burdened himself
with guilt by the time of his arrival at Munsalvæsche: his offences
against Herzeloyde, Jeschute and Ither are plain for all to see.
Wapnewski's argument, therefore, ends up by being a sophisticated elaboration of Chrétien's original motivation that Perceval
was unable to ask the question owing to the force of the sin against
his mother. This is, of course, not to be denied, but Wapnewski

---

[1] *Op. cit.*, p. 68. [2] *Ibid.*, p. 95. [3] *Ibid.*, p. 93.

rationalizes and theologizes this interpretation to such an extent that one wonders just how much of all this Wolfram really intended or was aware of. Can we really explain Wolfram justly through reference to so complex a pattern of sin, sinfulness, penance and satisfaction, especially when Wolfram's range of knowledge, vast though it may be, has all the impress of an enthusiastic layman and none of a religiously trained scholar? Wolfram's technique, as we may readily see from the prologue and from the so-called *Bogengleichnis*, is to illustrate his ideas by images, images, moreover, which cannot be resolved into straightforward propositions, but exert their power through ambiguous meanings and multivalent interpretations. Is it not then the case that the *Mitleidsfrage* falls into this same category? Is it not capable of a multiplicity of explanations, none of which wholly exhaust the possibilities of the motif, but each of which contributes towards an understanding of it? Parzival's failure at Munsalvæsche is the symbol of his total incapacity to attain the Grail, and as the Grail cannot be completely explained either, but remains invested with a certain impenetrable mystery, so Parzival's failure also proves resistant to a definitive analysis. This is surely the whole point of symbolism: a symbol in poetry is not susceptible of complete rational analysis or of being equated with one particular meaning—this would be represented by the one-to-one relationship of the first stages of allegory—but rather derives its power from the fact that it unites in itself a variety of levels of meaning, each of which is necessary to the whole. Thus, while the description of Parzival's development and the position within this of the *Mitleidsfrage* takes place on an individual level, the interpretation of this can follow an individual path for part of the way, but eventually ends with an acceptance of an underlying symbolic meaning which can only be pointed to, but not fathomed.

The religious element in Parzival's failure must be strongly emphasized, but is not the severity of the sin of not asking the question also illuminated by the fact of Parzival's predestination to the kingship of the Grail? For the whole of Parzival's history is teleologically orientated to the Grail, and a failure at the very point where the *telos* is within sight, if not within reach, justifies the depths of disgrace into which Parzival falls. For Wolfram the element of predestination is present from the beginning, but never stated in such a direct and blatant way as to render the events intervening between Parzival's childhood and eventual attainment of the Grail kingship nothing more than the storyteller's skilful technical manipulation of his material. His method is rather to drop brief hints at various stages in the poem and let the audience draw the conclusions. Thus, his first account of the poem's hero as being *træclîche wîs* (4.18) is no more than a vague indication that the audience can expect him to win through to his goal. Again, Karnahkarnanz' remarks to the boy Parzival are in a similar vein, but since they are phrased in the form of a conditional sentence, nothing very definite can be inferred from them: 'dir hete got den wunsch gegebn, / ob du mit witzen soldest lebn' (124.19 f.). It is interesting to note that in both these comments success is connected with being *wîs*, i.e. with the contrary of what causes Parzival's fall. The next indication has no specific connotations of this kind; Wolfram merely states in announcing Parzival's arrival at Artus' court: 'sus wart für Artûsen brâht / an dem got wunsches het erdâht' (148.29 f.). This is, admittedly, somewhat ambiguous, as it could very well refer only to Parzival's physical appearance, the excellence of which has just been described. But it could also indicate that God intended in the future to reveal perfection in him, i.e. in his attaining the Grail kingship.[1] But, despite the fact that these hints are slight, it is clear enough that the idea of predestination is continually in the background. It is, therefore, a calamity that Parzival's predestination to the Grail should apparently be so thoroughly thwarted by a failure for which he is judged fully responsible. This means that a method has to be found whereby Parzival can overcome the conditions by which the kingship of the Grail is ideally attained. The whole interest of the poem lies in Wolfram's treatment of this theme. How does Parzival conquer his disability and finally release Anfortas and become king of the Grail in his place?

[1] This latter view is sustained by Mockenhaupt (*op. cit.*, p. 59).

The ideal mode of releasing the Grail king from his misery consists in the spontaneous asking of a simple question, whereby the knight performing this deed attains without further ado and without the performance of any acts of valour to the Grail kingship. But as Parzival fails to do this, a second means is presented, consisting in the *erstrîten* of the Grail by someone who is called by God to this deed, and Trevrizent informs Parzival of this, though at a time when he is still unaware of the latter's identity (468.12 ff., cf. also 786.4 ff. and 798.24 ff.). This second method presupposes that the knight is free from any taint of *hôchvart*, as Trevrizent is at pains to point out to Parzival, after the knight has uttered the hope that God might call him to win the Grail through *strîten* (472.1 ff.). The course of Parzival's stay in the hermit's cell has, by the time the young knight confesses his offence, shown Trevrizent a change in Parzival's attitude to an acceptance of the principle of *diemüete*, so that the former can in all honesty point the way to a possible *erstrîten* of the Grail, though, as he says later, 'ez was ie ungewonheit, / daz den grâl ze keinen zîten / iemen möhte erstrîten' (798.24 ff.). Not that Trevrizent emphasizes this point of *erstrîten* in his remarks immediately following Parzival's confession (489.13 ff.). On the contrary, it is only casually slipped in; the real emphasis goes on *buoz*, a concern for the salvation of the soul and counsel to respect the priesthood for its power to perform the sacrament of the eucharist. Trevrizent then allows Parzival to take his leave, absolving him from his sin, reminding him about his advice and exhorting him to maintain a resolute will to do this (502.25 ff.).

By the end of book IX Trevrizent has succeeded in turning Parzival away from his one-sided pursuit of knightly achievement for its own sake and directed him to a course of conduct in which both the service of God and the service of the world have their due place. Parzival accepts the fifteen days of penitence with his uncle 'wand in der wirt von sünden schiet / unt im doch rîterlîchen riet' (501.17 f.) and then departs on his continued search for Munsalvæsche. The greater part of this search is merely reported to us, for the adventures of Gawan fill books X to XIII, and Parzival only appears as a background figure. But in the duel between Gawan and Parzival in book XIV and that between Parzival and Feirefiz in book XV Parzival demonstrates his suitability for the kingship of the Grail, and Cundrie is able to announce her triumphant confirmation of the fact:

zuo Parzivâle sprach si dô
'nu wis kiusche unt dâ bî vrô.
wol dich des hôhen teiles,
du krône menschen heiles!
daz epitafjum ist gelesen:
du solt des grâles hêrre wesen.'   (781.11 ff.)

Everything now progresses without any further hitch to the final scene, in which Parzival utters the question and thereby releases Anfortas from his suffering. Through this formal and ceremonious act the seal is set on Parzival's achievement. The new Grail king then takes it upon himself to tell the good news to Trevrizent, and this particular passage, as has already been mentioned,[1] is thick with problems on account of its inconsistency with what has been said in book IX.

Trevrizent, rejoicing at Anfortas' release (which we must constantly remember is his primary concern and the aim of his penitential life as a hermit), emphasizes to Parzival the mystery of God's ways with men and reiterates his faith in the Incarnation and the Trinity. He then goes on:

græzer wunder selten ie geschach,
sît ir ab got erzürnet hât
daz sîn endelôsiu Trinitât
iwers willen werhaft worden ist.
ich louc durch ableitens list
vome grâl, wiez umb in stüende.
gebt mir wandel für die süende:
ich sol gehôrsam iu nu sîn,
swester sun unt der hêrre mîn.

_____

[1] See above, pp. 340 ff.

[There then follows the revocation about the neutral angels, after which he continues:]

> mich müet et iwer arbeit:
> ez was ie ungewonheit,
> daz den grâl ze keinen zîten
> iemen möhte erstrîten:
> ich het iuch gern dâ von genomn.
> nu ist ez anders umb iuch komn:
> sich hât gehœhet iwer gewin.
> nu kêrt an diemuot iwern sin.'   (798.2 ff.)

This passage as a whole implies that Trevrizent deliberately led Parzival away from the idea of winning the Grail through *strîten*, presumably because this means of winning it has never been known before (798.24 ff.), and he accordingly considers it ill-advised to encourage Parzival in this direction, despite the fact that he knows this means to be a possibility. This sentiment does not in fact correspond with what Trevrizent actually does say about the Grail in book IX, since nothing of what he says contradicts the way in which Parzival attains his goal through being *benennet* and through *strîten*. One *can* say, however, that in terms of an over-all impression Trevrizent holds out little hope of Parzival's being able to undo the consequences of his failure and that it is this impression which is the subject of his present remarks. The passage can only be understood as the reaction of Trevrizent to a situation in which, subjectively, he feels himself to have been unjustifiably dampening. Apart from this there is no other explanation. With this episode Trevrizent's role in the poem is concluded. The action based on the Grail is completed, and Parzival makes his way to a reunion with Condwiramurs.

CONCLUSION

The preceding section of this chapter has of necessity been more concerned with the characterization of Parzival than with that of Trevrizent, and this fact is strongly illustrative of the relationship between the two characters. For, despite the other facets of his personality, Trevrizent is first and foremost the person through whom Parzival learns 'diu verholnen mære umben grâl' (452.30) and is turned to a right relationship with God. The accent is at all times laid on the problems confronting Parzival, and Trevrizent merely—if that is not an inappropriate word!—provides the answers.

A great deal of what Trevrizent says—and speaking is his chief means of expression—comes into the category of information imparted to Parzival. He is an encyclopedia of knowledge about the Grail, the Grail family, Anfortas, Parzival's background and moral theology. None of this information, however, is kept strictly within the bounds of the purely objective and functional, since at every point it emerges from Trevrizent's personal experience and acquaintance and is coloured by his own feelings and assessment of the matter in hand. It is also clearly shaped so as to speak to Parzival's immediate condition as Trevrizent sees it, and in this way the hermit appears as very much more than just a mine of information. Everything is tailored to the situation. Thus, for example, in telling Parzival all the relevant details about Anfortas' suffering and its history, Trevrizent betrays his own emotional participation:

> ieweder ouge im wiel,
> dô er an diz mære dâhte,
> daz er dâ mit rede volbrâhte.
> dô sprach er 'hêrre, ein künec dâ was:
> der hiez und heizt noch Anfortas.
> daz sol iuch und mich armen
> immer mêr erbarmen,
> umb sîn herzebære nôt,
> die hôchvart im ze lône bôt.' (472.18 ff.)

This inner participation of Trevrizent in the events and situations to which he refers provides a marked difference from the relative objectivity of Chrétien's sainz hermite, who remains an isolated and rather impersonal figure in the French poem, dealing virtually exclusively with Perceval's religious problems, while the germaine cousine relates all the information about the Grail king and his wound. Wolfram's Trevrizent, on the contrary, has his very

raison d'être in his penitential activity on behalf of Anfortas; this is
the motive force of his hermit existence:

> dâ lobet ich der gotes kraft,
> daz ich deheine rîterschaft
> getæte nimmer mêre,
> daz got durch sîn êre
> mînem bruoder hulfe von der nôt.
> ich verswuor ouch fleisch, wîn unde brôt,
> unt dar nâch al daz trüege bluot,
> daz ichs nimmer mêr gewünne muot.   (480.11 ff.)

The motivation for Chrétien's hermit remains at the most implicit,
for nothing very clear is ever said about it. But in Wolfram's
depiction of Trevrizent at this point alone there is also a much
more detailed portrait of the hermit uncle, a psychological motivation that Chrétien had not considered necessary in his characters
apart from Perceval, a more carefully thought out incorporation
of the hermit into the Grail family as a whole, the emergence of an
individualized, realistic, 'whole' character capable of a large range
of emotional reactions. Thus, in giving Parzival the information
he requires to be able to understand his own problems *vis-à-vis*
the Grail and his first visit to Munsalvæsche, Trevrizent gives a
great deal more and reveals a considerable amount of his own
character.

The scope of the hermit's character is enlarged by Wolfram so
as to concentrate the revelation of the secrets of the Grail in book
IX and at the same time to amplify them. But above and beyond
this Trevrizent has two further, decisive functions for Parzival's
development—(i) to absolve him from his sin, and (ii) to give him
knightly counsel (501.17 f.). The first of these is dealt with by
Wolfram at much greater length than Chrétien devotes to the
subject, but the process of question and answer, statement and
confession, with all its delicate probings and finely articulated
investigation, more properly contributes to the individualization
of Parzival than to that of Trevrizent. The second function, however, is directly concerned with the individualization of Trevrizent.
Because Trevrizent acts also as a guide to Parzival on matters of

chivalry and thus contributes positively to the realization of the theme of *gote und der werlde gevallen*, Wolfram sees fit to provide the hermit with a knightly background. Accordingly, Trevrizent himself gives an account of his earlier years and knightly exploits. In this way he gains a wider function in the poem as a whole through being given a history, through being given a past as well as a present, and it is through this history that he gains the experience the fruits of which he can pass on to Parzival. He meets Gahmuret, Parzival's father, in the course of chivalrous journeys which establish his reputation as a Grail knight; he is involved in the history of Anfortas' downfall; his own sinful conduct as a Grail knight enables him to speak from a similar experience to Parzival about the latter's problems. In addition, he is drawn into Parzival's previous history through being present at the occasion on which Parzival swears to Jeschute's innocence and reunites her with Orilus, and he is brought into Parzival's triumph in attaining the Grail kingship. Through all these details Trevrizent is given a story of his own, which is complete and forms a coherent, logical whole. He is in the poem not merely for the sake of Parzival in book IX (though this is plainly his chief function), but has an existence of his own which does not need Parzival as its justification. He is not solely the character of one episode. In this way Trevrizent becomes a clearly individualized figure, linked vitally not only with Parzival, but also with Anfortas and the Grail family, with Gahmuret, Ither, Orilus and Jeschute. He is no longer the isolated spiritual adviser of Chrétien's poem.

The problems of religion and chivalry are closely connected in Trevrizent's experience and in his instruction. His theological outlook goes a long way beyond that of the *sainz hermite*, and although this is orientated principally towards the individualization of Parzival's psychology, it also affects the characterization of Trevrizent. While the *sainz hermite* concerns himself chiefly with the practical details of the Christian life and its ecclesiastical setting, Trevrizent's remarks are more deeply rooted in Biblical examples and in the nature of God Himself. His approach is one which combines the tenets of faith with matters of personal experience, and although it in no way contravenes the claims of orthodox church life and teaching (apart from the question of the neutral angels), it does concentrate on the metaphysical foundation of religious experience rather than on formulations of doctrine arising from it. Trevrizent is concerned with a personal realization of spiritual truths, and in this he represents an individual and not an ecclesiastical approach and is in line with the development of medieval mystical writings. His theology is, accordingly, expressed with a view to the needs of the moment, of the individual problems with which he is confronted.

Trevrizent is far from being the typical figure of the medieval hermit, for whom the gulf between the ways of God and the way of the world is unbridgeable. To be sure, he himself has made a complete break with his knightly past in renouncing it, but he does not therefore view the world with completely negative eyes, nor does he seek to persuade Parzival to break with the world. His life as a hermit is led with one particular end in view—the salvation of Anfortas. It is not led from an inner conviction that to belong to the world necessarily endangers the soul. This means that the basis of his life is not a solely religious one, but an individual one combining a strict religious observance with devotion to the fortunes of the Grail community, in which chivalry and spirituality are united. It is only from a hermit with these characteristics that the particular problems of Parzival can receive proper treatment, and in this way it is clear that the individualization of Trevrizent serves the supreme individualization of Parzival.

VIII

GAWAN

INTRODUCTION

IN the second volume of his history of medieval German literature Helmut de Boor refers to the two-storeyed structure of Wolfram's *Parʒival*, in which the Gawan theme provides the storey of the Arthurian world through which Parzival goes to the storey of the Grail world.[1] It would be more accurate to talk of a four-storeyed structure, since Gahmuret and Feirefiz are also 'heroes' of the poem in much the same sense as Gawan. The adventures of Gahmuret introduce elements of the heroic life set mainly outside the Arthurian world and act as a prelude to the history of Parzival, and the action centred on Feirefiz brings in the theme of the 'noble heathen' and the extension of knightly and spiritual ideals to the East. Both Gahmuret and Feirefiz have their place in Wolfram's scheme. This proliferation of heroes represents an acceptance of the idea that each man has his own position in the world, his *ordo*, and that his task in life is to fulfil the claims of his position to the best of his ability; it expresses a limited recognition of individuality. Within this scheme, however, Parzival and Gawan have a particular place and are carefully balanced against each other, though Parzival always retains his pre-eminence in the poem and is referred to as *des mæres hêrre* (338.7) at the very beginning of the Gawan section; moreover, the last line of book XIII, when Gawan's part in the poem is approaching its conclusion, declares: 'an den rehten stam diz mære ist komn' (678.30), and Parzival re-enters the action. It is clear that Parzival's story is by far the most important part of the poem. It is equally clear, however, that Wolfram makes no judgements on the relative worth of his heroes' achievements. This is shown above all by the broken duels of Parzival with Gawan and with Feirefiz and by Gahmuret's

[1] De Boor, *op. cit.*, pp. 106 f.

epitaph (108.3 ff.) and the long eulogy which Parzival devotes to him (751.2 ff.).

The function of Gawan in the poem as a whole is to exemplify the standards of courtliness and act as a norm against which we can assess Parzival's achievements. The code of life which Gawan represents is not essentially different from that which Parzival follows, but less is required of him. The studies of Hildegard Emmel and Maria Bindschedler[1] have demonstrated that the various characteristics of individual knights, their accomplishments and proximity to or distance from their Arthurian community, are measured by comparison with the ideal conduct of Gawan. For this reason Gawan is never the main figure of a classical Arthurian romance and only occurs in this capacity in works such as Heinrich von dem Türlin's *Krône* and the Dutch *Walewein*, which show a degeneration from the classical pattern.[2] From this it follows that Gawan must be—if he conforms in *Parzival* to his role as indicated above—a conventional, idealized figure in whom little individuality need be expected. In many respects this is true, but the Gawan theme occupies books VII and VIII and X to XIV, in all seven out of a total of sixteen books, and the depiction of a merely conventional hero in such a large part of the poem would have detracted severely from the artistic merit of the work. In *Parzival* the Gawan story is carefully worked out in an elaborate series of adventures, partially balancing and partially contrasting with the Parzival story. A definite parallelism is certainly present, as, for example, in the testing points of the two heroes at Munsalvæsche and Schastel marveil, but the subordination of Gawan to Parzival in human experience means that his character is not highly individualized. In fact, the chief interest in Gawan's story lies in the characters whom he meets and the situations in which he finds himself; they, much more than

---

[1] Hildegard Emmel, *Formprobleme des Artusromans und der Graldichtung*; Maria Bindschedler, *Die Dichtung um König Artus und seine Ritter.*

[2] Bindschedler, *op. cit.*, p. 94. For the latest assessment of *Diu Krône* see Rosemary E. Wallbank, 'The Composition of *Diu Krône*: Heinrich von dem Türlin's Narrative Technique' in *Medieval Miscellany presented to Eugène Vinaver* (Manchester, 1965).

Gawan himself, are remarkably individualized. The Gawan theme is by no means a merely entertaining diversion, but fulfils a clear function in the poem as a whole so that the work would be considerably the poorer were it to have been omitted as being an inessential sideline detracting from the Parzival story proper. The purpose of this chapter is to investigate the significance of Gawan in the poem, bearing in mind the proposition that his function is to serve as a norm of courtliness.

SYNONYMS

As has been shown in the preceding chapters, the degree of individualization to be found in a character is reflected to a large extent in the range of the synonyms used to refer to him; and the synonyms used for Gawan are no exception to this. They express his various courtly attributes in a large combination of conventional words and phrases, some of which—such as the terms *wîgant* and *degen*—are coloured by Wolfram's delight in pre-courtly terminology and do not in fact represent Gawan as being in any way essentially different from the normal, idealized courtly knight. There is none of the rich differentiation of moods and stages of development to be found in the synonyms applied to Parzival.

Gawan is introduced into the poem as a boy—*der kleine* (66.18) —at the time of the tourney of Kanvoleis in book II. He is present with his father, Lot of Norway, and is referred to in the capacity of *suon* (66.15), a form of periphrasis which is continued throughout the poem. Thus, he is called *fil li roy Lôt* (314.11, 644.3), *des künec Lôtes sun,*[1] *des künec Lôtes kint* (351.14, 625.14), *Lôtes sun* (387.9), *des werden Lôtes kint* (401.27, 676.8), *des werden Lôtes sun* (422.29, 609.1). He is also called *von Norwæge Gâwân* (651.10) and *der von Norwæge* (387.14, 587.11, 676.3). Through these two name-patterns, which punctuate the whole of Gawan's adventures, we are continually reminded of Gawan's place within the great Arthurian family, since Lot was married to Sangive, the sister of Artus, and we also learn something of the knightly and courtly

[1] 300.23, 353.2, 368.3, 543.9, 597.26, 707.15, 709.19.

traditions in which Gawan was reared. Little is told us of King Lot except for the few remarks in book II and the unprepared-for statement of Gramoflanz in book XII that he killed Irot, Gramoflanz' father (608.11 f.), which then leads to Gawan's duel with Parzival and Parzival's with Gramoflanz, neither of which are fought out to the end. The few words about Lot do, however, give us a good idea of Gawan's background:

> der wol mit rîterschefte kan,
> Lôt von Norwæge,
> gein valscheit der træge
> und der snelle gein dem prîse,
> der küene degen wîse.   (66.10 ff.)

The characteristics mentioned here—knightly prowess, lack of deceit, praiseworthiness, courage and experience—are all marks of knightly excellence and are amplified later in the characterization of Gawan, who follows exactly this pattern of the knightly life without any significant modification in contrast to Parzival, whose character is clearly differentiated from that of his father and contains important changes of emphasis and a definite moral advance and development. This kind of differentiation between father and son is entirely lacking in the case of Lot and Gawan.

The references to Lot and Norway are supplemented by the mention of other relationships, which show varying aspects of Gawan's position within the Arthurian family. Thus, Artus calls him *mîner swester suon* (727.10) and *mîn werder swestersuon* (649.13), and Wolfram also refers to him as *Artûs(es) swester sun* (416.6). The term *neve* is used on several occasions by Artus[1] and by Parzival (689.22, 693.7); on one occasion Parzival qualifies it with *liep* (701.17), otherwise it appears either merely as *neve* or as *mîn neve*. In addition, Itonje, once she has realized Gawan's identity, refers to him as *bruoder* (710.28, 711.18.23), and Wolfram also once calls him *ir bruoder* (710.11). In this way Gawan is specifically linked with his father Lot, his mother Sangive, through her with Artus and Itonje, and lastly with Parzival. The relationships are

---

[1] 650.16, 671.7, 672.2.23, 677.6.8, 717.19, 719.5, 727.23, 785.5.

not as complex as those of Parzival, since they are confined—except for the distant one with Parzival himself—to the Arthurian circle, but they are important in establishing Gawan firmly in the Arthurian family and in giving him the proper context for his knightly and courtly activity.

The main way in which Wolfram refers to Gawan is either as *hêr Gâwan* or as *mîn hêr Gâwân*,[1] a usage which is almost entirely absent in the case of Parzival, who is only three times—so far as I have found—referred to as *hêr Parꝫivâl* (315.9.26, 316.26). This type of reference emphasizes that it is the courtly world in which Gawan moves, and Parzival is only named in this way at the very moment at which he is ejected from the courtly world on account of his defection at the Grail castle.

The many characteristics of the courtly world are well exemplified in the various nouns and adjectives applied to Gawan. First of all, the term *kurteis* (*kurtoys*) is employed three times—in the episode with Obie, Meljanz and Obilot (380.28), and twice in connexion with Orgeluse, the duchess of Logroys, rhyming with the name of her duchy (619.25, 672.25). In another instance Gawan is called *der höfsche man* (756.22). It is clear then that Gawan is looked upon as the representative of courtliness.

Werdekeit seems to be the chief feature of Gawan's personality, if we are to be guided by the number of times this and associated words occur with reference to him. Very often he is called *der werde Gâwân*,[2] once *der werde erkande Gâwân* (338.4), *der werde man* (646.18), *der werde helt* (397.29), *der werde muotes rîche* (538.16), *der werde degen balt* (339.15), *der degen wert* (541.12, 666.17), *der werde degen* (688.15), *der stolꝫe werde* (353.6), merely *der werde* (516.25), and he is also referred to as Vergulaht's *werder gast* (410.19) and, at his first meeting with Orgeluse, as *der edele werde gast* (530.26). At one point this excellence is affirmed by his being called *der man | der werdekeit ein bluome ie was* (598.6 f.).

---

[1] The number of occasions on which these synonyms are used is so great that it is unnecessary to detail them.

[2] 340.23, 366.4.19, 371.17, 392.17, 394.19, 402.14, 406.12, 624.21, 631.7. 652.5, 668.26, 677.23, 679.1, 684.5, 685.6, 689.3, 703.19.

The frequency with which this word occurs in contexts which stretch over the whole of that part of the poem in which Gawan appears indicates the importance of Wolfram's moral assessment of Gawan's character and shows that Gawan does not undergo any definite moral development, since at no time is he less worthy than at any other. This is underlined by the use of various phrases in which Gawan's innocence of the accusation brought against him by Kingrimursel is continually asserted. Book VII, for example, begins with the telling phrase *der nie gewarp nâch schanden* (338.1), and elsewhere Gawan is called *der ie was valsches vrî* (580.7) and *der valsches vrîe* (668.30), which contrasts strongly with Parzival's being enmeshed in *valsch*.[1] He is also referred to as *der êren rîche und lasters arm* (581.1), this occurring after the episode of Lit marveile. But connected with this complex of ideas Gawan is twice called a *valschære* (362.24, 363.16) and once a *trügenære* (363.14); these, however, all come into the same sphere as belonging to the various unjust calumniations which Obie directs against Gawan after his arrival at Lippaut's castle and which Wolfram shows to be unfounded, since he states immediately afterwards: 'unschuldec was hêr Gâwân' (363.17). Gawan's courtliness is brought out further by the use of several phrases indicating his noble birth, as *der wol geborne gast* (405.23, 522.17) and *der degen wol geborn* (299.30, 602.14). His praiseworthy nature is summed up in the terms *der prîss erkande* (558.1) and *der wol gelobte man* (299.13). Further specifically courtly attributes are shown in the use of the words and phrases *milte* (666.8), *sælden rîche* (670.21)— because of his alliance with Orgeluse— *der reht gemuote* (339.1), *der wol gevar* (375.25)—a phrase found much more frequently referring to Parzival— *er süeer man vil guoter* (374.22). It should be borne in mind, however, that these few phrases, which are rather more specific than those mentioned earlier in this paragraph, occur only once, or at the most twice, and therefore give only slight indications of other courtly characteristics. They would lead one to the conclusion that Gawan is a highly generalized character and appears much more as the ideal representative of Arthurian

[1] See above, pp. 169 f.

society, as *der werden tavelrunder bote* (380.11), than as a character with an independent existence.

One of the foremost features of Gawan's life is his attitude towards *minne*,[1] and a variety of synonyms cover this aspect of his life. Thus, he is referred to as *der minnen gernde* (503.15) and *der minne(n) gernde man* (512.19, 615.15), all of which occur in connexion with his attempts to win the favour of Orgeluse. Wolfram refers once to Gawan as Antikonie's *vriunt* (408.5), a term which is used in pre-courtly and early courtly literature and scarcely ever in courtly literature proper with the exception of Wolfram's works, but later he calls Gawan Orgeluse's *âmîs* (728.2), a word borrowed from the French vocabulary of courtliness and one which expresses all the attraction of a foreign fashion. Here, if anywhere, there is a difference which might have led one to conclude that Gawan, like Parzival, undergoes a development in his character, but this could only be asserted if further parallels could be found for the combination *vriunt* = *âmîs*; in the use of synonyms, however, this example remains isolated.[2] As it happens, Gawan's character is a function of the circumstances in which he finds himself.

The next group of synonyms covers Gawan's activity as a knight, and here, as in the case of all Wolfram's knights, we find a marked use of pre-courtly vocabulary. The word *ritter* is not the most frequently used term, though it does occur several times[3] and twice combined with the adjective *fremd* (368.17, 373.19) in the Obie-Meljanz episode. A more popular term with an archaic flavour is *degen*, of which many instances have already been given; in addition to them the following occur: (397.25); combined with the equally archaic *snel* (432.24, 503.20, 535.8), *balt* (397.25, 534.11, 601.14), *mære* (605.3), *ellenthaft* (418.3). *Ellens rîch* is also found independently (418.23, 429.12, 544.22, 602.12). An alternative to

---

[1] Wolfgang Mohr, *Parzival und Gawan* (*Euph.*, LII, 1958), pp. 5 f., considers that the part played in Gawan's story by the *minne*-episodes has been overstated and that *minne* is only a secondary theme in Gawan's as well as in Parzival's history. Gawan, like Parzival, has a task to fulfil.

[2] Gawan is, however, also called *geselle* in the Antikonie episode (410.5).

[3] 353.29, 358.2.4, 372.30, 574.7.15.

degen is *wîgant,* of which there are three examples (553.3, 588.11, 602.27). Then comes the more general term *helt,*[1] which on one occasion is amplified into *der helt unverʒagt* (582.8) when Gawan after his initial adventure at Schastel marveil is longing for Orgeluse, and the word connects Gawan also with the terminology of the prologue. In another place he is called *der wâre strîtes helt* (335.17). The descriptions *manlîch* (331.23), *stolʒ* (403.4, 705.11), *stark* (602.24) and *getriwe* (522.7) are also applied, but add nothing that is not implicit in the already mentioned terms. The word *gast* is used on many occasions[2] and merely indicates the itinerant nature of Gawan's life. It is combined with other words, as has been shown above, and it is, further, once elaborated by the addition of *fremd* (374.23). When Gawan eventually, after Artus' approval of all the various marriages at the end of book XIV, remains with the court and receives Parzival and Feirefiz, he is referred to as *der wirt* (764.1.8, 774.9). Nothing of any great moment is contained in all these references: they are solely of the conventional kind to be expected as describing any idealized courtly hero. Two more phrases remain, however: one of these is purely descriptive of Gawan after his encounter with the lion in Schastel marveil—*der sieche wunde* (584.30); the other is Orgeluse's contemptuous view of Gawan—*ir gans* (515.13)—which ties up with Obie's assessment of Gawan firstly as a *koufman* (352.16) and secondly as a *valschære* or *trügenære.* These last references are the only unexpected ones in the whole of the characterization of Gawan, since the pre-courtly terms do not constitute a mark of individuality in Gawan, but rather in Wolfram. The synonyms present us with a conventional, idealized knight with no significant distinguishing features. What distinguishing features there are are found in a different sphere.

DESCRIPTIVE PASSAGES

In the course of the poem several passages containing longer or shorter descriptions of Gawan occur sporadically in those books

---

[1] 339.21, 342.4, 411.19, 548.19, 567.28, 574.28, 581.12.19, 611.17.
[2] 363.24, 368.22, 372.3, 412.19, 422.21, 553.29, 557.24, 558.14, 572.5, 601.7.

in which he appears as the main character. The particular physical appearance of Gawan does not, however, seem to be very important in Wolfram's mind, since the features which he mentions are usually very general. Gawan is not deliberately introduced into the story with a descriptive passage, but emerges from the Arthurian background as a person who requires no introduction. It seems to be taken for granted that everyone knows who Gawan is and what function he fulfils in Arthurian romance. He is mentioned very early in the poem as having been present at the tourney of Kanvoleis as a boy. Next, Clamide speaks of him as a knight at Artus' court (221.2 ff.), to whom he, Clamide, would like to be commended. A third reference to him occurs when Orilus offers his *sicherheit* to Cunneware at Artus' court (277.4), and a fourth when Segramors exclaims in fury that Gawan's and Artus' dignity, and with them the whole of the Round Table, has been violated by the presence of Parzival in an attitude of battle (284.14 ff.). Nowhere, however, is any description given either of his physical appearance or of his representing the courtly ideal until Gawan discloses his name to Parzival after having broken his *minne*-trance. Then Parzival declares with great wonder that he has heard of Gawan's reputation: 'ich hôrte von dir sprechen ie, / du erbütesz allen liuten wol' (304.4 f.); but even here there is no more precise information. Everything points to the fact that the function and personality of Gawan in Arthurian romance in general was widely known and needed neither comment nor explanation. His role was not that of an individual knight, about whom a series of adventures was told, but on the contrary that of a figure who represented the courtly knight *par excellence*. The adventures in which Gawan is the hero are there to show how the perfect knight acts in particular situations; they do not have a function in showing the unfolding character of the knight, since, if he represents an ideal, by the nature of the case there can be no such development. It is the task of later sections in this chapter to discuss the purpose of the Gawan adventures both in the characterization of Gawan and in the scheme of the whole poem.

If Gawan had been too closely described, this would in large measure have removed his idealized character. We have already seen how this applies to the characterization of Condwiramurs, who is also described in merely general, idealized terms, all strictly individual features being omitted. The descriptions of Gawan which occur in the poem after Parzival's words of wonder do a little to clarify our picture of his physical appearance, but they are in terms of praise and idealization, and the main impression we receive is of Gawan's high moral worth. Thus, Kingrimursel, in challenging him to a duel on account of an alleged insult, refers to him as someone 'der dicke prîs hât getân / und hôhe werdekeit bezalt' (321.6 f.). Later, at Lippaut's castle, the reference is made more concrete and Wolfram describes him as

> ... Gâwân ...,
> der selten ellens ie vergaz;
> an dem er [sc. Scherules] vant krancheite flust,
> lieht antlütze und hôhe brust,
> und einen ritter wol gevar. (361.19 ff.)

The brightness of Gawan's face is mentioned again shortly afterwards by Obie and Obilot's mother, who declares: 'sîn blic ist reht ein meien glast' (374.24), which more than any other word or phrase places Gawan in the context of the ecstatic courtly love-lyric and the month of May which is its favourite season (cf. also the portrayal of Artus as *der meienbære man* (281.16)). The excellence of Gawan's character and his peculiar position within the company of the Round Table is indicated at the end of book VI, where his departure means that 'der werdekeit ein weise / wart nu diu tavelrunder' (335.8 f.), and also in book XII, where Gramoflanz states:

> nu ist Lôt erstorben,
> und hât Gâwân erworben
> solhen pris vor ûz besunder
> daz ob der tavelrunder
> im prîses niemen glîchen mac. (608.25 ff.)

These are the most important facts about Gawan, fundamental to an understanding of his character; the elaboration of them to be found in other places does not in any way lessen this ideal.

At the beginning of book VII Wolfram makes a few introductory remarks on the adventures of Gawan, which are now to come to the forefront of the poem, and suggests that the function of this part of the poem is to depict something which is not particularly important for the main hero Parzival, that is, the role of *âventiure*. I think it is somewhat misleading to assert, as Wapnewski has, that Gawan is Parzival's 'Darstellungsform' or 'Aktionsart',[1] though there is significance in this remark. Gawan is *not* a function of Parzival, as Wapnewski's comments imply, but has a career of his own, which forms a parallel to that of Parzival. The stories of the two heroes are complementary.[2] What leads Wapnewski to the above assertion is a feeling that the adventures of Gawan relate in detail something which is omitted from the history of Parzival or, rather, is only hinted at and never fully described. There is, however, a difference of plane between Parzival and Gawan, which makes an attempt to show Gawan as Parzival's 'Darstellungsform' illusory. The adventures of Gawan are not intended to expand, in the setting of the courtly world, those brief appearances of Parzival as the *rôter ritter* in the significant intervals between his first visit to the Grail castle, his sojourn with Trevrizent and his second visit to Munsalvæsche. They express a different level of human experience,[3] and it is important that this should be expressed as the highest in a particular station in life. The purpose of Gawan's life is in the fulfilment of the courtly ideal, not in the achievement of

---

[1] *Op. cit.*, p. 127.

[2] If we are to consider certain characters as functions of another, then Gawan, Gahmuret, Feirefiz *and* Parzival are all functions of the overall subject of the poem, which is man himself. In this way Gawan, Parzival and the rest become representatives of the general idea of man in particular times, places and circumstances. It is at this level of particular examples of the idea of man that the identification of Parzival with Gawan and Feirefiz is to be understood. Nevertheless, despite their definite dependence one on another, each of these characters maintains a certain independence and autonomy.

[3] Max Wehrli, *Wolfram von Eschenbach. Erzählstil und Sinn seines 'Parzival'* (*DU*, VI, V, 1954), p. 32.

the Grail (though this latter task is laid upon him also). He is, thus, in a sense a contrasting figure to Parzival, someone against whom Parzival can be measured, but he is not merely a function of Parzival or a stage in his development. If he were, then the duel would, clearly, have as a decisive outcome the victory of Parzival over Gawan, and Gawan, as Parzival's 'lower self', would be completely vanquished. As this does not happen, it is reasonable to assume that Gawan has a definite independence and function of his own.

The introductory lines of book VII, then, present Gawan prepared for all possibilities and able to cope with any knightly eventuality. He is depicted as being reliably valiant in battle, with a heart in battle like a fortress, impregnable to cowardice, an example of manly strength and courage. His knightly prowess is such that his battle-cry sounds loud in his favour however much Kingrimursel would have liked to deprive him of his reputation in battle. With such words Wolfram sets the scene for Gawan's adventures, and the ensuing episodes live up to the standard initially set for them.

Clothes, possessions, horses and the like also provide a medium for characterization, the external features pointing to states of mind and moods that lie behind them. This method we observed particularly with Gahmuret, in whose case it expressed what was not explicitly stated in direct terms on account of the necessary subordination of Gahmuret to Parzival, and also with Parzival, with whom the many ways of characterization open up different levels of his personality. But this indirect method of characterization is not extensively used with Gawan, and descriptions of his appearance, when they occur, are usually quite short and not clearly individualized.

The first passage which can be termed a description of his clothing and possessions is to be found at the end of book VI as Gawan departs from Artus' court, and this catalogues the various gifts which are showered on him by Artus and his followers. Artus himself gives him valuable presents, gold, jewels and silver, and from others and merchants he gets three well-tried, solid shields, seven battleworthy horses and twelve sharp spears from Angram, a land which is mentioned only in connexion with the quality of its spears, each fitted with strong wooden shafts from a *heidenschez muor* in Oraste Gentesin. The number of these knightly necessities must have been considered significant, though perhaps the interpretations of the numbers varied according to the interpreter. The attribution of any one particular association at this time does not entail that the objects to which the numbers refer then become symbols of higher powers throughout the rest of the poem. The three shields, for example, would naturally be connected in the medieval mind with the Trinity, faith in Whom would be defensive against the devil as the shields would be against a knightly opponent; and it is clear in the poem that Gawan has an unshaken faith in God and is never overcome by any other knight. The horses, by their being seven, would be aligned with the perfection implied in the seven days of creation, with the idea of the seven churches of the Book of Revelation, with the seven planets and the influence they were held to have over happenings in the world, and so forth. The twelve spears might be associated with the twelve apostles, to mention only the most obvious example. What is important about the actual numbers used, however, is not any *definite association* the purpose of which is immediately apparent and meaningful throughout the poem, but the *suitability* and the *evocativeness* of the numbers, which then enhances the description of Gawan's appearance.[1]

The gifts of the Arthurian court serve later as a pretext for Obie's attempts to calumniate Gawan, and she refers to the richness of his worldly possessions, his horses, silver and clothing, as the property of a deceiver (362.25 ff.). She sticks to her original impression that Gawan is a merchant, and Scherules has to protest on Gawan's behalf that he has never been the bearer of a money-bag or a coiner of money. Gawan's various possessions had been described a little before on the occasion of his arrival at Lippaut's castle (353.4 ff.),

---

[1] See Vincent Foster Hopper, *Medieval Number Symbolism* (New York, 1938), particularly the chapters on the Early Christian Writers and Medieval Number Philosophy, for a discussion of number symbolism in general.

the mattress and quilt for his bed being singled out for reference, though not for closer description.

After Gawan's debilitating adventure with the lion at Schastel marveil, the great testing point of his history is past and he is able to proceed, after having been healed from his wounds by the four queens, to marry Orgeluse. This turning point is marked, as the various stages in Parzival's career are, by a change in clothing. Gawan had been wearing armour in his fight with the lion, and the ladies in the castle relieve him of its weight and encumbrance (575.17 ff.). Under it they find that he is wearing a tunic of sable with two gampilûne[1] on it. This coat of arms was that of Ilinot and is mentioned also as belonging to him in 383.1 ff., though then each of the Britons in the battle wore it. It is not clear just what the significance, if any, of the recurrence of this motif is. It is, in any case, not a distinguishing feature of Gawan's, since the ladies in the castle remain ignorant of Gawan's identity until he reveals it to them on Artus' arrival at Schastel marveil. The most reasonable explanation would seem to be that as Ilinot was Artus' son the appearance of Gawan in Ilinot's coat of arms indicates that Gawan is in some way to be regarded as Artus' adoptive son in his quality of being the most perfect knight in the Round Table. Nevertheless, this is all put on one side when Gawan has recovered from his injury, and he receives a splendid new set of clothes (588.14 ff.) as a sign that he has proved his ability: shirt and trousers of buckeram, a sleeveless gown of marten's fur, a fur coat of the same, a scarlet cloak from Arras and new boots. At the beginning of book XIII, as all the strands of Gawan's adventures are beginning to be woven together, further magnificent clothes of pfelle embroidered with gold are mentioned (628.15 ff.), but apart from this there are no more specific references to clothing or changes of clothing.

The description of Gawan's bed in his lodging with Plippalinot and his daughter Bene can also be mentioned in connexion with the descriptions of Gawan's appearance (552.9 ff.). This passage is filled with the spirit of ironic belittlement, as Wolfram depicts the

[1] Lexer defines gampilûn as a 'wunderbares, drachenartiges thier'.

bed in some detail, but is at pains to note its inferior quality. In this way a deliberate contrast is made between this bed and Lit marveile of the next book, though it is clear that Plippalinot gives Gawan the best that is at his disposal—a feather bed covered with great satin (not of the highest quality, Wolfram points out, but artificial), a quilt without the gold embroidery that a noble knight might expect, but made of soft silk, and white linen sheets and a pillow. The reception, however, shows that Gawan is welcome in all kinds of society and that he is a guest who can suit himself to all occasions. This particular description obviously leads up to the episode of Lit marveile[1] and is just one of the many instances of the importance of gradation in the development of the story and in the relative significance of the various episodes.

The whole of book X, in which Orgeluse is introduced into the poem, is seen on one level in terms of the various characters' horses, and we have seen in the chapter on Parzival how Parzival's progress is illuminated with reference to the three horses he rides.[2] In the case of Gawan his story is in part seen as that of Gringuljete,[3] whose history previous to Gawan's ownership of him is detailed twice in slightly varying terms (339.26 ff. and 540.25 ff.). Originally Gringuljete was one of the Grail horses and is branded with the mark of the turtle-dove, the emblem of the Grail, on its hock (540.26 f.), a feature which enables Gawan to recognize him without any possibility of making a mistake when he gets him back after a period of absence. The horse was first in the possession of the Grail knight Lybbeals of Prienlascors, from whom Lähelin won it in a battle at the lake of Brumbane (473.22 ff. and 540.28 f.). Lähelin then passed it on to his brother Orilus, who still owns the horse when Parzival meets him for the second time in book V

---

[1] The significance of Lit marveile with regard to Gawan's character is closely connected, quite obviously, with the descriptive passages mentioned above, but a discussion of it is postponed until later in the section dealing with the episodes of Schastel marveil. See below, pp. 383 ff. and 431 f.

[2] See above, p. 125.

[3] The name of the horse comes from Chrétien's 'le Gringalet' (6209, 7136), which derives, according to Grandsaignes d'Hauterive, from the Welsh *Kein Kaled*, the name of Gauvain's horse.

(261.27 ff.), and Orilus presents Gringuljete to Gawan as he departs from Artus' court to re-establish his honour with Vergulaht (339.26 ff. and 540.30 ff.). The way in which Gawan, therefore, becomes the owner of Gringuljete connects him—at least implicitly —with Parzival, since we may assume that it was through Parzival's victory over Orilus and the condition he set that Orilus should tell Artus and Ginover of his activity in their service that Orilus came to be at the Arthurian court at the time when Gawan and Parzival were both compelled to forsake it. The fact that Gawan rides one of the Grail horses is an important aspect in the careful parallelism of the heroes.

Gringuljete is a powerful horse, a *kastelân* (522.27), and is known as 'mit den rôten ôren Gringuljete' (339.29) and 'von Munsalvæsche Gringuljete' (597.21), but nothing more is told us of his appearance, and indeed nothing more is necessary. It is his *part* in the action of book X that is important in pointing out Gawan's own fortunes. Orgeluse is determined to test Gawan to the uttermost, and this is reflected in what happens to Gringuljete, though indeed Orgeluse is not responsible for it. Thus, she pours scorn on Gawan for busying himself with medical matters and laughs at him when Urjans takes advantage of him, remembering his days with the dogs at Artus' court, which he attributes to Gawan's ill-will, and rides away on Gringuljete. Orgeluse declares with great spite:

> für einen rîter ich iuch sach:
> dar nâch in kurzen stunden
> wurdt ir arzet für die wunden:
> nu müezet ir ein garzûn wesn. (523.6 ff.)

And this is, to be sure, Gawan's position with respect to her, but he is not afraid of scorn and persists in offering his service:

> solt ich diens geniezen,
> iuch möhte spots verdriezen.
> ob ez mir nimmer wurde leit,
> ez krenket doch iur werdekeit. (524.5 ff.)

Later, Malcreatiure and his horse, a broken-down *runzît*, appear on the scene, and when Malcreatiure goes off on foot, Gawan takes his horse, but it is unfit for battle and so weak that Gawan nevertheless has to go on foot while taking the horse with him. Orgeluse, therefore, is seen to be in control of the situation and Gawan very much in a position of subordination and inferiority. Gawan's poor horse leads him into some embarrassment in his encounter with Lischoys Gwelljus (536.18 ff.), but after an initial joust, the duellers turn to swords on foot and Gawan eventually overcomes Lischoys, though he thinks better of killing him. It is at this point that Gawan realizes that he has won back Gringuljete, who must in the meantime have passed from Urjans' into Lischoys' hands. Gawan ascribes Gringuljete's return to God's action on his behalf, and he therefore must be regarded as having passed with honour through the period of Orgeluse's deliberately testing behaviour: 'ob duz bist, got hât dich wider / mir schône gesendet, / der dicke kumber wendet' (540.22 ff.). It is clear that Gawan's fortunes are paralleled by the descriptions of the horses which he rides, and the appearance and weakness of Malcreatiure's little *runzît*, of which Gawan for a time takes possession, shows the extent to which Gawan is degraded—innocently and unjustifiably, as Wolfram points out—by the actions of Urjans and Orgeluse. This is just one of the many ways in which external features are used to reinforce the exposition of a character.

All in all, however, the descriptions of Gawan's personal appearance tell us little specific about him, though the descriptions of clothing, possessions and the story of Gringuljete go a little, but certainly not very far, towards creating a slightly more individual picture. In no respect does Gawan become a serious rival to Parzival as *the* hero of the poem, as in all the episodes and descriptions in his story his character, in all its idealization, remains generalized and lacking the passion and depth of feeling that is characteristic of Parzival.

MONOLOGUES

Parzival's monologues are distributed fairly evenly over the whole of his story and illuminate his development at many stages. By contrast Gawan's are confined to a narrower range of episodes and consequently bring particular happenings into relief while the rest of his story continues on a uniform level. Emil Walker points out that the use of monologues is a fair indication of the participation of the author in the inward action of the poem and that the long passages (of 400 lines or above) in which no monologues occur tend to show the author's detachment from his subject.[1] The things which Wolfram, according to this view, wishes to emphasize are: (i) Gawan's participation in the *Blutstropfenepisode*; (ii) the demands of the knightly life as illustrated by the part that Gawan is called to play in the defence of Lippaut and the service of Obilot; (iii) the meeting with Urjans' lady and the encounter with Lischoys Gwelljus; (iv) the adventures of Schastel marveil; and (v) Gawan's love for Orgeluse. These are in fact the most important parts of Gawan's career, and the monologues are calculated to bring out some special aspect in Gawan's character which needs to be underlined at the time in question.

The total number of Gawan's monologues is nineteen, and of these fifteen have no corresponding monologue in the *Conte del Graal*.[2] This fact links up generally with the elaborations we have already noted in Wolfram's work, and it is interesting to note that the ideas of expansion and individualization apply to the character of Gawan as well as to that of Parzival. The findings of the previous sections of this chapter might well have led us not to expect any monologues at all, or at least a considerably smaller number than actually are found. We must now examine the various groups of monologues in turn.

(i) The incident of the drops of blood on the snow, present in Chrétien's poem, we have seen to be changed in emphasis by Wolfram, and the function that Gawan has in it is by virtue of his acknowledged position as the perfect example of courtliness. Gawan has already addressed Parzival and explained that his behaviour is an insult to the king before he realizes that Parzival

[1] Walker, *op. cit.*, pp. 22 ff.

[2] Walker, *op. cit.*, p. 238. The monologues with no correspondence in Chrétien are as follows: 301.22 ff., 339.24 f., 340.7 ff., 350.1 ff., 350.14 f., 351.17 ff., 504.15 ff., 536.18 ff., 539.26 ff., 540.17 ff., 542.9 f., 543.10 ff., 553.19 f., 571.7 ff., 587.15 ff.

has fallen into a *minne*-trance and is completely unaware of his, Gawan's, presence (300.24 ff.). He then remembers how he himself had been in virtually the same position with regard to Queen Inguse of Bahtarliez and uses this experience to imagine how Parzival feels:

> waz op diu minne disen man
> twinget als si mich dô twanc,
> und sîn getriulîch gedanc
> der minne muoz ir siges jehen? (301.22 ff.)

In this way Gawan's action in placing the cloth over the drops of blood as the best means of delivering Parzival from his trance is justified. The attempts of Segramors and Keie had failed because they did not understand the situation and also because they did not possess the experience and knightly perfection necessary to give authority to their actions. These soliloquizing words of Gawan show that he is in command of the situation, and he is thus able by a fitting action to release Parzival from the bonds of *minne*. The situation demands all Gawan's courtly tactfulness, and his monologue expresses how much he is involved in it. This is, in fact, Gawan's first significant appearance in the poem. It is important that Wolfram causes him to intervene in this episode instead of allowing the trance, as Chrétien does, to wane and finally disappear with the melting of the snow and the consequent vanishing of the drops of blood (4426 ff.).

(ii) Six monologues occur in book VII and cover the theme of the demands made upon the courtly knight by society.[1] Both the first three and the second three monologues are linked by certain words and ideas with the prologue and the theme of *zwîvel*. The book opens with a scene in which Gawan meets an unknown army, whose intentions may be friendly or unfriendly, so far as he knows, and he is in some doubt as to what to do. On consideration, however, he decides against making a detour because of the length of the way (339.24 f.) and resolves to approach the army and investigate the situation. He considers that a knight who is so

---

[1] 339.24 f., 340.7 ff., 340.22 ff., 350.1 ff., 350.14 f., 351.17 ff.

timid (*verzagt*) as to retreat before any attack is made is unworthy of praise, and he, Gawan, has in any case already been seen by the larger part of the army so that his avoidance of them would be ignominious on his part (340.7 ff.). He therefore decides, in case the army should have unfavourable intentions towards him, to take the initiative in a joust before they can turn against him (340.22 ff.).

The second group of monologues is found after Gawan has learnt from a *knappe* of Lisavander the significance of the army's approach to Bearosche, and the idea of *zwîvel* is twice explicitly mentioned with respect to what Gawan is to do (340.30, 350.30). Here the term *zwîvel* is connected with the necessity for deciding between alternative courses of action. Gawan is concerned in the first place with his knightly honour and reputation: if he remains aloof from the fighting, he will lose his honourable status; if he joins in and is injured, he will be in the same case; but he also considers the claims of his duel with Vergulaht and concludes that they are paramount at present (350.1 ff.). Nevertheless, he is sorely troubled by the problem and cannot really make up his mind either one way or the other, but puts the situation into God's hands: 'nu müeze got bewarn / die kraft an mîner manheit' (350.14 f.). Gawan is in a state of indecision about the whole affair and has no deep feelings as to the justness of either side's cause; he is merely concerned about the question of honour. Eventually he reaches the conclusion that he would be in a more favourable position in Bearosche than outside it. The idea of a reward is of no importance to him except in so far as fortune (*gelücke*) should bring it his way (351.17). He is a disinterested participant in the situation, concerned with the abstract claims of knighthood more than with the merits of the particular case. Despite the fact that it is only with him in *Parzival* that we find this type of monologue expressing the act of choice, first found in German literature in the courtly period and showing a trend towards self-consciousness,[1] I feel that it is the incident which shapes Gawan's character and not the character which determines the course of action. Gawan does not put himself

---

[1] Walker, *op. cit.*, pp. 181 ff.

in control of the situation, but allows himself to be drawn into it and yields to the power of *gelücke* and the appeal to God (350.14 f.). He does not make a free decision that would assert his moral sovereignty. Nevertheless, there is at this stage a definite attempt to portray the psychological side of Gawan's character, and this in itself is an advance on the characterization of pre-courtly literature.

(iii) Book X opens with the encounter of Gawan with Urjans' lady, in whose figure the idea of struggle, foreshadowing Gawan's troubled service of Orgeluse, and the power of Lischoys Gwelljus are introduced, since Lischoys has wounded Urjans and at the end of the book is overcome by Gawan. Gawan has no idea who the lady is, and we never learn her name, but his musings about her and comparison of her with Kamille, whom Veldeke depicts in his *Eneide* (8784 ff.) as fighting against the Trojans, plainly introduce the idea of the *minne*-encounter as a battle. The appearance of the lady makes Gawan consider how he would fare in battle against her. Here again, as in the previous monologues, Gawan's first thought is his knightly reputation and how he could prove and maintain his honour.

This preoccupation with honour in battle is pursued in the next monologue of this book, when Gawan meets Lischoys and is embarrassed by the weakness of his poor *runzît* (536.18 ff.), which would certainly be overcome by Lischoys' superior horse. But such is Gawan's devotion to Orgeluse, who has put him in the position of meeting Lischoys, that he is prepared to fight him on foot, even if he should never again receive Orgeluse's *gruoz*. But Gawan, as we might expect, overcomes Lischoys, and in his next monologue he queries whether he should kill him, this being the logical consequence of his action. However, the humanitarian spirit pervading the entire poem, which means that neither Parzival nor Gawan is shown taking an opponent's life (except for Parzival's killing of Ither), leads Gawan to the thought that he will allow Lischoys to escape with his life, if he will offer him his *sicherheit* (539.26 ff.). But Lischoys refuses this, takes advantage of Gawan's relaxation of his grip to regain his sword and join battle once more, which causes Gawan to think that he will make

Lischoys pay for his action (542.9 f.). Again Lischoys refuses to yield to Gawan's conditions and declares that Gawan will gain great honour in killing him. At this point Gawan remembers Orgeluse, on whose account they are fighting, and considers how he would lose her esteem if he were to kill unnecessarily this innocent knight. He muses how Lischoys too is constrained by love of Orgeluse and how the situation, if he is to win her, here invoking once more the power of *gelücke*, will not be affected by Lischoys' remaining alive. He considers that, if Orgeluse had been watching their fight, she would have had to acknowledge his worthiness to serve her, and this leads him to be merciful to Lischoys for Orgeluse's sake and say: 'ich wil durch die herzogîn / dich bî dem leben lâzen sîn' (543.10 ff., 25 f.).

The monologues of book X continue and extend the features of Gawan's personality already presented. The idea of honour is now explicitly connected with Orgeluse, and *minne*—not solely knightly reputation—becomes the most important aspect of Gawan's career. His power to reach decisions is now more apparent, but the idea of *gelücke*—the outside agency of fortune—persists.

(iv) After an unimportant monologue of two lines at the beginning of book XI, in which Gawan expresses his characteristic consideration for other people (553.19 f.), we come to a series in which the adventures of Schastel marveil, the parallel in Gawan's story of Parzival's adventures at Munsalvæsche, provide the focal point for Gawan's thoughts. These monologues deal in turn with Lit marveile, the *starker gebûr*, the lion and Gawan's resultant debilitated condition and correspond in the physical sphere to the spiritual experiences of Parzival at the Grail castle.

The adventure of Lit marveile has been connected by Bernard Willson with the prologue of *Parzival* and especially with 1.15 ff. and 2.5 ff.[1] I have pointed out elsewhere[2] that Gawan is involved in the complexities of the discussion on *zwîvel* and *triuwe*, but I

[1] Bernard Willson, *Wolframs Bîspel. Zur Interpretation des 1. Teils des Parzival-Prologs* (*Wolfram-Jahrbuch*, 1955), pp. 29 ff.
[2] See above, pp. 189 ff.

do not agree with Willson that it is due to Gawan's lack of *stæte* that he finds difficulty in jumping on to the bed, since the attack by Kingrimursel on Gawan's reputation in book VI is an unjust one.[1] In any case Gawan's supposedly blemished reputation has already been cleared at or before this stage of the poem. Nor can one assert that for Gawan to pursue *âventiure* is equivalent to his being characterized by *unstæte*, as Willson boldly states.[2] The prologue, after all, is cast in highly metaphorical and obscure language, and it would be unwise to press definite interpretations too far for particular passages. The prologue is meant, as well as referring primarily to Parzival, to have general relevance for the whole poem, but not necessarily for specific incidents so that particular words can be considered to illustrate, for example, *unstæte* or *stiure*. Nevertheless, Gawan is certainly involved in the ideas of the prologue, but the connexion of the adventure of Lit marveile with it is surely through the word *wenken*, 'vacillation' or 'instability', and not through *unstæte*, 'constancy in evil', which in any case is not mentioned in this adventure. Gawan is characterized by both *wenken* and *zwîvel*, but in a much more limited sense than Parzival, and this persists until the arrival of Artus for Gawan's duel with Gramoflanz, when 'Artûs Gâwâne den zwîvel brach' (661.19). The *zwîvel* to which Gawan is a prey is an uncertainty as to whether he will win Orgeluse for his bride, and the adventures of Schastel marveil are a testing ground for Gawan's worthiness to possess her, but not the final one. Gawan's task of looking for the Grail is, for him, a work of supererogation, since his task is fulfilled at Schastel marveil, and he has only to wait for Artus to be, as it were, formally pronounced free from *zwîvel*. It is surely the point of the first adventure of Schastel marveil that the bed represents in a completely transparent fashion the goal of Gawan's relationship with Orgeluse, and that its *wenken* parallels the many difficulties that Orgeluse puts in Gawan's way. Once Gawan has managed to jump on to the bed—whatever other terrors arise afterwards—he has in effect reached his goal and

---

[1] *Op. cit.*, p. 29. [2] *Ibid.*, p. 32.

overcome at least *wenken*, the liberation from *zwîvel* following as
a seal on his achievement.

The monologue in the Lit marveile incident (567.7 ff.) shows
Gawan before a task which he is conscious demands all his
resources, and it is followed by a second monologue on the
appearance of the dreadfully arrayed *gebûr*, whom Gawan manages
at first to bluff into retreat, thinking that, exhausted though he is by
the bitter struggle of Lit marveile, he might be able to defend
himself against a man without armour (570.10 f.). The irruption
of the lion into the room, however, makes him think again of his
plight, and he considers this the extremity of his position and
scarcely knows what to do next:

> waz sol mir geschehn?
> ich möhte nu wol kumbers jehn:
> wil sich mîn kumber mêren?
> ze wer sol ich mich kêren. (571.7 ff.)

Here we see Gawan in a situation bordering on despair (*zwîvel*, but
not a religiously conditioned *zwîvel*), but he does not actually
succumb to despair and consequent inaction, but springs to his
defence, weak though he feels himself to be, and despite everything he overcomes the *grôze nôt* by *strît*, by exercising his knightly
capabilities (572.22 f.). He then considers the bloody mess in
which he is and sees the bed as the means of escaping from it
(572.25 ff.), but he is by this time so weak that he cannot exert
himself to do any more and loses consciousness, lying with his
head on the dead lion.

In this most important of Gawan's adventures we find that
monologues provide a direct way of showing him in an exacting
and tense emotional situation unlike any previous one. Description on the part of the author recedes into the background at these
moments, and we are confronted with Gawan's immediate reactions. Almost more than anywhere else in his story the use of
monologues at this point emphasizes the significance of the episode
as Gawan voices his inmost feelings, of which we can be aware only
through the monologue form.

(v) Gawan's last soliloquy (587.15 ff.) deals with the theme of *minne* and depicts his feelings as he lies in bed recovering from the wounds of his adventures at Schastel marveil. He is tormented by sleeplessness and complains of Lit marveile, which broke him down physically, and of his second bed, which had increased his desire for *minne*. He declares that if he is to recover properly to his former state of joy, Orgeluse must be gracious to him and grant him her love. It is clear from this that Orgeluse is the key to the understanding of Gawan's character and his ultimate desire, since his only thought after having survived the rigours of Schastel marvel is of union with her.

There is, then, a noticeable progression through Gawan's monologues to this final position. First of all he is concerned entirely with the question of his knightly honour, which is only secondarily related to the fates of the various ladies with whom he comes into contact, but this moves into the field where *minne* and *âventiure* are interlinked, and at the end *minne* in the figure of Orgeluse becomes the all-important aspect of Gawan's life. To begin with Gawan has no particular destiny, but merely appears as 'the perfect knight' in a variety of incidents, but as the poem continues he becomes less 'the perfect knight' and more a knight with a destiny of his own, namely, the conquest of Schastel marveil and the winning of Orgeluse as his bride. The monologues are one medium through which this development, slight though it is in comparison with the thorough-going changes that Parzival undergoes, is portrayed. It would be ridiculous to claim any deep psychological treatment of Gawan's personality, as it is fundamentally so simple and Gawan's life has none of the ups and downs that feature in Parzival's, but the monologues do bring out this emergence of Gawan's somewhat tenuous individuality, and this should be noted.

THE THEME OF *MINNE*

In an article entitled *Parzival und Gawan*[1] Wolfgang Mohr argues against the viewpoint that the full meaning of Gawan's existence

---

[1] *Euph.*, LII, 1958, pp. 5 f.

is to be found in his *minne*-adventures and states his opinion that *minne* is 'wohl nur ein Nebenthema in seiner Lebenssinfonie' and plays scarcely a more important part for Gawan than for Parzival. To me this seems an overstatement of the case, as it is obvious that *minne* has a more important function in Gawan's life than in Parzival's merely to judge from the number of episodes in which it is the significant theme. There is, to be sure, a task in Gawan's history corresponding to the question Parzival has to ask of Anfortas, and the knightly exploits by which Gawan demonstrates his courage and ability should not be in any way undervalued in assessing his place in the poem; but this nonetheless means that the question of courtly love is the most important single theme in Gawan's life. It is, moreover, treated in a more detailed fashion than with Parzival, in whom it is confined to his uncouth meeting with Jeschute, his transitory feeling for Liaze and his lasting constancy towards Condwiramurs. The various episodes in Gawan's story in which *minne* figures show a careful gradation from the affection Gawan gives to Obilot through the sensuality and ambiguity which is found with Antikonie to the hardship and eventual fulfilment he experiences with Orgeluse. The atmosphere of these episodes and of Gawan's career in general is more obviously courtly than is the case with Parzival, and the theme of *minne*, though here as in most instances it culminates in marriage, comes closer to the norm of courtly love than in the relationship of Parzival and Condwiramurs.

The manner of gradation in the *minne*-episodes has been defined by Mergell[1] in the following terms: (i) the Obilot episode— 'Dienst ohne Minneerfüllung'; (ii) the Antikonie episode— 'Minneverlangen ohne Dienst'; (iii) the end of the process with Orgeluse—'Gleichgewicht von Dienst und Minne'. This broad statement will serve as a basis for further discussion of the problems involved.

(i) The events of book VII, so far as Gawan is concerned, deal primarily with *âventiure* and *strît*, and he is attracted into the battle because of his love of fighting and the need to preserve his knightly

---

[1] Mergell, *op. cit.*, pp. 266 f.

honour, not because of any compulsion by the power of *minne*. Indeed, the main protagonists of the action are Meljanz and Obie, and the book relates the story of their quarrel and eventual reconciliation. Nevertheless, the role of Obilot in the story as the counterpart of Obie and as the person through whom the quarrel is resolved requires that Gawan also should be involved, though when Wolfram comes to sharing out the palms for success in battle, he gives them to Obilot, into whose hands he entrusts the future of Meljanz, and to Parzival (388.6 ff.). Gawan is merely the servant who performs Obilot's wishes.

The idea of service (*dienst*) is paramount in the relationship between Gawan and Obilot and is present from the very beginning. Thus, Obilot, ridiculing her sister's illusion that Gawan is a merchant, immediately claims him as her knight and desires his service:

> er ist sô minneclîch getân,
> ich wil in zeime ritter hân.
> sîn dienst mac hie lônes gern:
> des wil ich in durch liebe wern. (352.23 ff.)

We should note that Obilot is attracted by Gawan's *minneclîch* appearance and that for her the two components of *minne* and *dienst* are present in the relationship in similar measure, while with Gawan service preponderates heavily. Obilot is conscious of the fact that the service of a knight involves a mutual commitment, and in talking to Obie she declares that she will increase Gawan's *freude* in return for his service (358.11 ff.). Later, when she is busy trying to implement her promises to Gawan and seeks assistance from her father, she again says that she is asking for Gawan's service in return for a reward, that is, the reward of *minne* (368.17 f.). In her anxiety to win Gawan's service, she uses the argument that in serving her Gawan is also coming to Lippaut's assistance in the battle with Meljanz:

> Ob ir manlîche site hât,
> sô wæne ich wol daz ir niht lât
> irn dient mir: ich pin diens wert.
> sît och mîn vater helfe gert

388

an friwenden unde an mâgen,
lât iuch des niht betrâgen,
irn dient uns beiden ûf mîn [eins] lôn.   (370.1 ff.)

But despite Obilot's promises and her recognition of the mutuality required in a *minne*-relationship, there are other factors which make this unlike any normal *minne*-relationship.

The situation is one of the utmost delicacy. Obilot's approach to Gawan is marked by her *ʒuht* (369.6), her *schamlîcher sin* (369.7) and by *mâʒe* (369.15), but the very thing she desires to grant Gawan, namely, *minne*, is something which Gawan declares she is not in a position to do because she is too young: 'ê daz ir minne megt gegebn, / ir müezet fünf jâr ê lebn: / deist iwerr minne zît ein zal' (370.15 ff.). This is not, however, what causes Gawan anxiety about the situation: he is thinking of the duel with Vergulaht to which he has been summoned. Nevertheless, encouraged by the thought of Parzival's service rendered to noble ladies in distress, he decides to enter the battle as Obilot's knight. It does not seem necessary to interpret Gawan's action in terms of devotion to *minne* as such, as Mohr has done,[1] shying away from the idea of Gawan's service to a little girl. It is surely the case that Gawan joins in Obilot's 'game' in all seriousness and treats her in the same way as he would a noble lady in whose service he was engaged. It remains, however, none the less a game, though a highly sophisticated and elaborate one at that. The episode continues in just the way that one would expect, had those involved in the *minne*-relationship been equals.[2]

Once Gawan has declared his willingness to serve Obilot, she launches into a catalogue of all that she will give and be to Gawan in return. She will have her part to play in the battle too, as Gawan had just indicated to her. It is she who gives him the strength to fight or rather she who is fighting in the person of Gawan. Thus, Obilot describes how she will be his defence and consolation in

[1] Wolfgang Mohr, *Obie and Meljanʒ. Zum 7. Buch von Wolframs Parʒival* in the Festschrift Günther Müller (Bonn, 1957), p. 15.

[2] Cf. Xenja von Ertzdorff, *Fräulein Obilot—Zum siebten Buch von Wolframs Parʒival* (*WW*, XII, 1962).

return for having been released from the pains of *zwîvel* (371.1 ff.). In addition to being his companion in danger, her *minne* will bring him *fride*, *gelücke*, *sælde* and *ellen*. Gawan then declares that he will take both her *minne* and the benefits of her consolation (371.18 ff.).

In order to give this new relationship a visible status in the courtly world, Obilot begs from her father new and more splendid clothes for herself and valuable gifts with which she can reward Gawan, since she and Clauditte have only dolls of their own that they could use as presents. Her feelings towards Gawan are of the highest, and she wishes to be able to act towards him as a courtly lady should:

> hân ich im niht ze gebenne,
> waz toug ich dan ze lebenne,
> sît er mir dienst hât geboten?
> sô muoz ich schämelîche roten,
> ob ich im niht ze gebne hân.
> nie magede wart sô liep ein man.   (373.21 ff.)

The importance of Obilot's new clothes is emphasized by the fact that one of the sleeves of her gown has been detached so that Gawan can wear it in battle.[1] When Gawan returns from battle, Obilot is given the sleeve to wear and gains great joy from it.

It is some indication of the role that Gawan has in this book, and indeed in other episodes too, that the successes of the battle are attributed by Wolfram to Obilot as the moral force behind Gawan's action and to the unknown Red Knight whom we know to be Parzival:

> inrehalp wart ez dâ guot getân
> durch die jungen Obilôt,
> und ûzerhalb ein ritter rôt,
> die zwêne behielten dâ den prîs,
> für si niemen keinen wîs.   (388.6 ff.)

Gawan in this instance is as it were merely the instrument of Obilot's will, and this is clear from the structure of the whole

---

[1] Gahmuret previously had worn a garment of Herzeloyde's in battle (101.9 ff.) and this type of action shows the erotic aspect of the tournament in courtly life.

episode. The interest of the author and of the audience lies not so
much in the way in which Gawan reacts, since this is in no way other
than one would have expected, as in the characters of Obie,
Meljanz, Lippaut and Obilot, whose lives provide the peculiar
situation into which Gawan irrupts. The actions and characterization of Gawan in this episode are not individualized, as the
emphasis in the story is not placed on him. The individualization
is to be found in the detailed treatment which Wolfram gives, as
far as the incidents of the story are concerned, to Obie and Meljanz
and, as far as the theme of *minne* is concerned in Gawan's life, to
Obilot. Obilot is put in complete control of the situation,
admittedly by Gawan, but she is none the less in control for that,
and it is she who resolves the quarrel between Meljanz and Obie by
commanding that Meljanz, whom Gawan had handed over into
her custody, should receive Obie as his *âmîe*. Meljanz had previously shown his contentment to be in the hands of Obilot and
had said that she was becoming the 'kranz aller wîplîchen güete'
(394.12 f.).

The significance of book VII for the theme of *minne* with respect
to Gawan and his individuality may be assessed as follows.
Mergell's slogan of 'Dienst ohne Minneerfüllung' stands up to
examination. The idea of *minne* is exemplified in all its outward
forms—the mutuality of the *minne*-relationship, the service and
the gifts, the moral strength that the knight is given by his lady,
all these are present. But physical consummation of the relationship is impossible on account of Obilot's sexual immaturity. So
far as Gawan is concerned here, he performs the *dienst* required in
the *minne*-situation as an elaborate game, which he is prepared to
play observing all the rules as if it were 'real life'. In this episode
he is showing that he is capable of perfection in courtly matters,
even where, by the nature of the case, there can be no real reward
of *minne*. It is a matter of fulfilling the form. In this situation
Gawan's actions are not individualized at all, since he is playing the
part of the perfect knight. The interest and individuality of the
theme of *minne* is found in the originality of the character of
Obilot, whom Gawan transforms into his lady for the purposes of

áventiure and of coming to the assistance of Lippaut. Gawan's chief concern at this time is to maintain his knightly reputation and to pursue the vocation of *strît*.

The fact that eroticism is excluded from Gawan's *minne* in this episode on account of Obilot's immaturity is interpreted by Emil Karl as an indication that Wolfram meant it to be understood that Gawan's service to ladies arises from a 'geistige Schätzung der Frau', which through the medium of the senses has the effect of ennobling the knight. This ennobling power Gawan feels also through Obilot, since his honouring of women has become a natural virtue in him.[1] This view, I feel, misses the sophistication of the game or 'conceit' of Gawan's relationship with Obilot and fails to do justice to the dialectical development of Gawan's progress in *minne*, which becomes readily apparent with the Antikonie episode of book VIII. There is a certain spirituality about Gawan's service to Obilot, but this is inherent in the particular details of the adventure and cannot therefore be evaluated in terms of the absolute primacy of spirituality in Gawan's understanding of *minne*. It is clear from the succeeding *minne*-adventures in Gawan's career that the physical senses are by no means neglected and are just as important as the spiritual side. Karl's assessment underestimates the idea of development, and particularly of dialectical development, in Gawan's approach to *minne* and places too great a stress on the spirituality of his first adventure.

(ii) The episode with Antikonie, which takes up virtually the whole of book VIII and which Mergell, as a generalized catchphrase, characterizes as 'Minneverlangen ohne Dienst', is by far the most difficult of all Gawan's adventures to interpret on account of its ambiguities, inconsistencies and obscurities. It forms an obvious contrast to the Obilot episode with its emphasis on the sensual aspect of courtly love, but the main difficulty lies in estimating how seriously Wolfram intended his depiction of Antikonie to be taken, and about this there is some argument and uncertainty. Scholars have seen a discrepancy between the actual

[1] Emil Karl, *Minne und Ritterethik bei Wolfram von Eschenbach* (Diss. Freiburg i. Br., 1952), p. 116.

conduct of Antikonie towards Gawan and the fulsome praise
which Wolfram at every opportunity bestows on her. Karl
Kinzel, in trying to explain the inconsistency, considered that
Wolfram himself was not sympathetically disposed towards the
character of Antikonie and excused the episode by frequent
references to his source, to which he was bound for his information.[1] This view is largely to be ascribed to the moralizing
attitude in which some nineteenth-century critics approached
episodes such as this in Wolfram's poem and neglects the passages
in which Wolfram eulogizes Antikonie independently of what he
found in his source.[2] For on the whole Chrétien is content to
describe briefly the course of the action—Gauvain's reception by
the sister of the king of Escavalon, their embraces, their discovery
by one of the king's knights and subsequent retreat into the tower,
the lady's defence of Gauvain and curse of the crowd and her
brother, and Gauvain's promise to seek *la lance qui saine* as a
condition of his liberation. Apart from this Chrétien says little but
that the king's sister (who remains nameless throughout) is
'molt ... cortoise et bele' (5820); he certainly does not pass any
moral judgements on her. Wolfram on the other hand gratuitously
inserts several passages describing Antikonie's virtue and high
moral worth (403.26 ff., 404.24 ff., 414.18 ff., 427.5 ff., 431.12 ff.).
In portraying her he goes far beyond what his source would have
justified; contrary to what Kinzel thought, he in fact enjoys the
story and feels a definite sympathy with Antikonie, otherwise why
should he have expanded the meagre data of Chrétien's poem and
come out so strongly in favour of her?

The episode as a whole defies conclusive interpretation, since
we cannot be absolutely certain what Wolfram's intentions were,
but I think there is some justification for regarding books VII and
VIII as being dialectically opposed and both with a certain element
of the game about them. If the events of book VIII do not fit
into the framework of Wolfram's view of life, as Rolf Weber says,[3]

[1] Karl Kinzel, *Antikonie* (*ZfdA*, xxx, 1886).
[2] Rolf Weber, *Askese und Quietismus bei Wolfram von Eschenbach* (*JEGP*,
xvii, 1918), p. 391.
[3] *Op. cit.*, pp. 390 f.

then neither do those of book VII in so far as *minne* is concerned. If we accept that Wolfram was attracted to the *story* of Antikonie, then we can also accept that he did not feel it necessary to condemn the relationship between her and Gawan out of hand. Indeed, as Wolfram was no prude about sexual matters and considered the physical consummation of *minne* both natural and desirable, it is likely that he did not consider the action of Gawan and Antikonie to be entirely reprehensible, or rather that he did not lay the blame entirely at Antikonie's door, if indeed he laid it anywhere. In any case, the action is one of mutual consent, as Wolfram clearly states: 'des willn si bêde wârn bereit' (407.9), so that any possible blame must be shared between them. It is not necessary to be as harsh on Antikonie as Kinzel was. But before going further, I shall need to examine the actual course of events in the episode a little more closely.

Vergulaht sends Gawan to Schampfanzun and *knowingly* commends him to the delights of his sister, expecting that he will receive such attention from her that he will not be over-anxious for the king's arrival:

> dâ ist mîn swester ûf, ein magt:
> swaz munt von schœne hât gesagt,
> des hât si volleclîchen teil.
> welt irz iu prüeven für ein heil,
> deiswâr sô muoz si sich bewegen
> daz se iwer unz an mich sol pflegen.
> ich kum iu schierre denn ich sol:
> ouch erbeit ir mîn vil wol,
> gesehet ir die swester mîn:
> irn ruocht, wolt ich noch lenger sîn.   (402.21 ff.)

The king sends a knight to Antikonie telling her to conduct herself so as to make the time pass quickly for Gawan, and she shows herself obedient to her brother's request (405.5 ff.). The key-word for the episode is *kurzewîle*, 'pleasure and entertainment', and is introduced first by Wolfram in an allusive description of Antikonie (404.5) and then taken up by the queen herself in her first speech to Gawan (405.8). In his speech she declares herself ready to kiss

Gawan, who immediately accepts her offer and plants 'ein kus ungastlîch' (405.21) on her lips. But Antikonie then refuses to go as far as Gawan presses her, saying that for her brother's sake she is doing better for him than Ampflise did for Gahmuret 'âne bî ligen' (406.6), and that she does not even know her suitor's name. Gawan prevaricates about this, since if Antikonie were to realize his identity as the alleged insulter of Vergulaht, she would have had reason to refuse his request once and for all, but he does not let this temporary disconcertment prevent him from making advances calculated to evoke a closer embrace. At this point of mutual consent the two are surprised by an old knight, who accuses Gawan of attempting to rape Antikonie and raises a hue and cry throughout the town. The two retreat into a tower, where they defend themselves and eventually are joined by Kingrimursel, whose popularity is such that Vergulaht's men forsake the battle and persuade the king to find a just solution to the whole situation.

Antikonie is nowhere blamed by Wolfram for her moral conduct, but is on the contrary praised for her lack of deceit (404.26, 413.2, 427.8 ff., 431.13), the most emphasized aspect of her character. Elsewhere she is characterized by *zuht* (405.15.22), *guot gebærde* (414.23), and particularly by *kiusche* (404.27, 414.23, 427.6). That *kiusche* is not necessarily exclusively linked with the idea of sexual morality is shown by comments of Wolfram on Antikonie's part in the battle. Action such as this, deplored by Wolfram in the case of the women of Tolenstein, is justified by the element of *triuwe* present in it:

> swâ harnaschrâmec wirt ein wîp,
> diu hât ir rehts vergezzen,
> sol man ir kiusche mezzen,
> sine tuoz dan durch ir triuwe. (409.12 ff.)

Wolfram's comments on Antikonie's character largely ignore her willingness to comply with Gawan's physical commands and concentrate on her defence of Gawan in the tower. To be sure, Gawan is called her *friunt*, i.e. a knight who has reached the position where he may expect sexual intercourse in courtly love (the equivalent of the Provençal *drutz*), and Wolfram connects this with the concepts of *liebe* and *stæte* in a highly approbatory manner when he describes Antikonie in battle: 'wol si daz bescheinde, / daz friwentlîch liebe ist stæte' (409.20 f.). The significant word, however, is *stæte*, highlighted as we have seen in the prologue to *Parzival* as one of the most important ideas of the poem and by no means confined to the sphere of sexuality. *Stæte* is a more general and widely applicable idea than that and refers to constancy in moral good. After the battle, in her furious verbal castigation of Vergulaht, Antikonie links the idea of *kiusche* with it, showing how closely it is bound up with the faithfulness of her defence of Gawan:

> guot gebærde und kiuscher site,
> den zwein wont vil stæte mite.
> den bôt ich für den ritter mîn,
> den ir mir sandet dâ her în.   (414.23 ff.)

And Wolfram in one of his eulogies states: 'lûter virrec als ein valkensehe / was balsemmæzec stæte an ir' (427.16 f.). From this it appears reasonably clear that Wolfram recognized the situation of Gawan and Antikonie as one which he need not judge from the standpoint of a strict morality. In the first place Antikonie has acted in accordance with the directions of her brother, who was well aware of her attractions, and therefore she incurs no blame; and in the second place her defence of Gawan receives nothing but approval for her loyalty to him in this difficult position. It is, on the contrary, Vergulaht who suffers the greatest censure, as Antikonie claims that a knight who flees to a lady gains the right of asylum with her (415.1 ff.).

In his treatment of *minne* elsewhere Wolfram, as we have seen, finds its fulfilment in the bond of marriage. In book VIII this is not the case, as Gawan leaves Antikonie and later meets Orgeluse.[1]

---

[1] Emil Karl's view (*op. cit.*, p. 126) of an 'Ehe post factum', possible because of a less rigorous understanding of the form of marriage in the Middle Ages, in order to save Antikonie from the accusation of being 'der Ausbund einer Heuchlerin', would bring with it the awkward question of a double marriage in its attempt to solve the first problem and is in any case unjustifiable.

But the relationship of Gahmuret and Ampflise presents a parallel which is all the stronger as Antikonie herself refers to it (406.3 ff.). We have seen in the chapter on Gahmuret[1] the high value which Wolfram set upon the episode *in its context*, and as Ampflise is characterized by the presence of *kiusche* too, so Antikonie fits in a similar way into the pattern of Wolfram's thinking, not as representing an absolute standard, but rather one which is in place at the time at which it occurs. If this is so, then the events of book VIII should be regarded as the dialectical counterpart of the Obilot adventure and be taken also in some sense as a 'game'. If they are looked upon in this light, there is no need whatsoever to expect exactly the same standard of morality here as elsewhere in the poem. The episode is an incident of entertainment, an interlude where Gawan's sensuality has its fling, and Wolfram no more expects it to be accepted as an aim or ideal than he does the episode with Obilot or the relationship of Gahmuret and Ampflise. Each episode represents an extreme of the *minne*-situation in itself unacceptable to Wolfram, but he was too involved in the delights which their plots offered to want to intersperse moralizing comments on his true views in either of them.

One important aspect of the problem, however, I have not yet mentioned—the connexion with Veldeke's *Eneide*. Three times in the course of book VIII Wolfram refers to Veldeke or the *Eneide*, and there are additional features which cause one to assume that Wolfram intended an analogy between Antikonie and Dido. In the first instance Wolfram compares Eneas' discovery of Carthage with Gawan's approach to Schampfanzun, and the adventure certainly has several traits in common with the first part of the *Eneide*. To correspond with the passage in which Antikonie says:

> ich erbiutz iu durch mîns bruoder bete,
> daz ez Ampflîse Gamurete
> mînem œheim nie baz erbôt;
> âne bî ligen   (406.3 ff.)

[1] See above, pp. 45 ff.

there are two relevant passages in the *Eneide*, where Dido offers
all that she has to Eneas, and these passages have certain verbal
similarities as well as the basic sense in common:

> ich wele em bieden âne nôt,
> dat ich manne gebôt
> in dirre werlde noch nie. (539 ff.)
>
> nie enwart van einen wîve
> bat ontvangen ein man. (570 f.)

Moreover, the lines describing Gawan's and Antikonie's amorous
embraces just before they are disturbed by the old knight (407.2 ff.)
are reminiscent of the scene in the wood when Eneas takes Dido
under his cloak to protect her from the wildness of the storm
(1834 ff.). These various references indicate a close connexion
between the ideas of Veldeke and those of Wolfram. The most
interesting of Wolfram's remarks, however, occurs immediately
after a description of Antikonie:

> sol wîplîch êre sîn gewin,
> des koufes het si vil gepflegn
> und alles valsches sich bewegn:
> dâ mite ir kiusche prîs erwarp.
> ôwê daz sô fruo erstarp
> von Veldeke der wîse man!
> der kunde se baz gelobet hân. (404.24 ff.)

The significant phrase is 'baz gelobet'. In view of the parallelism
existing between Antikonie and Dido one would expect a similar
assessment of their moral situation. But Veldeke disapproves of
Dido's *unmâze*, whereas Wolfram refrains from expressing such a
view, although the situations possess the same moral elements.
The purpose of the words 'baz gelobet' must then be taken in an
oblique and ironical sense and mean that Veldeke *could have given
a truer picture* of Antikonie than Wolfram actually does—from the
strictly moral angle. Veldeke could not have presented a more
lively, realistic or individualized character than Wolfram, but by
this double-edged reference to him Wolfram shows that by absolute standards, i.e. by his own standard that true *minne* is con-

summated in marriage, the relationship between Gawan and Antikonie is imperfect (as is the case also with Gahmuret and Ampflise). In doing this in an indirect manner Wolfram is able to concentrate on the vitality and sympathetic nature of the actual *story* and show the sensual side of Gawan's character unhampered by the judgements of conventional morality, which would undoubtedly have detracted from the aesthetic enjoyment of the episode had they been allowed to penetrate it. In this way the full poetic value of the story can be expressed, while the reference to Veldeke safeguards the deeper-going morality that pervades the poem as a whole as well as showing Wolfram's literary master.

I have written at some length about the character of Antikonie in this *minne*-episode, and it is clear that she stands out as a considerably individualized personality despite or rather because of the conventional laudatory epithets attached to her. As is the case with the Obilot episode, individuality is found in the interest of the plot and of the female counterpart to Gawan, not in any particular features of Gawan's own character, since he reacts in his capacity as the perfect courtly knight just as the individualized situation demands. So far as he is concerned, the episode illustrates his facility in the sensual aspects of courtly love. He falls in love at first sight with Antikonie,[1] obviously captivated by her physical attractions, and in their battle in the tower he is spurred on to brave deeds by the sight of her beauty and particularly by the sight of her slim waist: 'minne gerende gelust / kunde ir lîp vil wol gereizen' (409.30 f.); 'Gâwânen wac vil ringe / vînde haz, swenn er die magt erkôs' (410.10 f.). I think the images of the hare on the spit and of the ant are humorous, baroque images of Antikonie's beauty, bringing out her individuality, rather than indications of her dangerous capacity in battle, as J. K. Bostock suggests,[2] though this second idea would certainly be possible if the line of tradition and contamination from the *Iliad* to *Parʒival* could be shown. But it is a commonplace in courtly love that the lady emboldens the knight in battle and gives him strength to fight in

[1] Karl, *op. cit.*, p. 123.
[2] J. K. Bostock, *The Ant's Waist: A Query* (*Med. Aev.*, xxv, 1957), pp. 84 f.

her service, so that it is unnecessary to have recourse to the far-scattered references of Bostock's article in order to understand this section of the episode.

Mergell's formulation for this book—'Minneverlangen ohne Dienst'—is one which points out the dialectical progression of Gawan's career, but it is not completely true. There *is* an element of service in Gawan's relationship with Antikonie: the fighting in the tower is an instance of this, though perhaps an unusual one. Nevertheless it is an occurrence which binds the lovers together, and when Gawan prepares to depart from Schampfanzun at the end of book VIII, he approaches Antikonie to request her permission for his action and tells her that his adventures will be undertaken in her service:

> frouwe, hân ich sinne
> unt sol mir got den lîp bewaren,
> sô muoz ich dienstlîchez varen
> unt rîterlîch gemüete
> iwer wîplîchen güete
> ze dienste immer kêren. (431.6 ff.)

But this can be no more than a pious wish and conventional departure, as Antikonie is never again mentioned in the poem, and Gawan's adventures centre on his commission to seek the Grail on behalf of Vergulaht, his adventures at Schastel marveil and his wooing of Orgeluse. It nevertheless ties up with my previous remarks about Wolfram's double standard for the episode that it should be concluded in the spirit of conventional *minne* and that the values here described should then be allowed to recede into oblivion after having served their purpose. The main standard for judging book VIII is aesthetic; the moral standard is implied, but not permitted to become obtrusive didacticism.

(iii) With the person of Orgeluse, introduced into the poem near the beginning of book X, we reach the point where Wolfram expresses the synthesis of his dialectical exposition of Gawan's progress in *minne*. Quite obviously Orgeluse is portrayed as the counterpart in Gawan's life to Condwiramurs in Parzival's, and

Wolfram emphasizes this parallelism as soon as he first mentions her:

> ein brunne ûzem velse schôz:
> dâ vander, des in niht verdrôz,
> ein alsô clâre frouwen,
> dier gerne muose schouwen,
> aller wîbes varwe ein bêâ flûrs.
> âne Condwîrn âmûrs
> wart nie geborn sô schœner lîp.
> mit clârheit süeze was daz wîp,
> wol geschict unt kurtoys.
> si hiez Orgelûse de Lôgroys.
> och sagt uns d'âventiur von ir,
> si wære ein reizel minnen gir,
> ougen süeze ân smerzen,
> unt ein spansenwe des herzen.

The fact that Orgeluse and Condwiramurs are to be seen as the two ultimate examples of womanly perfection is brought out in a later passage, where Ginover promises Gawan's *knappe* to bring a large number of noble ladies to be present at Gawan's duel with Gramoflanz:

> âne Parzivâles wîp
> unt ân Orgelûsen lîp
> sone erkenne ich ûf der erde
> bî toufe kein so werde.   (645.27 ff.)

But as Gawan is differentiated from Parzival and represents Wolfram's view of courtliness, so also Orgeluse differs from Condwiramurs. We have already seen how Gawan is characterized as *kurtoys* and *höfsch*, epithets which never occur in connexion with Parzival. Similarly, the first passage quoted above shows that Orgeluse is singled out in the same way, though the physical description scarcely diverges from those in which Wolfram depicts Condwiramurs. This, however, is not the main significance of the parallelism, which derives its importance not from mere description, but from the moral contrast between the two heroines. The key-word for the relationship between Gawan and Orgeluse is *kurtoys*, and in their story Wolfram explores as thoroughly as he is able all the aspects and implications of the idea of *courtly* love, exemplifying the various stages of the *minne*-relationship from the knight's initial devotion to consummation in the bond of marriage.

If Gawan falls in love at first sight with Antikonie, then this is all the more true of his encounter with Orgeluse. Earlier Vergulaht had prepared Gawan for the delights that Antikonie could offer so that it was perfectly natural that a *minne*-adventure should follow. But in book X Gawan is on a different errand: he is in search of Lischoys Gwelljus and wishes to discover what has caused the dismal plight of the wounded knight to whom he has given assistance. The knight has warned him of the danger of meeting Lischoys, but Gawan is undeterred and in his search encounters, in a totally unexpected manner, a beautiful lady, who turns out to be Orgeluse de Logroys and with whom he immediately falls in love. This introduction of Orgeluse is, nonetheless, entirely appropriate, since the knight's warning about Lischoys is repeated by many others with reference this time to Orgeluse, so that it is clear that Gawan's intrepidity in pursuit of *âventiure* is matched by and closely linked with his perseverance in *minne* despite all attempts to disconcert him. In the story of Gawan and Orgeluse we are shown how closely knit the themes of *strît* and *minne* are. Here more than elsewhere in the poem Wolfram shows how the courtly knight has to undergo extreme trials on the part of his lady before he can win through to his reward. The resistance of the lady provides the means whereby the knight is educated to be worthy of her. About this Emil Karl writes:

Hier wird ganz klar, was Wolfram an der höfischen Minne reizt: es ist die ritterliche Freude an der Eroberung. Je stärker eine Frau durch Tugend gepanzert ist, umso mehr reizt sie ihn. Aber nicht in der niedern Absicht, ihr diese Tugend zu entreißen, sondern durch eigene Tüchtigkeit und Persönlichkeitskraft den gerechten Widerstand zu überwinden und so einen Bund vereinter Kraft zu schließen. Gawan weiß sich kraft seiner höfischen Tugend als der Mann, der es mit der Besten aufnehmen kann.[1]

[1] *Op. cit.*, p. 130.

All the disconcerting remarks and mockery of Orgeluse are calculated to test the reality of Gawan's *minne*, and only when he has subjected himself to their harshness and performed many feats demanding both courage and knightly ability, retaining all the while his dignity as a knight of the Round Table, does Orgeluse herself undergo a change of heart and accept him with a willing spirit.

On first seeing Orgeluse, Gawan is entirely captivated—primarily by her appearance and not by any awareness of her disposition—and is compelled by the power of *minne* that she possesses to declare that no knight could be happier than the one in her presence:

> ob ich iuch des willen schouwe
> daz ir mich gerne bî iu hât,
> grôz riwe mich bî freuden lât:
> sone wart nie rîter mêr sô frô.
> mîn lîp muoz ersterben sô
> daz mir nimmer wîp gevellet baz. (509.4 ff.)

Orgeluse reacts to this declaration by spurning Gawan in no uncertain terms and tells him to seek *minne* elsewhere. Like Antikonie, she lays stress on the fact that she has no knowledge of Gawan's identity. Gawan accepts the justice of her remarks, directed as they are against the *tumben*, among whom he is at this moment counted, but confesses that he can do nothing about it. His eyes have mediated the desire of his heart, and he is now Orgeluse's prisoner. It is she who has captured him in her heart and she alone who can release or bind him. Here are echoes of the motif found, among other places, in the Latin love-letter among the letters of Wernher von Tegernsee (*MF* 31), where the lover is locked in the heart of the beloved.

This passage in *Parzival* is the first instance of the compulsive power that *minne* exerts on Gawan through the person of Orgeluse. Gawan feels himself completely in her power and is *getwungen* by *minne* from the very beginning right through to the time when he and Orgeluse are finally united in a fully mutual relationship. This fact of *twingen* causes Gawan to release Lischoys because he too is a slave to Orgeluse's wishes (543.14 ff.). Plippalinot hears also of Gawan's troubles (548.1 f.). The thought of Orgeluse torments Gawan when he sits with the four queens at Schastel marveil (591.14 ff.), and in addition we hear of the manifold causes of his *kumber*:

> in twungen ouch wunden sêre,
> unt diu minne michels mêre,
> unt der vier frouwen riuwe:
> wand er sach an in triuwe. (595.5 ff.)

All the time that Gawan is undergoing a variety of adventures at Schastel marveil and while much that is pleasurable happens to him, he is never deserted by the thought of Orgeluse and his desire for her: 'doch muoser tougenlîchen sehen / an die clâren herzoginne: / diu twanc sîns herzen sinne' (637.28 ff.). The idea of *twingen* represents a force that is exerted on Gawan from outside, and such is its power that when Gawan perceives Orgeluse in the magic column at Schastel marveil, he becomes 'gein minne helfelôs' (593.19). But this state of *minne*-experience is also described as originating in Gawan with the idea of *senen*. Again this is brought out while he is in the company of the four queens at Schastel marveil (582.1 ff.) and when he is recovering from the wounds he received in his exploits there (587.15 ff.). Just before this passage Wolfram indulges in a long personal commentary on Gawan's state and the way in which even a knight so well able to defend himself as Gawan should have been vanquished by the power of a woman. At the same time he draws parallels with Parzival's *verdâhtheit* in the *Blutstropfenepisode*, with Galoes and Gahmuret, with Itonje and Gramoflanz, and Surdamur and Alexander, showing how *frou minne* has them all in her spell. These comments might lead one to suppose that Wolfram really disapproved of Orgeluse's power over Gawan in much the same way as he inveighs against the excessive power of *minne* over Parzival in the first half of book VI. It is, however, significant that Wolfram makes his most important remark on *minne* and its relation with the pervasive concept of *triuwe* in the midst of this first episode with Orgeluse: 'reht minne ist wâriu triuwe' (532.10). In a long excursus Wolfram declares his lack of sympathy with the idea that love is measured out by Amor, Cupid and Venus:[1]

> diu minne ist ungehiure.
> swem herzenlîchiu triwe ist bî,
> der wirt nimmer minne frî,
> mit freude, etswenn mit riuwe.
> reht minne ist wâriu triuwe.
>
> . . .
>
> sol ich der wâren minne jehn,
> diu muoz durch triwe mir geschehn.   (532.6 ff.)

Such remarks as these we might consider would be better placed in the context of Parzival's adventures. Wolfram evidently thought otherwise, and we must therefore assume that, despite the arrogance of Orgeluse's conduct, the essential features of Gawan's relationship with her deserved Wolfram's approval. He could not praise or understand that type of *minne* which occurred at the arbitrary will of the gods and was unconnected with the moral values of life, symbolized for him in the concept of *triuwe*. But he does not include Gawan among those affected by this strange type of *minne*. He is favourably disposed towards him and reiterates here the phrase that occurs many times elsewhere that Gawan is *âne schande*, even if he becomes caught in the bonds of *minne*. And this is surely because Gawan, in his capacity as the perfect knight, reacts in the correct way to all the various trials with which he is confronted by Orgeluse. He has developed beyond the stage of mere joy in knightly tactics (as with Obilot) and mere sensuality (as with Antikonie) to a perfect balance between the two, in which he is able to deal with the extreme demands of Orgeluse. It is a relationship which only slowly progresses towards maturity, but this is in no way due to Gawan's need for growth. From the beginning he presents the proper attitude of the courtly knight towards his lady. It is rather Orgeluse who requires to undergo

---

[1] Cf. James F. Poag, *Heinrich von Veldeke's* minne; *Wolfram von Eschenbach's* liebe *and* triuwe (*JEGP*, LXI, 1962), who discusses Wolfram's criticism of Veldeke with particular reference to this passage.

a change in her attitude towards Gawan, and this only takes place when she sees the hardships that Gawan is prepared to undergo in order to win her love. Her desire to avenge the death of her lover Cidegast is at this point assuaged, as she realizes that she can never exact what she requires. Gawan has suffered the greater part of her wrath, and the perfection of his character and willingness to do all that Orgeluse demands in some way modify her anger and bring her into a state of equilibrium. As Wolfgang Mohr writes:

> Gawan ist ein Ritter, durch dessen pures Dabeisein die Welt, wo er auch hinkommt, menschlicher wird. . . . Und schließlich Orgeluse— auch sie ein Mensch, der durch ein schlimmes Schicksal verhärtet wurde und sich in Prinzipien des Menschenhasses verbiß: Ihre Ver- krampfung löst sich durch Gawans beharrlichen Minnedienst. Ohne daß Gawan selbst viel dazu tut, wirkt er überall, wo er hinkommt, gleichsam als Katalysator der Menschlichkeit.[1]

This quotation serves as a brief summary of the relationship, but there is also a complexity about it which necessitates a closer examination. It is the most fully developed of all Gawan's relation- ships and gives more evidence for an individuality in his story than any other.

As has emerged from the whole of this chapter, it is the events and the other characters in Gawan's story which give it colour and individuality and this is no less the case with Orgeluse. Everything depends on her. Her character is strongly delineated and marked above all by a fidelity to her name, derived from the adjective that is used to describe her in the *Conte del Graal*, i.e. *l'Orgueil- leuse de Nogres* (8638). Her words and actions show an arrogant spirit and an unseemly determination to test to the uttermost those captivated by her *minne*. This cardinal feature of her character is, however, not fully explained and motivated—so far as the audience is concerned—until after Orgeluse has seen fit to accept Gawan's service (615.27 ff.), so that an atmosphere of some mystery surrounds her figure for the greater part of the time that she appears in the story. As Margaret Richey has pointed out, Orgeluse's character dominates all those around her by its subtlety and depth,

[1] Mohr, *Parzival und Gawan*, pp. 13 f.

and by comparison 'the brave and debonair Gawan, despite his prowess, is cast in too light a mould to sustain, in all seriousness, her task of vengeance'.[1] When Gawan first meets her, Orgeluse rejects all his advances with an abrupt decisiveness and warns him that persistence will bring him nothing but hardship and sorrow. Gawan is nonetheless undeterred and goes off at Orgeluse's command to fetch her horse from the orchard. During the course of this brief expedition her own warnings to Gawan are further underlined by remarks on the part of those who already know her. Those in charge of the orchard deplore her *trügeheit* that will lead Gawan astray into great hardship, and the knight in whose care Gawan finds Orgeluse's horse curses her for her power to ruin so many a worthy knight (513.12 ff. and 514.6 ff.). Later, Urjans reiterates this charge against Orgeluse, when Gawan comes with herbs to cure his wounds:

> du hâst eine frouwen brâht,
> diu dîns schaden hât gedâht.
> von ir schuldn ist mir sô wê:
> in Âv'estroit mâvoiê
> half si mir schärpfer tjoste
> ûf lîbs und guotes koste.
> wellestu behalten dînen lîp,
> sô lâ diz trügehafte wîp
> rîten unde kêr von ir.   (521.25 ff.)

Wolfram himself refers to Orgeluse's 'kampfbæriu lide' (515.4), and on other occasions there are comments on the fact that her sweetness is mingled with a considerable sourness. Thus, the knight in the orchard tells Gawan: 'diu ist bî der süeze al sûr, / reht als ein sunnenblicker schûr' (514.19 f.). None of this, however, has any effect on Gawan, who maintains an unflinching devotion to Orgeluse and even delights in her mockery and attacks:

> ir scharpfiu salliure
> in dûhte sô gehiure

---

[1] Margaret Fitzgerald Richey, *Studies of Wolfram von Eschenbach* (Edinburgh, 1957), p. 97.

daz ern ruochte waz si sprach:
wan immer swenner an si sach,
sô was sîn pfant ze riwe quît.
si was im reht ein meien zît,
vor allem blicke ein flôrî,
ougen süeze unt sûr dem herzen bî.
sît vlust unt vinden an ir was,
unt des siechiu freude wol genas,
daz frumt in zallen stunden
ledec unt sêre gebunden.   (531.19 ff.)

On another occasion, when Gawan is with Plippalinot before
crossing the ferry, he complains of the paradoxical effects that
Orgeluse's love can have:

diu mir dis ungemach gebôt,
diu kan wol süeze siuren
unt dem herzen freude tiuren
unt der sorgen machen rîche:
si lônet ungelîche.   (547.14 ff.)

Orgeluse treats Gawan with no respect at all, calls him a *gans*
(515.13) and laughs at every discomfiture that comes his way. Her
words and actions can be summed up in the word *hôchverteclîche*,
by which Wolfram characterizes her when she leaves Gawan before
the ultimate test of Schastel marveil (535.12). She scorns Gawan
for his solicitude about Urjans, is vastly amused when Urjans
rides away on Gringuljete and laughs in malicious delight when
Gawan wounds himself on Malcreatiure's hedgehog-like hair.

All this occurs despite the fact that from the beginning Gawan
declares himself ready to fulfil his obligations of *dienst* in the
minne-relationship. Orgeluse nonetheless fails to treat the affair
as something demanding reciprocity, and Gawan therefore undergoes a strenuous time of wooing. With Antikonie he had gained
what he desired without due consideration of his obligations
towards her. Indeed, the idea of service occurs to him more or
less as an afterthought when he is seeking to take his leave. Thus,
from his point of view, the relationship with Orgeluse marks a
definite advance, and he is able to say:

> wer mac minne ungedienet hân?
> muoz ich iu daz künden,
> der treit si hin mit sünden.
> swem ist ze werder minne gâch,
> dâ hœret dienst vor unde nâch. (511.12 ff.)

Orgeluse retorts to this that Gawan will have to live *werlîche*, may bring disgrace upon himself and must not be lacking in courage (511.17), and again she declares that he will have to endure mockery and attacks on his worthiness:

> solt ich diens geniezen,
> iuch möhte spots verdriezen.
> ob ez mir nimmer wurde leit,
> ez krenket doch iur werdekeit. (524.5 ff.)

To Gawan this is of no moment, and he asserts that he will serve Orgeluse whether his reward is *freude* or *nôt* (530.16 f.). Orgeluse makes sure that *nôt* and *arbeit* come Gawan's way, and the tasks which she sets him, as well as constituting a means by which she can in some fashion wreak vengeance on man for the enormity of Gramoflanz' crime against her, provide a *Läuterungsprozeß* for Gawan and a means whereby he can be educated through suffering to be worthy of Orgeluse's love.

The service which Gawan devotes to Orgeluse is bound up with *triuwe* and is ever-present in his thoughts of her (541.6 f. and 584.20 f.), and it is clear, as we have seen, that this link is fundamental in Wolfram's conception of the nature of *minne*. Gawan considers all his actions in the light of this relationship with Orgeluse, and when he is in a position to kill Lischoys, he refrains from doing so for Orgeluse's sake and muses that she would now concede to him that he had reached the stage of being able to serve for love (543.21 ff.). After the many adventures in Schastel marveil Gawan again thinks of his merits and pleads that Orgeluse should consider his *nôt*:

> ob iwer helfe kan gezemn
> daz ir mîn dienst ruochet nemn,
> sô wart nie nôt sô hert erkant,
> ine sî ze dienste iu dar benant. (599.17 ff.)

Orgeluse is now beginning to relent a little of the harshness she
has displayed to Gawan and promises him one more task, in which
she will accompany him. The way is now being paved for the
final adventure: if Gawan can secure a garland from a particular
tree in Clinschor's enchanted forest, she will grant him her love:

> do sprach si 'hêrre, jenen stam
> den heiet der mir freude nam:
> bringet ir mir drab ein rîs,
> nie rîter alsô hôhen prîs
> mit dienst erwarp durch minne.'   (601.25 ff.)

The point of this particular adventure is surely symbolic; it is
certainly not meaningless, as Margaret Richey says,[1] though why
it is hard to know. There is a certain sense in its decidedly un-
utilitarian nature: the act is something which demands merely
obedience on Gawan's part, and he does not need to see any clear
purpose in it apart from this. It is also a task of some considerable
difficulty, and if Gawan succeeds, he will have broken again the
power of Clinschor, in whose enchanted forest the tree stands, and
have flouted the authority of Orgeluse's arch-enemy Gramoflanz,
whose duty it is to protect the tree. In this way we can see the
completed task as the crown of Gawan's career in winning
Orgeluse. After Gawan has managed to secure the garland,
Orgeluse changes her former unrelenting attitude, feeling that
vengeance has been wrought on Gramoflanz and that Gawan has
proved himself utterly worthy of her love, and declares that she
will heal Gawan's wounds:

> si sprach 'an gîserten arm
> bin ich selten worden warm.
> dâ gein ich niht wil strîten,
> irn megt wol zandern zîten
> diens lôn an mir bejagn.
> ich wil iwer arbeit klagn,
> unz ir werdet wol gesunt
> über al swâ ir sît wunt,

[1] *Op. cit.*, p. 96.

unz daz der schade geheile.
ûf Schastel marveile
wil ich mit iu kêren.'   (615.3 ff.)

She then explains her history to Gawan, the reasons which led her
to hate Gramoflanz, and her baleful connexion with Anfortas, and
when they go together to Schastel marveil, her sensuous lips and
body overcome the pain from which Gawan is suffering. But there
are other things then with which Wolfram spins out the story—
the subplot with Gramoflanz and Itonje, the necessity for Artus and
his court to be present at Gawan's duel with Gramoflanz, his duel
with Parzival—before Gawan and Orgeluse can finally be united.
Artus gives his blessing to the several couples that are united at
the end of book XIV, and Orgeluse then says

daz Gâwân het ir minne
gedient mit prîse hôch erkant,
daz er ir lîbs und über al ir lant
von rehte hêrre wære.   (730.16 ff.)

To this declaration of Orgeluse's Artus, much later, in his conversation with Feirefiz, adds his own estimation of the service that
has been shown to her not only by Gawan, but by many other
knights too, and with this Orgeluse disappears from the story:

ich wil dich diens wizzen lân,
daz selten græzer ist getân
ûr erde decheinem wîbe,
ir wünneclîchem lîbe.
ich mein die herzoginne,
diu hie sitzet. nâch ir minne
ist waldes vil verswendet:
ir minne hât gepfendet
an freuden manegen rîter guot
und in erwendet hôhen muot.   (769.5 ff.)

More clearly than is the case with Parzival, Wolfram stresses the
physical side of *minne* and the fact that consummation is its only
aim. Gawan incarnates *l'homme moyen sensuel* whose whole nature

411

derives its driving power from sexuality. His adventures as well as his explicitly sexual exploits represent the erotic element that is always present in the idea of the tournament and the duel. Wolfram makes this perfectly plain in words, as if it were not already sufficiently clear from the course of the action: 'er wær immer unernert / sunder âmîen' (643.12 f.); 'âne wîplîch geselleschaft / sô müeser sîne schärpfe nôt / hân brâht unz an den sûren tôt' (643.24 ff.). From this it is reasonable to assert the primacy of the search for the true minne-partner in Gawan's life, despite the strictures of Mohr mentioned earlier. Once Gawan has battled through to a right relationship with Orgeluse, his problems are over; and it is of significance that the adventures of Schastel marveil are completed before Gawan and Orgeluse are united. It is the adventures displaying knightly ability which fit into the pattern of the minne-episodes rather than vice versa. Despite the fact that Gawan still has to face a duel with Gramoflanz after Orgeluse has surrendered to him, his troubles are over. The duel with Parzival takes place, and then Parzival assumes his troubles for him. Gawan recedes into the background of the story and allows Parzival to be once more the proper hero of the poem.

The idea of minne as shown in Gawan's career is not an extraordinary one, but—given the conclusion of marriage—expresses in a direct and extremely vivid way the manner in which the epitome of courtly knighthood works out his salvation. The character of Gawan himself is not particularly enriched thereby, though it undergoes some change in the dialectical processes shown. The main interest is in the clearly individualized characters of the three ladies with whom he has experiences of minne, and it is they who impart life to what might otherwise easily have been a second-rate part of the poem. This demonstrates more than anything else the fact that it is the portrayal of people that Wolfram is concerned with, and only incidentally with the exposition of ideas. We can see very clearly the interpenetration of minne and triuwe, of freude and arbeit, but it is through particular relationships and situations that Wolfram makes his audience understand what he is trying to say.

THE THEME OF KNIGHTHOOD

Gawan is the exemplary knight—of that there can be no doubt—and on this point rests the whole of his part in the poem. He has been reared at the Arthurian court (667.20 f.) and is its perfect representative. It is natural, therefore, that he should form a parallel figure to Parzival, and indeed their fortunes are closely interlinked from the time at which Parzival is admitted to membership of the Round Table.[1] Before this time there is no real parallel between their histories.

If we pass over the *Blutstropfenepisode*, the first important occasion on which Gawan is drawn into the basic framework of the poem after this is to be found when both he and Parzival are accused of having brought shame and dishonour on the Round Table, at the end of book VI. A parallel and a contrast are made between the two heroes. Both are accused of a crime, but while Parzival on the one hand we know to be guilty of it, Gawan on the other is innocent. This latter fact is emphasized with some force for a considerable section of the poem and makes clear the already obvious fact that Gawan's character and career are not filled with the same problematic features that create the psychological depth in Parzival. To begin with, Gawan from the first had been at home in the use of knightly weapons (66.19 ff.), which makes it unlikely that he should have committed a series of early crimes similar to those committed by Parzival. Gawan has no difficulties to overcome which lie within his own personality: everything is confined to the realm of the external world, and his character is essentially straightforward and unproblematic. He undergoes none of the religious anxieties that beset Parzival, and wherever there are references to God and to religious rituals in his story, they are of a conventional kind. This is not to say that they are hypocritical; the words of Wolfgang Mohr express very well Gawan's attitude in this particular case.

Gottes Hilfe ist für Gawan etwas, womit man notfalls rechnen kann und was nie ausbleibt (568.1 ff.). Wenn er sie erfahren hat, nimmt er

---

[1] Cf. Marianne Wynn, *Parzivâl and Gâwân—Hero and Counterpart* (*Beitr.* (Tübingen), LXXXIV, 1962).

sie dankbar, als etwas Selbstverständliches, zur Kenntnis (z.B. 392.30 ff.). Er macht es Gott nicht schwer, denn gewöhnlich kann er sich selber helfen. Irren und Schuld und Verzweiflung kennt er nicht. So verschließt sich ihm auch die Erfahrung, daß Gottes Hand sich dem Irrenden und Sündigen und Verzweifelnden entgegenstreckt. Gawan bewegt sich in immer der gleichen Distanz zu seinem ritterlichen Gott —und immer in Distanz. Er kennt nicht die Erfahrung des Wechsels von Gottnähe und Gottferne, das Grunderlebnis der religiösen Menschen.[1]

Gawan has a different part to play in the poem, which necessarily limits the psychological interest of his character. Innocence and normality tend not to be the themes which absorb the attention of the psychologist.

Although Wolfram continually insists on Gawan's innocence, he does not explain until half way through book VIII who it is that bears responsibility for the deed of which Gawan is accused. All we hear to begin with is Kingrimursel's words about Gawan:

> unpris sîn het aldâ gewalt,
> dô in sîn gir dar zuo vertruoc,
> ime gruozer mînen hêrren sluoc.
> ein kus, den Jûdas teilte,
> im solhen willen veilte.
> ez tuot manc tûsent herzen wê
> daz strenge mortlîche rê
> an mîme hêrren ist getân.   (321.8 ff.)

No further explanation is offered, and although Gawan himself does not know the reason for the duel—'ine weiz war umbe ich strîten sol' (323.27)—he accepts the challenge and departs from the court in order to fulfil it. Kingrimursel, however, while not elaborating the cause of the challenge, points out that Gawan's fundamental offence is one against *triuwe* and that the Round Table would be damaged by the presence of 'ein triwenlôser man' (322.6) at it. Artus immediately repudiates this accusation:

> wil glücke, iu sol Gâwânes hant
> mit kampfe tuon daz wol bekant
> daz sîn lîp mit triwen vert
> und sichs valsches hât erwert.   (322.19 ff.)

[1] Mohr, *Parzival und Gawan*, p. 15.

Beacurs also, Gawan's brother, comes to his defence and offers to
stand in on Gawan's behalf. But Gawan's honour is slighted by
Kingrimursel's attack, unjustified though it may be, and he
resolves then and there to accept the challenge and go to Schampfanzun at the appointed time. Despite everything the duel never
takes place, as other events and considerations supervene and
modify the situation. Vergulaht outrages the guarantees of
Kingrimursel that Gawan shall suffer no assault except at the time
of the duel and in some way has to make amends for this. The
result is that the duel is avoided and the theme of Gawan's search
for the Grail introduced. Meanwhile, Wolfram, again insisting
upon Gawan's innocence, mentions that the initial insult to
Vergulaht had been done by another man and that it was 'der
stolze Ehcunat' who had brought about Gawan's *nôt* (414.13 ff.).

The book which actually embarks on the narration of Gawan's
adventures opens with the lines:

> Der nie gewarp nâch schanden,
> ein wîl zuo sînen handen
> sol nu dise âventiure hân
> der werde erkande Gâwân. (338.1 ff.)

This serves as a slogan principally for the adventure with Obie,
Obilot and Meljanz, but also for Gawan's exploits in general. The
man who suffers most and unjustly in book VII is Lippaut, the
father of Obie and foster-father of Meljanz, and Wolfram informs
his audience of this several times (347.22.27, 367.6). It is thus
extremely appropriate and a reinforcement of this statement that
Gawan takes up Lippaut's case for the sake of Obilot.[1] His
innocence is reiterated on several occasions: he bears the hatred of
Obie *âne schulde* (360.8), and Scherules the burgrave defends him
against Obie's calumniations (363.17.24). Again Wolfram asserts
that Gawan bears the brunt of the quarrel between Obie and
Meljanz (365.18). This emphasis on Gawan's and Lippaut's
innocence in face of the assaults made upon them is particularly
significant in view of the fact that Parzival is their chief opponent

---

[1] Mohr, *Obie und Meljanz*, p. 13.

on Meljanz' side. He has arrived on the scene mysteriously and anonymously and takes a decisive part in the battle, so that Wolfram ascribes to him and to Obilot the credit for success:

> inrehalp wart ez dâ guot getân
> durch die jungen Obilôt,
> und ûzerhalb ein ritter rôt,
> die zwêne behielten dâ den prîs,
> für si niemen keinen wîs. (388.6 ff.)

This battle is in some measure a prefiguring of the duel between Parzival and Gawan described at the beginning of book XIV, and the fact that they do not come together in battle at this point is due to their being protected by God and by their *helendiu ʒuht* (392.30 ff.). Parzival manages to overcome three of Gawan's chief supporters—Marangliez, Schirniel and the king of Avendroyn—but Gawan himself, as the representative of Obilot, manages to capture Meljanz and so is able to put an end to the painful quarrel. It is surely part of the significance of the episode that Gawan's innocence is what creates his superiority over Parzival, since the latter at this time is still weighed down by the commission of many sins and therefore is unable to overcome the powers of good. Parzival at this point in the poem is fighting 'on the wrong side', but his capabilities are nonetheless of a very high order, though they do not as yet measure up fully to Gawan's.

This first adventure of Gawan's shows him in a most favourable light: it is his virtue and Obilot's which win the victory. Book VIII mentions once more that Gawan is innocent of Kingrimursel's allegation (398.13), but this is not the most important aspect of the episode. The conduct of Gawan and Antikonie is the focal point, and Wolfram maintains a rigorous silence on the question of Gawan's innocence so far as behaviour is concerned. It is unlikely that Wolfram considered Gawan to be 'guilty' here, as he is never shown in a situation where guilt has to be expiated, unless it should be that his acceptance of the task of seeking the Grail can be interpreted in this way as well as being a substitute for the duel with Vergulaht. This is not absolutely necessary, and

I am inclined to omit consideration of moral issues in the Antikonie episode for the reason that it is meant as a dialectical contrast with the 'game' of the Obilot adventure. The whole point about Gawan's career is its unsullied nature, its lack of spiritual problems and its exemplary purpose. To weigh down Gawan with moral responsibility for the Antikonie episode would be to place more strain on his character than it could bear.

Gawan's innocence is again to the fore in the short episode with Urjans at the beginning of book X, where a sharp contrast is made between the compassionate action of Gawan towards him and Urjans' despicable seizure of Gringuljete. The relationship between them goes back, however, to a more serious occasion when Urjans had been found guilty of raping a lady who had come as a messenger to the Arthurian court. When Urjans discovers Gawan's identity at the time of being healed by him, he reproaches him for the four weeks during which he ate with the dogs at Artus' court as a punishment for this rape. Gawan naturally protests his innocence (524.19 ff.) and explains how Urjans' punishment was completely justified in view of the enormity of his guilt. This occurs as an explanation for Orgeluse's benefit, and during it Urjans is characterized—in opposition to Gawan—as *der schuldehafte* (525.28) and *der schuldec man* (527.15).

A further reference to Gawan's unblemished character is found in the excursus on the nature of *minne* in book X, where Wolfram asserts his great sympathy for Gawan in his difficulties with Orgeluse and says: 'er ist doch âne schande, / lît er in minnen bande' (532.23 f.). Wolfram is anxious to point out here that Gawan is not a prey to the *ungehiure minne* meted out by Amor, Cupid and Venus. He thereby dissociates Gawan from that conception of *minne* as a purely external force which has no basis in the human personality, as it is shown, for example, in Eilhart's *Tristrant* and Veldeke's *Eneide*. *Minne* in Wolfram's eyes is intimately linked with the idea of *triuwe* and is therefore a moral responsibility for each person.

The last instance of Gawan's innocence occurs at the time of his duel with Parzival at the beginning of book XIV, and here again a definite contrast is made between the two heroes. It is Parzival's reactions which are the centre of interest, but they nonetheless bring out this constant element of innocence in Gawan. Parzival is ashamed to have been fighting against Gawan, who is to him the epitome of true knighthood, and cries out:

> schuldec ich mich geben wil.
> hie trat mîn ungelücke für
> unt schiet mich von der sælden kür. (688.28 ff.)

Thus, all the time Gawan maintains his honour intact and lives in a state of natural innocence. In this way he is able to serve as a measure of the stature of all other knights and, in particular, of Parzival. Were he not the paragon of knighthood and therefore of unsullied reputation, his position at the Round Table would be false and unjustified.

Loosely connected with the theme of Gawan's innocence is the *koufman* motif, which crops up on several occasions as a particular instance of the unjust accusations levelled against Gawan's character. It is introduced when Gawan arrives at Bearosche, as he appears on the scene in a somewhat mysterious fashion and no one is certain who he is and what rank he possesses. The old duchess first wonders what company he belongs to and is informed by Obie that he is a merchant. This remark forms the point on which the personalities of the two daughters are contrasted, as Obilot springs to Gawan's defence and, after her mother has made an objection to Obie's answer about the shields Gawan has with him, declares that Gawan could not possibly be a merchant and that what singles him out is the fact that he presents a *minneclîch* appearance (352.20). The duchess, having carefully watched Gawan's servants unload, realizes that a merchant could not act in such a manner and is again supported by Obilot, who uses this as an opportunity for expressing her disapproval of Obie's conduct towards Meljanz. Later on she humorously picks up Obie's originally disparaging comment when she claims Gawan as her knight for the ensuing battles: 'sît du gihst er sî ein koufman, / er sol mîns lônes market hân' (358.13). Obie nevertheless persists in her attitude towards Gawan and prosecutes three calumniations against him, all based on the idea that he is a merchant. In the first place, she sends a servant to buy his horses and coffers; secondly, she informs the burgrave Scherules that a merchant is trying to deceive them; and thirdly, she sends a *spilwîp* to her father to persuade him that Gawan is a *valschære*, an arch-deceiver, and that his possessions would provide sufficient plunder for seven soldiers to join battle. All these attacks on Gawan's honour are firmly repulsed: Gawan drives away the servant himself as an insolent lout; Scherules realizes on meeting him that he cannot be a merchant and is deserving of respect; and in the third instance Scherules again is able to show Lippaut the true state of affairs with respect to Gawan. And at the end of the episode Obilot triumphantly points out that Gawan has proved by his actions that he is not a merchant, as Obie had contested (396.5 ff.).

One might have thought that the *koufman* motif would have been exhausted at this point, but it is re-introduced in an extended form in the episode with Orgeluse in book X. The incident which provides the occasion for this is that in which Gawan turns doctor and looks for herbs to cure Urjan's wounds. Orgeluse finds this an amusing and degrading occupation and remarks derisively:

> kan der geselle mîn
> arzet unde rîter sîn,
> er mac sich harte wol bejagn,
> gelernt er bühsen veile tragn.   (516.29 ff.)

This recurrence of the motif must surely remind the audience of the earlier episode with Obie and suggest that as she was reunited with her lover Meljanz, so Gawan will be eventually united with Orgeluse despite the appearances at this moment in question. Moreover, Orgeluse does not relinquish the motif after having once used it: she emphasizes it again when Urjans takes unfair advantage of Gawan's assistance and rides away on his horse:

> ir süezer munt hin zim dô sprach
> 'für einen rîter ich iuch sach:
> dar nâch in kurzen stunden
> wurdt ir arzet für die wunden:
> nu müezet ir ein garzûn wesn.'   (523.6 ff.)

Gawan is unshaken by this attack and retaliates by telling Orgeluse
that her mockery will bring its own reward:

> nu nennt mich rîter oder kneht,
> garzûn oder vilân.
> swaz ir spottes hât gein mir getân,
> dâ mite ir sünde enpfâhet,
> ob ir mîn dienst smâhet. (523.30 ff.)

Orgeluse does not let the matter rest there, however, and indulges
in one more occasion of raillery before she forsakes Gawan at
Schastel marveil, when she reverts to the merchant motif in a
stronger form, though it is still allied with the doctor motif. It is
Gawan's action in binding his shield to his horse which occasions
the caustic remark, and this clearly links with the custom ascribed
to merchants by Obie at the very first use of the motif:

> si sprach 'füert ir krâmgewant
> in mîme lande veile?
> wer gap mir ze teile
> einen arzet unde eins krâmes pflege?
> hüet iuch vor zolle ûfem wege:
> eteslîch mîn zolnære
> iuch sol machen fröuden lære.' (531.12 ff.)

This is received by Gawan in a perfectly calm fashion. He no
longer troubles to retort to Orgeluse, but accepts her attacks with
joy because he is so deeply in love with her. The fact that she
notices him is sufficient; he does not care what it is that she says
(531.19 ff.).

The merchant motif, of which one further slight example occurs
when Plippalinot demands the toll from Gawan for ferrying him
across the water to Schastel marveil (544.23), is one of the
instances which add a genuine touch of individuality to Gawan's
story. It cannot be said that it helps to individualize Gawan's
character, since the accusations levelled against him are essentially
false and have therefore an ironic effect while not yet creating a
different aspect to his character. It is the way of looking at his
character from the point of view of some other personage of the

poem which creates the interest of the motif. The individuality thus occurs around the figure of Gawan and not actually in him. But it is none the less an individual feature for that. Moreover, the use of the motif at different parts of the poem helps to fashion a more lively, *vraisemblant* picture of Gawan in that the various episodes are connected not merely by the fact that they all have the same hero in name, but also by similar mistakes made about his character, even if they are not similar aspects of his own character. His adventures do not merely occur in a series, but are linked to each other in small, though significant ways.

The idea of calumniation, arising through a mistaken attitude towards Gawan, through ignorance of his identity or through the excess of avenging zeal, is closely connected with the idea of Gawan's anonymity. Parzival, as we know, travels about unknown to his fellow men or depicted solely as the *rôter ritter*; but Gawan also enjoys a considerable anonymity, which is a fundamental feature of his role in the poem. This may be forced upon him, as Mohr says,[1] but the alternation between the episodes in which Gawan is known to the other participants and those in which he conceals his identity provides one of the means of creating variation and interest in his story.

The first episode in which Gawan appears actively occurs when he intervenes to release Parzival from his *minne*-trance, and this constitutes his first meeting with Parzival, who does not realize his identity until Gawan reveals it to him (303.27 f.). Until the end of book VI, that is, so long as Gawan is still present at the Arthurian court and therefore in his accustomed setting, he remains a known figure, but after being accused and having departed from there, he sinks into an almost complete anonymity so far as those whom he meets are concerned. The whole of book VII passes in this manner: Lippaut and Obilot accept the services of the unknown knight without troubling to ascertain who he is, and Gawan certainly does not tell them himself. It is therefore possible for the various misunderstandings about his character to arise naturally. Gawan

---

[1] Mohr, *Parzival und Gawan*, p. 5.

takes no advantage from his reputation, but has to prove his worth in action. He is referred to by the other participants in this adventure as *der fremde ritter* (373.19) or *der fremde gast* (374.23), to mention only two of the ways in which he is called. The fact that his reputation has been questioned by Kingrimursel's challenge means that he can no longer travel about the courtly landscape as a recognized figure, to whom all honour is accorded, but instead he must go about unknown to others and merit his emergence from anonymity through being recognized for his noble acts. And this indeed does happen.

Book VIII presents a singular example of complexity in that to some of the characters Gawan is known, to others unknown. Both Vergulaht and Kingrimursel are perfectly aware of Gawan's identity in view of the arranged duel, but Antikonie is in the dark —and this has its point. She enquires Gawan's name when he demands her *minne*, and he evades the question by saying that he is 'mîner basen bruoder suon' (406.15), since this will then relieve Antikonie of the responsibility which would attach to her conduct if she were fully conscious of Gawan's identity and thus of the fact that he is to fight a duel with her brother. If Gawan had told her his name, she would have had an understandable reason for not granting Gawan's request. But though Antikonie must realize (though we are never explicitly told) from the time when Kingrimursel joins them in the tower that it is Gawan with whom she has been dealing, her loyalty towards him is unaffected and is indeed a powerful example of *wîbes stæte*.

After this episode Gawan returns once more to a state of anonymity. The beginning of book X is shrouded in mystery, so far as the characters' knowledge of each other's identity is concerned. The lady all equipped for battle whom Gawan first meets looking after Urjans is never actually named, and it is some time before he realizes that it is Urjans who is evoking his compassion. The way in which Urjans in the first place guesses Gawan's identity is extremely indirect. Orgeluse is also present when they meet the second time, and Gawan is attempting to counter her assaults on his knightly prowess. His remarks are such that it is implied that if Orgeluse chooses still to spurn his service, her own virtue will thereby be vitiated. From this Urjans jumps to the conclusion that it must be an extremely worthy knight who is in a position to say such a thing (this is implicit in the situation) and asks: 'bistuz Gâwân?' (524.10). Apart from this there is no other explanation of Urjans' guess. It is Gawan's *behaviour* which gives him the clue to his identity, and Gawan is then in a position to know who Urjans is also. Up to this point Orgeluse had also been unaware of Gawan's identity and had made a similar remark to Antikonie's when Gawan made his advances to her: 'ichn weiz niht, hêrre, wer ir sît' (509.25). It is strange, however, that after Gawan and Urjans have become acquainted she still says: 'ich pin nu iwer bêder vogt, / und enweiz doch wer ir bêdiu sît' (529.10 f.). Certainly it makes no difference to Orgeluse's conduct that she is dealing with Gawan, but it is difficult to know at what moment she becomes conscious of his identity, since when she finally accepts him he asks her not to reveal his name to anyone at Schastel marveil (620.1 ff.). It may be that it is only when Gawan meets Gramoflanz after having performed Orgeluse's last task that she realizes that she has met her match and that it is Gawan whom she has been testing. Perhaps the most important fact is that Wolfram's audience is aware of the identities involved and that Wolfram himself was not unduly worried about pinning down the moment of recognition to a particular time.

Gawan's anonymity is preserved for a considerably longer time in the poem, so that few of the characters are aware who it is with whom they are dealing. For many of them it appears irrelevant to know Gawan's name. Lischoys never discovers it, and it is sufficient to Plippalinot and Bene that they have the honour of lodging the conqueror of Lischoys in their house; they do not trouble to find out more. And the adventures which take place at Schastel marveil are perhaps even more mystifying because one or other of the characters is ignorant of what is happening. This in large measure constitutes a parallel to Parzival's visit to Munsalvæsche, where the visitor's identity also remains undiscovered. But Gawan visits Schastel marveil only on the one occasion and even after having succeeded in the tasks set him he does not reveal his identity. Arnive is consumed with curiosity about his actions, but she learns nothing until Artus and Ginover actually arrive on the scene at Gawan's request. Then it is by inference, albeit an obvious one, that Gawan's identity becomes clear. Gawan introduces the long-imprisoned queens to Artus in terms of family relationships, and in doing so he presents Sangive as 'diu muoter mîn' and Itonje and Cundrie as 'mîn swester' (672.11 ff.). There is now no need any longer for Gawan to remain anonymous; all his adventures except one have been completed, he has vindicated his knightly ability and honour (though in reality it was never otherwise than it is now) and won the hand of Orgeluse. All that remains is the duel with Gramoflanz, which never actually takes place, but is displaced by the duel between Gawan and Parzival. Here it is absolutely necessary that the two heroes should be ignorant of the other's identity, though it is amazing and inexplicable that Gawan should be unaware of the fact that the knight in red armour, mentioned time and again in this way throughout the poem and particularly during the siege of Bearosche, is in fact Parzival. But here again, as everywhere, it is the other person, i.e. Parzival, who discovers Gawan's identity. Then for Gawan everything is over: his part in the poem is finished, and Parzival is able to take over from him and fight the duel with Gramoflanz in his stead. Gawan is united with Orgeluse and becomes once more the epitome and, apart from Artus, the presiding genius of the courtly world, who fades into an honourable obscurity as the host while the careers of Parzival and Feirefiz progress towards their conclusion.

The main significance of Gawan's anonymity is to show that he cannot rely any longer on his reputation, especially when its purity has been questioned. Nothing can any more be taken for granted, but Gawan must prove his worth by his actions. Moreover, he has to do this afresh in each case, but his actions are so true to his established character that he never transgresses the bounds of courtly behaviour, and this shines through to the audience the whole of the time. The situation then appears that the conduct of Gawan is entirely constant, but must be discovered anew by the characters with whom he comes into contact at each individual encounter.

Gawan's character is shown in its essential simplicity, perfection and constancy through the various meetings which he has with others. So far as knightly (as opposed to courtly) affairs are concerned, his *character* does not undergo a perceptible development, but there is nonetheless a certain gradation in his *adventures* and meetings, which is displayed through the characters whom he encounters and not principally through his own actions and reactions, which themselves are characterized by an extreme constancy. Gawan never does anything totally unexpected.

If we examine the course of his adventures, we shall find that there is an increasing element of inward participation traceable in them. The initial episode of the quarrel between Meljanz and Obie is a matter in which Gawan's part is that of a disinterested person, of what Mohr calls a *Katalysator*, in whose presence everything becomes more human.[1] The fate of the two young lovers is of no vital importance to Gawan except as an occasion for him to exercise his knightly powers, and we have noticed that his chief concern is to preserve his honour while at the same time not failing to appear at the appointed time for his duel with Vergulaht. In this episode Gawan is not the central figure: he is merely the person through whom the complex relationships of Obie, Meljanz, Lippaut and Obilot are satisfactorily resolved. Moreover, the most developed relationship that he has in this book is with Obilot, and the fact that she is a little girl means that Gawan is not deeply and emotionally involved in the situation. His performance in battle is not unusual, and although he does capture Meljanz, Parzival takes several of his supporters prisoner and thus shows that Gawan is by no means in sole and complete control of the situation.

The next stage in Gawan's story, which fills out book VIII, deals with the immediate purpose of Gawan's journey away from the Round Table. It is an episode in which several themes are touched upon, but the main one—apart from the incidents with

[1] Mohr, *Obie und Meljanz*, p. 17; *Parzival und Gawan*, p. 14.

Antikonie, which have no consequences entirely in themselves—centres on Gawan's alleged insult of Vergulaht. This obviously involves Gawan to a much greater degree, as does also his second *minne*-relationship with Antikonie, since his reputation is at stake. However, Vergulaht's own arrogance and transgression of the rules of hospitality and sanctuary create a situation in which the duel becomes an impossibility on account of Vergulaht's insult of Gawan. A disagreement nonetheless remains, and Liddamus and Kingrimursel dispute the merits of the cases only to arrive at the conclusion that Gawan should take upon himself the task of searching for the Grail which was enforced upon Vergulaht by Parzival.[1] By this the dilemma is in some way resolved and a new theme introduced into Gawan's history. The question of Gawan's alleged insult of Vergulaht is not properly clarified, but the motif disappears from the poem and is replaced by that of the Grail.

By introducing the Grail motif into Gawan's story Wolfram underlines the parallelism of the two main heroes and thereby makes an attempt to unify their two careers. Vergulaht is extremely attached to his sister and cannot bear the thought of her condemnation (428.1 ff., especially 10 ff.), so that rather than lose her he will forgive Gawan for the alleged injury, if Gawan will guarantee to seek the Grail. This Gawan willingly undertakes and rides away on this errand at the end of the episode (432.19 f.). At this point the adventures of Parzival and the central importance of book IX intervene, but immediately Gawan returns Wolfram mentions that he is looking for the Grail and that this is his sole occupation:

> si fuoren beide sunder dan,
> Vergulaht unt Gâwân,

---

[1] This feature is emblematic of Wolfram's divergence from Chrétien, for in the French poem Gauvain accepts a commission from the king of Escavalon to seek *la lance qui saine* (6149 ff.) and bring it back within a year. Wolfram omits this entirely, but stresses the Grail theme through making Parzival demand of all his conquered opponents that they should help him in his task of finding it. Of course, Gawan does not find it, but his seeking for it is one of the means whereby Wolfram unifies the Gawan and Parzival sections of the poem.

an dem selben mâle
durch vorschen nâch dem grâle,
aldâ si mit ir henden
manege tjoste muosen senden.
wan swers grâles gerte,
der muose mit dem swerte
sich dem prîse nâhen.
sus sol man prîses gâhen. (503.21 ff.)

But though the search for the Grail is the purpose which lies behind the later part of Gawan's travels, it is peripheral to the actual happenings which make up his story. The aim of his travels changes from book to book: Gawan is very much a man who responds to the calls of the moment and can be deflected from his ostensible goal. As he goes from adventure to adventure, they join together in comprehensible, but largely fortuitous ways. Thus, his first adventure constitutes an interlude before his duel with Vergulaht, and then with Vergulaht he receives his commission to see the Grail, and in trying to fulfil this he meets those other characters who lead him bit by bit to the climax of his adventures, which occurs at Schastel marveil. There is, however, in contrast to Parzival, no definite purpose set out at the beginning of Gawan's travels. This only gradually becomes apparent, though the various adventures tie up in a more or less coherent whole.

Book X, then, opens with a short recapitulation of Gawan's and Vergulaht's task of seeking the Grail, and while Gawan is engaged on this highest of all errands, he is confronted with assault after assault on his personality and faced with a series of trials. Up to this time he has not himself been humiliated, though his reputation has been questioned. First of all he meets Urjans (though neither realizes who the other is) and ministers to his bodily needs. In doing this he encounters Orgeluse, and from this moment on he is tested with a savagery which scarcely knows any bounds. Everything conspires against him: Urjans rides off with his horse, he is wounded in trying to get the better of Malcreatiure, and Orgeluse continually inflicts hardship on him. Lischoys then refuses to surrender to him, and so Gawan for Orgeluse's sake grants him freedom. Then, after this, comes a moment of respite with Plippalinot and Bene before the adventures of Schastel marveil.

Schastel marveil occupies in Gawan's story an analogous position to that of Munsalvæsche in Parzival's, but with several striking differences. The adventures are not completely unheralded, though they are not quite set before Gawan as an aim like Parzival's through which he is to fulfil his destiny. In fact, at the same time as Cundrie pronounces her curse upon Parzival, she announces the extraordinary plight of Schastel marveil:

> si sprach 'ist hie kein rîter wert,
> des ellen prîses hât gegert,
> unt dar zuo hôher minne?
> ich weiz vier küneginne
> unt vier hundert juncfrouwen,
> die man gerne möhte schouwen.
> ze Schastel marveil die sint:
> al âventiure ist ein wint,
> wan die man dâ bezalen mac,
> hôher minne wert bejac.'   (318.13 ff.)

The reasons for this state of affairs are not explained now and indeed only emerge gradually in a not very precise manner after Gawan has released the queens and other inhabitants of the castle from the spell under which they have been living. There is an undefined relationship between Clinschor, the ruler of Schastel marveil, and Orgeluse, and this Wolfram is pleased to allow to remain in the aura of mystery with which he surrounds the entire episode. But the fact that 'al âventiure ist ein wint / wan die man dâ bezalen mac' is reinforced by the judgement of Plippalinot at the beginning of book XI before Gawan actually sets out:

> aller kumber ist ein niht,
> wan dem ze lîden geschiht
> disiu âventiure:
> diu ist scharpf und ungehiure
> für wâr und âne liegen.
> hêrre, in kan niht triegen.   (557.25 ff.)

By Cundrie's and Plippalinot's words the cardinal importance of this adventure is demonstrated, but it does not mean that Schastel marveil outweighs Munsalvæsche *except as an adventure*. Parzival's task at the Grail castle is of a different order, and we are told that although he has been near Schastel marveil he is unaware of the distress of the castle and, moreover, it is not for him to be turned away from his purpose of seeking the Grail (559.23 ff.). Gawan's history revolves around the themes of *minne* and *âventiure* in their more ordinary and more or less secular sense; Parzival's deals with things spiritual and, while including the themes of *minne* and *âventiure*, is not limited by them and finds fulfilment beyond them. With this in mind it can be said that Schastel marveil does constitute the ultimate in the sphere of *âventiure*.

A parallelism between Schastel marveil and Munsalvæsche is apparent in many respects. There is even at one point a subjective confusion between them in that Gawan, on receiving medical treatment at Schastel marveil, imagines that he is at Munsalvæsche (580.2 ff.). Both castles are afflicted with a great distress and ruled by kings suffering from a sexual injury. But while Anfortas' sin has brought a punishment on himself and the Grail castle, from which both are released by the action of Parzival, Clinschor is not relieved from misery by Gawan, though the ladies whom he held in Schastel marveil by his spell are indeed liberated. Thus, the action of Gawan is one of physical strength overcoming the powers of darkness, whereas that of Parzival is essentially an act of spiritual redemption. In any case, Clinschor is absent from the scene at Schastel marveil, so that it is the four queens and the other imprisoned noble ladies who must be the object of Gawan's action.

The question motif is also found in this adventure, but in a different form. In staying with Plippalinot Gawan has noted the presence of many ladies in the castle and enquires of Bene who they may be. Bene shrinks in terror and tells Gawan he ought not to ask such a question. Plippalinot then enters, and Gawan explains to him the reason for Bene's distress. Plippalinot reacts in exactly the same way: 'dô sprach er "vrâgets niht durch got: / hêr, dâ ist nôt ob aller nôt"' (556.15 f.). The asking of this question differentiates Gawan in the clearest possible way from Parzival. Both heroes in their respective places were confronted with a mysterious situation; but Parzival refrains from asking the question and thereby incurs guilt, whereas Gawan in all naturalness indulges his curiosity and is reprimanded for it. He speaks and acts free from all inhibitions and constraints. Schastel marveil is no *problem* for him; it is an *adventure* which has to be pursued and won. It is therefore only to be expected that he should fail to be content with Plippalinot's off-putting response and persist in his attempt to disperse the mystery. The ferryman complies with Gawan's request and tells him something of the position, mentioning Lit marveile and warning Gawan that he is risking his life in undertaking to enter the castle (557.1 ff.). The question motif is here much weaker than is the case with Parzival, where it has significance in itself and is all that is required of the hero. With Gawan the question, treated as a mirror image of Parzival's, has a more formal significance and implies no particular virtue in itself except as an instance of Gawan's natural behaviour. It is merely a prelude to the actual adventures of Schastel marveil and reinforces the parallelism of the two heroes, though by a definite contrast. The meaning of Gawan's life is to be found in his actions and not in the 'spiritual' state to which he has attained.

When Gawan arrives at Schastel marveil, having left his horse with the merchant at the gate, he finds his way into the deserted hall where Lit marveile stands. Compared with Chrétien (7692 ff.), Wolfram spends little time on pure description of the bed, but launches immediately into the feats of strength which it demands of Gawan. He stresses three times that Gawan's aim is to seek *âventiure*, twice on the part of the merchant at the gate (563.28 and 564.9) and once as a comment by the author (566.30); and thus the motifs of the bed and of Schastel marveil in general cannot be understood in a moral sense, as can the question which Parzival puts to Anfortas, but only as an aspect of performing a miracle through strength, which then acts as a release from a magic spell, a motif which is common in fairy-tales.

The question then arises: What does Lit marveile represent?

This could be asked of all the motifs of this kind that occur any-where, and surely here also the task of securing a garland from the tree that Gramoflanz guards must be included. It is not easy to answer questions of this sort, but it is certain that the power which the motifs exercise in the poem is related to their inexplicability. Motifs which can be fully explained tend to lose their fascination and depth and descend to the level of a superficial allegory. Their meaning is enhanced by their apparent meaninglessness by normal rational standards.

One of the possible 'meanings' of the adventure of Lit marveile is to be discovered in an elucidation of it as an obvious sex symbol. In this respect it is to be linked with Orgeluse, who has up to this time successfully resisted all Gawan's attempts to win her and now has sent him to the trials of Schastel marveil. This particular episode has been connected with the *bíspel* of the prologue to the whole poem and especially with the idea of *wenken*,[1] and the bed is indeed difficult to jump on to on account of the smooth slipperi-ness of the floor as well as because of its own swift motions. The parallel with the behaviour of Orgeluse is evident, and the rain of blows that Gawan receives and the noise that results are the equivalent of all the mockery and discomfiture that Gawan suffers while in the physical presence of Orgeluse. The stones and arrows that wound Gawan, the battles with the *starker gebûr* and the lion, all of which he manages in the end to win through, are the means whereby Orgeluse's humiliation of Gawan is effected, since she is in some undefined way in league with the sorcerer Clinschor. This adventure marks the climax of Gawan's career, though the episode with Gramoflanz' tree has yet to come and he never succeeds in finding the Grail. From now on, despite the fact that he has to be healed from his wounds by the four queens, Gawan is in control of the situation and no longer continues in a series of fortuitous adventures. His success in the castle has made him lord of it (594.15), and he is able to work out the destinies of the queens, uniting them once more with the Arthurian court and joining

---

[1] Bernard Willson, *Wolframs Bíspel*, pp. 30 f. See also above, pp. 383 ff.

Gramoflanz and Itonje in marriage. Arnive is incapable of penetrating the veil of mystery with which Gawan envelops his identity and actions and has eventually to yield to the realization that Gawan is master.

The adventures of Schastel marveil are the climax of Gawan's career, but his part in the poem continues for some considerable time afterwards, in a fashion which unduly delays the conclusion with Parzival and Feirefiz at Munsalvæsche. The action is held up by the last task that Orgeluse sets Gawan and the resulting complications in the relationship of Gramoflanz with Itonje.

The task of breaking a branch from the tree in Clinschor's forest which Gramoflanz guards has a similar quality to that of springing on to Lit marveile in that it is a feat of knightly ability demanding the utmost strength, but with little, if any, intrinsic significance. It emerges, however, from Gramoflanz' remarks to Gawan that it was he who killed Orgeluse's lover Cidegast, and so this task becomes a symbol of the revenge that Orgeluse determines to have upon him. Gawan's success in this last test is the seal upon a union that had already been decided at Schastel marveil. But in the course of Gramoflanz' conversation with Gawan it becomes clear that an ancient feud remains between Gramoflanz and Gawan's father Lot, who killed the former's father. This Gramoflanz relates quite unaware of Gawan's identity, only to be surprised by Gawan's acceptance of his duty towards Lot. A duel is arranged on the spot for sixteen days hence at Joflanze, but it is not Gawan, but on the contrary Parzival who undertakes it. Moreover, Parzival also has broken a garland from Gramoflanz' tree (679.14 ff.), so that with Gawan physically unable to enter into battle with the arrogant king, Parzival can justifiably take over his place in the plot and in the poem and allow Gawan to sink back, now united with Orgeluse, into the courtly setting from which he came.

In book XIV Gawan's part is largely passive, though nonetheless necessary. The theme of the book is the love of Itonje and Gramoflanz, which is in imminent danger of being thwarted by the duel outstanding between Gramoflanz and Gawan. Parzival's

attempt to undertake Gawan's responsibility in the matter is
broken off just at the point when he has almost defeated Gramoflanz (707.26 ff.), and Gawan, though not yet fully recovered from
his injuries sustained at Schastel marveil, promises to accept his
part in the duel, leaving Gramoflanz a day in which to recover
from Parzival's near-conquest of him. This situation is obviously
unsatisfactory: the love of Itonje and Gramoflanz is clearly
compatible with the vindication of knightly honour demanded
by the duel. Things have reached such a pass that Artus now comes
into his own and acts as arbitrator and mediator in the courtly
world. It is he who controls the outcome of the situation and
decides in consultation that *minne*—and above all the secret,
worthy love of Itonje and Gramoflanz which represents the height
of *hôhe minne* (724.23)—must take precedence over vengeance.
Artus declares that he can prevent the duel if he knows that Itonje
and Gramoflanz are really united by their love, but as Gramoflanz
insists on fighting Gawan, having been already thwarted in this
by the intervention of Parzival (717.5 ff.), Artus rules that the
problem can be solved only by Itonje's commanding Gramoflanz
to desist from battle for her sake (727.1 ff.). Thus, in the courtly
world the power of *minne* is seen to be pre-eminent, and a general
reconciliation takes place between all the parties to the dispute,
during which Orgeluse announces with finality that Gawan has
merited her love 'mit prîse hôch erkant' (730.17).

The Round Table is now united again except for the departure
of Parzival at the celebration of marriages, but soon he returns,
bringing with him his newly found brother Feirefiz, and the court
is once more fully gathered. Gawan has little to do in this part of
the poem. His own adventures are over, and he can only act as
host to Parzival and Feirefiz, encouraging them to turn their
opposition and hatred into friendship (760.6), a belated and unnecessary piece of advice. Gawan himself is in the midst of the
festivities of marriage, and everything now points to a happy
conclusion to the whole poem. Here at the Arthurian court, where
Parzival and Gawan were together accused of evil, they are once
more united in the reception of Feirefiz into the fraternity of the

knights of the Round Table and in hearing the news from Cundrie that Parzival's name has appeared on the Grail as its future lord. Gawan's part is completed; his own happiness with Orgeluse is assured and the rest of the poem belongs to Parzival and is beyond Gawan's reach. He has returned to the Arthurian court, his honour re-established and united with the lady of his choice. To say more is unnecessary.

CONCLUSION

The character of Gawan, as has emerged from the preceding pages, is essentially straightforward and unproblematic and as such contrasts vividly with Parzival's. It is indeed impossible to consider it without reference to Parzival, though it is not to be considered in opposition to it. Scholars as various as Gustav Ehrismann[1] and Georg Keferstein[2] have asserted from their researches that Parzival and Gawan must be understood as representing the same basic idea of life, but in different degrees. Thus, as Keferstein says, it is not the problems of an individual that Wolfram wishes to portray, but the problems of the great, inclusive knightly world,[3] and in this both Parzival and Gawan have their necessary part. Keferstein considers Parzival as the 'Heiliger' and Gawan as the 'Repräsentant' of this world,[4] and if one de-Nazifies and also corrects the one-sidedly religious bias of this view, there is a certain element of truth in it. The history of Parzival deals with the development of a knight with a particular vocation; the story of Gawan shows the actions of the perfect representative of the courtly world, who responds with the fulness of his being to the demands of whatever situation he is in. He is filled with no inward compulsion to perform particular acts or seek particular things, but accepts his commissions as they come and displays the expected courage, ability and temperament of the exemplary courtly knight in doing so. If Gawan is seen as the *Repräsentant* of

---

[1] Gustav Ehrismann, *Über Wolframs Ethik* (*ZfdA*, XLIX, 1905), p. 457.
[2] Georg Keferstein, *Die Gawanhandlung in Wolframs 'Parzival'* (*GRM*, XXV, 1937), p. 260.
[3] *Ibid.*, pp. 257 ff.
[4] *Ibid.*, pp. 262 f.

the Arthurian world, he cannot also be strongly individualized. His function is to express the fundamental, accepted ideals of courtliness as a kind of framework in which the actions of Parzival can be comprehended. 'Man muß sich hüten, Gawan als minderwertig anzusehen. Er ist eine edle natur mit denselben guten veranlangungen wie Parzival, nur hat er sie nicht zu dem sittlichen aufschwung gebracht wie dieser, denn er war nicht unter den berufenen. fast alle seine tugenden sind um einen grad geringer als die Parzivals.'[1] So Ehrismann. But is this true? There is surely a difference in quality between the two heroes, and it would be folly deliberately to ignore it. In the terms of Keferstein's analogy, the life of a saint (though I do not think this term can or should be applied literally to Parzival) is clearly superior to that of the ordinary Christian; but the fact that there are ordinary Christians, i.e. a setting for the religious life, if no more, makes it possible for the saint to pursue his vocation. The same applies *mutatis mutandis* to the entwined stories of Parzival and Gawan. Thus, from the point of view of this study, the tale of Gawan is 'inferior' to that of Parzival and is treated in a different fashion.

The character of Gawan is constant and undergoes no real development, except to a limited extent in his experience of *minne*. Here there is a dialectical progression, but we must be careful not to over-emphasize its importance. The progression is extremely simple in its basic structure and depends mainly on the circumstances of each episode to bring out a particular aspect of Gawan's character that is already present. Thus, the adventure with Obilot evokes his sense of service predominantly, that with Antikonie his sensual desire, and the various adventures with Orgeluse combine them. Gawan is a man who reacts directly to the situation, and, moreover, it is the situation which produces and shows his character and not his character which shapes the situation. Gawan never makes a decision which is not already called for by some outside act or circumstance.

It follows from this that the individuality which is found in his

---

[1] Ehrismann, *op. cit.*, p. 457.

story arises from the individuality of the characters with whom he comes into contact and of the adventures in which he takes part. Thus, in the sections of the poem in which Gawan is the main hero we find a large variety of highly individualized, lively figures and situations—the haughty, overweening Obie, who treats Gawan as a merchant; the despairing Lippaut, torn between love for his daughter and affectionate allegiance towards his lord, Meljanz; the little girl Obilot playing the part of the *grande dame* in every detail; the handsome, arrogant huntsman-king Vergulaht and his alluring sister Antikonie; the honest Kingrimursel, compelled by his promise to defend Gawan against the onslaught of Vergulaht's retinue; the ungrateful, devilish Urjans; the revengeful and passionate Orgeluse; Lischoys, who refuses ever to surrender in battle; the overbearing, *minne*-smitten Gramoflanz, who normally will only take on two opponents at a time; the devoted ferryman Plippalinot and his daughter Bene. It is these characters and their respective stories, each told in bright, evocative detail, which bring to life the travels of Gawan through the courtly landscape. He is the hero who connects their stories and brings a solution in times of trouble through the exercise of his knightly ability. Gradually the succession of adventures calls forth the utmost in Gawan's capabilities, until he reaches the final trials of Schastel marveil and Gramoflanz' tree. This does constitute a kind of development, but it is one of courage and ability and not of emotional or spiritual growth. If the latter were the case, then Gawan could not properly represent the norms and ideals of the courtly world. He has no problems of his own to solve: his task is to solve those of other people, and this is what divides him and his courtly background from the individual existence of Parzival.

There is a kind of individuality in Gawan, but it is of a mainly external nature and does not proceed directly from the workings of his own character. The nearest that we come to this is in the monologues, where there is a dim kind of development from *âventiure* for its own sake through to its fulfilment in the service of *minne*. In the earlier part of the poem Gawan is much concerned with his reputation as a knight and his honour in fighting, but this does progress into a communion of knightly prowess and courtly love. And this is the theme which Wolfram desires to stress: namely, that the ideas of *âventiure* and *minne* must be combined. In combining them in his service to Orgeluse, Gawan exemplifies and is the epitome of the courtly knight.

IX

FEIREFIZ

INTRODUCTION

O F all the multitudinous characters that Wolfram invented to people the pages of his romance, Feirefiz is, even more than Gahmuret, the most important and the most peculiarly Wolframian. It is his part in the poem which gives the story of the Grail a wider horizon and a broader basis than that of Chrétien's incomplete *Conte del Graal*. If the tale of Gahmuret forms the subject-matter of books I and II, then that of Feirefiz covers books XV and XVI, and the two provide a framework for the romance of the Grail proper and the parallel histories of Parzival and Gawan. There is, however, a fundamental difference between the functions of Gahmuret and Feirefiz in the poem. Gahmuret's problems furnish a courtly background that is both historically and geographically redolent of the age of the Crusades; they are the basis from which we can understand the significance of *schildes ambet* in Parzival's life. The story of Feirefiz, on the other hand, is *not* a background datum, but a necessary part of Wolfram's conception of the Grail theme, since it extends the relevance of the Grail beyond the narrow bounds of Christianity and foreshadows the ideas which Wolfram later developed in his *Willehalm*. It illustrates the idea of world redemption and presents a charitable assessment of the position of the heathen from the point of view of Christian tolerance. The magpie image of black and white, of good and evil, applies not merely to the Christian hero of the poem, but also to the heathen adventurer whose chequered body is the outward sign of the not completely unredeemable state of his soul. The story is not one of facile optimism, blurring the distinctions between good and evil and claiming that one faith is as good as another—it would be a false judgement of medieval Christianity to assert such a viewpoint.

In the final analysis Feirefiz has to accept Christian baptism in order to be able to see the Grail and become incorporated into the Grail family through his marriage with Repanse de schoye. But although he is frequently referred to as *der heiden* or *der ungetoufte*, he is not thereby degraded in his personal qualities, which remain of the very highest. It is this view of the 'edler Heide' which makes Wolfram's account of his story so significant.

The first mention of Feirefiz occurs at the end of book I, where his birth is described almost immediately after the passage in Gahmuret's letter about his genealogy. Feirefiz is from the beginning placed in the context of the Anschouwe family, and Belacane names him *Feirefîz Anschevîn* (57.21 f.). The main ideas in the poem relating to the House of Anjou have been fully discussed by Willem Snelleman[1] and bear chiefly on the characterization of Gahmuret, much of which is derived from the historical figure of Richard the Lionheart. As far as both Feirefiz and Parzival are concerned, the name of Anschevin is an inherited one and does not condition in any real way the shape of their characters. The point here is that this name provides the means whereby, at the end of the poem, Parzival and Feirefiz recognize each other. Anschouwe in its literal meaning is of no significance for either hero, but it is the point at which the two brothers meet. Feirefiz maintains the name of Anschevin[2] throughout the poem as a basic part of his varied inheritance, but it is not until after the duel with his brother that Parzival claims the name that is also his own inheritance (746.11 f.).[3] In this way the beginning and the end of the poem are bound together in a deep unity, and the figure of Feirefiz is seen to be of great importance merely through the medium of a name shared with his brother. Thus, the significance of the Anjou motif is extended beyond the glorification of Richard the Lionheart and woven into the fabric of the entire romance.

But the introduction of Feirefiz into the poem is not concluded

---

[1] *Das Haus Anjou und der Orient in Wolframs 'Parzival'*.

[2] He is referred to as *Feirefîz Anschevin* 745.28, 764.16, 765.28, 793.3, 794.6, 808.9, 812.2, 814.23, 815.26, 820.9.

[3] Snelleman, *op. cit.*, pp. 56 f.

with the mention of Anschouwe: emphasis is laid on his piebald appearance, which is then explicitly connected with the imagery of the prologue and praised as one of God's miraculous creations:

> diu frouwe an rehter zît genas
> eins suns, der zweier varwe was,
> an dem got wunders wart enein:
> wîz und swarzer varwe er schein.
>
> . . .
>
> als ein agelster wart gevar
> sîn hâr und och sîn vel vil gar.   (57.15 ff.)

The chequered appearance of Feirefiz has both a physical and a spiritual significance. Physically, it expresses the primitive, albeit strikingly imaginative, conception that Wolfram, in common with most of the people of his time, had of the distant and therefore mysterious Orient. Monsters, giants and all kinds of miraculous creatures were credited to the Eastern countries, which at this time were just beginning to be opened up to the West through the movement of the Crusades. The giants in *König Rother* are another example of the strangeness that the East possessed for the Christian West. As far as the *Rolandslied* was concerned, such an appearance was regarded as inhuman because divorced from God. Wolfram's Christian tolerance modifies this view (whereas in *König Rother* it is probably attenuated because religious problems are treated here in a not very detailed manner). Thus, Feirefiz' unusual appearance is not regarded as a monstrosity to be scorned and laughed at, but is to be understood as an example of the wonderful and praiseworthy in the creation, as well as demonstrating in a remarkable and memorable form his black and white ancestry. That Feirefiz is to develop great strength and prowess in battle is indicated in the same passage, which is a further early sign that his curious looks in no way detract from the noble qualities that he possesses:

> der wart ein waltswende:
> die tjoste sîner hende
> manec sper zebrâchen,
> die schilde dürkel stâchen.   (57.23 ff.)

On the spiritual plane Feirefiz' piebald skin links him with the metaphysical ideas of the prologue. The actual image of the magpie is taken up here and then not again until it provides the means whereby Feirefiz is recognized after the duel: 'der heiden schiere wart erkant: / wander truoc agelstern mâl' (748.6 f.). But the contrast of black and white is mentioned on several other occasions[1] throughout the course of the poem. It is in the figure of Feirefiz that this metaphysical image is most literally manifested, although the history of Parzival provides the most detailed expression of it. When therefore it comes to the duel between Parzival and Feirefiz, Wolfram presents us with an extremely striking resolution of the problem of good and evil in human experience. Parzival has reached the point where he is reconciled with God and thus finds himself in a position to attain to the kingship of the Grail, and his duel with his brother is the means by which this is expressed. Feirefiz here represents that part of Parzival's character which Parzival had to overcome in order to be worthy of the Grail. After the duel is interrupted and ended by the breaking of Parzival's sword, the one he had won from Ither, Feirefiz, on learning that he had been fighting with his brother, confesses to guilt at having done so. In other words, Feirefiz, as a heathen, shows a magnanimity which the young Parzival had *not* shown to Ither. Neither hero in fact wins the duel, but Parzival is tacitly assumed to be the victor. He has overcome the dichotomy of good and evil in the duel with Feirefiz, whose body pictographically expresses it.[2]

THE NAME 'FEIREFIZ' AND RELATED THEORIES

The preceding paragraphs have shown how much of a piece the various references to Feirefiz throughout the poem are and how closely the last two books are connected with the first and with the prologue. Everything goes to show how skilfully constructed

[1] 317.9 f., 328.17, 793.28.
[2] For a longer discussion of this duel and its relationship with the prologue see above, pp. 203 ff.

Wolfram's poem is and how a variety of strands of thought are woven into a single complex fabric. The same is true of the actual name 'Feirefiz' and the interpretations it has received.

Two theories have been advanced to explain the name. The first, propounded by Karl Bartsch,[1] sees it as a germanization of Old French *vaire fiz*, 'piebald son'. The second, suggested by A. N. Veselovsky,[2] understands it as derived from the French *voire fiz*, 'true son'.

The first theory fits the bill very well and gives a perfectly adequate explanation which is clearly supported by the text. Feirefiz is certainly described as piebald in a variety of places already mentioned, and in addition to these Wolfram refers to him as *dirre bunte man* (758.2), *der heiden bunt gevar* (764.14), *Feirefiz der vêch gevar* (781.6), *Feirefiz der vêch gemâl* (789.2) and *der heiden vêch gemâl* (810.10). In view of the obvious importance of colour in the magpie image, this theory suits the facts admirably.

The second theory seems to me to be less probable, though it is certainly possible and does not do violence to a proper understanding of the poem. Its main defect (if it can be called such) derives from the fact that the researches with which it is connected consist of exploration and suggestion rather than of proved facts. The extremely interesting work of Helen Adolf on possible Oriental sources for some of Wolfram's ideas, particularly on the Grail itself,[3] opens up a wide horizon for the subject, though it is difficult to see just how Wolfram might have had access to such ideas. The story of Gahmuret and Belacane and the subsequent birth of Feirefiz does bear a strong resemblance to the legend that Bilqis, the Queen of Sheba, bore to Solomon a son, Menelek, who afterwards became emperor of Ethiopia, and Helen Adolf quotes in support of her interpretation of the name Feirefiz the fact that in one version of the legend 'the young prince is acknowledged by

---

[1] Bartsch, *Eigennamen in Parzival und Titurel*, p. 138.

[2] Veselovsky, *On the Problem of the Origin of the Grail Legend (Journal of the Russian Ministry for Enlightenment of the People*, CCCLI, 1904), p. 452, quoted by Helen Adolf in the article listed in the following note.

[3] Helen Adolf, *New Light on Oriental Sources for Wolfram's Parzival and Other Grail Romances (PMLA*, LXII, 1947).

King Solomon with the very words: "My true son!"[1] Be this as it may, this investigation of sources is not decisive in coming to an appreciation of the actual character of Feirefiz as Wolfram portrays it. It may attempt to give an explanation of how Wolfram reached his formulation of Feirefiz' character, but it gives us no more than a legendary parallel for a personality and does not perceptibly deepen our assessment of that personality, which in fact depends on the role that he has in the poem and the way in which the author depicts him. In any case, the phrase 'true son' is likely to have been of such general use (unlike the use of 'piebald') that parallels such as have been cited cannot prove anything convincingly. Feirefiz is indeed the 'true son' of Gahmuret, a state which is emphasized by his use of the name 'Anschevin', but it is none-theless the visual image of his magpie-like skin and hair which is at the forefront of Wolfram's descriptions of him and of the role he has to play in the poem.

DESCRIPTIVE PASSAGES

After the first mention of Feirefiz at the end of book I a number of other references to and descriptions of him occur before he finally appears in person on the scene of battle in book XV. These descriptions are given by Eckuba, the heathen from Janfuse, and by Cundrie, also of Eastern origin, and there are other mentions midstream in the poem, which keep Feirefiz in our minds as an important participant in the action.

The first occurrence of Feirefiz' name and reputation is to be found in Cundrie's long tirade against Parzival at the Arthurian court, and immediately we see that he is being set up as a model of behaviour against which Parzival's action can be measured. Cundrie declares to Parzival that by not having asked Anfortas the fateful question at Munsalvæsche he has forfeited everything; the asking of the question would have been of greater worth and consequence than the pagan city of Tabronit, which contains all earthly perfection (316.29 ff.). She then continues by telling him that this city and the queen of the land were won by Feirefiz

[1] *Op. cit.*, p. 310.

443

through performing difficult knightly feats. He, the son of the king of Zazamanc, lacks nothing in manly virtue and presents a marvellous appearance with his black and white skin. It is illuminating that Parzival's conduct, as well as disgracing the Round Table, is considered as being far below that of his pagan brother and of his father. The emphasis is on *ritterschaft* and not on religious depth and experience at this stage, and Feirefiz is held up as an outstanding example of it. It therefore is a logical outcome of the construction of the poem that Parzival's final test consists in a duel with his brother, and when he has successfully completed it he can go on to the kingship of the Grail. Of Feirefiz no more is said here; there is merely enough to show that he is following in his father's footsteps and that he is a person to be reckoned with. It is not necessary for Wolfram to say more, and he pursues his usual technique of imparting information gradually in small doses.

A little later, on Cundrie's departure, the heathen queen of Janfuse takes it upon herself to enlarge on Feirefiz' position and achievements, and her comments are lent the more authority in that she is Feirefiz' aunt (*sîner muoter muomen tohter*). In this long passage (328.2–30) Eckuba concentrates on telling Parzival of his worldly splendour and power and of his excellence in the qualities of a courtly knight. His rule extends over the two kingdoms of Azagouc and Zazamanc, both powerful countries, and his power is such that only that of the *bâruc* and the land of Tribalibot exceed it and his people worship him like a god. Before she goes on to describe his moral virtues, Eckuba inserts her view of his extraordinary appearance, which she appends to her remark that his people worship him, unlike all other men as he is: the importance of his chequered skin is again brought out, though nothing further is said about its symbolic significance. He is characterized by magnificence, constant victory in jousting, high moral worth, generosity and complete lack of deceit. Finally, Eckuba names the king about whom she has been speaking and tells how he has learnt to suffer through his deeds on behalf of noble ladies. This passage has a particular purpose about it in that it is meant to be an encouragement to Parzival, since Eckuba considers that he possesses, at least in latent form, the very qualities she predicates of Feirefiz. Cundrie had exalted Feirefiz far above his delinquent brother, but Eckuba is quick to spur him on to a realization of the same virtues.

Until Feirefiz appears in book XV there is very little that expands our picture of him. What references there are connect him with the extraordinary and the miraculous that characterized the East in the medieval mind. In the middle of Wolfram's disquisition in book X on the curious people and things in creation, he mentions that Feirefiz had won Secundille as his wife and that her kingdom was full of these monstrosities (519.2 ff.). In a later place he notes that Clinschor brought the *wundersiule* from Feirefiz' kingdom (559.10 f.), adding a few lines further on that it was stolen from Tabronit from Queen Secundille herself (592.18 f.) This all forms part of Wolfram's deliberately close texture in the poem, and through it the marvellous character of Feirefiz is sustained until he steps forward into the main stream of the action.

When the poem finally centres on Feirefiz in book XV, Wolfram devotes a good deal of space to building up a more detailed picture of his pagan hero, but he refers to him by a series of synonyms,[1] which spotlight the various characteristics of his role, until when the duel is broken off Feirefiz announces with unconcealed pride and a sure awareness of his individuality:

> ich pin Feirefîz Anschevîn,
> sô rîche wol daz mîner hant
> mit zinse dienet manec lant.   (745.28 ff.)

With this Feirefiz emerges from his anonymity (though it is clear to Wolfram's audience the whole of the time who he is) and asserts with strength and conviction his far-famed achievement. He is not the perfect representative of courtliness, idealized like Gawan, but an Oriental potentate of magnificent appearance and strength, linked by clear family relationships with the other heroes of the poem and individualized by his particular conquests in battle, his aims in life and his uniquely patterned skin.

[1] See below, pp. 448 ff.

Wolfram spares no pains in painting a brilliant portrait of Feirefiz. It is his *ʒimierde*, the plumes and ornaments on his helmet and the rich decoration of his battle-dress, that most interest Wolfram, and he prefaces his remarks by saying that if he told his audience 'mêre denne genuoc' about it, there would still be very much more to say (735.9 ff.). He then launches forth into his description.

Feirefiz' *wâpenroc* is so richly sewn with precious stones that all Artus' subjects in Bertane and Engellant could not have paid for them; rubies and chalcedonies are the poorest among them (735.15 ff.). Great emphasis is laid on the variety and wealth of the precious stones, from which, together with his love for Secundille, Feirefiz derives his physical strength:

> der heiden truoc zwuo geselleschaft,
> dar an doch lac sîn meistiu kraft;
>
> . . .
>
> daz ander wâren steine,
> die mit edelem arde reine
> in hôchgemüete lêrten
> und sîne kraft gemêrten.   (743.1 ff.)

These gems are what to Wolfram signify the extreme opposite of poverty:

> es het ein armez wîp bevilt
> an dem wâpenrocke al eine:
> sô tiwer wârn die steine
> an den stücken allen vieren.   (757.20 ff.)

Indeed, they are so far removed from his own range of knowledge and experience that he twice insists that he is in no position to tell his audience what they are (735.30, 773.18 ff.), and thereupon he refers them to the authority of the ancients, Eraclius, Ercules, Alexander and Pictagoras (773.21 ff.). But although Wolfram admits his inability to do justice to the subject, he cannot refrain entirely from making the attempt and, when describing Feirefiz' shield, throws in for good measure the names of the five types of jewel that decorate it—turquoise, chrysoprase, emerald, ruby and carbuncle—the colours of which are generally known in their variety. The last-mentioned of these has assigned to it in addition the 'Oriental' name *antrax* (741.12 ff.).[1]

Feirefiz' glittering *wâpenroc* is itself made of soft asbestos, which the medievals imagined to be fashioned by salamanders (the name of the reptile being used by extension to mean the thing it actually made as well[2]), and his shield is of *aspindê*, i.e. ligneous asbestos. The peculiar properties of asbestos fit in well with the curious splendour and invulnerability with which Wolfram wishes to invest his hero. Apart from the bright array of jewels the *wâpenroc* itself is merely described as being shaggy and the colour of snow (757.1).

The *Helmschmuck* is the most important part of Feirefiz' attire and is a feature which he shares only with Gahmuret, Kaylet and Orilus, though other figures have their smaller plumes.[3] The distinguishing mark of his *Helmschmuck* is an *ecidemón*, which has been given to him by his queen, Secundille, as a part of his arms (741.15 ff.); it is referred to in this context as 'daz reine tier'. Elsewhere it is described in greater detail as a beast that has the power of killing snakes (736.9 ff.). From this it seems that it could be interpreted as a weasel, for which there is support in Isidore,[4] but which is a Western animal; or it might be a name invented to cover what was known of the Oriental animal, the mongoose. In either case, the originality of the decoration is striking and is a further mark of the individuality of Feirefiz. The only other Eastern ruler with whom he can be compared is the *bâruc* of Baldac, who is left undescribed in his magnificence and serves merely as a type of the powerful monarch, whereas Feirefiz is carefully delineated in a large number of clearly individualized ways.

This stress on Feirefiz' knightly prowess is shown also in the

---

[1] Actually the Greek ἄνθραξ. Cf. Isidore, *Etymologiae*, XVI, xiv.

[2] Snellemann, *op. cit.*, p. 153. See also 812.21.

[3] *Ibid.*, pp. 95 ff.

[4] *Etymologiae*, XII, iii: 'Mustela dicta, quasi mus longus; nam telum a longitudine dictum. Haec ingenio subdola in domibus, ubi nutrit catulos suos, transfert mutatque sedem. Serpentes etiam et mures persequitur. Duo autem sunt genera mustelarum; alterum enim silvestre est distans magnitudine, quod Graeci ἰκτίδας vocant; alterum in domibus oberrans.'

list of names of those knights whom he has vanquished in battle and which exceeds Parzival's list by seven or more (770.1 ff. and 772.1 ff.). It is not sufficient for Wolfram to give an undefined praise of Feirefiz: he has to furnish a precise catalogue of the achievements of both his heroes, and this, though it consists of fabulous and fantastic names, does make for a further crystallization of Feirefiz' character. The curious names add to the impression of extraordinariness which his appearance creates, while at the same time giving a sense of reality by their exactness, particularly as some of the geographical locations and conquered princes are known through other contexts, as for example Liddamus, Argemuntin, Assigarzionte, Killicrates, Orastegentesin, Arabie, Janfuse, Nourjente, Azagouc, Zazamanc, Gampfassasche.[1]

SYNONYMS

In the course of the last two books of the poem Feirefiz is referred to by a considerable number of synonyms, which reflect his position and role in the conclusion of the romance. The picture that emerges from them is one of a full character with many facets— genealogical links, geographical symbols, religion, and courtliness all come into it. Through them all his personality is defined and circumscribed.

Apart from the 'surname' *Anschevîn*[2] Feirefiz' courtly accomplishments and knightly prowess are mirrored in a variety of synonyms: *vogt* (734.30), *der selbe kurteise* (735.2), *ein rîcher gast* (735.8), *helt* (735.19), *ein helt unverʒagt* (746.14), *der selbe werlîche knabe* (736.25), *der küene rîche gast* (744.12), *der küene degen balt* (747.15), *der degen wert* (754.24), *diser rîter* (758.15). In this group it is the adjectives which lend colour to the picture; the nouns themselves are conventional and belong to Wolfram's normal usage. The word *kurteis*, however, is particularly significant in that it places Feirefiz, a pagan and an Oriental, firmly within the

---

[1] Very many of these names are taken from Solinus, for a discussion of which see Jean Fourquet, *Les Noms propres du Parʒival* in the Mélanges Ernest Hoepffner (Paris, 1949), pp. 252 ff.
[2] See above, p. 439.

context of Western cultural patterns. The fact that he is a heathen is of no importance in an evaluation of his knightly ability and in no way detracts from it. This idea is most highly developed in the courtly period in Wolfram's work, expecially in his *Willehalm*, but it does not arise suddenly with Wolfram, as Hans Naumann is at pains to point out.[1] Nevertheless, this glorification of Feirefiz as a courtly knight is a powerful contribution towards individualization.

The other adjectives used in the above group of synonyms are generally the same as might be applied to any hero with whom the poet's sympathy lay. The word *unverzagt* provides a slender connexion with the ideas of the prologue,[2] but the main emphasis lies on the power and wealth which Feirefiz enjoys. The word *rîch* is—apart from the religious vocabulary—the most frequent description applied to him. I have already noted two instances, but Feirefiz is referred to as *der rîche Feirefîz* or *Feirefîz der rîche* on eight other occasions.[3] Once the word *stolz* is combined with the phrase (757.27), and once *wert* (782.3)—in another instance he is called *der werde gast* (811.5). In two further cases he is called *der rîche heiden* (761.5, 774.12). The reiteration of Feirefiz' power-fulness through the adjective *rîch*, occurring at regular intervals throughout the course of the last two books, impresses the audience with the equality that Feirefiz shares with Parzival and saves him from ever falling into an inferior position on account of his religion.

As well as being integrated into courtly society, Feirefiz is on many occasions shown in his relationship with the other characters and given a clear position within the complex genealogical struc-ture. First of all, he is several times referred to as Parzival's *bruoder*,[4] the relationship which is of prime importance for the

---

[1] Naumann, *Der wilde und der edle Heide. Versuch über die höfische Toleranz* in the Festgabe Gustav Ehrismann (Berlin/Leipzig, 1925), *passim*.

[2] See above, p. 204.

[3] 747.19, 749.15, 757.27, 758.17, 763.12, 774.25, 782.3, 821.23.

[4] 749.24, 753.25, 754.23, 759.5.8, 760.10, 784.24, 792.13, 813.10, 816.24. When Parzival is explaining to Gawan about the duel, he in addition refers to Feirefiz as *dirre heinlîche gast* (759.11), which ties in with the various relationships in an oblique manner.

development of the poem's main theme and which gives Feirefiz his essential individuality. But the matter does not end here. Necessarily connected with his being Parzival's brother is the fact that he is the son of Gahmuret, and this is all the more important as Feirefiz' journeyings through the wide world are undertaken with the express purpose of discovering his father (750.27 ff.). Instead of finding him he meets the other son of Gahmuret and is joined by this into the extension of the Grail kingdom and family. Thus, he is referred to as *Gahmuretes kint* (785.27), *des stolzen Gahmuretes kint* (761.17), *der heiden, Gahmuretes kint* (814.3) and *Gahmurets sun von Zazamanc* (811.15). As Parzival is also referred to as Gahmuret's son, a distinction is usually made (though not always) by the addition of Feirefiz' name or a distinguishing feature, as in the last two instances quoted. The kingdom of Zazamanc is so closely linked with Gahmuret, who is several times called *der künec von Zazamanc* in book II, that it can also be used for Feirefiz as a reference to his being Gahmuret's son. He is called once simply *der von Zazamanc* (816.13) and once *der künec von Zazamanc* (758.13). A further example of his incorporation into the Grail family is given through his being called Loherangrin's *veter* (805.29).

In addition to this Feirefiz is connected with the Arthurian court. Gawan demands of Parzival who *der geselle dîn* (758.7) is, and after he has been informed of Feirefiz' identity, he refers to him as *sîn neve von Thasmê* (760.8). Artus similarly calls him *sîn neve der heiden* (762.5) and *sîn neve Feirefîz* (774.13), as does Ginover (765.18).

The most important set of synonyms is that which is used principally with respect to the duel between Feirefiz and Parzival and raises the complex question of religion. The whole of books XV and XVI are written in terms of the opposition between Christianity and paganism, and Feirefiz is therefore most frequently designated as *der heiden*.[1] This is qualified in a few instances

---

[1] 735.11, 736.4, 738.11, 739.7.23, 740.7.18.23, 741.1, 742.1.16, 743.1, 744.8.20.25, 745.13, 746.2, 747.29, 748.6.13, 750.14, 752.2, 753.1.16, 754.5, 756.9.26, 765.1.6.23, 767.30, 769.29, 773.1.9, 778.12, 785.21.24, 786.20, 806.3, 810.3, 813.4, 815.19, 817.2, 818.15.

which show that the word is used objectively to state a matter of fact and not to insinuate a moral deficiency on Feirefiz' part. Thus, twice it is amplified by the addition of *rîch* (761.5, 774.12), once by *wert* (793.15), and once by the formula *starc unde snel* (747.12). At the beginning of book XV he is first called *ein heidenischer man,* / *der toufes künde nie gewan* (735.3 f.) and shortly afterwards *der ungetoufte gehiure* (736.20) and *der heidenische man* (747.1), thus slightly varying this most constant of all the synonyms. On other occasions a geographical element is added, and Feirefiz is referred to as *der heiden von Thasmê* (745.25) and *der von Tribalibot* (750.1, 822.8). At the end of the poem Wolfram explains that 'wir heizenz hie Indîâ: / dort heizet ez Tribalibôt' (823.2 f.), and this fantastic name for India has its origin in the name Palibothra of Solinus[1] or Palibothri of Pomponius Mela's map of the Eastern world of *c.* 42 A.D.[2] This area is marked on the map both with this name and with *Indi,* which connects closely with Wolfram's explanation. Not that an exact geographical location is necessary for the name to have any significance, but the vast land of India could provide a plausible situation for a kingdom that only that of the *báruc* of Baldac rivalled. Feirefiz' pagan origin is the most important factor in his story and is accordingly underlined throughout the poem, but after his baptism this lack is completely remedied and he is immediately referred to as *der getoufte Feirefîz* (819.9).

RELIGION AND MINNE

Just as the themes of Condwiramurs and the Grail (and therefore of religion) are intertwined in Parzival's story, so also it is extremely difficult to separate Feirefiz' religious beliefs from his desire for *minne.* Here too we have an interesting contrast between the unresolved problems of Gahmuret at the beginning of the poem and the solution which Feirefiz reaches after his arduous travels in the entire world. (Of course Parzival's solution is more striking.) Gahmuret had deserted Belacane ostensibly on the

---

[1] Ernst Martin, *Kommentar zu Wolframs Parzival,* p. 274.
[2] Snellemann, *op. cit.,* p. 188 and the map opposite.

grounds that she was a pagan; Feirefiz, in the reverse situation (since it is he who is the pagan in this case), renounces his heathenism in order to marry Repanse de schoye. It does not affect the issue that Belacane had professed her willingness to become a Christian: the plain fact is that she did not, as the opportunity was not allowed her. Feirefiz, on the other hand, has the opportunity and makes the decision to be baptized, facing the issue fairly and squarely that Gahmuret ran away from. There are indeed humorous, perhaps even slightly ludicrous, overtones about Feirefiz' naïve impatience to do anything (i.e. to be baptized) so as to be able to marry Repanse, but this does not lessen the fact that he has to accept baptism as an essential condition for his entrance into the Grail family. All this, however, is concerned with the end of Feirefiz' religious career, and it is necessary to examine his pagan beliefs and practices before this.

Time and again, as we have seen, it is stressed that Feirefiz is a heathen, but this does not condemn him as a wicked being doomed to perdition. On the contrary, he is the person who, by virtue of his coloured skin, is most obviously connected with the images and ideas of the prologue and who 'mac dennoch wesen geil: / wand an im sint beidiu teil, / des himels und der helle' (1.7 ff.). Although he is a heathen, there still remains for him the possibility of salvation, which is mediated to him through the power of *minne* as manifested in the person of Repanse de schoye. This connexion of religion and *minne* has already been mentioned in discussing the relationship of Parzival with Condwiramurs, where Condwiramurs' constant love for her husband provides a point of security for Parzival in his search for the Grail.[1] Furthermore, it is the thought of Condwiramurs which finally gives him the strength to strike Feirefiz to the ground in their momentous duel (743.24 ff.). It is therefore clearly in line with Wolfram's way of thinking that Feirefiz, in his moment of crisis, afflicted by the sight of Repanse and his inability to perceive the Grail, is spurred on by the power of *minne* to renounce his paganism, which—however much he is praised as an *edler Heide*—is nonetheless a work of the devil

[1] See above, pp. 243 ff.

(817.12), accept the true religion of Christianity and be united into the Grail family.

Wolfram writes of Feirefiz' religion in general and conventionally medieval terms. The main thing to be emphasized is that he is a pagan, but there is no question of exploring the particular kind of pagan religion that he adheres to. Despite all the connexions with India, Ethiopia and Baldac that he has, Feirefiz remains depicted as a believer in the gods of ancient Rome. The names of Jupiter and Juno are continually on his lips, though he places his trust in other gods too. Certainly there is nothing of the stark monotheism that we nowadays think of as characterizing Islam. Pagans are polytheistic wherever they are found in this period of medieval German literature.[1]

Feirefiz' history, however, like Parzival's, contains an element of development, though it cannot be as fully described or motivated as Parzival's on account of Feirefiz' subsidiary role. A definite progression from enthusiastic polytheism to accepted Christianity, in which *minne* also has its part, is clearly discernible, though the psychology behind it may be somewhat naïvely and fragmentarily expressed. But at no time does Wolfram pour scorn on Feirefiz' original beliefs, however much he regards it as necessary that they should be superseded.

Feirefiz refers on a few occasions to 'al mîne gote' (748.16, 818.9), but the only ones that he actually mentions are Jupiter and Juno, to whom he at first ascribes his felicitous meeting with Parzival. He does not discriminate between the sphere of influence of the god and goddess, but praises them both for leading him to the West. But although he pays a particular devotion to Jupiter as the guardian of his good fortune (748.19 f. and 763.14 ff.) and to Juno

---

[1] Naumann, *Der wilde und der edle Heide*, p. 83: 'Alles Nichtchristliche ist miteinander schlechtweg als heidnisch identifiziert. Indem die antiken Heiden mit den Moslems gleichgestellt werden, überträgt sich von jenen auf diese die historisch gänzlich falsche Vorstellung von der Vielgötterei mitsamt den antiken Götternamen, wird aber auch ein sehr fester Grund zu ihrer späteren Rehabilitierung gelegt. Wenn das Bild des edlen dem Bilde des wilden Heiden schließlich die Wage hält, so liegt eine fortwirkende Ursache in der Zusammenfassung von Römern und Griechen mit den Sarazenen unter dem gemeinsamen Begriffe Heiden.'

for directing him westwards and breaking his chain of misfortune (767.2 ff.), the planets also he recognizes to have a power over his life (748.23 ff.). This astrological motif has a definite Oriental colouring about it and is emphasized by Cundrie's speech in book XV ('daz epitafjum ist gelesen'), in which she mentions the planets by recognizably Arabic names (782.6 ff.). Such is the basis of Feirefiz' religious faith to begin with.

Quite soon after the duel, whose fortunate outcome Feirefiz at first attributes to the power of Jupiter (752.20 ff.), his preoccupation with *minne* becomes evident, and when he finds himself in the middle of explaining his knightly feats and service of Secundille, he plays down the influence of Jupiter and praises Secundille instead:

> swâ ich sider kom in nôt,
> zehant so ich an si dâhte,
> ir minne helfe brâhte.
> diu was mir bezzer trôstes wer
> denne mîn got Jupiter. (768.26 ff.)

This is a parallel to Parzival's constancy towards Condwiramurs, which persists throughout all the time that he reacts against God, only for belief in God and faith in Condwiramurs to be united in the end. But at the end Feirefiz has to reject both Jupiter and Secundille (815.6 ff.) in order to achieve a greater vocation. At this point and in the course of events leading up to it the themes of religion and *minne* are inextricably bound together, and the parallelism with Parzival is very close.

Minne is an extremely powerful part of Feirefiz' life, even the most important of all. As he is introduced in book XV, we are told:

> sîn gir stuont nâch minne
> unt nâch prîss gewinne:
> daz gâbn ouch allez meistec wîp,
> dâ mite der heiden sînen lîp
> kostlîche zimierte.
> diu minne condwierte

in sîn manlîch herze hôhen muot,
als si noch dem minne gernden tuot.

. . .

der ungetoufte gehiure
ranc nâch wîbe lône:
des zimiert er sich sus schône.
sîn hôhez herze in des betwanc,
daz er nâch werder minne ranc.   (736.1 ff.)

In this respect Feirefiz is a true son of his father, and in his many
loves is merely following the pattern of relationships that Gahmuret
had with Belacane, Ampflise and Herzeloyde. Two queens,
Olimpie and Clauditte, were his mistresses before he married
Secundille (771.15 ff.), but it is through her that he is king of
Tribalibot and wields his power. She is the inspiration and the
source of strength for his knightly adventures. The *ecidemôn* of his
arms he bears at Secundille's desire (741.15 ff.), and *daz reine tier*
is an emblem that ties up with the *werde minne* for which Feirefiz
is striving, an enterprise that causes Secundille no explicitly
mentioned anxiety (in contrast to Herzeloyde *vis-à-vis* Gahmuret).
Whatever adventures Feirefiz may have with other noble ladies,
she remains his mistress and 'sîn schilt in nôt' (740.12). All that
she has is his:

                si liez in âventiure
                ir minne, ir lant unde ir lîp:
                dise zimierde im gab ein wîp
                (er leist ouch gerne ir gebot
                beidiu in freude und in nôt),
                diu küngîn Secundille.
                ez was ir herzen wille,
                daz se im gab ir rîcheit:
                sîn hôher prîs ir minne erstreit.   (757.6 ff.)

Nevertheless she is at the best a shadowy figure, and although she
may be better able to offer consolation than Jupiter, when Feirefiz
first catches sight of Repanse de schoye, all her power over him
vanishes, and he renounces her together with his pagan gods. The
news of her subsequent death (822.20) removes any trace of
blemish or reminiscence of Gahmuret's marriage with Herzeloyde

while Belacane was still alive from his marriage with Repanse. An entirely happy ending is thus secured.

Feirefiz' pagan religion and his *minne*-relationship with Secundille are considered as parallel phenomena, both unsatisfactory. When it comes to the point, Wolfram, however charitable he is towards his pagan characters on account of their undoubted excellence in courtliness and morality, insists on the religious superiority of Christianity. Feirefiz simply cannot be incorporated into the Grail family as a heathen; he has to be baptized in order to be able to perceive the Grail at all and in order to marry Repanse de schoye. This done, he is then in a position to respond to one of the highest of all vocations—the spreading of Christianity in India—through which the theme of Prester John and the vision of an *orbis christianus* are introduced.

The conversion of Feirefiz is effected through the power of *minne* in Repanse de schoye, to which Feirefiz reacts in a half-serious, half-comical way and one, moreover, which closely resembles the reaction of Parzival after his failure at the Grail castle, but with a twist in its significance. After having shown his interest in all women (754.5 ff.), Feirefiz is entirely captivated by the sight of Repanse and the attraction of the ladies at the Arthurian court immediately fades. He is afflicted with pain at the sight of her surpassing beauty:

> ir blic mir inz herze gêt.
> ich wânde sô starc wær mîn lîp,
> daz iemmer maget ode wîp
> mir freuden kraft benæme.
> mirst worden widerzæme,
> ob ich ie werde minne enpfienc.
> unzuht mir zuht underviene,
> daz ich iu künde mîne nôt,
> sît ich iu dienst nie gebôt.
> waz hilfet al mîn rîchheit,
> und swaz ich ie durch wîp gestreit,
> und op mîn hant ihr hât vergeben,
> muoz ich sus pîneclîche leben?
> ein kreftec got Jupiter,
> waz woltstu mîn zunsenfte her? (810.14 ff.)

Feirefiz is in such a state of torment that absolutely nothing can comfort him, not even the thought of Secundille (811.8 f.); he is completely in the power of Repanse. Anfortas realizes the pain that he is suffering, and Feirefiz declares to him the extent of his passion. He is fully conscious of himself and his feelings at this crucial moment, and the intensity of his emotion is no longer placed at one remove through Wolfram's narration: Feirefiz expresses himself directly in speech to Anfortas and thereby stresses his self-awareness and individuality. All that he desires is Repanse, and he wishes that any feat he has performed could have been done for her. He describes the occasion on which he fought a blazing knight outside Agremuntin and despite his asbestos protection was burnt in the jousting; his sorrow is that he could not have done this for Repanse's sake. Then Feirefiz assumes the same bargaining attitude towards God that Parzival uttered to Trevrizent (461.9 f.), the attitude of despair:

> Jupiter mîme gote
> wil ich iemmer hazzen tragn,
> ern wende mir diz starke klagn.   (812.28 ff.)

The god whom previously he had called *kreftec* (748.19) and actually meant it, he now characterizes in the same way with disillusion (810.27), but his situation is by no means as difficult as was Parzival's. The solution is all ready to hand; no long wandering expiation is required: all that is necessary is for him to be baptized. This is explained by Titurel from his sick-bed:

> der sprach 'ist ez ein heidensch man,
> sô darf er des niht willen hân
> daz sîn ougn âns toufes kraft
> bejagen die geselleschaft
> daz si den grâl beschouwen:
> da ist hâmît für gehouwen.'   (813.17 ff.)

Feirefiz' immediate reaction is to demand whether baptism will advance his desire for *minne*, and it is on this level that he understands it and not on a doctrinal one. Indeed, after the priest has given him brief instruction in Christianity, he admits his readiness

457

to believe anything, provided it eases his trouble and grants him *minne* (818.2 ff.). This attitude causes some amusement among the Grail family, but the high value that Wolfram sets on the concept of *minne* as a spiritual force within the bond of marriage renders Feirefiz' attitude both reasonable and not exceptional in the context of the whole poem. His desire for *minne* is impetuous and instinctive, and we may expect an element of sensuality about it from what we know of his previous experience (though this is not mentioned), but the explicit virtue of Repanse de schoye, the virgin most closely associated with the Grail and the pure bearer of it, is such that the power of *minne* she exercises must be understood in quasi-religious terms. In this way the themes of *minne* and religion are fused.

In the analysis of the religious aspect of Feirefiz' conversion the question of *triuwe* looms large and is complicated by the fact that Wolfram has two distinct kinds of *triuwe* in mind. The first kind is general in its nature and is shared by the two brothers; the second is specifically that of Christianity and is what separates them. The difference is that between natural and revealed religion.

It is in the duel that the first kind of *triuwe* is most taken note of, although the distinction between *heiden* and *getoufter* is never let out of sight. Thus, in his detailed preparation for the actual duel, Wolfram declares that both of the heroes are 'der geliutrten triwe fundamint' (740.6), and when the battle is being fiercely fought, he says again: 'dâ streit der triwen lûterheit: / grôz triwe aldâ mit triwen streit' (741.21 f.). In the same place, having mentioned that both knights are fighting for the sake of *minne* (even here it is impossible to avoid the close connexion), Wolfram writes that Parzival, since his departure from Trevrizent, 'wol getrûwet gote' (741.26) and thereby makes a transition to a more specific kind of *triuwe*, since he does not mention here that Feirefiz derives any real power from Juno and Jupiter. In the sphere of natural religion and basic morality, however, Feirefiz and Parzival are equals and, moreover, equated with each other, as Wolfram's treatment of the duel shows. Because of this it is impossible that either should physically triumph over the other.

The question of *triuwe* in its more restricted form cannot be solved through an unexpressed trust in the saving power of God and the forces of *minne*. The matter of baptism, as in the case of Belacane and Gahmuret, becomes all-important. After the duel is broken off, Feirefiz begins to cry, and Wolfram sees in his tears an analogy with Christian baptism:

> sîn heideschiu ougen
> begunden wazzer rêren
> al nâch des toufes êren.
> der touf sol lêren triuwe,
> sît unser ê diu niuwe
> nâch Kriste wart genennet:
> an Kriste ist triwe erkennet. (752.24 ff.)

Here it is the tears of one who has *triuwe* that are implicitly equated with the water of baptism.[1] For the time being, however, the matter rests. The idea of baptism has been introduced, but the moment at which it will be inevitable has not yet arrived. It is mentioned again *en passant* by Artus, when he praises Feirefiz as the only heathen coming 'ûf toufpflegenden landen' (766.27) whom he would be willing to serve, thus making the point that Feirefiz is now in a Christian society and hinting that he may have to conform to its ways. This occurs in book XVI, when Feirefiz realizes that in order to see the Grail and reap the benefits of Repanse's love he will have to accept baptism. At the same time Parzival recognizes him fully as his brother and begins at last to address him in the second person singular; this shows in an unmistakable fashion that Feirefiz possesses the spiritual qualities which make for a true kinship between the brothers. Feirefiz does not properly comprehend the religious significance of the act, thinking that it is something he can win by knightly prowess and not something which he has merely to accept, but this does not minimize his desire for it nor his response afterwards. This desire to gain baptism by his own effort constitutes a parallel to Parzival's

---

[1] Cf. Herzeloyde at the end of book II (111.3 ff.).

intention of winning the Grail (*bejagn* (468.12), *erstrîten* (798.26)), but in Feirefiz' case this is impossible.

The baptism takes place in the specific context of the Grail family with Parzival requiring of Feirefiz that he should renounce all his pagan gods and henceforth put all his strength into the defence of 'der hôhste got', if he wishes to marry Repanse. Feirefiz declares his willingness, the baptismal basin is inclined towards the Grail, and a grey-bearded priest takes charge of the ecclesiastical ceremony, beginning with the time-honoured first question of the renunciation of the devil. The rest of his speech outlines in the briefest of terms the doctrine of the Trinity, the example of Christ in being baptized and the power of water. In one place he gives an almost word-for-word reiteration of part of Trevrizent's conversation with Parzival at the beginning of book XVI (797.28 ff.); and the lines 817.23 f. are strongly reminiscent of other words of Trevrizent in book IX (464.28 f.). After this Feirefiz again plainly declares that he is receiving baptism and believing in Repanse's God in order to conquer his discomfort and win her love; these are the lengths he will go to in order to achieve his desire:

> ist ez mir guot für ungemach,
> ich gloub swes ir gebietet.
> op mich ir minne mietet,
> sô leist ich gerne sîn gebot.
> bruoder, hât dîn muome got,
> an den geloube ich unt an sie
> (sô grôze nôt enpfieng ich nie):
> al mîne gote sint verkorn.
> Secundill hab och verlorn
> swaz si an mir ie gêrte sich.
> durh dîner muomen got heiz toufen mich.   (818.2 ff.)

Moreover, Feirefiz is ready to exercise that *triuwe* that Parzival demands, if he is to have Repanse for his wife (817.1 ff.). The baptism then ensues, Feirefiz is able to see the Grail at last and proceeds to marriage.

The basis of Feirefiz' baptism is not simply that Christianity is better than paganism, firmly believed though this was by the Christian Church. It is rather a matter of ends and means, and as such it has to be considered as the action of an individual responding to an individual situation. The end is to marry Repanse and to see the Grail; the means necessary to accomplish this is Christian baptism. Accordingly, Feirefiz casts aside the paganism of which a gradual weakening has already been apparent—a further sign of more detailed psychological treatment and therefore of individuality—and he stakes everything on his love for Repanse. There is a likeable logicality about his actions.

A NOTE ON COURTLINESS

The basis of the concept of the 'edler Heide' lies in the acknowledgement of the pagan's knightly prowess as equal to the Christian's. In Feirefiz we find this together with considerable achievement in *minne*. I have already indicated the importance of the synonym *der selbe kurteise* for Feirefiz' character,[1] but other characters in the poem also emphasize it in what they say about Feirefiz. Jofreit speaks about him in the following terms at the Arthurian court:

> erst sô kurtoys,
> ir muget in alle gerne sehn:
> wan ir sult wunder an im spehn.
> er vert ûz grôzer rîcheit:
> sîniu wâpenlîchiu kleit
> nie man vergelten möhte:
> deheiner hant daz töhte.
> Löver, Bertâne, Engellant,
> von Pârîs unz an Wîzsant,
> der dergein leit al die terre,
> ez wærem gelte verre.   (761.20 ff.)

His achievement and courtly character are such that even Artus, *primus inter pares* of the knights of the Round Table, does not stint himself in praising God for Feirefiz' arrival in their lands. The two

---

[1] See above, pp. 448 f.

kings vie with each other in their esteem for the other's reputation, but this in no way detracts from the eulogy:

> Artûs sprach 'nu lob ichs got,
> daz er dise êre uns erbôt,
> daz wir dich hie gesehen hân.
> ûz heidenschaft gefuor nie man
> ûf toufpflegenden landen,
> den mit dienstlîchen handen
> ich gerner diens werte,
> swar des dîn wille gerte.' (766.23 ff.)

It is obvious from this that there will be little difficulty in admitting Feirefiz into the sodality of the Round Table. Indeed, nothing additional is required from him before this can happen, since he has already reached that pre-eminence in courtliness and knightly activity which is necessary for membership of the Round Table. This highest secular society is open to him by virtue of his noble deeds; it is an entirely different matter with the Grail community. Once Feirefiz becomes a knight of the Round Table, Wolfram follows up his extreme praise by declaring that he is now the most powerful of all the knights belonging to it (777.2 ff.). But all this splendour of achievement does not prevent Parzival's small son Loherangrin from shrinking back and refusing to kiss his strange-looking uncle. Feirefiz' appearance will always be unusual, and Loherangrin's action is a delightfully individualized touch that keeps this uniqueness of Feirefiz in the audience's mind.

The conclusion of the duel is also conducted in a courtly fashion and marked by the generosity of Feirefiz' spirit. In Wolfram's comment before his opening words to Parzival this is made quite clear by the fact that he speaks 'höfschlîche' and 'en franzois' (744.26 f.). His further actions, in particular the casting aside of his sword when Parzival's breaks, are additional expressions of this courtly code of behaviour that must appeal to any Englishman's sense of 'fair play' and 'what is cricket'. There is no uncouthness about Feirefiz' conduct, however odd his appearance may be.

CONCLUSION

The duel between Parzival and Feirefiz in book XV is the final climax of the poem, the point at which Parzival is tested for his fitness to attain the kingship of the Grail. Accordingly, his opponent must be an outstanding character with well-defined qualities. Feirefiz is portrayed in the poem as an extraordinary individual—extraordinary not only in personal appearance, but in physical strength, material power, generosity of spirit and in his great desire for *minne*. And since we may regard Feirefiz as a symbolic projection of Parzival's own character, it is appropriate that Parzival's supreme test should consist in fighting this pagan warrior whose qualities are nonetheless of the very highest. This individuality of his character as a pagan is brought out by his gradual introduction into the action of the romance and by the many descriptions of his physical appearance and personal splendour. The variety of synonyms applied to him extend this picture and keep the different aspects of his personality and role in the poem continually before the audience. The Eastern elements are exploited to the full, and Feirefiz' black and white skin and his unusual *zimierde* are given a strong emphasis. In this way the duel is heightened in its purely external aspect.

In the more spiritual side of Feirefiz' character, however, there is much less individualization. The presentation of his religious beliefs is both sketchy and conventional, though the way in which they are intimately bound up with his desire for *minne* belongs to Wolfram's general conception of the interdependence of religious faith and *minne*, which he illustrates clearly in the varying fortunes of Gahmuret, Gawan, Anfortas, Feirefiz and most of all Parzival. And since it is the spiritual problems of Parzival that are the central subject of the poem, the problems of even the immediately subordinate characters cannot be treated in detail, since this would unbalance the structure of the work. Instead the spiritual questions are merely outlined, as is the case here with Feirefiz, and the external, the physical, aspects of their histories and characters are individualized and developed. With Feirefiz this process goes perhaps furthest in the short space which is devoted to him (though certainly the refinements of courtly love are best dealt with in Gawan's adventures). His part in the poem is more closely integrated than Gawan's, and his personal characteristics are elaborated in a manner which connects up with the peculiarly Wolframian ideas of the prologue and which could scarcely be more individually worked out.

X

CONCLUSION

As each of the preceding chapters (excluding the Introduction) has ended with a conclusion about the degree of individuality present in the character under discussion, it would be otiose to repeat these remarks here. A number of points remain, however, to be drawn from the conclusions on each chapter.

The scope of Wolfram's poem is unrivalled by any other medieval German work. Only Gottfried's *Tristan* in any measure approaches it in intensity and accomplishment, but there the problems treated centre much more on the single question of *minne* than does *Parʒival*. Moreover, Wolfram's own personality emerges from his work more clearly than that of any other medieval German poet from his writings. He indulges in frequent personal comment on the action, relating it to his own circumstances, often in a humorous way. In poetic usage and language he is consciously idiosyncratic, and as his literary model he takes Heinrich von Veldeke, who had initiated the fashion of courtly romance in Germany some thirty years before Wolfram completed his *Parʒival* (cf. *Tristan* 4723 ff.), whilst Gottfried followed in the steps of Hartmann von Aue. Wolfram continually expresses his opposition to both Hartmann and Gottfried in their attitudes towards the problems of the day, emphasizing that *schildes ambet* and not literature is his profession. This consciousness of his own personality and his differences from the courtly society of his day is largely the origin of the individuality that Wolfram infuses into so many of his characters. Of course, a considerable measure of individuality is present in Gottfried and Hartmann, the *Nibelungenlied* and the outstanding *Minnesänger* up to Neidhart, where an awareness of the individual and personal experience (whether real or literary) is combined with high aesthetic sensibility. Wolfram shares something of this culturally current awareness, but he also deliberately diverges from fashion in such matters as vocabulary (his use of pre-courtly and early courtly terminology) and ideals of womankind. He is hostile to artificiality and pretentiousness and constantly shows his personal feelings and human sympathy, so that interjections, personal comments and reminiscences abound. Wolfram's own individuality is never hidden for very long behind the story that he is telling. There is little of the objectivity characteristic of the heroic epic in his work, though he is clearly attracted by its values. A firm basis is thus given to the individuality in characterization through Wolfram's own *Selbstherrlichkeit*.

Parzival is full of surprises, odd items of knowledge and gratuitous information. It is diversified in a remarkable manner. It contains material which fits happily into the conventional framework of the Arthurian romance (above all the Gawan episodes); the main body of Parzival's story is an elaboration and transmutation of subject-matter furnished by Chrétien de Troyes, but it also has long and important sections which lack any one coherent source and consist of Wolfram's own reworking of motifs known to him from a variety of disparate sources (principally the stories of Gahmuret and Feirefiz). Wolfram's inventiveness is unparalleled in the other authors of his time, but he controls his diversity in a far from haphazard way, as the studies of Mergell especially have shown (though one cannot always accept all Mergell's conclusions). This dexterity is apparent also in the elements and techniques of Wolfram's characterization, as the headings of the subsections in the chapters of this present study clearly show. Descriptions, synonyms and epithets, the use of speech and monologue, comparison, hyperbole and panegyric are all employed in differing measure for the many characters portrayed in the poem. Elements of idealization, symbolic devices and merely conventional characterization are found side by side and intertwined with the individualizing traits and techniques which are the principal subject of this study.

Chrétien's *Conte del Graal* provides a convenient starting-point for formulating more precisely the types and degrees of individuality to be found in Wolfram's poem. Above all, the first difference which strikes one in comparing Wolfram with Chrétien is the extent to which the German poet identifies the personages of the French poem more clearly through giving them names and also vastly increases the number of characters who people the pages of his romance. In this way, which is perhaps the least important of Wolfram's innovations *vis-à-vis* Chrétien, the trend towards individualization is apparent at a level which, though hardly profound, is nonetheless significant. Wolfram's whole attitude is geared to the identification and isolation of characters, while Chrétien is more concerned with the broad outlines of the story and concentrates, at least during the Perceval episodes, much more on the figure of Perceval than Wolfram does on Parzival. With Wolfram several of the main characters evolve a real individuality. Perceval's mother and only faintly sketched father become genuine characters in the persons of Herzeloyde and Gahmuret. Although Gahmuret's character owes much to historical and literary models (though not as much as Panzer claims), it represents a phenomenal expansion on that of Perceval's father, for he is presented with a history of his own, independent of the main stream of the poem, and despite the fact that this history contains many conventional features culled from elsewhere Wolfram's deployment of his motifs produces an individualized figure with clear characteristics and problems of his own. Gahmuret is a character for whom a certain slight *point de départ* was given in the *Conte del Graal,* but Wolfram went completely beyond Chrétien in the creation of Feirefiz, whose individuality is demonstrated through his not being a merely conventional depiction of an exotic heathen. He is extraordinary above all in appearance, but also in physical strength, material power, generosity of spirit and his varied *minne*-relationships. The creation of Feirefiz was a masterstroke of Wolfram's, for in this way the Grail world is shown to extend its significance beyond the bounds of Christendom pure and simple. Feirefiz has in the end to be converted from a conventionally and sketchily portrayed paganism to Christianity, but this is largely a formal matter and is hardly stressed as a real religious event. Indeed, since Feirefiz represents one aspect of Parzival's character, the religious element in the former cannot be stressed as it must remain subordinated to the spiritual development of Parzival. Nonetheless, Feirefiz is a figure such as only Wolfram could create from the vivid and encyclopedic enthusiasm of his imagination.

All the other main characters of Wolfram's poem have undergone some change in the transition from French to German. Herzeloyde emerges from the shadowy conventionality of Perceval's mother. Her former existence as a largely one-dimensional mother-figure in Chrétien is amplified from the bare hints that the French poet provides, and she thus takes on a more rounded existence in Wolfram's work. The traditional Church dogma is virtually omitted (though a certain delicate Marian symbolism is introduced), and what is left is generalized, while her experience of *minne* and her instruction to Parzival already express something of Wolfram's dissatisfaction with *hôhe minne*. Again, the conventional role of Blancheflor is significantly changed and fitted into the Grail atmosphere in Condwiramurs, whose very name indicates the importance that Wolfram attaches to her changed role. Condwiramurs is a highly idealized figure, but she is by no means a typical courtly lady. Both the hermit uncle and the Fisher King receive names at Wolfram's hand, while in each case much more information is given about them. In addition, the episode with the *sainz hermite*, with its traditional and straight-forwardly presented theology, becomes the pivot of the German poem, and Trevrizent's amplified role is tailored much more exactly to Parzival's transmuted history. Furthermore, the *germaine cousine*, whose part in Chrétien is restricted to one brief episode, becomes Sigune, whose history is closely interlinked with Parzival's and whom Wolfram found fascinating enough to treat in another poem. Gauvain also undergoes a certain change in that his story is more clearly integrated into the structure of the whole poem than is the case with Chrétien, but there is little that one could regard in his character as being obviously individualized.

The main change occurs, of course, in the character of Parzival, for Wolfram organizes and adds to the various traits of character supplied by Chrétien in such a way as to deepen the whole significance of the hero's career. This is evident at every turn and is most obvious in the treatment of the question motif in the two poems and in the theme of courtly love and the Grail. From being just another Arthurian knight with a series of adventures differentiated solely through their having the Grail as their goal, Parzival becomes a person whose struggles, failures and final success transcend the values of the courtly world and assume lasting human interest. The weight of his story is thrown more solidly on the religious-spiritual side of his career, and his adventures and encounters are articulated with this constantly in mind. It is impossible to discern exactly what Chrétien intended with Perceval's story on account of its being unfinished, but it is nonetheless patent that Wolfram's work is more than a mere Arthurian romance with religious episodes.

A further criterion of the individualization apparent in Wolfram's poem is provided by the degree of development to be found in many of the characters apart from Parzival. Few of them can be regarded as completely static, for Wolfram is at pains to present even minor characters, such as Lähelin and Orilus, more than once at different points in the unfolding of the plot so that the impression we receive is of figures whose role is not confined to one incident alone, but who also have an existence of their own apart from their relationship with Parzival. As far as the main characters are concerned, the degree of development depends on that of Parzival in so far as it must not begin to rival his. Thus, since Gawan is conceived as a parallel hero to Parzival, though subordinated, his history may express a development, but it must plainly be of a different order from Parzival's. Accordingly, Gawan's own *character*, with the perfection of chivalry as its norm, undergoes no development, since this would have endangered that of *des mæres hêrre* as well as contravening Gawan's position as the supreme representative of Arthurian society. But the *episodes* in his career do manifest a development, though this is external to him in that it is shown in the characters whom he encounters, and the dialectics of his *minne*-relationships is dependent on them and not on a genuine development within himself. Gawan takes no decisions of his own except when they are demanded by outward circumstances. He has no problems of his own (the accusation of Kingrimursel is unsubstantiated and therefore constitutes at most a pseudo-problem), but he takes on the problems of others and performs actions devoid of personal moral significance on their behalf. He has no real individuality as a result of his position as the embodiment of courtly excellence.

In the other main characters a more real development is shown. There are two main types—historical and actual. Into the historical category come Anfortas and Trevrizent, who are static as Parzival meets them, but whose former type of life and its change into the present are expressed in historical accounts. Anfortas' career provides an explanation for his maimed condition and proceeds naturally from his physical state. His final transfiguration is in fact no development of character, as it is solely a mechanical result of Parzival's action; it is a function of the latter's development, not of Anfortas'. The matter is somewhat different in Trevrizent's case, for his own history furnishes the necessary background for his second function towards Parzival, namely, that of giving knightly advice, which marks an important distinction between Chrétien's and Wolfram's conception of the hermit uncle. This knightly career furthermore provides a link with Gahmuret and, significantly, with Ither, so that Trevrizent gains an individuality beyond his role as a hermit figure; though even here he is individualized through not imposing a negative view of the world on Parzival. This kind of development is typically Wolframian and makes Trevrizent more than the character of one episode. His position in the poem reaches back into the past and modifies the meaning of important events in the poem, such as the death of Ither. Through the introduction of Trevrizent's personal history into the poem the whole emphasis of Wolfram's work is changed and the significance of Parzival's career illuminated. This type of individuality, therefore, serves the greater individuality of Parzival; it is not there for its own sake, but for the sake of Wolfram's new conception of Parzival.

In the sphere of actual development Herzeloyde and Sigune must above all be mentioned, though here again the individuality present forms part of Parzival's. Herzeloyde provides us with a thoroughgoing development, which is a function of the source story, and her reactions at Gahmuret's death are to be viewed as a logical, abrupt development of her love for him and her wish to protect his child from a similar fate. Her role as the *veve fame* in Chrétien is elaborated and properly motivated through the events of book II of *Parzival*, and we actually observe the change from her being the forceful queen of Waleis and wife of Gahmuret to the anxious, anti-courtly mother of Parzival. Herzeloyde cannot, of course, be separated in consideration from Gahmuret, and although Gahmuret presents no real development of character, Herzeloyde's position is conditioned by his, and both affect— through the forces of heredity as well as through environment— the career of their son. In any case, the individuality which Herzeloyde exhibits is very much a function of her relationship with Parzival.

Sigune perhaps presents the greatest degree of personal individuality among all the main characters, and this is shown among other things by the fact that Wolfram devotes a further romance to her story. The development which she shows in *Parzival* is independent of Parzival's career, but the various situations in which we see her are carefully aligned with Parzival's own development and heighten our understanding of what he also is experiencing, for Sigune acts as a mirror of Parzival's progress. But although she manifests a development in four stages, we do not witness the actual progress of it, as it is presented in a tableau form and not as a continuous process. In this way it is skilfully subordinated to Parzival's development, which we see actually happening. With Sigune each time we see the result of the development, not the development itself, so that again her individuality is carefully depicted so as not to detract from Parzival's.

Finally, it is necessary to characterize the various types and degrees of individuality present in Wolfram's poem.

(i) As Parzival's story forms the principal focus of interest in the poem, it is natural that his character should show the greatest degree of individuality. There are, of course, aspects of his career which may be found elsewhere in medieval romance, features which are typical in origin, and conventional traits, but Wolfram uses them in such a way as to portray his own view of life, which was consciously different from that of his contemporaries. Parzival is thus Wolfram's brain-child and displays a genuine personal individuality which reflects the poet's particular solution to the key problem of *gote und der werlde gevallen* and his view of the nature of *minne*, the ambiguity and complexity of human life, the questions of guilt and sin, forgiveness and reconciliation. Parzival's story is no ordinary one even from the point of view of external incidents, and Wolfram's genius is such that from these he creates a beautifully co-ordinated, coherent personality, whose innermost thoughts, emotions and reactions he most delicately and sympathetically investigates as they emerge from and inform the outward actions. Everywhere there is detail, refinement and subtlety, relating perfectly to the situation in hand. The external features of Parzival's individuality—his forest upbringing, his unsteady irruption into courtly society, his vist to Munsalvæsche and pursuit of the Grail above all—are underlined and supplemented with great complexity and skill in the sphere of human psychology, so that finally we see a genuine individual before us, whose individuality is such that it impinges on our own at many points and takes on that quality of eternal human interest which we find in those characters who speak most directly to us when they are most themselves.

(ii) The individuality discernible in most of the other main characters—Gahmuret, Herzeloyde, Sigune, Condwiramurs, Anfortas, Trevrizent, Feirefiz—has by and large a dual function. It is, in the first place, a means whereby the individuality of Parzival may be more lucidly expressed, for the individualizing elements are tailored to the development of *des mæres hêrre*. Thus, the extended role of Herzeloyde brings out further aspects of the boyhood episodes; Gahmuret provides an inherited basis of knightly talents and problems for Parzival's career; Sigune's history pinpoints Parzival's life at significant stages; Anfortas acts as an antithetical figure; Trevrizent's knightly background enables him to give his nephew chivalric as well as spiritual advice; Condwiramurs forms the culmination of Parzival's experience in *minne*; Feirefiz shows the extent of Parzival's knightly prowess and spiritual achievement. In this way, each of them has a function which serves the individuality of Parzival. *It is thus a dependent individuality they possess which derives from their relationship to Parzival.* But, secondly, they have a distinct individuality of their own in that, although their lives tend to affect Parzival's at one point in particular—their main function in the poem—they have an independent career of their own which continues after their contact with Parzival. Moreover, they are frequently mentioned in other sections of the poem in connexion with matters not immediately affecting the main pattern of the story. Of course, their own histories are not developed or portrayed in such detail as Parzival's, being definitely subordinated to him. But within bounds, provided that the individualization does not detract from the attention that must centre on Parzival, their characters are presented in far more than conventional, idealized or typical terms. None of them can be characterized as a mere type—not even Condwiramurs, who in many ways exemplifies the idealized *frouwe*, nor even Gahmuret with his deeds of chivalry and features culled from a variety of sources. Each of these characters possesses a vivid, though limited, personal individuality, developed in a relationship with Parzival, but moderated so as not to rival his individuality.

(iii) The minor characters present the widest range of possibilities in characterization. Many occur as mere names; some appear with a quite brief indication of their position and function; while others may play an important role in one particular episode. This last category, which has only been dealt with *en passant* in this study, exhibits a considerable degree of individualization, since as the characters are clearly minor or peripheral any details lavished on them do not constitute a threat to the main characters. The type of individuality to be found in them is largely of a descriptive nature. Their function must at all times be carefully geared to the aim and themes of the entire work, but descriptions are in order. Such is the case in the Parzival sections of the poem with characters like Jeschute, Cundrie and Kahenis' daughters, but with Artus and Keie their traditional roles are modified and questioned too. In the Gawan episodes it is the colour and individuality of the minor characters which maintain the interest of the reader. There is an individuality of function here, for Gawan cannot provide it on account of his traditional role in Arthurian romance. Obie and Obilot, Antikonie, Orgeluse (though she can scarcely be classed as a minor figure), Urjans, Clinschor and Gramoflanz provide the substance and brilliance of the Gawan episodes. They move in a world with which Parzival only comes into fleeting contact, and thus any individuality of theirs does not detract from his, but instead furnishes Gawan with what little individuality he has. They are characterized by an individuality of situation; they are what gives the *Abenteuerroman* its attraction. Otherwise the Gawan episodes would be a pallid counterpart to the sections centred on Parzival.

The degrees of individuality present in Wolfram's poem are varied and subtle and have to be suited to the other types of characterization also found. The individuality of any character is attuned to his function in the entire work and may thus be expressed in matters of detail, description or symbolism, or it may be shown in a more radical individuality of function or role in the poem. Variety is of the essence of Wolfram's art, and this is no more richly demonstrated than in his technique and types of characterization.

CARL F. BAYERSCHMIDT, *Wolfram von Eschenbach's Christian Faith* (GR, XXIX, 1954).

J. K. BOSTOCK, *The Ant's Waist: A Query* (Med. Aev., XXV, 1957).

—— *Der eilfte spân* (MLR, LV, 1960).

HANS EGGERS, *Literarische Beziehungen des Parzival zum Tristrant Eilharts von Oberg* (Beitr., LXXII, 1950).

—— *Strukturprobleme mittelalterlicher Epik, dargestellt am Parzival Wolframs von Eschenbach* (Euph., XLVII, 1953).

—— *Non cognovi litteraturam (zu Parzival 115, 27)* in the Festgabe Ulrich Pretzel (Berlin, 1963).

GUSTAV EHRISMANN, *Über Wolframs Ethik* (ZfdA, XLIX, 1908).

XENJA VON ERTZDORFF, *Fräulein Obilot—Zum siebten Buch von Wolframs Parzival* (WW, XII, 1962).

—— *Höfische Freundschaft* (DU, XIV, vi, 1962).

JEAN FOURQUET, *Les Noms propres du Parzival* in the Mélanges Ernest Hoepffner (Paris, 1949).

SIEGFRIED GROSSE, *Wis den wisen gerne bi. Die höfischen Lehren in Hartmanns Gregorius und Wolframs Parzival* (DU, XIV, vi, 1962).

HERMANN HECKEL, *Das ethische Wortfeld in Wolframs Parzival* (Würzburg, 1939).

URSULA HEISE, *Frauengestalten im 'Parzival' Wolframs von Eschenbach* (DU, IX, ii, 1957).

HEINRICH HEMPEL, *Der zwîvel bei Wolfram und anderweit* in the Festgabe Karl Helm (Tübingen, 1951).

—— *Der Eingang von Wolframs Parzival* (ZfdA, LXXXIII, 1951/2).

WALTER HENZEN, *Das 9. Buch des Parzival. Überlegungen zum Aufbau* in the Festgabe Karl Helm (Tübingen, 1951).

—— *Zur Vorprägung der Demut im Parzival durch Chrestien* (Beitr. (Tübingen), LXXX, 1958).

W. T. H. JACKSON, *The Progress of Parzival and the Trees of Virtue and Vice* (GR, XXXIII, 1958).

EMIL KARL, *Minne und Ritterethik bei Wolfram von Eschenbach* (Diss. Freiburg i. Br., 1952).

OSKAR KATANN, *Einflüsse des Katharertums auf Wolframs Parzival* (WW, VIII, 1957/8).

GEORG KEFERSTEIN, *Die Gawanhandlung in Wolframs Parzival* (GRM, XXV, 1937).

—— *Parzivals ethischer Weg* (Weimar, 1937).

—— *Zur Liebesauffassung in Wolframs 'Parzival'* in the Festschrift Albert Leitzmann (Jena, 1937).

BIBLIOGRAPHY

NOTE: This bibliography lists (i) dictionaries used; (ii) editions of medieval works from which quotations have been made; (iii) critical works on medieval literature and *Parzival* in particular which have been of use or relevant to the theme of this dissertation.

DICTIONARIES

R. GRANDSAIGNES D'HAUTERIVE, *Dictionnaire d'Ancien Français. Moyen Age et Renaissance* (Paris, 1947).

FR. KLUGE, *Etymologisches Wörterbuch* (Berlin, 1957).

MATTHIAS LEXER, *Mittelhochdeutsches Handwörterbuch* (Leipzig, 1872–8).

ALFRED SENN & WINFRIED LEHMANN, *Word-Index to Wolfram's Parzival* (Madison, 1938).

Trübners Deutsches Wörterbuch, ed. A. Götze & W. Mitzka (Berlin, 1939–57).

EDITIONS

WOLFRAM VON ESCHENBACH, ed. K. Lachmann (Berlin, 1891[5]), for quotations and normal use.

—— ed. K. Lachmann & E. Hartl (Berlin, 1926[6]), for the *Verzeichnis der Eigennamen*.

—— ed. Karl Bartsch & Marta Marti (Leipzig, 1927–9[4]).

—— ed. Ernst Martin (Halle, 1900–3).

EILHART VON OBERG, *Tristrant*, ed. Franz Lichtenstein (Strasbourg, 1877).

GOTTFRIED VON STRASSBURG, *Tristan und Isold*, ed. Fr. Ranke (Berlin/Frankfurt am Main, 1949).

HARTMANN VON AUE, *Erec*, ed. A. Leitzmann (Tübingen, 1957[2]).

—— *Gregorius*, ed. H. Paul & A. Leitzmann (Tübingen, 1953[8]).

—— *Der arme Heinrich*, ed. J. K. Bostock (Oxford, 1947).

—— *Iwein*, ed. G. F. Benecke, K. Lachmann & L. Wolff (Berlin/Leipzig, 1926[5]).

HEINRICH VON VELDEKE, *Eneide*, ed. O. Behaghel (Heilbronn, 1882).

PFAFFE KONRAD, *Das Rolandslied*, ed. Carl Wesle (Halle, 1955).

PFAFFE LAMPRECHT, *Alexander*, ed. K. Kinzel (Halle, 1885).

WALTHER VON DER VOGELWEIDE, *Gedichte*, ed. H. Paul & A. Leitzmann (Halle, 1945⁶).

WILLIRAM, *Das Hohelied*, ed. J. Seemüller (Strasbourg, 1878).

König Rother, ed. Th. Frings & J. Kuhnt (Halle, 1954).

Liederdichter des 13. Jahrhunderts, ed. Carl von Kraus (Tübingen, 1952).

Die Litanei, ed. Carl von Kraus in *Mittelhochdeutsches Übungsbuch* (Heidelberg, 1926²).

Des Minnesangs Frühling, ed. K. Lachmann, M. Haupt, Fr. Vogt & Carl von Kraus (Leipzig, 1954³¹).

Das Nibelungenlied, ed. K. Bartsch & H. de Boor (Wiesbaden, 1956¹³).

Orendel, ed. H. Steinger (Halle, 1935).

Das St. Trudperter Hohe Lied, ed. H. Menhardt (Halle, 1934).

CHRÉTIEN DE TROYES, *Conte del Graal*, ed. W. Roach (Geneva/Lille, 1956).

La Chanson de Roland, ed. J. Bédier (Paris, 1955¹⁹⁵).

ST. BERNARD OF CLAIRVAUX, in J. P. Migne, *Patrologia latina*, CLXXXIII.

ST. ISIDORE OF SEVILLE, *Etymologiae sive Origines*, ed. W. M. Lindsay (Oxford, 1911).

ST. PETER DAMIAN, in J. P. Migne, *Patrologia latina*, CXLIV.

The Mabinogion, tr. Gwyn Jones & Thomas Jones (London, 1957).

CRITICAL WORKS

(a) General

MARIA BINDSCHEDLER, *Die Dichtung um König Artus und seine Ritter* (*Dt. Vjs.* XXXI, 1957).

HELMUT DE BOOR, *Geschichte der deutschen Literatur von den Anfängen bis zur Gegenwart*. Bd. II. *Die höfische Literatur. Vorbereitung, Blüte, Ausklang. 1170–1250* (Munich, 1953).

HENNIG BRINKMANN, *Der Prolog im Mittelalter als literarische Erscheinung* (*WW*, XIV, 1964).

HILDEGARD EMMEL, *Formprobleme des Artusromans und der Graldichtung. Die Bedeutung des Artuskreises für das Gefüge des Romans im 12. und 13. Jh. in Frankreich, Deutschland und den Niederlanden* (Bern, 1951).

WERNER FECHTER, *Absalom als Vergleichs- und Beispielfigur im mhd. Schrifttum* (*Beitr.* (Tübingen), LXXXIII, 1961).

WOLFGANG HARMS, *Der Kampf mit dem Freund oder Verwandten in der deutschen Literatur bis um 1300* (Munich, 1963).

VINCENT FOSTER HOPPER, *Medieval Number Symbolism* (New 1938).

JOHAN HUIZINGA, *The Waning of the Middle Ages* (London, 1

FRIEDRICH MAURER, *Leid. Studien zur Bedeutungs- und F geschichte besonders in den großen Epen der staufischen Zei 1951).

WOLFGANG MOHR, *Wandel des Menschenbildes in der mittela Dichtung* (*WW*, III (Sonderheft), 1952/3).

HANS NAUMANN, *Der wilde und der edle Heide. Versuch über di Toleranz* in the Festgabe Gustav Ehrismann (Berlin 1925).

HANS NAUMANN, *Die Kultur im Zeitalter des Rittertums* (Pots [1938]).

NORA SCHNEIDER, *Erziehergestalten im höfischen Epos* (Di 1935).

JULIUS SCHWIETERING, *Typologisches in mittelalterlicher Dich Festgabe Gustav Ehrismann* (Berlin/Leipzig, 1925).

—— *Wandel des Heldenideals in der epischen Dichtung d (ZfdA, LXIV, 1927).

—— *Die deutsche Dichtung des Mittelalters* (Potsdam, n.d

—— *Natur und art* (*ZfdA*, XCI, 1961/2).

THEODOR STEINBÜCHEL, *Vom Menschenbild des christlichen (Basle, n.d.).

WILHELM WACKERNAGEL, *Die Farben- und Blumensprache alters* in *Kleinere Schriften* I (Leipzig, 1872).

EMIL WALKER, *Der Monolog im höfischen Epos. Stil- u geschichtliche Untersuchungen* (Stuttgart, 1928).

JESSIE L. WESTON, *From Ritual to Romance* (Cambridge,

ERNST WINDISCH, *Das keltische Britannien bis zu K (Abhandl. d. sächs. Ges. d. Wiss., phil.-hist. Kl.*, x

EVA MARIA WOELKER, *Menschengestaltung in vorhöfischer Jahrhunderts* (Berlin, 1940).

(b) Wolfram's 'Parzival'

HELEN ADOLF, *New Light on Oriental Sources for Wolf and Other Grail Romances* (*PMLA*, LXII, 1947).

—— *The Theological and Feudal Background of Wo (JEGP*, XLIX, 1950).

KARL BARTSCH, *Eigennamen in Parzival und Titurel i Studien*, II (Vienna, 1875).

GERHARD BAUER, *Parzival und die Minne* (*Euph.* LVII

KARL KINZEL, *Antikonie* (*ZfdA*, XXX, 1886).

—— *Frauen in Wolframs Parʒival* (*ZfdPh*, XXI, 1889).

WOLFGANG KLEIBER, *Zur Namenforschung in Wolframs Parʒival* (*DU*, XIV, vi, 1962).

ERICH KÖHLER, *Die drei Blutstropfen im Schnee: Bemerkungen ʒu einem neuen Deutungsversuch* (*GRM* (*NF*), IX, 1959).

HERBERT KOLB, *Schola Humilitatis. Ein Beitrag ʒur Interpretation der Gralerʒählung Wolframs von Eschenbach* (*Beitr.* (Tübingen) LXXVIII, 1956).

—— *Die Blutstropfen-Episode bei Chrétien und Wolfram* (*Beitr.* (Tübingen), LXXIX, 1957).

HANS-JOACHIM KOPPITZ, *Wolframs Religiosität. Beobachtungen über das Verhältnis Wolframs von Eschenbach ʒur religiösen Tradition des Mittelalters* (Diss. Bonn, 1954).

WILLY KROGMANN, *wunsch von pardîs* (*ZfdA*, LXXXV, 1954/5).

HUGO KUHN, *Parʒival. Ein Versuch über Mythos, Glaube und Dichtung im Mittelalter* (*Dt. Vjs.*, XXX, 1956).

K. LUCAE, *Über den Traum der Herʒeloyde im Parʒival* (*ZfdPh*, IX, 1877).

BODO MERGELL, *Wolfram von Eschenbach und seine französischen Quellen. II. Teil. Wolframs Parʒival* (Münster, 1943).

BENEDIKT MOCKENHAUPT, *Die Frömmigkeit im Parʒival Wolframs von Eschenbach* (Bonn, 1941/2).

WOLFGANG MOHR, *Parʒivals ritterliche Schuld* (*WW*, II, 1951/2).

—— *Hilfe und Rat in Wolframs Parʒival* in the Festschrift Jost Trier (Meisenheim, 1954).

—— *Obie und Meljanʒ. Zum 7. Buch von Wolframs Parʒival* in the Festschrift Günther Müller (Bonn, 1957).

—— *Parʒival und Gawan* (*Euph.*, LII, 1958).

HANS NAUMANN, *Doch ich ein leie wære* (*Arch.*, CLXXXVIII, 1951).

ALBERT NOLTE, *Die composition der Trevriʒent-scenen. Parʒ. IX 452, 13–502* (*ZfdA*, XLIV, 1900).

FRIEDRICH PANZER, *Gahmuret. Quellenstudien ʒu Wolframs Parʒival* (*SB d. Heidelberger Akad. d. Wiss., phil.-hist. Kl.*, 1939/40).

JAMES F. POAG, *Heinrich von Veldeke's minne; Wolfram von Eschenbach's liebe und triuwe* (*JEGP*, LXI, 1962).

CARL PSCHMADT, *Jeschute* (*ZfdA*, LV, 1917).

MARIE RAMONDT, *Zur Jugendgeschichte des Parʒival* (*Neoph.* IX, 1924).

FRIEDRICH RANKE, *Zur Symbolik des Grals bei Wolfram von Eschenbach* (*Triv.*, IV, 1946).

MARGARET F. RICHEY, *Ither von Gaheviez* (*MLR*, XXVI, 1931).

—— *Studies of Wolfram von Eschenbach* (Edinburgh, 1957).

WERNER RICHTER, *Wolfram von Eschenbach und die blutende Lanze* (*Euph.*, LIII, 1959).

MARTÍN DE RIQUER, *Perceval y las gotas de sangre en la nieve* (*Rev. fil. esp.*, XXXIX, 1955).

HEINZ RUPP, *Die Funktion des Wortes tump im ' Parzival' Wolframs von Eschenbach* (*GRM* (*NF*), VII, 1957).

—— *Wolframs Parzival-Prolog* (*Beitr.* (Halle), LXXXII (Sonderband), 1961).

HERMANN SCHNEIDER, *Parzival-Studien* (*SB d. Bayr. Akad. d. Wiss., phil.-hist. Kl.*, 1944/6).

WALTER JOHANNES SCHRÖDER, *Der dichterische Plan des Parzival-romans* (*Beitr.*, LXXIV, 1952).

—— *Die Soltane-Erzählung in Wolframs Parzival* (Heidelberg, 1963).

WERNER SCHRÖDER, *Zum Wortgebrauch von riuwe bei Hartmann und Wolfram* (*GRM* (*NF*), IX, 1959).

JULIUS SCHWIETERING, *Sigune auf der Linde* (*ZfdA*, LVII, 1919/20).

—— *Der Fischer vom See Brumbane* (*ZfdA*, LX, 1923).

—— *Parzivals Schuld* (*ZfdA*, LXXXI, 1944).

WILLEM SNELLEMAN, *Das Haus Anjou und der Orient in Wolframs Parzival* (Nijkerk, 1941).

HILDA SWINBURNE, *Parzival's Crisis* (*MLR*, L, 1955).

—— *Gahmuret and Feirefiz in Wolfram's Parzival* (*MLR*, LI, 1956).

GEORGE F. TIMPSON, *The Heraldic Element in Wolfram's ' Parzival'* (*GLL* (*NS*), XIII, 1960).

M. O'C. WALSHE, *Der Künec von Kukumerlant* (*Lond. Med. St.*, I, 1937/9).

PETER WAPNEWSKI, *Wolframs Parzival. Studien zur Religiosität und Form* (Heidelberg, 1955).

GOTTFRIED WEBER, *Parzival. Ringen und Vollendung* (Oberursel, 1948).

ROLF WEBER, *Askese und Quietismus bei Wolfram von Eschenbach* (*JEGP*, XVII, 1918).

MAX WEHRLI, *Wolfram von Eschenbach. Erzählstil und Sinn seines ' Parzival'* (*DU*, VI, V, 1954).

HERMANN J. WEIGAND, *Wolfram's Grail and the Neutral Angels: A Discussion and a Dialogue* (*GR*, XXIX, 1954).

—— *Three Chapters on Courtly Love in Arthurian France and Germany. Lancelot—Andreas Capellanus—Wolfram von Eschenbach's Parzival* (Chapel Hill, 1956).

CARL WESLE, *Zu Wolframs Parzival* (*Beitr.*, LXXII, 1950).

P. B. WESSELS, *Wolfram zwischen Dogma und Legende* (*Beitr.* (Tübingen), LXXVII, 1955).

H. BERNARD WILLSON, *Wolframs Bîspel. Zur Interpretation des 1. Teils des Parzivalprologs* (*Wolfram-Jb.*, 1955).

—— *The Symbolism of Belakâne and Feirefîz in Wolfram's 'Parzival'* (*GLL* (*NS*), XIII, 1960).

—— *The Grail King in Wolfram's 'Parzival'* (*MLR*, LV, 1960).

—— *Das Fragemotiv in Wolframs Parzival* (*GRM* (*NF*), XII, 1962).

—— *Wolframs neutrale Engel* (*ZfdPh*, LXXXIII, 1964).

MAURICE WILMOTTE, *Le Poème du Gral et ses auteurs. Le Parzival de Wolfram d'Eschenbach et ses sources françaises* (Paris, 1933).

LUDWIG WOLFF, *Die höfisch-ritterliche Welt und der Gral in Wolframs Parzival* (*Beitr.* (Tübingen), LXXVII, 1955).

MARIANNE WYNN, *The Poetic Structure of Wolfram von Eschenbach's 'Parzival'. A Study of the Natural Setting* (Diss. Cambridge, 1953).

—— *Geography of Fact and Fiction in Wolfram von Eschenbach's 'Parzivâl'* (*MLR*, LVI, 1961).

—— *Scenery and Chivalrous Journeys in Wolfram's Parzival* (*Spec.*, XXXVI, 1961).

—— *Parzivâl and Gâwân—Hero and Counterpart* (*Beitr.* (Tübingen) LXXXIV, 1962).

EDWIN H. ZEYDEL, *Wolframs Parzival, 'Kyot' und die Katharer* (*Neoph.*, XXXVII, 1953).

(c) Wolfram's Dawnsongs

A. T. HATTO, *On Beauty of Numbers in Wolfram's Dawnsongs* (*MLR*, XLV, 1950).

(d) Hartmann von Aue

K. C. KING, *Zur Frage der Schuld in Hartmanns Gregorius* (*Euph.* LVII, 1963).

HILDEGARD NOBEL, *Schuld und Sühne in Hartmanns 'Gregorius' und in der frühscholastischen Theologie* (*ZfdPh*, LXXVI, 1957).

GABRIELE SCHIEB, *Schuld und Sühne in Hartmanns Gregorius* (*Beitr.*, LXXII, 1950).

H. B. WILLSON, *Sin and Redemption in Hartmann's Erec* (*GR*, XXXIII, 1958).

—— *Love and Charity in Hartmann's 'Iwein'* (*MLR*, LVII, 1962).

(e) Minnesänger

HANS FURSTNER, *Studien zur Wesensbestimmung der höfischen Minne* (Groningen/Djakarta, 1956).

MARGARET F. RICHEY, *Essays on the Mediaeval German Love-Lyric* (Oxford, 1943).

EDUARD WECHSSLER, *Das Kulturproblem des Minnesangs* (Halle, 1909).

(f) Grail Literature

RETO R. BEZZOLA, *Le Sens de l'aventure et de l'amour* (Paris, 1947).

JEAN FRAPPIER, *Le Graal et l'hostie. Conte del Graal*, v. 6413–6431 in *Les Romans du Graal aux XIIe et XIIIe siècles. Colloques internationaux du Centre National de la Recherche Scientifique* (Paris, 1956).

STEFAN HOFER, *Chrétien de Troyes. Leben und Werke des altfranzösischen Epikers* (Graz/Cologne, 1954).

PAUL IMBS, *L'Elément religieux dans le Conte del Graal de Chrétien de Troyes* in *Les Romans du Graal aux XIIe et XIIIe siecles* (Paris, 1956).

WILHELM KELLERMANN, *Aufbaustil und Weltbild Chrestiens von Troyes im Percevalroman* (Halle, 1936).

INDEX